Children's Memorial Hospital (CMH)
Children's Memorial Medical Center (CMMC)
Chrysler
Chubb
Cincinnati Sport Service
Circuit City
Cisco
Cisneros Group
Citations
Citibank
Citicorp
Clorox
CNN
Coca-Cola
Colgate-Palmolive
Columbia/CBS Records
Columbia /HCA
Columbia Studios
Comdisco
Compaq
Connecticut General
Conoco
Conseco
Constantin Vacheron
Consumer Reports
Continental Airlines
Continental Can
Cook
Cooper Tire
Coors
Corning Inc.
Cray Research
Crest Toothpaste
Crown, Cork and Seal
Crown Holdings
CSX
Cummins Engine

Daimler-Benz
Daimler-Chrysler
Danskin
Daum
Dean Witter Brokerage Services
DeBeers
Deere & Company
Dell
Delta Airlines
Deltona Corporation
Denon
Detroit Diesel Corporation
Deutsche Post
Disney
Disney-ABC

DLJ Direct
Dollar
Dollar General
Dow Chemicals
Dow Corning
Dow Jones and Co.
Dr. Pepper
Dresser Industries
drsfosterandsmith
Duke Energy
DuPont

E-Land
Eastman Kodak
eBay
Edward Hospital
Eli Lilly
Embraer
Emerald Airlines
Emerson Electric
Emriates Air
EMI
Enron
Enterprise Rent-A-Car
Epson
Ericsson
ESPN
Estee-Lauder Companies
Exxon Mobil

Fairchild Semiconductor
Family Dollar
Federal Express
Ferrari
Filene's Basement
Fingerhut
Finnish Cable Works
Finnish Rubber Works
First USA/Bank One
Fischer-Price
Fleischmann's
Fluky's
Fluor
Ford
Freeport-McMoRan
Frito-Lay
Fujitsu

Gannett
Garan Inc.
Gateway
Genentech Inc.
General Dynamics
General Electric
General Foods

General Mills
General Motors
Genetics Institute
Georgia-Pacific
Giant
Gillette
Glaxo
Global Relationship Bank
Goodyear
Google
Great Atlantic and Pacific Tea
Great Lakes Refining Company
Gucci
Gulf and Western
Gulfstreams

H&R Block
Harley-Davidson
Hasbro
HBO
Hertz
Hewlett-Packard
Hit de Venezuela
Hitachi
Hollywood Video
Home Box Office
Home Depot
Honda
Hudepohl
Human Genome Sciences
Hyundai

IBM
ICI
Incyte Genomics
Intel
Interbrand
International Harvester
International Nickel
Internet Auction Co
ITT

J.B. Hunt
J.C. Penny
Jeep
JetBlue Airways
Jiffy Lube
John Fairfax and Sons
Johnson and Johnson
Johnson Controls
JVC

Kasper Instruments
Kawasaki
Kazi Foods Inc.

(list continues at back of book)

ECONOMICS OF STRATEGY

ECONOMICS
OF STRATEGY
Fourth Edition

David Besanko / *Northwestern University*

David Dranove / *Northwestern University*

Mark Shanley / *Purdue University*

Scott Schaefer / *University of Utah*

JOHN WILEY & SONS

ASSOCIATE PUBLISHER   Judith Joseph
SENIOR PRODUCTION EDITOR   Valerie A. Vargas
MARKETING MANAGER   Christopher Ruel
CREATIVE DIRECTOR   Harry Nolan
SENIOR DESIGNER   Hope Miller
PRODUCTION MANAGEMENT SERVICES   Ingrao Associates
EDITORIAL ASSISTANT   Emily Horowitz
MEDIA EDITOR   Allison Morris
COVER PHOTO   The yellow Iris (oil on canvas) by Monet, Claude (1840–1926) © Musee Marmattan, Paris, France/out of copyright.

This book was set in 10/12 Janson Text by GGS Information Services and printed and bound by R. R. Donnelley. The cover was printed by Phoenix Color.

This book is printed on acid-free paper. ∞

To order books or for customer service, please call 1-800-CALL WILEY (225-5945).

Library of Congress Cataloging-in-Publication Data

Economics of strategy / David Besanko . . . [et al.].--4th ed.
    p. cm.
    Includes index.
    ISBN 978-0-471-67945-5 (cloth)

    1. Strategic planning--Economic aspects. 2. Managerial economics. I. Besanko, David, 1955-

    HD30.28.B4575 2006
    658.4′012--dc22

                                                2006042641

10 9 8 7 6 5 4 3

PREFACE

A lot has happened to the business landscape in the 10 years since we began writing the first edition of *The Economics of Strategy*. Several years of steady but unspectacular economic growth culminated with the dot com bubble and subsequent global recession. Most markets have since recovered, and many firms in both the "old" and "new" economies are enjoying unprecedented profitability.

How often over the past decade did we hear from strategy gurus that "the rules of business had changed"?[1] Managers and investors who bought into the hysteria of the new economy did so at their own risk. Ignoring the old joke about selling high volumes but losing money on every sale, investors staked and lost billions on Internet retailers. Dismissing the dangers of competing in a market with homogeneous products and extremely high fixed costs, firms laid thousands of miles of transatlantic fiber-optic cable in the futile hope of becoming global telecom giants. Seemingly oblivious to the dangers of far-ranging integration, movie studios instead followed the mantra of convergence, creating entertainment supergiants that failed to deliver shareholder value. Hospitals made the same mistake, pursuing the holy grail of integrated health care and losing billions of dollars in the process.

The bear market of the early 2000s was a wakeup call to managers in these and other industries who had neglected business fundamentals in favor of the latest fads. The fourth edition of this text reaffirms what we have preached all along: there are a set of business principles that apply at all times, to all sectors of the economy. Sound strategic management requires mastery of these principles, not blind adherence to the "strategy du jour."

By their nature, principles are enduring. But they are not always well-understood. Consider that Michael Porter's classic treatment of the principles of competition, *Competitive Strategy*, was not published until 1980. Porter's book provides an important illustration of how economic reasoning can inform practicing managers, particularly with regard to strategies for dealing with a firm's external environment. Following on the heels of Porter, we joined with other business school economists in a search for a textbook that might provide a broader and deeper economic foundation for strategic analysis.

What we found was at first discouraging. Most of the available texts in strategic management lacked disciplinary grounding. Few contained serious discussions of economics principles that are essential to strategy, such as economies of scale, transactions-cost economics, oligopoly theory, entry, commitment, incentives for innovation, and agency. Moreover, most of these books were targeted at more general audiences than what one finds at a business school such as Kellogg. We learned that we were not the only ones struggling to find an appropriate text for teaching business strategy. Indeed the choice of a text for the core strategy course appeared to be problematic at many business schools.

Seeking to expand on Porter's contributions to taking an economics-based approach to teaching strategy, we considered possible solutions. One possibility was to use a microeconomics text, such as Robert Pindyck and Daniel Rubinfeld's *Microeconomics*, which offers many real-world examples to demonstrate the practical importance of economics. But this represents at best a compromise between traditional microeconomics and management strategy.

In the years immediately preceding our work on the first edition of *Economics of Strategy*, two important books appeared. Sharon Oster's *Modern Competitive Analysis* was remarkable for its breadth, covering most of the topics that we had identified as important to teach in a management strategy class. Paul Milgrom and John Roberts's *Economics, Organization, and Management* was remarkable for its depth. Milgrom and Roberts provided a deep theoretical basis for understanding issues involving organization, incentives, and hierarchy. Our objective in writing *Economics of Strategy* was, in part, to capture the breadth of Oster at a level of analysis approaching Milgrom and Roberts, while offering the kinds of illustrative examples that appear in both books.

The first three editions of *Economics of Strategy* largely met our objectives and have been warmly received by Kellogg students (and students around the world; the book has been translated into at least four other languages!) We are especially pleased with the response to the material on human resources management (sometimes called personnel economics) that was added for the third edition. This edition further expands on this material.

We have made a few other notable changes in this edition. The chapter on business history has been updated to include the recent dot-com bubble. The chapters on entry and positioning have undergone thorough overhauls. There have been noticeable renovations in most other chapters, notably those on diversification, dynamics of competition, and sustaining advantage. There are many new example boxes, and most of the carryovers have been brought up to date. As always, we have strived to make *The Economics of Strategy* reflect the cutting edge of academic thinking about business strategy.

ORGANIZATION OF THE BOOK

This book is organized in four parts. Part One focuses on the boundaries of the firm. Major topics include economies of scale and scope, vertical integration, and diversification. Part Two covers competitive strategy from the perspective of industrial organization (IO) economics. It includes traditional IO topics such as market structure and entry and modern IO topics such as dynamic pricing rivalry. It concludes with a discussion of Porter's Five Forces, which we view as a systematic framework for assessing the IO issues presented in the preceding chapters. Part Three of the book covers strategic positioning and dynamics. The chapters in this section provide an economic foundation for understanding competitive advantage, how it might be diagnosed, the conditions under which it might be sustained, and how it might be acquired in the first place. This portion of the book draws from modern literature in both economics and strategy. Part Four covers topics associated with internal organization, including two chapters on personnel economics, organization structure, and strategic fit. The final chapter ties the book together, arguing that a crucial role of the general manager is to make the strategic decisions that we detail throughout the book.

The book is liberally interspersed with real-world examples that bring the economic models to life. The examples are drawn from throughout the world and cover business practice from the eighteenth century to the present day. The business world is ever changing, and by the time this book hits the market, some of our references to organizations and individuals will be obsolete. We hope that the lessons learned from them will endure.

We believe that this book can be used as a text either in a core strategy course or in a business economics course that focuses on the economics of industry and the economics of the firm. In our 10-week strategy course for first-year MBA students at Kellogg, we typically assign the following chapters:

Chapter 1 The Evolution of the Modern Firm
Chapter 2 The Horizontal Boundaries of the Firm: Economies of Scale and Scope
Chapter 3 The Vertical Boundaries of the Firm
Chapter 10 Industry Analysis
Chapter 11 Strategic Positioning for Competitive Advantage
Chapter 12 Sustaining Competitive Advantage

If we had an entire semester for our strategy course, we would add Chapter 6 (Competitors and Competition), Chapter 13 (The Origins of Competitive Advantage: Innovation, Evolution, and the Environment), and Chapter 15 (Incentives in Firms). A more organizations-focused course might replace Chapters 6 and 13 with Chapters 5 (Diversification), 14 (Agency and Performance Measurement), 16 (Strategy and Structure), and/or 17 (Environment, Power, and Culture).

Our placement of the boundaries of the firm chapters (2–5) before the strategy chapters (10–13) may strike some as atypical. However, it is not at all essential that instructors follow this ordering. As along as students understand the material in the Economics Primer and the material on economies of scale and scope in Chapter 2, the strategy chapters can be taught before the chapters on the boundaries of the firm.

The set of Chapters 7–9 relating to commitment, dynamic competition, and entry/exit are the most "game theoretic" of the chapters in the book. This set of chapters is the most demanding one for students with weaker economic backgrounds (though the introduction to game theory in the primer coupled with material in Chapter 6 should be sufficient for students to understand this material). Because students in our basic strategy course at Kellogg have not yet taken economics, we do not cover these chapters until the advanced class in Competitive Strategy. The material in Chapters 11 and beyond does not depend on the material in Chapters 7–9, so these chapters can be easily skipped without any loss in continuity.

The book can also be used in a strategy or managerial economics course that emphasizes competitive strategy and modern industrial organization. For a one-quarter course, we recommend use of these chapters:

Chapter 2 The Horizontal Boundaries of the Firm: Economies of Scale and Scope
Chapter 6 Competitors and Competition
Chapter 7 Strategic Commitment
Chapter 8 The Dynamics of Pricing Rivalry

For a one-semester course, one could add Chapter 5 to the above list and supplement the material from all the chapters with advanced readings on competitive strategy, industrial organization, and game theory.

SUPPLEMENTARY MATERIALS

Instructor's Manual
This Instructor's Manual provides several valuable resources that enhance each chapter of the text, including a list of the chapter contents, a chapter summary, approaches to teaching the chapter, suggested Harvard Business School Case Studies that complement the chapter, suggested extra related readings, and answers to all of the end-of-chapter questions.

PowerPoint Presentations: Prepared by Richard PonArul of California State University, Chico
PowerPoint Slides of text art and lecture outlines for each chapter are provided on the companion web site and can be viewed or downloaded to a computer.

ACKNOWLEDGMENTS

Many individuals helped make the fourth edition of *The Economics of Strategy* possible. We are especially grateful to Judith Joseph of Wiley for the substantial work she did in coordinating the development of the book. We want to also thank Valerie A. Vargas of Wiley and Suzanne Ingrao of Ingrao Associates for so ably keeping the production of this book on track.

Many of the improvements in the fourth edition are the result of comments received by instructors who used the third edition. Thanks to our colleagues who so kindly pointed out the problem areas and suggested ways to improve them. Considerable gratitude also goes to Dean Emeritus Donald Jacobs and to (former) Associate Dean Mark Satterthwaite of the Kellogg School for giving us the opportunity to develop Kellogg's basic strategy course and for the enthusiasm and support they showed for us in writing the first and second editions of this book. We would also like to thank current Kellogg dean, Dipak Jain, for his support for us in writing this edition and for the enthusiasm he has shown in promoting the importance of this book among various members of the Kellogg community: students, alumni, and corporate partners.

We are also grateful for the comments we received from those who reviewed the book, including

* Gautam Gowrisankaran, Washington U

* Mark Funk, U of Arkansas at Little Rock

- Darren Filson, Claremont Graduate U

- Martin Robson, U of Durham, UK

- Kenneth Zapp, Metropolitan State U

- John Sellers, Lincoln Memorial U

We were pleased by the many substantive suggestions they offered for a book that has already been through three editions.

A number of Kellogg Masters of Managements students provided valuable assistance for specific parts of the book. They are individually acknowledged in footnotes that accompany their contributions. Finally, we want to thank all of the Kellogg students who have used previous editions of the book. They faithfully identified typographical and factual errors, while suggesting ideas for new examples. In these and many other ways, they left their mark on the third edition. The origin of this book lay in our desire to develop a challenging, principle-based strategy course for students at Kellogg. As was the case with previous editions, we are pleased to say that our students have had a significant impact on the final product.

David Besanko

David Dranove

Mark Shanley

Scott Schaefer

Evanston, Illinois

ENDNOTE

[1] A Google search of "the rules have changed" comes up with hundreds of business-related hits. We wonder how they can be rules if they are constantly changing.

Brief Contents

PART FOUR: INTERNAL ORGANIZATION

CONTENTS

INTRODUCTION: STRATEGY AND ECONOMICS

WHY STUDY STRATEGY? ◆ ◆ ◆ ◆ ◆

To answer this question, we first have to understand what strategy is. Consider how three leading contributors to the field define the concept of strategy:

> ... the determination of the basic long-term goals and objectives of an enterprise, and the adoption of courses of action and the allocation of resources necessary for carrying out these goals.—Alfred Chandler.[1]
>
> ... the pattern of objectives, purposes or goals, and the major policies and plans for achieving these goals, stated in such a way as to define what business the company is in or should be in and the kind of company it is or should be.—Kenneth Andrews.[2]
>
> ... what determines the framework of a firm's business activities and provides guidelines for coordinating activities so that the firm can cope with and influence the changing environment. Strategy articulates the firm's preferred environment and the type of organization it is striving to become.—Hiroyuki Itami.[3]

These definitions have much in common. Phrases such as "long-term goals" and "major policies" suggest that strategy has to do with the "big" decisions a business organization faces, the decisions that ultimately determine its success or failure. The emphasis on the "pattern of objectives" and "the framework of a firm's business" suggests that strategy is revealed in terms of consistent behavior, which in turn implies that strategy, once set, is not easy to reverse. Finally, the idea that strategy defines "what business the company is in or should be in" suggests that strategic decisions shape the firm's competitive persona, its collective understanding of how it is going to succeed within its competitive environment.

In short, strategy is fundamental to an organization's success, which is why the study of strategy can be both profitable and intellectually engaging. The objective of this book is to study and analyze strategy primarily (though not exclusively) from the perspective of economics. Our central theme is that much can be learned by uncovering durable economic principles that are applicable to many different strategic situations. This value shows up in two fundamental ways: one, by gaining a better understanding of how firms compete and organize themselves, and two, by developing a more secure foundation for making good strategic decisions.

♦ ♦ ♦ ♦ ♦ WHY ECONOMICS?

The study of strategy can be approached in many ways. It can be studied from the perspective of mathematical game theory by which one seeks to discover the logic of choice in situations that involve rivalry. Strategy can also be studied from the perspective of psychology, focusing on how the motivations and behaviors of individual decision makers shape the direction and performance of their organizations. Finally, strategy-related questions can be studied from an organizational perspective, political science, or even anthropology.

Much can be said for viewing strategy from the perspective of multiple disciplinary lenses. But depth of strategic knowledge is as important as breadth. Deep knowledge of a discipline permits the formulation of subtle and powerful hypotheses that generate rich strategies. An advantage of economics, and one reason for its widespread use for analyzing individual and institutional decision making, is that it requires the analyst to be explicit about the key elements of the process under consideration. Economic models must carefully identify each of the following:

- *Decision makers*. Who are the active players? Whose decisions are "fixed" in the situation at hand?

- *Goals*. What are the decision makers trying to accomplish? Are they profit maximizing, or do they have nonpecuniary interests?

- *Choices*. What actions are under consideration? What are the strategic variables? What is the time horizon over which decisions can be made?

- *Relationship between choices and outcomes*. What is the mechanism by which specific decisions translate into specific outcomes? Is the mechanism complicated by uncertainty regarding such factors as taste, technology, or the choices of other decision makers?

Although other social sciences often address the same questions, economic theory is distinctive, we think, in that the answers to these questions are nearly always explicitly obtained as part of the development of the theory. The advantage to this is that a clear link exists between the conclusions that can be drawn from the application of economic reasoning and the assumptions used to motivate the analysis. This leaves what Garth Saloner has called an "audit trail" that allows one to be able to distinguish between logically derived propositions and unsupported conjectures.[4] We will not provide the detailed audit trails that support our propositions, for this would require countless pages and advanced mathematics. But we will provide the intuition behind each of the propositions that we advance.

Economic modeling, by its very nature, abstracts from the situational complexity that individuals and firms face. Thus, the application of economic insights to specific situations often requires creativity and a deft touch. It also often requires explicit recognition of the constraints imposed on firms by mistakes, history, and organizational and political factors. Nor does economics fully address the *process* by which choices are made and translated into actions and outcomes. The process of managing the implementation of a competitive strategy decision or a change in the nature of internal organization is often fundamental to a firm's success. Our emphasis on economics in this book is not intended to downgrade the importance of process; it is simply beyond the scope of our expertise to say much about it.

THE NEED FOR PRINCIPLES ◆ ◆ ◆ ◆ ◆

Serious observers of business understandably have a keen interest in understanding the reasons for profitability and market success. They often leap uncritically to the conclusion that the keys to success can be identified by watching and imitating the behaviors of successful firms. A host of management prescriptions by consultants and in the popular business press is buttressed by allusions to the practices of high-performing firms and their managers.

A classic example of this type of analysis is provided by the famous 1982 book, *In Search of Excellence*, by Thomas Peters and Robert Waterman.[5] Peters and Waterman studied a group of 43 firms that were identified as long-term superior performers on dimensions such as profitability and growth. The study concluded that successful firms shared common qualities, including "close to the customer," "stick to the knitting," and "bias for action."

Another example is provided by Fred Wiersema in *The New Market Leaders*.[6] Wiersema identified the behaviors of leading firms in the "new economy," with a focus on Internet, technology, and telecom firms. The average annual return for investors in these firms was 48 percent. In explaining their success, Weirsema's findings mirror those of Peters and Waterman. New market leaders are close to their customers and skilled at segmenting markets. They develop new products, advertise intensively, and outsource core activities, so as to better concentrate on what they do best.

A final example is *Good to Great*, by Jim Collins.[7] Collins studied the characteristics of firms that broke a long pattern of good (above-average) performance and entered into a 15-year period of great performance (cumulative stock return three times that of the general market). Only 11 firms met this demanding hurdle, including such well-known firms as Walgreens, Wells Fargo, Philip Morris, and Abbott. Collins finds several characteristics that help explain his group's performance. These firms possess leaders who shun the spotlight and work for the firm. Performance shifts at these firms begin with management staffing, so that the "right" people are put in place. The firms use technology to support rather than determine their strategies. Managers at these firms can "confront the brutal facts" of their situation and decide what to do about it.

So What's the Problem?

All of these studies assess the past performance of successful firms. Using currently successful firms as a standard for action assumes that other firms can achieve similar successful results by mimicking their actions. We do not believe that firms succeed randomly, but we are convinced that using a given firm's experiences to understand what would make all firms successful is extremely difficult.

For one thing, the reasons for success are often unclear and are likely to be complex. We can think of no better example than Enron. As Example I.1 details, Enron

The rapid fall of Enron easily ranks as one of the most astonishing business stories of recent times. In August 2000, Enron stock hit its all-time-high price of $90.56, and the firm was praised by major business publications as one of the most admired and innovative in the nation. Any struggling manager could surely look to Enron for clues about how to turn a business around. Little more than a year later (January 2002), Enron, in Chapter 11 bankruptcy, ceased trading on the New York Stock Exchange at a share price of $0.67. The bankruptcy was the biggest in U.S. history (until WorldCom's 2002 bankruptcy). Thousands of Enron's employees lost their jobs and their retirement savings as the share price plummeted. Enron's auditor, Arthur Andersen, was indicted and convicted, effectively ending its history as a major accounting firm.

Enron was born in 1985, during the deregulation of natural gas pipelines, from the merger of Houston Natural Gas and Inter-North. The merger produced a large debt load for the new firm, which had lost exclusive rights to its pipelines during deregulation. It was this necessity that induced Enron to become more inventive in its strategies. Enron's CEO Kenneth Lay hired McKinsey and Company, which assigned Jeffrey Skilling, a consultant with banking and asset management experience, to assist Enron in developing new strategies. The resulting strategy, in which Enron assumed a trading role to make a market in natural gas, was the key to the firm's meteoric growth.

Enron's success with its "gas bank" strategy made Lay and Skilling powerful men in the firm. Skilling, who rose to be president and CEO, along with his young CFO Andrew Fastow, hired the best finance MBAs from major business schools, often in competition with Wall Street firms. Enron's finance group grew in size and prestige and began to mimic the culture and norms of Wall Street firms regarding credentials, hours worked,

performance standards, rewards, and risks. There were virtually no limits to bonuses in a corporate culture that allowed star traders to "eat what they could kill." Enron and its executives were also well connected politically, through widespread contributions to prominent elected officials. Other high-flying companies, including ill-fated Global Crossing and WorldCom, followed similar paths to success. Companies that did business another way were operating like firms in the "old economy" and would surely be left behind.

Skilling increasingly applied Enron's trading strategy to other commodity areas besides natural gas, such as electricity, coal, steel, and water. Enron's growth became linked to the Internet and telecommunications boom in 1999 and early 2000, with the formation of EnronOnline and the start of a major broadband venture. Enron's growth seemed to fit perfectly with the times. The high point of this expansion came in July 2000, with the announcement of a venture with Blockbuster to provide video-on-demand service over high-speed Internet connections.

As Enron expanded out of its more familiar businesses, its deals became riskier and its accounting became more complex. While fraud has not yet been proven, it is clear that accounting norms for such items as "special-purpose entities" were stretched beyond accepted limits. But even the most complicated accounting could not cover up the fact that intense competition in what were essentially commodity businesses, combined with massive investments in capital, was taking its toll on Enron's bottom line. Lay, Skilling, and Fastow could not alter the underlying economics of competition, no matter how widely they were admired or how wealthy they had become on paper. When some of the riskier deals began to go bad, confidence in the firm started to erode among analysts and institutional investors and the stock price began a steep decline. After announcing its first quarterly loss in four years and taking a $1 billion charge in October 2001, Enron's decline accelerated until the bankruptcy declaration in December. It was during this time that Security and Exchange Commission (SEC) investigations began, documents were shredded, and employee 401(k) holdings were locked up.

In the wake of the bankruptcy, the U.S. Justice Department and SEC opened nationwide investigations. The matter has been the subject of multiple congressional inquiries. Numerous civil lawsuits have been filed or are pending. Financial institutions that provided funding to Enron, including J.P. Morgan and Citigroup, have come under fire for their exposure. The conviction of Arthur Andersen for destroying Enron documents has forced many of its audit clients to reexamine their books and secure new auditors. Enron had built its empire on a house of cards. Managers and investors who ignored business principles in the belief that the rules of the "new economy" had changed did so at their own risk.

was once held up as an exemplar of how to conduct business in the New Economy but was ultimately revealed to be a company that relied on accounting shell games to appear profitable. Many other, less pernicious examples of this complexity can be cited. The internal management systems of a firm may spur product innovation particularly well and not be apparent to individuals unfamiliar with how the firm operates. In addition, the industry and market conditions in which successful firms operate may differ greatly from the conditions faced by would-be imitators. Success may also be due in part to a host of idiosyncratic factors that will be difficult to identify and impossible to imitate.

Finally, there may be a bias resulting from trying to understand success solely by examining the strategies of successful firms. Strategies associated with many successful firms may have been tried by an equally large number of unsuccessful firms. Successful firms may pursue several strategies, only some of which contribute to their success. Successful firms may possess proprietary assets and know-how that allow them to succeed where imitators would fail. A strategy of "monkey see, monkey do" is no guarantee of success.

To further understand the potential bias, consider that it is easy, after the fact, to say that successful firms put the right people in place or developed products that customers valued. The choices of successful firms always seem correct in hindsight, but managers cannot always determine which strategic choices will work in advance. Consider a firm investing in a risky new technology. If it gambles correctly, then the technology will appear to "support its strategy," a good thing according to the strategy gurus. If it gambles incorrectly, it may be optimal to stick with the technology, especially if the costs are sunk and cannot be recovered. In examining this firm, the gurus might conclude that it let technology determine its strategy. But the real mistake was in selecting the wrong technology to begin with, not its ongoing application.

Managers cannot wait until after the fact to determine what technologies to adopt, which employees to hire, or which customers to cultivate. This is what makes managerial work risky. We do believe that it is useful to study the behaviors of firms. The value of this study, however, lies in helping us identify the general principles explaining why firms behave as they do, not in trying to develop lists of characteristics that lead to automatic success. *There is no such list.* A strategy textbook can provide the general principles that underlie strategic decisions. Success depends on the manager who must match principles with conditions.

To see this point, consider the variety of practices that a serious observer of business faces today in attempting to identify success strategies. He or she would encounter a broad range of management practices among firms. Take, for example, three highly regarded and successful firms: Trek, Usiminas, and Wal-Mart.[8] Each of them has a different organizational structure and corporate strategy. Trek performs few of the functions traditionally associated with large industrial firms and instead uses independent contractors for much of its production, distribution, and retailing. Trek's success is built largely on low-cost outsourcing of bicycle production and careful brand management. Usiminas is a traditional, vertically integrated steel firm best known for its operational excellence in manufacturing. That excellence, coupled with its access to Brazil's low-cost labor and abundant energy supplies, has made Usiminas one of the lowest-cost producers of steel in the world. Unlike the first two, Wal-Mart is a distributor and retailer. It relies on the initiative of its local store managers, combined with sophisticated purchasing and inventory management, to keep its retailing costs below those of its rivals.

Making sense of this variety of strategies can be frustrating, especially because, within most industries, we see poorly performing firms employing the same strategies and management practices as industry exemplars. For every Trek, there is a Raleigh. For every Usiminas, there is a Bethlehem Steel. For every Wal-Mart, there is a Kmart. If we find this variety of management practices bewildering, imagine the reactions of a manager from 1910, or even 1960, who was transported ahead in time. The large hierarchical firm that dominated the corporate landscape until the 1970s seems out of place today. General Motors received its share of criticism in the wake of the oil shortages and the Japanese invasion of the 1970s, but its structure and strategy were models for manufacturing from the 1920s through the 1960s. United States Steel (now USX), the first firm in the world to achieve annual sales of one billion dollars at the time of its inception in 1901, has greatly declined in relative size and now must rely on selling oil to remain one of the 25 largest U.S. industrial firms. The list of once-admired firms that today are struggling to survive is a long one.

This bewildering variety and evolution of management practice can be interpreted in two ways. The first is to believe that the development of successful strategies is so complicated as to be essentially a matter of luck. The second interpretation presumes that successful firms succeeded because the strategies their managers chose best allowed them to exploit the potential profit opportunities that existed at the time or to adapt to changing circumstances. We believe in this second interpretation. Although luck, both good and bad, no doubt plays a role in determining the success of firms, we believe that success is often no accident. We believe that we can better understand why firms succeed or fail when we analyze decision making in terms of consistent principles of market economics and strategic action. And we believe that the odds of competitive success increase when managers try to apply these principles to the varying conditions and opportunities they face. Although these principles do not uniquely explain why firms succeed, they should be the basis for any systematic examination of strategy.

◆ ◆ ◆ ◆ ◆ A FRAMEWORK FOR STRATEGY

In our opening discussion of what strategy is, we asserted that strategy is concerned with the "big" issues that firms face. But what specifically does this mean? What are these "big" issues? Put another way, to formulate and implement a successful strategy, what does the firm have to pay attention to? We would argue that to successfully formulate and implement strategy, a firm must confront four broad classes of issues:

- *Boundaries of the firm.* What should the firm do, how large should it be, and what businesses should it be in?

- *Market and competitive analysis.* What is the nature of the markets in which the firm competes and the nature of competitive interactions among firms in those markets?

- *Position and dynamics.* How should the firm position itself to compete, what should be the basis of its competitive advantage, and how should it adjust over time?

- *Internal organization.* How should the firm organize its structure and systems internally?

Boundaries of the Firm

The firm's boundaries define what the firm does. Boundaries can extend in three different directions: horizontal, vertical, and corporate. The firm's horizontal boundaries refer to how much of the product market the firm serves, or essentially how big it is. The firm's vertical boundaries refer to the set of activities that the firm performs itself and those that it purchases from market specialty firms. The firm's corporate boundaries refer to the set of distinct businesses in which the firm competes. All three boundaries have received differing amounts of emphasis at different times in the strategy literature. The Boston Consulting Group's emphasis on the learning curve and market growth in the 1960s gave prominence to the firm's horizontal boundaries. Formal planning models organized around tools, such as growth-share matrices, gave prominence to the firm's corporate boundaries. More recently, such concepts as network organizations and the virtual corporation have given prominence to the firm's vertical boundaries. Our view is that all are important and can be fruitfully analyzed through the perspectives offered by economics

Market and Competitive Analysis

To formulate and execute successful strategies, firms must understand the nature of the markets in which they compete. As Michael Porter points out in his classic work *Competitive Strategy*, performance across industries is not a matter of chance or accident.[9] There are reasons why, for example, even mediocre firms in an industry such as pharmaceuticals have, by economy-wide standards, impressive profitability performance, while the top firms in the airline industry seem to achieve low rates of profitability even in the best of times. The nature of industry structure cannot be ignored either in attempting to understand why firms follow the strategies they do or in attempting to formulate strategies for competing in an industry.

Position and Dynamics

Position and dynamics are shorthand for how and on what basis a firm competes. Position is a static concept. At a given moment in time, is the firm competing on the basis of low costs or because it is differentiated in key dimensions and can thus charge a premium price? Position, as we discuss it, also concerns the resources and capabilities that underlie any cost or differentiation advantages that a firm might have. Dynamics refers to how the firm accumulates resources and capabilities, as well as to how it adjusts over time to changing circumstances. Fundamentally, dynamics has to do with the process emphasized by the economist Joseph Schumpeter, who argued that "the impulse of alluring profit," even though inherently temporary, will induce firms and entrepreneurs to create new bases of competitive advantage that redefine industries and undermine the ways of achieving advantage.

Internal Organization

Given that the firm has chosen what to do and has figured out the nature of its market, so that it can decide how and on what basis it should compete, it still needs to organize itself internally to carry out its strategies. Organization sets the terms by which resources will be deployed and information will flow through the firm. It will also determine how well aligned the goals of individual actors within the firm are with the overall goals of the firm. How the firm organizes itself—for example, how it structures its organization, the extent to which it relies on formal incentive systems as opposed to informal influences—embodies a key set of strategic decisions in their own right.

The remainder of this book is organized along the lines of this framework. Chapters 1 through 5 have to do with the firm's boundaries. Chapters 6 through 10 deal with industry structure and market analysis. Chapters 11 through 13 address position and dynamics. Chapters 14 through 18 deal with internal organization.

ENDNOTES

[1]Chandler, A., *Strategy and Structure: Chapters in the History of the American Industrial Enterprise*, Cambridge, MA, MIT Press, 1962, p. 13.

[2]Andrews, K., *The Concept of Corporate Strategy*, Homewood, IL, Irwin, 1971.

[3]Itami, H., *Mobilizing Invisible Assets*, Cambridge, MA, Harvard University Press, 1987.

[4]Saloner, G., "Modeling, Game Theory, and Strategic Management," *Strategic Management Journal*, 12, Winter 1991, pp. 119–136.

[5]Peters, T. J. and R. H. Waterman, *In Search of Excellence*, New York, Harper and Row, 1982.

[6]Wiersema, F., *The New Market Leaders*, New York, Free Press, 2001.

[7]Collins, J. C., *Good to Great*, New York, Harper Business, 2001.

[8]The full name of Usiminas is Usinas Siderurgicas de Minas Gerais.

[9]Porter, M., *Competitive Strategy*, New York, Free Press, 1980.

Primer: Economic Concepts for Strategy

*I*n 1931 conditions at the Pepsi-Cola Company were desperate.[1] The company had entered bankruptcy for the second time in 12 years and, in the words of a Delaware court, was "a mere shell of a corporation." The president of Pepsi, Charles G. Guth, even attempted to sell Pepsi to its rival Coca-Cola, but Coke wanted no part of a seemingly doomed enterprise. During this period, Pepsi and Coke sold cola in 6-ounce bottles. To reduce costs, Guth purchased a large supply of recycled 12-ounce beer bottles. Initially, Pepsi priced the 12-ounce bottles at 10 cents, twice the price of 6-ounce Cokes. However, this strategy failed to boost sales. But, then, Guth had an idea: Why not sell 12-ounce Pepsis for the same price as 6-ounce Cokes? In the Depression, this was a brilliant marketing ploy. Pepsi's sales shot upward. By 1934 Pepsi was out of bankruptcy. Its profit rose to $2.1 million by 1936, and to $4.2 million by 1938. Guth's decision to undercut Coca-Cola saved the company.

This example illustrates an important point. Clearly, in 1931 Pepsi's chief objective was to increase profits so it could survive. But merely deciding to pursue this objective could not make it happen. Charles Guth could not just order his subordinates to increase Pepsi's profits. Like any company, Pepsi's management had no direct control over its profit, market share, or any of the other markers of business success. What Pepsi's management did control were marketing, production, and the administrative decisions that determined its competitive position and ultimate profitability.

The link between the decisions managers control and a firm's profitability is mediated by a host of economic relationships. The success of any strategy depends on whether the firm's decisions are compatible with these relationships. Pepsi's success in the 1930s can be understood in terms of a few key economic relationships. The most basic of these is the law of demand. The law of demand says that, all other things being the same, the lower the price of a product, the more of it consumers will purchase. Whether the increase in the number of units sold translates into higher sales revenues depends on the strength of the relationship between price and the quantity purchased. This is measured by the price elasticity of demand. As long as Coke did not respond to Pepsi's price cut with one of its own, we would expect that the demand for Pepsi would have been relatively sensitive to price, or in the language of economics, price elastic. As we will see later in this chapter, price-elastic demand implies that a price cut translates not only into higher unit sales, but also into higher sales revenue. Whether Coke is better off responding to Pepsi's price cut depends on another relationship, that between the size of a competitor and the profitability of price matching. Because Coke had such a large share of the market, it was more profitable to keep its price high (letting Pepsi steal some of its market) than to respond with a price cut of its own.[2] Finally, whether Pepsi's higher sales revenue translates into higher profit depends on the economic relationship between the additional sales revenue that Pepsi's price cut generated and the additional cost of producing more Pepsi-Cola. That profits rose rapidly after the price reduction suggests that the additional sales revenue far exceeded the additional costs of production.

The importance of economic relationships for strategy is a central theme of this book. Most of the important contributions to the literature on strategy in the past 25 years, such as Michael Porter's "Five Forces" framework or C. K. Prahalad and Gary Hamel's concept of "core competencies," are based on well-developed ideas from economics. As we argue throughout this book, understanding robust economic relationships can help us understand why some strategies are well suited to one set of conditions but not to others. The judicious application of economic principles to a firm's circumstances can increase the odds of formulating and executing a successful business strategy.

This chapter lays out the basic economic tools that we will use to develop the principles you will study in this book. We focus here on those parts of intermediate microeconomics that are relevant for understanding business strategy. Most of the elements that contributed to Pepsi's successful price-cutting strategy in the 1930s will be on display here. An understanding of the language and concepts in this chapter will, we believe, "level the playing field," so that students with little or no background in microeconomics can navigate most of this book just as well as students with extensive economics training.

This chapter has five main parts: (1) costs; (2) demand, prices, and revenues; (3) the theory of price and output determination by a profit-maximizing firm; (4) the theory of perfectly competitive markets; and (5) game theory.[3]

◆ ◆ ◆ ◆ ◆ Costs

A firm's profit equals its revenues minus its costs. We begin our economics primer by focusing on the cost side of this equation. We discuss four specific concepts in this section: cost functions; economic versus accounting costs; long-run versus short-run costs; and sunk costs.

Cost Functions

Total Cost Functions

Managers are most familiar with costs when they are presented as in Tables P.1 and P.2, which show, respectively, an income statement and a statement of costs of goods manufactured for a hypothetical producer during the year 2008.[4] The information in

TABLE P.1
INCOME STATEMENT: 2008

(1) Sales Revenue		$35,600
(2) Cost of Goods Sold		
Cost of Goods Manufactured	$13,740	
Add: Finished Goods Inventory 12/31/07	$3,300	
Less: Finished Goods Inventory 12/31/08	$2,950	
		$14,090
(3) Gross Profit: (1) minus (2)		$21,510
(4) Selling and General Administrative Expenses		$8,540
(5) Income from Operations: (3) minus (4)		$12,970
Interest Expenses		$1,210
Net Income Before Taxes		$11,760
Income Taxes		$4,100
Net Income		$7,660

All amounts in thousands.

these tables is essentially retrospective. It tells managers what happened during the past year. But what if management is interested in determining whether a price reduction will increase profits, as with Pepsi? The price drop will probably stimulate additional sales, so a firm needs to know how its total costs would change if it increased production above the previous year's level.

This is what a total cost function tells us. It represents the relationship between a firm's total costs, denoted by TC, and the total amount of output it produces in a given time period, denoted by Q. Figure P.1 shows a graph of a total cost function. For each level of output the firm might produce, the graph associates a unique level of

TABLE P.2
STATEMENT OF COST OF GOODS MANUFACTURED: 2008

Materials:		
Materials Purchases	$8,700	
Add: Materials Inventory 12/31/07	$1,400	
Less: Materials Inventory 12/31/08	$1,200	
(1) Cost of Materials		$8,900
(2) Direct Labor		$2,300
Manufacturing Overhead		
Indirect Labor	$700	
Heat, Light, and Power	$400	
Repairs and Maintenance	$200	
Depreciation	$1,100	
Insurance	$50	
Property Taxes	$80	
Miscellaneous Factory Expenses	$140	
(3) Total Manufacturing Overhead		$2,670
Total Cost of Manufacturing: (1) + (2) + (3)		$13,870
Add: Work-in-Process Inventory 12/31/07		$2,100
Less: Work-in-Process Inventory 12/31/08		$2,230
Cost of Goods Manufactured		$13,740

All amounts in thousands.

FIGURE P.1
TOTAL COST FUNCTION

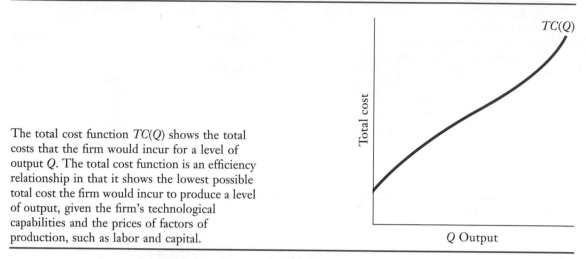

The total cost function $TC(Q)$ shows the total costs that the firm would incur for a level of output Q. The total cost function is an efficiency relationship in that it shows the lowest possible total cost the firm would incur to produce a level of output, given the firm's technological capabilities and the prices of factors of production, such as labor and capital.

total cost. Why is the association between output and total cost unique? A firm may currently be producing 100 units of output per year at a total cost of $5,000,000, but if it were to streamline its operations, it might be able to lower costs, so that those 100 units could be produced for only $4,500,000. We resolve this ambiguity by defining the total cost function as an efficiency relationship. It represents the relationship between total cost and output, assuming that the firm produces in the most efficient manner possible given its current technological capabilities. Of course, firms do not always produce as efficiently as they theoretically could. The substantial literature on total quality management and reengineering attests to the attention managers give to improving efficiency. This is why we stress that the total cost function reflects the current capabilities of the firm. If the firm is producing as efficiently as it knows how, then the total cost function must slope upward: The only way to achieve more output is to use more factors of production (labor, machinery, materials), which will raise total costs.[5]

Fixed and Variable Costs

The information contained in the accounting statements in Tables P.1 and P.2 allows us to identify the total cost for one particular level of annual output. To map out the total cost function more completely, we must distinguish between fixed costs and variable costs. Variable costs, such as direct labor and commissions to salespeople, increase as output increases. Fixed costs, such as general and administrative expenses and property taxes, remain constant as output increases.

Three important points should be stressed when discussing fixed and variable costs. First, the line dividing fixed and variable costs is often fuzzy. Some costs, such as maintenance or advertising and promotional expenses, may have both fixed and variable components. Other costs may be *semifixed*: fixed over certain ranges of output but variable over other ranges.[6] For example, a beer distributor may be able to deliver up to 5,000 barrels of beer a week using a single truck. But when it must deliver between 5,000 and 10,000 barrels, it needs two trucks, between 10,000 and 15,000, three trucks, and so forth. The cost of trucks is fixed within the intervals (0, 5,000), (5,000, 10,000), (10,000, 15,000), and so forth, but is variable between these intervals. Second, when we say that a cost is fixed, we mean that it is invariant to the firm's output. It does not mean that it cannot be affected by other dimensions of the firm's operations or decisions the firm might make. For example, for an electric utility, the cost of stringing wires to hook up houses to the local grid depends primarily on the number of subscribers to the system, and not on the total amount of kilowatt-hours of electricity the utility generates. Other fixed costs, such as the money spent on marketing promotions or advertising campaigns, arise from management decisions and can be eliminated should management so desire.[7] Third, whether costs are fixed or variable depends on the time period in which decisions regarding output are contemplated. Consider, for example, an airline that is contemplating a one-week-long fare cut. Its workers have already been hired, its schedule has been set, and its fleet has been purchased. Within a one-week period, none of these decisions can be reversed. For this particular decision, then, the airline should regard a significant fraction of its costs as fixed. By contrast, if the airline contemplates committing to a year-long reduction in fares, with the expectation that ticket sales will increase accordingly, schedules can be altered, planes can be leased or purchased, and workers can be hired. In this case, the airline should regard most of its expenses as variable. Whether the firm has the freedom to alter its physical capital or other elements of its operations has important implications for its cost structure and the nature of its decision making. This will be covered in more detail below when we analyze the distinction between long-run and short-run costs.

Average and Marginal Cost Functions

Associated with the total cost function are two other cost functions: the average cost function, $AC(Q)$, and the marginal cost function, $MC(Q)$. The average cost function describes how the firm's average or per-unit-of-output costs vary with the amount of output it produces. It is given by the formula

$$AC(Q) = \frac{TC(Q)}{Q}$$

If total costs were directly proportional to output—for example, if they were given by a formula, such as $TC(Q) = 5Q$ or $TC(Q) = 37,000Q$, or more generally, by $TC(Q) = cQ$, where c is a constant—then average cost would be a constant. This is because

$$AC(Q) = \frac{cQ}{Q} = c$$

Often, however, average cost will vary with output. As Figure P.2 shows, average cost may rise, fall, or remain constant as output goes up. When average cost decreases as output increases, there are economies of scale. When average cost increases as output increases, there are diseconomies of scale. When average cost remains unchanged with respect to output, we have constant returns to scale. A production process may exhibit economies of scale over one range of output and diseconomies of scale over another. Figure P.3 shows an average cost function that exhibits economies of scale, diseconomies of scale, and constant returns to scale. Output level Q' is the smallest level of output at which economies of scale are exhausted and is thus known as the minimum efficient scale. The concepts of economies of scale and

FIGURE P.2
AVERAGE COST FUNCTION

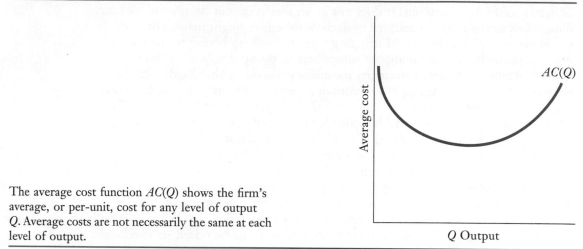

The average cost function $AC(Q)$ shows the firm's average, or per-unit, cost for any level of output Q. Average costs are not necessarily the same at each level of output.

minimum efficient scale are extremely important for understanding the size and scope of firms and the structure of industries. We devote all of Chapter 2 to analyzing economies of scale.

Marginal cost refers to the rate of change of total cost with respect to output. Marginal cost may be thought of as the incremental cost of producing exactly one more unit of output. When output is initially Q and changes by ΔQ units and one knows the total cost at each output level, marginal cost may be calculated as follows:

$$MC(Q) = \frac{TC(Q + \Delta Q) - TC(Q)}{\Delta Q}$$

For example, suppose when $Q = 100$ units, $TC = \$400,000$, and when $Q = 150$ units, $TC = \$500,000$. Then $\Delta Q = 50$, and $MC = (\$500,000 - \$400,000)/50 = \$2,000$.

FIGURE P.3
ECONOMIES OF SCALE AND MINIMUM EFFICIENT SCALE

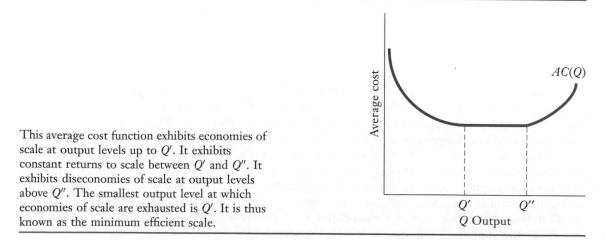

This average cost function exhibits economies of scale at output levels up to Q'. It exhibits constant returns to scale between Q' and Q''. It exhibits diseconomies of scale at output levels above Q''. The smallest output level at which economies of scale are exhausted is Q'. It is thus known as the minimum efficient scale.

Thus, total cost increases at a rate of $2,000 per unit of output when output increases over the range 100 to 150 units.

Marginal cost often depends on the total volume of output. Figure P.4 shows the marginal cost function associated with a particular total cost function. At low levels of output, such as Q'', increasing output by one unit does not change total cost much, as reflected by the low marginal cost. At higher levels of output, such as Q', a one-unit increase in output has a greater impact on total cost, and the corresponding marginal cost is higher.

Businesses often use information about average cost to estimate the marginal cost of a change in output. But average cost is generally different from marginal cost. The exception is when total costs vary in direct proportion to output, $TC(Q) = cQ$. In that case,

$$MC(Q) = \frac{c(Q + \Delta Q) - cQ}{\Delta Q} = c$$

which, of course, is also average cost. This result reflects a more general relationship between marginal and average cost (illustrated in Figure P.5):

- When average cost is a decreasing function of output, marginal cost is less than average cost.

- When average cost neither increases nor decreases in output—because it is either constant (independent of output) or at a minimum point—marginal cost is equal to average cost.

- When average cost is an increasing function of output, marginal cost is greater than average cost.

FIGURE P.4
RELATIONSHIP BETWEEN TOTAL COST AND MARGINAL COST

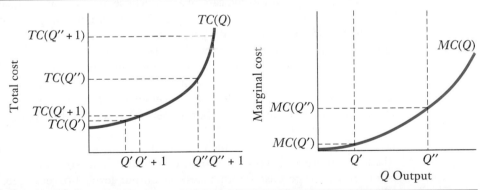

The marginal cost function $MC(Q)$ on the right graph is based on the total cost function $TC(Q)$ shown in the left graph. At output level Q', a one-unit increase in output changes costs by $TC(Q' + 1) - TC(Q')$, which equals the marginal cost at Q', $MC(Q')$. Since this change is not large, the marginal cost is small (i.e., the height of the marginal cost curve from the horizontal axis is small). At output level Q'', a one-unit increase in output changes costs by $TC(Q'' + 1) - TC(Q'')$, which equals the marginal cost at Q''. This change is larger than the one-unit change from Q', so $MC(Q'') > MC(Q')$. Because the total cost function becomes steeper as Q gets larger, the marginal cost curve must increase in output.

When average cost is decreasing (e.g., at output Q'), $AC > MC$ (i.e., the average cost curve lies above the marginal cost curve). When average cost is increasing (e.g., at output Q''), $AC < MC$ (i.e., the average cost curve lies below the marginal cost curve). When average cost is at a minimum, $AC = MC$, so the two curves must intersect.

These relationships follow from the mathematical properties of average and marginal cost, but they are also intuitive. If the average of a group of things (costs, test scores, or whatever) increases when one more thing is added to the group, then it must be because the value of the most recently added thing—the "marginal"—is greater than the average. Conversely, if the average falls, it must be because the marginal is less than the average.

The Importance of the Time Period: Long-Run versus Short-Run Cost Functions

We emphasized the importance of the time horizon when discussing fixed versus variable costs. In this section, we develop this point further and consider some of its implications.

Figure P.6 illustrates the case of a firm whose production can take place in a facility that comes in three different sizes: small, medium, and large. Once the firm commits to a production facility of a particular size, it can vary output only by varying the quantities of inputs other than the plant size (e.g., by hiring another shift of workers). The period of time in which the firm cannot adjust the size of its production facilities is known as the short run. For each plant size, there is an associated short-run average cost function, denoted by SAC. These average cost functions include the annual costs of all relevant variable inputs (labor, materials) as well as the fixed cost (appropriately annualized) of the plant itself.

If the firm knows how much output it plans to produce before building a plant, then to minimize its costs, it should choose the plant size that results in the lowest short-run average cost for that desired output level. For example, for output Q_1, the optimal plant is a small one; for output Q_2, the optimal plant is a medium one; for output Q_3, the optimal plant is a large one. Figure P.6 illustrates that for larger outputs, the larger plant is best; for medium-output levels, the medium plant is best; and for small-output levels, the small plant is best. For example, when output is Q_1, the reduction in average cost that results from switching from a large plant to a small plant is $SAC_L(Q_1) - SAC_S(Q_1)$. This saving not only arises from reductions in the fixed costs of the plant, but also because the firm can more efficiently tailor the

FIGURE P.6
SHORT-RUN AND LONG-RUN AVERAGE COST FUNCTIONS

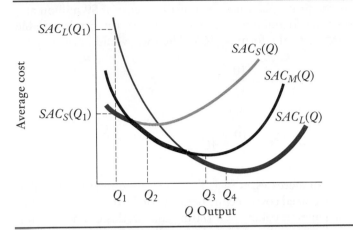

The curves labeled $SAC_S(Q)$, $SAC_M(Q)$, and $SAC_L(Q)$ are the short-run average cost functions associated with small, medium, and large plants, respectively. For any level of output, the optimal plant size is the one with the lowest average cost. For example, at output Q_1, the small plant is best. At output Q_2, the medium plant is best. At output Q_3, the large plant is best. The long-run average cost function is the "lower envelope" of the short-run average cost functions, represented by the bold line. This curve shows the lowest attainable average cost for any output when the firm is free to adjust its plant size optimally.

rest of its operations to its plant size. When the firm produces Q_1 in the large plant, it may need to utilize more labor to assure steady materials flows within the large facility. The small plant may allow flows to be streamlined, making such labor unnecessary.

The long-run average cost function is the lower envelope of the short-run average cost functions and is depicted by the bold line in Figure P.6. It shows the lowest attainable average cost for any particular level of output when the firm can adjust its plant size optimally. This is the average cost function the firm faces before it has committed to a particular plant size.

In this example, the long-run average cost function exhibits economies of scale. By operating with larger plant sizes, the firm can lower its average costs. This raises a deceptively simple but extremely significant point. To realize the lower average costs, the firm must not only build a large plant but must also achieve sufficient output, so that the large plant is indeed the optimal one. It would be disastrous for the firm to build a large plant if it only achieved an output of, say, Q_1. The firm would be saddled with an expensive underutilized facility. If we were to observe a firm in this situation, we might be tempted to conclude that the scale economies inherent in the production process were limited or nonexistent. This would be incorrect. Scale economies exist, but the firm is not selling enough output needed to exploit them.

It is often useful to express short-run average costs as the sum of average fixed costs (AFC) and average variable costs (AVC):

$$SAC(Q) = AFC(Q) + AVC(Q)$$

Average fixed costs are the firm's fixed costs (i.e., the annualized cost of the firm's plant plus expenses, such as insurance and property taxes, that do not vary with the volume of output) expressed on a per-unit-of-output basis. Average variable costs are the firm's variable costs (e.g., labor and materials) expressed on a per-unit-of-output basis. For example, suppose the firm's plant has an annualized cost of $9 million and other annual fixed expenses total $1 million. Moreover, suppose the firm's variable costs vary with output according to the formula $4Q^2$. Then we would have

$$AFC(Q) = \frac{10}{Q}$$

$$AVC(Q) = 4Q$$

$$SAC(Q) = \frac{10}{Q} + 4Q$$

Note that as the volume of output increases, average fixed costs become smaller, which tends to pull down SAC. Average fixed costs decline because total fixed costs are being spread over an ever-larger production volume. Offsetting this (in this example) is the fact that average variable costs rise with output, which pulls SAC upward. The net effect of these offsetting forces creates the U-shaped SAC curves in Figure P.6.

Sunk versus Avoidable Costs

When assessing the costs of a decision, the manager should consider only those costs that the decision actually affects. Some costs must be incurred no matter what the decision is and thus cannot be avoided. These are called *sunk costs*. The opposite of sunk costs is *avoidable costs*. These costs can be avoided if certain choices are made. When weighing the costs of a decision, the decision maker should ignore sunk costs and consider only avoidable costs.

To illustrate the concept of sunk costs, take the case of a mail-order merchandiser of laser printers. The merchandiser traditionally purchased large quantities of printers from the manufacturer, so that it could satisfy rush orders. Increasingly, though, the merchandiser was carrying high inventories, including some lines that the manufacturer no longer produced and would not repurchase. A natural response to this problem would be to put the discontinued lines on sale and reduce inventory. However, the firm's managers were reluctant to do this. They felt that even in the best of times the margins on their products barely covered their overhead, and by cutting the price, they would be unable to cover their cost of the goods they sold.

This argument is wrong. The cost incurred to purchase the laser printers is a sunk cost as far as pricing is concerned. Whether or not the merchandiser cuts price, it cannot avoid these costs. If it believes that a seller should never price below average cost, the merchandiser will end up with large losses. Instead, it should accept that it cannot undo past decisions (and their associated sunk costs) and strive to minimize its losses.

It is important to emphasize that whether a cost is sunk depends on the decision being made and the options at hand. In the example just given, the cost of the discontinued lines of printers is a sunk cost with respect to the pricing decision today. But before the printers were ordered, their cost would not have been sunk. By not ordering them, the merchandiser would have avoided the purchase and storage costs.

Students often confuse sunk costs with fixed costs. The two concepts are not the same. In particular, some fixed costs need not be sunk. For example, a railroad serving Chicago to Cleveland needs a locomotive and a crew whether it hauls 1 carload of freight or 20. The cost of the locomotive is thus a fixed cost. However, it is not necessarily sunk. If the railroad abandons its Chicago-to-Cleveland line, it can sell the locomotive to another railroad, or redeploy it to another route.

Sunk costs are important for the study of strategy, particularly in analyzing rivalry among firms, entry and exit decisions from markets, and decisions to adopt new technologies. For example, the concept of sunk costs helps explain why an established American steel firm would be unwilling to invest in a new technology, such as continuous casting, while a new Japanese firm building a "greenfield" facility from scratch would adopt the new technology. The new technology has higher fixed costs, but lower variable operating costs. For the established American firm, the fixed cost of its old technology is sunk. This firm will adopt the new technology only if the savings in operating costs exceed the fixed cost of the new technology. Starting from scratch, the Japanese firm can avoid the fixed cost of the old technology by adopting the new technology. Thus, this firm will adopt the new technology if the savings in operating costs exceed the *difference* between the fixed costs of the new and old technologies. The American firm thus requires a larger cost savings than the Japanese firm to induce it to adopt the new technology. We will return to the concept of sunk costs in our discussions of commitment in Chapter 7, entry and exit in Chapter 9, sustainable advantage in Chapter 12, and innovation in Chapter 13.

ECONOMIC COSTS AND PROFITABILITY ◆ ◆ ◆ ◆ ◆

Economic versus Accounting Costs

The costs in Tables P.1 and P.2 reflect the accountant's concept of costs. This concept is grounded in the principles of accrual accounting, which emphasize historical costs. Accounting statements—in particular, income statements and balance sheets— are designed to serve an audience outside the firm—for example, lenders and equity investors. The accounting numbers must thus be objective and verifiable, principles that are well served by historical costs.

However, the costs that appear in accounting statements are not necessarily appropriate for decision making inside a firm. Business decisions require the measurement of economic costs, which are based on the concept of opportunity cost. This concept says that the economic cost of deploying resources in a particular activity is the value of the best foregone alternative use of those resources. Economic cost may not correspond to the historical costs represented in Tables P.1 and P.2. Suppose, for example, that the firm purchased its raw materials at a price below their current market price. Would the costs of goods manufactured in Table P.2 represent the economic cost to the firm of using these resources? The answer is no. When the firm uses them to produce finished goods, it forsakes the alternative of reselling the materials at the market price. The economic cost of the firm's production activities reflects this foregone opportunity.

At a broader level, consider the resources (plant, equipment, land, etc.) that have been purchased with funds that stockholders provide to the firm. To attract these funds, the firm must offer the stockholders a return on their investment that is at least as large as the return that they could have received from investing in activities of comparable risk. To illustrate, suppose that at the beginning of 2009, a firm's assets could have been liquidated for $100 million. By tying their funds up in the firm, investors lose the opportunity to invest the $100 million in an activity providing an 8 percent return. Moreover, suppose because of wear and tear and creeping obsolescence of plant and equipment, the value of the assets declines by 1 percent over the year 2009. The annualized cost of the firm's assets for 2009 is then $(0.08 + 0.01) \times \$100$ million $= \$9$ million per year. This is an economic cost, but it would not appear in the firm's income statement.

In studying strategy, we are interested in analyzing why firms make their decisions and what distinguishes good decisions from poor ones, given the opportunities and the constraints firms face. In our formal theories of firm behavior, we thus emphasize economic costs rather than historical accounting costs. This is not to say that accounting costs have no place in the study of business strategy. Quite the contrary: In assessing the past performance of the firm, in comparing one firm in an industry to another, or in evaluating the financial strength of a firm, the informed use of accounting statements and accounting ratio analysis can be illuminating. However, the concept of opportunity cost provides the best basis for good economic decisions when the firm must choose among competing alternatives. A firm that consistently deviated from this idea of cost would miss opportunities for earning higher profits. In the end, it might be driven out of business by firms that are better at seizing profit-enhancing opportunities, or it may find itself starved for capital as investors bid down its stock price Whenever we depict a cost function or discuss cost throughout this book, we have in mind the idea of costs as including all relevant opportunity costs.

Economic Profit versus Accounting Profit

Having distinguished between economic cost and accounting cost, we can now distinguish between economic profit and accounting profit:

- Accounting Profit = Sales Revenue − Accounting Cost.
- Economic Profit = Sales Revenue − Economic Cost
  = Accounting Profit − (Economic Cost − Accounting Cost).

To illustrate the distinction between the two concepts, consider a small software development firm that is owner operated. In 2008, the firm earned revenue of $1,000,000 and incurred expenses on supplies and hired labor of $850,000. The owner's best outside employment opportunity would be to earn a salary of $200,000 working for Microsoft. The software firm's accounting profit is $1,000,000 − $850,000 = $150,000. The software firm's economic profit deducts the opportunity cost of the owner's labor services and is thus $1,000,000 − $850,000 − $200,000 = −$50,000. This means that the owner made $50,000 less in income by operating this business than she could have made in her best outside alternative. The software business "destroyed" $50,000 of the owner's wealth in that, by operating the software business, she earned $50,000 less income than she might have otherwise.

As discussed earlier, an important cost excluded from a firm's accounting costs is the opportunity cost of its capital assets, such as its plant and equipment. When a firm's accounting earnings do not cover this opportunity cost, the firm will earn a positive accounting profit but a negative economic profit. For example, in 2002 McDonald's had positive accounting income of more than $2 billion, but it had a negative economic profit of $124 million.[8] (Table P.3 shows McDonald's economic profit, and that for other selected food and beverage chains, between 1997 and 2004.) What does this negative $124 million mean? Just as with the owner of our software firm, a negative

TABLE P.3

ECONOMIC PROFIT FOR SELECTED U.S. FOOD AND BEVERAGE CHAINS, 1997–2004 ($ MILLIONS)

Company	2004	2003	2002	2001	2000	1999	1998	1997
McDonald's	551	172	−124	30	240	407	452	250
Starbucks	151	71	30	19	10	−8	−4	−1
Outback Steakhouse	68	90	113	90	104	96	73	61
Brinker Int'l	58	47	47	44	31	22	3	−16
Wendy's	15	31	36	17	10	−1	−22	7
Jack In The Box	7	6	23	22	26	39	18	−1
Cheesecake Factory	12	10	11	7	4	2	−3	−3
Applebee	48	48	36	35	32	25	27	16

Source: Stern Stewart Performance 1000.

accounting profit indicates that McDonald's assets, when liquidated and deployed elsewhere, would have earned $124 million more in income for its owners than McDonald's earned in 2002. In this sense, in 2002 McDonald's "destroyed" $124 million of its owners' wealth because its owners could have earned $124 million more that year by deploying the funds they had invested in McDonald's in their best alternative use. Not all firms, of course, make a negative economic profit. In 2004, Starbucks earned an accounting profit of slightly over $390 million and a positive economic profit of $151 million. This positive economic profit means that Starbucks created $151 million more in income for its owners than its sources would have created for themselves if they liquidated Starbucks's assets and invested them in their best alternative use. In this sense, in 1999 Starbucks "created" an additional $151 million in wealth for its owners that they could not have gotten elsewhere.

Economic Profit and Net Present Value

Economic profit is closely related to the concept of net present value from finance. We will use an example to illustrate net present value and the relationship between it and economic profit.

Consider a firm that contemplates constructing a plant with capacity to produce 100,000 units per year. The firm's production expenses when it produces at capacity are $5 per unit of output. The cost of building the plant is $15 million. To make the example as simple as possible, assume that the plant has an infinitely long life (i.e., it does not depreciate). Suppose, finally, that the firm's cost of capital is 10 percent. This rate reflects what the firm's investors could make from alternative investments and thus reflects the appropriate opportunity cost for evaluating the investment in the plant.

Now suppose that the market price is currently $25 per unit and is expected to remain at that level for the foreseeable future. Should the firm build the plant? We can look at this decision in two seemingly different, but (as it turns out) equivalent, ways. First, we could calculate an annual economic profit in the way we just discussed. Total revenues would be $2.5 million per year. Total production costs that would show up on the firm's accounting statements would be $500,000 per year. The annualized opportunity cost of the plant would be the 10 percent cost of funds times the investment of $15 million, or $1.5 million per year. Economic profit would thus be $2.5 - 0.5 - 1.5 = \$0.5$ million per year. Since the investment in the plant is expected to yield a positive economic profit year after year, the firm should build it. Put another way, by investing in the plant, the firm delivers to its owners $500,000 per year above and beyond what they could earn from their best alternative investment.

The second way to analyze this decision is to use net present value analysis. To explain this approach, we must first introduce the concept of present value. The present value of a cash flow C received in t years at an interest rate i is equal to the amount of money that must be invested today at the interest rate i, so that in t years the principal plus interest equals C.[9] Mathematically, present value would be given by

$$PV = \frac{C}{(1+i)^t}$$

The present value of a stream of cash flows received over a period of years is the sum of the present value of the individual sums. Thus, the present value of cash flows C_1, $C_2, \ldots C_T$ received one year from now, two years from now, $\ldots$, T years from now, is

$$PV = \frac{C_1}{(1+i)} + \frac{C_2}{(1+i)^2} + \cdots + \frac{C_T}{(1+i)^T}$$

which can be written more compactly as

$$\sum_{t=1}^{T} \frac{C_t}{(1+i)^t}$$

The net present value (*NPV*) of an investment is simply the present value of the cash flows the investment generates minus the cost of the investment.

Given the assumptions that the investment has an infinite life and that the price and revenues are expected to remain the same over the foreseeable future, the *NPV* of the investment in the plant is given by

$$NPV = \sum_{t=1}^{\infty} \frac{2,000,000}{(1.10)^t} - \$15,000,000$$

This looks intimidating, but fortunately the term in the summation is the present value of a perpetuity. A perpetuity is a level cash flow C received each year forever. The present value of a perpetuity has a convenient formula: It is equal to the cash flow divided by the interest rate, C/i. With this formula, we can rewrite *NPV* as

$$NPV = \frac{2,000,000}{0.10} - 15,000,000 = 5,000,000$$

Since the net present value is positive, the firm should undertake the investment.

Note that the calculations of *NPV* and economic profit are similar. Indeed, with a constant annual cash flow and an infinitely lived investment, economic profit is simply equal to the *NPV* times the cost of capital, or put another way, *NPV* is equal to the present value of economic profit generated by the investment over its (infinite) lifetime. When cash flows are not constant and/or when the investment has a finite life, these relationships between *NPV* and economic profit are more complicated to illustrate, but they still hold. In particular, it can be shown that the collective *NPV* of the firm's investments is equal to the present value of the economic profit those investments generate over their useful lives. Given this, economic profit can be thought of as an annualized *NPV* calculation. The concept of zero economic profit thus begins to make more sense. It does not mean that the firm's net cash flows are zero. Instead it means that the present value of these cash flows just covers the cost of the firm's investments, or equivalently, the net present value of the firm's investments is zero.

DEMAND AND REVENUES   ◆ ◆ ◆ ◆ ◆

The second component of profit is sales revenue, which is intimately related to the firm's pricing decision. To understand how a firm's sales revenue depends on its pricing decision, we will explore the concept of a demand curve and the price elasticity of demand.

Demand Curve

The demand function describes the relationship between the quantity of product that the firm is able to sell and all the variables that influence that quantity. These variables include the price of the product, the prices of related products, the incomes and tastes of consumers, the quality of the product, advertising, product promotion, and many other variables commonly thought to make up the firm's marketing mix. With so many variables, it would be difficult to depict the demand function on a graph.

Of special interest is the relationship between quantity and price. To focus on this important relationship, imagine that all the other variables that influence the quantity demanded remain fixed, and consider how the quantity demanded would change as the price changes. We can show this simple relationship on a graph. Figure P.7 depicts a demand curve. We would expect the demand curve to be downward sloping: the lower the price, the greater the quantity demanded; the higher the price, the smaller the quantity demanded. This inverse relationship is called the *law of demand*.

The law of demand may not hold if high prices confer prestige or enhance a product's image. If a seller of fine Scotch or crystal lowered its price, it might diminish its prestige value, and thus sell less rather than more. A related phenomenon would occur when consumers cannot objectively assess the potential performance of a product and use price to infer quality. A lower price might signal low quality, reducing rather than increasing sales. Both prestige and signaling effects could result in demand curves that slope upward for some range of prices. Even so, personal experience and countless studies from economics and marketing confirm that the law of demand applies to most products.

As Figure P.7 shows, the demand curve is typically drawn with price on the vertical axis and quantity on the horizontal axis. This may seem strange because we think that price determines the quantity demanded, not the other way around. However, this representation emphasizes a useful alternative interpretation for a demand

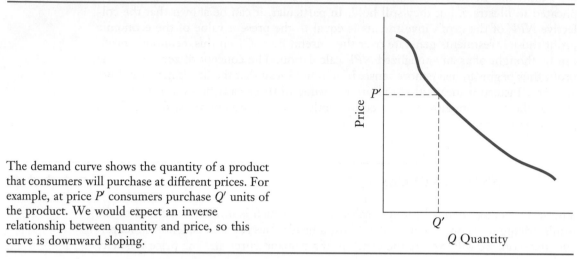

The demand curve shows the quantity of a product that consumers will purchase at different prices. For example, at price P' consumers purchase Q' units of the product. We would expect an inverse relationship between quantity and price, so this curve is downward sloping.

curve. Not only does the demand curve tell us the quantity consumers will purchase at any given price, it also tells us the highest possible price that the market will bear for a given quantity or supply of output. Thus, in Figure P.7, if the firm sets a target of selling output level Q' (which might be what it can produce by running at full capacity), the demand curve tells us that the highest price the firm can charge is P'.

The Price Elasticity of Demand

Look at a firm that is considering a price increase. The firm understands that according to the law of demand, the increase in price will result in the loss of some sales. This may be acceptable if the loss in sales is not "too large." If sales do not suffer much, the firm may actually increase its sales revenue when it raises its price. If sales drop substantially, however, sales revenues may decline, and the firm could be worse off.

Figure P.8 illustrates the implications of the firm's pricing decision when its demand curve has one of two alternative shapes, D_A and D_B. Suppose the firm is currently charging P_0 and selling Q_0, and is considering an increase in price to P_1. If the firm's demand curve is D_A, the price increase would cause only a small drop in sales. In this case, the quantity demanded is not very sensitive to price. We would suspect that the increase in price would increase sales revenue because the price increase swamps the quantity decrease. By contrast, if the firm's demand curve is D_B, the increase in price would cause a large drop in sales. Here, the quantity demanded is very sensitive to price. We would expect that the price increase would decrease sales revenues.

As this analysis shows, the shape of the demand curve can strongly affect the success of the firm's pricing strategy. The concept of the price elasticity of demand summarizes this effect by measuring the sensitivity of quantity demanded to price. The price elasticity of demand, commonly denoted by η, is the percentage change in quantity brought about by a 1 percent change in price. Letting subscript "0"

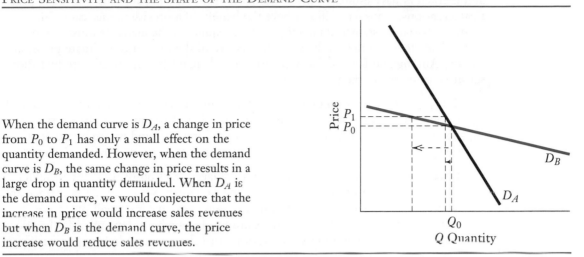

When the demand curve is D_A, a change in price from P_0 to P_1 has only a small effect on the quantity demanded. However, when the demand curve is D_B, the same change in price results in a large drop in quantity demanded. When D_A is the demand curve, we would conjecture that the increase in price would increase sales revenues but when D_B is the demand curve, the price increase would reduce sales revenues.

represent the initial situation and "1" represent the situation after the price changes, the formula for elasticity is

$$\eta = -\frac{\Delta Q/Q_0}{\Delta P/P_0}$$

where $\Delta P = P_1 - P_0$ is the change in price, and $\Delta Q = Q_1 - Q_0$ is the resulting change in quantity.[10] To illustrate this formula, suppose price is initially $5, and the corresponding quantity demanded is 1,000 units. If the price rises to $5.75, though, the quantity demanded would fall to 800 units. Then

$$\eta = -\frac{\dfrac{800 - 1000}{1000}}{\dfrac{5.75 - 5}{5}} = -\frac{-0.20}{0.15} = 1.33$$

Thus over the range of prices between $5.00 and $5.75, quantity demanded falls at a rate of 1.33 percent for every 1 percent increase in price. The price elasticity η might be less than 1 or greater than 1.

- If η is less than 1, we say that demand is *inelastic*, which is the situation along demand curve D_A for the price change being considered.

- If η is greater than 1, we say that demand is *elastic*, which is the situation along demand curve D_B for the price change being considered.

Given an estimate of the price elasticity of demand, a manager could calculate the expected percentage change in quantity demanded resulting from a given change in price by multiplying the percentage change in price by the estimated elasticity. To illustrate, suppose management believed $\eta = 0.75$. If it contemplated a 3 percent increase in price, then it should expect a $3 \times 0.75 = 2.25$ percent drop in the quantity demanded as a result of the price increase.[11]

Price elasticities can be estimated using statistical techniques, and economists and marketers have estimated price elasticities for many products. But in most practical situations, managers will not have the benefit of a precise numerical estimate of elasticity based on statistical techniques. Consequently, the manager must rely on his or her knowledge of the product and the nature of the market to estimate price sensitivity. Among the factors that tend to make demand for the firm's product more sensitive to price are the following:

- The product has few unique features that differentiate it from rival products, and buyers are aware of the prices and features of rival products. Airline service is a good example of a product that is hard to differentiate and where consumers can easily inform themselves of the range of prices that exist in a particular market.

- Buyers' expenditures on the product are a large fraction of their total expenditures. In this case, the savings from finding a comparable item at a lower price are large, so consumers tend to shop more than when making small purchases. Refrigerators and washing machines are products whose demand is fairly price sensitive because consumers are motivated to shop around before purchasing.

- The product is an input that buyers use to produce a final good whose demand is itself sensitive to price. In this case, if buyers tried to pass through to their customers even small changes in the price of the input, demand for the finished good could decrease dramatically. The input buyers will thus be very sensitive to price. For example, a personal computer manufacturer's demand for components and materials is likely to be highly price elastic because consumer demand for personal computers is highly price elastic.

Among the factors that tend to make demand less sensitive to price are the following:

- Comparisons among substitute products are difficult. This could be because the product is complex and has many performance dimensions; because consumers have little or no experience with substitute products and thus would face a risk if they purchased them; or because comparison shopping is costly. Items sold door-to-door, such as Avon cosmetics, have traditionally been price inelastic because, at the time of sale, most consumers lack good information about the prices of alternatives.

- Because of tax deductions or insurance, buyers pay only a fraction of the full price of the product. Health care is an excellent example.

- A buyer would incur significant costs if it switched to a substitute product. Switching costs could arise if the use of a product requires specialized training or expertise that is not fully transferable across different varieties of the product. For example, to the extent that a consumer develops expertise in using a particular word processing package that is incompatible with available alternatives, switching costs will be high, and price sensitivity for upgrades will be low.

- The product is used in conjunction with another product that buyers have committed themselves to. For example, an owner of a copying machine is likely to be fairly insensitive to the price of toner, because the toner is an essential input in running the copier.

Brand-Level versus Industry-Level Elasticities

Students often mistakenly suppose that just because the demand for a product is inelastic, the demand facing each seller of that product is also inelastic. Consider, for example, cigarettes. Many studies have documented that the demand for cigarettes is price inelastic, with elasticities well below 1. This suggests that a general increase in the price of all brands of cigarettes would only modestly affect overall cigarette demand. However, if the price of only one brand of cigarettes increases, the demand for that brand would probably drop substantially because consumers would switch to the now lower-priced brands. Thus, while demand can be inelastic at the industry level, it can be highly elastic at the brand level. Research by Frank Irvine nicely illustrates this difference for the automobile industry.[12] While estimates of the industry-level price elasticity for automobiles are on the order of 1 to 1.5, Irvine found that the average price elasticity for individual makes of automobiles ranged from 6 to 10.

Brand-level elasticities are higher than industry-level elasticities because consumers can purchase other brands when only one brand raises its price. Brand-level elasticities should also increase as more firms enter the market and more brands are offered. A study of the personal computer industry by Joanna Stavins illustrates this point.[13] She finds that the average brand-level elasticity rose over time from 5.0 in 1977 to 12.4 in 1988 as new firms entered the market. These elasticity estimates highlight an important reason for the increasing price competitiveness in that industry.

Should a firm use an industry-level elasticity or a brand-level elasticity in assessing the impact of a price change? The answer depends on what the firm expects its rivals to do. If a firm expects that rivals will quickly match its price change, then the industry-level elasticity is appropriate. If, by contrast, a firm expects that rivals will not match its price change (or will do so only after a long lag), then the brand-level elasticity is appropriate. For example, Pepsi's price cut succeeded because Coke did not retaliate. Had Coke cut its price, the outcome of Pepsi's strategy would have been different. Making educated conjectures about how rivals will respond to pricing moves is a fascinating subject. We will encounter this subject again in Chapter 8.

Total Revenue and Marginal Revenue Functions

A firm's total revenue function, denoted by $TR(Q)$, indicates how the firm's sales revenues vary as a function of how much product it sells. Recalling our interpretation of the demand curve as showing the highest price $P(Q)$ that the firm can charge and sell exactly Q units of output, we can express total revenue as

$$TR(Q) = P(Q)Q$$

Just as a firm is interested in the impact of a change in output on its costs, it is also interested in how a change in output will affect its revenues. A firm's marginal revenue, $MR(Q)$, is analogous to its marginal cost. It represents the rate of change in total revenue that results from the sale of ΔQ additional units of output:

$$MR(Q) = \frac{TR(Q + \Delta Q) - TR(Q)}{\Delta Q}$$

It seems plausible that total revenue would go up as the firm sells more output, and thus MR would always be positive. But with a downward-sloping demand curve, this is not necessarily true. To sell more, the firm must lower its price. Thus, while it generates revenue on the extra units of output it sells at the lower price, it loses revenue on all the units it would have sold at the higher price. For example, a compact disc store may sell 110 compact discs per day at a price of $11 per disc and 120 discs at $9 per disc. It gains additional revenue of $90 per day on the extra 10 discs sold at the lower price of $9, but it sacrifices $220 per day on the 110 discs that it could have sold for $2 more. The marginal revenue in this case would equal −$130/10 or −$13; the store loses sales revenue of $13 for each additional disc it sells when it drops its price from $11 to $9.

In general, whether marginal revenue is positive or negative depends on the price elasticity of demand. The formal relationship (whose derivation is not important for our purposes) is

$$MR(Q) = P\left(1 - \frac{1}{\eta}\right)$$

For example, if $\eta = 0.75$, and the current price $P = \$15$, then marginal revenue $MR = 15(1 - 1/0.75) = -\$5$. More generally,

- When demand is elastic, so that $\eta > 1$, it follows that $MR > 0$. In this case, the increase in output brought about by a reduction in price will raise total sales revenues.

- When demand is inelastic, so that $\eta < 1$, it follows that $MR < 0$. Here, the increase in output brought about by a reduction in price will lower total sales revenue.

Note that this formula implies that $MR < P$. This makes sense in light of what we just discussed. The price P is the additional revenue the firm gets from each additional unit it sells, but the overall change in revenues from selling an additional unit must factor in the reduction in revenue earned on all of the units that would have sold at the higher price, but are now being sold at a lower price.

FIGURE P.9
THE MARGINAL REVENUE CURVE AND THE DEMAND CURVE

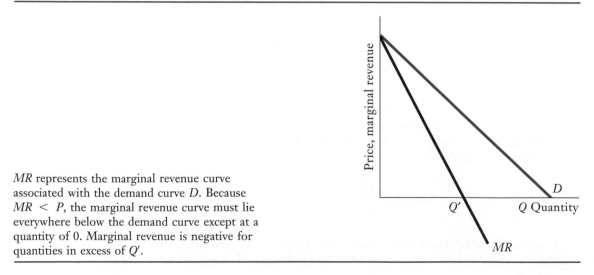

MR represents the marginal revenue curve associated with the demand curve D. Because $MR < P$, the marginal revenue curve must lie everywhere below the demand curve except at a quantity of 0. Marginal revenue is negative for quantities in excess of Q'.

Figure P.9 shows the graph of a demand curve and its associated marginal revenue curve. Because $MR < P$, the marginal revenue curve must lie everywhere below the demand curve, except at a quantity of zero. For most demand curves, the marginal revenue curve is everywhere downward sloping and at some point will shift from being positive to negative. (This occurs at output Q' in the figure.)

THEORY OF THE FIRM: PRICING AND OUTPUT DECISIONS ◆ ◆ ◆ ◆ ◆

Part Two of this book studies the structure of markets and competitive rivalry within industries. To set the stage for this analysis, we need to explore the theory of the firm, a theory of how firms choose their prices and quantities. This theory has both explanatory power and prescriptive usefulness. That is, it sheds light on how prices are established in markets, and it also provides tools to aid managers in making pricing decisions.

The theory of the firm assumes that the firm's ultimate objective is to make as large a profit as possible. The theory is therefore appropriate to managers whose goal is to maximize profits. Some analysts argue that not all managers seek to maximize profits, so that the theory of the firm is less useful for describing actual firm behavior. An extensive discussion of the descriptive validity of the profit-maximization hypothesis would take us beyond this primer. Suffice it to say that a powerful "evolutionary" argument supports the profit-maximization hypothesis: if, over the long haul, a firm's managers did not strive to achieve the largest amount of profit consistent with industry economics and its own particular resources, the firm would either disappear or its management would be replaced by one that better served the owners' interests.

Ideally, for any given amount of output the firm might want to sell, it would prefer to set price as high as it could. As we have seen, though, the firm's demand curve limits what that price can be. Thus, when determining the amount it wants to sell, the firm simultaneously determines the price it can charge from its demand curve.

How, then, is the optimal output determined? This is where the concepts of marginal revenue and marginal cost become useful. Recalling that "marginals" are rates of change (change in cost or revenue per one-unit change in output), the change in revenue, cost, and profit from changing output by ΔQ units (where ΔQ can either represent an increase in output, in which case it is a positive amount, or a decrease in output, in which case it is a negative amount) is

$$\text{Change in Total Revenue} = MR \times \Delta Q$$
$$\text{Change in Total Cost} = MC \times \Delta Q$$
$$\text{Change in Total Profit} = (MR - MC) \times \Delta Q$$

The firm clearly would like to increase profit. Here's how:

- If $MR > MC$, the firm can increase profit by selling more ($\Delta Q > 0$), and to do so, it should *lower* its price.

- If $MR < MC$, the firm can increase profit by selling less ($\Delta Q < 0$), and to do so, it should *raise* its price.

- If $MR = MC$, the firm cannot increase profits either by increasing or decreasing output. It follows that output and price must be at their optimal levels.

FIGURE P.10
OPTIMAL QUANTITY AND PRICE FOR A PROFIT-MAXIMIZING FIRM

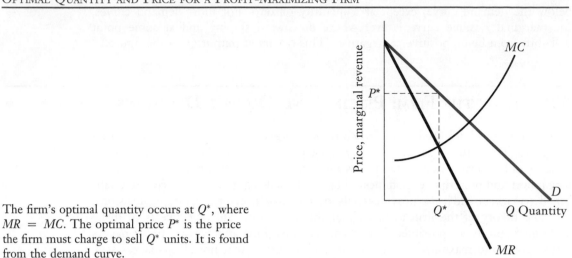

The firm's optimal quantity occurs at Q^*, where $MR = MC$. The optimal price P^* is the price the firm must charge to sell Q^* units. It is found from the demand curve.

Figure P.10 shows a firm whose output and price are at their optimal levels. The curve D is the firm's demand curve, MR is the marginal revenue curve, and MC is the marginal cost curve. The optimal output occurs where $MR = MC$, that is, where the MR and MC curves intersect. This is output Q^* in the diagram. The optimal price P^* is the associated price on the demand curve.

An alternative and perhaps more managerially relevant way of thinking about these principles is to express MR in terms of the price elasticity of demand. Then the term $MR = MC$ can be written as

$$P\left(1 - \frac{1}{\eta}\right) = MC$$

Let us now suppose, that as a first approximation, the firm's total variable costs are directly proportional to output, so that $MC = c$, where c is the firm's average variable cost. The percentage contribution margin or PCM on additional units sold is the ratio of profit per unit to revenue per unit, or $PCM = (P - c)/P$. Algebra establishes that

$$MR - MC > 0 \text{ as } \eta > 1/PCM$$
$$MR - MC < 0 \text{ as } \eta < 1/PCM$$

which implies that

- A firm should lower its price whenever the price elasticity of demand exceeds the reciprocal of the percentage contribution margin on the additional units it would sell by lowering its price.

- A firm should raise its price when the price elasticity of demand is less than the reciprocal of the percentage contribution margin of the units it would not sell by raising its price.

These principles can guide pricing decisions even though managers do not know the firm's demand curve or marginal cost function. Managers have only to make educated conjectures about the relative magnitude of elasticities and contribution margins.[14] An example may help cement these concepts. Suppose $P = \$10$ and $c = \$5$, so $PCM = 0.50$. Then the firm can increase profits by lowering its price if its price elasticity of demand η exceeds $1/0.5 = 2$. If, instead, $P = \$10$, and $c = \$8$, so that $PCM = 0.2$, the firm should cut its price if $\eta > 5$. As this example shows, the lower a firm's PCM (e.g., because its marginal cost is high), the greater its price elasticity of demand must be for a price-cutting strategy to raise profits.

PERFECT COMPETITION ◆ ◆ ◆ ◆ ◆

A special case of the theory of the firm is the theory of perfect competition. This theory highlights how market forces shape and constrain a firm's behavior and interact with the firm's decisions to determine profitability. The theory deals with a stark competitive environment: an industry with many firms producing identical products (so that consumers choose among firms solely on the basis of price) and where firms can enter or exit the industry at will. This is a caricature of any real market, but it does approximate an industry, such as aluminum smelting or copper mining, in which many firms produce nearly identical products.

Because firms in a perfectly competitive industry produce identical products, each firm must charge the same price. This market price is beyond the control of any individual firm; it must take the market price as given. For a firm to offer to sell at a price above the market price would be folly because it would make no sales. Offering to sell below the market price would also be folly because the firm would needlessly sacrifice revenue. As shown in Figure P.11, then, a perfectly competitive firm's demand curve is perfectly horizontal at the market price, even though the industry demand curve is downward sloping. Put another way, the firm-level price elasticity of demand facing a perfect competitor is infinite, even though the industry-level price elasticity is finite.

Given any particular market price, each firm must decide how much to produce. Applying the insights from the theory of the firm, the firm should produce at the point where marginal revenue equals marginal cost. When the firm's demand

FIGURE P.11
DEMAND AND SUPPLY CURVES FOR A PERFECTLY COMPETITIVE FIRM

A perfectly competitive firm takes the market price as given and thus faces a horizontal demand curve at the market price. This horizontal line also represents the firm's marginal revenue curve MR. The firm's optimal output occurs where its marginal revenue equals marginal cost. When the market price is P_0, the optimal output is Q_0. If the market price were to change, the firm's optimal quantity would also change. At price P_1, the optimal output is Q_1. At price P_0, the optimal output is Q_0. The firm's supply curve traces out the relationship between the market price and the firm's optimal quantity of output. This curve is identical to the firm's marginal cost curve.

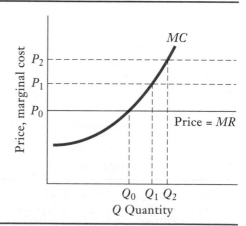

curve is horizontal, each additional unit it sells adds sales revenue equal to the market price. Thus, the firm's marginal revenue equals the market price, and the optimal output, shown in Figure P.11, is where marginal cost equals the market price. If we were to graph how a firm's optimal output changed as the market price changed, we would trace out a curve that is identical to the firm's marginal cost function. This is known as the firm's supply curve. It shows the amount of output the perfectly competitive firm would sell at various market prices. Thus, the supply curve of a perfectly competitive firm is identical to its marginal cost function.

If we aggregate over the firm supply curves of all active producers in the industry, we get the industry supply curve, depicted in Figure P.12 as SS. This figure shows an industry with 1,000 identical active firms. At any price, the industry supply is 1,000 times the supply of an individual firm. Given the industry supply curve, we can now see how the market price is determined. For the market to be in equilibrium, the market price must be such that the quantity demanded equals the quantity supplied by firms in the industry. This situation is depicted in Figure P.13, where P^* denotes the price that "clears" the market. If the market price was higher than P^*, then more of the product would be offered for sale than consumers would like to buy. The excess supply would then place downward pressure on the market price. If the market price was lower than P^*, then there would be less of the product offered for sale than consumers would like to buy. Here, the excess demand would exert upward pressure on the market price. Only when the quantities demanded and supplied are equal—when price equals P^*—is there no pressure on price to change.

The situation shown in Figure P.13 would be the end of the story if additional firms could not enter the industry. However, in a perfectly competitive industry, firms can enter and exit at will. The situation in Figure P.13 is thus unstable because firms in the industry are making a profit (price exceeds average cost at the quantity q^* that each firm supplies). Thus, it will be attractive for additional firms to enter and begin selling. Figure P.14 shows the adjustment that occurs. As more firms enter,

FIGURE P.12
FIRM AND INDUSTRY SUPPLY CURVES UNDER PERFECT COMPETITION

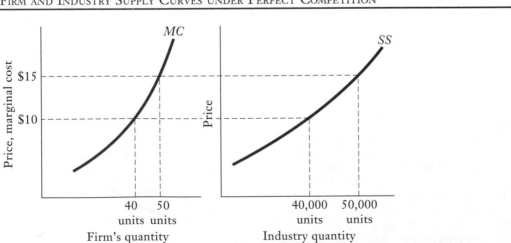

A single firm's supply curve is shown in the graph on the left. The industry's supply curve SS is shown in the graph on the right. These graphs depict an industry of 1,000 identical firms. Thus, at any price the industry supply is 1,000 times the amount that a single firm would supply.

FIGURE P.13
PERFECTLY COMPETITIVE INDUSTRY PRIOR TO NEW ENTRY

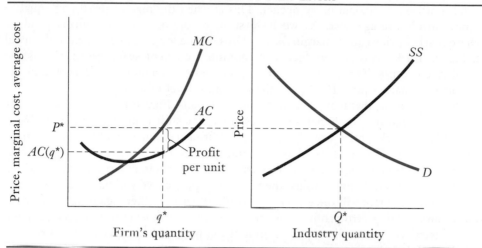

At the price P^*, each firm is producing its optimal amount of output q^*. Moreover, the quantity demanded equals the quantity Q^* supplied by all firms in the industry. However, each firm is earning a positive profit because at q^*, the price P^* exceeds average cost $AC(q^*)$, resulting in a profit on every unit sold. New firms would thus want to enter this industry.

FIGURE P.14
PERFECTLY COMPETITIVE INDUSTRY AT LONG-RUN EQUILIBRIUM

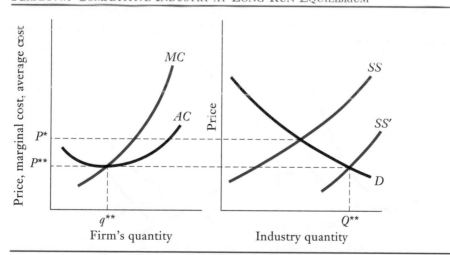

At price P^*, new entrants are attracted to the industry. As they come in, the industry's supply curve shifts to the right, from SS to SS', resulting in a reduction in market price. Entry ceases to occur when firms are earning as much inside the industry as they can earn outside it. Each firm thus earns zero economic profit, or equivalently, price equals average cost. Firms are choosing the optimal output and earning zero economic profit when they produce at the point at which market price equals both marginal cost and average cost. This occurs when the price is P^{**} and firms produce q^{**}. Firms are thus at the minimum point on their average cost function.

the supply curve *SS* shifts outward to *SS'*. As this happens, the quantity supplied exceeds the quantity demanded, and there is pressure on price to fall. It will continue to fall until no additional entry occurs. This is when the market price just equals a typical firm's average cost. As we have seen, to optimize output, firms produce where market price equals marginal cost. Thus, in the long-run equilibrium depicted in Figure P.14, firms are producing at minimum efficient scale (recall, this is the quantity corresponding to the minimum point on the average cost curve), and the equilibrium market price P^{**} equals the minimum level of average cost.

Suppose, now, that market demand suddenly falls. Figure P.15 shows what happens. The fall in market demand is represented by a shift from demand curve D_0 to D_1. Initially, market price would fall to P', and firms' revenues would not cover their economic costs. The industry "shakeout" then begins. Firms begin to exit the industry. As this occurs, the industry supply curve shifts to the left, and price begins to rise. Once the "shakeout" fully unfolds, the industry supply curve will have shifted to SS', and the market price will once again reach P^{**}. Firms are then again optimizing on output and earning zero profit. Thus, no matter what the level of industry demand, the industry will eventually supply output at the price P^{**}.[15]

This theory implies that the free entry exhausts all opportunities for making profit. This implication sometimes troubles management students because it seems to suggest that firms in perfectly competitive industries would then earn zero net income. But remember the distinction between economic costs and accounting costs. Economic costs reflect the relevant opportunity costs of the financial capital that the owners have provided to the firm. Zero profits thus means zero economic profit, not zero accounting profit. Zero economic profit simply means that investors are earning returns on their investments that are commensurate with what they could earn from their next best opportunity.

FIGURE P.15

EFFECT OF A REDUCTION IN DEMAND ON THE LONG-RUN PERFECTLY COMPETITIVE EQUILIBRIUM

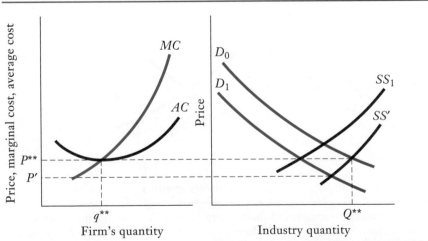

When demand falls, the demand curve shifts from D_0 to D_1, and price would initially fall to P'. Firms would earn less than they could elsewhere and would eventually begin to leave the industry. As this happens, the supply curve shifts to the left from SS' to SS_1. The industry shakeout ends when price is again P^{**}.

That free entry dissipates economic profit is one of the most powerful insights in economics, and it has profound implications for strategy. Firms that base their strategies on products that can be easily imitated or skills and resources that can be easily acquired put themselves at risk to the forces that are highlighted by the theory of perfect competition. To attain a competitive advantage, a firm must secure a position in the market that protects itself from imitation and entry. How firms might do this is the subject of Chapters 11, 12, and 13.

GAME THEORY ◆ ◆ ◆ ◆ ◆

The perfectly competitive firm faces many competitors, but in making its output decision, it does not consider the likely reactions of its rivals. This is because the decisions of any single firm have a negligible impact on market price. The key strategic challenge of a perfectly competitive firm is to anticipate the future path of prices in the industry and maximize against it.

In many strategic situations, however, there are few players. For example, four producers—Kellogg, General Mills, Post (owned by Kraft Foods), and Quaker Oats (owned by Pepsico)—account for more than 90 percent of sales in the ready-to-eat breakfast cereal market. In the market for commercial airframes, there are just two producers: Boeing and Airbus. In these "small numbers" situations, a key part of making strategic decisions—pricing, investment in new facilities, and so forth—is anticipating how rivals may react.

A natural way to incorporate the reactions of rivals into your analysis of strategic options is to assign probabilities to their likely actions or reactions and then choose the decision that maximizes the expected value of your profit, given this probability distribution. But this approach has an important drawback: How do you assign probabilities to the range of choices your rivals might make? You may end up assigning positive probabilities to decisions that, from the perspective of your competitors, would be foolish. If so, then the quality of your "decision analysis" would be seriously compromised.

A more penetrating approach would be to attempt to "get inside the minds" of your competitors, figure out what is in their self-interest, and then maximize accordingly. However, your rivals' optimal choices will often depend on their expectations of what you intend to do, which, in turn, depend on their assessments of your assessments about them. How can one sensibly analyze decision making with this circularity?

Game theory is most valuable in precisely such contexts. It is the branch of economics concerned with the analysis of optimal decision making when all decision makers are presumed to be rational, and each is attempting to anticipate the actions and reactions of its competitors. Much of the material in Part Two on industry analysis and competitive strategy draws on basic game theory. In this section, we introduce these basic ideas. In particular, we discuss games in matrix and game tree form, and the concepts of a Nash equilibrium and subgame perfection.

Games in Matrix Form and the Concept of Nash Equilibrium

The easiest way to introduce the basic elements of game theory is through a simple example. Consider an industry that consists of two firms, Alpha and Beta, that produce identical products. Each must decide whether to increase its production capacity in the upcoming year. We will assume that each firm always produces at full capacity. Thus, expansion of capacity entails a tradeoff. The firm may achieve a larger share of the market, but it may also put downward pressure on the market price. The consequences of each firm's choices are described in Table P.4. The first entry is Alpha's annual economic profit; the second entry is Beta's annual economic profit.

Each firm will make its capacity decision simultaneously and independently of the other firm. To identify the "likely outcome" of games like the one shown in Table P.4, game theorists use the concept of a Nash equilibrium. At a Nash equilibrium outcome, each player is doing the best it can, given the strategies of the other players. In the context of the capacity expansion game, the Nash equilibrium is that pair of strategies (one for Alpha, one for Beta) such that

• Alpha's strategy maximizes its profit, given Beta's strategy.

• Beta's strategy maximizes its profit, given Alpha's strategy.

In the capacity expansion game, the Nash equilibrium is (EXPAND, EXPAND); that is, each firm expands its capacity. Given that Alpha expands its capacity, Beta's best choice is to expand its capacity (yielding profit of 16 rather than 15). Given that Beta expands its capacity, Alpha's best choice is to expand its capacity.

In this example, the determination of the Nash equilibrium is fairly easy because for each firm, the strategy EXPAND maximizes profit no matter what decision its competitor makes. In this situation, we say that EXPAND is a dominant strategy. When a player has a dominant strategy, it follows (from the definition of the Nash equilibrium) that that strategy must also be the player's Nash equilibrium strategy. However, dominant strategies are not inevitable; in many games players do not possess dominant strategies (e.g., the game in Table P.5).

Why does the Nash equilibrium represent a plausible outcome of a game? Probably its most compelling property is that it is a self-enforcing focal point: If each party expects the other party to choose its Nash equilibrium strategy, then both parties will, in fact, choose their Nash equilibrium strategies. At the Nash equilibrium, then, expectation equals outcome—expected behavior and actual behavior converge. This would not be true at non-Nash equilibrium outcomes, as the game in Table P.5 illustrates. Suppose Alpha (perhaps foolishly) expects Beta not to expand capacity and refrains from expanding its own capacity to prevent a drop in the industry price level. Beta—pursuing its own self-interest—would confound Alpha's expectations, expand its capacity, and make Alpha worse off than it expected to be.

TABLE P.4
CAPACITY GAME BETWEEN ALPHA AND BETA

| | | Beta | |
		Do Not Expand	Expand
Alpha	DO NOT EXPAND	$18,$18	$15,$20
	EXPAND	$20,$15	$16,$16

All amounts are in millions per year. Alpha's payoff is first; Beta's is second.

TABLE P.5
MODIFIED CAPACITY GAME BETWEEN ALPHA AND BETA

		Beta Do Not Expand	Small	Expand
Alpha	DO NOT EXPAND	$18, $18	$15, $20	$9, $18
	SMALL	$20, $15	$16, $16	$8, $12
	LARGE	$18, $9	$12, $8	$0, $0

All amounts are in millions per year. Alpha's payoff is first; Beta's is second.

The "capacity expansion" game illustrates a noteworthy aspect of a Nash equilibrium. The Nash equilibrium does not necessarily correspond to the outcome that maximizes the aggregate profit of the players. Alpha and Beta would be collectively better off by refraining from the expansion of their capacities. However, the rational pursuit of self-interest leads each party to take an action that is ultimately detrimental to their collective interest.

This conflict between the collective interest and self-interest is often referred to as the prisoners' dilemma. The prisoners' dilemma arises because in pursuing its self-interest, each party imposes a cost on the other that it does not take into account. In the capacity expansion game, Alpha's addition of extra capacity hurts Beta because it drives down the market price. As we will see in Chapters 6 and 8, the prisoners' dilemma is a key feature of equilibrium pricing and output decisions in oligopolistic industries.

Game Trees and Subgame Perfection

The matrix form is particularly convenient for representing games in which each party moves simultaneously. In many situations, however, decision making is sequential rather than simultaneous, and it is often more convenient to represent the game with a game tree instead of a game matrix.

To illustrate such a situation, let us modify the capacity expansion game to allow the firm to choose among three options: no expansion of current capacity, a small expansion, or a large expansion. For contrast, let us first examine what happens when both firms decide simultaneously. This game is represented by the 3 by 3 matrix in Table P.5. We leave it to the reader to verify that the Nash equilibrium in this game is (SMALL, SMALL).

But now suppose that Alpha seeks to preempt Beta by making its capacity decision a year before Beta's. Thus, by the time Beta makes its decision, it will have observed Alpha's choice and must adjust its decision making accordingly.[16] We can represent the dynamics of this decision-making process by the game tree in Figure P.16.

In analyzing this game tree, we see what is known as a subgame perfect Nash equilibrium (SPNE). In an SPNE, each player chooses an optimal action at each stage in the game that it might conceivably reach and believes that all other players will behave in the same way.

To derive the SPNE, we use the so-called fold-back method: We start at the end of the tree, and for each decision "node" (represented by squares), we find the optimal decision for the firm situated at that node. In this example, we must find Beta's

FIGURE P.16

GAME TREE FOR SEQUENTIAL CAPACITY EXPANSION GAME

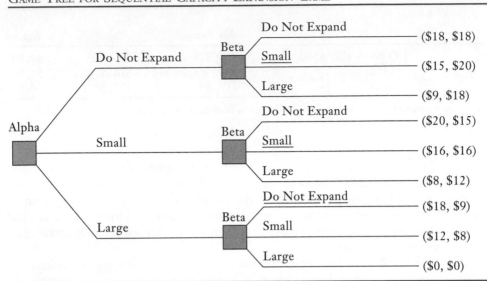

Alpha has three choices: DO NOT EXPAND, SMALL, and LARGE. Given Alpha's choice, Beta must then choose among DO NOT EXPAND, SMALL, LARGE. For whatever choice Alpha makes, Beta will make the choice that maximizes its profit. (These are underlined.) Given Beta's expected choices, Alpha's optimal choice is LARGE.

optimal decision for each of the three choices Alpha might make: DO NOT EXPAND, SMALL, and LARGE:

• If Alpha chooses DO NOT EXPAND, Beta's optimal choice is SMALL.

• If Alpha chooses SMALL, Beta's optimal choice is SMALL.

• If Alpha chooses LARGE, Beta's optimal choice is DO NOT EXPAND.

(Beta's optimal choices are underlined.)

By folding back the tree in this fashion, we assume that Alpha anticipates that Beta will choose a profit-maximizing response to any strategic move Alpha might make. Given these expectations, we can then determine Alpha's optimal strategy. We do so by mapping out the profit that Alpha gets as a result of each option it might choose, given that Beta responds optimally. The fold-back analysis tells us:

• If Alpha chooses DO NOT EXPAND, then given Beta's optimal reaction, Alpha's profit will be $15 million.

• If Alpha chooses SMALL, then given Beta's optimal reaction, Alpha's profit will be $16 million.

• If Alpha chooses LARGE, then given Beta's optimal reaction, Alpha's profit will be $18 million.

The SPNE is thus for Alpha to choose LARGE. Beta responds by choosing DO NOT EXPAND.

Note that the outcome of the sequential-move game differs significantly from the outcome of the simultaneous-move game. Indeed, the outcome involves a strategy for Alpha (LARGE) that would be dominated if Alpha and Beta made their capacity choices simultaneously. Why is Alpha's behavior so different when it can move first? Because in the sequential game, the firm's decision problems are linked through time: Beta can see what Alpha has done, and Alpha can thus count on a rational response by Beta to whatever action it chooses. In the sequential-move game, Alpha's capacity choice has commitment value; it forces Beta into a corner. By committing to a large-capacity expansion, Alpha forces Beta into a position where Beta's best response yields the outcome that is most favorable to Alpha. By contrast, in the simultaneous-move game, Beta cannot observe Alpha's decision, so the capacity decision no longer has commitment value for Alpha. Because of this, the choice of LARGE by Alpha is not nearly as compelling as it is in the sequential game. We discuss commitment in detail in Chapter 7.

ENDNOTES

[1]This example is drawn from Richard Tedlow's history of the soft drink industry in his book, *New and Improved: The Story of Mass Marketing in America*, New York, Basic Books, 1990.

[2]We will discuss this relationship in Chapter 8.

[3]The third, fourth, and fifth sections of this chapter are the most "technical." Instructors not planning to cover Chapters 6–9 can skip this material.

[4]The first part of this section closely follows the presentation of cost functions on pp. 42–45 of Dorfman, R., *Prices and Markets*, 2nd ed., Englewood Cliffs, NJ, Prentice-Hall, 1972.

[5]Students sometimes confuse total costs with average (i.e., per unit) costs, and note that for many real-world firms "costs" seem to go down as output goes up. As we will see, average costs could indeed go down as output goes up. The total cost function, however, always increases with output.

[6]This term was coined by Thomas Nagle in *The Strategy and Tactics of Pricing*, Englewood Cliffs, NJ, Prentice-Hall, 1987.

[7]Some authors call these *programmed costs*. See, for example, Rados, D. L., *Pushing the Numbers in Marketing: A Real-World Guide to Essential Financial Analysis*, Westport, CT, Quorum Books, 1992.

[8]The specific measure of accounting profit used is operating profit before taxes. The specific measure of economic profit used is called Economic Value Added (EVA), a term developed and trademarked by the financial consulting firm Stern Stewart & Company. See Stewart, G. Bennett, *The Quest for Value: A Guide for Senior Managers*, New York, Harper Business, 1991, for an extensive discussion of how EVA is calculated.

[9]For a good introduction to the basic concepts of present value, see Brealey, R. A. and S. C. Myers, *Principles of Corporate Finance*, 3rd ed., New York, McGraw-Hill, 1988.

[10]It is customary to put the minus sign in front, so that we convert what would ordinarily be a negative number (because ΔQ and ΔP have opposite signs) into a positive one.

[11]One complication should be noted: A given product's price elasticity of demand is not the same at all price levels. This means that an elasticity that is estimated at a price level of, say, $10 would be useful in predicting the impact of an increase in price to $11, but it would not accurately predict the impact of an increase to, say, $50, a price that is far outside the neighborhood of the price at which the elasticity was originally estimated. This is due to the properties of percentages, which require dividing by base amounts. If the price is so high that the quantity demanded is close to zero, even small absolute increases in quantity can translate into huge percentage increases.

[12]Irvine, F. O., "Demand Equations for Individual New Car Models Estimated Using Transaction Prices with Implications for Regulatory Issues," *Southern Economic Journal*, 49, January 1983, pp. 764–782.

[13]Stavins, J., "Estimating Demand Elasticities in a Differentiated Product Industry: The Personal Computer Market," *Journal of Economics and Business*, 49, July–August 1997, pp. 347–367.

[14]The use of this formula is subject to the caveat expressed earlier about the use of elasticities. It is useful for contemplating the effects of "incremental" price changes rather than dramatic price changes.

[15]This result is subject to the following qualification. If certain key inputs are scarce, the entry of additional firms bids up the prices of these inputs The firm's average and marginal cost functions then shift upward, and in the long run, the market price will settle down at a higher level. An industry in which this happens is known as an increasing-cost industry. The case we focus on in the text is known as a constant-cost industry.

[16]To keep the example as simple as possible, we will assume only two stages of decision making: Alpha makes its choice first, and then Beta responds. We do not consider the possibility that Alpha might respond to the capacity decision that Beta makes.

PART ONE

FIRM BOUNDARIES

THE EVOLUTION OF
THE MODERN FIRM

1

*T*his book identifies general economic principles behind the strategic decisions of firms. These principles should prove useful to managers across a wide range of business conditions and situations. They will clearly benefit managers trying to improve results that have been below expectations. Managers often can make immediate improvements in performance by better matching their firm's strategy to the demands of the business environment. Learning about principles, however, can also benefit managers of the most successful firms. As most managers should know, conditions change over time and industry contexts evolve. Strategies that are appropriate for today's business environment may evolve into arrangements that are inappropriate and out of touch with competitive conditions. Sometimes conditions that influence the business environment change gradually, as with the growth of suburban areas in the United States after 1950. Sometimes changes come more quickly, such as with the rapid improvements in communications, information processing, and networking technology during the 1990s. Some changes with major business repercussions seem to occur overnight, as with the privatization of businesses in Eastern Europe and the former Soviet Union after 1989 or the skepticism over accounting practices that emerged after the bankruptcy and scandal revelations at Enron in 2001. Armed with some general principles, however, the manager will be better prepared to adjust his or her firm's business strategy to the demands of its ever-changing environment and will have less need for relying on good luck.

We begin with a brief historical analysis to demonstrate the applicability of economic principles to widely disparate business conditions. This chapter examines the evolution of the modern business firm by focusing on economic activity and business organization at three points in time: 1840, 1910, and today. For each, we discuss the infrastructure of business and market conditions that firms faced, how those conditions affected the size and scope of the activities of the firm, and how business organizations responded to environmental conditions. We concentrate on developments in the U.S. economy, although parallel lines of development occurred in

43

Great Britain, France, and Germany.[1] We conclude more broadly by considering conditions in developing nations.

We chose our dates carefully. Although some aspects of a national infrastructure developed prior to 1840, limited transportation and communications constrained firms to operate in small localized markets. Changes in infrastructure between 1840 and 1910 encouraged the growth of national and international markets and such corporate giants as Standard Oil, U.S. Steel, and DuPont. Even the largest and best-managed firms, however, were still constrained by problems of coordination and control—how to gain sufficient information on a timely basis to manage large-scale operations and adapt to market changes. Since 1910, and particularly in the last 30 years, changes in communications, data processing, and networking have revolutionized firms' abilities to control their operations and interact with suppliers, customers, competitors, and other stakeholders.

◆ ◆ ◆ ◆ ◆ THE WORLD IN 1840

Doing Business in 1840

Before 1840, businessmen[2] managed their own firms in ways that their counterparts today would find unfamiliar. The experience of John Burrows was typical.[3] Burrows was an Iowa merchant who bought potatoes from nearby farmers and cleaned and packaged them. Hearing that potatoes were fetching $2 a bushel in New Orleans, he loaded an Illinois River flatboat and floated downstream. On the trip, he was offered 50 cents a bushel for his potatoes but rejected it in hope of getting a better price at New Orleans. While floating south, he was joined by other potato merchants seeking the same high prices. Soon, the New Orleans market was glutted. Supply and demand dictated that potato prices would plummet. After a six-week journey, Burrows sold his potatoes to a Bermuda ship captain for 8 cents a bushel.

Burrows was a merchant known as a "factor." Farmers in the United States sold their output to factors like Burrows, who brought the goods to major markets, such as New Orleans or New York, in search of buyers. Some of these buyers were local merchants, looking to stock their grocery stores. Most buyers, however, were "agents" representing out-of-town merchants, including some from Europe. Factors and agents rarely dealt directly with each other. Instead, they enlisted the help of "brokers." Brokers served as matchmakers between factors and agents. Brokers possessed specialized knowledge of market conditions (knowledge that individual factors and agents lacked), including the names of factors and agents, the availability of supplies, and the magnitude of demand.

Selling was informal. Transactions were relatively infrequent, the cast of potential transaction partners changed constantly, and timely information about the sales of comparable goods and the prices obtained for them was often unavailable. These problems increased with the geographic distance between buyers and sellers. As a result, factors and agents sought out brokers with whom they had done business before. Terms were rarely set in advance or specified in a contract. Instead, the brokers tried to arrange a price that best balanced supply and demand for a given situation. This was how most business was transacted in 1840. The brokerage arrangement no longer dominates the American business landscape, but it does survive in various forms in businesses such as real estate. An important modern example of the broker role is the "market maker" in securities transactions. Market makers in the New York Stock Exchange (NYSE) match the buy and sell orders of parties who do not know each other, facilitating transactions that would otherwise be difficult to complete.

Buy and sell orders for shares traded on the NYSE are filled almost immediately, so that both parties to a given transaction can be reasonably certain about the price at which the exchange will occur. John Burrows's experience shows that this was not the case in 1840. Factors and agents faced considerable price risk—that is, the price that they received when the transaction took place may have been different from what they expected when they began doing business (e.g., when John Burrows started floating downstream). This risk obviously increased with the distance between the site of production and its final destination. Thus, European merchants trading with the United States ran even larger risks than those Mr. Burrows faced.

The lack of knowledge about prices, buyers and sellers, and the associated risks dramatically shaped the nature of business. Farmers faced the most risk, and they relied on factors like Burrows to assume some of it by selling different farm products at different times of the year and by selling specific products at various times on the way to market. Presumably, Burrows was more willing to bear risk than most farmers, which may have been why he became a factor rather than a farmer. Once Burrows reached the market himself, he relied on brokers to find buyers for his goods, a task that he could not easily perform himself.

Bearing risk in these conditions could prove very profitable. In the early 1800s, for example, John Jacob Astor amassed a fortune in the fur trade that accounted for one-fifteenth of the personal wealth in the United States at the time. But even Astor's willingness to bear risk had its limits. He diversified his activities by investing in general trade with Europe and China (including the opium trade). He also knew when to quit the business. When he saw the imminent decline of the fur trade, he sold out his interest in American fur and invested instead in Manhattan real estate.[4]

Problems of limited information and increased transaction risk affected the size and structure of business during this period in other ways. With few exceptions, such as in the textiles, clockmaking, and firearms industries, small family-operated "firms" produced most goods and services. This stands in stark contrast to today, where a firm employing 100 workers is considered very small, and often a clear distinction exists between owners (shareholders), managers, and employees. Given the local nature of markets and the uncertainty about the market value of output, it is not surprising that individuals in 1840 were reluctant to use their own limited resources to expand the productive capabilities of their businesses. For similar reasons, banks were also unwilling to finance business expansion, leading to underdeveloped capital markets. Because of the problems with transportation and communication, which we describe below, family firms could not justify investing in the acquisition of raw materials or the distribution of final products, even though such investments might have allowed them to more efficiently coordinate the production process. The production and distribution of products involved many local firms of limited scale that needed to coordinate with each other in extended sequences of interaction. Market conditions at the time made any other system impractical.

Conditions of Business in 1840: Life Without a Modern Infrastructure

The dominance of the family-run small business in 1840 was a direct consequence of the *infrastructure* that was then in place. Infrastructure refers to those assets that assist in the production or distribution of goods and services that the firm itself cannot easily provide. Infrastructure facilitates transportation, communication, and financing. It includes basic research, which can enable firms to find better production techniques. The government has a key role in a nation's infrastructure because it affects the conditions under which firms do business (e.g., by regulating telecommunications) and often supplies infrastructure investments directly (e.g., the interstate highways). Government investments in infrastructure are necessary because individual firms making investments in public goods must bear the full costs of such investments but are seldom able to capture more than a fraction of their benefits. As a result, they lack the incentives to provide these investments on their own.

By modern standards, the infrastructure of 1840 in Europe and America was poorly developed. Limitations in transportation, communications, and finance created the business environment with which John Burrows and others of his time had to cope. While we discuss the situation in America in this and subsequent sections, European businessmen faced similar limitations, often made worse by political factors. Given these limitations, it is apparent that the ways in which business was conducted in 1840, though alien to us today, were appropriate for the time.

Transportation As a result of the harnessing of steam power, transportation was undergoing a revolution in the first half of the nineteenth century. Although the Romans had attempted to develop roadbeds by means of rails of different sorts, the modern railroad did not add value to commerce until the introduction of the steam engine and the use of iron and steel rails. By 1840, the railroads began to replace the horse and wagon for the shipment of raw materials and consumer goods. Rails in the United States took time to develop, however. As late as 1836, only 175 miles of railroad track were laid in one year.[5] By 1850, U.S. railway systems were still too fragmented to foster the growth of national markets. Few rails ran west of the Appalachian Mountains, "connecting" lines often had different gauges, and schedules were seldom coordinated. The development of an integrated transportation infrastructure through railroads in the United States would not be complete until after 1870.

Until the railroads developed, manufacturers used the waterways to transport goods over long distances, even though water transportation left much to be desired. For example, although the new steamships plied major American rivers and the Great Lakes as early as 1813, no direct route connected the major cities in the east to the Great Lakes until the completion of the Erie Canal in 1825. Steamships could not unload in Chicago until the 1840s. The trip from New York to Chicago was both lengthy and risky, especially during bad weather. Possible waterway routes were limited, and constructing and maintaining canals was expensive. Nonetheless, the opening of the Erie Canal led to startling growth. For example, between 1830 and 1840, the population of Illinois tripled, from 157,000 to 476,000, and the population of Chicago grew eight times, from 500 to more than 4,000.[6] While canals and railroads spurred growth, in 1840 they were still in their initial stages of development. Ocean transport at this time was still dominated by sailing ships, and innovations such as the steam engine and the screw propeller were new to this mode of travel. The White Star line, the famous British steamship firm and eventual owner of the *Titanic*, was founded during this time (1845).

Without safe and reliable means of transporting large volumes of goods, producers were reluctant to make the investments needed to expand their production capabilities or to acquire raw materials. Firms doing business in rapidly expanding markets also needed consistent communications with increasingly far-flung employees. An economy centered on large industrial firms would have to wait for the completion of the railroad system and the development of effective communications via the telegraph system.

Communications The local scale of business activities in 1840 was partially attributable to the lack of a modern communications infrastructure. A businessman transacting with distant trading partners needed to be able to respond if market conditions changed. Without adequate communication, businessmen preferred to delegate responsibility for the transaction to agents or factors, such as Mr. Burrows, rather than assume the risk themselves. If a businessman did establish separate facilities in different locations, he would need to communicate with each facility and coordinate their activities. Again, inadequate communication made this impossible. A lack of communications also affected transportation. Without regular communications, railroads could not schedule trains reliably and safely. This interfered with the flow of goods over long distances and made large-scale production and distribution more risky.

The primary mode of long-distance communication in 1840 was the public mail. The U.S. Postal Service had its beginnings in 1775 and had developed into the largest postal system in the world by 1828. Although the postal service may have served everyone, it was slow and expensive. The bulk of materials sent through the mail consisted of newspapers, whose postal rates were subsidized by the government. As late as 1840, the postal service depended almost exclusively on the horse and stagecoach, and had difficulty adjusting to the volume of communication that followed western U.S. expansion. It was not until the establishment of the Railway Mail Service in 1869 that the postal service shifted to railroads as the principal means for transporting mail nationally. This was hardly the instantaneous communication we have come to associate with a modern infrastructure.

Using the mails for business correspondence proved expensive and unpredictable. For example, correspondence from the Waterbury, Connecticut, headquarters of the Scovill Company in the 1840s took one day to reach New York City and two days to reach Philadelphia in good weather. In bad weather, it could easily take a week. To send a one-sheet letter from Waterbury cost 12.5 cents to New York and 18.5 cents to Philadelphia. The absence of postmarks on some letters from this time suggests that high postage rates encouraged Scovill owners and their agents to hand-carry items. Business mail volume increased after the U.S. Postal Service significantly lowered its rates twice, in 1845 and 1851, in response to the growth of competition from private delivery services.[7]

The first modern form of communications was the telegraph, which required laying wires between points of service. In 1844, Samuel Morse linked Baltimore and Washington by telegraph on a project funded by the U.S. Congress. While Morse's venture quickly proved unprofitable, other telegraph lines soon flourished. By 1848, New York was linked to both Chicago and New Orleans. By 1853, a total of 23,000 miles of line had been strung. Transatlantic cables soon connected the United States and Europe. These cables and their descendants remain important infrastructure elements today. After a period of explosive growth, the industry consolidated around a dominant firm—Western Union. By 1870, Western Union was one of the largest firms in the United States, and the telegraph industry provided the communications infrastructure for a growing industrial economy.

Even when modern communication capabilities became available, firms did not always adopt them, since their potential value was unclear at first while their start-up costs were high. Firms initially used the telegraph for its value in bridging distances with agents over matters such as pricing. Although using the telegraph was expensive, important time-sensitive messages justified the cost. Railroads used the telegraph for these reasons but were slow to adopt it for regular scheduling. The New York and Erie Railroad was the first to do this in the United States in 1851, following the example of British railroads.[8] In time, however, telegraph lines came to parallel most major train lines and proved indispensable for railroad scheduling and operations. Some modern telecommunications firms, such as Sprint, saw their beginnings in these types of arrangements.

Finance   Few individuals could afford to build and operate a complex firm themselves. Financial markets bring together providers and users of capital. They enable buyers and sellers to smooth out cash flows and reduce the risk of price fluctuation. In the first half of the nineteenth century, however, financial markets were less developed than they are today. Most businesses at the time were partnerships and found it difficult to obtain long-term debt. In addition, stocks were neither easily nor widely traded, which diluted their value and increased the cost of equity capital. Investors also found it hard to protect themselves against the increased risks of larger capital projects.

The major role of private banks at this time was the issuance of credit. By 1820, there were more than 300 banks in the United States; by 1837, there were 788. By offering short-term credit, banks smoothed the cash flows of buyers and sellers and facilitated reliable transactions, although considerable risk from speculation and inflation continued throughout the nineteenth century. There was a recurring pattern of boom and bust, with periodic major depressions, such as the Panic of 1837.

Many smaller firms had difficulty getting credit, however, and if it was available at all, credit was often granted informally on the basis of personal relationships. Government or private consortia—groups of private individuals brought together to finance a specific project—funded larger projects, such as the Erie Canal. As the scale of capital projects increased after 1840, government support or larger public debt or equity offerings by investment banks increasingly replaced financing by private individuals and small groups of investors as the principal sources of capital funds for businesses.

Financial institutions also reduce business risks. The mechanism for reducing the risk of price fluctuation is the futures market, in which individuals purchase the right to buy and/or sell goods on a specified date for a predetermined price. Futures markets require verification of the characteristics of the product being transacted. They also require that one party to the transaction is willing to bear the risk that the "spot" (i.e., current) price on the date the futures transaction is completed may differ from the transacted price. In 1840, no institutional mechanisms were available that reduced the risk of price fluctuation. The first futures market was created by the Chicago Board of Trade in 1858 and profoundly affected the farming industry, as we discuss in Example 1.1.

Production Technology   Production technology means the application of scientific or technical knowledge to production processes. Firms often direct resources toward internal innovation and toward stimulation of demand for new products from the market. Both of these activities may help spur eventual technological

EXAMPLE 1.1 THE EMERGENCE OF CHICAGO[9]

The emergence of Chicago as a major commercial center in the 1800s illustrates the core concepts that we have discussed, albeit for a city rather than a business. In the 1840s, growing cities in the Midwest, including Cincinnati, Toledo, Peoria, St. Louis, and Chicago, were all competing, as vigorously as firms in any other markets might compete, to become the region's center of commerce. Their success would ultimately be decided by the same conditions that determined the horizontal and vertical boundaries of business firms. Significant changes in *infrastructure* and *technology* enabled Chicago's business organizations, and with them the city's financial fortunes, to outstrip other cities. For example, by 1860, the Chicago Board of Trade bought and sold nearly all the grain produced in the Midwest. Similarly, two Chicago meatpackers, Armour and Swift, dominated their industry.

Chicago prospered because it conducted business differently from competing commercial centers. Chicago businesses were the first to take advantage of new technologies that reduced costs and risks. For example, Swift and Armour simultaneously adopted the refrigerated train car, which had first been used by Illinois fruit growers. (Lining a standard freight car with ice from Lake Michigan produced the refrigerator car.) This allowed cattle and hogs to be butchered in Chicago, before they lost weight (and value) on the way to market. Cyrus McCormick and others took advantage of the recently invented grain elevator to inexpensively sort, store, and ship grain bought from midwestern farmers. They reduced the risk of dealing with large quantities of grain by buying and selling grain futures at the newly founded Chicago Board of Trade.

The businesses run by Swift, Armour, McCormick, and other Chicago entrepreneurs required substantial investments in rail lines, icing facilities, grain elevators, the futures market, and so forth. These businessmen recognized that they could not recoup their investments without high volumes of business. This would require *throughput*: the movement of inputs and outputs through a production process. The meatpacking and grain businesses of Chicago required large supplies of ice and large assured movements of grain and livestock from the farmlands and grain and butchered meat to eastern markets. The need for throughput explains why Chicago emerged as the business center of the Midwest. Only Chicago, with its unique location as the terminus of rail and water routes from the East and West, had the transportation infrastructure necessary to assure throughput. Chicago thus emerged during the mid-1800s and remains today the "market leader" among midwestern cities.

Figure 1.1 shows the American railroad system in 1840, 1870, and 1890. As the figure shows, Chicago became the hub of significant East/West and North/South rail lines. This was in part due to the efforts of local business leaders to promote the city's growth. Once Chicago started to appear as a hub, however, it became reasonable for other railroad lines to pass through the city, making it an even larger transportation center. Only St. Louis could have competed in terms of rail throughput. But St. Louis lacked quick access to the Great Lakes—the preferred shipping route for grain during summer and fall and the principal source of ice for meatpackers.

development. At any given time, however, a single firm or group of firms has only a limited ability to change general levels of production technology and the current state of technology inevitably constrains the expansion of business activity. Technological constraints were substantial in 1840.

Technology was relatively undeveloped in 1840. Where factories existed at all, they produced goods in much the same way they had been produced in the previous

FIGURE 1.1
GROWTH OF AMERICAN RAILROADS FROM 1840 TO 1890

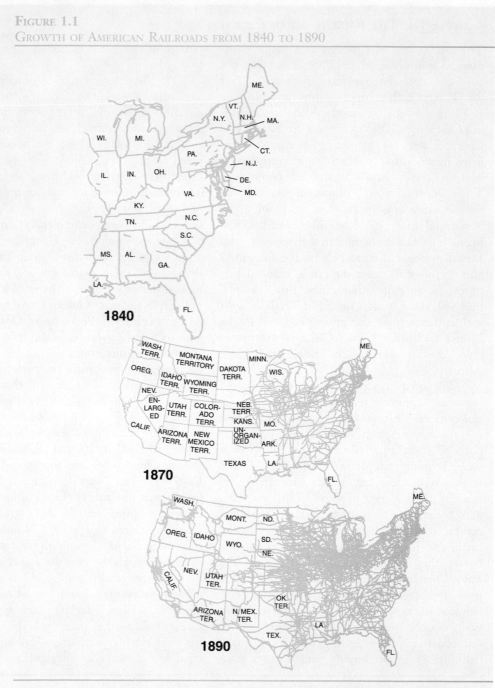

Chicago became the hub of significant East/West and North/South rail lines. This was in part due to the efforts of local business leaders to promote the city's growth. Once Chicago started to appear as a hub, however, it was increasingly reasonable to have further railroad lines pass through the city, making it an even larger transportation center.

Source: Association of American Railroads. Reprinted from Beniger, J. R., *The Control Revolution*, Cambridge, MA, Harvard University Press, 1986, p. 212.

century. Even the most advanced factories of the time lacked the ability to produce standardized goods at the high volumes that would become common by 1910. Even though textile plants had begun to be mechanized before 1820 and standardization was common in the manufacture of clocks and firearms, the "American System" of manufacturing through the use of interchangeable parts was only just beginning to be adopted. Until the 1870s, factories largely operated on the basis of internal contracting, in which their facilities were leased to a supervisor who in turn hired workers and produced goods. Even those factories that produced more standardized items with interchangeable parts produced small amounts of goods and made little use of inanimate sources of power, which would have accelerated production and required new forms of factory organization. While some large enterprises, such as Western Union and the Pennsylvania Railroad, were exploiting economies of scale by the 1860s, many of the scale-intensive industries most associated with industrial growth in the United States, such as steel, oil, chemicals, or automobiles, developed volume production only in the late nineteenth or early twentieth century.

Government Government resolves commercial disputes and sets the rules under which businesses operate. It also participates directly in economic activity through the purchase of goods and services, tax policies, or regulation. Historically, most infrastructure investments are left to the public sector. Private investors are reluctant to invest in infrastructure because while they would bear the cost, their competitors would share in the benefits. Government agencies do not compete with private firms, so they are better suited to develop the public infrastructure assets, such as canals and railroads, that serve the common good. For example, from 1820 until 1838, 18 states advanced credit of $60 million for canals, $43 million for railroads, and $4.5 million for turnpikes.[10]

Apart from large, fixed-cost infrastructure resources and wartime purchases, the government was not much involved in the U.S. economy around 1840, especially when compared with what government involvement in the economy would be by the 1930s and afterwards. Given the state of local markets at the time, this lack of involvement probably inhibited economic expansion, although this would change as government involvement increased. The government sponsored the competition between the Union Pacific and Central Pacific Railroads to build the first transcontinental railroad, which was completed in 1869. Today the role of the government in fostering the Internet is often noted; it is arguable that government sponsorship of transcontinental railroads had an equal or greater effect on the economy of the late nineteenth century in terms of improving communications and spurring private investment. The first major industry regulatory agency, the Interstate Commerce Commission, was created in 1887 to regulate the railroads. Other areas, such as the telegraph, remained largely self-regulated, through consensual industry standards.

A final but less well-known example of government involvement in building commercial infrastructure during this time occurred in 1884, when the U.S. government hosted the Prime Meridian Conference in Washington, D.C. This led to the nearly worldwide adoption of a system of standard time, including the now familiar 24 standard time zones, the location of the Prime Meridian in Greenwich, England, and the adoption of an International Date Line. This system was necessary to meet the demands for coordination in transportation, communication, and contracting that arose out of the worldwide expansion of markets owing to improvements in transportation and communications. When communication became nearly instantaneous and great distances could be traveled in a matter of days rather than weeks or months, a common standard of time was needed to coordinate the expanded volume of commerce that resulted.

Summary

The lack of a modern infrastructure limited economic activity in 1840. Firms were small and informally organized. Technology prevented production from expanding much beyond traditional levels in local markets. Even with a sophisticated technology, however, the limited transportation infrastructure, coupled with difficulties in obtaining accurate and timely information, would have made investments in volume production and distribution capabilities too risky for businessmen in 1840. There were no professional managers; owners ran their own enterprises. Market demand and technological development were needed before high-speed and high-volume production and distribution could occur. This required an expanded infrastructure. There were forces in play, however, that would change the conditions in which business operated and greatly increase its scale of operations and quality of management.

◆ ◆ ◆ ◆ ◆ THE WORLD IN 1910

Doing Business in 1910

Business changed greatly from 1840 to 1910, and the business practices and organizations of 1910 would seem much more familiar to the modern businessperson than those of 1840. In some sectors, such as farming and textiles, small firms still predominated, but they faced a well-developed set of buyers, suppliers, and service providers. Other sectors, such as chemicals, steel, and transportation, were increasingly dominated by large firms that not only produced finished goods, but also acquired raw materials and distributed end products. Because these firms were too large for their owners to be effectively involved in everyday decisions, a new class of "professional" managers emerged with little ownership interest in the firms they guided. These firms had internal hierarchies in which lower-level managers supervised day-to-day activities and reported to upper management, which attempted to shape the departments and divisions of the firm into a cohesive enterprise.

The evolution of these firms resulted from changes in infrastructure and technology. No change was more important than the development of mass-production technologies, such as the Bessemer process for making steel or the continuous-process tank furnace that facilitated the mass production of many products, such as plate glass. These new technologies enabled goods to be produced at costs far below what firms using older technologies could achieve. To exploit these production opportunities, firms needed reliable supplies of inputs, as well as access to widespread distribution and retail outlets. The fixed investments required to develop these outlets were justified only when large volumes of goods flowed through them. In short, firms needed to assure a sufficiently large *throughput* to make the expansion of productive capacity economical. The needed throughput was assured by the development of the infrastructure: railroads for shipping inputs and finished goods; telegraph and telephone for communication, control, and coordination of materials over expanded areas; and banking and accounting practices to provide the investment capital needed to finance production and distribution facilities. Businessmen like

Andrew Carnegie quickly appreciated the potential benefits of reorganizing production to increase volume and reach many more customers at lower costs per customer than their smaller competitors.

Historian Alfred Chandler has noted how businessmen reorganized their firms to take advantage of new production technologies.[11] The owner-operator who invested in a new technology found that he needed to increase production substantially to recoup his investment. This required a tremendous increase in throughput. This increased the owner-operator's responsibilities in functional areas of business, such as purchasing, sales, distribution, and finance. These all needed to be coordinated by a central office to assure that production runs went smoothly and finished goods found their way to market.

Product line and volume expansion altered relationships among manufacturers, their suppliers, and their distributors. Manufacturing firms increasingly chose to *vertically integrate*; that is, they chose to produce raw materials and/or distribute finished goods themselves rather than rely on independent suppliers, factors, and agents for these tasks. Chapter 3 discusses the costs and benefits of vertical integration in depth, but briefly, manufacturing firms in 1910 found it desirable to vertically integrate because the high volume of production made them more vulnerable to gaps in the chain of supply and distribution. This explains why vertical integration occurred in some industries, such as steel, chemicals, and machinery, but not in others, such as textiles and furniture. Vertical integration made sense only when firms could exploit new technologies to achieve cost savings from high-volume production. In industries such as furniture and textiles, few technological breakthroughs occurred that permitted volume-based economies. High-volume firms in these industries had no advantages over low-volume firms, so vertical integration to assure throughput did not occur there.

New production technologies also allowed firms to exploit *scope economies* by producing a wider range of products at lower costs than if they were produced separately. In the years immediately following 1910, many firms, such as DuPont, General Motors, and Alcoa, expanded horizontally by offering a wider variety of products. Some firms in newer sectors, such as General Electric, had little choice but to embrace scope. These firms found that the increased size and complexity of multiproduct operations necessitated a further reorganization into semiautonomous divisions. Each division in these firms made the principal operating decisions for their own businesses, while a separate corporate office made decisions that affected the entire corporation. For example, the divisions of General Motors made operating decisions for each car line, while corporate management controlled corporate finance, research and development, and new model development. This organizational form, known as the multidivisional or *M-form*, became characteristic of the largest industrial firms until the 1960s.

The expansion of mass production was also associated with the subsequent growth of mass-distribution firms in such sectors as groceries, apparel, drugstores, and general variety merchandising. Although chain stores dated to the mid-nineteenth century, they greatly expanded in number and market share after World War I. From 1920 to 1930, the 20 leading chains in the United States nearly quadrupled their numbers of stores (to over 37,000). The number of A&P food stores tripled during this time, as did J.C. Penney stores, while the number of Walgreen's drugstores increased twentyfold. By 1929, the national market share of the top three grocery chains (A&P, Kroger, and Safeway) approached 40 percent.

The growth of vertically and horizontally integrated firms often reduced the number of firms in an industry and increased the potential for collusion to restrict competition and increase profits. Mergers and informal associations of firms to restrict competition were common in such industries as tobacco, steel, aluminum, and oil. These anticompetitive activities generated resistance among competitors, buyers, suppliers, consumers, and the public at large, which ultimately resulted in government action. During the period around 1910, the U.S. government directed antitrust activities toward breaking up firms that appeared to be national monopolies. Among the major cases during this time were those involving Standard Oil (1911), American Tobacco (1911), DuPont (1912), International Harvester (1918), and Eastman Kodak (1920).

Integrated firms employed more individuals in more complex and interrelated tasks than had earlier firms, in both production and distribution. They also implemented systematic approaches to managing employees to standardize jobs and tasks, monitor worker compliance with management directives, appraise worker performance, test and train employees, and conduct the other functions that have come to be associated with personnel administration. These approaches spread widely among large firms, under the influence of a new type of specialist, the management consultant. Perhaps the best known of these approaches was Scientific Management, developed by Frederick W. Taylor, which sought to identify the most efficient ways of performing tasks through "time-and-motion" studies and then motivate workers to adopt these ways of working through the use of incentives, rewards, and sanctions.[12]

Besides vertical and horizontal integration, large firms needed managerial hierarchies. As Alfred Chandler describes, these hierarchies substituted the *visible* hand of management for the *invisible* hand of the market.[13] Managers coordinated across the various functions that had been brought inside the firm. Hierarchy was needed because of the greater volume of throughput needing coordination, the larger workforce required for mass production and distribution, and the enlarged markets that these large firms served.

The growth of managerial hierarchies fostered the emergence of a class of professional managers, many of whom owned little or no share of the business. These individuals tended not to have worked their way up in a particular business, but rather had been trained as engineers or in newly founded schools of business. On behalf of the owners, these managers applied their expertise in control and coordination to the firm and its business units. In doing so, they pioneered the standardized collection of data on a firm's operations, and with it the beginnings of cost accounting.

These changes in the nature of the firm and its managers caused problems and conflicts. Since there was little precedent for the rapid growth of firms at this time, growth of volume and expansion into new markets could easily lead to overexpansion and overcapacity. The development of internal controls needed for coordination and efficiency could easily turn into excessive bureaucracy. Newly expanded workforces resisted the controls on their behavior and the standardization of their work habits that were needed to foster greater and more predictable throughput. This aided the growth of unions and with them increased labor-related conflicts.

Finally, the increased size and complexity of these new large firms, coupled with their ability to persist beyond the lifetimes of their founders as legal corporations, raised new issues regarding the effective governance of and continuity of skilled leadership in these entities. While founders might wish to pass their ownership interests on to their children, it became increasingly unlikely that these heirs would have the skills or motivation to take over the family business and run it effectively. Yet, the very skill that new professional managers exhibited in guiding the growth of their firms raised issues regarding their motivation as well. Problems of ensuring that managers work in the best interests of owners (what we call governance problems) first appeared on a wide scale during this time. Public scrutiny of governance increased in periods of economic downturn and unemployment, such as during the Great Depression of the 1930s.

Business Conditions in 1910: A "Modern" Infrastructure

A substantially new infrastructure for business had emerged by 1910, notably in transportation and communications. These developments fostered the growth of national markets by enabling firms to count on the fast and reliable movements of goods, along with instantaneous and accurate communication over vast areas.

Production Technology   Technology developed greatly between 1840 and 1910, which promoted the growth of mass production. Most people did not begin to hear about mass production until after 1913, the year in which Henry Ford began producing the Model T. Mass-production processes permitted high volume, low-cost manufacturing of many products, including steel, aluminum, automobiles, and chemicals, to name only a few. These products proved to be of more than sufficient quality to compete with the lower-volume custom products they replaced. Along with production technology, the technology of managing new organizations also developed. The new managerial hierarchies led to innovations in document production (typewriters), copying (carbon paper; photocopying), analysis (adding machines; punched-card tabulators), and organization (vertical file systems) that enabled managers to coordinate the increased volume of transactions. Supplying these products spurred the growth of such firms as IBM, Burroughs, and Remington Rand.

Transportation   For mass production and distribution to be viable, producers needed assured throughput, which was permitted by the continued consolidation and rationalization of the railroads after the initial period of growth. By 1910, railroads dominated passenger and freight transportation. Travel by rail became faster, safer, and more reliable. The railroads became efficient and even profitable under the leadership of such managers as Edward H. Harriman of the Union Pacific. Manufacturers could obtain raw materials from distant sources and could swiftly ship their product to customers hundreds or even thousands of miles away. Smaller manufacturers sold to the new mass-distribution firms, such as Sears, which could cheaply distribute via the rails vast arrays of goods to scattered customers. Motorcars were also developing as a fundamental means of transportation, but trucks would not displace the U.S. railroads until the development of an extensive system of interstate highways following World War II.

Communications   The infrastructure in 1910 enabled businesses to communicate more accurately and quickly and allowed managers of growing firms to feel more confident in expanding their volume of transactions beyond traditional levels. The main components of the communications infrastructure in 1840—the postal system and the telegraph—were still important in 1910 and were increasingly becoming part of the management and communications systems of large firms. During this time, however, the telephone grew more important. Phone calls to suppliers and distributors could instantly assure managers that large production runs were feasible and that there were markets for their output.

The growth of American Telephone and Telegraph (AT&T) illustrates how the development of large firms depended on market and technological conditions. When the telephone was invented in 1876, its technological potential (and hence its profitability) was uncertain because some devices essential for telephone service as we know it, such as the switchboard, were unknown. The market conditions facing the telephone were also uncertain because of patent conflicts. This led to local competition to provide service. By the 1880s, patent conflicts had been resolved, and new technology made consolidation possible. In 1883, under the leadership of Theodore Vail, AT&T adopted a strategy of merging local telephone companies into a national system. The resulting network reduced the costs of interconnecting large numbers of users, and the telephone quickly replaced the telegraph as the communications technology of choice.[14] The telephone also had implications for how the emerging firms of this era were organized. For example, it is hard to imagine the growth of the multistory headquarters office building without the telephone to connect all headquarters employees with each other and with field offices.[15]

Finance   In 1910, securities markets publicly traded the shares of the largest industrial firms. Since the 1860s, large investment banking houses had been underwriting most stock transactions that were essential for financing large firms. Investment bankers like J. P. Morgan were among the most powerful businessmen in the world in 1910. The development of a financial infrastructure was further aided during this period by the systematization and circulation of credit information (credit bureaus), the availability of installment financing, and the development of the communications infrastructure. During this time, owners, managers, and investors realized that the growing scope of business required new ways of keeping track of a firm's activity and reporting its results. New accounting techniques were developed, and mandatory reporting standards for public firms became law. The new large firms developed these techniques to solve recordkeeping problems occasioned by their size and scope. For example, the railroads produced major innovations in cost accounting to manage their requirements of operating efficiencies. The newly formed mass-marketing firms, such as Sears, developed new accounting concepts, such as inventory turnover, to link profits to fluctuations in sales volume, while large industrial firms, such as DuPont, pioneered cost accounting.

Accounting developments also focused on the idea of public accounting—the public disclosure of details of a firm's operations to ensure that investors were not being cheated by managers and that capital was being maintained. In England, for example, laws enacted between 1844 and 1900 required the presentation of a "full and fair" balance sheet at shareholders' meetings, the payment of dividends out of profits, the maintenance of a firm's capital stock, and the conduct of compulsory and uniform audits of all registered firms. Similar developments occurred in the United States. For example, by the 1860s, the railroads employed more accountants than the U.S. government. The first U.S. independent accounting firm was founded in New York in 1883, and the American Association of Public Accountants was formed in 1886.

Government   Government regulation of the conditions under which business was conducted, in such areas as corporate law and governance, antitrust, provisions for disability insurance and worker safety, and insurance for widows and children, increased during this period. (Securities markets and labor relations were not fully regulated until the 1930s.) This increased regulation affected not only how firms

EXAMPLE 1.2 EVOLUTION OF THE STEEL INDUSTRY

Nowhere has change had more effect than in the American steel industry. In the first half of the twentieth century, success in the steel industry required both horizontal and vertical integration. Traditionally, the leading firms, such as U.S. Steel, Bethlehem Steel, and Republic Steel, produced a wide array of high-volume steel products and controlled the production process, from the mining of ore through the production of the finished steel products to marketing and distribution. But in the early 1950s, changes in market demand and technology transformed the industry.

The most significant change in market demand was driven by shifts in the economy. In the 1950s, "lighter" products, such as strips and sheets used to produce appliances, automobiles, and computers, became relatively more important than "heavier" products, such as rails and plates used for railroad and ship building. But the large steel producers, particularly U.S. Steel, were committed to the "heavy" products. Much of the steel makers' capacity was also poorly located to meet the new demands for lighter products. These factors allowed foreign producers to penetrate American markets.

The most notable technological advances were the basic oxygen furnace, the continuous casting process, and scrap metal processing with the electric arc furnace. The basic oxygen furnace, which was commercialized in 1950 by an Austrian firm, Linz-Donawitz, replaced the open-hearth process as the fastest way to convert iron into raw steel. Continuous casting, a German invention that was perfected in the early 1960s by a small American company, Roanoke Electric, allowed steel producers to bypass the costly process of pouring molten steel into ingots and reheating them for milling and finishing. The electric arc furnace was available before World War II but was little used before 1960. However, the increasing availability of scrap steel from discarded automobiles changed that, and by 1970, the electric arc furnace had become a viable way of producing nonalloy steel.

These technological advances had two profound effects. First, in postwar Japan and Germany, and later in Brazil and South Korea, start-up steel firms quickly adopted the basic oxygen furnace and continuous casting. By contrast, in the United States, the established integrated mills had made nonrecoverable investments in the older technologies, both in terms of physical capital and expertise. These firms were therefore reluctant to shift to the new technologies. As late as 1988, 93 percent of all Japanese firms and 88 percent of South Korean steel firms had adopted continuous casting, while only 60 percent of American firms had done so, and nearly half of these U.S. firms had made the changes only in the 1980s.[16] (U.S. Steel still does not have continuous casting at two of its major steel-producing plants.[17]) This allowed foreign producers to become competitive threats to the large integrated American producers.

Second, the new technology spurred the development of *minimills*, small nonintegrated producers that convert scrap metal into finished steel products. The success of minimill producers, such as Nucor, Chapparal, and North Star, is emblematic of the significance of this new way of producing steel. Minimills have eliminated the advantages of high-volume manufacturing in product lines, such as steel bars, structural shapes, and wire rods, and with Nucor's recent breakthrough in thin-slab casting, they may also take away the advantages of scale in the production of hot- and cold-rolled sheet. Although the large integrated producers have not disappeared, their importance has clearly diminished. From 1970 to 1990, American integrated producers retired nearly 40 percent of their capacity (55 million tons), while in the same period minimills increased their capacity from 4.5 million tons to 29 million tons.[18] Faced with strong competition from abroad and at home, the older, integrated steel makers have been forced to become more efficient, but they are still barely profitable. Not surprisingly, they have turned to government trade regulations for relief.

behaved toward competitors and employees, but also how they were managed, since government forced managers to collect detailed data on their operations that had not been gathered before and that were useful to professional managers. Nearly universal mandatory secondary school education also became the norm for industrialized nations in the first half of the twentieth century. This produced a workforce able to meet the specialized needs of large bureaucratic firms. Finally, through continued infrastructure investments, along with increasing military and shipbuilding expenditures, government became an important customer and partner of industry. These different roles embodied numerous potential conflicts and did not always fit together well in the new economic terrain.

Summary

The business infrastructure in 1910 made it efficient for firms to expand their markets, product lines, and production quantities. It is not surprising that the U.S. capital stock grew at a faster rate than the gross national product in the second half of the nineteenth century as businessmen invested in new technologies.[19] New technologies permitted a higher volume of standardized production, while the growth of the rail system permitted the reliable distribution of manufactured goods to a national market. The telegraph enabled large firms to monitor and control geographically separate suppliers, factories, and distributors. The growth of futures markets, capital markets, insurance companies, investment banks, and other financial institutions enabled business to be transacted on a scale that would have been impossible in 1840. By one estimate, the "transaction-processing sector," which included transportation, communication, and financial institutions, had become one-third of the U.S. economy by 1910.[20] To achieve the cost savings afforded by mass production and distribution, many firms reorganized and became more vertically and horizontally integrated firms. Increasingly, a new class of professional managers developed during this period and made critical decisions for firms. These managers became expert in functions that had not previously been handled by individual owners and entrepreneurs, and their skills became a source of competitive advantage for firms in industries that could benefit from expansion.

◆ ◆ ◆ ◆ ◆ ◆ THE WORLD TODAY

Doing Business Today

Since 1910, and particularly in the last 30 years, the ways of doing business have changed profoundly. Business practices that evolved in an era of political and economic stability can no longer be taken for granted when change is rapid and unpredictable. Globalization has presented threats and opportunities to firms that were accustomed to competing against domestic rivals. Computerized production processes allow specialized niche firms to offer tailor-made products at costs previously enjoyed only by larger firms exploiting scale economies. This is leading the large firms that once dominated the economy to increasingly prefer alliances and joint ventures to mergers and acquisitions.

The twentieth century witnessed several waves of diversification. Although some firms had begun to diversify beyond traditional product lines as early as 1890, the pace of diversification increased significantly after World War II, as firms discovered that their capabilities and skills were not exhausted by their historical product mix. Some of this diversification may have been the result of antitrust pressures that prevented large firms from growing even larger by acquiring rivals in the same industry. It also occurred because new opportunities opened in related markets and distribution channels. For example, consumer products companies like Philip Morris (Altria) and Quaker Oats believed that they could distribute a wide range of products through their traditional distribution channels. Technology-oriented companies, such as United Technologies or 3M, realized that they could apply skills mastered in an underlying technology or for a government customer, such as jet engines or adhesive chemistry, to a group of related business units operating in more traditional markets.

Other firms, such as ITT and Textron, acquired portfolios of unrelated businesses. Senior management ran these firms as holding companies and delegated most strategic and operating decisions to the individual business units. Although diversification was initially popular during the 1960s, the subsequent performance of conglomerates disappointed investors, and in some cases, such as RCA, excessive diversification appeared to ruin the company. Movements toward conglomeration eased in the 1970s, and the trend of subsequent mergers and acquisitions has been toward "deconglomeration" and a focus on core markets and enhanced linkages among business units.

Even with reduced conglomeration, firms have continued to form linkages across diverse businesses. The difference between the 1960s and today, however, is that diversification now takes place by strategic alliances and joint ventures as well as by merger and acquisition. This is in part because of the questionable performance of diversifying mergers. It has also occurred because the growth of data processing, telecommunications, and networking capabilities, as well as the growth of open standards in some industries, has made participation in alliances and joint ventures less costly and more predictable, relative to mergers. Antitrust authorities have also tended to not exhibit the same scrutiny toward alliances and joint ventures than they have toward mergers and acquisitions.

Firms have also taken a fresh look at their internal structure and the organization of the vertical chain of production. Until the 1960s, most large diversified firms followed the General Motors model and employed the M-form. But as these firms diversified into less related businesses, they eliminated layers of hierarchy and reduced corporate staffs. Even within firms with related product lines, the M-form became increasingly outdated. Some firms, such as Dow Corning, Amoco, and Citibank, had difficulty coordinating complicated production processes across different customer groups and market areas using traditional multidivisional structures. These firms adopted complex matrix structures, in which two or more overlapping hierarchies are used simultaneously. Other firms, including Benetton, Nike, and Harley-Davidson, simplified their internal hierarchies, controlling product design and brand image but leaving most other functions, including manufacturing, distribution, and retailing, to independent market specialists.

As firms focused on core businesses, market specialists performed more activities in the vertical chain. Firms like EDS, Accenture, and Servicemaster perform management functions that were previously done within hierarchical firms. Those functions that are not returning to the market via outsourcing are being automated, so managers can focus on a mix of technical, specialized, coordinative tasks and broader management duties.

Changes in industry conditions, organizational structures, and the balance of activities done inside the firm have together changed the job of the general manager.

In the large hierarchical firm that dominated the industrial landscape through the 1970s, a manager's power came from the chain of command. The manager's career path was usually within a particular functional department, and evaluations were based on contributions to departmental objectives. The organization was controlled through highly structured administrative systems, highly circumscribed job descriptions, and hierarchical relationships involving "bosses" and "subordinates." In many firms today, however, traditional hierarchies are weakening, and managers frequently switch companies. Decentralization, combined with rapid change, places a premium on the ability of managers to anticipate market shifts and quickly transform ideas into products.

The Infrastructure Today

Infrastructure today is marked by communications, transportation, and computing technologies that ensure coordination of extensive activities on a global scale. This, in turn, increases the interdependence of geographical markets and has magnified the costs of infrastructure failure. The interdependence of contemporary infrastructure was made tragically apparent in the aftermath of the September 11, 2001, terrorist attacks on New York and Washington. These attacks simultaneously halted two critical infrastructure sectors of the world economy—financial markets and air traffic. In addition, the attacks placed huge strains on other sectors whose influence cuts across the world economy, for example, insurance and leisure resorts.

Transportation   Automobile and air travel transformed the transportation infrastructure. The enormous increase in the number of motor vehicles, aided by national highway systems, also created a major industry in its own right. Interstate trucking has become a competitor to the railroads in the shipment of freight. Fast and reliable transportation of both passengers and freight by air has also profoundly changed the nature of business. Air, rail, and ground travel have become better coordinated. Increasing demands from shippers of large volumes of goods for efficient and reliable transportation over long distances, coupled with more sophisticated communications and data processing technology, has allowed goods to be shipped in containers that move from ships to railroads to trucks. The widespread use of air travel for both freight and passengers has reduced the need for cities and firms to be close to railroads and waterways. What Chicago was to the second half of the nineteenth century, Atlanta was to the second half of the twentieth, despite its relatively poor rail and water connections.

Communications   The twentieth century has seen the development of mass communications media, most notably radio and television, as well as the continuing development of the communications infrastructure initiated by the telegraph and the telephone and enhanced by data processing and networking technologies. The development of mass communications media has enabled business to create value through advertising and branding, public relations, and market research. Although fundamental developments in broadcasting, telecommunications, and computer technology occurred before World War II, many observers argue that the growth of these areas since 1950 has defined the economic infrastructure in the late twentieth century and set the stage for the twenty-first century. Observers struggle with how to characterize this new infrastructure, a recent effort being Thomas Friedman's discussion of a "flat" world that combines globalization, technological change, and post 9/11 world politics.[21]

In particular, telecommunications technologies, such as the fax or the modem, have made possible the nearly instantaneous transmission and reception of large amounts of complex information over long distances, creating global markets for a wide range of products and services. This technology, coupled with continuing improvements in data processing, has also drastically increased worker productivity, and has made the paper-based coordination and control of older integrated firms obsolete. The Internet has increased the possibilities for interfirm coordination via contracts, alliances, and joint ventures, although the ways in which the Internet will ultimately change how firms operate are unclear.[22]

Finance   The failure of financial markets in 1929, followed by worldwide recession in the 1930s, led to the creation of the modern financial infrastructure, through the separation of commercial and investment banking, the enhanced role of central banks, and the increased regulation of securities markets. The result was a stable financial services sector that supplied firms with equity and debt funding that the firms themselves could not provide through their retained earnings.

Deregulation of financial services in the 1970s and 1980s changed the role of the financial sector in the economic infrastructure. Since 1980, capital markets have more actively evaluated firm performance. The ready availability of large funds through so-called junk bonds allowed mergers and acquisitions (M&A) to multiply in number and dollar amount per deal. Globalization of financial markets facilitated many notable mergers and acquisitions such as Chrysler's merger with Daimler-Benz, Sony's acquisition of Columbia Studios, and German publisher Bertelsmann's acquisitions of Random House and Bantam Doubleday Dell. The dizzying pace of mergers and leveraged buyouts (LBOs) in the 1980s and 1990s, followed by the rush of Internet IPOs (initial public offerings), elevated finance from a support service to a central focus of many large firms. The success of such LBO firms as KKR seemed to challenge traditional notions of corporate governance and debt. The poor performance of M&As and the bursting of the Internet bubble, followed by some highly publicized bankruptcies, has raised harsh criticisms of recent corporate financial practices and spurred new governance legislation (such as the Sarbanes-Oxley Act of 2002) along with calls for greater transparency of financial reporting and greater accountability of managers to shareholders.

Financial accounting developed in the twentieth century to cope with the increased complexity of multidivisional firms, a process that began with the consolidation of General Motors in the 1920s and has continued with the creation of revised accounting procedures for mergers and acquisitions, restructuring, and partnerships. Cost or managerial accounting also provides managers with timely and accurate information on which to base their decisions. These developments were often made in conjunction with advances in data processing and statistical quality control. The most recent manifestation of this is the growth of activity-based accounting.

Production Technology   Computerization, the Internet, and other innovations have increased the sophistication of production technology, although with complex economic implications. Changes in production technology, such as the development of computer-aided design and manufacturing (CAD/CAM), have changed traditional ideas of price/quality tradeoffs and allowed the production of high-quality, tailor-made goods at low cost. In using new technologies, however, managers in the

2000s must choose between reformulating their strategies and reorganizing around new information and production technologies or using these technologies incrementally to reinforce traditional modes of production and organization.

Government Since 1910, the role of government in the economic infrastructure has become more complex. Government regulation of economic activities increased in the first half of the twentieth century, in response to two world wars and the Great Depression. The government also spent vast sums on the military and public works. The government's needs during World War II spread knowledge of differentiated personnel practices across many industries. Federal antitrust activity after World War II constrained competition by limiting horizontal mergers.

One area where the government has influenced infrastructure has been in support of Research and Development (R&D). Throughout the twentieth century, U.S. antitrust policy encouraged firms to develop new capabilities internally, through R&D efforts, rather than through M&As. Since World War II, a complex R&D establishment has developed that involves extensive government funding of basic research priorities in partnership with major research universities and private firms. Government policy has encouraged the diffusion and commercialization of R&D projects as well. While much of this research had military origins, this government support has greatly influenced such industries as computers, commercial aviation, and health care. The growth of the Internet out of the U.S. Defense Department and National Science Foundation is just a recent instance of the importance of government support of infrastructure R&D.

Since the 1960s, the government has relaxed many of the traditional regulations on some industries while increasing them on others. The breakup of the Bell System, the deregulation of airline, trucking, financial services, and health care industries, and the weakening of banking regulations have been major influences in the economy since 1970. Intergovernmental treaties and agreements on the development of regional free trade zones, such as with North American Free Trade Agreement (NAFTA) or the European Community, have greatly affected how firms compete in an increasingly global marketplace. Regulation of workplace safety, discrimination, and the environment became common in the 1960s and 1970s.

Infrastructure in Emerging Markets

Developed nations may possess modern infrastructures. Indeed, that is what makes them seem developed. Firms doing business today in the global economy, however, must contend with nations that lack modern infrastructure, and must adjust their business practices to the demands of such situations. The technologies that have revolutionized modern infrastructure are widely accessible, yet infrastructure hinders economic development in many emerging markets. The quality of transportation systems varies from nation to nation. Central Africa, for example, has few highways and its rails have deteriorated since colonial days. South Korea, on the other hand, boasts ultramodern rail lines and seaports. Transportation within urban business centers of developing nations can be particularly difficult. Example 1.3 describes the worst-case scenario—the near-complete gridlock that has plagued Bangkok, Thailand.

Developing nations may also lack other forms of infrastructure. Their businesses and consumers have limited access to the Internet, particularly through high-speed Integrated Services Digital Network or broadband connections. Their finance

EXAMPLE 1.3 ECONOMIC GYRATIONS AND TRAFFIC GRIDLOCK IN THAILAND

Thailand's economic growth during the last 25 years demonstrates the power of the big push. Thailand's growth began after its government liberalized investment and export policies and promoted a laissez-faire mentality. Many investors expected Thailand to become an economic tiger, and those expectations fed upon themselves. Banks granted credit, which fueled economic growth, which in turn encouraged even more liberal credit. Industrial plants proliferated, producing textiles, chemicals, oil, and plastics for export to developed nations. Between 1975 and 1995, Thailand's economy grew at an annual rate of 8 percent.

As the Western experience illustrates, economic growth must be accompanied by a well-developed infrastructure and managers able to handle the complex transactions that growth requires. Thailand lacks both, and the results have been dire. By 1996, Thailand's economic growth had faltered. Investment credit dried up, recently constructed office towers stood empty, and thousands of workers were laid off. In 1997, the government devalued the baht (the Thai unit of currency) to maintain the competitiveness of manufacturing plants, whose costs were higher than in nations such as China and Vietnam.

The Thai bubble has burst. The reasons why are a lesson in the importance of infrastructure. While the Thai economy was growing, its government adopted a laissez-faire approach. This encouraged foreign investment but discouraged investment needed for infrastructure. The main infrastructure problem in Thailand—especially in Bangkok—is one that we often take for granted in the West—traffic. Bangkok's roads are based on a traditional Asian pattern in which many small roads feed into a few large arteries that flow through the central city. During Thailand's boom, high-rise office buildings replaced the small dwellings that lined Bangkok's feeder roads. Construction was so dense that existing roads could not be widened. To add to traffic

problems, Bangkok does not have a subway. The result has been traffic gridlock in Bangkok beyond anything imaginable (even for New Yorkers). It can take more than an hour to drive less than 1 kilometer. Individuals who live outside of Bangkok and work or attend school in the city must allow six hours for the round-trip commute. About 300 women a year give birth in Bangkok taxis and rickshaws. Gas stations sell portable toilets. Traffic is so bad that in 1997 international business leaders cited it as the major reason they were reluctant to continue doing business in Bangkok.

Traffic is not the only infrastructure problem. Bangkok also suffers from periodic flooding during monsoon season due to unlimited development on the floodplains of the Zhao Phaya River. Pollution is also rampant, in part because the government does not regulate emissions. Finally, the absence of financial oversight for business loans has destabilized Thailand's banks and its currency. This combination of problems has soured overseas investors on Thailand. With many investment alternatives available across Asia, it is not surprising that the Thai bubble economy burst.

The Thai government has been aware of this problem and has tried to address it. For example, in 2003, the Thai Transport Ministry announced detailed new plans to address traffic problems. These measures ranged from stepped-up enforcement of traffic and parking regulations to a multibillion baht construction project to create new underpasses and overpasses (flyovers), double the size of the expressway system, and expand mass transit routes. These projects had been under consideration for years but had been postponed due to the downturn in the Thai economy, which also likely reduced the number of cars on the road in Bangkok. There is also a growing awareness that the traffic problems that plagued Bangkok are common ones for developing cities throughout Asia.

infrastructure is especially limited. In the past two decades, there have been substantial loans to businesses throughout Southeast Asia without the usual checks and balances provided by a diligent independent banking sector. Many analysts believe that this precipitated the Asian economic collapse of 1997. The economies of many developing nations have been crippled by their own governments. Businesses have been reluctant to invest in central and east Africa, for example, because of government corruption, cronyism, and civil war. Similar concerns arose just before President Haji Mohammad Soeharto's government in Indonesia fell in May 1998.

A nation's success in developing an infrastructure may lead to other problems, since it exposes the population to the pressures of the world economy and thus may strain the political consensus behind the economic system. For example, in Poland after the new millennium, nearly a decade of growth ended as the country fell victim to a European recession that interrupted plans to join the European Union. While many are doing well in Poland, many others are not, including older workers and farmers, and there is persistent high unemployment. In May 2002, the Polish government announced a heretofore unthinkable step—it intended to *renationalize* the Szczecin shipyard, which had been closed since March 2002, leaving 6,000 workers unpaid.

Summary

While the first half of the twentieth century was the era of the large hierarchical firm, changes in market conditions and infrastructure in the last 30 years have made smaller and flatter (and sometimes even virtual) business organizations the preferred structure in many industries. This change has come about for many reasons. The globalization of markets, facilitated by improvements in transportation, communications, and financial structures, has increased competition in many industries, which in turn has placed a premium on quickness and flexibility in responding to shifts in market demand. Changes in technology have reduced the advantages of large-scale production in many production processes. Advances in communications and computing, along with the development of industry standards, have enabled independent market specialists to coordinate complex activities over great distances, thus reducing the need for vertical integration. These changes have altered the role of the general manager and will continue to do so.

◆ ◆ ◆ ◆ ◆ THREE DIFFERENT WORLDS:
CONSISTENT PRINCIPLES, CHANGING CONDITIONS,
AND ADAPTIVE STRATEGIES

The enormous differences in business practices and infrastructure among the three periods surveyed in this chapter illustrate a key premise of this book: *Successful strategy results from applying consistent principles to constantly changing business conditions.* Strategies are—and should be—the adaptive, but principled, responses of firms to their surroundings. The infrastructure and market conditions of business do not uniquely determine the strategies that firms choose. In all three of our periods, there was considerable experimentation by firms, and various types of firms succeeded and failed. But market conditions and infrastructure do constrain how business can be conducted and the strategic choices that most managers can make. For example, by

1910 the railroad, telegraph, and telephone doomed most of the factors, agents, and brokers who facilitated trade so successfully in the 1840s.

Because circumstances change, one might conclude that no business strategy endures. Whatever one learns is bound to become obsolete as markets change or infrastructure evolves. This is true if one is looking for recipes for success under *any* conditions. If the survey in this chapter suggests nothing else, it is that recipes that purport to work under any market conditions or within any infrastructure (e.g., "Divest any business that does not have the largest or second-largest share in its market") are bound to fail eventually. Principles, however, are different from recipes. Principles are economic and behavioral relationships that apply to wide classes of circumstances. Because principles are robust, organizing the study of strategy around principles allows us to understand why certain strategies, business practices, and organizational arrangements are appropriate under one set of conditions but not others. Consider a simple, yet important, principle that has helped firms decide throughout business history whether to produce some good or service themselves or purchase it from another firm (the so-called make-or-buy decision):

> A production technology that involves a large upfront investment in facilities and equipment will have a cost advantage over a technology that involves a small upfront investment only if the firm can achieve a sufficiently large level of throughput.

This principle is as valid today as it was in 1840 or 1910. Applying this principle to the different conditions that existed in 1840, 1910, and today explains why large, vertically integrated firms were appropriate in 1910 but not in 1840 or, perhaps, today. In 1910, firms in industries such as steel, farm machinery, chemicals, and cigarettes could make their investments in new capital-intensive production techniques pay only if they could achieve sufficiently large throughput. These firms could have relied on independent market specialists to produce key inputs and components and bring their finished products to market. But the rudimentary communications and transportation infrastructure, though vastly more developed than that of the 1840s, would have prevented independent firms from coordinating the procurement, production, distribution, and marketing functions to achieve the needed throughput. In many industries, it was better to bring all of these critical functions inside a single vertically integrated firm and build a managerial hierarchy to coordinate them.

Vertical integration was unnecessary in 1840 because many of the technologies offering efficiencies from mass production did not exist. Even if they had existed, the undeveloped transportation and communications infrastructure would have limited the size of markets, constraining firms from achieving the throughput needed to take advantage of the new technologies. Vertical integration is less beneficial in today's business environment but for different reasons. Modern communications and computing technologies have reduced the costs of coordinating complex transactions. Independent suppliers and purchasers can work together to plan production runs and set delivery schedules more easily than they could have in 1910. As a result, transactions that in 1910 were most efficiently guided by the "visible hand" of hierarchy now can be carried out in the marketplace between independent specialists.

Recent changes in market conditions, infrastructure, and ways of doing business have created both opportunities and constraints for firms. For example, the growth of global markets has increased the potential sales of key products but has also produced powerful foreign competition. Similarly, changes in capital markets have made huge resources available to firms that could not have previously obtained them, but have

EXAMPLE 1.4 INFRASTRUCTURE AND EMERGING MARKETS:
THE RUSSIAN PRIVATIZATION PROGRAM[23]

Infrastructure generally develops over an extended time and in a largely incremental manner. That need not always be the case, however. In times of great change, an infrastructure may become obsolete overnight. The situation in Russia after 1989 provides an opportunity to see how decision makers developed a property rights infrastructure for a market economy.

Ideally, in an efficient property rights regime, the owners of productive assets will have the rights to control those assets and enjoy the gains (or suffer the losses) from their business decisions. This does not always occur, of course, in market economies—for example, when the owners of large public corporations (shareholders) are not the individuals (managers) who control those corporations. Even less-than-ideal arrangements can still be fairly efficient, however, if the parties involved in transactions can contract around imperfect arrangements and use incentives and sanctions. These conditions prevail in Western economies.

In the Soviet system before Premier Mikhail Gorbachev, there were three nominal holders of property rights in firms: politicians, managers, and the public. Most control rights were shared by a wide array of politicians, Communist Party officials, and enterprise managers. The public, via the Treasury, held cash flow rights (rights to capture gains and losses). The total control exercised by the Communist Party kept bureaucrats and managers from claiming cash flows for themselves (i.e., from profiting from the enterprise they regulated or managed). This system gave decision makers few incentives to make efficient decisions and forced the Soviet people to bear the costs of inefficiency.

Gorbachev and others, recognizing the inefficiency of the system, initiated reforms in 1986 that reallocated control rights from the Communist Party to the heads of government agencies and public enterprises, while maintaining public control over cash flows (i.e., profits and losses). As a result, managers could now decide how their enterprises would be run, but they would still not earn profits or suffer losses. By failing to link cash flow rights with control rights, however, Gorbachev's reforms, though well intended, increased inefficiencies by removing the constraints that kept politicians from appropriating cash flows from enterprises for themselves in pursuit of inefficient and politically based objectives. This exacerbated theft and bribery without solving the fundamental problem of the separation of control and cash flow rights.

Following the dissolution of the Soviet Union and the election of Boris Yeltsin as president of Russia in 1991, reformers pursued a privatization program that attempted to align cash flow rights and control rights in firms. They thus sought to resolve the fundamental property rights problem that had plagued the Soviet system. The privatization program had three parts. The first involved taking control rights away from the politicians and managers. The second involved transferring these rights to shareholders, who could exercise their control the way stockholders in Western economies do. Third, cash flow rights over privatized firms were granted directly to the public in the form of vouchers that were distributed to all citizens for a nominal fee. These vouchers could then be traded on an open market or used to purchase shares in privatized firms. The program was implemented quickly and on a large scale. Speed and scope were seen as necessary to minimize political interference with the program that would have perpetuated economic stagnation. By the end of 1994, over 16,000 midsized and large firms and nearly 100,000 small firms (including many local retail shops) had been privatized. In addition, over 750,000 new small businesses had been started. The ultimate results of the program are unclear, and the program did not escape political interference and its associated corruption. Advocates, however, claim that rapid privatization programs like those in Russia and Poland will eventually outperform more gradual programs, such as occurred in Hungary, as well as liberalization programs that the central government controls, or strong control, such as is being tried in China.

EXAMPLE 1.5 BUILDING NATIONAL INFRASTRUCTURE: THE TRANSCONTINENTAL RAILROAD[24]

The transcontinental railroad was built between 1863 and 1869, and connected Omaha (the eastern end of the Union Pacific Railroad) with Sacramento (the western home of the Central Pacific Railroad). This project was the Internet of its time. Together with the telegraph, which accompanied it along the route, the transcontinental railroad reduced the time and expense of moving people, goods, and information from the population centers in the East to California. Before its completion, trips to California took months by sea or over land, cost thousands of dollars, and were fraught with risks from disease to Indian attacks. Within months of its completion, a trip from New York to San Francisco took seven days, was much safer, and cost under a hundred dollars. Mail to California, which had been priced at dollars per ounce before 1869, cost pennies per ounce shortly afterward. The railroad fostered the growth of a national and continental perspective, such that a national stock market and national commodity markets developed, all working on a system of "standard" time, the impetus for which came from the railroads. This set the stage for the growth of national retail markets by the early years of the twentieth century.

The U.S. government heavily subsidized the builders of the railroad with financing and land grants. Since it crossed the continent in advance of settlement, this railroad was an infrastructure project that individual firms would not have found profitable to undertake on their own. Literally everything associated with the railroad had to be brought to the construction site as part of the venture. To ensure completion of the railroad, Congress structured the venture as a race between two firms (Central Pacific and Union Pacific) that started from opposite ends of the country and were built toward each other. The more miles of track that each firm graded and laid, the more the government would reimburse them for their costs. As one firm completed more of the route, there was less available to the other firm for reimbursement. Competing this way forced each firm to choose its strategies to lay the most track mileage in the shortest time. Managers emphasized speed at the expense of building the best or highest quality road.

As is also the case with the Internet today, managers, investors, government officials, and others were very uncertain regarding how to harness the commercial and transformative potential of the transcontinental railroad so that it could become profitable. Public optimism about the growth prospects of the railroads made financing available in the early years, and overbuilding of railroad lines was common. In 1872, a major scandal erupted over the financing of the transcontinental railroad and the misuse of funds for securing political influence regarding it. This was followed by a major national recession, the Panic of 1873, during the course of which sources of financing for railroads dried up. In the course of the 1870s, many of the major railroads went bankrupt and fell under the control of speculators, such as Jay Gould.

It was not until the 1890s that the transcontinental railroad was rationalized, unprofitable operations were closed, and remaining operations were upgraded and standardized by such general managers as E. H. Harriman. This allowed economies of scale in railroad network operations to be better realized. The result was an efficient and profitable industry that dominated transportation until the advent of the automobile.

also reduced the discretion of entrepreneurs. Technological innovation has given firms more control over production processes than ever before, but also allows smaller firms to compete on even or better terms with larger firms, who had previously been the primary beneficiaries of production improvements. Finally, at a time

EXAMPLE 1.6 THE RISKS OF MODERNITY: THE HALIFAX EXPLOSION OF 1917[25]

Living and working in a high-volume and high-speed economy not only offers great benefits but also poses considerable risks that were foreign to more traditional and less concentrated economies. One only need consider the attacks of 9/11 or the fears of "weapons of mass destruction" in advance of the Iraq War of 2003 to appreciate these risks. While weather threats, such as those from Hurricane Katrina, have become easier to anticipate through technological advances in radar and satellite-based warning systems, man-made threats, such as from terrorist attacks, have remained difficult to handle, owing to the inherent difficulties of predicting and detecting such threats in a free society.

A taste of modern vulnerability came to Halifax, Nova Scotia, on December 6, 1917. Halifax was a busy seaport that was enjoying a resurgence in prosperity as a result of wartime business supplying the Allied armies in Europe. Early that morning in the narrow waterway separating the harbor from more open waters, the Belgian relief ship *Imo* collided with *Mont Blanc*, a French munitions ship carrying hundreds of tons of picric acid, gun cotton, and TNT, an unstable high explosive. *Mont Blanc* was bound for Europe and had just sailed to Halifax from New York. Normally, a ship carrying high explosives would not be permitted in the harbor. However, wartime rules applied, German submarines were a threat in open waters, and secrecy was necessary.

The collision started fires on *Mont Blanc*, which ran aground 20 minutes later. The scene caught the attention of many Haligonians (as Halifax residents were known), who became spectators and victims of the events that followed. The fires ignited the TNT, which led to a blast that flattened everything within 2,600 feet and caused damage for a mile. *Mont Blanc* had become the largest bomb ever exploded (until Hiroshima). The explosion vaporized the 3,121-ton ship, sent a cloud more than 2,000 feet into the air, and showered the city with black residue. This was followed moments later by a *tsunami* that flooded both sides of the waterway, damaging and grounding dozens of ships, and washing hundreds of victims out to sea. Whole sections of the Halifax and nearby Dartmouth were destroyed in an instant. A few hurried emergency telegrams were sent in the wake of the disaster. One reached Boston, a city with ties to Halifax going back to the Revolutionary War. The Massachusetts Public Safety Committee was able to put several hundred volunteers on a train to Halifax by nightfall. That same night, however, snow began to fall from a major blizzard along the eastern coast that lasted for six days and isolated Halifax from other help.

The consequences were staggering. In a city of 60,000, over 2,000 were killed and over 9,000 injured, including many blinded after they had turned to look at the ship collision and fire. Another 6,000 people were made homeless in advance of a snowstorm, while 25,000 suffered from inadequate housing. Doctors who worked on relief would prove instrumental in developing the field of pediatric surgery in North America. Government inquiries about the blast and the response of authorities led to the development of national emergency plans in Canada. The blast itself was so powerful that J. Robert Oppenheimer, the lead scientist on the Manhattan Project in 1942 to develop the atomic bomb, used data from the Halifax explosion to predict the effects of the first atomic bombs. For the past 30 years, the people of Nova Scotia have sent the people of Boston a Christmas tree in remembrance of their assistance in 1917.

EXAMPLE 1.7 PARTIES, SCANDALS, AND DIRECTORS BEHAVING BADLY: AFTER THE BALL[26]

Since 2001, there has been a steady stream of instances of executive bad behavior ranging from poor judgment to outright criminality in such scandals as Enron and WorldCom. Perhaps one of the most publicized examples concerned a birthday party thrown by former Tyco CEO L. Dennis Kozlowski for his wife's fortieth birthday on the Mediterranean island of Sardinia. The party featured a Roman Empire theme and was part of a six-day event whose overall cost exceeded $2 million. The party featured dancing women, half-naked male models, and 75 toga-clad guests—all entertained by pop star Jimmy Buffett, whose band was flown in for the occasion. The party was featured in a 2003 indictment of Kozlowski and Mark Swartz, Tyco's former CFO, on charges that they looted the firm of $600 million by having the firm pay their private expenses. The first trial ended in a mistrial, but the two were eventually convicted and sentenced to long prison terms.

These types of scandalous displays are not new to American business. Indeed, they have been around as long as there have been large public firms under the control of professional managers or of the heirs of the initial founders and whose decisions affect thousands of employees and shareholders. One of the most notorious examples is the Hyde Park ball of 1905, thrown by James Hazen Hyde, the 28-year-old heir to the majority shareholder of the Equitable Life Assurance Society. The costume party's theme was French eighteenth-century nobility. It was held in the Hotel Sherry in Manhattan on two floors of mirrored ballrooms decorated to suggest the gardens of the Versailles Palace. Six hundred guests attended the party, whose centerpiece was a full play especially written for the occasion to feature the most famous French actress of the day, Rejane. The details of the party were widely reported the next day, and rumors spread that the ball had cost $200,000 and that Hyde had billed the Equitable for the costs. (The truth was that Hyde had paid for the party himself and that the cost was closer to $50,000.)

The scandal over the party set off a battle for control of the Equitable that was featured in 115 front-page articles in the *New York Times* in a single year. The battle would eventually lead Hyde to sell his interest in the Equitable and lead to reform legislation considerably limiting the discretion of insurance company managers. This battle was not just about the lavish tastes of the young heir. It was also concerned with the relationship between large insurance companies, their policyholders, and the business interests that sought investment funds from these firms. The firms seeking investment were largely associated with the railroads and steel companies, which were becoming quite profitable at the time through consolidation and rationalization. This brought names like Harriman, Frick, and Morgan onto the Equitable board. It was also a time when the rules governing how firms made their investments were just being formed and were rudimentary at best. Thus, a whole host of practices that would be illegal today were commonly practiced at the time. The investigation of the Hyde Park Ball allowed these practices to be exposed to the public, with the resulting cries of outrage and calls for reform.

when management skills are becoming more important for firms, pressures to outsource and downsize are thinning management ranks and making the jobs of managers who remain more complex. Managers have to decide how best to balance these tensions in ways that increase the adaptability of their firms.

EXAMPLE 1.8 BLAMING WAL-MART: THE PREQUEL[27]

The year 2005 witnessed a wide range of efforts by a diverse set of actors all focused on challenging the economic power of Wal-Mart, currently one of the largest corporations in the world and boasting more employees than the U.S. Army. The company is widely criticized for low wages, stingy benefits, and opposition to unions. Groups like Wal-Mart Watch have grown to monitor the company and expose its practices, such as by releasing an internal company memo recommending that the company start "discouraging unhealthy people from working at Wal-Mart" to stem rising health care costs. The company is regularly attacked in bestselling books, on such television shows as *South Park*, and on web sites like www.jibjab.com. Even a documentary film about Wal-Mart was released to theaters (*Wal-Mart: The High Cost of Low Price*). Wal-Mart, for its part, has tried to respond to criticisms vigorously and has even sponsored a conference for academics and journalists to examine the firm's impact on the U.S. economy.

This critical focus on one firm may seem unprecedented, but it is not. Seventy-five years before the latest in the anti–Wal-Mart campaign, a huge campaign was launched against a mass-market retailing firm that had become the fifth largest firm in America (with $1 billion in sales) and that was opening stores at an unheard of rate. The store was the Great Atlantic and Pacific Tea Company, a grocery chain known more commonly as A&P. In 1930, the *New York Times* called the company "the world's greatest retailing machine," and the firm's president attributed its success to a policy "of immediately passing on reductions in wholesale commodity prices to the consumer."

A&P's success, however, often came at the expense of others. Wages were kept low; wholesalers were squeezed and sometimes kept out of the supply chain altogether. When A&P entered a local market, it was not unusual for the smaller "mom and pop" stores in that market to go out of business, since they could not match A&P's prices or its large scale of operations.

These effects prompted reactions not unlike those that have greeted Wal-Mart. Unions agitated and sought to organize A&P workers. Laws were passed to keep the chains from getting discounts from manufacturers, and several states enacted "chain taxes." Independents organized the National Association of Retail Grocers and the National Association of Retail Druggists to lobby against A&P. Populist efforts to boycott the chain flourished. There was even a 1930 muckraking documentary film (*Forward America*) that parallels the Wal-Mart documentary.

The anti-A&P campaign fizzled when consumers continued to respond to lower prices and kept shopping at the chain. Unions also shifted their support from efforts to legislate against the chain to organizing efforts. While it is still too soon to tell with the campaign against Wal-Mart, the same outcome appears to be likely. Aggressive pursuit of low costs and low prices appears to be a way to succeed in mass-market retailing.

This book is about principles, not recipes. In the remaining chapters, we develop principles that pertain to the boundaries of the firm, the nature of industry structure and competition, the firm's strategic position within an industry, and the internal organization and management of the firm. Through the study of these principles, we believe that students of management can understand why firms and industries are organized the way they are and operate the way they do. We also believe that by judiciously applying these principles, managers can enhance the odds of successfully adapting their firms' strategies to the environments in which they compete.

CHAPTER SUMMARY

◆ A historical perspective demonstrates that while the nature of business has changed dramatically since 1840, successful businesses have always applied consistent principles to their business conditions.

◆ In 1840, communications and transportation infrastructures were poor. This increased the risk to businesses of operating in too large a market and mitigated against large-scale production. Business in 1840 was dominated by small, family-operated firms that relied on specialists in distribution as well as market makers who matched the needs of buyers and suppliers.

◆ By 1910, improvements in transportation and communications made large-scale national markets possible

◆ By 1910, innovations in production technology made it possible to greatly reduce unit costs through large-scale production. Mass distribution firms developed along with the growth in mass production.

◆ Businessmen in 1910 who invested in these new technologies needed to assure a sufficient throughput to keep production levels high. This led them to vertically integrate into raw materials acquisition, distribution, and retailing.

◆ Manufacturing firms also expanded their product offerings, creating new divisions that were managed within an "M-form" organization.

◆ These large hierarchical organizations required a professional managerial class. Unlike managers in 1840, professional managers in 1910 generally had little or no ownership interest in their firm.

◆ Continued improvements in communications and transportation have made the modern marketplace global. New technologies have reduced the advantages of large-scale production and vertical integration and promoted the growth of market specialists.

◆ In many industries, small manufacturers can meet the changing needs of their clients better than large hierarchical firms. In other industries, market specialists use computers, facsimile machines, and modems to coordinate activities that used to require a single integrated firm.

◆ Limited infrastructure hinders growth in many developing economies. The growing interconnectedness of firms in developed economies makes them increasingly vulnerable to global events and discontinuities beyond their normal scope of business.

◆ The continued importance of large firms means that the top managers of those firms remain important and highly visible. Concerns about managers range from the best incentive and compensation schemes, to their contributions to the firm and its owners, to the standards of behavior to which they should be held.

QUESTIONS

1. Why is infrastructure essential to economic development?

2. What is throughput? Is throughput a necessary condition for the success of modern business?

3. In light of recent downsizing and restructuring of Corporate America, was Chandler's explanation of benefits of size incorrect?

4. The technology to create a modern infrastructure is more widely available today than at any time in history. Do you think this will make it easier for developing nations to create modern economies that can compete with the economies of developed nations?

5. Two features of developing nations are an absence of strong contract law and limited transportation networks. How might these factors affect the vertical and horizontal boundaries of firms within these nations?

6. Many analysts say that the infrastructure of Eastern Europe today resembles that of the United States at the start of the twentieth century. If this is true, then what patterns of industrial growth might you expect in the next decade in the context of contemporary competitive forces?

7. How might U.S. industry have evolved differently if strong antitrust laws had been in place as of 1900?

8. In the past half-century, several American cities have been identified with specific industries: Akron/tires; Macon/carpets; Sunnyvale/computer chips; Orlando/tourism. Why do such centers emerge? Given evolving technology, what is their future?

9. The advent of professional managers was accompanied by skepticism regarding their trustworthiness and ethics in controlling large corporate assets on behalf of the shareholders. Today, this skepticism remains and has changed little since the founding of the managerial class a century ago and new laws concerning appropriate governance, such as Sarbanes-Oxley, continue to be introduced. Why has this skepticism remained so strong?

10. The Internet boom of the late 1990s was hailed as the advent of a "new economy" that would radically alter the face of business firms. By 2002, however, it was clear that the new economy had not arrived on schedule. With the advent of the Internet, digitization, and related innovations, what fundamental aspects of the economy have changed? Which aspects have remained the same? Why has the "new economy" been so slow to arrive?

11. There is considerable disagreement as to whether government regulation has largely positive or negative influences on economic growth. Compare and contrast the ways in which government involvement in particular industries may positively or negative influence the evolution of those industries.

12. Some firms seem to last forever. (For an extreme example, go to www.hbc.com.) In some industries, however, even the most effective firms may expect short lifetimes (lawn crews; Thai restaurants). Size certainly has something to do with longevity, but are other factors involved? How does size help larger firms or imperil smaller ones? What other factors besides size contribute to longevity?

13. How would you expect the business environment and the tasks of management to change over the next 30 or more years, given the aging of the baby boom, increasing life spans, the move toward service businesses, and other macro trends?

ENDNOTES

[1]For comparisons of Europe and America on these issues, see Chandler, A. D. and H. Daems (eds.), *Managerial Hierarchies: Comparative Perspectives on the Rise of the Modern Industrial Enterprise*, Cambridge, MA, Harvard University Press, 1980. For issues concerning industrialization within Europe, see Pollard, S., "Industrialization and the European Economy," *Economic History Review*, 26, November 1973, pp. 636–648. For international comparisons on the development of ideas about organizations and management, see Guillen, M. F., *Models of Management: Work, Authority, and Organization in a Comparative Perspective*, Chicago, University of Chicago Press, 1994.

[2]We use the term *businessmen* literally. Few, if any, women were involved in business in 1840. This had not changed much by 1910.

[3]This example comes from William Cronon's excellent history of the city of Chicago, *Nature's Metropolis*, New York, Norton, 1991.

[4]Madsen, A., *John Jacob Astor: America's First Multimillionaire*, New York, John Wiley, 2001.

[5]Cochran, T. C. and W. Miller, *The Age of Enterprise: A Social History of Industrial America*, New York, Harper & Row, 1961, p. 45.

[6]Cochran and Miller, *The Age of Enterprise*, p. 42.

[7]Yates, J., *Control Through Communication: The Rise of System in American Management*, Baltimore, MD, Johns Hopkins University Press, 1989, pp. 160–161.

[8]Yates, *Control Through Communication*, pp. 22–23.

[9]This example draws from Cronon, W., *Nature's Metropolis*, New York, Norton, 1991.

[10]Cochran and Miller, *The Age of Enterprise*, p. 42.

[11]Chandler, A. D., *Scale and Scope: The Dynamics of Industrial Capitalism*, Cambridge, MA, Belknap, 1990.

[12]Kanigel, R., *The One Best Way: Frederick Winslow Taylor and the Enigma of Efficiency*, New York, Viking, 1997.

[13]Chandler, A. D., *The Visible Hand*, Cambridge, MA, Belknap, 1977.

[14]For details, see Garnet, R. W., *The Telephone Enterprise: The Evolution of the Bell System's Horizontal Structure, 1876–1909*, Baltimore, MD, Johns Hopkins University Press, 1985. Also see Smith, G. D., *The Anatomy of a Business Strategy: Bell, Western Electric, and the Origins of the American Telephone Industry*, Baltimore, MD, Johns Hopkins University Press, 1985.

[15]John, Richard R., "Recasting the Information Infrastructure for the Industrial Age," pp. 55–105 in *A Nation Transformed by Information: How Information Has Shaped the United States from Colonial Times to the Present*, A. D. Chandler Jr. and J. W. Cortada, eds., Oxford, UK, Oxford University Press, 2000.

[16]Adams, W. and H. Mueller, "The Steel Industry," in W. Adams (ed.), *The Structure of American Industry*, 8th ed., New York, Macmillan, 1988, p. 90.

[17]Barnett, D. F. and R. W. Crandall, "Steel: Decline and Renewal," in L. L. Deutsch (ed.), *Industry Studies*, Englewood Cliffs, NJ, Prentice-Hall, 1993.

[18]Barnett and Crandall, "Steel: Decline and Renewal," p. 143.

[19]See Gallman, R. E., "The United States Capital Stock in the Nineteenth Century," Chap. 4 in Engerman, S. L. and R. E. Gallman (eds.), *Long-Term Factors in American Economic Growth*, Chicago, University of Chicago Press, 1986, pp. 165–214.

[20]Wallis, J. J. and D. C. North, "Measuring the Transaction Sector in the American Economy, 1870–1970," Chap. 3 in Engerman, S. L. and R. E. Gallman (eds.), *Long-Term Factors in American Economic Growth*, Chicago, University of Chicago Press, 1986, pp. 95–161.

[21]Chandler, A. D., *Inventing the Electronic Century*, New York, Free Press, 2001; Friedman, T. L., *The World Is Flat: A Brief History of the Twenty-First Century*, New York, Farrar, Straus, & Giroux, 2005.

[22]For a discussion of these interrelated issues, see Baldwin, C. Y. and K. Clark, *Design Rules: The Power of Modularity*, Cambridge, MA, MIT Press, 2000.

[23]This example is adapted from Boycko, M., A. Shleifer, and R. Vishny, *Privatizing Russia*, Cambridge, MA, MIT Press, 1996, Chaps. 2, 3, and 4. For additional details on the Russian program, see Blasi, J. R., M. Kroumova and D. Kruse, *Kremlin Capitalism: Privatizing the Russian Economy*, Ithaca, NY, ILR Press/Cornell, 1997. For details on the Polish privatization program, see Sachs, J., *Poland's Jump to the Market Economy*, Cambridge, MA, MIT Press, 1994.

[24]This example is based on information from Ambrose, S. E., *Nothing Like it in the World*, New York, Touchstone, 2000; and Bain, D. H., *Empire Express*, New York, Penguin, 1999.

[25]Information for this example comes from MacDonald, L. M., *Curse of the Narrows*, New York: Walker & Co., 2005.

[26]Materials for this example on the Hyde Park Ball are from Beard, P., *After the Ball*, New York: Harper Collins, 2003. Materials related to the Kozlowski party and indictment are from wire service accounts.

[27]Materials for this example are taken from Nocera, J., "To Change Wal-Mart, First Change America," *New York Times*, November 4, 2005; and from Mattera, P. Fighting Chain Stores Past and Present: The Roots of the Campaign Against Wal-Mart. Unpublished copy, 2005.

2

THE HORIZONTAL BOUNDARIES OF THE FIRM: ECONOMIES OF SCALE AND SCOPE

A firm's *horizontal boundaries* identify the quantities and varieties of products and services that it produces. Horizontal boundaries differ markedly across industries and across the firms within them. In some industries, such as microprocessors and airframe manufacturing, a few large firms (e.g., Intel and Airbus) account for an extremely large share of industry sales, and there are few viable small firms. In other industries, such as apparel design and management consulting, small firms predominate. Even the largest firms in these industries (e.g., Gucci, Accenture Consulting) are small by most conventional measures of business size. In still other industries, such as beer and computer software, small firms (Boston Beer Company, Blizzard Entertainment) and corporate giants (Anheuser-Busch, Microsoft) coexist successfully. And in a range of industries that include telecommunications and retailing, firms merge with the belief that bigger is better.

Why do giants dominate some industries and not others? When are mergers likely to generate efficiencies? The optimal horizontal boundaries of firms depend critically on *economies of scale and scope*. Economies of scale and scope are present whenever large-scale production, distribution, or retail processes have a cost advantage over smaller processes. Economies of scale and scope are not always available, however. Many activities, such as landscaping, tailoring, and the preparation of gourmet food, do not appear to enjoy substantial scale economies. Not surprisingly, these activities are typically performed by individuals or relatively small firms.

Economies of scale and scope not only affect the sizes of firms and the structure of markets, but they are also central to many issues in business strategy. Economies of scale and scope are fundamental to merger and diversification strategies. They affect pricing, entry and exit, and the ability of the firm to secure a long-term sustainable advantage. Thus, an understanding of the sources of economies of scale and scope is critical for formulating and assessing competitive strategy. This chapter identifies the key sources of economies of scale and scope and provides approaches for assessing their importance.

WHERE DO ECONOMIES OF SCALE COME FROM?

◆ ◆ ◆ ◆ ◆

Informally, when there are economies of scale and scope, "bigger is better." To facilitate identification and measurement, it is useful to define economies of scale and scope more precisely.

Definition of Economies of Scale

The production process for a specific good or service exhibits *economies of scale* over a range of output when average cost (i.e., cost per unit of output) declines over that range. If average cost (*AC*) declines as output increases, then the marginal cost of the last unit produced (*MC*) must be less than the average cost.[1] If average cost is increasing, then marginal cost must exceed average cost, and we say that production exhibits *diseconomies of scale*.

An *average cost curve* captures the relationship between average costs and output. Economists often depict average cost curves as U-shaped, as shown in Figure 2.1, so that average costs decline over low levels of output but increase at higher levels of output. A combination of factors may cause a firm to have U-shaped costs. A firm's average costs may decline initially as it spreads *fixed costs* over increasing output. Fixed costs are insensitive to volume; they must be expended regardless of the total output. Examples of such volume-insensitive costs are manufacturing overhead expenses, such as insurance, maintenance, and property taxes. As output increases, these costs are averaged over greater volumes, tending to drive down average costs. Firms may eventually see an upturn in average costs if they bump up against capacity constraints, or if they encounter bureaucratic and agency problems. We will develop most of these ideas in this chapter. Bureaucracy and agency problems are addressed in Chapter 3.

If average cost curves are U-shaped, then small and large firms would have higher costs than medium-sized firms. In reality, very large firms rarely seem to be at a substantial cost disadvantage relative to smaller rivals. The noted econometrician

FIGURE 2.1
A U-SHAPED AVERAGE COST CURVE

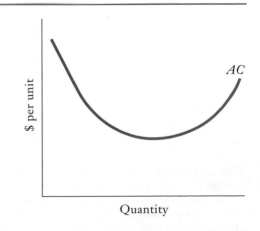

Average costs decline initially as fixed costs are spread over additional units of output. Average costs eventually rise as production runs up against capacity constraints.

John Johnston once examined production costs for a number of industries and determined that the corresponding cost curves were closer to L-shaped than U-shaped. Figure 2.2 depicts an L-shaped cost curve. When average cost curves are L-shaped, average costs decline up to the *minimum efficient scale (MES)* of production. When average cost curves are L-shaped, all firms operating at or beyond MES have similar average costs. Firms producing well past MES can avoid diseconomies of scale by increasing their productive capacity. Sometimes, they merely replicate the productive facilities of the minimum MES plant (as when cement companies build MES plants in multiple locations).

Definition of Economies of Scope

Economies of scale are related to economies of scope, and the two terms are sometimes used interchangeably. Economies of scale exist if the firm achieves unit-cost savings as it increases the production of a given good or service. *Economies of scope* exist if the firm achieves savings as it increases the variety of goods and services it produces. Whereas economies of scale are usually defined in terms of declining average cost functions, economies of scope are usually defined in terms of the relative total cost of producing a variety of goods and services together in one firm versus separately in two or more firms.

Because it is difficult to show scope economies graphically, we will instead introduce a simple mathematical formulation. Formally, let $TC(Q_x, Q_y)$ denote the total cost to a single firm producing Q_x units of good X and Q_y units of good Y. Then a production process exhibits scope economies if

$$TC(Q_x, Q_y) < TC(Q_x, 0) + TC(0, Q_y)$$

This formula captures the idea that it is cheaper for a single firm to produce both goods X and Y than for one firm to produce X and another to produce Y. To provide another interpretation of the definition, note that a firm's total costs are zero if it produces zero quantities of both products, so $TC(0, 0) = 0$. Then, rearrange the preceding formula to read:

$$TC(Q_x, Q_y) - TC(0, Q_y) < TC(Q_x, 0) - TC(0, 0)$$

FIGURE 2.2
AN L-SHAPED AVERAGE COST CURVE

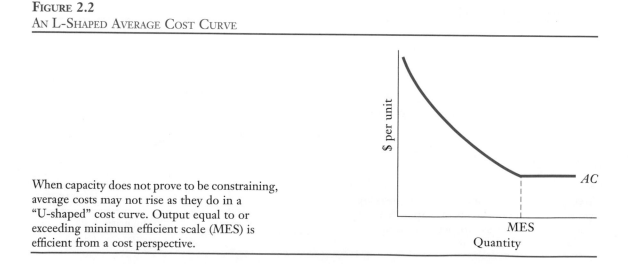

When capacity does not prove to be constraining, average costs may not rise as they do in a "U-shaped" cost curve. Output equal to or exceeding minimum efficient scale (MES) is efficient from a cost perspective.

This says that the incremental cost of producing Q_x units of good X, as opposed to none at all, is lower when the firm is producing a positive quantity Q_y of good Y.

The cost implications of economies of scope are shown in Table 2.1, which shows the production costs of a hypothetical manufacturer of adhesive message notes (good X) and tape (good Y). To produce tape, the firm must spend \$100 million to perfect the process of working with chemical adhesives, attaching these adhesives to cellophane, and manufacturing and packaging tape. Once this setup cost is incurred, each roll of tape can be produced at a cost of \$.20 each. Thus, we can write $TC(0, Q_y) = \$100m + .20Q_y$. For example, if $Q_y = 600$ million rolls of tape, total cost is \$220 million.

Now, given that the firm has made the investment in developing the know-how for manufacturing tape, much of that know-how can be applied to producing related products, such as adhesive message notes. Suppose that the additional investment needed to ramp up production of message notes, given that the upfront setup costs in tape production have already been incurred, is \$20m. Suppose also that the cost per ream of message notes is \$.05. Then $TC(Q_x, Q_y) = \$120m + .05Q_x + .20Q_y$. For example, if $Q_y = 600$ million and $Q_x = 100$ million, then total cost is \$245m. The cost to the firm of adding message notes to its production line is only \$245m − \$220m = \$25m.

By contrast, if the firm did not produce tape, much of the upfront investment in developing the know-how for working with chemical adhesives would have to be made just to get the expertise needed to make message notes. If developing this know-how requires an investment of \$50m, then with a per-ream cost of \$.05, $TC(Q_x, 0) = \$50m + .05Q_x$. Thus, if $Q_x = 100m$, total cost would equal \$55m. This more than doubles the additional cost to the tape manufacturer to add message notes to its production line.

This example illustrates the economic logic of exploiting economies of scope. This logic is often known as "leveraging core competences," "competing on capabilities," or "mobilizing invisible assets."[2] In this example it makes much more sense for the tape manufacturer to diversify into the production of message notes than it would for a firm producing unrelated products, such as a prepared-food manufacturer.

Economies of scale and scope may arise at any point in the production process, from acquisition and use of raw inputs to distribution and retailing. Although business managers often cite scale and scope economies as justifications for growth activities and mergers, they do not always exist. In some cases, bigger may be worse! Thus, it is important to identify specific sources of scale economies and, if possible, measure their magnitude. The rest of this chapter shows how to do this.

TABLE 2.1
COSTS TO PRINT MESSAGE NOTES AND TAPE

Q_x	Q_y	$TC(Q_x,Q_y)$
100m	0	\$55m
0	600m	\$220m
100m	600m	\$245m
200m	0	\$60m
0	1200m	\$340m
200m	1200m	\$370m

◆ ◆ ◆ ◆ ◆ WHERE DO SCALE ECONOMIES COME FROM?

There are four major sources of scale and scope economies:

1. Indivisibilities and the spreading of fixed costs
2. Increased productivity of variable inputs (mainly having to do with specialization)
3. Inventories
4. Engineering principles associated with the "cube-square rule"

We discuss each in detail.

Indivisibilities and the Spreading of Fixed Costs

The most common source of economies of scale is the spreading of fixed costs over an ever-greater volume of output. Fixed costs arise when there are *indivisibilities* in the production process. Indivisibility simply means that an input cannot be scaled down below a certain minimum size, even when the level of output is very small.

Web-based grocery stores such as Peapod and defunct Webvan have struggled to overcome the challenge of indivisibilities. Webvan once shipped groceries from its Chicago warehouse to suburbs throughout Chicagoland. To ship to a suburb such as Highland Park, Webvan required a truck, driver, and fuel. The amount that Webvan paid for these inputs was largely independent of whether it delivered to one household or 10. Webvan was unable to generate substantial business in Highland Park (or other Illinois communities, for that matter), so it sent its trucks virtually empty. Webvan was unable to charge enough to recoup its fixed costs. Peapod faces the same problem today but does enough business in densely populated neighborhoods in downtown Chicago to survive.

Indivisibilities may give rise to fixed costs, and hence scale and scope economies, at several different levels: the product level, the plant level, and the multiplant level. The next few subsections discuss the link between fixed costs and economies of scale at each of these levels.

Economies of Scale Due to Spreading of Product-Specific Fixed Costs

The production of a specific product often involves fixed costs. Product-specific fixed costs may include special equipment such as the cost to manufacture a special die used to make an aircraft fuselage. Fixed costs may also include research and development expenses such as the estimated $500 million or more required to develop a new pharmaceutical product; training expenses such as the cost of a one-week training program preceding the implementation of a total quality management initiative; and the costs necessary to set up a production process such as the time and expense required to set up a textbook before printing it.

Even a simple production process may require substantial fixed costs. The production of an aluminum can involves only a few steps. Aluminum sheets are cut to size, formed into a rounded shape, and then punched into the familiar cylindrical can shape. A lid with an opener is then soldered on top. Although the process is simple, a single line for producing aluminum cans can cost about $50 million. If the opportunity cost of tying up funds is 10 percent, the fixed costs expressed on an annualized basis could amount to about $5 million per year.[3]

The average fixed cost of producing aluminum cans falls as output increases. To illustrate, suppose that the peak capacity of a fully automated aluminum can plant is 500 million cans annually (or about 1 percent of the total U.S market). The average fixed cost of operating this plant at full capacity for one year is determined by dividing the annual cost ($5 million) by total output (500 million). This works out to 1 cent per can. On the other hand, if the plant only operates at 25 percent of capacity, for total annual production of 125 million cans, then average fixed costs equal 4 cents per can. The underutilized plant is operating at a 3-cent cost differential per can. In a price-competitive industry like aluminum can manufacturing, such a cost differential could make the difference between profit and loss.

Economies of Scale Due to Tradeoffs among Alternative Technologies

Suppose that a firm is considering entering the can manufacturing business but does not anticipate being able to sell more than 125 million cans annually. Is it doomed to a 3-cent per can cost disadvantage? The answer depends on the nature of the alternative production technologies and the planned production output. The fully automated technology described previously may yield the greatest cost savings when used to capacity, but it may not be the best choice at lower production levels. There may be an alternative that requires less initial investment, albeit with a greater reliance on ongoing expenses. A firm choosing this "partially automated" technology may be able to enjoy fairly low average costs even if it produces 125 million cans annually.

Suppose that the fixed costs of setting up a partially automated plant are $12.5 million, annualized to $1.25 million per year. The shortcoming of this plant is that it requires labor costs of 1 cent per can that are not needed at the fully automated plant. The cost comparison between the two plants is shown in Table 2.2.

Table 2.2 shows that while the fully automated technology has lower average total costs at high production levels, it is more costly at lower production levels. This is seen in Figure 2.3, which depicts average cost curves for both the fully and partially automated technologies. The curve labeled SAC_1 is the average cost curve for a plant that has adopted the fully automated technology; the curve labeled SAC_2 is the average cost curve for a plant that has adopted the partially automated technology. At output levels above 375 million, the fully automated technology has lower average total costs. At lower output levels, the partially automated technology is cheaper.

The aluminum can example demonstrates the difference between economies of scale that arise from increased capacity utilization with a given production technology and economies of scale that arise as a firm chooses among alternative production technologies. Reductions in average costs due to increases in capacity utilization are *short-run* economies of scale in that they occur within a plant of a given size. Reductions due to adoption of a technology that has high fixed costs but lower variable costs are *long-run* economies of scale. Given time to build a plant from scratch, a firm

TABLE 2.2
COSTS OF PRODUCING ALUMINUM CANS

	500 Million Cans per Year	*125 Million Cans per Year*
Fully Automated	Average fixed costs = .01 Average labor costs = .00 Average materials costs = .03 Average total costs = .04	Average fixed costs = .04 Average labor costs = .00 Average materials costs = .03 Average total costs = .07
Partially Automated	Average fixed costs = .0025 Average labor costs = .01 Average materials costs = .03 Average total costs = .0425	Average fixed costs = .01 Average labor costs = .01 Average materials costs = .03 Average total costs = .05

FIGURE 2.3
AVERAGE COST CURVES FOR CAN PRODUCTION

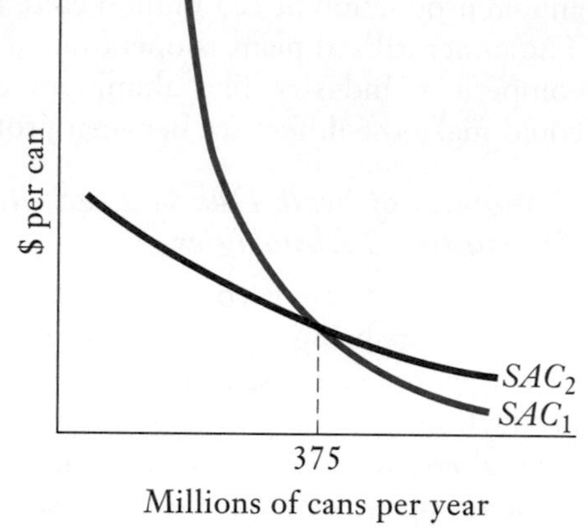

SAC_1 represents a high fixed/low variable cost technology. SAC_2 represents a low fixed cost/high variable cost technology. At low levels of output, it is cheaper to use the latter technology. At high outputs, it is cheaper to use the former.

can choose the plant that best meets its production needs, avoiding excessive fixed costs if production is expected to be low and excessive capacity costs if production is expected to be high.

Figure 2.4 illustrates the distinction between short-run and long-run economies of scale. (The Primer discusses this distinction at length.) SAC_1 and SAC_2, which duplicate the cost curves in Figure 2.3, are the short-run average cost curves for the partially automated and fully automated plants, respectively. Each decreases because, as output within each plant grows, fixed costs are spread over more and more units. If we trace out the lower regions of each curve, we see the long-run average cost curve. The long-run average cost curve is everywhere on or below each short-run average cost curve. This reflects the flexibility that firms have to adopt the technology that is most appropriate for their forecasted output.

Indivisibilities are More Likely When Production Is Capital Intensive

When the costs of productive capital such as factories and assembly lines represent a significant percentage of total costs, we say that production is *capital intensive*. Much

FIGURE 2.4
SHORT-RUN VERSUS LONG-RUN AVERAGE COST

In the long run, firms may choose their production technology as well as their output. Firms planning to produce beyond point X will choose the technology represented by SAC_1. Firms planning to produce less than point X will choose the technology represented by SAC_2. The heavy "lower envelope" of the two cost curves represents the lowest possible cost for each level of production, and is called the *long-run average cost curve*.

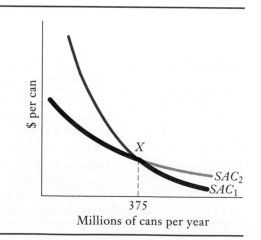

EXAMPLE 2.1 HUB-AND-SPOKE NETWORKS AND ECONOMIES OF SCOPE IN THE AIRLINE INDUSTRY

An important example of multiplant economies of scope arises in a number of industries in which goods and services are routed to and from several markets. In these industries, which include airlines, railroads, and telecommunications, distribution is organized around "hub-and-spoke" networks. In an airline hub-and-spoke network, an airline flies passengers from a set of "spoke" cities through a central "hub," where passengers then change planes and fly from the hub to their outbound destinations. Thus, a passenger flying from, say, Omaha to Boston on United Airlines would board an United flight from Omaha to Chicago, change planes, and then fly from Chicago to Boston.

Recall that economies of scope occur when a firm producing many products has a lower average cost than a firm producing just a few products. In the airline industry, it makes economic sense to think about individual origin–destination pairs (e.g., Omaha to Boston, Chicago to Boston) as distinct products. Viewed in this way, economies of scope exist if an airline's average cost is lower the more origin–destination pairs it serves.

To understand how hub-and-spoke networks give rise to economies of *scope*, it is first necessary to explain *economies of density*. Economies of density are essentially economies of scale along a given route, that is, reductions in average cost as traffic volume on the route increases. (In the airline industry, traffic volume is measured as revenue-passenger miles [RPM], which is the number of passengers on the route multiplied by the number of miles, and average cost is the cost per revenue passenger mile.) Economies of density occur because of spreading flight-specific fixed costs (e.g., costs of the flight and cabin crew, fuel, aircraft servicing) and because of the economies of aircraft size. In the airline industry, traffic-sensitive costs (e.g., food, ticket handling) are small in relation to flight-specific fixed costs. Thus, as its traffic volume increases, an airline can fill a larger fraction of its seats on a given type of aircraft (in airline industry lingo, it increases its *load factor*—the ratio of passengers

to available seats), and because the airline's total costs increase only slightly, its cost per RPM falls as it spreads the flight-specific fixed costs over more traffic volume. As traffic volume on the route gets even larger, it becomes worthwhile to substitute larger aircraft (e.g., 300-seat Boeing 767s) for smaller aircraft (e.g., 150-seat Boeing 737s). A key aspect of this substitution is that the 300-seat aircraft flown a given distance at a given load factor is less than twice as costly as the 150-seat aircraft flown the same distance at the same load factor. The reason for this is that doubling the number of seats and passengers on a plane does not require doubling the sizes of flight and cabin crews or the amount of fuel used, and that the 300-seat aircraft is less than twice as costly to build as the 150-seat aircraft, owing to the cube-square rule, which will be discussed below.

Economies of scope emerge from the interplay of economies of density and the properties of a hub-and-spoke network. To see how, consider an origin–destination pair such as Omaha to Boston. This pair has a modest amount of daily traffic. An airline serving only this route would use small planes and operate with a relatively low load factor. But now consider United's traffic on this route. United offers daily flights from Omaha to Chicago. It not only draws passengers who want to travel from Omaha to Chicago, but it would also draw passengers traveling from Omaha to all other points accessible from Chicago in the network, including Boston. By including the Omaha–Chicago route as part of a larger hub-and-spoke network, United can operate a larger airplane at higher load factors than can an airline serving only Omaha–Chicago. United benefits from economies of density to achieve a lower cost per RPM along this route. Moreover, because there will now be passengers traveling between Chicago and other spoke cities in this network, the airline's load factors on these other spokes will increase somewhat, thereby lowering the costs per RPM on these routes as well. This is precisely what is meant by economies of scope.

As more travelers take to the skies, and as smaller and more efficient jet aircraft reach the market, it is becoming possible to fly efficient nonstop flights between what were previously spoke cities. For example, Jet Blue flies nonstop from Fort Lauderdale to Long Beach; previously, this trip required flying on another carrier and changing at a hub city. This trend is reducing the economic advantages that were previously enjoyed by the major hub-and-spoke carriers.

productive capital is indivisible and therefore a source of scale economies. As long as there is spare capacity, output can be expanded at little additional expense. As a result, average costs fall. Conversely, cutbacks in output may not reduce total costs by much, and so average costs rise. When most production expenses go to raw materials or labor, we say that production is *materials* or *labor intensive*. Because materials and labor are divisible, they usually change in rough proportion to changes in output, with the result that average costs do not vary much with output. It follows that substantial product-specific economies of scale are more likely when production is capital intensive, and minimal product-specific economies of scale are likely when production is materials or labor intensive.

"The Division of Labor Is Limited by the Extent of the Market"

Economies of scale are closely related to the concept of specialization. To become specialists, individuals or firms must often make substantial investments. They will not do so unless demand justifies it; if demand is inadequate, they will not recover their costs and they will be reluctant to specialize. This is the logic underlying Adam Smith's famous theorem, "The division of labor is limited by the extent of the market." (Adam Smith is the father of laissez-faire economics. His best-known work, *Wealth of Nations*, was published in 1776.) The *division of labor* refers to the specialization of productive activities, such as when a financial analyst specializes in the analysis of start-up biotech companies. As suggested, this usually requires upfront investments—the analyst must do considerable research on the biotech industry before having the credibility to compete for clients. The *extent of the market* refers to the magnitude of demand for these activities, such as the demand for financial advice about start-up biotech companies. Although Smith referred mainly to specialization by individuals, his ideas apply equally well to specialization by firms.

Smith's theorem states that individuals or firms will not make specialized investments unless the market is big enough to support them. Indeed, growing prospects for start-up biotech companies during the late-1980s did cause some financial analysts to specialize in this sector. One additional implication of Smith's theorem is that larger markets will support a more specialized array of activities than smaller markets can. A small town may have a pet store that caters to owners of all kinds of critters. In the big city, one can find dog groomers, salt-water aquarium boutiques, and stores that sell nothing but exotic birds.

Smith's theorem also sheds light on the growth of the hierarchical firm described in Chapter 1. In a small market, the entrepreneurial firm must perform all of the tasks in the vertical chain because the market cannot support specialists in accounting, marketing, distribution, and such. Specialists emerge in larger markets, and the growing firm can use them for many activities. When the market gets even larger, the demand for the firm's product may become so great that the firm can produce enough of its inputs in-house to fully exploit available economies of scale. The firm makes the

EXAMPLE 2.2 THE DIVISION OF LABOR IN MEDICAL MARKETS

An interesting application of Smith's theorem involves the specialization of medical care. Physicians may practice general medicine or specialty medicine. Generalists and specialists differ in both the amount of training they receive and the skill with which they practice. Take the case of surgery. To become general surgeons, medical school graduates spend three to four years in a surgical residency. They are then qualified to perform a wide variety of surgical procedures. Because their training is broad, general surgeons do all kinds of surgery with good, but not necessarily great, skill.

Contrast this with the training and skills of a thoracic surgeon. Thoracic surgeons specialize in the thoracic region, between the neck and the abdomen. To become a thoracic surgeon, a medical school graduate must complete a residency in general surgery, and then an additional two year residency in thoracic surgery. Figure 2.5 depicts average "cost" curves for thoracic surgery performed by a general surgeon and a thoracic surgeon. We use "cost" in quotes because it represents the full cost of care, which is lower if the surgery is successful. (Successful surgery usually implies fewer

complications, shorter hospital stays, and a shorter period of recuperation.) The average cost curves are downward sloping to reflect the spreading out of the initial investments in training. The cost curve for the thoracic surgeon starts off much higher than the cost curve for the general surgeon because of the greater investment in time. However, the thoracic surgeon's cost curve eventually falls below the cost curve of a general surgeon because the thoracic surgeon will perform thoracic surgery more effectively than most general surgeons.

According to Smith's theorem, when the demand for thoracic surgery in a market is low, then the market will not support a specialized surgeon. Instead, thoracic surgery will be performed by a general surgeon, who may also perform other kinds of surgery. This may be seen in Figure 2.6, which superimposes demand curves over cost curves. For low levels of demand, such as at D_1, the market can support a general surgeon. A general surgeon who charges a price for thoracic surgery above P_1 can more than cover average costs. When demand is D_1, the market cannot support a thoracic surgeon. There is no price high enough to enable thoracic surgeons to recoup their costs.

FIGURE 2.5
COST CURVES FOR GENERAL AND THORACIC SURGEONS

General surgeons incur lower training costs than do thoracic surgeons, but usually are less efficient in performing thoracic surgery. Thus, the general surgeon's average cost curve is below the thoracic surgeon's for low volumes (reflecting lower average fixed costs) but above the thoracic surgeon's for high volumes (reflecting higher average variable costs).

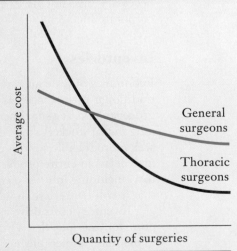

FIGURE 2.6

COST AND DEMAND FOR THORACIC SURGERY

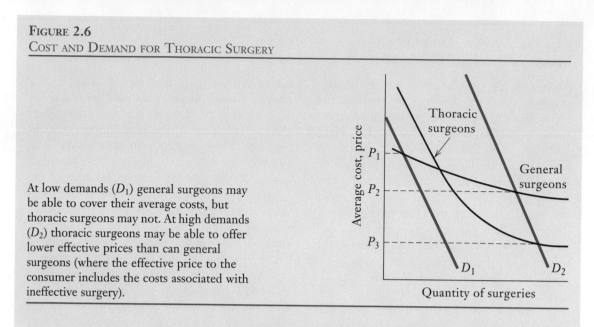

At low demands (D_1) general surgeons may be able to cover their average costs, but thoracic surgeons may not. At high demands (D_2) thoracic surgeons may be able to offer lower effective prices than can general surgeons (where the effective price to the consumer includes the costs associated with ineffective surgery).

When demand increases to D_2, the market can support a thoracic surgeon. A thoracic surgeon who charges a price above P_3 can cover average costs. Moreover, at prices between P_2 and P_3, the thoracic surgeon can make a profit, but the general surgeon cannot. Thus, at this high level of demand, the thoracic surgeon can drive the general surgeon from the market for thoracic surgery.

The same logic should apply to other specialized surgical and medical services. Thus, in large markets, we may expect to see a range of specialists and few or no generalists.

Researchers at the RAND Corporation documented this pattern of the division of labor in medical markets.[4] They found that general practitioners are disproportionately located in smaller towns—they do not appear to fare well in larger markets, which have a wider assortment of specialists. James Baumgardner also found that physicians who practice in small towns treat a wider range of illnesses than do their big-city counterparts.[5]

necessary investments to develop human and physical capital, thereby adding to its corporate hierarchy.

Inventories

Economies of scale may arise when firms carry inventories. Inventory may include the traditional variety, such as parts at an auto repair shop, and nontraditional, such as grocery clerks at a supermarket. Firms carry inventory to minimize the chances of running out of stock. A stock-out can cause lost sales and can lead potential customers to seek more reliable sources of supply. For a manufacturer, a stock-out for a single part may delay an entire production process. Of course, there are costs to carrying inventory, including interest on the expenses borne in producing the inventory and the risk that it will depreciate in value while waiting to be used or sold.

Inventory costs drive up the average costs of the goods that are actually sold. Suppose, for example, that a firm needs to hold inventories equal to 10 percent of its sales to maintain a tolerable level of expected stock-outs. This will increase its average cost of goods sold by as much as 10 percent. (The increase will be smaller if, at the end of the selling season, the firm can sell its inventories at some fraction of original cost.) Inventory costs are so important in some sectors, such as mass merchandising, that firms like Wal-Mart and Target are able to outcompete their rivals largely on their ability to manage inventories.

In general, inventory costs are proportional to the ratio of inventory holdings to sales. The need to carry inventories creates economies of scale because firms doing a high volume of business can usually maintain a lower ratio of inventory to sales while achieving a similar level of stock-outs. This reduces their average cost of goods sold. A full justification for this statement requires an extensive foray into the complex topic of *queuing theory*. This is well beyond the scope of this text, so instead we will offer an illustrative example.

Consider two equal-sized hospitals stocking a blood substitute that must be discarded after one month. Each hospital expects to use 20 liters per month. However, to ensure that there is only a 5 percent chance of running out, each holds 50 liters in inventory. If the blood substitute costs $100 per liter, then each hospital has an expected average cost of $250 per liter actually used. Suppose that the two hospitals share inventories (as they might if they merged). If one hospital runs out of the blood substitute, it can obtain it from the other. This implies that if the two hospitals maintain their present inventories of 50 liters apiece, their outage rates will be much less than 5 percent. It follows that they can maintain the desired 5 percent outage rate with lower inventories and, therefore, lower inventory holding costs. William Lynk has estimated the potential economies from hospitals sharing supplies and equipment in this way.[6] The potential savings is as large as 10 percent in some departments.

The Cube-Square Rule and the Physical Properties of Production

Economies of scale also arise because of the physical properties of processing units. An important example is the *cube-square rule*, well known to engineers.[7] It states that as we increase the volume of the vessel (e.g., a tank or a pipe) by a given proportion (e.g., we double it), the surface area increases by less than this proportion (e.g., it less than doubles).

What does the cube-square rule have to do with economies of scale? In many production processes, production capacity is proportional to the *volume* of the production vessel, whereas the total cost of producing at capacity is proportional to the *surface area* of the vessel. This implies that as capacity increases, the average cost of producing at capacity decreases because the ratio of surface area to volume decreases. More generally, the physical properties of production often allow firms to expand capacity without comparable increases in costs.

Oil pipelines are an excellent example of this phenomenon. The cost of transporting oil is an increasing function of the friction between the oil and the pipe. Because the friction increases as the pipe's surface area increases, transportation costs are proportional to the pipe's surface area. By contrast, the amount of oil that can be pumped through the pipe depends on its volume.[8] Thus, the average cost of a pipeline declines as desired throughput increases. Other processes that exhibit scale economies owing to the cube-square rule or related properties include warehousing (the cost of making the warehouse is largely determined by its surface area) and brewing beer (the volume of the brewing tanks determine output).

◆ ◆ ◆ ◆ ◆ SPECIAL SOURCES OF ECONOMIES OF SCALE AND SCOPE

The sources of economies of scale in the previous section related mainly to production. This section describes three special sources of economies of scale and scope that have to do with areas other than production:

1. Economies of scale and scope in purchasing
2. Economies of scale and scope in advertising
3. Economies of scale and scope in research and development

Economies of Scale and Scope in Purchasing

Most of us have purchased items in bulk. Whether we are buying gallon containers of milk or six-packs of soda, the price per unit of many items falls as the amount we purchase increases. Big businesses that make large purchases from their suppliers may also obtain discounts, enabling them to enjoy a cost advantage over smaller rivals.

There is no requirement that big buyers obtain bulk discounts. A supplier might not care whether its sales of X units come from a single buyer or from X different buyers. A supplier would care, for three possible reasons:

1. It may be less costly to sell to a single buyer. If each sale requires some fixed cost, say in writing a contract, setting up a production run, or delivering the product, then it truly is less costly to sell in bulk.
2. A bulk purchaser has more to gain from getting the best price and therefore will be more price sensitive. For example, someone purchasing hundreds of computer printers for a university is more likely to switch vendors over small price differences than someone else buying one printer for personal use.
3. The supplier may fear a costly disruption to operations, or in the extreme case, bankruptcy, if it fails to do business with a large purchaser. The supplier may offer a discount to the large purchaser so as to assure a steady flow of business.

If these conditions do not hold, then purchasing economies may be nonexistent. For example, small firms may form purchasing alliances that buy in bulk in order to obtain quantity discounts. As illustrated by the independent hardware stores described in Example 2.3, alliances can nullify the erstwhile purchasing advantages of larger rivals. To take another example, consider wholesale pricing of prescription drugs. Relatively small mail-order pharmacies often do not stock drugs for which they are unable to obtain favorable wholesale prices, whereas some pharmacy chains stock and sell drugs with little regard to their wholesale prices. This reverses condition 2. Drug manufacturers sometimes extend favorable pricing terms to the price-sensitive smaller pharmacies and not to the relatively price-insensitive chains.

Economies of Scale and Scope in Advertising

The advertising cost per consumer of a product may be expressed by the following formula:

$$\frac{\text{Cost of sending a message}}{\text{Number of potential consumers receiving the message}} \div \frac{\text{Number of actual consumers as a result of message}}{\text{Number of potential consumers receiving the message}}$$

EXAMPLE 2.3 THE ACE HARDWARE CORPORATION

With the recent growth of national hardware "superstore" chains such as Home Depot and Lowes, it might seem that "neighborhood" hardware stores will be unable to stay in business. After all, the chains enjoy economies of scale that local, independently owned stores could not hope to match. In fact, thousands of independently owned hardware stores do enjoy many of the same scale economies realized by national giants, by virtue of membership in hardware purchasing groups. Thanks to these groups, independent hardware stores continue to thrive.

One of the two largest purchasing groups is the Ace Hardware Corporation. Ace began as a hardware wholesaler and distributor based in the Midwest. A dealer buyout in 1974 led to a national expansion. Today, the Ace cooperative is jointly owned by its 4,800 member stores spanning 70 countries. (The 8,500 members of the other large cooperative, TruServ Corporation, operate under the True Value name.) Ace purchases in bulk from more than 4,000 suppliers, including Stanley Tools, Toro (lawnmowers), and Weber (grills). This gives individual store owners access to the same distribution channels as Home Depot and Lowes. Ace employs its own buyers, who obtain quantity discounts that are then passed on to individual stores. Ace suppliers manufacture high quality products that are sold under the Ace label. (Ace makes its own paint—about the only product that it makes itself.) Ace provides its members with other benefits as well. It places national advertising and coordinates national marketing campaigns. It provides information about local marketing practices and new products. It developed and supervised the installation of electronic systems for store owners, allowing them to rapidly check on inventories and prices (this is especially helpful for products such as lumber, which experience volatile price movements), place special orders, and communicate by e-mail with other stores. Finally, Ace used its clout to push suppliers to adopt bar codes to facilitate pricing and inventory maintenance.

Individual Ace hardware stores can match the purchasing and marketing economies of national chains. At the same time, they enjoy the benefits of independence. Store owners face hard-edged market incentives that limit their ability to shirk in areas such as customer service. (Market analysts often comment about how Home Depot and Lowes employees are working hard to develop the same "small-town" friendliness that is often the norm at Ace and True Value.) Stores can tailor their prices and supplies to local needs, and the typical Ace store obtains a large fraction of its merchandise from outside the purchasing group. Indeed, whereas many Ace stores are prototypical hardware stores, others look more like department stores sans clothing, stocked with appliances, televisions, cutlery, bicycles, bedding, and the occasional hammer.

The cooperative concept has disadvantages, however. Absent direction from a central office, individual stores may cannibalize each other through aggressive pricing and marketing practices. Store locations are not chosen with a mind toward inventory management. Key decisions regarding inventories, purchasing, and marketing can be delayed owing to the democratic nature of the cooperative. And Ace lacks the standardization that assures a Home Depot customer of consistent selection and pricing at all stores.

Larger firms may enjoy lower advertising costs per consumer either because they have lower costs of sending messages per potential consumer (the first term) or because they have higher advertising *reach* (the second term).

Costs of Sending Messages per Potential Consumer

Larger firms often enjoy lower advertising costs per potential consumer. This is because important fixed costs are associated with placing an ad, including preparation of the ad and negotiation with the broadcaster. If ad preparation costs and the costs of negotiating a single national and local advertising "buy" are about the same, the national advertiser will have a lower cost per potential consumer because these fixed costs get spread over a larger base of potential consumers.

To illustrate, suppose that Anheuser-Busch places an ad in *USA Today* and pays Gannett (the publisher of *USA Today*) $10 per thousand papers sold to run this ad. Because *USA Today* has a daily circulation of about two million, the direct costs of this ad to Anheuser-Busch would be $10 × (2,000,000/1000) or $20,000. The same day, Hudepohl, a local brewery in Cincinnati, Ohio, places an ad in the *Cincinnati Enquirer* (the local paper) and, let's say, pays the same rate of $10 per thousand papers sold. The *Enquirer* has a daily circulation of about 250,000, so the direct cost to Hudepohl would be $10 × (250,000/1,000) or $2,500. Finally, suppose that for both companies the cost of preparing the ad is $4,000.

Let us now look at the advertising cost per potential consumer for Anheuser-Busch and Hudepohl:

- Anheuser-Busch advertising cost per potential consumer = ($20,000 + $4,000)/2,000,000 = $.012 per potential consumer, or $12.00 per 1,000 potential consumers.

- Hudepohl advertising cost per potential consumer = ($2,500 + $4,000)/250,000 = $.026 per potential consumer, or $26.00 per 1,000 potential consumers.

This example illustrates the approximate difference in the cost per potential consumer between national and local advertising.

The logic underlying this example illustrates why national firms, such as McDonald's, enjoy an advertising cost advantage over their local counterparts, such as Fluky's (a chain of hot dog restaurants in Chicago).

Advertising Reach and Umbrella Branding

Even when two firms have national presences, the larger one may still enjoy an advantage. Suppose that Wendy's and McDonald's both place advertisements on rival television networks to air at the same time. The ads are seen by audiences of equal sizes and cost the same to place. Both ads are equally persuasive—20,000 viewers of the McDonald's ad have an urge to visit McDonald's; 20,000 viewers of the Wendy's ad are motivated to visit Wendy's. Despite these similarities, the cost per effective message is much lower for McDonald's. The reason is that there are about three times as many McDonald's in the United States as there are Wendy's. Almost all of the 20,000 viewers craving McDonald's can find one nearby, but many of the 20,000 who crave Wendy's cannot. They will go elsewhere or go unsatisfied.

The effectiveness of a firm's ad may be higher if that firm offers a broad product line under a single brand name. For example, an advertisement for a Samsung big-screen television may encourage customers to consider other products made by Samsung, such as DVD players. This is known as *umbrella branding*. Umbrella branding is effective when consumers use the information in an advertisement about one product to make inferences about other products with the same brand name, thereby reducing advertising costs per effective image. When Samsung advertises its big-screen television, consumers may infer that Samsung is on the cutting edge of technology, and therefore that its other high-tech products are also good.

Umbrella branding may also reduce the riskiness of new-product introductions. If consumers infer product quality from the brand name, firms may leverage the reputation of an existing brand name to help launch a new product. Disney used its brand appeal to launch a television network for kids. Nike leveraged its brand name to launch a new line of golf balls.

Umbrella branding has some risks. Some conglomerates have been unable to create an overall corporate brand identity. One example is Beatrice, which during the 1980s attempted but failed to stamp the Beatrice brand on an array of products that included Levelor blinds, Danskin exercise clothes, and Butterball turkeys. Sometimes firms prefer to keep brand identities separate—witness how Toyota launched the Lexus nameplate to avoid "tarring" its luxury cars with the mass-market reputation of their less costly brethren. Some brands are not meant to share the same image. In the 1970s, British conglomerate EMI introduced its new CT scanner medical diagnostic equipment. Potential buyers were shocked when EMI's music division signed a contract with punk pioneers the Sex Pistols. The corporate parent quickly dumped the Pistols (though lead single Johnny Rotten wrote a song entitled "EMI" about the incident). Although EMI salvaged its CT sales, it suffered in the music market. It was unable to sign any significant "new wave" performers for many years thereafter.

Economies of Scale in Research and Development

R&D expenditures exceed 5 percent of total sales revenues at many companies, including Intel, Microsoft, Glaxo, and GE. The nature of engineering and scientific research implies that there is a minimum feasible size to an R&D project as well as an R&D department. For example, researchers at Tufts University have carefully measured the costs of developing new pharmaceutical products for the U.S. market.[9] They estimate that drug companies must spend upwards of $500 million to successfully develop a new drug. This is a substantial indivisible investment, implying that average fixed costs will decline rapidly as sales of a particular drug increase.

R&D may also entail economies of scope. Economies of scope may result when ideas developed in one research project create positive spillovers to another another project. Using detailed R&D data, Rebecca Henderson and Iain Cockburn looked for evidence of scope economies in pharmaceutical firms.[10] They measured productivity as the number of patents per dollar of R&D. They found that an average firm with 19 research programs was 4.5 percent more productive than a firm with 17 programs. However, they also found that when a particular firm changed its scope, productivity was unchanged. The most likely explanation for this combination of facts is that firms with broader scope are more productive for other reasons and that changing scope will not, by itself, improve productivity. Nor do Henderson and Cockburn find any evidence that sheer corporate size contributes to R&D productivity.

Decades of research show that there is no clear-cut relationship among scale, scope, and R&D productivity. As we have discussed above, large firms may enjoy lower average R&D costs, but, as discussed below, small firms may be better able to motivate researchers. Firms of different sizes may also face different incentives to innovate. Finally, smaller firms may take a variety of independent approaches to tackling research problems, whereas a large firm may pursue a narrow agenda more aggressively. Depending on the nature of the science, either approach may be quicker to yield fruitful outcomes. We elaborate on these ideas in Chapter 14. Suffice it to say that economic theory and empirical evidence are ambiguous about whether big firms are more innovative than small firms.

<u>EXAMPLE 2.4</u> THE PHARMACEUTICAL MERGER WAVE

Beginning in the 1990s, pharmaceutical companies faced an unprecedented strategic challenge. The growth of managed care in the United States and the tightening of government health care budgets in other nations forced manufacturers to lower prices on many drugs. Traditional research pipelines began to dry up, while the advent of biotechnology promised new avenues for drug discovery coupled with new sources of competition. In response to these pressures, the pharmaceutical industry underwent a remarkable wave of consolidation, with the total value of merger and acquisition activity exceeding $500 billion. As a result, the combined market shares of the 10 largest firms has grown from 20 percent to more than 50 percent. Using almost any yardstick, we can view Glaxo's 2000 acquisition of SmithKline Beecham and Pfizer's 2003 acquisition of Pharmacia as among the largest in business history.

Industry analysts point out three potential rationales for consolidation. One cynical view is that executives at struggling pharmaceutical companies are buying the research pipelines of more successful rivals merely to save their jobs. We explore such managerial rationales for merger in Chapter 5.

Another potential rationale is to make more efficient use of sales personnel. Many pharmaceutical firms spend more money on sales than they do on R&D. Although pharmaceutical "direct to consumer" advertising has received a lot of attention lately, drug makers spend much more money on traditional advertising in medical journals and especially on "detailing." Detailing is when sales personnel visit doctors and hospitals to describe the benefits of new drugs and share data on efficacy and side effects. Detailers spend most of their time on the road, creating an obvious opportunity for scale economies. A detailer who can offer several cardiovascular drugs to a cardiologist will have a much higher ratio of selling time to traveling time. Why have two detailers from two companies visiting the same cardiologist when one will do?

Perhaps the most common explanation offered for the merger wave is to exploit economies of scale in R&D. As we discuss in the accompanying text, there are conflicting theories as to whether bigger firms will be more innovative or will innovate at lower cost. The theoretical considerations apply especially well in pharmaceutical R&D, and those in the industry who bank on achieving greater research effectiveness through scale economies in R&D may not have solid footing.

Recent research by Patricia Danzon, Andrew Epstein, and Sean Nicholson examines some of these potential scale economies.[11] Looking at financial and sales data for over 200 pharmaceutical companies spanning the time period 1988–2000, they found that acquirers tended to have older drug portfolios, lending some support to the cynical explanation for acquisitions. In contrast, targets had average-to-possibly-slightly-younger portfolios. Combined sales after the merger seem to be slightly below premerger sales levels, which may reflect the weak portfolios of the acquirers. Addressing scale economies, they find that two years after a merger, the number of employees has fallen by about 6 percent. This finding is consistent with economies of scale in sales. R&D spending does not change postmerger. Because of the long lag between R&D spending and new products reaching the market, it is too soon to tell if R&D productivity has increased.

Complementarities and Strategic Fit

Economists generally use the concept of scope economies to describe the synergies enjoyed by a firm that produces an array of complementary products and services. Paul Milgrom and John Roberts coined the term *complementarities* to describe synergies among organizational practices.[12] Practices display complementarities when the benefits of introducing one practice are enhanced by the presence of others. For example, Southwest Airlines strives for the fastest turnaround of any airline, often landing a plane and departing within 60 minutes. To accomplish this goal, Southwest uses several complementary practices. It does not cater its flights; it uses a single type of plane (Boeing 737), thereby simplifying baggage handling, refueling, and maintenance procedures; it does not fly into congested airports. Each of these practices makes the others more effective by eliminating potential bottlenecks. Thus, the reduction in maintenance time afforded by the use of a single type of plane would be wasted if Southwest took the time to cater meals.

The concept of complementarities is better known in the strategy literature as *strategic fit*. Harvard Business School Professor Michael Porter has forcefully argued that strategic fit among processes is essential to firms seeking a long-term competitive advantage over their rivals. Through strategic fit, the "whole" of a firm's strategy exceeds the "sum of the parts" of its organizational processes. Moreover, it is difficult for other firms to copy the strategy. Firms that have pursued an entirely different set of processes could not just copy one at a time. They would have to copy them all at once. For example, United Airlines could switch to a single type of plane, or stop onboard catering, but unless it moved out of its congested Chicago hub, it could not hope to match Southwest's operational efficiencies.

The power of strategic fit can been seen by a simple mathematical exercise. Suppose that a firm like Southwest has successfully implemented 10 different organizational practices. Its rivals can observe these practices and tries to emulate them. But suppose that the probability of successfully copying any one practice is only .80, either because Southwest possesses unique skills or, what is more likely, the history of the competition restricts what they can do. In this case, the probability of copying all 10 practices equals $.80^{10} = .11$, or 11 percent. Not only are Southwest's rivals unlikely to copy all 10 practices, complementarity among the 10 practices implies that there is a substantial disadvantage to firms that can copy even eight or nine of them.

SOURCES OF DISECONOMIES OF SCALE ◆ ◆ ◆ ◆ ◆

Given the attention we have paid to scale and scope economies, we might expect some colossal "megafirm" to dominate production across all industries. Antitrust laws may place some limits to firm growth. More likely, however, firms understand that there are limits to economies of scale, so that beyond a certain size, bigger is no longer better and may even be worse. Diseconomies of scale may arise for a number of reasons; here are some of the most important.

Labor Costs and Firm Size

Larger firms generally pay higher wages and provide greater benefits. Evidence from the 1980s showed a substantial wage premium paid to workers in large manufacturing firms compared with smaller firms.[13] Many recent studies confirm that the wage and benefit premium persists. Even if one controls for other determinants of wages such as work experience and job type, a wage gap of 10 percent or more between large and small firms is not unusual.

Labor economists offer several possible reasons for the wage gap. Large firms are more likely to be unionized than small firms. Workers in smaller firms may enjoy their work more than workers in large firms, forcing large firms to pay a *compensating differential* to attract workers. Large firms may need to draw workers from greater distances, forcing them to pay a compensating differential to offset transportation costs. Some economists speculate that the wage premium reflects hard-to-measure aspects of worker quality, such as their skill and experience in capital-intensive production processes. According to this view, size itself does not handicap larger firms. Instead, large firms are merely paying a premium to workers with unique and highly valued skills.

Two factors work in favor of larger firms. First, worker turnover at larger firms is generally lower. Since it can cost thousands of dollars to recruit and train new employees, lower turnover may offset some of the added costs due to higher wages. Second, large firms may be more attractive to highly qualified, upwardly mobile workers who want to move up the corporate ladder.

Spreading Specialized Resources Too Thin

Many talented individuals believe that having achieved success in one venue, they can duplicate it elsewhere. Sometimes this is sheer hubris, such as when Donald Trump felt that lending his name, but not his personal attention, to Atlantic City casinos would be enough to assure their success. (Trump Hotel & Casino Resorts filed for bankruptcy in November 2004.) Others fail because they lack the skills necessary to translate their success to a new situation, such as when basketball superstar Michael Jordan failed to turn his on-court heroics into success as a general manager. Some individuals simply spread themselves too thin. There are many stories of successful chef/owners opening a second and third restaurant, only to see the performance of all of their restaurants decline. When the key to a professional's success is the dedication of many hours to a single activity, performance may suffer across the board if he or she tries to devote time to several activities.

The same lessons also apply to specialized capital inputs, such as computers, tools and dies, or assembly lines. If a specialized input is a source of advantage for a firm, and that firm attempts to expand its operations without duplicating the input, the expansion may overburden the specialized input. The Kellogg School of Management avoided just such a problem during a recent expansion. Kellogg expanded its successful Kellogg Information Systems department (responsible for assisting students and faculty with computing needs) at the same time that the overall school expansion took place.

"Conflicting Out"

With the continued growth and consolidation of professional services firms in fields such as marketing, accounting, consulting, and law, it is important to consider another source of diseconomies of scale—*conflicting out*. When a potential client approaches a professional services firm with new business, it may be concerned about whether the firm is already doing business with one or more of its competitors and may wrong about the resulting potential conflict of interest. Sensitive competitor information might leak out. The firm might not take its client's interests fully to heart. Faced with these concerns, the client may take its business elsewhere. The professional services firm will have been conflicted out. The possibilities for conflict place a natural limit on the market share that any one professional services firm can achieve. For example, the marketing firm Chiat/Day lost its Coke account in 1995 when it was

<u>EXAMPLE</u> 2.5 THE AOL TIME WARNER MERGER AND
ECONOMIES OF SCOPE[14]

When AOL and Time Warner announced their merger in January 2000, Wall Street analysts rejoiced at the possibilities as potential synergies abounded. At the tail end of the technology boom, the merger was served up as the penultimate marriage between the Old Economy and the New Economy.

Less than one year after the merger hoopla, it was already obvious that AOL Time Warner could not immediately deliver on promises of 12 to 15 percent annual growth. The failure to meet projections was partially attributed to the failing economy. Two years later, AOL was still struggling to meet expectations, and CEO Stephen Case had been forced to resign. Today, the merger is regarded as a poster child for the unrealistic expectations of the "dot com" era.

By joining forces, AOL Time Warner had hoped to be the leader among companies striving for convergence among media, technology, and communications. Entering the merger, AOL had a dominant on line presence. The leading Internet service provider in the world, AOL had 29 million subscribers, who accounted for 33 percent of all time spent on the Internet. This figure was greater than that of any other service or content provider, as second and third place MSN and Yahoo each accounted for 7 percent.[15] In fact, AOL had already become somewhat of a pop icon, and its robotically voiced e-mail delivery tagline "You've got mail" was featured in the hit movie of the same name. Even so, the growing popularity of broadband was slowly cutting AOL's business, and the effort to integrate with Time Warner may have slowed AOL's move to broadband. As broadband competition grew, AOL contemplated moving its business model from one driven by subscriber revenue to one driven by free access to content combined with advertising revenue.

Before the merger, Time Warner also exhibited a strong off-line franchise in multiple distribution channels. At the time, it was the nation's second-largest cable operator. Time Warner cable networks like CNN, HBO, TBS, and TNT accounted for 25 percent of cable viewers. Its publishing arm included 35 magazines with a circulation of 200 million. Time Warner also owned the rights to multiple hit TV shows like ER and Friends. Lastly, the company also owned top-flight movie studios in Warner Brothers and New Line Cinema.

In the years immediately after the merger, the merged company hoped to bundle top-quality content supplied by Time Warner with its service provider franchise. The company also hoped to cross-promote its various media content, activities, events, and releases across the Internet, cable, television, publication, and film. Although these ideas sounded good on paper, the reality was that many of the expected scope economies were illusory. Cross-promotional activities may boost demand, but they come at the expense of selling promotional space to outside entities. Consumers preferred the freedom to download whatever content they wished (and the freedom to do so offered by broadband providers), rather than be force-fed whatever their service provider offered. The popularity of music downloads was an especially big blow to AOL Time Warner's dream of dominating through content.

While synergies proved to be few and far between, AOL Time Warner struggled with traditional merger issues: Whose interests would the CEO represent? Could the two cultures coexist? Would independent firms prove more flexible, beating AOL Time Warner to new market opportunities? By 2002, it was apparent that the merger was failing and that AOL was proving to be a drag on its old economy partner. Stephen Case, AOL's billionaire founder who had taken over as CEO of the merged entity resigned and was replaced by Richard Parsons, who had previously overseen Time Warner's content businesses. The company may not have downsized since then, but the name has—it is now known once again as Time Warner.

acquired by the Omnicom Group, which already owned BBD&O, the main ad agency for Pepsi. (The Omnicom Group was the ill-fated holding company formed when Saatchi and Saatchi attempted to become the largest marketing firm in the world. It failed, partly because of problems with conflicts such as these.)

Incentive and Bureaucracy Effects

In the next chapter, we describe a number of incentive and bureaucracy effects that make it difficult for firms to expand their vertical boundaries. The same problems emerge as firms expand their horizontal boundaries. In larger firms, compensation is much less likely to be tied to the worker's contribution toward firm profit. Larger firms may also have a more difficult time monitoring and communicating with workers, further leading to difficulties in promoting effective worker performance. Chapters 14 and 15 discuss a variety of potential solutions to these incentive issues.

◆ ◆ ◆ ◆ ◆ THE LEARNING CURVE

Medical students are encouraged to learn by the axiom "See one, do one, teach one." This axiom grossly understates the importance of experience in producing skilled physicians. Experience is an important determinant of ability in many jobs, and in the past three decades strategists have discovered the significance of experience for firms. The importance of experience is conveyed by the idea of the learning curve.

The Concept of the Learning Curve

Economies of scale refer to the advantages that flow from producing a larger output at a given point in time. The *learning curve* (or experience curve) refers to advantages that flow from accumulating experience and know-how. It is easy to find examples of learning by workers and firms. Workers often improve their performance of specific tasks as they gain experience. A manufacturer can learn the appropriate tolerances for producing a key system component. A retailer can learn about community tastes. An accounting firm can learn the idiosyncrasies of its clients' inventory management. The benefits of learning manifest themselves in lower costs, higher quality, and more effective pricing and marketing.

The magnitude of learning benefits is often expressed in terms of a *slope*. The slope for a given production process is calculated by examining how far average costs decline as cumulative production output doubles. It is important to use cumulative output rather than output during a given time period to distinguish between learning effects and other scale effects. As shown in Figure 2.7, suppose that a firm has cumulative output of Q_x with average cost of production of AC_1. Suppose next that the firm's cumulative output doubles to $2Q_x$ with average cost of AC_2. Then the slope equals AC_2/AC_1.

Slopes have been estimated for hundreds of products.[15] The median slope appears to be about .80, implying that for the typical firm, doubling cumulative output reduces unit costs by about 20 percent. Slopes vary from firm to firm and industry to industry, however, so that the actual slope enjoyed by any one firm for any given production process generally falls between .70 and .90 and may be as low as .6 or as high as 1.0 (e.g., no learning). Note that although an industry may have a slope of, say, .75,

FIGURE 2.7
THE LEARNING CURVE

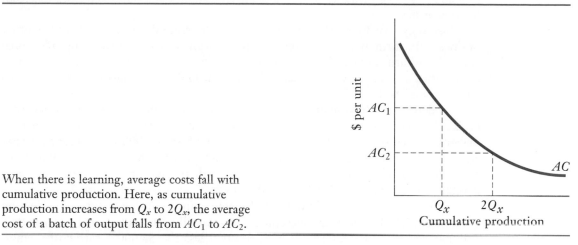

When there is learning, average costs fall with cumulative production. Here, as cumulative production increases from Q_x to $2Q_x$, the average cost of a batch of output falls from AC_1 to AC_2.

this does not imply that continual doubling of output inexorably leads to further and further 25 percent cost reductions. Estimated slopes usually represent averages over a range of outputs and do not indicate whether or when learning economies are fully exploited.

Although most studies of the learning curve focus on costs, some studies have documented the effects of learning on quality. There is a considerable literature on the relationship between experience and quality in medicine, for example. Some studies show that physicians who encounter a disease for the second or third time provide much more effective treatments than they did when they encountered the same disease the first time. Learning in medicine continues even after hundreds of encounters with the same disease. The obvious lesson for patients is to seek out physicians who have considerable experience treating their specific symptoms. A corollary of this idea is that patients should avoid teaching hospitals during the week when residents begin their new rotations. Studies of the learning curve in medicine bolster efforts to develop regional referral centers for the provision of highly specialized medical care.

Expanding Output to Obtain a Cost Advantage

When firms benefit from learning, they may want to ramp up production well past the point where the additional revenues offset the added costs. This strategy makes intuitive sense, because it allows the firm to move down the learning curve and realize lower costs in the future. Although it might seem to violate the cardinal rule of equating marginal revenue to marginal cost (see the Primer), the strategy is in fact completely consistent with this rule if one properly construes the cost of current production in the presence of learning. To see why this is so, consider the following example:

Suppose that a manufacturer of DRAM chips has cumulative production of 10,000 chips. The cost to manufacture one additional chip is $2.50. The firm believes that once it has produced 100,000 chips its unit costs will fall to $2.00, with no further learning benefits. The company has orders to produce an additional 200,000 chips when it unexpectedly receives an offer to bid on an order for 10,000 chips to be filled immediately. The firm must determine the lowest price it would be willing to accept for this order.

Assuming that filling the new order does not create delays that jeopardize other business, the firm need only compute the marginal cost of producing additional chips. If the firm myopically ignores learning effects, it would accept the order only if the price was at least $2.50 per chip. This would be wrong—the true marginal cost is not $2.50.

To determine the true marginal cost, the chip maker must consider how its accumulated experience will affect future costs. Before it received the new order, the chip maker had planned to produce 200,000 chips. The first 100,000 would cost $2.50 per chip, and the remaining 100,000 would cost $2.00 per chip, for a total of $450,000 for 200,000 chips. If the firm takes the new order, then the cost of producing the next 200,000 chips is only $445,000 (90,000 chips @ $2.50 + 110,000 chips @ $2.00).

By filling the new order, the DRAM manufacturer reduces its future production costs by $5,000. In effect, the incremental cost of filling the additional order is only $20,000, which is the current costs of $25,000 less the $5,000 future cost savings. Thus, the true marginal cost per chip is $2.00. The firm should be willing to accept any price over this amount, even though a price between $2.00 and $2.50 per chip does not cover current production costs.

In general, when a firm enjoys the benefits of a learning curve, the marginal cost of increasing current production is the expected marginal cost of the last unit of production the firm expects to sell. (This formula is complicated somewhat by discounting future costs.) This implies that learning firms should be willing to accept short-run prices that are below short-run costs. They may even earn negative accounting profits in the short run but will prosper even more in the long run.

Managers who are rewarded on the basis of short-run profits may be reluctant to exploit the benefits of the learning curve. Firms could solve this problem by directly accounting for learning curve benefits when assessing profits and losses. Few firms that aggressively move down the learning curve have accounting systems that properly measure marginal costs, however, and instead rely on direct growth incentives while placing less emphasis on profits.

Learning and Organization

The variation in slopes across firms and products shows that learning occurs at different rates for different organizations and different processes. While there has been little systematic study of the determinants of learning, some common sense helps us to identify situations in which learning is likely to be important.

Although much emphasis is placed on organizational learning, the obvious fact is that it is individuals who learn. Complex tasks, such as the design and production of statistical software, offer especially good opportunities for individuals to learn on their own and from their coworkers. While individuals do the learning, firms can take steps to improve learning and the retention of knowledge in the organization. Firms can facilitate the adoption and use of newly learned ideas by encouraging the sharing of information, establishing work rules that include the new ideas, and reducing turnover. Lanier Benkard argues that labor policies at Lockheed prevented the airframe manufacturer from fully exploiting learning opportunities in the production of the L-1011 TriStar.[18] Its union contract required Lockheed to promote experienced line workers to management, while simultaneously upgrading workers at lower levels.

EXAMPLE 2.6 THE BOSTON CONSULTING GROUP GROWTH/SHARE PARADIGM

The Boston Consulting Group (BCG) had a major impact on corporate strategy beginning in the 1970s when it introduced the *growth/share matrix*, an outgrowth of its success advocating learning curve strategies. Figure 2.8 depicts a typical BCG matrix. The matrix allows firms to distinguish their product lines on two dimensions: growth of the market in which the product is situated, and the product's market share relative to the share of its next-largest competitors. A product line was classified into one of four categories. A *rising star* is a product in a growing market with a high relative share. A *cash cow* is a product in a stable or declining market with a high relative share. A *problem child* is a product in a growing market with a low relative share. A *dog* is a product in a stable or declining market with a low relative share.

The BCG strategy for successfully managing a portfolio of products was based on taking advantage of learning curves and the *product life cycle*. BCG had observed that learning curves offered significant cost advantages in many markets. They also felt that most products had a characteristic life cycle, as shown in Figure 2.9.[16] According to this product life-cycle model, demand for the product is low just after it is introduced. The product then enters a phase in which demand grows rapidly. As demand becomes increasingly driven by replacement sales rather than sales to new

customers, demand growth levels off, and the product reaches its maturity stage. Finally, as superior substitute products eventually emerge, demand for the product will begin to decline. BCG felt that its clients should increase production in the early stages of the product's life-cycle in order to secure learning economies. Firms could use profits from cash cow products to fund increased production of problem child and rising star products. Learning economies would cement the advantages of rising stars while enabling some problem children to become more competitive. As their markets matured and demand slackened, these products would then become cash cows to support learning strategies in new emerging markets.

BCG deserves credit for recognizing the strategic importance of learning curves, and many firms have prospered by utilizing the growth/share matrix framework. However, it would be a mistake to apply the BCG framework without considering its underlying principles. As we have discussed, learning curves are neither ubiquitous nor uniform where they do occur. At the same time, product life cycles are easier to identify after they have been completed than during the planning process. Many products ranging from nylon to dedicated word processors that were forecast to have tremendous potential for growth did not meet expectations. Firms that invested

FIGURE 2.8
THE BCG GROWTH/SHARE MATRIX

The growth/share matrix divides products into four categories according to their potential for growth and relative market share. Some strategists recommended that firms use the profits earned from cash cows to ramp up production of rising stars and problem children. As the latter products move down their learning curves, they become cash cows in the next investment cycle.[17]

		Relative Market Share	
		High	Low
Relative Market Growth	High	Rising star	Problem child
	Low	Cash cow	Dog

FIGURE 2.9
THE PRODUCT LIFE CYCLE

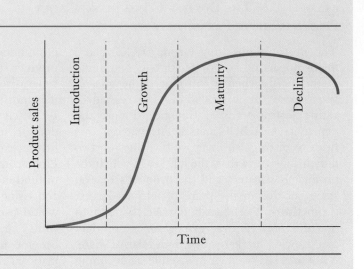

Product demand is thought to move through four stages. When the product is first introduced, sales and growth are low. Product demand then grows rapidly, but sales level off, and the industry enters a maturity phase. Eventually, demand declines as other superior products or technologies supplant it. It can be difficult to predict when each stage will begin.

heavily in them to secure learning advantages were losers. We conclude that one needs to do careful research about the learning curves and markets for the specific products in question before applying a learning curve strategy. Finally, the role of the firm as "banker"— using retained earnings to fund new ventures—is questionable. The emergence of venture capitalists has enabled independent firms with potential stars of their own to obtain financing without being part of a conglomerate. However, firms may sometimes be unable to convince skeptical external capital markets to fund good projects. When this occurs, those firms with free internal capital may have an advantage. We pursue this idea in more detail in Chapter 5, where we discuss diversification.

This produced a domino effect whereby as many as 10 workers changed jobs when one was moved to a management position. As a result, workers were forced to relearn tasks that their higher-ranking coworkers had already mastered. Benkard estimates that this and related policies reduced labor productivity at Lockheed by as much as 40 to 50 percent annually.

Codifying work rules and reducing job turnover facilitates retention of knowledge, but it may stifle creativity. At the same time, worker-specific learning is sometimes too complex to transmit across the firm. Examples include many professional services, in which individual knowledge of how to combine skills in functional areas with specific and detailed knowledge of particular clients or markets may give individuals advantages that they cannot easily pass along to others. Clearly, an important skill of managers is to find the correct balance between stability and change so as to maximize the benefits of learning.

Managers should also draw a distinction between firm-specific and task-specific learning. If learning is task-specific rather than firm-specific, then workers who acquire skill through learning may be able to shop around their talents and capture the value for themselves in the form of higher wages. When learning is firm-specific, worker knowledge is tied to their current employment, and the firm will not have to raise wages as the workers become more productive. Managers should encourage firm-specific learning but must usually rely on their judgment to determine if learning is firm- or task-specific. Research on learning curves in medicine suggests that for surgery, learning is largely firm-specific. It seems that experienced surgeons have better surgical outcomes, but only when they treat patients at the hospital where they perform most of their procedures. Health services researchers surmise that the surgeon's skill is tied to the experience of the entire surgical team.

The Learning Curve versus Economies of Scale

Economies of learning differ from economies of scale. Economies of scale refer to the ability to perform an activity at a lower unit cost when it is performed on a larger scale at a particular point in time. Learning economies refer to reductions in unit costs due to accumulating experience over time. Economies of scale may be substantial even when learning economies are minimal. This is likely to be the case in simple capital-intensive activities, such as two-piece aluminum can manufacturing. Similarly, learning economies may be substantial even when economies of scale are minimal. This is likely to be the case in complex labor-intensive activities, such as the practice of antitrust law.

Figure 2.10 illustrates how one can have learning economies without economies of scale. The left side of the figure shows a typical learning curve, with average costs declining with cumulative experience. The right side shows two average cost curves, for different experience levels. Both average cost curves are perfectly flat, indicating that there are no economies of scale. Suppose that the firm under consideration enters a given year of production with cumulative experience of Q_1. According to the learning curve, this gives it an average cost level of AC_1. This remains constant regardless of current output because of constant returns to scale. Entering the next

FIGURE 2.10
LEARNING ECONOMIES WHEN SCALE ECONOMIES ARE ABSENT

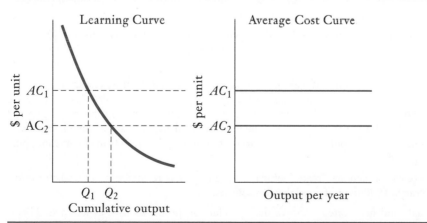

It is not necessary to have economies of scale to realize learning economies. The production process depicted here shows constant returns to scale, as evidenced by the flat average cost curves, which show output *within a given year*. The level of average cost falls with cumulative experience *across several years*, however, as shown by the learning curve.

year of production, the firm has cumulative output of Q_2. Its experiences in the previous year enable the firm to revamp its production techniques. In thus moving down the learning curve, it can enjoy an average cost level of AC_2 in the next year of production.

Managers who do not correctly distinguish between economies of scale and learning may draw incorrect inferences about the benefits of size in a market. For example, if a large firm has lower unit costs because of economies of scale, then any cutbacks in production volume will raise unit costs. If the lower unit costs are the result of learning, the firm may be able to cut current volume without necessarily raising its unit costs. To take another example, if a firm enjoys a cost advantage due to a capital-intensive production process and resultant scale economies, then it may be less concerned about labor turnover than a competitor that enjoys low costs due to learning a complex labor-intensive production process.

CHAPTER SUMMARY

◆ A production process exhibits economies of scale if the average cost per unit of output falls as the volume of output increases. A production process exhibits economies of scope if the total cost of producing two different products or services is lower when they are produced by a single firm instead of two separate firms.

◆ An important source of economies of scale and scope is the spreading of indivisible fixed costs. Fixed costs do not vary as the level of production varies.

◆ In general, capital-intensive production processes are more likely to display economies of scale and scope than are labor- or materials-intensive processes.

◆ In some industries, such as food retailing, firms may make expenditures to create scale economies that previously did not exist, such as expenditures to create and reinforce brand image.

◆ There are economies of scale in inventory management so that processes with large volumes need to carry less inventory on a percentage-of-output basis than similar processes with small volumes.

◆ The physical property known as the cube-square rule confers scale economies on processes, such as warehousing, where costs are related to the geometric volume of the production "vessel."

◆ There are often economies of scale associated with marketing expense, research and development, and purchasing. Large-scale marketing efforts often have lower costs per message received than do smaller-scale efforts. The costs of large research ventures may be spread over greater output, although big size may be inimical to innovation. Small firms may obtain purchasing discounts comparable to those obtained by large firms by forming purchasing groups.

◆ Large size can sometimes create inefficiencies. These may result from higher labor costs, bureaucracy, or dilution of specialized resources.

◆ Individuals and firms often improve their production processes with experience. This is known as learning. In processes with substantial learning benefits, firms that can accumulate and protect the knowledge gained by experience can achieve superior cost and quality positions in the market.

◆ (Appendix) Regression analysis that compares costs and outputs of firms of varying sizes and experience may be used to identify scale economies and the learning curve.

QUESTIONS

1. A firm produces two products, X and Y. The production technology displays the following costs, where $C(i, j)$ represents the cost of producing i units of X and j units of Y:

    $$
    \begin{aligned}
    C(0, 50) &= 100 & C(5, 0) &= 150 \\
    C(0, 100) &= 210 & C(10, 0) &= 320 \\
    C(5, 50) &= 240 & C(10, 100) &= 500
    \end{aligned}
    $$

    Does this production technology display economies of scale? of scope?

2. Economies of scale are usually associated with the spreading of fixed costs, such as when a manufacturer builds a factory. But the spreading of fixed costs is also important for economies of scale associated with marketing, R&D, and purchasing. Explain.

3. What is the difference between economics of scale and learning economies? If a larger firm has lower average costs, can you conclude that it benefits from economies of scale? Would a small firm necessarily enjoy the same cost position if it were to duplicate the size of its larger rival?

4. A firm contemplating entering the breakfast cereal market would need to invest $100 million to build a minimum efficient scale production plant (or about $10 million annually on an amortized basis). Such a plant could produce about 100 million pounds of cereal per year. What would be the average fixed costs of this plant if it ran at capacity? Each year U.S. breakfast cereal makers sell about 3 billion pounds of cereal. What would be the average fixed costs if the cereal maker captured a 2 percent market share? What would be its cost disadvantage if it only achieved a 1 percent share? If prior to entering the market, the firm contemplates achieving only a 1 percent share, is it doomed to such a large cost disparity?

5. The European Union has banned virtually all tariffs for trade among member nations. How is this likely to affect specialization by firms located in EU countries?

6. Historically, product markets were dominated by large firms and service markets by small firms. This seems to have reversed itself somewhat in recent years. What factors might be at work?

7. Best Buy stores have recently redesigned their stores so that customers waiting to make purchases must stand in a single queue and wait for the next available cashier, rather than queue up at separate cashiers. How does this relate to inventory economics of scale? (*Hint:* What is inventoried?)

8. In the past few years, several American and European firms opened "hypermarts," enormous stores that sell groceries, household goods, hardware, and other products under one roof. What are the possible economies of scale that might be enjoyed by hypermarts? What are the potential diseconomies of scale?

9. Some state governors have proposed purchasing prescription drugs on behalf of state residents, on the grounds that by pooling purchasing power, they can obtain deep discounts. What advice would you give to governors to improve their chances of obtaining low prices?

10. Suppose you wanted to quantify a firm's learning experience. One possible measure is the firm's lifetime cumulative output. What are the advantages and disadvantages of this measure? Can you offer a superior alternative measure?

11. During the 1980s, firms in the Silicon Valley of northern California experienced high rates of turnover as top employees moved from one firm to another. What effect do you think this turnover had on learning-by-doing at individual firms? What effect do you think it had on learning by the industry as a whole?

◆ ◆ ◆ ◆ ◆ APPENDIX

Using Regression Analysis to Estimate the Shapes of Cost Curves

Suppose that you had the following cost and output data for three chain saw manufacturing plants:

Plant	Annual Output	Average Cost
1	10,000	$50
2	20,000	$47
3	30,000	$45

Average costs apparently fall as output increases. It would be natural to conclude from this pattern that there are economies of scale in chain saw production. One might be tempted to recommend to the managers of plants 1 and 2 that they expand output (perhaps by building larger plants) so as to lower their average costs.

Just how confident should we be about the presence of scale economies in this instance? Put another way, what if the differences in costs at the three plants have nothing to do with scale economies? For example, plant 3 may be located in a region where labor costs are unusually low. If this is the case, then the other plants may have nothing to gain by expanding at their present locations. To be confident that the cost/output relationship truly reflects scale economies, alternative explanations need to be ruled out.

These are the ideas underlying *regression analysis of cost functions*. Regression analysis is a statistical technique for estimating how one or more factors affect some variable of interest. For cost functions, the variable of interest is average cost, and the factors may include output, wage rates, and other input prices.

To illustrate, suppose that we suspect that the average cost function is a quadratic function of the volume of output:

$$AC = \beta_0 + \beta_1 Q + \beta_2 Q^2 + \beta_3 w + noise$$

where Q denotes production volume (e.g., number of standard-size chain saws produced per year), w denotes the local wage rate, and *noise* represents all of the other factors that affect the level of cost that cannot be measured and that are not explicitly included in the analysis.

We can interpret the cost function as follows: the average cost at any particular plant is equal to some function of plant output, plus a function of wage rates, plus "noise." We expect β_3 to be positive as higher wages contribute to higher costs. We expect β_1 to be negative, suggesting that as output rises, average costs fall. We expect β_2 to be small and positive. Thus, at large levels of output (and therefore at very large levels of output squared), average costs may start to level off or even increase, as the positive effect of $\beta_2 Q^2$ offsets or dominates the negative effect of $\beta_1 Q$. It is the combination of β_1, whose negative slope indicates economies of scale, and β_2, whose positive slope indicates diseconomies of scale, that produces the characteristic parabolic or U shape of the average cost function.

Finally, the noise term represents variation in costs due to factors other than size and wage rates. If we had good information about sources of that variation, we could directly include additional variables in the cost function. Otherwise, we are forced to accept the notion that our cost function is necessarily imprecise. Regression analysis "fits" the cost function to actual cost/output data. In other words, regression provides estimates of the parameters β_1, β_2, and β_3 as well as the precision of these estimates.

There is a large literature on the estimation of cost functions. Cost functions have been estimated for various industries, including airlines, telecommunications, electric utilities, trucking, railroads, and hospitals.[19] Most of these studies estimate functional forms for the average cost function that are more complicated than the simple quadratic functions discussed here. Nevertheless, the basic ideas underlying these more sophisticated analyses are those described here, and these studies can be used to derive estimates of minimum efficient scale.

Estimating Learning Curves

Regression analysis may also be used to estimate learning curves. To do so, it is often convenient to estimate an equation with the following functional form:

$$\log AC = \alpha + \varepsilon \log E + \gamma \log X_1 + \ldots + \gamma_n \log X_n + noise$$

where log represents the natural logarithm, E denotes cumulative production volume, $X_1, \ldots, X_n$ denote the levels of cost drivers other than cumulative production volume that affect average cost (e.g., scale, capacity utilization, input prices, and so forth), and *noise* denotes the impact of factors that cannot be measured and are thus not included in the analysis. These other cost drivers are included in the equation to distinguish between cost reductions that are due to learning and cost reductions that are due to economies of scale or favorable positions on other cost drivers. The parameter ε is the percentage change in average cost per 1 percent change in cumulative experience, and γ_i is the percentage change in average cost per 1 percent change in cost driver X_i. Logarithms are used in the preceding equation, so that the estimated coefficients are elasticities.

ENDNOTES

[1]If you do not understand why this must be so, consider this numerical example. Suppose that the total cost of producing five bicycles is $500. The *AC* is therefore $100. If the *MC* of the sixth bicycle is $70, then total cost for six bicycles is $570 and *AC* is $95. If the *MC* of the sixth bicycle is $130, then total cost is $630 and *AC* is $105. In this example (and as a general rule), when *MC* < *AC*, *AC* falls as production increases, and when *MC* > *AC*, *AC* rises as production increases.

[2]Prahalad, C. K. and G. Hamel, "The Core Competence of the Corporation," *Harvard Business Review*, May–June 1990, pp. 79–91; Stalk, G., P. Evans, and L. Shulman, "Competing on Capabilities: The New Rules of Corporate Strategy," *Harvard Business Review*, March–April 1992, pp. 57–69; Itami, H., *Mobilizing Indivisible Assets*, Cambridge, MA, Harvard University Press, 1987.

[3]The opportunity cost is the best return that the investor could obtain if he or she invested a comparable amount of money in some other similarly risky investment. In this example, we have assumed, for simplicity, that the production line never depreciates and thus lasts forever. See the Economics Primer for further discussion.

[4]Newhouse, J. et al., "Does the Geographic Distribution of Physicians Reflect Market Failure?" *Bell Journal of Economics*, 13(2), 1982, pp. 493–505.

[5]Baumgardner, J., "What Is a Specialist Anyway?" Mimeo, Duke University, 1991.

[6]Lynk, W., "The Creation of Economic Efficiency in Hospital Mergers," *Journal of Health Economics*, 14(6), 1995, pp. 507–530.

[7]The name cube-square rule comes from the fact that the volume of a cube is proportional to the cube of the length of its side, whereas the surface area is proportional to the square of that length.

[8]See Cockenboo, L., "Production Functions and Cost Functions: A Case Study," in Mansfield, E. (ed.), *Managerial Economics and Operations Research*, 5th ed., New York, Norton, 1987.

[9]DiMasi, J. et al., "Cost of Innovation in the Pharmaceutical Industry," *Journal of Health Economics*, 10(2), 1991, pp. 107–142.

[10]Henderson, R. and I. Cockburn, "Scale, Scope, and Spillovers: Determinants of Research Productivity in the Pharmaceutical Industry," *RAND Journal of Economics*, 27(1), 1996, pp. 32–59.

[11] Danzon, P., Epstein, P. and S. Nicholson, 2004, "Mergers and Acquisitions in the Pharmaceutical and Biotech Industries," NBER Working Paper 10536.

[12]Milgrom, P. and J. Roberts, "The Economics of Modern Manufacturing: Technology, Strategy, and Organization," *American Economic Review*, 80(6), 1990, pp. 511–528.

[13]For a comprehensive discussion of size effects on workers, see Brown, C., J. Hamilton, and J. Medoff, *Employers Large and Small*, Cambridge, MA, Harvard University Press, 1990.

[14]Much of the information in this example was obtained from Hsieh, Jennifer and Rice, Andrea W., "AOL Time Warner Inc.: Piecing Together an Integrated Media Platform," Deutsche Banc Alex Brown, *Equity Research*, June 2001, p. 2.

[15]See, for example, *Perspectives on Experience*, Boston, Boston Consulting Group, 1970, for estimates of progress ratios for over 20 industries. See Lieberman, M., "The Learning Curve and Pricing in the Chemical Processing Industries," *RAND Journal of Economics*, 15(2), 1984, pp. 213–228, for learning curve estimates for 37 chemical products.

[16]The product life-cycle model has its origins in the marketing literature. See, for example, Levitt, T., "Exploit the Product Life Cycle," *Harvard Business Review*, November–December 1965, pp. 81–94.

[17]For a discussion of their treatment of the learning curve, see *Perspectives on Experience*, Boston, Boston Consulting Group, 1970.

[18]Benkard, C. L., "Learning and Forgetting: The Dynamics of Aircraft Production," mimeo, New Haven, CT, Yale University, 1998.

[19]John Panzar's article, "Determinants of Firm and Industry Structure," in Schmalensee, R. and R. D. Willig (eds.), *Handbook of Industrial Organization*, Amsterdam, North Holland, 1989, pp. 3–59. Reviews some of the work on estimation of cost functions and provides many references to the literature.

THE VERTICAL
BOUNDARIES
OF THE FIRM

3

*I*n early 2000, Internet service provider AOL stunned the business community by acquiring entertainment giant Time Warner. AOL's president, Stephen Case, boasted of the synergies that the two companies would realize under a single corporate umbrella. A year later, AOL Time Warner sought to exploit these synergies by promoting a new girl band called Eden's Crush.[1] Warner Music produced their debut album, "Popstars," the WB network aired a program documenting the band's tryouts and rehearsals, and the band was heavily promoted by AOL. The album was not a success, however, with sales falling short of gold-record status (under 500,000 copies sold). In contrast, another teen group called O-Town debuted at about the same time as Eden's Crush but worked with several independent companies. They released their eponymous debut record on BMG, Disney broadcast the obligatory documentary, and they received heavy publicity from MTV. This seemingly fragmented strategy paid off—their debut album went platinum, with sales exceeding 1.5 million copies.

The production of any good or service, from pop recordings to cancer treatment, usually requires many activities. The process that begins with the acquisition of raw materials and ends with the distribution and sale of finished goods and services is known as the *vertical chain*. A central issue in business strategy is how to organize the vertical chain. Is it better to organize all of the activities in a single firm, as AOL attempted, or is it better to rely on independent firms in the market? There are many examples of successful vertically integrated firms, such as Scott Paper, which cuts its own timber, mills it, makes paper products, and distributes them to the market. Other successful firms, such as Nike, are vertically "disintegrated": they outsource most of the tasks in the vertical chain to independent contractors. Former Hewlett-Packard CEO John Young described outsourcing by his firm as follows: "We used to bend all the sheet metal, mold every plastic part that went into our products. We don't do those things anymore, but somebody else is doing it for us."[2] The *vertical boundaries* of a firm define the activities that the firm itself performs as opposed to purchases from independent firms in the market. Chapters 3 and 4 examine a firm's choice of its vertical boundaries and how they affect the efficiency of production.

◆ ◆ ◆ ◆ ◆ MAKE VERSUS BUY

A firm's decision to perform an activity itself or to purchase it from an independent firm is called a *make-or-buy* decision. "Make" means that the firm performs the activity itself; "buy" means it relies on an independent firm to perform the activity, perhaps under contract. A firm that acquires an input supplier is now "making" the input, because it is performing the activity in-house. Typical make-or-buy decisions for a manufacturer include whether to develop its own source of raw materials, provide its own shipping services, or operate its own retail web site. Of course, a raw materials supplier might integrate forward, as when Alcoa began manufacturing aluminum foil in the 1920s. Distributors and retailers can also integrate backward, as when Home Box Office began producing its own programming.

Make and buy are two extremes along a continuum of possibilities for vertical integration. Figure 3.1 fills in some of the intermediate choices. Close to "make," integrated firms can spin off partly or wholly owned subsidiaries. Close to "buy," market firms can enter into a long-term contract, tying their interests for several years. In between are joint ventures and strategic alliances, in which two or more firms establish an independent entity that relies on resources from both parents. To illustrate the key economic tradeoffs associated with integration decisions, we will focus on the extreme choices of "make" and "buy." As we will discuss in Chapter 4, intermediate solutions share many of the benefits and costs of both the make and buy extremes.

Upstream, Downstream

In general, goods in an economy "flow" along a vertical chain from raw materials and component parts to manufacturing, through distribution and retailing. Economists say that early steps in the vertical chain are upstream in the production process, and later steps are downstream, much as lumber flows from upstream timber forests to downstream mills. Thus, cable sports channel ESPN, which assembles a package of sports entertainment programming, is downstream from the National Football League (a content "producer") but upstream to Comcast and other cable companies (content "retailers").

Figure 3.2 depicts a vertical chain for the production and sale of furniture. The vertical chain includes activities directly associated with the processing and handling of materials from raw inputs (e.g., wood) through the finished product. Processing activities include raw materials acquisition, goods processing, and assembly. Handling activities include all associated transportation and warehousing. When we discuss

FIGURE 3.1
MAKE OR BUY CONTINUUM

Arm's-length market transactions	Long-term contracts	Strategic alliances and joint ventures	Parent/ subsidiary relationships	Perform activity internally
Less integrated		→ → →		More integrated

Different ways of organizing production lie on a make/buy continuum.

EXAMPLE 3.1 VERTICAL DISINTEGRATION IN THE PHARMACEUTICAL INDUSTRY

Pharmaceutical companies have traditionally been vertically integrated firms, concerned with the entire drug discovery value chain from the generation of drug leads to drug production and marketing. In fact, these firms were given the moniker FIPCO, short for fully integrated pharmaccutical corporation, which once seemed an apt descriptor of their business model. Now, traditional pharmaceutical firms like Pfizer and Eli Lilly routinely outsource a number of their functions. Indeed, a major paradigm shift has occurred in this industry.

John Hagel III and Marc Singer argue that traditional pharmaceutical firms have come "unbundled" into three core businesses.[3] These three core businesses consist of a customer relationship business, a product innovation business, and an infrastructure business. The customer relationship business is responsible for finding customers and building relationships with them. Product innovation businesses create new products and services and bring them to market. An infrastructure business builds and manages facilities for high-volume, repetitive operational tasks such as manufacturing and communications.

The customer relationship business in the life science industry includes the marketing and selling of drugs. This domain has remained the province of pharmaceutical firms. In recent years, biotechnology firms have taken on the mantle for the product innovation business. Biotechnology specialist firms now focus on developing technologies that speed the drug discovery process for pharmaceutical firms. In addition, pharmaceutical firms now outsource part of their infrastructure to contract research organizations (CROs). These companies contract the clinical testing phase of the drug discovery process for pharmaceutical firms. By "unbundling" services, companies are able to specialize in a particular field. In turn, more specialized firms can react more quickly to the changing business landscape.

Technological advances have catalyzed the unbundling of the product innovation business from the traditional pharmaceutical firm. Traditionally, FIPCOs used an uneconomical trial-and-error process to screen new drug leads. However, the landmark sequencing of the human genome allows the genes themselves to become the new targets of disease research, resulting in more focused and economical approaches to drug discovery. Although technological breakthroughs like genomics may expedite the drug discovery process, they have also, paradoxically, increased its complexity. Smaller biotech companies are more adept in understanding and adapting to changes in technology than are larger pharmaceutical companies. Companies like Millennium Pharmaceuticals, Celera, Incyte Genomics, and Human Genome Sciences are examples of biotechnology companies that have thrived in the New World.

The pharmaceutical industry has also tried to decouple the testing phase of drug development with the intent of gaining economies of scope and scale from outsourcing this business.[4] Research and testing is a highly capital-intensive business, and large specialized research firms have greater incentives to make the required capital investments necessary to sustain this function. As pharmaceutical firms outsource research, capital that would have been spent on testing infrastructure can be spent on other activities. It is clear that CROs have become well entrenched in the infrastructure space. Until recently, the contract research industry was growing at a 20 percent clip per year. It is estimated that one-fifth of overall pharmaceutical development budgets were captured by these independent firms, which perform over half of all human trials.

Some biotechnology firms are seeking to reverse this disintegration trend with announced ambitions of becoming FIPCOs themselves. Only time will tell whether they are successful. Nonetheless, the fully integrated model has become less relevant for well-established pharmaceutical firms. They have turned to biotechnology firms to gain access to technologies that can speed the discovery process. Outsourcing testing to CROs also reduces the costs of discovery for these pharmaceuticals. Ultimately, this shift in paradigm has also allowed firms in the specialized spaces to develop and focus on their core competencies,[5] creating much greater long-term value for them.

activities that are upstream or downstream in a production process, we are usually referring to these processing and handling activities.

The vertical chain also involves many specialized support activities, such as accounting, finance, human resources management, and strategic planning. We place these services outside the vertical chain in Figure 3.2 to indicate that they support each step along the chain. As described in Chapter 1, large hierarchical enterprises in the early 1900s performed these support activities themselves to coordinate the flow of production through the vertical chain. Sometimes, these support activities became principal sources of value creation in integrated firms. Good examples include

FIGURE 3.2
THE VERTICAL CHAIN OF PRODUCTION FOR FURNITURE

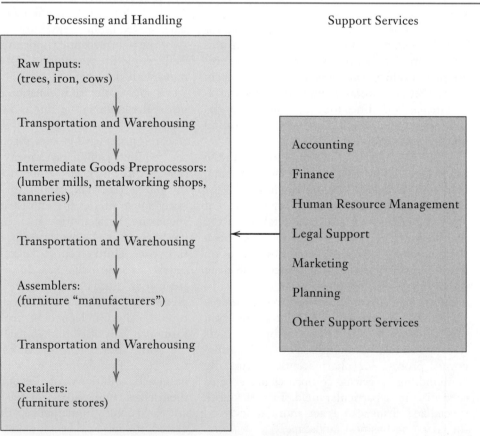

The materials necessary to make furniture are processed and handled through each step of the vertical chain. Professional support services are provided all along the chain.

General Electric in strategic planning, Pepsi in marketing, and Wal-Mart in distribution. In entire industries, such as athletic footwear, support activities like marketing are the lifeblood of the major players.

While many firms have succeeded by performing their own processing, handling, and support activities, others buy them from specialists in the market, or what we call *market firms*. Market firms specializing in these activities include many recognized leaders in their fields. Examples include Leo Burnett, which created Tony the Tiger and other brand icons for consumer products companies worldwide; United Parcel Service, which distributes products to customers of many manufacturers and retailers; and EDS, which provides software solutions for manufacturing, distribution, and warehousing problems. By using these firms, a manufacturer can obtain a superior marketing program, rapid, low-cost distribution, and accurate reports about payroll, sales, and inventories without having to perform any of these tasks itself.

It is not always desirable to use the market, however. A critical task for any firm is to "define its boundaries" by determining what tasks to make and what others to buy.

Defining Boundaries

Regardless of a firm's position along the vertical chain, it needs to define its boundaries. To resolve the associated make-or-buy decisions, the firm must compare the benefits and costs of using the market as opposed to performing the activity in-house. Table 3.1 summarizes the key benefits and costs of using market firms. These are discussed in detail in the remainder of this chapter.

Some Make-or-Buy Fallacies

Before detailing the critical determinants of make-or-buy decisions, we need to dispense with five common, but *incorrect*, arguments:

1. Firms should make an asset, rather than buy it, if that asset is a source of competitive advantage for that firm.
2. Firms should buy, rather than make, to avoid the costs of making the product. (This fallacy is often expressed this way: "By outsourcing an activity, we will eliminate the cost of that activity and thereby increase earnings.")

TABLE 3.1
BENEFITS AND COSTS OF USING THE MARKET

Benefits
- Market firms can achieve economies of scale that in-house departments producing only for their own needs cannot.
- Market firms are subject to the discipline of the market and must be efficient and innovative to survive. Overall corporate success may hide the inefficiencies and lack of innovativeness of in-house departments.

Costs
- Coordination of production flows through the vertical chain may be compromised when an activity is purchased from an independent market firm rather than performed in-house.
- Private information may be leaked when an activity is performed by an independent market firm.
- There may be costs of transacting with independent market firms that can be avoided by performing the activity in-house.

3. Firms should make, rather than buy, to avoid paying a profit margin to independent firms. (This fallacy is often expressed this way: "Our firm should backward integrate to capture the profit of our suppliers for ourselves.")

4. Firms should make, rather than buy, because a vertically integrated producer will be able to avoid paying high market prices for the input during periods of peak demand or scarce supply. (This fallacy is often expressed this way: "By vertically integrating, we obtain the input 'at cost,' thereby insuring ourselves against the risk of high input prices.")

5. Firms should make to tie up a distribution channel. They will gain market share at the expense of rivals. This claim has merit on some occasions, but it used to justify acquisitions on many other occasions when it lacks merit.

Though widely held, the first argument is easy to reject. If it is cheaper to obtain an asset from the market than to produce it internally, the firm should do the former. If the firm believes that the asset is a source of competitive advantage, yet it is easily obtained from the market, then the firm should reconsider its beliefs!

The second argument is also easy to reject. Consider an activity on the vertical chain, say the distribution of finished goods from a manufacturer to retailers. The manufacturer could distribute the goods itself or use an independent distributor. If the firm uses an independent distributor, it will not have to purchase trucks, hire drivers, and so forth. Instead, the independent distributor will have to purchase the trucks and hire the drivers and will then charge the manufacturer to cover the associated expenses. Choosing to buy, rather than make, does not eliminate the expenses of the associated activity. Make-or-buy choices can, however, affect the efficiency with which the activity is carried out, which is the central argument of this chapter.

There are two potential flaws in the third argument. The first flaw stems from the difference between *accounting profit* and *economic profit* discussed in the Economics Primer. Accounting profit is the simple difference between revenues and expenses. Economic profit, by contrast, represents the difference between the accounting profits from a given activity and the accounting profits from investing the same resources in the most lucrative alternative activity. In general, accounting profits exceed economic profits. Because economic profit speaks to the relative profitability of different investment decisions, it is more useful than accounting profit when making business decisions. Even if an upstream supplier is making accounting profits this does not imply that it is making economic profits or that a downstream manufacturing firm could increase its own economic profits by internalizing the activity.

The third argument may be flawed even if the upstream supplier's profits are high enough to generate substantial positive economic profits. The downstream manufacturer might believe that it could make an input at a cost below the "exorbitant" supply price. Before doing so, however, the manufacturer should ask itself the following: "If the supplier of the input is so profitable, why don't other firms enter the market and drive the price down?" The answer to this question will often dissuade the manufacturer from choosing to vertically integrate. Perhaps it is difficult to obtain the expertise needed to make the desired input, or maybe the existing supplier is the only one large enough to reap economies of scale. In these circumstances, the manufacturer would likely find it cheaper to pay the supplier's high price rather than make the input itself.

To illustrate the subtle issues raised by the fourth fallacy, consider a fictitious manufacturer of log homes, Rustic Homes. Rustic Homes sells log cabins that it assembles from specially milled lumber. The market price of this lumber varies from year to year, and for this reason, Rustic's managers are contemplating backward integration into the raising and milling of trees. This is a tempting but fallacious reason for vertical integration.

To see why, suppose that Rustic sells its log cabins for $10,000 each. Besides the costs of milled lumber, it incurs $4,000 in labor costs for every cabin it assembles. During the next year, Rustic has 100 confirmed orders for log cabins. It contemplates two options for its raw materials needs:

1. It can purchase lumber in the open market. Rustic believes that there is a chance that the price of the lumber needed to build one cabin will be $7,000, a chance that the price will be $5,000, and a chance that the price will be $3,000.
2. It can backward integrate by purchasing forest land and a lumber mill. To finance the purchase, Rustic can obtain a bank loan that entails an annual payment of $350,000 (or $3,500 per cabin). In addition, the cost of harvesting timber and milling it to produce the finished lumber for one cabin is $1,500. Thus, the effective cost of timber would be $5,000 per cabin.

Table 3.2 illustrates Rustic's annual income under these options. Under the vertical integration option, Rustic has an assured annual profit of $100,000. Under the nonintegration option, Rustic's net income is uncertain: it could be $300,000, it could be $100,000, or it could be −$100,000. The expected value of this uncertain income is $100,000.[6]

Even though the vertical integration and nonintegration options entail the same expected profit, it is tempting to argue in favor of vertical integration because it eliminates Rustic's risk of income fluctuations. This is an especially tempting argument if management is concerned that when lumber prices are high ($7,000), Rustic will not have enough cash to cover its loss and thus will go bankrupt. If Rustic is committed to being an ongoing business concern, according to this argument it should vertically integrate to eliminate the risk of being unable to pay its bills.

Rustic does not, however, need to vertically integrate to eliminate its income risk. It could counteract price fluctuations by entering into long-term (i.e., futures) contracts with lumber suppliers. This is a practice known as *hedging*, and businesses whose products depend on raw materials that are subject to price fluctuations employ it all the time. For example, a key input in the production of margarine is soybean oil (it represents 80 percent of total materials costs), and manufacturers of margarine, such as Nabisco (producer of Blue Bonnet and Fleischmann's) and Unilever (producer of Shedd's) hedge against price fluctuations by purchasing soybean oil through futures

TABLE 3.2
RUSTIC LOG HOMES

	Vertical Integration	Nonintegration and Lumber Price Is...		
		$3,000	$5,000	$7,000
Revenue	$1,000,000	$1,000,000	$1,000,000	$1,000,000
Cost of Goods Sold				
Lumber	$150,000	$300,000	$500,000	$700,000
Assembly	$400,000	$400,000	$400,000	$400,000
Total	$550,000	$700,000	$900,000	$1,000,000
Interest Expense	$350,000	—	—	—
Profit	$100,000	$300,000	$100,000	($100,000)

EXAMPLE 3.2 SELF-INSURANCE BY BRITISH PETROLEUM

Many firms face potentially large financial losses because of events beyond their control, such as workplace accidents or acts of God. Most firms can easily bear the expense of small losses and thus "self-insure" against them. By self-insure we mean that the firm might take steps to reduce the probability or size of an adverse event, but that it bears the expense out of its operating revenues should an event occur. A large expense can threaten the viability of the firm. For this reason, most firms purchase insurance to hedge against large potential losses.

Insurance sellers, such as Chubb, are famous for covering the costs of catastrophic events such as the World Trade Center disaster. It is more efficient for firms to purchase insurance against large losses from Chubb, rather than self-insure. Chubb can exploit economies of scale by (a) pooling insurance purchases from many firms, thereby spreading the risk, and (b) accessing capital from its many wealthy investors. Given the economic rationale for self-insuring small losses and outsourcing insurance against large losses, it was surprising when, in the early 1990s, British Petroleum purchased insurance to protect against losses under $10 million and self-insured against larger losses. In an interesting case study, Neil Doherty and Clifford Smith used a make-or-buy framework to explain this contrarian strategy.[7]

British Petroleum (BP) is one of the largest industrial firms in the world. Doherty and Smith observe that BP's size enables it to bear most risks without jeopardizing its viability. BP also has sufficient assets to obtain a line of credit to pay off large one-time expenses. Thus, the two main rationales for buying insurance against large losses—risk sharing and access to capital—do not apply to BP. But why does BP buy insurance against smaller losses?

Insurers do more than bear risk and provide capital; they also process and service claims, design and implement loss prevention programs, and challenge questionable claims in court. Most insurers have large databases that enable them to efficiently assess risk and evaluate loss prevention strategies. They also have experienced legal teams to challenge questionable claims. Insurance purchasers, even those as large as BP, lack these capabilities.

Insurers will have a cost advantage over BP if they have experience in the kinds of small losses that BP is likely to incur. BP may experience relatively minor losses (under $10 million) owing to vehicle accidents, small fires, and industrial injuries, for example. BP estimates that it experiences nearly 2,000 such events each year, with the average event costing $30,000. Because these events occur with great frequency, and because firms in the petroleum and other industries are likely to experience similar events, independent insurers can develop expertise in dealing with them. Thus, it makes sense for BP to purchase insurance against minor risks from independent market experts. BP may also experience large financial losses (above $10 million) owing to refinery explosions, oil spills, or tanker accidents. BP estimates that it will experience fewer than two such accidents annually and that each accident will be unique. The infrequency and uniqueness of large accidents suggests that independent insurers will not develop expertise in handling major claims.

Doherty and Smith point out two additional reasons why BP self-insures large losses. First, few insurers are willing to cover large losses, and pricing appears to be noncompetitive. As evidence, Doherty and Smith point out that during the 1980s, BP paid more than $1 billion and recovered only $250 million in claims. This suggests that insurers maintained high markups (although BP may have had unexpectedly few claims during this period). Second, insurers may be unwilling to cover large losses owing to concerns that firms seeking such coverage expect the risks to be relatively high. This is known as the *adverse selection* problem and is discussed in Chapter 14.

contracts. Even if Rustic could not hedge, the argument for vertical integration is still flawed. After all, if Rustic could raise the capital to purchase the forest land, it could instead create a capital reserve to weather short-term fluctuations in lumber prices (e.g., perhaps through a line of credit from the same bank that was willing to loan it the money to buy the land and the lumber mill).

Acquiring vertical partners to tie up channels seems to offer an easy way to increase profits: an upstream firm acquires a monopoly downstream supplier and then refuses to sell to its rivals (or sets a very high price.) This strategy has a number of limitations. First, it may run afoul of antitrust laws, which prohibit many forms of vertical foreclosure. Second, the upstream firm must be careful not to pay too much for the acquisition; after all, the downstream firm already has monopoly power and will presumably command a correspondingly high price. Third, the acquirer must consider how difficult it is for competitors to open new channels of distribution. Vertical foreclosure is clearly no panacea.

Economists have identified a number of special cases in which foreclosure may succeed. One example involves an upstream monopoly supplier that is unable to commit to a high price when selling to downstream firms. This could occur if, after selling at a high price to one downstream firm, it realizes that it can increase its profits by setting a lower price to other, more price sensitive buyers. As a result, all buyers, including the first one, may become leery of accepting the monopoly supply price. By forward integrating, the supplier can fully commit to limiting both input supply and output, thereby increasing its profits. Another example is when an upstream firm is "rolling up" (i.e., acquiring) several downstream firms to create a network. (See Chapter 13 for more on the value of networks.) As the network grows, the remaining firms then may accept lower prices rather than be left out of the network altogether.

REASONS TO "BUY" ◆ ◆ ◆ ◆ ◆

Firms use the market (or "buy") primarily because market firms are often more efficient. Market firms enjoy two distinct types of efficiencies: they exploit economies of scale and the learning curve, and they eliminate "bureaucracy."

Exploiting Scale and Learning Economies

It is conventional wisdom that firms should focus their activities on what they do best and leave everything else to independent outsourcing partners. There are several reasons for this. First, market firms may possess proprietary information or patents that enable them to produce at lower cost. Second, they might be able to aggregate the needs of many firms, thereby enjoying economies of scale. Third, they might exploit their experience in producing for many firms to obtain learning economies.

The first argument requires no additional analysis; the last two arguments are more subtle. Recall from Chapter 2 that when economies of scale or learning economies are present, firms with low production levels or little experience in production may be at a severe cost disadvantage relative to their larger, more experienced rivals. Market firms can often aggregate the demands of many potential buyers, whereas a vertically integrated firm typically produces only for its own needs. Market firms can therefore often achieve greater scale, and thus lower unit costs, than can the downstream firms that use the input.

FIGURE 3.3
PRODUCTION COSTS AND THE MAKE-OR-BUY DECISION

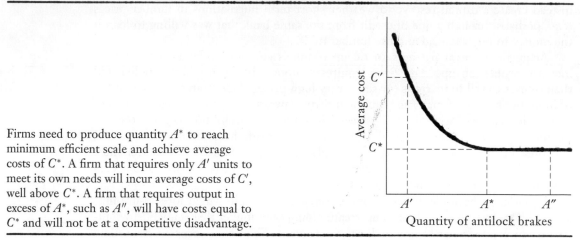

Firms need to produce quantity A^* to reach minimum efficient scale and achieve average costs of C^*. A firm that requires only A' units to meet its own needs will incur average costs of C', well above C^*. A firm that requires output in excess of A^*, such as A'', will have costs equal to C^* and will not be at a competitive disadvantage.

To illustrate this point, consider automobile production. An automobile manufacturer requires a vast variety of upstream inputs: steel, tires, antilock brakes, stereos, computer equipment, and so forth. A manufacturer, Chrysler, for example, could backward integrate and produce inputs such as antilock brakes itself, or it could obtain them from an independent supplier, such as LucasVarity or Robert Bosch Corporation. Figure 3.3 illustrates an average cost function for antilock brakes. According to the figure, the production of antilock brakes displays L-shaped average costs, indicating that there are economies of scale in production. In this example, the minimum efficient scale of production—the smallest level of output at which average cost is minimized—is output level A^*, with resulting average cost C^*.

Suppose that Chrysler expects to sell A'' automobiles with antilock brakes, where $A'' > A^*$. Thus, Chrysler expects to sell enough automobiles to achieve minimum efficient scale in the production of antilock brakes by producing for its own needs alone. This is seen in Figure 3.3, where the average cost of output A'' roughly equals C^*. From a cost perspective, Chrysler gets no advantage by using the market.

Suppose instead that Chrysler expects to sell A' automobiles with antilock brakes, where $A' < A^*$. In this case, Chrysler cannot achieve minimum efficient scale by producing only for its own needs. This is seen in Figure 3.3, where the average cost associated with output A', denoted C', exceeds the minimum average cost C^*. Chrysler could try to expand antilock brake output to A^*, thereby achieving scale economies. However, it would be producing more brakes than cars; it would have to convince other car makers to buy some of its brakes. This seems unlikely. Rivals may fear that Chrysler will withhold supplies during periods of peak demand or that Chrysler might gain vital information about planned production levels. Rivals may simply be unwilling to provide financial support to Chrysler operations. These concerns notwithstanding, competitors sometimes do buy inputs from each other. For example, the Taiwanese firm Giant makes frames for its own bicycles as well as for competitors such as Trek.

Alternatively, Chrysler could purchase antilock brakes from an independent manufacturer such as LucasVarity. LucasVarity would reach production of A' in Figure 3.3 just from its sales to Chrysler. Because there are many more car manufacturers than there are antilock brake makers, LucasVarity will probably sell its antilock brakes to other car makers. This will allow it to expand output beyond A', thereby exploiting scale economies.

It may be more efficient if LucasVarity produces the brakes, but Chrysler benefits only if LucasVarity passes along some of the cost savings. Under what circumstances will this occur? A basic tenet in microeconomics is that if markets are competitive, prices will approach average cost.[8] With only four major competitors, the antilock brake market probably falls somewhere between perfect competition and monopoly. LucasVarity may be able to charge a price in excess of C^*, but it could not charge a price above C'. If it did so, Chrysler could produce the antilock brakes itself at a lower cost. It is likely that Chrysler would be able to negotiate a price somewhere between C^* and C', so that LucasVarity earned positive profits while Chrysler enjoyed some of the benefits of using an efficient market supplier.

Bureaucracy Effects: Avoiding Agency and Influence Costs

Analysts often state that large firms suffer from "bureaucracy." This catchall term includes a number of specific problems associated with agency and influence costs.

Agency Costs

Managers and workers make many decisions that contribute to the profitability of a firm. Examples include how hard to work, how much to invest in innovation, and how many employees to keep on the payroll. Managers and workers who knowingly do not act in the best interests of their firm are *slacking*. *Agency costs* are the costs associated with slack effort and with the administrative controls to deter it. Chapter 14 provides a detailed analysis of agency costs in large organizations. For now, we provide a few salient examples.

A vivid example of agency costs is provided by the case of Crown, Cork and Seal, a producer of metal cans. When John Connelly became an outside director of Crown, Cork and Seal in 1956, he found an organization full of slack. According to one story, Connelly was escorted through a Crown manufacturing plant by a foreman who sang as they walked. The singing alerted workers, who were all hard at work when Connelly greeted them. Connelly asked the foreman to stop singing and continued the tour alone. He found some workers asleep; those who were not were playing cards. The next year Connelly took over the presidency of Crown, Cork and Seal, and promptly laid off nearly a fourth of the workers.[9]

Agency costs may be as simple as overstaffing or using express mail when regular mail will do. Such costs may be unnoticed—and therefore undeterred—by top management in large vertically integrated firm. One reason is that most large firms have common overhead or joint costs that are allocated across divisions. This makes it difficult for top management to measure an individual division's contribution to overall corporate profitability. A second reason is that in-house divisions in many large firms serve as *cost centers*. Cost centers perform activities solely for their own firms and generate no outside revenue. An example of a cost center would be the laundry service in a hospital or the data processing department in a bank. Cost centers are often insulated from competitive pressures because they have a committed "customer" for their inputs. Moreover, it can be difficult to evaluate the efficiency of cost centers because there is often no obvious market test for judging their performance. The absence of market competition, coupled with difficulties in measuring divisional performance, makes it hard for top management to know just how well an internal division is doing relative to its best achievable performance. This, in turn, gives division managers the latitude to engage in behavior that cuts into corporate profits.

Even when management is aware of agency costs, it may prefer to ignore them than to eliminate them. Many firms are unwilling to endure the ill-will generated by firing a nonproductive worker or ending a costly perk that has pervaded the organization. This is particularly likely if the firm possesses some inherent advantages in the market that insulates it from competition and relieves top management from the pressure of controlling agency costs. The famous economist Frederick von Hayek pointed out, "How easy it is for an inefficient manager to dissipate the differentials on which profitability rests."[10]

In principle, one could replicate internally the incentives of market firms by judiciously designing contracts that tie employees' pay and/or department budgets to specific measures of performance or effort. Chapter 14 explores the role of incentives contracts in eliminating slack. Incentive-based pay has become increasingly common in U.S. firms. Top managers in large U.S. firms may receive bonuses and long-term incentives (e.g., stock options) that exceed their base pay. As we will see in Chapter 14, however, these bonuses are not always closely tied to the managers' own performance. Another limitation is that managers (like most people) are risk averse; that is, they do not like the fluctuations in year-to-year income that incentive pay can produce. Thus, in exchange for facing "higher-power" incentives, risk-averse managers may also demand higher base-level compensation and may resist efforts to fully tie pay to performance.

Influence Costs

Another class of costs that arise when transactions are organized internally is what Paul Milgrom and John Roberts have called *influence costs*.[11] Milgrom and Roberts observe that firms allocate financial and human resources to internal divisions and departments through "internal capital markets." If internal capital is scarce, then when resources are allocated to one division or department, fewer resources are available to be allocated to others. Naturally, managers will attempt to influence this allocation. Influence costs include not only the direct costs of influence activities (e.g., the time wasted when a division manager lobbies central management to overturn a decision that is unfavorable to his or her division), they also include the costs of bad decisions that arise from influence activities (e.g., resources that are misallocated because an inefficient division is skillful at lobbying for scarce resources). As with agency costs, a large, vertically integrated firm may be prone to influence costs that a smaller, independent firm might avoid.

Supply relationships within General Motors nicely illustrate how influence activity can harm a vertically integrated firm. We'll imagine the program manager for a new GM product is unhappy with the in-house supplier's bid—it's too high, and in the past the supplier had quality and delivery problems. No sooner does the manager identify an alternative bidder outside the company than the in-house supplier goes to corporate headquarters and explains that the loss of business on his part will require an increase in the costs of similar parts already being supplied by other GM products. Why? Because economies of scale will be lost and the in-house supplier will have excess capacity.

Headquarters, always respectful of scale-economy and capacity-utilization justifications in a mass-production firm such as GM, then has a talk with the program manager. The in-house supplier makes solemn promises to try harder to reduce costs while improving quality and delivery reliability—and gets the business. In this way, the internal market, which supposedly keeps the in-house supply divisions honest, is gradually diluted. This process explains how GM managed to have both the world's highest production volume and the world's highest costs in many of its components supply divisions.[12]

EXAMPLE 3.3 GETTING "CONNECTED" AT SONY[13]

Sony is one of the most recognizable brand names in the world. Long a leader in home electronics, Sony vertically integrated into "software" (music and movies) with its 1988 acquisition of Columbia/CBS Records, which it rechristened Sony Home Entertainment. The partnership between the Sony hardware and software divisions helped the firm in the late 1990s when Sony joined other hardware makers in launching the DVD technology. While most independent movie studios sat on the fence, Sony Home Entertainment (SHE) released several popular titles from the massive Columbia movie library. In the early 2000s, Sony tried a similar strategy to support the new high-resolution Super Audio CD audio format, this time releasing hundreds of classical and jazz titles from its Columbia Records library.

The partnership between hardware and software divisions has not always gone smoothly. In 1998, Sony considered developing digital music technology through the integrated efforts of its hardware and software divisions. From the beginning of this endeavor, conflicts between divisions were the norm. Sony's personal computer and Walkman groups each had their own technologies to push. SHE opposed any effort, fearful that it would encourage illegal downloading that would eat into software sales. Sony allowed each of its groups to take a separate path; the PC and Walkman groups released rival products while SHE launched an online music portal that was not integrated with either hardware offering.

In the meantime, Apple had launched its iPod. Soon to be an icon of twenty-first century technology, the iPod offered seamless integration of hardware and software. In early 2003, Sony responded by launching the Connect project, to be headed by Howard Stringer and Philip Wiser, two executives from Sony USA. Connect would be a joint effort of Sony's top hardware makers, programmers, and SHE. Unfortunately, Wiser and Stringer did not control the hardware, programming,

or SHE groups. The hardware designers were skeptical of Connect, fearing that opposition from SHE would eventually block the entire project. But there were many, more practical problems.

Stringer and Wiser were aware that Sony's software for downloading and playing digital music paled beside Apple's iPod, yet Sony's software division refused to make improvements. Wiser and Stringer wanted Connect to be based on the Walkman design, storing music in MP3 format on a hard disk, a la the iPod. But the hardware folks in Japan's Walkman division opted for the proprietary Atrac format to be stored on minidiscs (a smaller version of the CD that was popular in Japan). The Walkman division eventually gave in on the hard disc, though not the MP3 formatting, but only after the division head complained that hard drives "aren't interesting because anyone can make them." The lack of interest showed in the quality of the finished product. Reviewers of Sony's digital Walkman complained about the Atrac format and the user-unfriendly software interface. To make matters worse, Sony's PC division had launched its own digital music player without any coordination with Connect.

In November 2004, Sony pulled the plug on Connect only to set up Connect 2.0—a new division within Sony that would have its own hardware and software groups. The new Connect turned to a Sony software team in San Jose to revamp the user interface. After some resistance, Connect was also able to recruit a team of flash memory designers from the Walkman group. Sony's PC group even pulled its digital music player from the market. In May 2005, Sony released its new MP3 digital player in Japan and followed up with summer 2005 releases in the United States and Europe. Sony's Connect music store features SME and many independent labels unavailable at the iTunes store. Early reviews have been positive, with sales in Japan running ahead of iPod sales.

◆ ◆ ◆ ◆ ◆ REASONS TO "MAKE"

The three major costs associated with using the market include the costs of poor coordination between steps in the vertical chain, the reluctance of trading partners to develop and share valuable information, and transactions costs. Each of these problems can be traced to costs associated with writing and enforcing contracts. Thus, we motivate our discussion of reasons to make by exploring the limitations of contracts.

The Economic Foundations of Contracts

Contracts define the conditions of exchange. They may take standardized forms, such as the "conditions of contract" on the back of an airline ticket or the terms and conditions of purchase printed on the back of a company's purchase order. Or they may be lengthy and complicated because they are carefully tailored to a specific transaction. For example, the contract for the sale of the Empire State Building in the 1960s involved more than 100 attorneys and was over 400 pages long.[14]

To understand the importance of contracts in the make-or-buy decision, it is useful to ask why firms use contracts. Contracts are valuable, in part, because they list the set of tasks that each contracting party expects the other to perform. But contracts also specify remedies in the event that one party does not fulfill its obligations. If necessary, an injured party may go to court to enforce the contract. This suggests another reason for contracts—firms do not completely trust their trading partners. Otherwise, there would be no need to specify penalties in the event that a firm failed to meet its obligations.

Contracts, then, protect parties to a transaction from opportunistic behavior. However, contracts are not equally effective in all circumstances. Their effectiveness depends on (1) the "completeness" of the contract and (2) the available body of contract law. We discuss each of these factors in turn.

Complete versus Incomplete Contracting

A *complete contract* eliminates opportunistic behavior. A complete contract stipulates each party's responsibilities and rights for each and every contingency that could conceivably arise during the transaction. A complete contract binds the parties to particular courses of action as the transaction unfolded. Neither party could exploit weaknesses in the other's position while the transaction was in progress.

The requirements for complete contracting are severe. Parties to the contract must be able to contemplate all relevant contingencies and agree on a "mapping" that specifies for each possible contingency a set of actions that each party must take. The parties must also be able to stipulate what constitutes satisfactory performance and must be able to measure performance. Finally, the contract must be enforceable. This implies that an outside party, such as a judge or an arbitrator, must be able to observe which contingencies occurred and whether each party took the required actions. For example, a contract in which the price of an item is tied to the seller's production costs might not be enforceable without an independent auditing mechanism that could verify those costs.

As might be imagined, virtually all real-world contracts are incomplete: they do not fully specify the "mapping" from every possible contingency to enforceable rights, responsibilities, and actions. Incomplete contracts involve some degree of open-endedness or ambiguity; there are circumstances under which neither party's rights and responsibilities are clearly spelled out. Consider, for example, the case *Cook v. Deltona Corp.*[15] In 1971 Deltona Corporation, a land developer, sold Cook a piece of property in Marco Shores, Florida. The land was under water at the time of the sale. The title to the land was to be delivered in 1980, by which time Deltona was to have dredged and filled the land. However, during the 1970s changes in federal policy toward wetlands made it difficult for developers to obtain dredge-and-fill permits from the Army Corps of Engineers. In 1976, after failing to obtain permits on nearby land, Deltona gave up trying to obtain a permit for Marco Shores. The sales contract did not specify the buyer's rights and the developer's responsibilities under these circumstances, so the contract was incomplete. Because the contract was silent on this unanticipated turn of events, it was not clear whether Deltona had breached the contract by not delivering the land in the condition promised. The outcome was a lawsuit that took nine years to resolve. (Cook won.)

Three factors prevent complete contracting:

1. Bounded rationality
2. Difficulties specifying or measuring performance
3. Asymmetric information

We will discuss each in turn.

Bounded Rationality

Bounded rationality refers to limits on the capacity of individuals to process information, deal with complexity, and pursue rational aims. Boundedly rational parties cannot contemplate or enumerate every contingency that might arise during a transaction. As a result, they cannot write complete contracts. In *Cook v. Deltona Corp.*, Deltona offered a defense based on bounded rationality. It argued that changes in regulatory requirements by the Army Corps of Engineers seemed so unlikely when the contract was written as to be unforeseeable. The court acknowledged that, in principle, this could be a valid defense, but it held that evidence that the Army Corps of Engineers had begun to toughen its policy meant that Deltona should have accounted for this risk in the contract.

Difficulties Specifying or Measuring Performance

When performance under a contract is complex or subtle, not even the most accomplished wordsmiths may be able to spell out each party's rights and responsibilities. Language in contracts is thus often left so vague and open-ended that it may not be clear what constitutes fulfillment of the contract. For example, a standard clause in lease contracts for new cars allows the company to bill the lessee for "excess wear and tear." However, the contract does not specify what this means. Some leasing companies have used this clause to charge customers who return the car in less-than-showroom condition.

A related problem is that performance may be ambiguous or hard to measure. For example, in relationships between airframe manufacturers and engine suppliers, engine thrust is the subject of much contention. Thrust cannot be measured exactly, and each engine supplier uses a different methodology. John Newhouse, in *The Sporty Game*, writes of Boeing engineers who "speak astringently about a Hartford pound of thrust [Pratt & Whitney], a Cincinnati pound of thrust [GE], and a Derby pound of thrust [Rolls-Royce].[16]

Asymmetric Information

Even if the parties can foresee the contingencies and specify and measure the relevant performance dimensions, a contract may still be incomplete because the parties do not have equal access to all contract-relevant information. If one party knows something that the other does not, then information is *asymmetric*, and the knowledgeable party may distort or misrepresent that information. For example, suppose a contract stipulates that a manufacturer is to receive a bonus if it maintains stringent quality control to assure the durability of its product. Because the manufacturer is responsible for quality control, it is the only one that can verify that appropriate quality control measures have been taken. The manufacturer would want to claim that it took the required steps to assure durability, even when it did not. Understanding the manufacturer's self-interest, the buyer might protest these claims. To enforce this contract, a court would have to look at evidence (e.g., an independent quality audit or testimony from each party) to ascertain whether the contract was fulfilled. But if the item being produced is complex or unique, this evidence may well be inconclusive, and the court would have little basis on which to resolve the dispute. Under these circumstances, the two parties may be unable to contract for "quality control."

The Role of Contract Law

A well-developed body of contract law makes it possible for transactions to occur smoothly when contracts are incomplete. In the United States, contract law is embodied in both common law and the *Uniform Commercial Code (UCC)*, the law governing contracts in all states except Louisiana. The doctrines of contract law specify a set of "standard" provisions applicable to wide classes of transactions. These doctrines eliminate the need for parties to specify these provisions in every single transaction. However, contract law is not a perfect substitute for complete contracting for two important reasons. First, the doctrines of contract law are phrased in broad language ("reasonable time," "reasonable price") that is open to differing interpretations when applied to specific transactions. Uncertainty about how particular doctrines will be applied raises the costs of transacting the exchange relative to an ideal world in which complete contracting is possible.

Second, litigation can be a costly way of "completing" contracts. A vivid illustration of this occurred in the mid-1970s when Westinghouse invoked the doctrine of *commercial impracticability* to justify reneging on contracts to deliver 70 million pounds of uranium.[17] This doctrine excuses a seller from performing its obligations under a sales contract if "performance has been made impracticable by the occurrence of a contingency the nonoccurrence of which was a basic assumption on which the contract was made" (UCC 2–504). In the early 1970s, Westinghouse had agreed to sell uranium at $10 per pound to a group of electric utilities. Soon after signing the contracts, the price of uranium increased dramatically, to $26 per pound in 1975. Westinghouse argued that the price increase was the result of unforeseeable events (the Arab oil embargo and the subsequent runup of oil prices) and that it could not deliver the uranium without incurring serious financial harm—losses of more than $1 billion on the contracts. The subsequent breach-of-contract litigation took over three years to resolve. Eventually, most of the cases were settled out of court, but the utilities accepted payments that were smaller than the value of the uranium they would have received under the original contracts.

Litigation can also weaken or destroy business relationships. As Stewart Macauley writes, "A breach of contract suit may settle a particular dispute, but such action often results in 'divorce,' ending the 'marriage' between two businesses, since a contract action is likely to carry charges with at least overtones of bad faith."[18] The termination of longstanding business relationships as a result of a breach-of-contract suit can be especially costly if the parties have invested in the relationship and become mutually dependent on one another. Establishing new relationships that are equally beneficial to both parties may be difficult or even impossible.

Coordination of Production Flows Through the Vertical Chain

Contracts between independent firms are often essential for assuring the coordination of production. For coordination to succeed, players must make decisions that depend, in part, on the decisions of others. Working together, firms can assure a good fit along all dimensions of production. Examples include:

- *Timing Fit.* The launch of a Heinekin marketing campaign must coincide with increased production and distribution by its bottlers.

- *Size Fit.* The sun roof of an automobile must fit precisely into the roof opening.

- *Color Fit.* The tops in Benetton's spring lineup must match the bottoms.

- *Sequence Fit.* The steps in a medical treatment protocol must be properly sequenced.

Without good coordination, bottlenecks may arise. The failure of one supplier to deliver parts on schedule can shut down a factory. A failure to coordinate advertising images across local markets can undermine a brand's image and dampen sales.

Firms often rely on contracts to assure coordination. Contracts may specify delivery dates, design tolerances, or other performance targets. If a supplier fails to meet the specified targets, it might have to pay a penalty. Alternatively, if they exceed expectations, they might receive a bonus. For example, construction firms often receive a bonus if they finish their work ahead of schedule. Firms may also assure coordination in the vertical chain by relying on *merchant coordinators*, independent firms that specialize in linking suppliers, manufacturers, and retailers.

The use of contracts and middlemen clauses is widespread, yet in some circumstances the protections afforded by contracts and middlemen may be inadequate. Paul Milgrom and John Roberts explain that coordination is especially important in processes with *design attributes*, which are attributes that need to relate to each other in a precise fashion; otherwise they lose a significant portion of their economic value.[19] Table 3.3 lists activities that are design attributes and those that are not.

TABLE 3.3
EXAMPLES OF DESIGN ATTRIBUTES

Are Design Attributes	*Are Not Design Attributes*
Timely delivery of part necessary for manufacturing process to begin	Timely completion of building construction
Sequencing of courses in MBA curriculum	Sequencing of sports activities in summer camp
Fit of automobile sunroof glass in opening of auto roof	Fit of bicycle handlebar covers on handlebars
Matching colors of sportswear ensembles within narrow tolerances	Matching sizes of sportswear ensembles within narrow tolerance

What the former have in common but the latter lack is that small errors can be exceptionally costly. For example, a slight delay in delivering a critical component can shut down a manufacturing plant. On the other hand, a slight delay in delivering landscaping supplies is unlikely to be critical to completing construction of an office tower.

Because contracts are incomplete, firms cannot rely on them to assure adequate coordination of design attributes. Whether by accident or design, an upstream supplier may fail to take the steps necessary to assure a proper fit. If the resulting cost is substantial, then even if the downstream firm seeks compensation in court, it may be unable to recover full economic damages. Confronting such a possibility, the downstream firm may wish to integrate all critical activities and rely on administrative control to achieve the appropriate coordination.

Many firms bring design attributes in-house. Benetton dyes its own fabrics, because slight mismatches of color can ruin a production run. Caremark, which provides home intravenous drug infusion therapy for patients with AIDS, cancer, and other illnesses, writes its own applications software so as to beat its competitors to the market with new drug therapies. Silicon chip makers make both the wiring and the wafers in order to assure a precise fit. In each example, the cost of a small error along the critical design attribute can be catastrophic.

Leakage of Private Information

A firm's *private information* is information that no one else knows. Private information may pertain to production know-how, product design, or consumer information. When firms use the market to obtain supplies or distribute products, they risk losing control of valuable private information. Speaking about relying on outside Japanese suppliers, a vice president of technology and market development for Xerox once stated, "It's not a game for the naïve player. It demands careful study. If you bungle a relationship with the Japanese, you can lose your technology, your business."[20]

Well-defined and well-protected patents afford research-driven organizations the ability to outsource downstream activities from production through marketing without compromising the principal source of their competitive advantage. But patents are not foolproof. Concern about sharing critical information that is seemingly protected by patent plays a central role in dictating the boundaries of firms in the pharmaceutical industry. Independent research companies, such as fledgling biotech firms, are often reluctant to license their discoveries to larger drug makers for fear of losing control over proprietary technology. One particular fear: to convince the big drug makers to pay for a license, the smaller companies must reveal some of their technological secrets. If they reveal too much, the drug makers can walk away from the deal without the need to purchase the license. This is one reason smaller companies attempt to bring their products through the drug review process despite the scale and experience advantages enjoyed by larger drug makers.

Firms may find it especially difficult to protect critical information that it must share with employees. Urban legend has it that the secret formula to Coca-Cola is known to only two executives, and each only knows one-half! (The reality is that a small handful of Coke execs know the entire formula.) Professional services firms that jealously guard privileged information about research, data, and even client lists often require new workers to sign noncompete clauses. These clauses state that should the individual leave the firm, he or she may not directly compete with it for several years. Protected by the noncompete clause, the firm can reveal important competitive information. In practice, many firms find it difficult to enforce noncompete clauses, making employment hardly more effective at protecting information than contracting with independent workers.

Transactions Costs

The concept of transactions costs was first described by Ronald Coase in his famous paper, "The Nature of the Firm."[21] Coase raised the following question: in light of the efficiencies of the competitive market mechanism emphasized in economic theory, why does so much economic activity take place within firms in which market transactions are replaced by centralized direction? Coase concluded that there must be costs to using the market that can be eliminated by using the firm. These have come to be known as *transactions costs*.

Transactions costs include obvious things like the time and expense of negotiating, writing, and enforcing contracts. They also include subtle and potentially far greater costs that arise when one or more firms exploits incomplete contracts to act opportunistically (i.e., seek private gain at the expense of the greater good). The adverse consequences of opportunistic behavior, as well as the costs of trying to prevent it, are the main focus of transactions costs economics.

Contract law might ameliorate the opportunism that can arise under incomplete contracting, but it is unlikely to eliminate it. Thus, incomplete contracting will inevitably entail some transactions costs. To help explain more precisely the nature of these transactions costs and how they might influence decisions to integrate, this section introduces three important theoretical concepts from transactions-cost economics: *relationship-specific assets*, *quasi-rents*, and the *holdup* problem. The following subsections define these concepts and explain their significance.

Relationship-Specific Assets

A relationship-specific asset is an investment made to support a given transaction. They are often essential for the efficiency of a particular transaction. However, a relationship-specific asset cannot be redeployed to another transaction without some sacrifice in the productivity of the asset or some cost in adapting the asset to the new transaction. Firms that have invested in relationship-specific assets cannot switch trading partners without seeing a decline in the value of these assets. This implies that investments in relationship-specific assets lock the parties into the relationship to some degree.

Forms of Asset Specificity   Asset specificity can take at least four forms:

1. Site specificity
2. Physical asset specificity
3. Dedicated assets
4. Human asset specificity

Site Specificity   Site specificity refers to assets that are located side-by-side to economize on transportation or inventory costs or to take advantage of processing efficiencies. Traditional steel manufacturing offers a good example of site specificity. Side-by-side location of blast furnaces, steelmaking furnaces, casting units, and mills saves fuel costs, as the pig iron, molten steel, and semifinished steel do not have to be reheated before being moved to the next process in the production chain.

Physical Asset Specificity Physical asset specificity refers to assets whose physical or engineering properties are specifically tailored to a particular transaction. For example, glass container production requires molds that are custom tailored to particular container shapes and glass-making machines. Physical asset specificity inhibits customers from switching suppliers.

Dedicated Assets A dedicated asset is an investment in plant and equipment made to satisfy a particular buyer. Without the promise of that particular buyer's business, the investment would not be profitable. The government-run Associated British Ports (ABP) often invests in dedicated facilities to serve the specific needs of import and/or export customers. For example, one facility might be designed with specialized bagging equipment to accommodate construction materials, whereas another may be equipped with concrete batching machines to handle marine aggregates (sand and gravel). ABP usually requires long-term contracts from its customers before making these multimillion pound investments.

Human Asset Specificity Human asset specificity refers to cases in which a worker, or group of workers, has acquired skills, know-how, and information that are more valuable inside a particular relationship than outside it. Human asset specificity not only includes tangible skills, such as expertise with company-specific software, but it also encompasses intangible assets. For example, every organization has unwritten "routines" and "standard operating procedures." A manager who has become a skillful administrator within the context of one organization's routines may be less effective in an organization with completely different routines. As hospitals develop new treatment protocols, the training of nurses and other specialized staff will become more firm-specific. Training of aides and orderlies, on the other hand, will remain transferable to other hospitals.

The Fundamental Transformation The need to create relationship-specific assets transforms the relationship as the transaction unfolds. Before individuals or firms make relationship-specific investments, they may have many alternative trading partners and can choose to partner with those that afford the highest possible profit. But after making relationship-specific investments, they will have few, if any, alternative trading partners. Their profits will be determined by bilateral bargaining. In short, once the parties invest in relationship-specific assets, the relationship changes from a "large numbers" bargaining situation to a "small numbers" bargaining situation. Oliver Williamson refers to this change as the *fundamental transformation*.[22]

Rents and Quasi-Rents

The fundamental transformation has significant consequences for the economics of bargaining between buyer and seller, which in turn affects the costs of arm's-length market exchange. To set the stage for our discussion of these costs that follows, we must first define and explain *rent* and *quasi-rent*.

These are hard concepts. To explain them we will walk through a numerical example about a hypothetical transaction. Suppose your company contemplates building a factory to produce cup holders for the Ford Taurus automobile. The factory can make up to 1 million holders per year at an average variable cost of C dollars per unit. You finance the construction of your factory with a mortgage from a bank that requires an annual payment of I dollars. The loan payment of I dollars thus represents your

EXAMPLE 3.4 THE FUNDAMENTAL TRANSFORMATION IN THE U.S. AUTOMOBILE INDUSTRY[23]

A real-life example of the fundamental transformation is the relationship between U.S. automobile assemblers and their component suppliers. Assemblers generally use competitive bidding for outside suppliers. The assembler solicits bids for short-term (usually one-year) supply contracts. These contracts specify price, quality (e.g., no fewer than two bad parts per thousand), and a delivery schedule. Before the contract, there are many potential bidders. Once the contract is let, however, specific investments on both sides bind the assembler and supplier in a mutually dependent relationship. For some components, the assembler must invest in specific production tooling. The supplier must invest in equipment that is tailored to the assembler's specifications. Because of asset specificity, suppliers and assemblers understand that suppliers are often bidding not just for a one-year contract but for a long-term business relationship.

The fundamental transformation makes the relationship between assemblers and suppliers contentious. Because suppliers often hope to enter a long-term relationship with an assembler, they will sometimes bid below cost to win the contract, a strategy known as buy-in. A supplier knows from experience that it might be able to renegotiate with the assembler based on claims that unanticipated events (e.g., poorer than expected qualities of key materials)

have raised costs. Because changing suppliers at this stage is costly, the assembler may acquiesce. On the other hand, the assembler's procurement managers are under tremendous pressure to hold costs down. At the competitive bidding stage, assemblers will routinely share production drawings with several potential suppliers. Thus, although it may be costly for an assembler to replace a supplier once the component goes into production, it can still do so. Assemblers do threaten to replace suppliers to hold component prices down. Because a supplier makes investments that are specific to its relationship with an assembler, termination of a supply contract can harm it severely. The supplier thus cannot take these threats lightly. The upshot is that once the fundamental transformation occurs, the relationship between the assembler and its suppliers often becomes one of distrust and noncooperation. Suppliers are reluctant to share information on their production operations or their production costs with the assembler for fear that the assembler will use this information to bargain down the contract price in subsequent negotiations. As Womack, Jones, and Roos express it, a supplier's attitude is "what goes on in my factory is my own business."[24] This greatly impedes the ability of the assembler and a supplier to work together to enhance production efficiencies and develop new production technologies.

(annualized) cost of investment in this plant. Note that this is an unavoidable cost: You have to make your mortgage payment even if you do not do business with Ford.[25] Your total cost of making 1 million cup holders is thus $I + 1,000,000C$ dollars per year.

You will design and build the factory specifically to produce cup holders for the Ford Taurus. Your *expectation* is that Ford will purchase your holders at a profitable price. But if you build the factory and *do not* end up selling cup holders to Ford, you still have a "bail-out" option: You can sell the holders to jobbers who, after suitably modifying them, will resell them to other automobile manufacturers. The "market price" you can expect to get from these jobbers is P_m. If you sell your cup holders to jobbers, you would thus get total revenue of $1,000,000P_m$.

Suppose that $P_m > C$, so the market price covers your variable cost. Thus, you are more than willing to sell to the jobbers if you had no other option. Ignoring the investment cost I for a moment, your profit from selling to the jobbers is $1,000,000(P_m - C)$. Suppose also that the annual investment cost $I > 1,000,000(P_m - C)$, implying that you will not recover your investment cost if you sell only to jobbers. In this sense, a portion of your investment is specific to your relationship with Ford. In particular, the difference $I - 1,000,000(P_m - C)$ represents your company's *relationship-specific investment (RSI)*.

- The RSI equals the amount of your investment that you cannot recover if your company *does not* do business with Ford.

- For example, if $I = \$8,500,000$, $C = \$3$, and $P_m = \$4$, then the RSI is $\$8,500,000 - 1,000,000(4 - 3) = \$7,500,000$. Of your $\$8,500,000$ investment cost, you lose $\$7,500,000$ of it if you do not do business with Ford and sell to jobbers instead.

We can now explain rent and quasi-rent. First, let us explain rent. Suppose that before you take out the loan to invest in the cup holder plant, Ford agreed to buy 1 million sets of cup holders per year at a price of P^* per unit, where $P^* > P_m$. Thus, your company expects to receive total revenue of $1,000,000P^*$ from Ford. Suppose that $I < 1,000,000(P^* - C)$, so that given your expectation of the price Ford will pay, you should build the plant. Then,

- Your *rent* is $1,000,000(P^* - C) - I$.

- In words: Your rent is simply the profit you expect to get when you build the plant, assuming all goes as planned.[26]

Let us now explain quasi-rent. Suppose, after the factory was built, your deal with Ford falls apart. You can still sell cup holders to the jobbers. Should you do so? The answer is yes. Even though sales to jobbers do not cover your investment cost I, once you have built the factory, the cost I is unavoidable—remember, you still have to pay your mortgage! Thus, I is a sunk cost and does not affect decision making. You should sell to the jobbers because $1,000,000(P_m - C) > 0$; that is, sales to distributors cover your variable costs.

- Your quasi-rent is the difference between the profit you get from selling to Ford and the profit you get from your next-best option, selling to jobbers. That is, quasi-rent is $[1,000,000(P^* - C) - I] - [1,000,000(P_m - C) - I] = 1,000,000(P^* - P_m)$.

- In words: Your *quasi-rent* is the *extra* profit that you get if the deal goes ahead as planned, versus the profit you would get if you had to turn to your next-best alternative (in our example, selling to jobbers).

It seems clear why the concept of rent is important. Your firm—indeed any firm—must expect positive rents to induce it to invest in an asset. But why is quasi-rent important? It turns out that quasi-rent tells us about the possible magnitude of the holdup problem, a problem that can arise when there are relationship-specific assets.

The Holdup Problem

If an asset was *not* relationship-specific, the profit the firm could get from using the asset in its best alternative and its next-best alternative would be the same. Thus, the associated quasi-rent would be zero. But when a firm invests in a relationship-specific asset, the quasi-rent must be positive—it will always get more from its best alternative than from its second-best alternative. If the quasi-rent is large, a firm stands to lose a lot if it has to turn to its second-best alternative. This opens the possibility that its trading partner could exploit this large quasi-rent, through *holdup*.[27]

- A firm *holds up* its trading partner by attempting to renegotiate the terms of a deal. A firm can profit by holding up its trading partner when contracts are incomplete (thereby permitting breach) and when the deal generates quasi-rents for its trading partner.

To see how this could happen, let's return to our example of Ford and your cup holder company. Ford could reason as follows: You have already sunk your investment in the plant. Even though Ford "promised" to pay you P^* per cup holder, it knows that you would accept any amount greater than P_m per unit and still sell to it. Thus, Ford could break the contract and offer you a price *between* P^* and P_m; if you accept this renegotiation of the deal, Ford would increase its profits.

Could Ford get away with this? After all, didn't Ford sign a contract with you? Well, if the contract is incomplete (and thus potentially ambiguous), Ford could assert that, in one way or another, circumstances have changed and that it is justified breaking the contract. It might, for example, claim that increases in the costs of producing the Taurus will force it to discontinue the model unless suppliers, such as yourself, renegotiate their contracts. Or it might claim that the quality of your cup holders fails to meet promised specifications and that it must be compensated for this lower quality with lower prices.

Unless you want to fight Ford in court for breach of contract (itself a potentially expensive move), you are better off accepting Ford's revised offer than not accepting it. By reneging on the original contract, Ford has "held you up" and has transferred some of your quasi-rent to itself. To illustrate this concretely, suppose $P^* = \$12$ per unit, $P_m = \$4$ per unit, $C = \$3$ per unit, and $I = \$8,500,000$.

- At the original expected price of $12 per unit, your rent is
  $(12 - 3)1,000,000 - 8,500,000 = \$500,000$ per year.

- Your quasi-rent is $(12 - 4)1,000,000 = \$8,000,000$ per year.

- If Ford renegotiates the contract down to $8 per unit, Ford will increase its profits by $4 million per year and it will have transferred half of your quasi-rents to itself.

Note that after the holdup has occurred, you realize that you are getting a profit of $(8 - 3)1,000,000 - 8,500,000 = -\$3,500,000$. You are losing money on your investment in the factory! This tells us that if, instead of trusting Ford, you had anticipated the prospect of holdup, then you would not have made the investment to begin with. This situation is especially problematic because your rent was small but your quasi-rent was large. When Ford holds you up and extracts a portion of your quasi-rent, you end up with losses that dwarf the expected profits. This example shows why we talk about the holdup problem in the context of vertical integration. If you are afraid of being held up, you might be reluctant to invest in relationship-specific assets in the first place, forcing Ford either to find another supplier of cupholders *or to make them itself*.

The Holdup Problem and Transactions Costs

The holdup problem raises the cost of transacting arm's-length market exchanges in four ways. It can lead to:

1. More difficult contract negotiations and more frequent renegotiations
2. Investments to improve *ex post* bargaining positions

EXAMPLE 3.5 POWER BARGES

How do you deal with trading partners who are reluctant to make investments that have a high degree of site specificity? This is the problem that many developing nations face in convincing foreign corporations to construct power plants. Power plants are usually highly specialized assets. Once a firm builds a power plant in a developing nation, the associated investment undergoes the "fundamental transformation" and becomes a site-specific asset. If the purchasing government defaults on its payments, the manufacturer has few options for recovering its investment. (The firm could route the power to consumers in other nations, but the defaulting government could easily prevent it.) Even though no manufacturer has had to repossess a plant, the fear of default has scared them off. As a result, growing economies in developing nations may be slowed by power shortages.

The solution to the problem is ingenious. Manufacturers have eliminated the geographic asset specificity associated with power generation! They do this by building power plants on floating barges. During the 1990s, companies such as Raytheon, Westinghouse, Smith Cogeneration, and Amfel built floating power plants (which can generate upward of 500 megawatts of power and cost as much as $500 million). Customers include countries such as Bangladesh, Ghana, Haiti, Kenya, and Malaysia, as well intermediaries such as the Power Barge

Corporation. Power barges are moored on one or more barges in safe harbors and "plugged into" land-based transformers that send electricity to domestic consumers. If the purchaser defaults, the manufacturer or intermediary can tow the barge(s) away and sell the plant to another customer.

Floating power plants are not new. Since the 1930s, U.S. Navy battleships have used their turboelectric motors to provide emergency power to utilities. Consolidated Edison operates a gas-turbine generator that is housed on a barge in the Gowanus Canal in Brooklyn. Recent innovations have reduced the size and increased the reliability of gas turbines, making it possible to house large-capacity generators on a small number of barges. This is especially attractive to nations such as Ghana that have their own natural gas reserves. (Some floating power plants use oil or geothermal energy.)

Floating power plants can also be assembled off-site and then towed to the purchasing nation. This lowers labor costs because the manufacturers do not have to pay their skilled workers to go to a distant site for a long time. One final incentive for floating power plants: a recent amendment to the 1936 U.S. Merchant Marine Act provides substantial financing advantages for vessels constructed in the United States but documented under the laws of another nation. Floating barges fit this description, and enjoy favorable financing.

3. Distrust
4. Reduced investment in relationship-specific investments

Contract Negotiation and Renegotiation

The most obvious way in which the holdup problem raises the costs of market transactions is by increasing the difficulty of contract negotiations and the frequency of contract renegotiations. When each side anticipates the possibility of holdup, the initial contract negotiations are likely to be time consuming and costly, as each party attempts to protect itself against being held up later on. But if the relationship is sufficiently complex, the ability to write complete contracts that safeguard each party is limited, and as circumstances change in unanticipated ways, the temptation for a party to hold up its trading partner is likely to lead to frequent renegotiations of contracts. This, too, raises the direct costs of carrying out the transaction. In addition, more frequent renegotiations are likely to be associated with more frequent delays or disruptions in the exchange, raising production costs and impeding delivery of products to customers.

Investments to Improve Ex Post *Bargaining Positions*

The possibility of holdup may also lead parties to make investments that improve their postcontractual bargaining positions. This can take several forms. A manufacturer may acquire a standby production facility for a key input as a hedge against contractual holdup by the input supplier. A firm might also seek a second source for an input to reduce the risk of holdup by a sole supplier. For example, in the early 1980s, Intel's customers (including IBM) pressured it to provide second sources for its 8088 and 80286 microprocessors. Although standby facilities and second sources can reduce the possibility of holdup, they are not without cost. A standby facility that duplicates the production facility of the input supplier may stand idle much of the time, thus representing costly excess capacity that will eventually be borne by the buyer.

Distrust

A less tangible, but real, cost of holdup is the distrust that can arise between parties in the relationship. Distrust raises the costs of contracting in two ways. First, it raises the direct costs of contract negotiation as parties insist that more formal safeguards be written into the contract. Second, distrust impedes sharing information or ideas to achieve production efficiencies or quality improvements. (As discussed in Example 3.4, distrust characterizes the relationship between U.S. auto assemblers and their suppliers.) Industry experts cite it as a reason for high production costs and the less-than-satisfactory quality of components.

Reduced Investment

Finally, and perhaps worst of all, the possibility of holdup can reduce incentives to invest in specific assets. Underinvestment could occur in several ways. A firm might reduce the scale of its investment in relationship-specific assets. For example, an alumina producer might build a small refinery rather than a large one. Or a firm might substitute general-purpose assets for more specific ones. Continuing the example, the alumina producer might build a refinery that can process many different grades of bauxite, instead of just one grade.

The tendency to underinvest in relationship-specific assets causes problems because relationship-specific investments usually allow firms to achieve efficiencies that they cannot achieve with general-purpose investments. An alumina refinery that is set up to accommodate more than one grade of bauxite is generally more costly to operate than one that is designed to accommodate a particular type of bauxite. When the holdup problem leads to underinvestment in relationship-specific assets, the result is likely to be lower productivity and higher production costs.

Recap: From Relationship-Specific Assets to Transactions Costs

Because the ideas developed in this section are complex and subtle, let's recap the main lines of argument:

- A relationship-specific asset is an asset that supports a particular transaction. Redeploying a relationship-specific asset reduces its productivity or entails extra costs.

EXAMPLE 3.6 UNDERINVESTMENT IN RELATIONSHIP-
SPECIFIC ASSETS BY BRITISH SUBCONTRACTORS[28]

Bruce Lyons recently studied investments in relationship-specific assets by British subcontractors. His study focused on small firms (those employing 110 or fewer workers) that produced components for British manufacturers. The firms studied by Lyons included both low-tech firms making products such as metal casings, and high-tech firms producing items such as microprocessors and computer software. In all cases, the firms manufactured products that were customized to individual buyers. Many of the subcontractors in Lyons's sample did not use formal contracts in their transactions with their principal customers. The subcontractors who did employ formal contracts were those whose principal buyer accounted for a large fraction of the subcontractors' sales revenues, who produced a highly customized product, and who made significant relationship-specific investments. These subcontractors faced the greatest risks of holdup and, perhaps not surprisingly, sought to protect themselves through formal contracts.

Resorting to formal contracts was not the only way, or even the main way, that the subcontractors studied by Lyons protected themselves against potential holdup. Many underinvested in relationship-specific assets. Half of the subcontractors in Lyons' sample indicated that an "ideal" relationship-specific production technology was available to support their transactions with their primary customer. However, only 40 percent of this group said they were using this technology or planning to do so. The subcontractors who were most likely to avoid investing in the relationship-specific technology saw themselves as vulnerable to opportunistic behavior by their principal customer and characterized their relationship with that customer as involving a high degree of distrust. These subcontractors refrained from investing in the ideal production technology because they were afraid that they would be held up.

- A relationship-specific asset gives rise to quasi-rents. The quasi-rent in a transaction with relationship-specific assets equals the *extra profit* a firm gets when it deploys its relationship-specific assets in their intended use and the transaction goes ahead as planned, as opposed to deploying those assets in their best alternative use.

- When a party has quasi-rents, it can be held up by its trading partner. When this happens, the trading partner transfers some of the quasi-rents to itself. Holdup is especially tempting when contracts are highly incomplete, so that proving breach of contract is difficult.

- The potential for holdup raises the cost of market transaction by making contract negotiations more contentious, by inducing parties to invest in "safeguards" to improve postcontractual bargaining positions, by engendering distrust, and by leading to underinvestment in relationship-specific assets.

Double Marginalization: A Final Consideration

When a firm with market power contemplates vertical integration with another firm with market power, it needs to consider one additional benefit, known as double marginalization. Double marginalization results when an upstream firm exploits its market power by setting a price that exceeds marginal cost. The downstream firm purchases these marked-up inputs and then exploits its own market power by applying its own markup—effectively marking up twice the marginal cost of the upstream supplier. This causes the price of the finished good to be too high—higher than the price that would maximize the joint profits of the supplier and buyer. Through integration, the downstream firm can set prices based on the actual marginal costs of production, rather than artificially inflated market costs for inputs. This will lead to lower retail prices and higher profits for the integrated firm.

SUMMARIZING MAKE-OR-BUY DECISIONS: THE MAKE-OR-BUY DECISION TREE

◆ ◆ ◆ ◆ ◆

The make-or-buy decision involves a calculated balancing of several benefits and costs of integration. A manager can easily get lost in the complexity of this balancing act. Figure 3.4 provides a series of questions to guide the manager through the decision-making process. The manager must first assess whether the market provides any

FIGURE 3.4
SUMMARIZING THE FRAMEWORK: AN ISSUE TREE

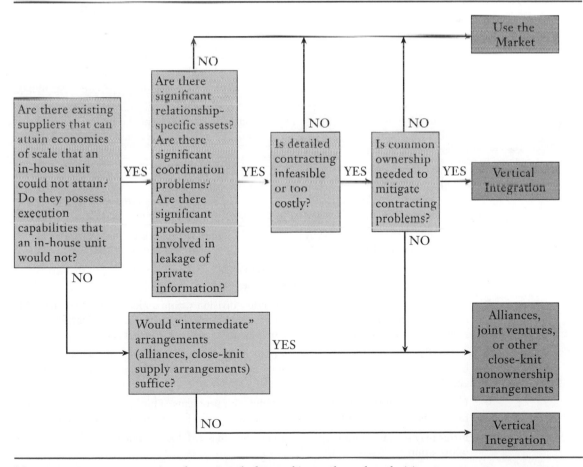

Managers must answer a series of questions before making make-or-buy decisions.

alternative to vertical integration. If the answer is no, then the firm must either take on the task itself or prop-up a quasi-independent supplier through a joint venture or strategic alliance. If the market does offer alternatives to vertical integration, then the manager must determine whether market relationships will be impeded by information, coordination, or holdup problems. If such problems do not exist, then the firm should use the market. But if they do exist, the manager must finally determine whether these problems can be prevented either through contract (favoring the use of the market) or through internal governance (favoring integration). Though not shown in the decision tree, managers should also consider whether special circumstances of market power are causing double marginalization and whether profits are suffering as a result.

CHAPTER SUMMARY

◆ The production of any good or service usually requires a range of activities organized in a vertical chain. Production activities flow from upstream suppliers of raw inputs to downstream manufacturers, distributors, and retailers.

◆ The vertical chain includes processing and handling activities associated directly with the processing and distribution of inputs and outputs, and professional support activities, such as accounting and planning.

◆ A fundamental question is which activities in the vertical chain a firm should perform itself and which it should leave to independent firms in the market. This is known as the "make-or-buy" problem.

◆ A fallacious make-or-buy argument is that firms should buy to avoid incurring the associated costs. The firm it buys from will have to incur these costs and will charge accordingly.

◆ A second fallacy is that firms should make, rather than buy, to keep for themselves the profits earned by independent firms. These profits usually represent the returns necessary to attract investment and would be required of the firm that "makes" just as they are required of independent firms.

◆ A third fallacy is that vertically integrated firms can produce an input at cost and thus have an advantage over nonintegrated firms that must buy inputs at market prices. This argument ignores a hidden opportunity cost to the vertically integrated firm: By using the input to produce its final output, it forgoes outside sales in the open market.

◆ The solution to the make-or-buy decision depends on which decision leads to the most efficient production. This is determined by assessing the benefits and costs of using the market.

◆ Market firms can often achieve economies of scale in production of an input that firms that choose to make the input themselves cannot.

◆ Market firms offer other advantages. While a division within a hierarchical firm may hide its inefficiencies behind complex monitoring and reward systems, independent firms must survive market competition. This encourages efficiency and innovation.

◆ Vertically integrated firms can try to replicate market incentives but may encounter problems associated with motivation (agency costs) and internal lobbying for resources (influence costs).

◆ Use of market firms often presents coordination problems. This is especially problematic for inputs with design attributes that require a careful fit between different components.

◆ Firms may be reluctant to use the market when they risk losing control of valuable private information.

◆ Use of market firms may entail transactions costs.

QUESTIONS

1. Describe the vertical chain for the production of computer games. Describe the extent of vertical integration of the steps in this chain.

2. A manufacturer of pencils contemplates backward integration into the production of rapeseed oil, a key ingredient in manufacturing the rubberlike material (called factice) that forms the eraser. Rapeseed oil is traded in world commodity markets, and its price fluctuates as supply and demand conditions change. The argument that has been made in favor of vertical integration is this: "Pencil production is very utilization-sensitive (i.e., a plant that operates at full capacity can produce pencils at much lower cost per unit than a plant that operates at less than full capacity). Owning our own source of supply of rapeseed oil insulates us from short-run supply–demand imbalances and therefore will give us a competitive advantage over rival producers." Explain why this argument is wrong.

3. Matilda Bottlers bottles and distributes wines and spirits in Australia. Big Gator is a conglomerate that manufactures, among other things, a popular lager beer. By virtue of a lifetime contract, Mathilda has exclusive rights to bottle and distribute Big Gator Beer in New South Wales, the largest state in Australia. Matilda uses its monopsony power to pay a lower price for Big Gator Beer than do bottlers in other states. Is this sufficient justification for Big Gator to buy out Matilda Bottlers?

4. In each of the following situations, why are firms likely to benefit from vertical integration?
   (a) A *grain elevator* is located at the terminus of a *rail line*.
   (b) A *manufacturer* of a product with a national brand name reputation uses *distributors* that arrange for advertising and promotional activities in local markets.
   (c) A *biotech firm* develops a new product that will be produced, tested, and distributed by an established *pharmaceutical company*.

5. Consider the following pairs of situations. In each pair, which situation is more likely to be susceptible to *coordination* problems?
   (a) Maintenance of *corporate landscaping* by a gardening company versus maintenance of a *football or soccer stadium's grass turf* by a gardening company.
   (b) Design of a *toolbox* to hold *tools* versus design of a *wafer* to hold the wires of a microscopic *silicon chip*.

6. Universities tend to be highly integrated—many departments all belong to the same organization. There is no technical reason why a university could not consist of freestanding departments linked together by contracts or other market arrangements. Why do you suppose that universities are not organized in this way?

7. Why does asymmetric information lead to inefficient actions?

8. Some contracts, such as those between municipalities and highway construction firms, are extremely long, with terms spelled out in minute detail. Others contracts, such as those between consulting firms and their clients, are short and fairly vague about the division of responsibilities. What factors might determine such differences in contract length and detail?

9. "If the corporate governance function cannot protect specific assets, then firms may as well transact at arm's is length." Discuss.

10. Suppose that Governor Arnold Schwarzenegger (GAS) pays Besanko, Dranove, Shanley, and Schaefer (BDS^2) an advance of $5 million to write the script for *Incomplete Contract*, a movie version of their immensely popular text on business strategy. The movie contract includes certain script requirements, including the one that AS gets to play a strong, silent, business strategist with superhuman analytic powers. BDS^2 spend $100,000 worth of their time to write a script that is tailor-made for the ex-Terminator (GAS, that is). When they turn in the script to GAS, he claims that it fails to live up to the contractual requirement that he have several passionate love scenes, and so he attempts to renegotiate. Given the ambiguity over what constitutes passion, BDS^2 are forced to agree.
    (a) What was BDS^2's rent?

    (b) What is their quasi-rent? What assumptions do you have to make to compute this?

    (c) Could BDS^2 have held up GAS? Explain

11. In many modern U.S. industries the following patterns seem to hold:

    (a) Small firms are more likely to outsource production of inputs than are large firms.

    (b) "Standard" inputs (such as a simple transistor that could be used by several electronics manufacturers) are more likely to be outsourced than "tailor-made" inputs (such as a circuit board designed for a single manufacturer's specific needs).

    What factors might explain these patterns?

ENDNOTES

[1]The information is taken from Orwall, B. and M. Peers, "The Message of Media Mergers: So Far, They Haven't Been Hits," *Wall Street Journal*, May 10, 2002, p. A1.

[2]From *Chicago Tribune*, February 21, 1993, section 1, p. 15.

[3]Hagel, John and Marc Singer, "Unbundling the Corporation," *The McKinsey Quarterly*, 3, 2000.

[4]Azoulay, Pierre, "The Many Faces of Outsourcing," MIT Sloan School of Management, June 13, 2001.

[5]Doz, Yves L. and Gary Hamel, *Alliance Advantage: The Art of Creating Value Through Partnering*, Boston, Harvard Business School Press, 1998.

[6]Expected value is found by multiplying the probability of an event by the payoff associated with that event. In this case, the expected value is

$$(\tfrac{1}{3}) \times (-100,000) + (\tfrac{1}{3}) \times -100,000 + (\tfrac{1}{3}) \times 300,000 = 100,000$$

[7]Doherty, N. and C. Smith, "Corporate Insurance Strategy: The Case of British Petroleum," *Journal of Applied Corporate Finance*, Fall 1993, 10, pp. 84–96.

[8]See the Economics Primer for a discussion of perfectly competitive markets.

[9]"The Unoriginal Ideas that Rebuilt Crown Cork," *Fortune*, October 1962, pp. 118–164.

[10]Von Hayek, F., "The Use of Knowledge in Society," *American Economic Review*, 35, September 1945, pp. 519–530.

[11]Milgrom, P. and J. Roberts, "Bargaining Costs, Influence Costs, and the Organization of Economic Activity," in Alt, J. and Shepsle, K. (eds.), *Perspectives on Positive Political Economy*, Cambridge, Cambridge University Press, 1990.

[12]Womack, J., D. Jones, and D. Roos, *The Machine that Changed the World: The Story of Lean Production*, New York, HarperCollins, 1990, p. 143.

[13]Much of the information for this example is taken from Dvorak, P., "Out of Tune: At Sony, Rivalries Were Encouraged; Then Came iPod," *Wall Street Journal*, June 29, 2005, p. A1.

[14]Macauley, S., "Non-Contractual Relations in Business: A Preliminary Study," *American Sociological Review*, 28, 1963, pp. 55–67.

[15]*Cook v. Deltona Corp.*, 753 F2d 1552 (1985) United States Court of Appeals, Eleventh Circuit.

[16]Newhouse, J., *The Sporty Game*, New York, Knopf, 1982, pp. 53–54.

[17]Joskow, P., "Commercial Impossibility, the Uranium Market, and the Westinghouse Case," *Journal of Legal Studies*, 6, 1977, pp. 119–176.

[18]Macauley, S., "Non-contractual Relations in Business."

[19]Milgrom, P. and J. Roberts, *Economics, Organization and Management*, Englewood Cliffs, NJ, Prentice-Hall, 1992.

[20]Excerpted from the *Wall Street Journal*, July 29, 1992, p. A5.

[21]Coase, R., "The Nature of the Firm," *Economica*, 4, 1937, pp. 386–405.

[22]Chapter 2 of Williamson, O., *The Economic Institutions of Capitalism*, New York, Free Press, 1985.

[23]This discussion draws from Chapter 6 of Womack, J., D. Jones, and D. Roos, *The Machine that Changed the World: The Story of Lean Production*, Cambridge, MA, MIT Press, 1991.

[24]Womack, Jones, and Roos, *The Machine that Changed the World*, p. 144.

[25]We assume that default or declaring "bankruptcy" is not an option. Once you build the factory, you have to make your mortgage payment no matter what. To justify this assumption, imagine that your company has many other profitable business activities that generate enough cash to cover your mortgage payment on this factory under all circumstances. You would thus be legally obligated to pay your mortgage no matter how unprofitable the factory proves to be.

[26]Rent is synonymous with economic profit, and we will often use the terms interchangeably. To relate this to an important concept from corporate finance, when an investment has a positive rent, it will have a positive net present value. See the Economics Primer for net present value.

[27]The expression "holdup problem" was coined by Victor Goldberg in his article, "Regulation and Administered Contracts," *Bell Journal of Economics*, 7, Autumn 1976, pp. 426–448.

[28]Lyons, B., "Contracts and Specific Investment: An Empirical Test of Transaction Cost Theory," *Journal of Economics and Management Strategy*, 3, Summer 1994, pp. 257–278.

4

ORGANIZING VERTICAL BOUNDARIES: VERTICAL INTEGRATION AND ITS ALTERNATIVES

*I*n Chapter 3, we argued that the organization of the vertical chain is a matter of choice. Firms can organize exchange around arm's-length market transactions, or they can organize exchange internally; that is, they can vertically integrate. Although we discussed factors that affect the relative efficiency of market exchanges versus vertical integration—scale economies, incentives, coordination, leakage of private information, and the transactions costs of market exchange—we have not yet systematically studied how these factors trade off against one another in particular circumstances. We must do this to understand why vertical integration differs across industries (e.g., firms in the aluminum industry are generally more vertically integrated than firms in the tin industry), across firms within the same industry (e.g., GM is more vertically integrated than Ford), and across different transactions within the same firm (e.g., U.S. firms tend to outsource transportation services to a much greater degree than warehousing or inventory management).

The first part of this chapter assesses the merits of vertical integration as a function of the industry, firm, and transactions characteristics. It then discusses vertical integration in specific industries, including automobiles, aerospace, and electric utilities. We also examine whether other factors besides those discussed in Chapter 3 affect a firm's decision to vertically integrate. We focus in particular on how ownership of relationship-specific assets affects vertical integration. Finally, we explore other ways of organizing exchange besides arm's-length market contracting and vertical integration.

◆ ◆ ◆ ◆ ◆ TECHNICAL EFFICIENCY VERSUS AGENCY EFFICIENCY

Economizing

The costs and benefits of relying on the market can be classified as relating to either *technical efficiency* or *agency efficiency*. Technical efficiency has several interpretations in economics. A narrow interpretation is that it represents the degree to which a firm produces as much as it can from a given combination of inputs.[1] A broader interpretation—the one used in this chapter—is that technical efficiency indicates whether the firm is using the least-cost production process. For example, if efficient production of a particular good required specialized engineering skills, but the firm did not invest enough to develop those skills, then the firm has not achieved full technical efficiency. The firm could achieve technical efficiency by purchasing the good in question from a market firm, or by investing to develop the skills itself.

Agency efficiency refers to the extent to which the exchange of goods and services in the vertical chain has been organized to minimize the coordination, agency, and transactions costs discussed in Chapter 3. If the exchange does not minimize these costs, then the firm has not achieved full agency efficiency. To the extent that the process of exchange raises the costs of production (e.g., when the threat of holdup leads to reductions in relationship-specific investments and increases in production costs), we would classify this as an agency inefficiency rather than a technical inefficiency.

The make-or-buy decision often has conflicting implications for agency and technical efficiency. For example, when a computer maker obtains memory chips from the market, the firm may improve its technical efficiency by buying from specialized chip manufacturers. But this arrangement may reduce agency efficiency by necessitating detailed contracts that specify performance and rewards. The appropriate vertical organization of production must balance technical and agency efficiencies. Oliver Williamson uses the term *economizing* to describe this balancing act.[2]

Williamson argues that the optimal vertical organization minimizes the sum of technical and agency inefficiencies. That is, parties undertaking an exchange along the vertical chain arrange their transactions to minimize the sum of production and transactions costs. To the extent that the market is superior for minimizing production costs but vertical integration is superior for minimizing transactions costs, tradeoffs between the two costs are inevitable. Even the best organized firms confront the effects of this tradeoff, in the form of higher production costs, bureaucracy, breakdowns in exchange, and litigation.

The Technical Efficiency/Agency Efficiency Tradeoff and Vertical Integration

Figure 4.1 provides a useful way to think about the interplay of agency efficiency and technical efficiency.[3] The figure illustrates a situation in which the quantity of the good being exchanged is fixed at a particular level. The vertical axis measures cost *differences* between internal organization and market transactions. Positive values indicate that costs from the internal organization exceed costs from the market transactions. The horizontal axis measures asset specificity, denoted by k. Higher values of k imply greater asset specificity.

The curve ΔT depicts the differences in technical efficiency. It measures the differences in production costs when the item is produced in a vertically integrated firm and when it is exchanged through an arm's-length market transaction. We exclude any differences in production costs that result from differences in incentives to control costs or to invest in cost-reducing process improvements across the two modes of organization. ΔT is positive for any level of asset specificity because outside suppliers can aggregate demands from other buyers and thus can take better advantage of economies of scale and scope to lower production costs than firms that produce those inputs themselves. The cost difference declines with asset specificity because greater

FIGURE 4.1

TRADEOFF BETWEEN AGENCY EFFICIENCY AND TECHNICAL EFFICIENCY

The curve ΔT represents the minimum cost of production under vertical integration minus the minimum cost of production under arm's-length market exchange; that is, it reflects differences in technical efficiency. The curve ΔA represents the transactions costs when production is vertically integrated minus the transactions costs when it is organized through an arm's-length market exchange. (This difference includes any increases in production costs over their minimum level that are due to poor incentives or investments that are not made because of the holdup problem.) This curve reflects differences in agency efficiency. The curve ΔC is the vertical sum of ΔT and ΔA and represents the overall cost difference between vertical integration and market exchange.

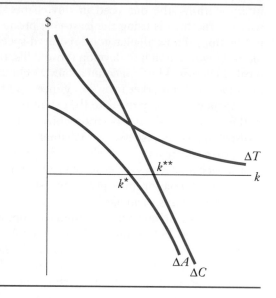

asset specificity implies more specialized uses for the input and thus fewer outlets for the outside supplier. As a result, with greater asset specificity, the scale- and scope-based advantages of outside suppliers are likely to be weaker.

The curve ΔA reflects differences in agency efficiency. It measures differences in exchange costs when the item is produced internally and when it is purchased from an outside supplier in an arm's-length transaction. When the item is purchased from an outside supplier, these costs comprise the direct costs of negotiating the exchange; the costs of writing and enforcing contracts; and the costs associated with holdup and underinvestments in relationship-specific assets that we discussed in Chapter 3. They also include the costs of breakdowns in coordination and leakage of private information, also discussed in Chapter 3. When the item is produced internally, these costs include the agency and influence costs discussed in Chapter 3. In short, the ΔA curve reflects differences in agency efficiency between the two modes of organizing transactions.

The ΔA curve is positive for low levels of asset specificity ($k < k^*$) and negative for high levels of asset specificity. When asset specificity is low, holdup is not a significant problem. In the absence of significant holdup problems, market exchange is likely to be more agency efficient than vertical integration because, as discussed in Chapter 3, independent firms often face stronger incentives to innovate and control production costs than divisions of a vertically integrated firm. As asset specificity increases, the transactions costs of market exchange also increase, and beyond a critical level, k^*, these costs are so large that vertical integration is more agency efficient than market exchange.

The curve ΔC is the vertical summation of the ΔA and ΔT curves. It represents production and exchange costs under vertical integration minus production and exchange costs under market exchange. If this curve is positive, then arm's-length market exchange is preferred to vertical integration. If the curve is negative, the exchange costs of using the market more than offset the production costs savings, and vertical integration is preferred. As shown in Figure 4.1, market exchange is preferred when asset specificity is sufficiently low ($k < k^{**}$). When asset specificity is greater than k^{**}, vertical integration is the preferred mode of organizing the transaction.

Vertical integration becomes increasingly attractive as the economies of scale in production become less pronounced. To see this point, recall that the height of the ΔT curve reflects the ability of an independent producer to achieve scale economies in production by selling to other firms. Weaker economies of scale would correspond to a downward shift in ΔT and ΔC, which in turn results in a wider range in which vertical integration is preferred to arm's-length market contracting. In the extreme case, as economies of scale disappear, the ΔT curve coincides with the horizontal axis, and the choice between vertical integration and market procurement is determined entirely by agency efficiency, that is, the ΔA curve.

Figure 4.2 shows what happens to the choice between market contracting and vertical integration as the scale of the transaction increases. There are two effects. First, the vertically integrated firm could now take fuller advantage of scale economies because it produces a higher output. This reduces the production-cost disadvantage of internal organization and shifts the ΔT curve downward. Second, increasing the scale of the transaction accentuates the advantage of whichever mode of production has lower exchange costs. Thus, the ΔA curve would "twist" clockwise through the point k^*. The overall effect of these two shifts moves the intersection point of the ΔC curve to the left, from k^{**} to k^{***}. (The solid lines are the shifted curves; the dashed lines are the original curves.) This widens the range in which vertical integration is the preferred mode of organization. Put another way, as the scale of the transaction goes up, vertical integration is more likely to be the preferred mode of organizing the transaction for any given level of asset specificity.

FIGURE 4.2
THE EFFECT OF INCREASED SCALE ON TRADEOFF BETWEEN
AGENCY EFFICIENCY AND TECHNICAL EFFICIENCY

As the scale of the transaction increases, the firm's demand for the input goes up, and a vertically integrated firm can better exploit economies of scale and scope in production. As a result, its production cost disadvantage relative to a market specialist firm will go down, so the curve ΔT will shift downward. (The dashed lines represent the curves at the original scale of the transaction; the solid lines represent the curves when the scale of the transaction increases.) At the same time, increased scale accentuates the advantage of the organizational mode with the lowest exchange costs. Thus, curve ΔA twists clockwise through point k^*. As a result, the intersection of the ΔC curve with the horizontal axis moves leftward, from k^{**} to k^{***}, expanding the range in which vertical integration is the least-cost organizational mode.

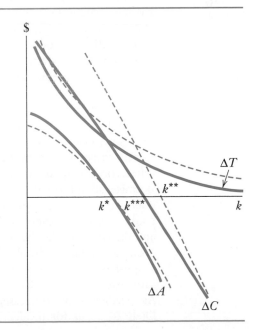

Figures 4.1 and 4.2 yield three powerful conclusions about vertical integration:

1. *Scale and Scope Economies:* We know that a firm gains less from vertical integration when outside market specialists are better able to take advantage of economies of scale and scope. We also know from Chapter 2 that a key source of economies of scale and scope is "indivisible," up-front "setup" costs, such as investments in physical capital or in the development of production know-how. It follows that *if the firm is considering whether to make or buy an input requiring significant upfront setup costs, and there is a large market outside the firm for the input, then the firm should buy the input from outside market specialists.* This will often be the case for routine products and services that are capital intensive or benefit from a steep learning curve.

2. *Product Market Share and Scope:* The more the firm produces, the more its demand for inputs grows. This increases the likelihood that in-house input production can take as much advantage of economies of scale and scope as an outside market specialist. It follows that *a firm with a larger share of the product market will benefit more from vertical integration than a firm with a smaller share of the product market.* It also implies that *a firm with multiple product lines will benefit more from being vertically integrated in the production of components for those products in which it can achieve significant market scale.* It will benefit less from being vertically integrated in the production of components for "boutique" or "niche" items that it produces on a small scale.

3. *Asset Specificity: A Firm Gains More from Vertical Integration When Production of Inputs Involves Investments in Relationship-Specific Assets:* If asset specificity is significant enough, vertical integration will be more profitable than arm's-length market purchases, even when production of the input is characterized by strong scale economies or when the firm's product market scale is small.

Real-World Evidence

Evidence suggests that many real-world firms behave in accordance with these principles. The evolution of the hierarchical firm discussed in Chapter 1 is certainly consistent with the product market scale and the asset-specificity effects. A key step in the growth of the modern firm was forward integration by manufacturers into marketing and distribution.[4] Between 1875 and 1900, technological breakthroughs allowed for unprecedented economies of scale in manufacturing industries. This, coupled with improvements in transportation and communication that expanded the scope of markets, led to vast increases in the size of firms in capital-intensive industries, such as steel, chemicals, food processing, and light machinery.

As these firms grew, they vertically integrated. Before 1875, most manufacturers relied on independent commercial intermediaries to distribute their products. Because an intermediary could aggregate the demands of many manufacturers, it could sell and distribute at a lower cost per unit than any individual manufacturer could. However, there were limits to the economies of scale and scope in selling and distribution. As the scale of the manufacturers in the capital-intensive industries grew, independent wholesaling and marketing agents lost much of their scale- and scope-based cost advantages. As this happened, manufacturers forward integrated into marketing and distribution, a result consistent with the firm-size hypothesis. As predicted by the asset-specificity hypothesis, forward integration was most likely to occur for products that required specialized investments in human capital

EXAMPLE 4.1 VERTICAL INTEGRATION IN A MOUNTAIN PARADISE

Strategy gurus often say that firms should "stick to their knitting," taking on only those activities they know best. But asset specificity often requires firms to perform activities that are far removed from their core competencies. One happy example took place a century ago in isolated, cold, rugged, and beautiful terrain.

The Banff/Lake Louise region of the Canadian Rockies is truly among the natural wonders of the world. The combination of snow-capped peaks, floral-laden mountain valleys, ice fields, and glacier-fed clear blue lakes is breathtaking. Many travelers believe that Lake Louise is the most picturesque spot on earth, and the mountains near Banff have some of the world's best skiing.

Every year, tens of thousands of tourists visit the region from all over the world. Many are fortunate to stay at the Chateau Lake Louise and the Banff Springs Hotel. The two resorts are situated less than an hour apart and have a combined 1,270 beds. They are frequently listed among the finest resorts in the world and for good reason. Not only do they offer spectacular natural scenery, but both resorts have several fine restaurants, spa facilities, horseback riding, hiking trails, and everything else required for a complete vacation. A popular vacation package includes a three-night stay at each resort. Golfers are especially attracted by the prospect of launching 300+ yard drives from the mile-high tees in Banff.

Until the late nineteenth century, the region around Banff/Lake Louise was known only to a few intrepid explorers and naturalists. The area is accessible by the Bow River, which is fed by Lake Louise glacial waters and flows 400 miles past Calgary before feeding the Saskatchewan River (and eventually Hudson Bay). During the 1880s, the Bow River valley proved to be a perfect location for the Canadian Pacific (CP) Railroad as it laid a section of the transcontinental railroad between Calgary (just east of the Canadian Rockies) and Vancouver. In 1883, CP railway workers discovered natural hot springs at the base of Sulphur Mountain, near the

conjuction of the Bow and Spray rivers. Shortly thereafter, Canada established Banff National Park—the nation's first—including the hot springs and the surrounding region. Today, Banff National Park stretches for 2,564 square miles and includes all of Banff and Lake Louise.

Once the CP rail line was complete, the region was open to tourists. Few tourists came, however, because there was no place for them to stay. William Van Horne, the general manager of the Canadian Pacific, struck on a novel idea. Fueled by the philosophy, "If we can't export the scenery, we will import the tourists," he ordered the construction of the Banff Springs Hotel at the base of Sulphur Mountain, as well as a series of other resorts on or near the rail line, to include the Chateau Lake Louise. With CP controlling access to the region, it had no choice but to build these hotels itself. No one else would risk such massive investments when the rail line owned the only means of access.

Once Van Horne's vision was realized, the trains and the resorts filled up. Through the mid-twentieth century, CP continued to build new resorts in the Rockies, as well as expand its flagship resorts in Banff and Lake Louise. The Trans-Canada Highway opened in 1962, creating new opportunities for tourists to access the Canadian Rockies. New motels and hotels sprung up in Banff. (The area around Lake Louise is not large enough to support additional development.) As Calgary boomed following the 1988 Olympics (and its airport began handling more flights), tourism to the region skyrocketed. Today, the town of Banff has 7,500 year-round residents and dozens of motels, hotels, and resorts.

Forced to develop its own expertise in operating luxury hotels, Canadian Pacific has become a leading hotelier worldwide. Now a free standing subsidiary (in accordance with the advice of the gurus!), Canadian Pacific Hotels acquired the CN hotel chain in 1988 and the world famous Fairmont chain in 1999. Today, the Banff Springs Hotel and the Chateau Lake Louise operate under the Fairmont name.

(e.g., George Eastman's marketing of cameras and film) or in equipment and facilities (e.g., Gustavus Swift's refrigerated warehouses and boxcars). For those industries in which manufacturers remained small (e.g., furniture or textiles) and/or marketing and distribution did not rely on specialized assets (e.g., candy), manufacturers continued to rely on independent commercial intermediaries to distribute and sell their products.

Statistical evidence on vertical integration from a variety of industries is also consistent with the theory developed earlier. Consider these examples from strategy research:

Automobiles   In a classic and oft-cited study, Kirk Monteverde and David Teece examined the choice between vertical integration and market procurement of components by General Motors and Ford.[5] Monteverde and Teece surveyed design engineers to determine the importance of applications engineering effort in the design of 133 different components. Greater applications engineering effort is likely to involve greater human asset specificity, so Monteverde and Teece hypothesized that car makers would be more likely to produce components that required significant amounts of applications engineering effort and more likely to buy components that required small amounts of applications engineering effort. Their analysis of the data confirmed this hypothesis. They also found that GM is more vertically integrated than Ford on components with the same asset specificity. This is consistent with the firm-size hypothesis.

Aerospace Industry   Scott Masten studied the make-or-buy decision for nearly 2,000 components in a large aerospace system.[6] He asked procurement managers to rate the design specificity of the components, that is, the extent to which the component was used exclusively by the company or could be easily adapted for use by other aerospace firms or firms in other industries. A transistor or resistor would be an example of a nonspecific item; a circuit board designed to individual specifications would be an example of a component with high design specificity. Consistent with the asset-specificity hypothesis, Masten found that greater design specificity increased the likelihood that production of the component was vertically integrated. He also studied the effect of the complexity of the component, that is, the number of relevant performance dimensions and the difficulty in assessing satisfactory performance. He found that more complex components were more likely to be manufactured internally. When the item being purchased is complex or it is not easy to measure performance, contracts become more difficult to write. As a result, parties in an arm's-length market transaction find it hard to protect themselves with contracts, increasing the risk of holdup.

Electric Utility Industry   Paul Joskow studied the extent of backward integration by electric utilities into coal mining.[7] Coal-burning electricity-generating plants are sometimes located next to coal mines. This minimizes the costs of shipping coal and maximizes the operating efficiency of the generating plant. A utility that makes a "mine-mouth" investment will typically design its boilers with tight tolerances to accommodate the quality of coal from that particular mine. The utility may also make large investments in rail lines and transmission capacity, and the mine will often expand its capacity to supply the on-site utilities. The relationship between the utility and the mine thus involves both site and physical-asset specificity. Joskow found that mine-mouth plants are much more likely to be vertically integrated than other plants. Where mine-mouth plants were not vertically integrated, Joskow found that coal suppliers relied on long-term supply contracts containing numerous safeguards to prevent holdup. Mine-mouth plants rarely relied on short-term arm's-length contracts with the coal mine.

Electronic Components   Erin Anderson and David Schmittlein studied vertical integration between electronics manufacturers and sales representatives.[8] Manufacturers' reps operate like the sales department of a firm except that they usually represent more than one manufacturer and work on a commission. Anderson and Schmittlein surveyed territory sales managers in 16 major electronics component manufacturers to determine the extent to which they relied on independent reps or on their own sales forces in a given sales territory for a given product. The survey measured the amount of asset specificity in the selling function and the degree of difficulty in evaluating a salesperson's performance. The measure of asset specificity embraced such factors as the amount of time a salesperson would have to spend learning about the company's product, the extent to which selling the product would necessitate extra training, and the importance of the personal relationship between the salesperson and the customer. Anderson and Schmittlein found that greater asset specificity in the selling function was associated with a greater likelihood that firms rely on their own sales forces rather than manufacturers' reps. They also found that holding asset specificity constant, larger manufacturers were more likely to use a direct sales force than smaller firms. Finally, they found that the more difficult it was to measure performance, the more likely manufacturers were to rely on direct sales forces. The latter result is consistent with the notion that when the transaction environment is less amenable to contractual safeguards (e.g., because contracting on performance is more difficult), arm's-length market contracting becomes a relatively more costly form of organizing an exchange.

Vertical Integration and Asset Ownership

The basic argument of the preceding section is that the interplay of technical and agency efficiency (which is influenced by the factors discussed in Chapter 3) determines the relative desirability of vertical integration versus arm's-length market contracting. Sanford Grossman, Oliver Hart, and John Moore (GHM) have developed a different theory for comparing vertical integration with market exchange.[9] Their theory focuses on the importance of asset ownership and control and makes the critical observation that the resolution of the make-or-buy decision determines ownership rights. The owner of an asset may grant another party the right to use it, but the owner retains all rights of control that are not explicitly stipulated in the contract. These are known as residual rights of control. When ownership is transferred, the residual rights of control are transferred as well.

To clarify the concept of residual rights of control, consider the relationship between PepsiCo and its bottlers. PepsiCo has two types of bottlers: independent and company owned. An independent bottler owns the physical assets of the bottling operation and the exclusive rights to the franchise territory. PepsiCo has no direct authority over how the independent bottler manages its operations. If a bottler refuses to stock particular stores or participate in a national campaign like the Pepsi Challenge, PepsiCo can only try to persuade the bottler to cooperate. Suppose, however, that PepsiCo acquires one of its independent bottlers. PepsiCo could choose to cede to the bottler specific forms of authority over the assets. However, unless stated

EXAMPLE 4.2 AN APPLICATION OF THE MAKE-OR-BUY
FRAMEWORK TO CHILDREN'S MEMORIAL HOSPITAL

Although the trend in most industries is to "buy" rather than "make," there has been substantial vertical integration in the health care industry. Integrated health care systems like the Henry Ford Clinic in Michigan or the Sutter system in California have consolidated the vertical chain, placing hospitals, physician offices, home health care, pharmacies, health insurance, and diagnostic imaging facilities in a single corporate entity. Increasingly, however, health care systems recognize that full integration is not always optimal, and many are evaluating each link in the vertical chain to determine which activities to make and which to buy.

In 1993, Children's Memorial Hospital (CMH) used the framework developed in this chapter to assess the make or buy decision for home health care. Industry experts believe that home health care—including home nursing, therapy, and housemaking services—is a cost-effective alternative to institutional care. There were dozens of home care agencies in Chicago in 1993, including CM Health Care Resources (CMHR), which was wholly owned by Children's Memorial Medical Center (CMMC), the parent of CMH. Most CMH patients who received home care got it from CMHR. On the other hand, CMHR received more than half of its patients from hospitals other than CMH.

CMMC pondered whether to make CMHR a fully independent firm or to keep it as a wholly owned subsidiary. By spinning off CMHR, CMH would have more flexibility to refer patients to other independent home care agencies. Independent agencies would be unlikely to enjoy significant scale economies, however, because home care is labor intensive. Transportation costs were another matter. As a tertiary-care children's hospital, CMH gets patients from throughout the Chicago area. Thus, it might make sense for CMH to use independent home care agencies rather than CMHR to service distant communities. These agencies could combine patients from hospitals in their local areas with CMH patients to reduce transportation costs. CMHR could then redeploy its nurses more efficiently to serve nearby communities with an adequate patient density.

Using the market would also be attractive if the market provided discipline and sharp incentives for efficiency that CMH cannot instill in an integrated CMHR. CMHR was at best an average-cost supplier in the market, as indicated by the fact that several insurers directed CMH to discharge patients to less costly home care agencies. Perhaps CMHR felt complacent: many CMH physicians were loyal to CMHR and referred patients to them without considering alternatives. Thus, CMHR had some guaranteed sales regardless of its efficiency.

Still, CMHR was probably not grossly inefficient. Most of its business came from other hospitals, and CMHR had to provide a competitive cost/quality mix. In fact, CMH encouraged CMHR to compete for non-CMH patients, in part to assure that CMHR faced market incentives.

This discussion suggests that the advantages to CMH from using the market were probably not overwhelming. Still, unless there were offsetting advantages to keeping CMH and CMHR vertically integrated, a case could be made to spin CMHR off. One benefit to integration came from enhanced coordination in delivering patient care. Nurse training, drug use, and therapy must be coordinated between the hospital and home care agency. CMHR worked with CMH to develop protocols to assure coordination. There are also critical timing decisions involved in discharging a patient from the hospital. Poor coordination between CMHR and an independent home care agency delays a patient's discharge from the hospital and drives up costs.

Common ownership also helped align incentives in a subtle but important way. Most CMH patients are on Medicaid, which is a notoriously stingy payer. CMH would like to discharge Medicaid patients as soon as it is safe to do so, allowing it to admit more privately insured patients. Many independent home care agencies are reluctant to accept Medicaid patients, because payments are so low. But CMHR accepts them from CMH. This reduces CMHR's profits but increases CMH's.

Joint ownership of CMH and CMHR may also encourage investments in relationship-specific assets such as nurse training. CMHR trains nurses who work full-time at CMH. This improves the discharge process and training of home caregivers. However, the profitability of this training depends on the fact that CMHR receives most of the patients that CMH discharges to home care. CMHR would be reluctant to make these investments if it could not count on receiving the bulk of CMH's business.

To summarize, vertical integration of CMH and CMHR reduced CMH's flexibility to use other home care agencies, which may raise the cost of delivering home care because it sacrificed scale economies. It may also have partially shielded CMHR from market forces, making it somewhat less efficient. However, CMH and CMHR probably gained significantly from being vertically integrated. These gains are attributable to the benefits from coordinated discharge and treatment protocols and from CMHR's willingness to accept Medicaid patients. Vertical integration has probably also created stronger incentives for CMHR to train nurses at CMH. After balancing these concerns, CMMC chose to keep CMHR as part of the integrated organization, where it has continued to thrive.

otherwise in a contract, PepsiCo has the ultimate authority over how the bottling assets are deployed and how the bottler's territory is managed. If the management of the bottling subsidiary refused to participate in a national advertising campaign, that PepsiCo could replace them with a more cooperative team.

If contracts were complete (i.e., if they specified every action under every contingency), it would not matter who owned the assets. The contract would spell out exactly what actions should be taken at all times and how all parties were to be compensated. In other words, *complete contracts would render make-or-buy decisions inconsequential*.[10] As we discussed in Chapter 3, virtually all real-world contracts are incomplete.

Taking incomplete contracting as a starting point, the GHM theory analyzes how ownership affects the willingness of parties to invest in relationship-specific assets. The theory considers a situation in which two units enter a transaction with each other. For simplicity, think of unit 1 being upstream from unit 2 in the vertical chain. To carry out the transaction, the parties must jointly make an array of operating decisions. The theory assumes that the parties cannot write a contract that specifies these operating decisions in advance. Instead, they must bargain over them once the transaction is underway.

We can imagine three alternative ways to organize the transaction:

1. *Nonintegration:* The two units are independent firms, each with control over its own assets.
2. *Forward Integration:* Unit 1 owns the assets of unit 2 (i.e., unit 1 forward integrates into the function performed by unit 2 by purchasing control over unit 2's assets).
3. *Backward Integration:* Unit 2 owns the assets of unit 1 (i.e., unit 2 backward integrates into the function performed by unit 1 by purchasing control over unit 1's assets).

The GHM theory establishes that the form of integration affects the incentives of parties to invest in relationship-specific assets. Generally speaking, by having control

EXAMPLE 4.3 VERTICAL INTEGRATION OF THE SALES FORCE IN THE INSURANCE INDUSTRY

In the insurance industry, some products (e.g., whole life insurance) are usually sold through in-house sales forces, while other products (e.g., fire and casualty insurance) are mainly sold through independent brokers. The Grossman/Hart/Moore (GHM) theory helps us understand this pattern. Relying on independent agents versus in-house sales employees is essentially a choice by the insurance firm for nonintegration versus forward integration into the selling function. This choice determines the ownership of an extremely important asset in the process of selling insurance: the list of clients. Under nonintegration, the agent controls this key asset; under forward integration, the insurance firm controls it.

If the agent owns the client list, the agent controls access to its clients; they cannot be solicited without the agent's permission. A key role of an insurance agent is to search out and deliver dependable clients to the insurance company, clients who are likely to renew their insurance policies in the future. To induce an agent to do this, the commission structure must be "backloaded," for example, through a renewal commission that exceeds the costs of servicing and re-signing the client. When the insurance company owns the client list, however, this commission structure creates incentives for the company to hold up the agent. It could threaten to reduce the likelihood of renewal (e.g., by raising premiums or restricting coverage) unless the agent accepts a reduced renewal commission. Faced with the possibility of this holdup problem, the agent would presumably underinvest in searching out and selling insurance to repeat clients. By contrast, if the agent owned the client list, the potential for holdup by the insurance company would be much weaker. If the company did raise premiums or restrict coverage, the agent could invite its client to switch companies. Threats by the company to jeopardize the agent's renewal premium would thus have considerably less force, and underinvestment in the search for persistent clients would not

be a problem. In some circumstances, the holdup problem could work the other way. Suppose the insurance company can engage in list-building activities such as new product development. The agent could threaten not to offer the new product to the customer unless the insurance company paid the agent a higher commission. Faced with the prospect of this holdup, the company is likely to underinvest in developing new products. By contrast, if the insurance company owned the list, this type of holdup could not occur, and the insurance company's incentive to invest in new product development would be much stronger.

This suggests that there are tradeoffs in alternative ownership structures that are similar to those discussed above. According to the GHM theory, the choice between an in-house sales force versus independent agents should turn on the relative importance of investments in developing persistent clients by the agent versus list-building activities by the insurance firm. Given the nature of the product, a purchaser of whole life insurance is much less likely to switch insurance companies than, say, a customer of fire and casualty insurance. Thus, the insurance agent's effort in searching out persistent clients is less important for whole life insurance than it is for fire and casualty insurance. For whole life insurance, then, backloading the commission structure is not critical, which diminishes the possibility of contractual holdup when the insurance company owns the client list. The GHM theory implies that whole life insurance would typically be sold through an insurance company's in-house sales force. This is consistent with industry practice: most companies that offer whole life insurance have their own sales forces. By contrast, for term life or substandard insurance, the agent's selling and renewal-generation efforts are relatively more important. Consistent with the GHM theory, many insurance companies rely on independent agents who own the client list to sell these products.

over the other unit's assets, a unit has a better bargaining position when it negotiates with the other unit over the operating decisions that they could not contract on. With a better bargaining position, the unit can capture more of the economic value created by the transaction, thus boosting its willingness to make relationship-specific investments. The theory implies that *vertical integration is desirable when one unit's investment in relationship-specific assets has a significantly greater impact on the value created in the vertical chain than the other's investment does.* When the investments of both units are of comparable importance, nonintegration is the best arrangement.

By emphasizing asset ownership, the GHM theory identifies an important dimension of vertical integration. It also suggests that there are degrees of vertical integration, depending on the extent to which one party or the other controls specialized assets. This helps us understand certain real-world arrangements that fall between vertical integration and arm's-length market contracting. For example, General Motors and Ford often own their own specialized tooling and dies, even though an independent firm produces body parts and components. This is especially likely for components, such as radiators and starters, that require specialized physical assets but do not require much specialized engineering or operational know-how.[11] Similarly, in the glass bottle industry, large buyers will often retain ownership of specialized molds, even though an independent manufacturer produces the jars and bottles. The GHM theory implies that this is a form of vertical integration and is distinct from the situation in which the independent supplier carries out production and owns the physical asset.

PROCESS ISSUES IN VERTICAL MERGERS ◆ ◆ ◆ ◆ ◆

The principles presented in this chapter thus far provide a basis for assessing the desirability of vertical mergers: firms should merge if it improves the net balance of technical and agency efficiency. The decision as to whether to vertically merge is not so simple, however. Merging on the vertical chain is not a clear make-or-buy decision, but more a matter of "buying" an opportunity to "make." Whether that opportunity will be productive depends on how governance arrangements between the two merging firms develop.

Governance arrangements delegate decision rights and the control of assets within firms. (Compare this with contracts, which delegate decision rights and control of assets between firms.) If an integrated firm does not get the governance right, then the benefits of integration may be lost.

The GHM theory discussed in the previous section suggests a criterion for judging which governance arrangements will be efficient. It addresses situations in which the specialized human capital of an acquired firm's managers and employees may be important for the success of a merger. The acquiring firm may gain governance rights over physical assets, but it can never gain full governance rights over human capital—it is up to each employee to decide how hard to work, regardless of whom he or she works for. If a worker's specialized human capital is not employed in the interests of the acquiring firm, the merged firm will be less profitable. A governance arrangement that does not grant acquired workers decision-making rights commensurate with their control over specialized resources thus risks being inefficient.

This suggests that decision-making rights for an activity should be given to those managers whose decisions will have the greatest impact on the performance of the activity and ultimately on the profitability of the firm. For example, if the success of a merger depends largely on synergies associated with the combined physical assets of two firms, such as through the resolution of coordination problems between a buyer and a supplier, then decision-making authority should be centralized. If, however, success depends on the specialized knowledge of acquired managers, such as their knowledge of key contacts in local markets, then decision authority should be decentralized.

Who will actually exercise decision-making authority in the combined firm? What governance arrangements will develop between formerly independent firms? It is not clear in advance which of several possible governance arrangements will develop after a merger. On the one hand, managers at the acquiring firm could delegate significant decision-making authority to unit managers and grant them an autonomy that parallels their prior independent state. On the other hand, managers at the acquiring firm may assume authority for most decisions themselves. In between are numerous arrangements in which authority is delegated on some decisions and not on others. The actual arrangements that develop may or may not be efficient, in that they will not necessarily reflect the transactions-cost requirements suggested by GHM. The process by which governance develops can also exhibit *path dependence*. That is, past circumstances could exclude certain possible governance arrangements in the future. For example, if the period following a merger is marked by conflict, an efficient governance structure requiring cooperation between acquired and acquiring firm managers might not be feasible.

These same considerations will also apply to vertical disintegration. At first glance, a vertically related unit of a firm that was spun off to the market as an independent firm would appear to be a market actor. Initially, however, managers in that unit will not be used to making decisions as an autonomous market actor and may continue to rely on associations with managers in the former parent firm. This would make the relationship between the two firms after a spinoff not a market transaction, but rather a long-term informal association, which is somewhere between being part of an integrated firm and a specialized market actor.

The path-dependent nature of the processes by which firms develop can also affect vertical relationships by affecting the firm's capacity to sell the products of a unit to other downstream buyers besides itself. In Chapter 3, we suggested that market specialists could be more efficient sources of an input for a firm than self-manufacture, since specialists could gain economies of scale by selling to multiple downstream buyers that were not available to a firm that self-manufactured. Firms manufacturing for internal uses would typically not sell excess output to other firms because this would be both a distraction and an activity for which the firm lacked the requisite skills. If a firm acquired rather than built its supply capacity, however, the situation would be different. The acquired firm would know how to sell to multiple buyers. This marketing capacity would presumably be one of the resources acquired by the parent through the merger. In such a situation, selling product produced primarily for internal uses to outside firms would be neither a distraction nor an activity for which the firm lacked resources. The firm's opportunities for selling to other users of the product could still be limited by competitive conditions, however.

♦ ♦ ♦ ♦ ♦ ALTERNATIVES TO VERTICAL INTEGRATION

This chapter poses the problem of the firm's vertical boundaries rather starkly—the firm must either make an input or purchase it from an independent firm through an arm's-length market transaction. A variety of in-between alternatives may capture the best of both worlds. In this section we consider four "hybrid" ways of organizing exchange: (1) tapered integration, in which the firm both makes and buys a given input; (2) strategic alliances and joint ventures; and (3) close-knit semiformal relationships among buyers and suppliers, often based on long-term implicit contracts that are supported by reputations for honesty, cooperation, and trust.

Tapered Integration: Make *and* Buy

Tapered integration represents a mixture of vertical integration and market exchange. A manufacturer might produce some quantity of an input itself and purchase the remaining portion from independent firms. It might sell some of its product through an in-house sales force and rely on an independent manufacturers' representative to sell the rest. Examples of tapered integration include such retailers as Blockbuster Video and Wendy's, which own some of their retail outlets but award franchises for others; Coca-Cola and Pepsi, which have their own bottling subsidiaries, but also rely on independently owned bottlers to produce and distribute their soft drinks in some markets; and General Motors, which has its own market research division but also purchases market research from independent firms.

Tapered integration offers three benefits. First, it expands the firm's input and/or output channels without requiring substantial capital outlays. This is helpful to growing firms, such as fledgling retail chains. Second, the firm can use information about the cost and profitability of its internal channels to help negotiate contracts with independent channels. The firm can threaten to use the market further to motivate the performance of its internal channels, and it can use the threat of self manufacture to discipline its external channels. Third, the firm may also develop internal input supply capabilities to protect itself against holdup by independent input suppliers.

Oil refiners provide a classic example of tapered integration. The largest refiners, such as Exxon Mobil and Shell, explore for and produce crude oil. Because they can refine twice as much oil as they internally produce, they make substantial purchases of oil in the open market. This forces their internal production divisions to stay competitive with independent oil producers.

If tapered integration offers the best of both the make-and-buy worlds, it may also offer the worst. Forced to share production, both the internal and external channels may not achieve sufficient scale to produce efficiently. Shared production may lead to coordination problems because the two production units must agree on product specifications and delivery times. Moreover, a firm's monitoring problems may be exacerbated. Not only must the firm duplicate contracting and monitoring efforts, it cannot be certain that its production units are producing efficiently. For example, the firm may mistakenly establish the performance of an inefficient internal supplier as the standard to be met by external suppliers. Finally, managers may maintain inefficient internal capacity rather than close facilities that had formerly been critical to the firm. An example of this approach is the excess capacity for internal productions that major movie studios maintain.

Strategic Alliances and Joint Ventures

Since the 1970s, firms have increasingly turned to strategic alliances as a way to organize complex business transactions collectively without sacrificing autonomy. To illustrate the ubiquity of alliances, Table 4.1 lists the pharmaceutical and biotechnology firms that have been most active in strategic alliances between 1973 and 2001. All of these firms have entered into over 100 alliances!

EXAMPLE 4.4 TAPERED INTEGRATION IN GASOLINE RETAILING

Gasoline retailing offers an interesting example of tapered integration.[12] Most of the gasoline stations that sell major brands of gasoline (i.e., a gasoline station that sells the product of a major refiner such as Shell or Chevron Texaco) are operated by independent dealers. These independent dealers sign long-term contracts to purchase their gasoline from a single refiner and use that refiner's brand name. They are otherwise free to set the retail price of gasoline, the hours of business, and employ their own staff. Major refiners own and operate a sizable number of their own service stations. At these refiner-owned stations, the refiner sets the hours of business and retail prices, and employs the personnel. Independent stations that carry their own brand names and purchase gas from a wide variety of refiners make up the rest of the stations. (This includes the small but steadily growing number of Wal-Mart gas stations.)

Tapered integration by refiners was not always commonplace. In the 1920s and 1930s, most large oil companies were fully integrated at the retail level: they owned almost all the stations that sold their gasoline. In the mid-1930s, the possibility that Iowa might impose a "chain-store" tax led the major refiners to experiment with sales through independent franchised dealers. The oil companies soon found that this arrangement had significant advantages. Selling gasoline through independent dealers gave the major refiners access to many local markets without having to make substantial capital investments. Independent operation also relieves the refiner of having to monitor and evaluate the activities of the service station and instead subjects dealers to the discipline of the market forces. But sales through independent dealers also have a significant disadvantage. The refiners cannot set retail prices,

and imperfect competition in downstream markets often leads independent dealers to impose high markups over the wholesale price of gasoline. The resulting decrease in volume hurts the refiner by reducing the profit from its markup over the unit cost of production. (This is the double marginalization problem we discussed in Chapter 3.)

Because vertical integration has advantages as well as disadvantages, the major oil companies continue to own and operate their own stations. What is interesting is that changes in how gasoline is sold at the retail level have altered the balance between the costs and benefits in a way that seems to favor vertical integration. Traditionally, most gasoline stations not only sold gasoline, but also automobile maintenance and repair services, such as oil changes or brake replacement. For these stations, the cost of monitoring salaried employees was likely to be substantial because many repair tasks were nonroutine and the quality of a worker's output was difficult to measure. Thus, in most cases the optimal arrangement for these stations was likely to be independent operation. Since 1980, however, the traditional service station has given way to large "pumper" stations—gasoline stations with 10 or 12 self-service pumps staffed by a single cashier—and maintenance and repair business is increasingly being done by specialized outlets such as Jiffy Lube and Midas Muffler.[13] The result has been a shift in the relative proportion of independently operated and company-operated gasoline stations. Between 1980 and 1990 alone, the number of major-brand, independently operated stations declined from about 180,000 to 110,000, whereas the number of company-operated stations grew from about 8,000 to 11,000.

In a strategic alliance, two or more firms agree to collaborate on a project or to share information or productive resources. Firms may rely on a contract to spell out specific responsibilities for investing in assets as well as the distribution of earnings, but the contracts may be largely silent about the details of the collaborative

TABLE 4.1

PHARMACEUTICAL AND BIOTECH FIRMS MOST ACTIVE IN STRATEGIC
ALLIANCES, 1973-2001

Pharma Firms	Number of Alliances
GlaxoSmithKline	373
Pharmacia*	370
Pfizer	287
Novartis	230
Elan	228
Biotech Firms	
Applera	214
Chiron	172
Genentech	124
Genzyme	122
Shire	119

*Pharmacia was acquired by Pfizer in 2003.
Source: Baker, G., R. Gibbons, and K. Murphy, 2002, "Relational Contracts in Strategic Alliances"
Unpublished Working Paper.

effort. For example, in biotech/pharma alliances, contracts detail the division of revenues if the product reaches the market, but may say little about the required scientific input from each partner.

Allying partners usually are involved in multiple market activities. Some firms have alliance partners in many different markets while remaining fully integrated in others. Alliances may be horizontal, involving collaboration between two firms in the same industry, as when United Technologies and Daimler Benz teamed up to cooperate on a range of engine development activities. They may be vertical, such as Intel and Oracle's efforts to develop software for Intel's 64-bit Itanium chip. Or they may involve firms that are neither in the same industry nor related through the vertical chain, as when Toys "R" Us and McDonald's of Japan formed a venture to build Toys "R" Us stores in Japan that would include a McDonald's restaurant.

A joint venture is a particular type of strategic alliance in which two or more firms create, and jointly own, a new independent organization. The new organization may be staffed and operated by employees of one or more parent firms, or it may be staffed independently of either. Examples of joint ventures include Coca-Cola's and Cadbury Schweppes' agreement to bottle and distribute Coca-Cola in Great Britain; Merck's and Johnson & Johnson's venture to market over-the-counter medicines such as Pepcid, an anti-ulcer treatment; and Genetics Institute's (one of the largest U.S. biotech companies) and Wellcome's (at one time the largest British pharmaceuticals company) agreement to manufacture products based on recombinant DNA.

Alliances and joint ventures fall somewhere between arm's-length market transactions and full vertical integration. As in arm's-length market transactions, the parties to the alliance remain independent. However, an alliance typically involves more cooperation, coordination, and information sharing than would occur in an arm's-length transaction. Kenichi Ohmae has likened a strategic alliance to a marriage: "There may be no formal contract.... There are few, if any, rigidly binding provisions. It is a loose, evolving kind of relationship."[14] Like a marriage, the participants in an alliance rely on norms of trust and reciprocity rather than on contracts to govern their relationship, and they resolve disputes through negotiation rather than through litigation.

What kinds of business transactions should be organized through alliances? The most natural candidates for alliances are transactions for which, using the framework in Chapter 3, there are compelling reasons to both make *and* buy. Specifically, transactions that are natural candidates for alliances have all or most of the following features:

1. The transaction involves impediments to comprehensive contracting. For example, the transacting parties know that as their relationship unfolds, they will need to perform a complex set of activities. But because of uncertainty and the parties' bounded rationality, the parties cannot write a contract that specifies how decisions about these activities are supposed to be made.
2. The transaction is complex, not routine. Standard commercial and contract law could not easily "fill the gaps" of incomplete contracts.
3. The transaction involves the creation of relationship-specific assets by both parties in the relationship, and each party to the transaction could hold up the other.
4. It is excessively costly for one party to develop all of the necessary expertise to carry out all of the activities itself. This might be due to indivisibilities (developing the expertise to operate on even a small scale requires significant upfront investments in information acquisition and training) and the presence of an experience curve (the cost of developing incremental expertise becomes less costly the more expertise that is acquired). These considerations make it difficult for a single firm to organize the transaction internally.
5. The market opportunity that creates the need for the transaction is either transitory, or it is uncertain that it will continue on an ongoing basis. This makes it impractical for the independent parties to merge or even commit themselves to a long-term contract.
6. The transaction or market opportunity occurs in a contracting or regulatory environment with unique features that require a local partner who has access to relationships in that environment. For example, the strong role that the Chinese government plays in regulating foreign investment requires that nearly all foreign ventures in China are joint ventures with Chinese partners.

To illustrate some of these points, consider the alliance between McDonald's-Japan and Toys "R" Us mentioned earlier.[16] Toys "R" Us formed this alliance with McDonald's of Japan in 1990 to facilitate its entry into the Japanese market.[17] Japan's Large-Scale Retail Store Law required that Toys "R" Us be approved by Japan's Ministry of International Trade and Industry (MITI) before building its stores. This law, which protected Japan's politically powerful small merchants, made it difficult even for Japanese retailers, such as supermarket operator Daiei, to open large-scale establishments. Toys "R" Us concluded that it had to find a local partner.

The alliance with McDonald's-Japan was formed to help Toys "R" Us navigate the politically charged entry process. McDonald's-Japan's president, Den Fujita, was politically well-connected and understood the ordeal Toys "R" Us faced, having built McDonald's-Japan into the largest fast-food operator in the country. He also had a remarkable knowledge of Japanese real estate. "If you name a city," he bragged, "I can see the post office, train station, everything." In 1990, Toys "R" Us and McDonald's-Japan formed an alliance in which McDonald's took a 20 percent stake in the Toys "R" Us Japanese unit, Toys "R" Us Japan. As part of the alliance, 9 of the 11 Toys "R" Us stores would have a McDonald's restaurant on the premises.

This transaction was a good candidate for an alliance both because it pertained to a small and specific element of both companies' overall business, but also because it

EXAMPLE 4.5 AMICORE COMES TO THE AID OF PHYSICIANS[15]

On October 10, 2001, three of the world's largest companies, Microsoft, IBM, and Pfizer, announced an ambitious and unusual joint venture. Together, they launched Amicore, an independent company to help physicians with web-enabled software and devices to reduce physicians' paperwork.

Physicians spend an unusually large amount of time dealing with paperwork. They must submit bills to insurance companies, complete medical charts and examine medical histories, request lab tests, and retrieve test results. This is an age-old problem, and many companies offer solutions. For example, physicians can purchase dedicated hardware and software for billings and medical recordkeeping. Some physicians contract with physician practice management (PPM) companies, which provide all administrative services in exchange for a share of practice revenues. WebMD, a onetime high-flying dot-com company founded by Internet guru Jim Clark, offers physicians a complete web-based approach for reducing paperwork.

Pfizer's interest in reducing physician paperwork dates back to the early 1990s. At that time, physicians were frequently complaining to Pfizer's sales representatives about a rising sea of paperwork that was taking time away from patient care. In 1995, Pfizer founded Pfizer Health Solutions, which provides electronic medical records to physicians. But this did little to eliminate the paperwork problem.

The problem persisted for several reasons. First, the marketplace of potential solutions was diverse and growing. But to many physicians such diversity was a hindrance, not a help. There was no standard for billing or medical records. This meant that physicians could not merge records with other providers, so that medical records remained disjointed. One physician treating a patient on referral from another might well have to receive and review a hard-copy record, even if both had electronic systems. The lack of standards for billing could be even more problematic. If

two physicians merged, there might be no way to integrate their billing records. Either they would continue to maintain different systems, or they would sacrifice billing history. Physicians were also unhappy with PPMs. PPMs charged high fees and helped with billing, but did little to streamline day-to-day practice operations. PPMs also proved to be financially unstable, and most physicians were unwilling to sell off part of their practice to firms whose futures were in doubt. The same uncertainty plagued WebMD, which promised to streamline billing, prescriptions, and medical records through the Internet, but was slow to achieve the scale necessary to be effective.

Pfizer recognized that a successful business model to facilitate paperwork reductions would require standardization across practices. Moreover, physicians would be unwilling to invest in yet another dedicated billing or medical records system. Any solution would have to build off of traditional PC-based computing, in conjunction with the Internet. Pfizer understood the opportunity but lacked the expertise to create the necessary software and devices, and the clout to create a standard. Microsoft and IBM had what Pfizer lacked.

It was not too difficult for Pfizer to envision the kind of products that would have to be developed. But how could Pfizer get Microsoft and IBM to participate? Outright merger was out of the question. But why couldn't Pfizer enter into an arm's-length arrangement under which it would pay Microsoft and IBM to develop appropriate software and devices? Though feasible, this approach had several significant problems. From Pfizer's point of view, it would be difficult to specify performance standards in the contract. Pfizer could pay Microsoft and IBM a share of the profits, but this would expose Microsoft and IBM to risk. After all, both firms would undoubtedly need to make substantial relationship-specific investments. If Pfizer was wrong about the size of the market, or if Pfizer attempted to renegotiate contracts, IBM and Microsoft would be in a vulnerable position.

Given these problems, a joint venture makes sense. With a joint venture, Pfizer could not unilaterally attempt to renegotiate the terms of the deal; this served to increase Microsoft and IBM's commitment to the venture. At the same time, Pfizer's sales reps would be promoting the new venture, demonstrating Pfizer's commitment to the deal.

As of 2005, Amicore had over 1,000 physician customers. Amicore's electronic medical records, patient messaging, and practice management systems streamline scheduling, billing, and recordkeeping. Amicore products even help physicians navigate complex insurer reimbursement rules that sometimes depend on meeting a variety of performance objectives. But given its pedigree and a potential market in the 100,000s, Amicore still has much room to grow. It faces competition from WebMD and others, as well as a reluctant physician marketplace that seems content to pair twenty-first century medical technology with twentieth century management tools.

had elements that strongly argued for both "buying" and "making." Toys "R" Us needed to obtain McDonald's political know-how, site selection expertise, and business connections to enter the Japanese market. It would have been extremely costly, perhaps even impossible, for Toys "R" Us to have developed this know-how on its own. These considerations argued for Toys "R" Us "buying" the political and site selection services from the market rather than "making" them itself.

Toys "R" Us could have conceivably signed a contract with McDonald's (or perhaps even a public relations or consulting firm) to lobby on its behalf, select sites, and help negotiate deals with suppliers. However, Toys "R" Us would have been contracting for difficult-to-measure services. For example, measuring the efficacy of behind-the-scenes help to lobby government officials is not easy. This was especially problematic given Toys "R" Us's inexperience with the Japanese political economy. It was also problematic because, at the time, Japan's retail store laws were in flux. By 1990, momentum was already building to overhaul them. McDonald's, or some other market firm, might have promised to perform the political services Toys "R" Us needed, but reneged by secretly shirking, and then (assuming a change in the law) claimed credit for actions it promised to take but didn't. Considerations such as these complicated the ability of Toys "R" Us to "buy" the political know-how and lobbying services it needed to attain government approval to enter the Japanese market.

By taking a stake in the success of Toy's "R" Us's Japanese venture—through both its 20 percent ownership of the venture and the colocation of the Toys "R" Us stores and McDonald's restaurants—McDonald's faced hard-edged incentives to carry out its part of the bargain. For example, McDonald's-Japan estimated that a McDonald's restaurant located inside a Toys "R" Us store would generate three times more customers than a standalone restaurant would. The potential payoff from this venture gave McDonald's-Japan a strong incentive to work hard on behalf of Toys "R" Us. The alliance enabled Toys "R" Us to obtain the political services and site selection know-how it needed without having to make costly investments of its own. The alliance also avoided the difficult incentive problems that might have arisen had Toys "R" Us relied on traditional market contracting to obtain the services and know-how it needed.

Although alliances can combine the best features of buying and making, they can also suffer from the drawbacks of both buying and making. For example, just as traditional market transactions can involve a risk of leakage of private information, independent firms that collaborate through alliances also risk losing control over proprietary information. In fact, the risk of information leakage can often be more severe in an alliance than in a traditional market transaction because the conditions that tend to make an alliance desirable (complex, ambiguous transactions that do not lend themselves to comprehensive contracting) often force the parties to exchange a considerable amount of closely held information.

In addition, although the loose, evolving governance structure of an alliance can help the parties adapt to unforeseen events, it may also compromise coordination between the firms. Unlike an "inside-the-firm" transaction, in an alliance there are often no formal mechanisms for making decisions or resolving disputes expeditiously. The "footprints" of this are delay and lack of focus, problems that plagued the highly publicized alliances between IBM and Apple in the early 1990s to develop a new operating system, a multimedia software language, and the PowerPC. Indeed, by 1994 IBM's senior management had become so frustrated in its protracted negotiations with Apple over the operating system for the PowerPC that it concluded it would have been better off acquiring Apple rather than dealing with it through an alliance.

Finally, just as agency costs can arise within departments of firms that are not subject to market discipline, alliances can also suffer from agency and influence costs. Agency costs in alliances can arise because the fruits of the alliance's efforts are split between two or more firms. This can give rise to a *free-rider problem*. Each firm in the alliance is insufficiently vigilant in monitoring the alliance's activities because neither firm captures the full benefit of such vigilance. Firms that repeatedly engage in alliances may be less prone to free ride, lest they establish a reputation for free riding that precludes them from finding future partners. Influence costs can arise because the absence of a formal hierarchy and administrative system within an alliance can encourage employees to engage in influence activity, such as lobbying, to augment their resources and enhance their status.

Collaborative Relationships

In the past few years, large firms throughout North America and Europe have increasingly focused on a core set of activities, outsourcing the rest to specialized trading partners in the vertical chain. These companies are following the lead of their East Asian counterparts for whom vertical disintegration has been the normal way of doing business for decades.[18] Japanese and South Korean firms do not organize the vertical chain through arm's-length contracts. Instead, they rely on a labyrinth of long-term, semiformal relationships between firms up and down the vertical chain. Next we consider two closely related types of relationships: subcontractor networks and Japanese *keiretsu*. (Hong Kong and South Korean also have large *keiretsu*; in South Korea they are known as Chaebol.)

Subcontractor Networks

Many Japanese manufacturers make extensive use of networks of independent subcontractors with whom they maintain close long-term relationships. Unlike the relationships many American and European firms have with their subcontractors, in Japan these relationships typically involve a much higher degree of collaboration between the manufacturer and the subcontractors and the delegation of a more sophisticated set of responsibilities to the subcontractor. Toshihiro Nishiguchi's study of Japanese and British subcontracting in the electronics industry illustrates these differences.[19] In Great Britain, electronics manufacturers typically rely on subcontractors for specific, narrowly defined jobs. Their relationship is mediated by contractual agreements on price and performance and often does not persist beyond a few clearly defined transactions. Subcontractors are much less dedicated to the needs of particular buyers, and

EXAMPLE 4.6 INTERFIRM BUSINESS NETWORKS IN THE
UNITED STATES: THE WOMEN'S DRESS INDUSTRY IN NEW
YORK CITY[20]

Business networks based on social ties and governed by norms of trust and reciprocity exist outside Japan. As Brian Uzzi has shown, they even exist in New York City. Uzzi recently studied business networks in the "better dress" segment of the women's apparel industry in New York City. This is a highly fragmented industry, with low barriers to entry and intense competition, both domestic and international. One might expect that in such a context, arm's-length contracting would be the norm and social ties would not count for much. Uzzi's research demonstrates that this is not the case. He shows that many business relationships in this industry are characterized by what he calls *embedded ties*: relationships characterized by trust and a willingness to exchange closely held information and work together to solve problems.

The design and marketing of women's dresses is carried out by firms called *jobbers*. Working with in-house or freelance designers, these firms design dresses and market these designs to retail buyers, who then place orders. Most jobbers do not manufacture the dresses themselves. Instead, they manage a network of subcontractors, including grading contractors, who size the dress patterns, cutting contractors, who cut the fabric, and sewing contractors, who sew the dresses. The jobbers also manage the flow of raw materials in the production process. For example, they purchase fabric from converters and send it to the cutting contractors, who cut the fabric to make the pieces of the dress.

Uzzi observed two main ways of organizing exchange in this industry: arm's-length ties, or what the participants called market relationships, and embedded ties, which they called close or special relationships. Market relationships were characterized by a lack of reciprocity between the parties in the exchange. "It's the opposite of a close tie," one participant reported to Uzzi. "One hand doesn't wash the other." They also lacked social content. "They're relationships that are like far away," according to one manager. "They don't consider the feeling for the human

being." Many exchanges in this industry were governed by arm's-length relationships. However, for major transactions that participants considered for the company's overall success, the exchange was often governed by embedded ties.

The "close" or "special" relationships that Uzzi observed were characterized by a high degree of trust. Such trust often developed when one party voluntarily did a favor for another that was then reciprocated later. For example, a subcontractor might work overtime so that a jobber could fill a rush order. Later, the jobber might place an order to help the subcontractor keep its shop running when demand was slow. According to Uzzi, trust gave the parties access to resources and information that improve efficiency, but would have been difficult to acquire through arm's-length contracts. It also promoted collaborative problem solving. One manufacturer told Uzzi, "When you deal with a guy you don't have a close relationship with, it can be a big problem. Things go wrong, and there's no telling what will happen. With my guys [his key contractors], if something goes wrong, I know we'll be able to work it out. I know his business and he knows mine."

Relationships in this industry based on trust could be extremely powerful. In one instance, according to Uzzi, a jobber was moving its production to Asia and would thus be ending its relationship with its New York City subcontractors. This jobber had strong incentives *not* to inform its subcontractors that it was going to leave. By doing so, it risked provoking opportunistic behavior by its subcontractors (e.g., shirking on quality) to take advantage of what they would now regard as a temporary relationship. Yet, the CEO of this firm personally informed the subcontractors with whom he had a special relationship, and he promised to help them adapt to the loss of his business. In turn, those subcontractors continued to provide high-quality services. This firm did *not* inform the subcontractors with whom it had market relationships that it was planning to close its New York operation.

the customer base of a particular supplier is usually much larger than a Japanese subcontractor of comparable size.

By contrast, the relationship between a Japanese electronics manufacturer and its suppliers can persist for decades. Subcontractors generally perform more sophisticated and comprehensive tasks than their British counterparts. For example, rather than just fabricating a component, a subcontractor might also be involved in its design and the testing of prototypes. In addition, subcontractors typically see their role as not just to fill the buyer's orders, but more generally, to closely integrate their operations with the buyer's, for example, by dedicating assembly lines to the buyer's product, by developing special-purpose machines that can produce to the buyer's specifications more efficiently, or by working closely with the customer to improve production. Nishiguchi concludes that the relationship between electronics manufacturers and subcontractors in Japan involves significantly more asset specificity than the corresponding relationship in Britain.

Keiretsu

Ever since the 1960s, business strategists have alternately admired and criticized Japanese *keiretsu*. These systems are closely related to subcontractor networks, but they supposedly involve more formalized institutional linkages, as depicted in Figure 4.3. Based on data on banking patterns, corporate board memberships, and social affiliations such as executive "lunch clubs," analysts identified six large *keiretsu*—Mitsubishi, Sumitomo, DKB, Mitsui, Fuyo, and Sanwa. Each has more than 80 members. All have core banks that facilitate relationships among members, and nearly all have members in key industries such as steel, life insurance, and chemicals. It is generally thought that each member of a *keiretsu* is the first choice of another *keiretsu* member in future business dealings. This formalization of the subcontractor relationships described above was supposed to be one of the reasons Japanese corporations outperformed U.S. corporations during the crucial period of 1970–1990. Critics counter that the *keiretsu* concentrate corporate power among a few banks and their business partners, and harm the competitiveness of firms that do not belong. Analysts now believe that the power of *keiretsu* is in decline, perhaps due to the partial opening of trade barriers, and that *keiretsu* members no longer earn above-average profits.

Recent research by Yoshior Miwa and J. Mark Ramseyer cast doubt on the very existence of *keiretsu*.[21] Miwa and Ramseyer acknowledge that executives at firms identified as belonging to *keiretsu* do belong to the same lunch clubs and meet at other business events. They also show that otherwise, their business relationships are quite ordinary. Members of a *keiretsu* borrow substantial amounts from their central bank, but they borrow nearly as much from other banks. They go outside of the *keiretsu* for other business dealings as well. Miwa and Ramseyer agree that *keiretsu* profits today are quite average, but they revisit the data to show that *keiretsu* profits have always been quite average. With this and other data, Miwa and Ramseyer show that the tight-knit and highly profitable structure of the Japanese *keiretsu*—held up as an exemplar of vertical organization—is a myth that has been perpetuated for 40 years. Not only do these firms have extensive outside business dealings, but the members of the *keiretsu* never outperformed other firms that were excluded from *keiretsu*.

Despite their mytical status, Western firms have generally avoided the kinds of close entanglements that supposedly characterized the *keiretsu*, partly because of legal restrictions on interlocking boards of directors and other antitrust issues. But Western firms recognize the importance of the implicit contracts and long-term relationships that have made *keiretsu* so successful.

FIGURE 4.3
DEBT, EQUITY, AND TRADE LINKAGES IN JAPANESE *KEIRETSU*

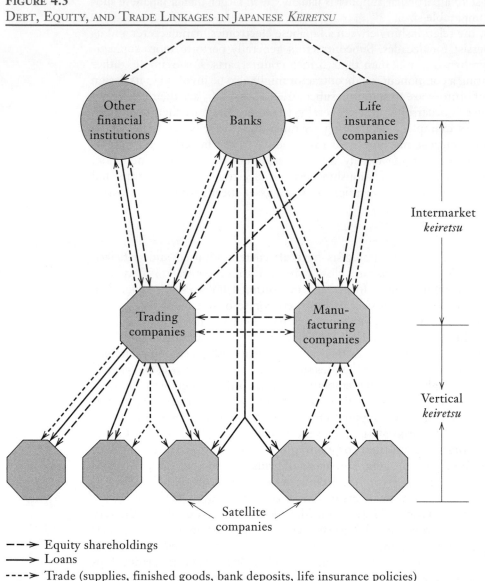

Source: Gerlach, M. L. and J. Lincoln, "The Organization of Business Networks in the United States and Japan," in Nigria, N. and R. G. Eccles (eds.), *Networks and Organizations: Structure, Form, and Action*, Boston, Harvard Business School Press, p. 494. The dashed lines show equity holdings within a typical *keiretsu*, the solid lines show loans, and the small dashed lines show the patterns of exchange within the *keiretsu*.

Implicit Contracts and Long-Term Relationships

An implicit contract is an unstated understanding between parties in a business relationship. The understandings that exist among members of the *keiretsu* are implicit contracts. But implicit contracts are generally not enforceable in court, so parties to an implicit contract must rely on alternative mechanisms to make the understanding viable. A powerful mechanism that makes implicit contracts viable is the threat of losing future business if one party breaks the implicit contract for its own gain.[22]

To see why the threat to withdraw future business can be so powerful, imagine two firms in the vertical chain that routinely transact business with each other. Their longstanding relationship has enabled them to coordinate their activities through formal planning and monitoring of product quality, and as a result, both firms have profited significantly. In particular, suppose that the upstream firm sells inputs to the downstream firm for a $1 million profit every year, and the downstream firm processes the inputs and sells a finished product to consumers for a $1 million profit of its own. Each firm has an alternative trading partner, but each would only reap profits of $900,000 per year if forced to switch.

Although each firm apparently has no reason to switch, in fact the relationship has a potential complication. Each firm could increase its profit at the expense of the other by performing less of the planning and monitoring that make the relationship successful. Specifically, suppose that the upstream firm estimates that by breaking its implied commitments to the downstream firm, it could boost its annual profits to $1.2 million. If it does this, however, the downstream firm will learn that it has broken its commitments, and the relationship will end. Each firm would then be forced to do business with another trading partner.

How much does the upstream firm benefit by honoring its implicit contract indefinitely? In one year, it earns $100,000 more by transacting with the downstream firm than with its alternative trading partner. If the firm's discount rate is 5 percent, the net present value of honoring the implicit contract indefinitely would be $2 million.[23] This far exceeds the short-term (i.e., one-year) increase in profit of $200,000 from breaking the contract. Indeed, to make breaking the implicit contract worthwhile, the discount rate would have to be 50 percent! This high hurdle for switching helps sustain the implicit contract.

Thomas Palay's study of rail freight contracting illustrates the power of long-term relationships in sustaining cooperative behavior.[24] He discusses a railroad that purchased specially designed auto-rack railcars to move a particular make of automobile for a major auto manufacturer. Soon after the railroad made the investment, however, the manufacturer changed the design of the car, making the auto racks obsolete. Even though it was not contractually obligated to do so, the manufacturer compensated the railroad for more than $1 million to cover the unamortized portion of the investment. The director of shipping at the automobile manufacturer alluded to the importance of maintaining a long-term relationship as the basis for this action. "We've got to keep them healthy, viable, and happy to guarantee that we'll get the equipment we need, when we need it."

CHAPTER SUMMARY

◆ The advantages and disadvantages of relying on the market versus relying on internal organization can be expressed in terms of a tradeoff between technical efficiency and agency efficiency. Technical efficiency occurs if the firm is using least-cost production techniques. Agency efficiency refers to the extent to which the firm's production and/or administrative costs are raised by the transactions and coordination costs of arm's-length market exchanges or the agency and influence costs of internal organization.

◆ Vertical integration is preferred to arm's-length market exchange when it is less costly to organize activities internally than it is to organize them through arm's-length market exchange. This cost difference will reflect differences in both technical efficiency and agency efficiency across the two modes of organization.

◆ Vertical integration is relatively more attractive (a) when the ability of outside market specialists relative to the firm itself to achieve scale or scope economies is limited; (b) the larger the scale of the firm's product market activities; and (c) the greater the extent to which the assets involved in production are relationship-specific.

◆ Vertical integration changes the pattern of asset ownership and control, and thus alters the bargaining power between parties in a vertical relationship. This, in turn, affects incentives to invest in relationship-specific assets. Vertical integration will be attractive when there are large asymmetries in the importance of relationship-specific investments in achieving the full efficiencies from the exchange, and where it is important for one party to control the use of those assets.

◆ Vertical integration and arm's-length market exchange are not the only ways to organize transactions. A firm may pursue tapered integration, in which it supplies part of its input requirement itself and relies on market exchanges for the remainder.

◆ Firms may undertake strategic alliances or joint ventures. Although the transacting parties remain legally separate under these modes of organization, they typically entail much closer cooperation and coordination than an arm's-length exchange between two independent firms.

◆ Firms may also be bound together in cooperative relationships in long-lasting networks, such as the Japanese *keiretsu*. Finally, long-term, arm's-length market relationships can provide strong incentives for cooperative behavior and can thus achieve the advantages of vertical integration (e.g., avoidance of transactions costs, flexibility in governance) without incurring the disadvantages (e.g., softening incentives for innovation).

QUESTIONS

1. Why is the "technical efficiency" line in Figure 4.1 above the *x*-axis? Why does the "agency efficiency" line cross the *x*-axis?

2. Explain why the following patterns seem to hold in many industries:
   (a) Small firms are more likely to outsource production of inputs than are large firms.
   (b) "Standard" inputs (such as simple transistors that could be used by several electronics manufacturers) are more likely to be outsourced than "tailor-made" inputs (such as a circuit board designed for a single manufacturer's specific needs).

3. Use the argument of Grossman, Hart, and Moore to explain why stockbrokers are permitted to keep their client lists (i.e., continue to contact and do business with clients) if they are dismissed from their jobs and find employment at another brokerage house.

4. Analysts often array strategic alliances and joint ventures on a continuum that begins with "using the market" and ends with "full integration." Do you agree that these fall along a natural continuum?

5. What does the *keiretsu* system have in common with traditional strategic alliances and joint ventures? What are some of the differences?

6. The following is an excerpt from an actual strategic plan (the company and product name have been changed to protect the innocent):

   Acme's primary raw material is pvc sheet that is produced by three major vendors within the United States. Acme, a small consumer products manufacturer, is consolidating down to a single vendor. Continued growth by this vendor assures Acme that it will be able to meet its needs in the future.

   Assume that Acme's chosen vendor will grow as forecast. Offer a scenario to Acme management that might convince them that they should rethink their decision to rely on a single vendor. What do you recommend Acme do to minimize the risk(s) that you have identified? Are there any drawbacks to your recommendation?

7. Shaefer Electronics is a medium-size producer (about 18 million in sales in 1993) of electronic products for the oil industry. It makes two main products—capacitors and integrated circuits. Capacitors are standardized items. Integrated circuits are more complex, highly customized items made to individual customer specifications. They are designed and made to order, require installation, and sometimes require postsale servicing. Shaefer's annual sales are shown in the table below.

Shaefer relies entirely on manufacturers' representatives (MRs) located throughout the United States to sell its products. MRs are independent contractors who sell Shaefer's products in exchange for a sales commission. The company's representatives are not exclusive—they represent manufacturers of related but noncompeting products, such as circuit breakers, small switches, or semiconductors. Often a customer will buy some of these related products along with integrated circuits or an order of capacitors. MRs have long experience within local markets, close ties to the engineers within the firms that buy control systems, and deep knowledge of their needs. In the markets in which they operate, MRs develop their own client lists and call schedules. They are fully responsible for the expenses they incur in selling their products.

Once an order for one of Shaefer's products is taken by the MR, Shaefer is responsible for any installation or postsale servicing that is needed.

Shaefer recently hired two different marketing consultants to study its sales force strategy. Their reports contained the conclusions reported below. Please comment on the soundness of each conclusion.

(a) "Shaefer should continue to sell through MRs. Whether it uses MRs or an in-house sales force, it has to pay commissions. By relying on MRs, it avoids the variable selling expenses (e.g., travel expenses for salespeople) it would incur if it had its own sales force. As a result, Shaefer's selling expenses are lower than they would be with an in-house sales force of comparable size, talent, and know-how."

(b) "Selling through MRs made sense for Shaefer when it was first getting started and specialized in capacitors. However, given its current product mix, it would not want to set itself up the way it is now if it were designing its sales force strategy from scratch. But with what it has got, Shaefer should be extremely cautious about changing."

SHAEFER ANNUAL SALES ($000)

	1990	1995	1999	2000	2001	2002	2003
Capacitors	$5,568	6,488	7,131	7,052	7,043	7,360	8,109
Integrated circuits	$678	1,679	4,651	6,245	7,363	8,589	9,508
Total	$6,246	8,167	11,782	13,297	14,406	15,959	17,617

ENDNOTES

[1]Caves, R. and D. Barton, *Efficiency in U.S. Manufacturing Industries*, Cambridge, MA, MIT Press, 1990.

[2]See Williamson, O., "Strategizing, Economizing and Economic Organization," *Strategic Management Journal*, 12, Winter 1991, pp. 75–94, for a complete explanation of this concept along with a brief discussion of its intellectual history.

[3]This figure has been adapted from Oliver Williamson's discussion of vertical integration in *The Economic Institutions of Capitalism*, New York, Free Press, 1985, chap. 4.

[4]Chandler, A. D., Jr., *Scale and Scope: The Dynamics of Industrial Capitalism*, Cambridge, MA, Belknap, 1990.

[5]Monteverde, K. and D. Teece, "Supplier Switching Costs and Vertical Integration in the Automobile Industry," *Bell Journal of Economics*, 13, Spring 1982, pp. 206–213.

[6]Masten, S., "The Organization of Production: Evidence from the Aerospace Industry," *Journal of Law and Economics*, 27, October 1984, pp. 403–417.

[7]Joskow, P., "Vertical Integration and Long-Term Contracts: The Case of Coal-Burning Electric Generating Plants," *Journal of Law, Economics, and Organization*, 33, Fall 1985, pp. 32–80.

[8]Anderson, E. and D. C. Schmittlein, "Integration of the Sales Force: An Empirical Examination," *RAND Journal of Economics*, 15, Autumn 1984, pp. 385–395.

[9]Grossman, S. and O. Hart, "The Costs and Benefits of Ownership: A Theory of Vertical and Lateral Integration," *Journal of Political Economy*, 94, 1986, pp. 619–719; Hart, O. and J. Moore, "Property Rights and the Nature of the Firm," *Journal of Political Economy*, 98, 1990, pp. 1119–1158.

[10]Grossman and Hart point out the need to be able to enforce the contracts in a court of law. This includes the ability to collect penalties for breach of contract.

[11]See Masten, S., J. W. Meehan, and E. A. Snyder, "Vertical Integration in the U.S. Auto Industry: A Note on the Influence of Transactions Specific Assets," *Journal of Economic Behavior and Organization*, 12, 1989, pp. 265–273.

[12]This example draws heavily from Borenstein, S. and R. Gilbert, "Uncle Sam at the Gas Pump: Causes and Consequences of Regulating Gasoline Distribution," *Regulation*, 1993, pp. 63–75.

[13]Another increasingly common arrangement is convenience stores that sell gasoline on a self-service basis. However, the gasoline sold at these outlets is usually not produced by the major brand-name refiners.

[14]Ohmae, K., "The Global Logic of Strategic Alliances," *Harvard Business Review*, March–April 1989, pp. 143–154.

[15]This example was developed by Jondy Syjuco and Li Liu, Kellogg MBA class of 2002.

[16]McDonald's-Japan is a joint venture between McDonald's and Fujita & Company.

[17]See "Guess Who's Selling Barbies in Japan Now?" *Business Week*, December 9, 1991, p. 60.

[18]See Clark, R., *The Japanese Company*, New Haven, CT, Yale University Press, 1979, or Nishiguchi, T., *Strategic Industrial Sourcing: The Japanese Advantage*, New York, Oxford University Press, 1994.

[19]Nishiguchi, T., *Strategic Industrial Sourcing: The Japanese Advantage*, New York, Oxford University Press, 1994.

[20]This example is based on Uzzi, B., "Social Structure and Competition in Interfirm Networks: The Paradox of Embeddedness," *Administrative Sciences Quarterly*, 42, 1997, pp. 35–67.

[21]Miwa, Y. and J. M. Ramseyer, 2002, "The Fable of the Keiretsu," *Journal of Economics and Management Strategy*, 11(2), 169–224.

[22]The idea that future flows provide firms with incentives to maintain ongoing relationships was initially developed by Benjamin Klein and Keith Leffler in the article, "The Role of Market Forces in Assuring Contractual Performance," *Journal of Political Economy*, 89, 1981, pp. 615–641.

[23]If the discount rate is i, then an infinite-lived stream of X dollars per year is worth X/i in today's dollars. See the Economics Primer for a fuller discussion of present value.

[24]Palay, T., "Comparative Institutional Economics: The Governance of Rail Freight Contracting," *Journal of Legal Studies*, 13, 1984, pp. 265–287.

DIVERSIFICATION

5

*M*any well-known firms are diversified—that is, they produce for numerous markets. For example, Philips is a diversified manufacturer of home electronics equipment, and Wal-Mart is diversified both in its product line and in the local markets its stores serve. Through diversification within their areas of business, these and other firms hope to reduce costs and improve market effectiveness by exploiting economies of scale and scope.

Since about 1950, many large firms have expanded beyond the boundaries of any particular business area. Careful readers of Chapter 2 may wonder how economies of scope can be derived from combining the production of medical equipment and popular music, as did EMI. In analyzing broadly diversified firms (sometimes called conglomerates), it is often difficult to specify what businesses the firm is in, what its key resources are, and what services corporate management contributes to individual business units.

This chapter examines corporate diversification. We first discuss the history of diversification in the United States, and then we turn our attention to the question of why firms diversify. We discuss how diversification may affect a firm's owners, identifying both potential benefits and potential costs. We observe that owners of publicly held firms are rarely involved in decisions regarding corporate diversification. Instead, managers (mostly chief executive officers) make these choices. Diversification decisions therefore may reflect the preferences of these individuals rather than those of shareholders. We discuss a number of reasons why a firm's managers may prefer to diversify even if shareholders do not benefit. Finally, we review the performance of diversified firms. The evidence here is clear: successful diversification combines businesses that can exploit economies of scope. Diversification for other reasons tends to be less successful.

A BRIEF HISTORY

We begin by discussing research on patterns in corporate diversification in the United States over the past 120 years. We first discuss historical variation in the level of corporate diversification, and we then address variation in rates of merger and acquisition activity.

To measure how diversified a firm is at a given point in time, Richard Rumelt developed the notion of *relatedness*. This measure depends on how much of a firm's revenues are attributable to product market activities that have shared technological characteristics, production characteristics, or distribution channels. Rumelt focused on three characteristics of firms: the proportion of a firm's revenues derived from (1) its largest business, (2) its largest group of related businesses, and (3) the stages of a vertically integrated production process.[1]

Rumelt then classified firms into four groups, based on the relatedness of the firms' businesses. A *single-business firm* is one with more than 95 percent of its business in a single activity or line of business. Examples of such firms include W. R. Wrigley in chewing gum, DeBeers in diamonds, and Daimler-Chrysler in motor vehicles. A *dominant-business firm* obtains between 70 and 95 percent of its annual revenues from a principal activity. Examples include Nestlé in food products and the Tribune Company (publisher of the *Chicago Tribune* and *Los Angeles Times*) in publishing. A *related-business firm* derives less than 70 percent of its revenue from a primary area but has other lines of business related to the primary area. Examples include Abbott Laboratories, H&R Block, and Bausch & Lomb. Finally, an *unrelated-business firm* derives less than 70 percent of its business from a primary area and has few related business lines. The Indian firm Tata Sons is an example, as are American firms such as 3M and General Electric. Firms such as these are commonly called conglomerates.

Rumelt also documented a trend toward diversification among U.S. businesses after World War II. In 1949, 70 percent of major firms were classified as single-business or dominant-business firms. By 1969, only 35 percent of his sample showed a similar focus. In contrast, the proportion of unrelated-business firms increased from 3.4 percent in 1949 to 19.4 percent in 1969.

A number of authors have updated Rumelt's work. They have found that the postwar trend toward diversification appears to have reversed. Gerald Davis, Kristina Dieckman, and Catherine Tinsley, for example, have devised a measure of diversification called entropy.[2] Entropy equals 0 for a firm that derives all of its sales from a single four-digit SIC category; it increases as the firm's sales are spread across more categories. For Fortune 500 firms, entropy fell from an average of 1.00 in 1980 to .67 in 1990; that is, these firms had become less diversified. (As a benchmark, a firm that derives 5 percent of its sales from each of 20 different lines of business has entropy of 3.) Similarly, Robert Comment and Gregg Jarrell report that the fraction of U.S. firms with a single-business segment increased from 36.2 percent in 1978 to 63.9 percent in 1989.[3]

Although firms can diversify in a number of ways, including internal development of new business areas and joint ventures with other firms, it is perhaps easiest to measure diversifying activity by examining mergers and acquisitions. Merger activity seems to occur in waves, with periods of high activity followed by lulls during which few firms are bought or sold. There have been five such merger waves in the United States in the last 120 years.[4]

The first merger wave began after the worldwide depression of 1883, which left many capital-intensive industries with overcapacity, and ended in the early 1900s. This wave involved roughly one-sixth of all U.S. manufacturing firms. Some combinations that arose at this time, such as Standard Oil and United States Steel, were able to monopolize their industries. A second, smaller merger wave occurred in the early

EXAMPLE 5.1 CHANGES IN DIVERSIFICATION, FROM
AMERICAN CAN TO PRIMERICA

The history of business is filled with examples of firms that have reinvented themselves, sometimes more than once. When confronted with changes in technological and market conditions, the managers of these firms refocused their businesses into areas that were less subject to environmental threats, or else entered new businesses that forced them to acquire new organizational capabilities that would enable their firms to compete under changed conditions.[5]

Among contemporary businesses, American Can provides one of the most interesting examples of such refocusing. American had long manufactured tin cans and other metal containers for buyers that included major food and beverage companies. In Rumelt's typology, it was a single-product firm. The can industry, however, became increasingly unfavorable during the 1950s and 1960s, for several reasons. First, the technology for making cans was simple, so American Can had many competitors. Second, forward integration by aluminum producers and backward integration by food companies eroded American's market share and limited its ability to raise prices. Finally, plastic containers threatened the marketability of cans because plastics could be used in ways that cans could not.

Beginning in the 1950s, American Can diversified into businesses unrelated to can manufacturing, including paper products and printing. In 1977, the company acquired Pickwick International, a record distributor, and its retail subsidiary Musicland. In 1978, it purchased the direct-mail marketer Fingerhut. By 1980, American Can was an unrelated-business firm.

In 1980, American Can began to refocus its entire portfolio of businesses. The first move was to acquire Associated Madison, a life insurance company. During the 1980s, American proceeded to acquire several other financial services businesses, including Barclays Bank and Smith Barney. In 1986, American Can sold off its can business, and it has since sold off other businesses. The restructuring of American Can was crowned in 1987 when the firm changed its name to Primerica, indicating that it had become a financial services firm. In 1993, Primerica merged with Travelers, adopting its partner's well-known name and umbrella logo. The evolution of the firm culminated with its 1997 acquisition of Salomon for $9.2 billion—the second largest acquisition of a securities brokerage firm to date—and its 1998 merger with Citicorp.

American Can is not the only firm to diversify away from the business around which it was built and refocus on another business. USX, formally U.S. Steel, today derives most of its revenue from oil; it remains in the steel business largely because of labor considerations. International Harvester (IH), once focused on farm equipment, diversified in the 1930s and 1940s into trucks and construction equipment. Facing bankruptcy in the 1980s, IH sold its farm equipment business (and the rights to the "International Harvester" name) to Tenneco and its construction equipment business to Dresser Industries. The firm that remained is called Navistar and is a world leader in medium and heavy truck production.

1920s. Antitrust laws such as the Sherman Act and the Federal Trade Commission Act discouraged mergers designed to grab monopoly power rather than promote efficiency. As a result, many combinations stopped short of achieving 50 percent market share, and their industries resembled oligopolies instead of monopolies. Other combinations involved vertical, rather than horizontal, integration. The formation and growth of General Motors during this time displayed both types of integration.

The reasons for the first two merger waves are easy to understand. Firms in the same market combined in horizontal mergers to reduce competition and achieve economies of scale. The emergence of manufacturing giants tilted the calculus of the make-or-buy decision in favor of vertical integration, as explained in Chapter 1. Hence, these merger waves did not lead to increases in corporate diversification, as measured by Rumelt's concept of relatedness.

The Great Depression of the 1930s and American participation in World War II put a damper on U.S. merger activity until 1950. New antitrust laws, notably the Celler-Kefauver Act, further hindered both horizontal and vertical mergers. By the late 1950s and early 1960s, managers understood that diversified combinations of businesses were legal, whereas horizontal and vertical mergers were likely to encounter resistance from antitrust officials.

By 1960, the pace of merger activity had again quickened. Unlike the previous waves, this third wave featured increased levels of unrelated diversification and produced large conglomerates selling extensive product lines in diverse markets. Mergers in the 1960s resulted in firms such as American Can, which sold cans, clothing, and financial services, and ITT, whose business portfolio included life insurance, car rental, hotels, and vending machines.

There was scarcely a lull between this wave of conglomerate mergers and the fourth merger wave, which occurred in the 1980s. The mergers of the 1980s again differed markedly from their predecessors. Some cash-rich firms, lacking solid investments in their own businesses, instead attempted to grow through acquisition. Philip Morris, flush with cash from the tobacco business, bought 7-Up in 1978, General Foods in 1985, and Kraft in 1988. The merger wave of the 1980s also saw the emergence of the leveraged buyout, in which a company was purchased by not another firm but by a group of private investors, often with the assistance of incumbent management. These transactions were notable for their heavy reliance on debt as a means of financing the transaction. Frequently, the debt was retired in part by selling off portions of the acquired firm—usually portions that were unrelated to the firm's core business.

The fifth merger wave began in the mid-1990s and, despite a lull in 2001 and 2002, continued through 2005. Deals made during this wave included Exxon-Mobil, Procter & Gamble-Gillette, and Oracle-PeopleSoft. It is too early to evaluate the impact of these transactions, but they seemed to be motivated by one of two factors: (1) Firms desired to establish dominant market shares within specific industries; and (2) firms desired access to international markets. In either case, the merging firms were usually "related" businesses.

◆ ◆ ◆ ◆ ◆ WHY DO FIRMS DIVERSIFY?

Firms may choose to diversify for either of two reasons. First, diversification may benefit the firm's owners by increasing the efficiency of the firm. Second, if the firm's owners are not directly involved in deciding whether to diversify, diversification decisions may reflect the preferences of the firm's managers.

In this section we explore both possibilities. First we discuss how diversification may affect corporate efficiency and thereby affect the value accruing to the firm's owners. We discuss ways in which diversification can both enhance and reduce efficiency. We then discuss how a firm's manager may benefit from diversifying the firm, why shareholders may be unable to prevent diversification that does not create value, and what forces constrain management's ability to diversify firms.

Efficiency-based Reasons for Diversification

We begin by discussing both the benefits and the costs of corporate diversification to a firm's shareholders. We first present each potential benefit and discuss the extent to which it is likely to underlie observed patterns of diversification. We then describe some potential costs associated with diversification.

Economies of Scale and Scope

Chapter 2 suggests that one motive for diversification may be to achieve economies of scale and scope. A study by Thomas Brush supports the plausibility of scale and scope economies as a starting point for understanding the performance of diversified firms.[6] Brush conducted a large-sample longitudinal analysis of mergers in 356 manufacturing industries. He reasoned that if mergers are associated with operational synergies, the market share of merged firms should increase following a combination. Brush sought to determine whether mergers were more likely when there was an expectation of positive changes in market share. He found that they were and that the gains expected from mergers were substantial. He also examined whether these performance expectations, on average, were realized. Later changes in market share were, in fact, explained by expectations from mergers.

If firms diversify in order to pursue economies of scope, we might also predict that large firms would offer a related set of products to a narrow population of consumers. Historical analyses, such as the work of Daniel Nathanson and James Cassano, have found that this happens only occasionally.[7] Nathanson and Cassano classified more than 180 U.S. firms from the 1970s according to the degree of their *product diversity* and *market diversity*. Some firms, such as Schlitz, Maytag, and Zenith, were undiversified on both dimensions. They may be seen as pursuing economies of scale and scope in narrow markets with a common technology. At least as many firms, however, were highly diversified on both dimensions. Firms such as Union Carbide, Allis-Chalmers, and Gulf and Western produced goods that shared little technology and were sold to consumer groups that had little in common. Thus, it does not appear that economies of scope from shared technologies or shared consumer groups can explain observed patterns of diversification.

Economies of scope can, however, come from other sources. Edith Penrose, a founder of the resource-based view of the firm, argues that scope economies can come from spreading a firm's underutilized organizational resources to new areas.[8] At any given time, a firm may possess specific resources that it cannot fully utilize in its current product market. Such resources might be effectively applied in other product markets, and doing so would give rise to economies of scope. In a similar vein, C. K. Prahalad and Richard Bettis suggest that managers of diversified firms may spread their own managerial talent across nominally unrelated business areas. They call this a "dominant general management logic," which comprises "the way in which managers conceptualize the business and make critical resource allocations— be it in technologies, product development, distribution, advertising, or in human resource management."[9]

This logic applies most directly when managers develop specific skills—say, in information systems or finance—and seemingly unrelated businesses rely on these skills for success. Managers sometimes mistakenly apply this logic when they develop particular skills but diversify into businesses that do not require them. For example, some observers of the 1995 Disney-ABC merger wondered whether Michael Eisner's ability to develop marketing plans for Disney's animated motion pictures would translate into skill at scheduling of network television programming. The dominant general management logic is more problematic when managers perceive themselves to possess superior general management skills with which they can justify any diversification. Without detailed knowledge about the particular businesses involved in a diversification initiative, one cannot know at the time of the diversification whether the new business fits the dominant logic or whether the general manager involved is above average. In the absence of obvious relationships between businesses, such as those identified by Nathanson and Cassano, it is difficult to defend claims that economies of scope are derived from the dominant general management logic.

Economizing on Transaction Costs

The issue of transaction costs developed in conjunction with our discussion of vertical integration in Chapters 3 and 4 is also relevant if diversification occurs through mergers or acquisitions. A merger or acquisition is only a legal basis for combining firms. If the firms involved can exploit economies after the legal change in ownership, why couldn't they do so before the change? David Teece asked why economies of scope cannot be achieved by coordinating several independent firms; that is, why must business units be brought into a firm for economies to be realized?[10]

Teece argues that the multiproduct firm is an efficient choice when transaction costs complicate coordination among independent firms. Recall from Chapters 3 and 4 that transaction costs are more likely to arise in relationships with independent firms when the production process involves specialized assets, such as human capital, organizational routines, or other forms of proprietary knowledge. In the absence of specialized assets, transactions costs are not likely to be a problem. In this case, market coordination may provide superior incentives and flexibility.

Many decisions regarding whether to diversify or operate as independent firms follow the logic of minimizing transaction costs. Consider how higher education is organized. Undergraduate universities represent the "merger" of separate schools and departments, each of which could, in principle, offer educational programs located contiguously but operated independently of each other. Undergraduate students tend to take courses in many departments, however, and this creates economies of scale in locating the departments near each other and near common dormitory, library, athletic, and other facilities. The common location of these facilities means that any investments by any department are, in part, relationship specific. In other words, the value of one department's investments depends on the actions of other departments. For example, even if the Department of Economics at Northwestern University recruits several prize-winning teachers, their value in the classroom will not be fully realized if the university cannot attract high-quality students. This might happen if, say, the other departments were of low quality or refused to support actions aimed at enhancing the educational experience, such as funding for the library, computer labs, and residence halls. Common ownership of Northwestern's various departments allows for a single policy regarding hiring and promotion, as well as specialized investments.

Contrast the organization of undergraduate education into "diversified firms" with the way many paraprofessional training schools, such as schools for legal assistants or medical technicians, are organized. Such schools tend to be narrowly focused, offering training in only one field. Students interested in paraprofessional training generally do not require courses in other areas, so there is no need to assure access to them. The paraprofessional school reaps the full benefits of its investments in plant and labor, and it does not have to fear holdup by other schools that share in

EXAMPLE 5.2 ACQUIRING FOR SYNERGY: PROCTER & GAMBLE BUYS GILLETTE

An example of strategic diversification is the acquisition of Gillette by Procter & Gamble, which was announced in January 2005. Although both corporations operated in the consumer packaged goods industry, this acquisition represents a diversification strategy due to the rather limited overlap of their brands. While P&G's historical strengths have been in women's personal care, Gillette was a global leader in the men's personal care segment. P&G paid $57 billion in stock for Gillette, making the deal the largest global merger in the first half of 2005. A premise of this chapter has been that in order to create economics of scale and scope, businesses have to be related in either products or markets. The Gillette/P&G combination fits into both rationales.

Procter & Gamble, a Cincinnati-based firm founded in 1837, is a global leader in the consumer packaged goods industry. Its leading brands include Crest toothpaste, Pampers diapers, Tide laundry detergent, and Charmin toilet paper. The firm grew rapidly after its accidental invention, in 1878, of a bar soap that floats in water. This product, named "Ivory Soap" and marketed as "99 and 44/100 percent pure", was among the first personal care products to be marketed directly to consumers, as opposed to wholesalers. P&G is widely credited with having invented most modern brand management practices. By 2004, the firm had built a stable of more than 300 brands, with 16 brands each accounting for $1 billion or more in sales. Worldwide sales totaled more more than $51 billion, with approximately half this sales volume coming from outside the United States. The firm is also an extremely aggressive advertiser and ranked number one in global ad spending in both 2002 and 2003. Procter & Gamble has developed a unique corporate culture. Lifetime jobs, conservative dress, and a unique vocabulary set "Proctoids" apart from typical employees.

Boston-based Gillette was founded in 1901 to market the safety razor, which was invented by the firm's founder King C. Gillette. Building on this early innovation, the company remained a leader in shaving technology. It introduced the first razor specifically designed for women (1916), the first with stainless steel blades (1963), and the first double-blade razor (1971). While the firm grew to be the number 1 global maker of shaving supplies, it nevertheless remained far smaller than its suitor. The firm's 2004 sales were just over $10 billion, with more than half this total coming from its own set of five $1 billion brands—Oral B, Mach 3, Braun, Gillette, and Duracell.

In considering the synergies between the two firms, it is instructive to focus on both the firms' products and their customers. As noted above, P&G is credited with having invented modern brand management, a set of practices used to maintain the quality and price premium of branded products over non-branded competitors. While there are no obvious technological synergies between the manufacture of P&G's Tide detergent and Gillette's Mach 3 razor, these products do share the characteristic of being widely known consumer brands. If P&G holds a unique expertise in managing branded products (as some observers believe it does), then the acquisition of Gillette will allow P&G to apply its expertise to a broader group of products, and thus increase profits.

The two firms also have many common customers. Large retailers, such as Wal-Mart and Target, comprise a large and growing share of sales for consumer packaged goods firms. In 2004, more than 18% of P&G's global sales were to Wal-Mart. To manage this important relationship, P&G assigns 250 employees to its dedicated "Wal-Mart team" and stations them in Arkansas near Wal-Mart headquarters. Gillette allocated significant resources to managing its Wal-Mart relationship as well, and the newly combined firm would likely be able to economize on such costs. Indeed, the combined firm expects to lay off around 6000 employees—about 4 percent of the total company workforce—and realize cost savings of about $1 billion yearly.

Some observers, however, wondered whether the deal was instead intended to increase the combined firm's market power. P&G and Gillette did compete head-to-head in a number of markets. P&G's Old Spice and Gillette's Right Guard men's deodorants, for example, were direct competitors. The merger therefore presented the possibility of reduced price competition, at least in some markets. This could lead to higher profits for the merging firms, but at consumer expense. Another power-based explanation for the deal hinges on the growing importance of large buyers like Wal-Mart. If scale allows the large retailers to demand price reductions from smaller manufacturers, then one logical response of manufacturers is to increase their own scale. If P&G's broader product line allows it to extract higher prices from Wal-Mart (by, for example, threatening to restrict access to popular brands such as Tide unless Wal-Mart offers a higher unit price on Mach 3 razors), then the deal could again lead to higher profits for P&G, but with no gains for consumers.

Antitrust regulators, in both the United States and the European Union, followed the merger closely. The European Commmission approved the deal in July 2005 but only after requiring the firm to sell some brands in the battery-powered toothbrush market. In the United States, approval by the Federal Trade Commision hinged on divestitures of teeth-whitening products and men's deodorants.

As seems to be the case in most mergers, shareholders of the target firm gained most from the deal. On the day the merger was announced, Gillette stock rose more than 12 percent, while P&G's shares fell 2 percent. The newly combined firm faces a number of challenges. While there may indeed be synergistic gains to be had from this deal, the newly combined firm will likely need to reorganize to achieve these gains. P&G managers are unaccustomed to thinking about how their decisions affect Gillette-owned brands. In order to realize the full synergies available in the deal, the firm must find some way of motivating these managers to consider such cross-brand effects. Doing this may involve changing the way performance is measured and evaluated inside the firm. Another challenge will be to integrate long-time Gillette employees into the conservative P&G corporate culture. Such organizational issues often limit the success of synergistic mergers.

the student population. Given the absence of transaction costs for paraprofessional schools, it is not surprising that many of them are freestanding.

Internal Capital Markets

Combining unrelated businesses may also allow a firm to make use of an internal capital market. Consider the combination of a cash-rich business and a cash-constrained business to create a single firm. Through cross-subsidization, the proceeds from the cash-rich business can be used to fund profitable investment opportunities in the cash-constrained business. This strategy can increase overall value, but only if it allows the cash-constrained business to make profitable investments *that would not otherwise be made*. Given the sophistication of modern financial markets, it is worthwhile to ask what frictions might affect such markets. Is it reasonable to expect that firms would be unable to finance profitable projects from external sources?

As Jeremy Stein recounts, the answer to this question may well be yes.[11] It might be costly for firms to raise capital from external sources. First, transactions in financial markets may suffer from incomplete information. Firms have a clear incentive to issue new equity when their shares are overvalued and to issue new debt when the terms of the loan are especially attractive given the risks associated with new investment. Given this informational disadvantage, providers of capital will be reluctant to purchase equity or to lend. Second, firms with existing debt may have difficulty obtaining new loans, especially if the new debt is junior to the existing debt. Any proceeds from new investment must go, in part, to existing bondholders, and this limits the amount that new lenders are willing to provide. Third, external finance consumes monitoring resources, for bond and equity holders must ensure that managers take actions that serve their interests.

If external finance is costly, there may indeed be profitable projects that cannot be funded by external sources. Note that unlike the two preceding explanations for diversification, this rationale does not require that the two businesses be related in any way. There need not be shared production technology, customer groups, or organizational resources. In fact, the only requirement is that one business has cash in excess of its investment opportunities while the other has investment opportunities in excess of its available cash. Hence, the logic of internal capital markets may provide the best efficiency-based explanation for observed diversification in completely unrelated activities.

Diversifying Shareholders' Portfolios

This rationale for diversification begins with the observation that individual shareholders benefit from investing in a diversified portfolio. By purchasing small holdings in a broad range of firms, investors can reduce the chance of incurring a large loss due to the failure of any single firm and thus insulate themselves from risk. A broadly diversified firm may receive only a small percentage of its revenues from any one line of business. Hence, a shareholder seeking to avoid large swings in value can invest in a single diversified firm and achieve the benefits of portfolio diversification.

Note, however, that most shareholders can diversify their own personal portfolios and seldom need corporate managers to do so on their behalf. For example, shareholders of Philip Morris could easily have purchased shares of Kraft Foods and did not need Philip Morris to acquire Kraft in order to diversify in this way. Indeed, many shareholders may have preferred *not* to be diversified in this particular way, which implies that the acquisition of Kraft may have made them worse off (in the absence of other efficiency gains from the purchase).

One might argue that a corporation may be able to diversify more extensively or more inexpensively than shareholders themselves can. This is questionable, however, especially given the ready availability of mutual funds to today's individual investors. Hence, this rationale for diversification is sensible only if investors are, for some reason, unable to diversify their portfolios on their own. This may occur if investors with large ownership blocks in a firm are unable to fully diversify their holdings themselves.[12]

Identifying Undervalued Firms

Finally, a firm's shareholders may benefit from diversification if its managers are able to identify other firms that are undervalued by the stock market. Suppose, for example, that firm B's stock is currently trading at $80 per share, but the manager of firm A determines that firm B is actually worth $100 per share. If firm A can purchase firm B for $80 per share, firm A will profit by $20 for each share of firm B purchased, even if no gains in efficiency are realized through the merger.

One can be somewhat skeptical of this justification for corporate diversification, especially when the business of the acquired firm is unrelated to that of the acquiring firm. First, this argument requires that the market valuation of the target firm (that is, the firm being purchased) is incorrect *and* that no other investors have yet identified this fact. Given that speculators, fund managers, and other investors are constantly scouring the market in search of undervalued stocks, it seems hard to believe that a CEO whose attention is largely consumed by running his or her own firm could easily identify valuation errors that these other market participants have missed, unless the target firm is in a closely related business.

Second, announcements of merger proposals attract attention, frequently leading other potential acquirers to bid for the target firm. Bidding wars are not uncommon, and they serve to reduce the profits an acquiring firm can hope to earn through a merger. Consider Verizon's February 2005 offer to purchase MCI for $6.75 billion. A rival telecom firm, Qwest, quickly entered the bidding with an even higher offer. After a protracted struggle, with offers and counter-offers going back and forth several times, Verizon purchased MCI for $8.5 billion. It is possible that MCI was a bargain at $6.75 billion, but the $1.75 billion premium Verizon paid may have significantly cut into its profit from the deal.

Third, and perhaps most troubling, is the observation that successful bidders in auctions and similar sales arrangements tend to suffer from the "winner's curse." Consider a group of acquiring firms bidding for a target. Each bidder may have an estimate of the value of the target, and each will drop out of the bidding as the price surpasses that estimate. The firm with the most optimistic assessment of the target's value will win the bidding. Has the winner paid a price low enough so that it can earn a profit from the purchase? Given that all other bidders' estimates of the target's value are below the final purchase price, it is likely that the winner has overpaid. As Max Bazerman and William Samuelson point out in their article "I Won the Auction but Don't Want the Prize," unless the diversifying firm knows much more about the target than other bidders do, it will probably pay too much to "win" the bidding.[13]

Potential Costs of Diversification

Expanding the scope of the firm may be costly for shareholders. First, combining two businesses in a single firm is likely to result in substantial influence costs. In a diversified firm, corporate management evaluates each division to determine where to allocate resources. This evaluation is generally performed during the firm's strategic planning and capital budgeting processes. The success of these processes depends on the quality of information received from division heads and the ability of corporate management to evaluate information objectively rather than let personal feelings affect decisions. To the extent that these decisions are affected by internal lobbying, resource allocations may be inefficient.

Margaret Meyer, Paul Milgrom, and John Roberts argue that influence costs may explain why some firms elect to sell unprofitable divisions, either by conducting an initial public offering (IPO) or by issuing shares in the division to its existing shareholders.[14] Meyer, Milgrom, and Roberts point out that if a struggling division is contained within a larger firm, managers of that division may lobby for resources that are best spent on growing divisions. This results in both direct costs of lobbying and the potential for misallocation of resources. Overall value, they argue, may be highest if the unprofitable division is a separate entity, competing for resources through market means.

Second, corporate management of diversified firms must use costly control systems that reward division managers on the basis of division profits and that discipline managers by tying their pay and promotions to business unit objectives. This assumes, of course, that corporate management has the proper incentives to work on behalf of shareholders. Capital markets also provide incentives for managers to act in the interests of shareholders (e.g., to reward superior returns and penalize inferior returns). They do this without the need for costly internal control systems.

Third, recent evidence suggests that internal capital markets may not work very well in practice. Because oil operations generate a lot of cash, Owen Lamont suspected that oil firms with nonoil subsidiaries may be engaging in cross-subsidization.[15] To examine the efficacy of this practice, he studied how investment in the nonoil subsidiaries changed when the price of oil fell dramatically in the mid-1980s.

Assuming that (1) managers are investing only in profitable projects all the time and (2) the number of profitable projects in the nonoil subsidiaries is not affected by the price of oil, investment by oil firms in the nonoil subsidiaries should be completely unaffected by the drop in the price of oil. After carefully removing those subsidiaries where one might think investment would be affected by oil prices, Lamont found that investment in nonoil subsidiaries fell sharply after the drop in oil prices. This means one of two things: either the oil companies were investing *too much* in their nonoil subsidiaries before the drop in oil prices, or they were investing *too little* after the drop in prices. Lamont was unable to determine which of these two possibilities obtains. However, his evidence suggests that the internal capital market is not serving its intended purpose of facilitating investment in profitable projects in cash-poor businesses.

Why might this have happened? If, as we discuss in the next section, managers have a strong preference for corporate growth even if such growth is unprofitable, they may overinvest (that is, invest in all profitable projects and some unprofitable ones) when the firm has a lot of cash. This could explain possible overinvestment in nonoil subsidiaries prior to the drop in oil prices. Alternatively, underinvestment in nonoil subsidiaries may be a response to increased influence activity on the part of oil subsidiary managers after the drop in oil prices. In order to limit the incentives for these executives to lobby for investment in their parts of the firm, top managers may elect to engage in a form of investment socialism, simply making across-the-board cuts in investment.

MANAGERIAL REASONS FOR DIVERSIFICATION ◆ ◆ ◆ ◆ ◆

We have discussed how corporate diversification might generate benefits and costs that are felt by a firm's owners. If shareholders were making decisions regarding corporate diversification, we could conclude our discussion here. We could assert that economic theory suggests firms should diversify when the benefits to shareholders exceed the costs, and then we could examine empirical evidence on this point.

As Adolph Berle and Gardiner Means pointed out in 1932, however, a key feature of large corporations in modern economies is the separation of ownership and control.[16] That is, the owners of large firms are rarely (if ever) involved in making decisions that affect the firm's profits. Such decisions are delegated to managers. Although managers may own some shares in their firms, they typically do not bear the full wealth consequences associated with their actions. As such, managers' preferences regarding corporate actions may conflict with those of shareholders. Hence, it is important to consider how diversification might affect a firm's managers and whether managers may undertake diversifying acquisitions that do not generate net benefits for the firm's shareholders. Here, we describe how managers may benefit from undertaking acquisitions, why problems with corporate governance may make it difficult for shareholders to stop such activity, and what mechanisms constrain managers to act in the interests of shareholders.

Benefits to Managers from Acquisitions

We identify three potential reasons why a firm's managers may benefit from undertaking acquisitions, even if shareholders do not. First, as Michael Jensen argues, managers may simply enjoy running larger firms:

> Corporate growth enhances the social prominence, public prestige, and political power of senior executives. Rare is the CEO who wants to be remembered as presiding over an enterprise that makes fewer products in fewer plants in fewer countries than when he or she took office.[17]

One might wonder whether this is a bad thing; after all, don't shareholders want their firms to grow and prosper? Of course they do, but it is important to realize that growth can be either profitable or unprofitable. Shareholders want their firms to grow only if such growth leads to increases in profits. Jensen's claim is that managers value growth whether or not it is profitable.

To see how a preference for growth may lead a manager to undertake acquisitions that are not in shareholders' interests, consider a CEO who values growth for its own sake and is engaged in a negotiation over a potential acquisition. Assume that the CEO believes the target firm to be worth $1 billion. If the CEO agrees to pay $1.1 billion for the target, is the CEO made better or worse off? The fact that the CEO overpays for the acquisition makes shareholders worse off by $100 million. However, the CEO may own only a small fraction of the firm's shares. If the CEO owns 1 percent of the firm's shares, the transaction will cause the value of his or her personal holdings to fall by $1 million. If, however, the CEO receives great personal value (more than $1 million) from the prospect of running a larger firm, he or she may be willing to undertake this acquisition even though it does not benefit shareholders. The key point here is that if CEOs hold small equity stakes in their firms, the personal benefits to CEOs of undertaking bad acquisitions (arising from prominence or prestige) may outweigh the personal costs (stemming from the lost value of the CEO's shareholdings).

Although it is difficult to devise precise measures of such abstract notions as social prominence and public prestige, researchers have identified some ways in which CEOs who undertake acquisitions appear to benefit. Chris Avery, Judy Chevalier, and Scott Schaefer, for example, found that CEOs who undertake acquisitions are more likely to be appointed to *other firms'* boards of directors.[18] If CEOs value such appointments, they may wish to pursue acquisitions in order to secure them.

Second, others have argued that managers may pursue unrelated acquisitions in order to increase their compensation. Robert Reich wrote:

> When professional managers plunge their companies deeply into debt in order to acquire totally unrelated businesses, they are apt to be motivated by the fact that their personal salaries and bonuses are tied to the volume of business their newly enlarged enterprise will generate.[19]

Evidence on this point is mixed. The fact that executives of larger firms earn higher compensation does not by itself imply that a given executive can increase the size of his or her paycheck simply by increasing the size of the firm.[20] Avery and colleagues could find no difference in growth of pay between CEOs who undertook acquisitions and those whose firms grew organically. In contrast, Richard T. Bliss and Richard J. Rosen found that CEOs of banks that undertook acquisitions did receive large increases in compensation.[21]

Third, Yakov Amihud and Baruch Lev suggest that managers may pursue unrelated acquisitions in order to shield themselves against risk.[22] They observe that shareholders are unlikely to replace top management unless the firm performs poorly relative to the overall economy. To reduce the risk of losing their jobs, managers must reduce the risk of poor performance. One way to do so is through unrelated acquisitions. Simple statistics tell us that the performance of a highly diversified firm is likely to mirror that of the overall economy and therefore is less likely to lead shareholders to fire management. To support their point, Amihud and Lev show that manager-controlled firms engage in more conglomerate acquisitions than owner-controlled firms. Although these acquisitions reduce the risk of job loss for top management, they may not benefit shareholders, who may easily reduce their own financial risk by managing their portfolio of investments (e.g., by purchasing mutual funds).

AOL's acquisition of Time Warner in 2000 may have been motivated by then-CEO Steve Case's desire to shield himself against risk. As an owner of nearly 1 percent of AOL's shares—a stake worth more than $1 billion at the time—Case was subject to considerable AOL-specific risk. By purchasing Time Warner, he spread his holdings over an Internet business and a broadcast and print media business, reducing his exposure to the ups and downs of the technology sector.[23] While Case and his Time Warner counterpart Gerald Levin emphasized the many synergies that would result from the combination of television and Internet channels, the first several years of the combination produced little more than numerous cross-promotional efforts. AOL, for example, broadcast previews of Time Warner's film *The Lord of the Rings* to subscribers, while Time Warner offered trips to see the film's premiere to AOL subscribers who upgraded to a new version of the software.[24] Even if such cross-promotional efforts do create value, it is clearly not necessary for the firms to merge in order to undertake them.

Problems of Corporate Governance

All these managerial motives for diversification rely on the existence of some failure of *corporate governance*—that is, the mechanisms through which corporations and their managers are controlled by shareholders. If shareholders could (1) determine which acquisitions will lead to increased profits and which ones will not and (2) direct management to undertake only those that will increase shareholder value, the possibility of managerially driven acquisitions would disappear.

In practice, however, neither condition (1) nor condition (2) is likely to hold. First, it is unlikely that shareholders can easily determine which acquisitions will increase profits and which ones will not. Typically, shareholders have neither the expertise nor the information to make such determinations. Second, even if shareholders do disagree with management's decisions, they may find it difficult to change those decisions. Formally, boards of directors are charged with the responsibility of monitoring management to ensure that actions are taken to increase shareholder value. However, many authors, including Benjamin Hermalin and Michael Weisbach, have suggested that CEOs may exercise considerable control over the selection of new directors.[25] A CEO who packs the board with supporters may have little reason to fear that his or her decisions will be subject to close scrutiny. Although shareholders do hold formal control over the board through their power to elect directors, it is quite rare for incumbent directors to be voted out of office. Moreover, most shareholders in

EXAMPLE 5.3 THE RISE AND FALL OF AN INDUSTRIAL CONGLOMERATE: THE STRANGE CASE OF TYCO INTERNATIONAL

One of the most spectacular business rise-and-fall tales of recent years is that of Tyco International, an industrial conglomerate. Founded in 1960 as a government-funded research laboratory, Tyco showed a taste for acquisitions almost from the beginning. The firm went public in 1964 and had completed 16 acquisitions by 1968. The firm grew rapidly between 1982 and 1992 under CEO John Fort, who perfected the firm's growth-by-acquisition strategy.

Dennis Kozlowski, the son of a Newark, New Jersey, police detective, was appointed to the CEO job in mid-1992. Kozlowski pursued Fort's acquisition methods with unheard-of zeal. He employed an in-house team of M&A specialists, who scoured the business world for potential targets. Tyco looked for solid firms with strong management teams, and deals had to be friendly and have an immediate positive impact on Tyco's earnings. The firm completed literally hundreds of acquisitions in the 1990s under Kozlowski, and the firm's market value grew more than fiftyfold between 1992 and 2001. By mid-2001, the firm was worth more than General Motors and Ford Motor Company combined. The firm's six divisions—Electronics, Health Care, Fire and Security Systems, Tycom Telecom, CIT Financial Group, and Flow Control—operated independently, with top management taking a very hands-off approach and using high-powered incentives tied to earnings growth to motivate the divisional managers.

The zenith of the firm's success under Kozlowski was a May 28, 2001 *Business Week* cover story that proclaimed him "The Most Aggressive CEO" and lauded his growth-by-acquisition strategy. Despite the firm's success, some observers continued to question the logic of Tyco's strategy. While it was clear that acquisitions within each of the firm's six industry groups were directed at exploiting economies of scale and scope, it was unclear what the sources of across-business-unit value creation

were. How does Tyco's Flow Control Division, which makes fire sprinkler systems for commercial buildings, benefit by being under the same corporate umbrella as Tyco's Health Care Division? To put this question succinctly, why is this one firm instead of six?

As if to prove the old maxim that "the bigger they are, the harder they fall," Kozlowski's 2002 fall was very hard indeed. In June of that year, he was indicted by the state of New York for sales tax evasion. Kozlowski was fired from Tyco just before this news broke, but things got even worse for "The Most Aggressive CEO" in September of that year. Kozlowski and former Tyco CFO Mark Swartz were named in both a state fraud indictment and a civil lawsuit by the SEC. The pair was accused of essentially looting $600 million from the firm while the board of directors looked the other way. According to prosecutors, Kozlowski and Swartz funded their lavish lifestyles out of the firm's coffers and hid these expenses from shareholders and most directors by using secret bonuses and forgivable loans. Kozlowski famously billed the firm $1 million for his wife's fortieth birthday party, which was held on the Italian island of Sardinia and featured toga-clad gladiators, risqué ice sculptures, and a live performance by pop musician Jimmy Buffett. In 2005, Kozlowski and Swartz were convicted on the fraud charges and were each sentenced to 8 1/2 to 25 years in state prison.

Given the deception and accounting sleight-of-hand that obviously contributed to the firm's purported success, one might have expected Tyco to be split apart after Kozlowski's firing. If the firm's complexity was in place only to facilitate management's thievery, then presumably a simpler structure would be appropriate post-Kozlowski. New CEO Ed Breen, a veteran manager who had previously been president of Motorola, did fire the firm's entire board of directors and all of Kozlowski's

50 top managers He sold some assets, notably the CIT Financial Group and the Tyco Global Network of undersea cables. However, even with these divestitures the firm remains very much an industrial conglomerate. As of October 2005, the firm still operated five divisions—Electronics, Fire and Security, Healthcare, Plastics & Adhesives, and Engineered Products and Services—and still employed a hands-off management style. And despite the sharp drop in the firm's share prices in early 2002 as news of Kozlowski's misdeeds spread, Tyco stock still beat the S&P 500 over the 10 years preceding September 30, 2005. The question of whether, and if so why, Tyco

is better off as one firm instead of five is very much an open one.

One potential answer is suggested by the discussion of internal capital markets in this chapter. If Tyco's strategy is to purchase small industrial concerns that lack access to capital, then Tyco's strong balance sheet may allow it to make positive NPV investments that might not otherwise be made. Target firms may therefore be worth more under Tyco's ownership than they would as standalone entites. Without detailed access to the firm's business-unit by business unit investment figures, it is difficult to say for certain whether Tyco is pursuing such a cross-subsidization strategy.

large corporations own a very small fraction of the firm's shares. Thus, if any one shareholder were to invest considerable time and energy in monitoring management, that shareholder would receive at most a small fraction of the resulting benefits.

There is ample evidence that diversifying acquisitions are driven, at least in part, by managerial motives facilitated by problems of corporate governance. As we discuss shortly, a large number of studies have found that the share prices of firms making acquisitions tend to fall when the acquisition is announced. If acquisitions benefit shareholders of the acquiring firm, one would expect the reverse.

The Market for Corporate Control and Recent Changes in Corporate Governance

If diversification is driven in part by managerial objectives, what forces work to keep managers focused on the goals of owners? Henry Manne suggests that the "market for corporate control" serves as an important constraint on the actions of managers.[26]

Manne's argument is as follows. Managers who undertake acquisitions that do not serve the interests of shareholders will find that their firms' share prices fall, for two reasons. First, if a manager overpays for a diversifying acquisition, the value of his or her firm will fall by the amount of the overpayment. Second, if the stock market expects the firm to overpay for additional acquisitions in the future, the market price of the firm's shares will fall today in expectation of these events. This disparity between the firm's *actual* and *potential* share prices presents an opportunity for another entity (either an individual, another firm, or a specialist investment bank) to try a takeover. A potential acquirer can purchase control of the firm simply by buying its shares on the market. With a sufficiently large block of shares, the acquirer can vote in its own slate of directors and appoint managers who will work to enhance shareholder value. The acquirer profits by purchasing shares at their actual value and then imposing changes that return the shares to their potential value. Note that the market for corporate control can serve to discipline managers even *without* takeovers actually occurring. If an incumbent manager is concerned that he or she may lose his or her job if the firm is taken over, he or she may work to prevent a takeover by keeping the firm's share price at or near its potential value.

Michael Jensen argues that Manne's reasoning underlies the wave of leveraged buyout (LBO) transactions observed in the 1980s. Jensen claims that firms in many U.S. industries had free cash flow—that is, cash flow in excess of profitable investment opportunities—during this period. Managers elected to invest this free cash flow to expand the size of the business empires they controlled, both by undertaking unprofitable acquisitions and by overexpanding core businesses. Given that these investments were unprofitable, Jensen reasons that shareholders would have been better served had the free cash flow been paid out to them in the form of dividends. In an LBO, a corporate raider borrows against the firm's future free cash flow and uses these borrowings to purchase the firm's equity. Such a transaction helps the firm realize its potential value in two ways. First, since the number of shares outstanding is greatly reduced, it is possible to give the firm's management a large fraction of its equity. This improves incentives for management to take actions that increase shareholder value. Second, since the debt must be repaid using the firm's future free cash flow, management no longer has discretion over how to invest these funds. Management must pay these funds out to bondholders or risk default. This limits managers' ability to undertake future acquisitions and expand core businesses.

Critics of the LBO merger wave have raised questions about the effects of such transactions on parties *other* than shareholders, such as employees, suppliers, and bondholders. Andrei Shleifer and Lawrence Summers, for example, speculate about the effects of LBOs on long-run economic efficiency.[27] They argue that redistribution of wealth may adversely affect economic efficiency when the acquired wealth is in the form of quasi-rents extracted from stakeholders who have made relationship-specific investments in the target firm. Recall from Chapter 3 that after making a relationship-specific investment, an individual expects to receive quasi-rents that exceed the amount of the investment. These may take the form of wages in excess of what the worker could earn elsewhere, opportunities for promotion, or perquisites such as a company car. Once the investments have been made, however, the person will proceed with the deal if quasi-rents are positive. Firms facilitate relationship-specific investments. A relative benefit of firms over markets is the ability of workers and managers to rely on implicit versus explicit contracts in settling disputes within the firm. Indeed, it is precisely the inability to forge sufficiently complete contracts that makes firms necessary in the first place.

As an example, suppose that a firm's long-term employees develop assets that are valuable chiefly to their firm, such as knowledge of how to operate the firm's specialized equipment or how best to use the firm's administrative procedures. These resources are not readily saleable in the job market because other firms have their own specialized equipment and practices. A new owner could break long-standing assurances of job security and reduce wages significantly before the employee would find it worthwhile to look for a new job. Although takeovers motivated by redistribution may benefit an acquirer in the short term, they may have long-term adverse consequences for firms. In the short term, the raider gains from redistribution. In the long term, employees, as well as other parties who do business with the firm, will be aware of the firm's past behavior and are unlikely to invest in firm-specific assets in the future unless they are adequately compensated for their risk of future redistribution. Shleifer and Summers point out that the damage of LBO transactions need not be limited to the firms undergoing LBOs; if employees of any firm suspect that their firm may eventually be an LBO target, they may become more reluctant to make relationship-specific investments. This could damage long-run growth rates throughout the economy.

Researchers have found that, although there was some redistribution of wealth surrounding LBO transactions, gains in efficiency were substantial as well. Steven Kaplan and Jeremy Stein show that significant gains in operating performance were associated with LBOs.[28] During the early 1980s, LBO firms made substantial profits and were unlikely to default on their debt. Although defaults became more common in later years, these were due not to a lack of efficiency improvements but to high debt burdens brought about by the competition among LBO acquirers. According to Kaplan and Bengt Holmstrom, "the reason for the defaults was not that profits didn't improve, but that they didn't improve by enough to pay off the enormous quantities of debt."[29] Even for those firms that defaulted, the net effect of the transaction was beneficial. Other authors asked specifically whether raiders targeted firms that had previously made diversifying acquisitions. In a paper titled "Do Bad Bidders Make Good Targets?" Mark Mitchell and Kenneth Lehn found that corporate raiders profited by acquiring and splitting up firms that had previously pursued unprofitable diversification strategies.[30]

The LBO merger wave ended rather abruptly around 1990. Holmstrom and Kaplan attribute this to changes in corporate governance practices since the mid-1980s. They point out that firms increased CEO ownership stakes (dramatically, in many cases) and introduced new performance measures that forced an accounting for the cost of capital (such as Economic Value Added). In addition, large shareholders such as pension funds began to take a more active role in monitoring managers. Given Shleifer and Summers's arguments, researchers have concluded that the market for corporate control postulated by Manne is a fairly costly way of motivating managers to work for shareholders' interests. These recent changes in corporate governance practices may serve to constrain managers' actions without incurring the possibility of efficiency-reducing redistributions in wealth or costly defaults on debt. If these changes in governance are intended to limit unrelated diversification, they appear to be working—the merger wave of the 1990s included few cases of diversification into unrelated activities.

PERFORMANCE OF DIVERSIFIED FIRMS

Although we have discussed why diversification may be profitable, many academics and practitioners remain skeptical of the ability of diversification strategies to add value. Perhaps Michael Goold and Kathleen Luchs, in their review of 40 years of diversification, best sum up the skeptic's viewpoint:

> Ultimately, diversity can only be worthwhile if corporate management adds value in some way and the test of a corporate strategy must be that the businesses in the portfolio are worth more than they would be under any other ownership.[31]

Studies of the performance of diversified firms, undertaken from a variety of disciplines and using different research methods, have consistently found that although diversification can create value up to a point, the sources of performance gains for diversified firms are unclear. It can also be difficult to realize efficiencies from diversification. Extensive diversification into unrelated areas is often associated with poorer performance.

In this section we review some of the findings that led Goold and Luchs and others to question the value of diversification. The general picture that emerges from this body of research is unfavorable to diversification (especially unrelated diversification) as a means of creating value.

Studies of Operating Performance

Many researchers have studied how diversified firms compare to undiversified firms in terms of operating performance, as measured by accounting profits or productivity. They have found the relationship between performance and corporate diversity to be unclear. Profits were more likely to be determined by industry profitability, coupled with how the firm related new businesses to old ones, rather than by diversification per se.[32] These results have persisted despite methodological differences associated with the measurement of diversification and performance, as well as the time frame used to assess changes in performance.

Some examples of these studies may be helpful. Richard Rumelt found several systematic relationships between diversification and firm performance. Moderately diversified firms had higher capital productivity. Firms with moderate to high levels of unrelated diversification, however, had moderate or poor productivity. Cynthia Montgomery reconfirmed Rumelt's results for more recent years, using different measures of diversification.[33] Noel Capon and his colleagues found that firms that restricted their diversification to narrow markets performed better than did broader firms, presumably because of their learning particular market demands.[34] Leslie Palich, Laura Cardinal, and Chet Miller confirmed this finding in their synthesis of 55 studies over the past 30 years.[35] They concluded that firms pursuing related diversification outperformed those choosing either narrower or broader strategies. Finally, Antoinette Schoar collected detailed information on plant-level productivity and found that diversification led to a destructive "new toy" effect.[36] After an acquisition, newly acquired plants saw an average productivity increase of 3 percent. This improvement, however, occurred at the expense of the firm's other plants. Incumbent plants' productivity fell by 2 percent on average, and since there are typically far more incumbent plants than new ones, this decline implies an overall reduction in efficiency.

Valuation and Event Studies

Two streams of research rely on evidence from firms' stock prices to assess the success of diversification. Research of the first type—known as *valuation studies*—compares market valuations of diversified firms to those of undiversified firms. The second type—*event studies*—looks at the changes in market valuations in response to the announcement of diversifying acquisitions.

Valuation studies consistently show that the shares of diversified firms trade at a discount relative to those of their undiversified counterparts. Typically, these studies proceed by comparing the relationships between market value and assets (or sales) at diversified and undiversified firms. Consider a conglomerate that receives half its earnings from selling automobiles and half from selling televisions. By examining the share price and the book value of assets of an undiversified automobile firm, researchers can estimate what "price" the market places on one dollar of an automobile firm's assets. An undiversified television firm can provide an estimate of the price of each dollar of television-producing assets. These figures can be used to predict the value of each half of the conglomerate. This predicted value can then be compared to the conglomerate's actual market value. Two pathbreaking studies in this area, one by Larry Lang and Rene Stulz and the other by Philip Berger and Eli Ofek, both found that the share prices of diversified firms are depressed relative to those of their undiversified counterparts.[37] The magnitude of this effect is large: diversified firms' share prices appear to be lower by as much as 15 percent.

The weight of evidence clearly indicates that the so-called diversification discount is present, but it is less clear *why* it is present. Is it because combining two unrelated businesses reduces value in some way? Or is it because the unrelated businesses that *elect to combine* tend to be those that had low market values even before the combination? Some recent evidence suggests that at least part of the diversification discount can be explained by this latter effect; that is, firms that elect to combine appear to be those whose shares traded at discounts even before the combination. John Graham, Michael Lemmon, and Jack Wolf found that the shares of many targets of diversifying acquisitions traded at a discount before those firms were acquired.[38] Similarly, Jose Campa and Simi Kedia found that acquirers' shares trade at a discount before those firms undertake unrelated diversification.[39] In contrast, subsequent work by Berger and Ofek showed that diversified firms with shares trading at the largest discounts were more likely to be taken over.[40] This finding is consistent with the assertion that diversification does destroy value and that the market for corporate control works to counteract it.

Another group of studies has considered the reaction of the stock market to the announcement of diversifying events. Event studies presume that stock markets are efficient at assimilating new information about firms into share prices. Under this assumption, the market value of a firm at any point in time is the best estimate of that firm's future stream of profits. The change in the value of a firm's shares in response to any event is therefore indicative of how stock market participants believe the event will affect the firm's future profits.

Two key findings emerge from the event study literature on diversifying acquisitions. First, as noted earlier, returns to acquirers are negative, on average. This is strong evidence that shareholders of firms that undertake diversifying acquisitions do not benefit from those acquisitions. This finding has been made repeatedly by a large number of researchers over a broad range of time periods. Randall Morck, Andrei Shleifer, and Robert Vishny, for example, found that the returns to bidding shareholders are lower when their firm diversifies and when the firm's managers performed poorly before the acquisition.[41] Wilbur Lewellen, Claudio Loderer, and Ahron Rosenfeld found that these negative effects on the value of the acquiring firm are more pronounced when the CEO holds a smaller share of the firm's equity.[42]

Second, shares of target firms tend to rise when an acquisition is announced. Acquirers typically must pay more than the preacquisition market value of the target, which suggests a transfer of value from the shareholders of the acquiring firm to the shareholders of the target. Of particular interest, however, is the finding that, on average, the increase in the market value of the target is greater than the reduction in the market value of the acquirer.[43] This pair of findings is perhaps most consistent with the assertion that diversifying acquisitions do create value in some way, but that either overconfidence or the winner's curse causes acquiring firms' managers to pay too much.[44]

Building on these main findings, other event studies seek to identify how different types of diversification might lead to different allocations of wealth between acquirers and targets. Harbir Singh and Cynthia Montgomery found that acquirers had greater returns when they targeted related firms than they did from unrelated acquisitions.[45] Indeed, the gains to unrelated acquirers appeared to be completely bid away during the auction for the target. Anju Seth studied the abnormal stock price returns for 102 deals between 1962 and 1979 to discover whether there were synergistic gains from acquisitions and whether returns differed between related and unrelated acquisitions. She found that mergers produce synergistic gains but that one could not clearly associate gains with mergers.[46] Lois Shelton obtained similar results, using a

EXAMPLE 5.4 THE SEARCH FOR SYNERGY IN NEW MARKETS: EBAY'S ACQUISITION BINGE

The experience of eBay, the world leader in on-line auctions, illustrates the difficulty of identifying potential synergistic merger targets when the technologicial and market environment is changing rapidly. As we shall discuss in Chapter 12, the on-line auction market features strong network externalities. Buyers prefer to log on to the site that has the most sellers, and vice versa. Founded in 1995, the firm quickly grew to dominate this form of internet commerce, beating out other firms (such as Yahoo!) that had been early rivals. eBay went public in 1998 and was one of the few Internet firms to develop a reliable business model in time to survive the dot-com shakeout in 2000 and 2001. eBay's market position was so strong, in fact, that it was able not only to survive, but also to undertake a series of acquisitions. Although some of eBay's deals have succeeded, others have not.

One of eBay's first major acquisitions was that of Billpoint, an on-line credit card payment service, in May 1999. By allowing individuals to use their credit cards to pay for merchandise purchased on-line, such services reduce the cost to consumers of buying and selling on the net and thus increase demand for eBay's auction services. Common ownership of the auction site and payment service could presumably reduce transaction costs by limiting the parties' incentive to hold each other up. Despite partnering Billpoint with powerhouse financial institutions like Wells Fargo and Visa, eBay was never able to make its $86 million investment pay off. eBay was slow to integrate Billpoint onto its auction site, with beta tests delayed until the fourth quarter of 1999. This lag allowed an upstart on-line payment service, PayPal, to gain market acceptance. eBay traders with good experiences using PayPal saw no reason to switch to Billpoint, and as a result eBay's in-house service never took off. PayPal grew rapidly, however, and was eventually purchased by eBay in 2002 for $1.5 billion. eBay shuttered Billpoint shortly thereafter. In 1999,

eBay also purchased Butterfield and Butterfield, a global appraisal and auction house, for $260 million. Butterfield and Butterfield specialized in the authentication, appraisal, and marketing of high-end items such as jewelry, art, and furniture. Here, it seems eBay was exploring the possibility of synergies between on-line auctions and traditional, off-line auctions for such collectibles. It appears, however, that serious art collectors were unwilling to purchase big-ticket items online, and the combination soured as a result. eBay sold Butterfield to rival off-line auctioneer Bonhams in 2002, reportedly at a large discount relative to the original purchase price.

On the plus side, eBay's purchases of non-U.S.-based Internet auctioneers have worked out reasonably well. The firm has made a number of such investments over the years, including the purchase of South Korea's Internet Auction Company and Latin America's Mercado Libre in 2001, and India-based Baazee.com in 2004. Such deals leverage the network externalities underlying eBay's business model. If buyers in one country value access to sellers in another, then eBay's acquisition strategy facilitates this cross-border trade and increases the value of the firm's services in both countries. The transactions may also allow eBay to realize scale economies in the development of the latest Internet-auction software.

In September 2005, eBay announced its largest deal to date. The firm agreed to buy Skype, a British Internet telephone firm, in a transaction valued between $2.6 and 4.1 billion. Many analysts immediately questioned the rationale for this combination. How, some asked, are Internet auctions and Internet telephony related? A press release posted on the eBay's Investor Relations web site suggests that the deal is attractive because Skype is a great standalone business and because Skype/eBay integration can facilitate buyer/seller commmunication regarding items up for bid on eBay. Furthermore, eBay can use its market penetration to sign up new Skype users. Skeptical analysts suggested that while Skype was growing rapidly, $4.1 billion seemed like a hefty price tag. Others wondered why common ownership was needed to achieve the cross-fertilization aims. Couldn't eBay sign up new Skype users and receive, say, a fixed fee per transaction from Skype? Why does common ownership improve on such a contract in this case?

Reviewing eBay's acquisition history, it seems that the firm is engaged in a constant search for synergies but is uncertain about which activities will best complement its existing businesses. This difficulty in understanding how activities can fit together to exploit new technologies and new markets is by no means unique to the Internet age. eBay's experience is not unlike that of another still-prominent firm that grew by capitalizing on new technologies—the Ford Motor Company. After Henry Ford's development of the assembly line and mass production in the early part of the twentieth century, the firm embarked on a costly and, in the end, unsuccessful strategy of diversification by vertical integration. By 1927, the firm made its own steel, glass, and plastic, only to divest these holdings as it became apparent that transactions inside the firm did not improve on market exchange.

more refined measure for relating acquisitions to gains.[47] In one of the most comprehensive stock price studies of diversification, Sayan Chatterjee and Birger Wernerfelt found that firms with highly specialized resources engage in more related diversification strategies and achieve superior results compared to firms that use unspecialized resources, such as cash, to diversify.[48]

Long-Term Performance of Diversified Firms

Another set of studies followed merging firms over long periods and also compared the success of mergers that took place during different merger waves. Authors of these studies typically assert that the true time horizon for assessing the results of diversification is longer than is commonly measured in research, and they report that the longer-term performance of diversified firms has been poor.

David Ravenscraft and F. M. Scherer studied nearly 6,000 mergers and acquisitions made between 1950 and 1977 and found that performance, whether measured by changes in stock prices or by accounting results, was poor. Moreover, the larger the merger, the more likely returns were to be negative.[49] Michael Porter considered the corporate portfolios of 33 major diversified firms and found that between one-third and one-half of all acquisitions made by firms in his sample between 1950 and 1986 were eventually divested.[50] More than half of the acquisitions into new businesses were eventually divested. Since divestiture is usually carried out as a result of poor performance, this indicated the failure of acquisition policies. Similar poor results were obtained for joint ventures and strategic alliances.

Andrei Shleifer and Robert Vishny have summarized and compared the evidence on the merger waves of the 1960s and 1980s.[51] They conclude that the merger wave of the 1980s, which was characterized by more related acquisitions and by corporate refocusing, can best be understood as a broad correction to the conglomerate mergers of the 1960s. This implies that the capital market imperfectly evaluated conglomerate mergers in the 1960s. It also highlights the importance of antitrust policy in merger activity, since the mergers of the 1980s coincided with a period of relaxed antitrust enforcement that permitted a degree of horizontal and vertical combination that had not been possible in the 1960s.

In a related study, Constantinos Markides looked at mergers in the 1980s and identified overdiversified firms.[52] The returns to these firms from refocusing were significant and positive, consistent with Shleifer and Vishny's conclusion that the mergers of the 1980s corrected the mistakes of the 1960s and refocused overdiversified firms. Robert Hoskisson and Michael Hitt echo this idea of refocusing by arguing that diversified firms need to reduce their scope of activities in order to reach a point at which profitable diversification is possible.[53]

In summary, three different lines of research on the performance of diversified firms have led to similar overall conclusions. Diversification can create value, although its benefits relative to nondiversification are unclear. Among diversifying firms, no clear association exists between simple measures of diversity within a business portfolio and overall corporate performance. However, firms that diversify according to a core set of resources, and with an eye toward integrating old and new businesses, tend to outperform firms that do not work toward building interrelationships among their units. This is consistent with the generally accepted idea that defensible diversification will combine some basis in economies of scope with transaction cost conditions that make it efficient to organize diverse businesses within a single firm, relative to joint ventures, contracts, alliances, or other governance mechanisms.

CHAPTER SUMMARY

◆ A firm is diversified if it produces for numerous markets. Most large and well-known firms are diversified to some extent. Broadly diversified firms (conglomerates) have portfolios of businesses that go beyond conventional ideas of economies of scope. In these firms it is often difficult to identify the corporation's core skills.

◆ Firms can diversify in several ways, ranging from internal growth to strategic alliances, to joint ventures, to formal combinations via merger or acquisition. Merger and acquisition have been the principal modes of diversification, although alternative modes, such as alliances and joint ventures, became increasingly popular in the 1980s and 1990s.

◆ It is difficult to measure the extent of diversification. Most approaches have considered the similarity of businesses in a firm's portfolio according to some measure of technological or market relatedness—that is, according to how similar the businesses are in terms of products sold or customers served.

◆ Corporate diversification in the United States increased dramatically between 1950 and 1980, and then fell. These changes occurred largely in two merger waves—the first, in the 1960s, highlighting the growth of conglomerates, and the second, in the 1980s, highlighting more closely related combinations of activities and the deconglomeration of broadly diversified firms.

◆ Economies of scope provide the principal rationale for diversification. These economies can be based on market and technological factors as well as on managerial synergies due to a dominant general management logic. Financial synergies, such as risk reduction or increased debt capacity, comprise a related rationale that emphasizes corporate management's role as a banker and financial adviser to its business units.

◆ Economizing on transaction costs is another important rationale for diversification. This is because the diversifier must consider the costs of a particular mode of diversification in addition to the benefits to be obtained from it. Common ownership, for example, is justified only when transaction costs make less formal combinations, such as strategic alliances, infeasible.

◆ Firms may diversify in order to make use of an internal capital market. Combining a cash-rich business and a cash-poor business into a single firm allows profitable investments in the cash-poor business to be funded without accessing external sources of capital. If there are frictions in capital markets, this strategy can create value. Evidence suggests that internal capital markets may not always function effectively.

◆ Diversification may also reflect the preferences of a firm's managers rather than those of its owners. If problems of corporate governance prevent shareholders from stopping value-reducing acquisitions, managers may diversify in order to satisfy their preference for growth, to increase their compensation, or to reduce their risk.

◆ The market for corporate control limits managers' ability to diversify unprofitably. If the actual price of a firm's shares is far below the potential price, a raider can profit from taking over the firm and instituting changes that increase its value. This reasoning may explain the wave of leveraged buyout transactions that occurred in the 1980s. In recent years, firms' corporate governance practices have changed in such a way as to align CEO interests more closely with those of shareholders.

◆ Research on the performance of diversified firms has produced mixed results. Where diversification has been effective, it has been based on economies of scope among businesses that are related in terms of technologies or markets. More broadly diversified firms have not performed well, and many conglomerates refocused their business portfolios during the 1980s. Although mergers have increased shareholder value, these increases have largely gone to the shareholders of acquired firms. Over a longer time frame, active diversifiers have divested many of their acquisitions.

QUESTIONS

1. The main reason that firms diversify is to achieve economies of scope. Discuss.
2. Is relatedness necessary for success in the market for corporate control?
3. How is expansion into new and geographically distinct markets similar to diversification? How is it different?
4. The following is a quote from a GE Medical Systems web site: "Growth Through Acquisition—Driving our innovative spirit at GE Medical Systems is the belief that great ideas can come from anyone, anywhere, at any time. Not only from within the company, but from beyond as well . . . . This belief is the force behind our record number of acquisitions." Under what conditions can a growth-through-acquisition strategy create value for shareholders?
5. With the growing number of firms that specialize in corporate acquisitions (e.g., Berkshire Hathaway, KKR), a very active market for corporate control appears to have developed. As the number of specialist firms expands, will control arguments be sufficient to justify acquisitions? Do you think that relatedness will become more or less important as competition in the market for corporate control intensifies?
6. In rapidly developing economies—such as India and South Korea—conglomerates are far more common than they are in the United States and Western Europe. Using the logic of internal capital markets, explain why this organizational form may be more suitable for nations where financial markets are less well developed.
7. Pharmaceutical companies are diversified firms. They sell products in many different therapeutic categories, and they engage in a variety of vertical activities ranging from research and development to sales and marketing. Many pharmaceutical companies spend a fixed percentage of their sales revenues on R&D. Do you think this simple rule of thumb is a good idea?
8. Professor Dranove's son has been shoveling snow for his neighbors at $5 per hour since last year, using his dad's shovel for the job. He hopes to save up for a bicycle. The neighbors

decided to get a snow blower, leaving the boy a few dollars short and sorely disappointed. (He knows that his dad will not contribute a penny!) How is this situation different from that described by Shleifer and Summers? Is there an efficiency loss as a result of the neighbors' actions?

9. Suppose that you observed an acquisition by a diversifying firm and that the aftermath of the deal included plant closings, layoffs, and reduced compensation for some remaining workers in the acquired firm. What would you need to know about this acquisition to determine whether it would be best characterized by value creation or value redistribution?

10. How would you tell if the businesses owned by a diversified firm would be better off if they were independent?

ENDNOTES

[1]This discussion of Rumelt's work is based on Rumelt, R., *Strategy, Structure, and Economic Performance*, Boston, Division of Research, Harvard Business School, 1974. For a review of research that builds on Rumelt's work, see Galbraith, J. R. and R. K. Kazanjian, *Strategy Implementation*, 2nd ed., St. Paul, MN, West Publishing, 1986.

[2]Davis, G. F., K. A. Dieckman, and C. H. Tinsley, "The Decline and Fall of the Conglomerate Firm in the 1980s: The De-Institutionalization of an Organizational Form," *American Sociological Review*, 59, August 1994, pp. 547–570.

[3]Comment, R. and G. Jarrell, "Corporate Focus, Stock Returns and the Market for Corporate Control," *Journal of Financial Economics*, 37, 1995, pp. 67–88.

[4]For discussions of these waves, see Fligstein, N., *The Transformation of Corporate Control*, Cambridge, MA, Harvard University Press, 1990.

[5]Best, M., *The New Competition: Institutions of Industrial Restructuring*, Cambridge, MA, Harvard University Press, 1990, chap. 1.

[6]Brush, T. H., "Predicted Change in Operational Synergy and Post-Acquisition Performance of Acquired Businesses," *Strategic Management Journal*, 17, 1996, pp. 1–24.

[7]Nathanson, D. and J. Cassano, "Organization, Diversity, and Performance," *The Wharton Magazine*, Summer 1982, pp. 19–26.

[8]Penrose, E., *The Theory of the Growth of the Firm*, 3rd ed., Oxford, Oxford University Press, 1995.

[9]Prahalad, C. K. and R. A. Bettis, "The Dominant Logic: A New Linkage Between Diversity and Performance," *Strategic Management Journal*, 7, 1986, pp. 485–501.

[10]Teece, D., "Toward an Economic Theory of the Multiproduct Firm," *Journal of Economic Behavior and Organization*, 3, 1982, pp. 39–63.

[11]Stein, J., "Agency, Information and Corporate Investment," in Constantinides, G., M. Harris, and R. Stulz (eds.), *Handbook of the Economics of Finance*, North-Holland, Amsterdam, 2003.

[12]For a discussion of this possibility, see Shleifer, A. and R. W. Vishny, "Large Shareholders and Corporate Control," *Journal of Political Economy*, 1986, pp. 461–468.

[13]Bazerman, M. and W. Samuelson, "I Won the Auction but Don't Want the Prize," *Journal of Conflict Resolution*, 1983, pp. 618–34.

[14]Meyer, M., P. Milgrom, and J. Roberts, "Organizational Prospects, Influence Costs and Ownership," *Journal of Economics and Management Strategy*, 1, 1992, pp. 9–35.

[15]See Lamont, O., "Cash Flow and Investment: Evidence from Internal Capital Markets," *Journal of Finance*, 52, 1997, pp. 83–109.

[16]Berle, A. and G. Means, *The Modern Corporation and Private Property*, New York, Macmillan, 1932.

[17]Jensen, M. C., "The Eclipse of the Public Corporation," *Harvard Business Review*, September–October 1989, pp. 61–74.

[18]Avery, C., J. C. Chevalier, and S. Schaefer, "Why Do Managers Undertake Acquisitions? An Analysis of Internal and External Rewards for Acquisitiveness," *Journal of Law, Economics & Organization*, 14, 1998, pp. 24–43.

[19]Reich, R., *The Next American Frontier*, New York, Times Books, 1983.

[20]See, for example, surveys by Sherwin Rosen, "Contracts and the Market for Executives," in L. Werin, and H. Wijkander (eds.), *Contract Economics*, Cambridge, MA; Blackwell, 1992, and Kevin J. Murphy, "Executive Compensation," in O. Ashenfelter and D. Card (eds.), *The Handbook of Labor Economics*, Vol. 3, Amsterdam; North-Holland, 2000.

[21]Bliss, R. and R. Rosen, "CEO Compensation and Bank Mergers," *Journal of Financial Economics*, 61, 2001, pp. 107–138.

[22]Amihud, Y. and B. Lev, "Risk Reduction as a Managerial Motive for Conglomerate Mergers," *Bell Journal of Economics*, 12, 1981, pp. 605–617.

[23]The motivation for diversification here is somewhat complicated, for Case was both a major shareholder of AOL and the firm's CEO. A mixture of managerial risk reduction and diversification on behalf of shareholders may have been the motivation for this deal. Had Case attempted to diversify his portfolio in other ways, perhaps by selling AOL shares, the market might have inferred that Case had received unfavorable information about the firm's future prospects. Note that shareholders other than Case could surely have invested directly in Time-Warner stock on their own had they wanted to do so; thus, they did not benefit from risk reduction as a result of the merger.

[24]See "Who's Afraid of AOL Time Warner?" *The Economist*, January 24, 2002.

[25]Hermalin, B. E. and M. S. Weisbach, "Endogenously Chosen Boards of Directors and Their Monitoring of the CEO," *American Economic Review*, 88, 1998, pp. 96–118.

[26]Manne, H., "Mergers and the Market for Corporate Control," *Journal of Political Economy*, 73, 1965, pp. 110–120.

[27]Shleifer, A. and L. H. Summers, "Breach of Trust in Hostile Takeovers," in Auerbach, A. J. (ed.), *Corporate Takeovers: Causes and Consequences*, Chicago, University of Chicago Press, 1988, pp. 33–68.

[28]See Kaplan, S., "The Effects of Management Buyouts on Operations and Value," *Journal of Financial Economics*, 24, 1989, pp. 217–254, or Kaplan, S. and J. Stein, "The Evolution of Buyout Pricing and Financial Structure in the 1980s," *Quarterly Journal of Economics*, 108, 1993, pp. 313–358.

[29]Holmstrom, B. and S. Kaplan, "Corporate Governance and Merger Activity in the U.S.: Making Sense of the 1980s and 1990s," *Journal of Economic Perspectives*, Spring 2001, pp. 121–144.

[30]Mitchell, M. and K. Lehn, "Do Bad Bidders Make Good Targets?" *Journal of Political Economy*, 98, 1990, pp. 372–392.

[31]Goold, M. and K. Luchs, "Why Diversify? Four Decades of Management Thinking," *Academy of Management Executive*, 7, 1993, pp. 7–25.

[32]The classic study on this point is Christensen, H. K. and C. A. Montgomery, "Corporate Economic Performance: Diversification Strategy versus Market Structure," *Strategic Management Journal*, 2, 1981, pp. 327–343. See also Bettis, R. A., "Performance Differences in Related and Unrelated Diversifiers," *Strategic Management Journal*, 2, 1981, pp. 379–383.

[33]Montgomery, C. A., "The Measurement of Firm Diversification: Some New Empirical Evidence," *Academy of Management Journal*, 25, 1982, pp. 299–307.

[34]Capon, N., J. M. Hulbert, J. U. Farley, and L. E. Martin, "Corporate Diversity and Economic Performance: The Impact of Market Specialization," *Strategic Management Journal*, 9, 1988, pp. 61–74.

[35]Palich, L., L. Cardinal, and C. Miller, "Curvilinearity in the Diversification—Performance Linkage: An Examination of over Three Decades of Research," *Strategic Management Journal*, 21, 2000, pp. 155–174.

[36]Schoar, A., "Effects of Corporate Diversification on Productivity," *Journal of Finance*, 57, 2002, pp. 2379–2493.

[37]See Lang, L. H. P. and R. Stulz, "Tobin's q, Corporate Diversification and Firm Performance," *Journal of Political Economy*, 102, 1994, pp. 1248–1280, and Berger, P. and E. Ofek, "Diversification's Effect on Firm Value," *Journal of Financial Economics*, 37, 1995, pp. 39–65.

[38]Graham, J. R., M. Lemmon, and J. Wolf, "Does Corporate Diversification Destroy Value?" *Journal of Finance*, 57, 2002, pp. 695–720.

[39]Campa, J. M. and S. Kedia, "Explaining the Diversification Discount," *Journal of Finance*, 57, 2002, pp. 1731–1762.

[40]Berger, P. and E. Ofek, "Diversification's Effect on Firm Value," *Journal of Financial Economics*, 37, 1995, pp. 39–65.

[41]Morck, R., A. Shleifer, and R. Vishny, "Do Managerial Objectives Drive Bad Acquisitions?," *Journal of Finance*, 45, 1990, pp. 31–48.

[42]Lewellen, W., C. Loderer, and A. Rosenfeld, "Merger Decisions and Executive Stock Ownership in Acquiring Firms," *Journal of Accounting and Economics*, 7, 1985, pp. 209–231. See also Jensen, M. and R. Ruback, "The Market for Corporate Control: The Scientific Evidence," *Journal of Financial Economics*, 11, 1983, pp. 5–50; and Denis, D. J., D. K. Denis, and A. Sarin, "Agency Problems, Equity Ownership, and Corporate Diversification," *Journal of Finance*, 52, 1997, pp. 135–160. Jeremy Stein (see footnote 11) offers a recent summary of this literature.

[43]See, for example, Chevalier, J., "What Do We Know about Cross-Subsidization? Evidence from the Investment Policies of Merging Firms," *Advances in Economic Analysis and Policy*, 4, 2004.

[44]Richard Roll suggests that managerial "hubris" may drive acquisitive behavior. See Roll, R., "The Hubris Hypothesis of Corporate Takeovers," *Journal of Business*, 59, 1986, pp. 197–216. Combining this idea with Schoar's new toy effect, many managers correctly assess their ability to create value in acquired plants but for some reason ignore the opportunity cost associated with reducing efforts toward increasing productivity in incumbent facilities.

[45]Singh, H. and C. A. Montgomery, "Corporate Acquisitions and Economic Performance," *Strategic Management Journal*, 8, 1987, pp. 377–386.

[46]Seth, A., "Sources of Value Creation in Acquisitions: An Empirical Investigation," *Strategic Management Journal*, 11, 1990, pp. 431–446.

[47]Shelton, L. M., "Strategic Business Fits and Corporate Acquisition: Empirical Evidence," *Strategic Management Journal*, 9, 1988, pp. 278–287.

[48]Chatterjee, S. and B. Wernerfelt, "The Link Between Resources and Type of Diversification," *Strategic Management Journal*, 12, 1991, pp. 33–48.

[49]Ravenscraft, D. J. and F. M. Scherer, *Mergers, Sell-Offs, and Economic Efficiency*, Washington, DC, Brookings Institution, 1987.

[50]Porter, M. E., "From Competitive Advantage to Corporate Strategy," *Harvard Business Review*, May–June 1987, pp. 43–59.

[51]Shleifer, A. and R. W. Vishny, "Takeover in the '60s and the '80s: Evidence and Implications," *Strategic Management Journal*, 12, Special Issue, 1991, pp. 51–60.

[52]Markides, C. C., "Consequences of Corporate Refocusing: Ex Ante Evidence," *Academy of Management Journal*, 35, 1992, pp. 398–412.

[53]Hoskisson, R. E. and M. A. Hitt, *Downscoping: How to Tame the Diversified Firm*, New York, Oxford University Press, 1994.

PART TWO

MARKET AND COMPETITIVE ANALYSIS

COMPETITORS AND COMPETITION

6

$\mathcal{T}$he domestic U.S. airline industry has experienced its ups and downs during the past two decades. The 1990s began with a mild recession that left carriers with empty seats. The airlines recognized that the marginal cost of filling an empty seat was negligible, and some carriers slashed prices in the hopes of filling their planes. The resulting price war took a heavy toll, with aggregate industry losses exceeding $4 billion in 1992. The economic recovery of the mid-1990s lifted the industry. Flying at or near capacity, the carriers raised prices for all passenger classes. When an airline did have empty seats, it utilized computerized pricing algorithms to selectively reduce prices on a short-term basis rather than slash them across the board. By the late 1990s, record losses had given way to record profits, with the industry earning a combined $4 billion in 1999. As the economy softened in 2000 and especially in 2001, the airlines once again struggled to fill planes and resist the temptation to discount their airfares. The September 11 attack threatened the solvency of many of the major airlines and necessitated a government bailout to keep them flying. Today, the major carriers face growing threats from new entrants, even as they struggle to avoid repeating the damaging price wars of the past. The fate of several big carriers, including United and Delta, is in doubt.

This brief history illustrates the interplay among competitors in a concentrated market. The major players understand the need to avoid deep discounting, but they also understand the economics of empty seats. As demand rises and falls, their ability to avoid price wars rises and falls with it. Threats from new competitors may prove even more damaging than the losses that occurred after September 11.

Chapters 6–10 of this book are concerned with competition. The present chapter introduces basic concepts in competitive analysis. The first part discusses competitor identification and market definition. The second part considers four different ways in which firms compete: perfect competition, monopoly, monopolistic competition, and oligopoly. Chapters 7 through 9 present advanced concepts, including the effect of commitments on competition, the dynamics of competition, and entry. Chapter 10 discusses how to use the material in these chapters to assess competition in specific markets.

◆ ◆ ◆ ◆ ◆ COMPETITOR IDENTIFICATION AND MARKET DEFINITION

Most managers can readily identify competitors. Competitors are the firms whose strategic choices directly affect one another. For example, if Mercedes reduced the price on its sports coupe, BMW would have to consider a pricing response—Mercedes coupes and BMW coupes are direct competitors. Firms also compete indirectly, when the strategic choices of one affect the performance of the other, but only through the strategic choices of a third firm.[1] For example, if Mercedes reduced the price on its station wagons, Volvo might do the same. This might cause Jeep to change price on its Grand Cherokees—Mercedes wagons and Jeep Grand Cherokees are indirect competitors.

Although managers are conversant with these ideas, it is worthwhile to develop methods to systematize competitor identification. These methods force managers to carefully identify the features that define the markets they compete in, and often reveal aspects of competition that a "quick and dirty" analysis might miss.

The first step in identifying competitors is market identification, that is, naming the markets in which the firm competes. A firm may compete in both input and output markets simultaneously. It is important to analyze each market separately because the competitors and the nature of competition may be quite different in each one. For example, a coal mining operation in a small town in northern England may have little or no competition in the market for labor, an input, but may face many competitors in the market for coal, its output.

The Basics of Competitor Identification

Antitrust agencies, such as the U.S. Department of Justice (DOJ), are responsible for preventing anticompetitive conduct. They examine whether merging firms will monopolize a market and whether existing monopolists are abusing their power. To make these judgments, the DOJ uses a simple conceptual guideline to identify potential competitors whose presence might limit bad conduct. According to the DOJ, all of the competitors in a market have been identified if a merger among them would lead to a *small but significant nontransitory increase in price*. This is known as the *SSNIP* criterion. "Small" is usually defined to be "more than 5 percent," and "nontransitory" is usually defined to be "at least one year." For example, suppose Audi believed it competed only against BMW and Mercedes. According to the SSNIP criterion, Audi would be correct if, in the event the three German car makers merged, they would collectively boost their prices for at least one year by 5 percent. If they would not raise prices by 5 percent for fear that they would lose market share to other luxury name plates, then the list of competitors would need to be expanded.

Putting Competitor Identification into Practice

The SSNIP criterion is sensible, but it is often impractical. Audi should not have to merge with BMW and Mercedes in order to identify its competitors. Even so, the SSNIP criterion points to the kind of evidence needed for competitor identification. Specifically, the SSNIP criterion suggests that two firms directly compete if a price increase by one causes many of its customers to do business with the other. This is the essence of the economic concept of *substitutes*.

In general, two products X and Y are substitutes if, when the price of X increases and the price of Y stays the same, purchases of X go down and purchases of Y go up. When asked to identify competitors, most managers would probably name substitutes. For example, a manager at Mercedes would probably name BMW, Audi, Volvo, Lexus, and Acura as competitors. In fact, when Lexus and Acura entered the 1980s with relatively low prices, they took considerable business away from Mercedes. When Mercedes and other European luxury car makers reduced their prices in the early 1990s, they regained market share from Lexus and Acura.

At an intuitive level, products tend to be close substitutes when three conditions hold:

1. They have the same or similar *product performance characteristics*.
2. They have the same or similar *occasions for use*.
3. They are sold in the same *geographic market*.

A product's performance characteristics describe what it does for consumers. Though highly subjective, listing product performance characteristics often clarifies whether products are substitutes. Mercedes and Volvo sedans have the following product performance characteristics in common:

- Ability to seat five comfortably

- High "curb appeal" and prestigious name

- High reliability

- Powerful acceleration and sure handling and braking

- Plenty of features, such as leather seats and a compact disc player

Based on this short list, we can assume that the products are in the same market. We would probably exclude Jeeps from this market, however.

A product's occasion for use describes when, where, and how it is used. Both orange juice and cola quench thirst, but because orange juice is primarily a breakfast drink, they are probably in different markets.

Products with similar characteristics and occasions for use may not be substitutes if they are in different geographic markets. In general, two products are in different geographic markets if (a) they are sold in different locations, (b) it is costly to transport the goods, and (c) it is costly for consumers to travel to buy the goods. For example, a company that mixes and sells cement in Mexico City is not in the same geographic market as a similar company in Oaxaca. The cost of transporting cement over long distances is so large relative to its price that it would not be economical for the Oaxaca cement seller to ship its product to Mexico City, even if cement prices in Mexico City are higher.

Empirical Approaches to Competitor Identification

Although the intuitive approach to competitor identification is often sufficient for business decision making, it can be subjective. When possible, it is helpful to augment the intuitive approach with data. As pointed out in the Economics Primer, the degree to which products substitute for each other is measured by the cross-price elasticity of demand. If the products in question are X and Y, then the cross-price elasticity measures the percentage change in demand for good Y that results from a 1 percent change in the price of good X. Formally, if η_{yx} denotes the cross-price elasticity of

EXAMPLE 6.1 SUBSTITUTES AND COMPETITION IN THE POSTAL SERVICE

One of the few constants about international business is that the postal service is a government-regulated or government-owned monopolist. Among the developed countries, only Holland has fully privatized its postal service. Advocates of maintaining government monopoly control of the postal service claim that it is in their nation's best interest to assure that all residents, regardless of location, have equal access to communication by post. Another justification for government-sponsored postal monopoly is that it is unnecessarily costly for two or more firms to deliver mail to the same addresses.

As monopolies, postal services have operated with legendary inefficiency. In the early 1990s, Chicago newspapers reported bags of undelivered mail found abandoned in unlikely places, such as under highway overpasses and in workers' garages. (Fortunately for Chicagoans, the media attention brought substantial improvements in service.) But changes in technology and global competition are beginning to catch up with postal services, and their protected status is at risk.

Government regulations do not limit all forms of competition to the postal service. Businesses routinely use private express mail service. Most big cities have private courier services that offer same-day delivery between downtown office buildings. Electronic mail, fax, and interactive television have siphoned off billions of dollars of business from European postal services alone. (Following the dictum "If you can't beat 'em, join 'em," the British Post Office once experimented with an "electronic post office." Rather than use "snail mail," individuals could have letters copied and e-mailed to recipients. After just 11 transactions in 12 months, the idea was abandoned.)

Faced with these competitive pressures, national postal services are seeking to operate more like private businesses, especially in the fiercely competitive international parcel post market. Germany's Deutsche Post went public in the year 2000, acquired international parcel post carrier DHL in 2001, and never looked back. After a string of acquisitions that included India's Blue Dart parcel delivery company, Deutsche Post has become the world's largest air freight company.

Deutsche Post has even considered diversifying into distribution of electricity, gas, and water. Other national postal services have sales offices throughout Europe to compete for international parcel post, and New Zealand's postal service has sales teams that travel the world in search of business. New Zealand's post office has diversified in its home country, opening a bank and funding a venture-capital arm that has invested in several e-commerce firms.

As nations liberalize their postal services and state-owned post offices begin to operate like other big conglomerates, the post offices may eventually lose their protected status for local service. Already, private postal services in Europe including Spain's Unipost and England's Speedmail (both owned in part by Deutsche Post) may compete with national postal services on business bulk mail and personal mail meeting minimum weight requirements. Some foresee the elimination of all barriers to competition, with private carriers delivering residential mail. We may even see national postal services competing head to head for local and international business.

demand of product Y with respect to product X, Q_y the quantity of Y sold, and P_x the price of product X, then

$$\eta_{yx} = (\Delta Q_y \mid Q_y)/(\Delta P_x \mid P_x)$$

When η_{yx} is positive, it indicates that consumers increase their purchases of good Y as the price of good X increases. Goods X and Y would thus be substitutes. Thanks to the growing availability of retail scanner pricing data, it is increasingly possible for the makers of consumer products to directly measure cross-price elasticities of demand.

There are other quantitative approaches to competitor identification. One might observe how prices of different firms change over time—the prices of close competitors tend to be highly correlated. One might obtain data about the purchase patterns of individual consumers to predict where they would turn if their present seller were to raise prices.[2] Finally, one could identify firms in the same Standard Industrial Classification (SIC) as defined by the U.S. Bureau of the Census. SIC codes identify products and services by a seven-digit identifier, with each digit representing a finer degree of classification. For example, within the two-digit category 35 (industrial and commercial machinery and computer equipment) are four-digit categories 3523 (farm machinery and equipment) and 3534 (elevators and moving stairways). Within 3534 are six-digit categories for automobile lifts, dumbwaiters, and so forth. One should use caution when using SIC codes to identify competitors. Although products with the same SIC code may often be classified as competitors, this is not always so. For example, category 2834 includes all pharmaceuticals, but not all drugs substitute for each other. Conversely, some four-digit categories are too narrow. Firms in the four-digit categories for variety stores (5331), department stores (5311), and general merchandise stores (5399) may all compete against each other.

Geographic Competitor Identification

The government census provides a good starting point for identifying geographic competitors. City, county, and state lines often provide an adequate first step for delineating the scope of competition. But such *ad hoc* boundaries are only a first step. For example, it is unlikely that all the grocery stores in Chicago compete with one another. By the same token, grocers in the Illinois town of Glencoe in Cook County surely compete with grocers in the neighboring town of Highland Park in Lake County.

Rather than rely on *ad hoc* market boundaries, it is preferable to identify competitors by directly examining the flow of goods and services across geographic regions. To illustrate this approach, consider how a hypothetical sporting goods store in the Sunset section of San Francisco—Bay City Sports—might try to identify its competitors. Bay City Sports might assume that its competitors are the other sporting goods stores in the Sunset. This is mere guesswork and is probably wrong.

Bay City Sports might survey its customers to find out where else they shop. This would certainly identify some competitors, but it might miss others. To identify all of its competitors, Bay City Sports should first ask its customers where they live. The store can identify the contiguous area from which it draws most of its customers, sometimes called the *catchment area*. If most of its customers live in the Sunset, then Bay City should definitely list among its competitors other sporting goods stores in the Sunset. But suppose, as seems likely, that some local residents shop at sporting goods stores located outside of the Sunset. To identify these competitors, Bay City Sports should perform a second survey of Sunset residents (not just its own customers) to find out where they shop for sporting goods.

This is an example of *flow analysis*—examining data on consumer travel patterns. Although flow analysis is a good starting point for identifying geographic competitors, it is not foolproof. It may turn out that few customers currently leave the Sunset, but this does not imply that they would not leave if stores in the Sunset were to raise their prices. Or it may be that many customers who currently shop outside the Sunset do so for idiosyncratic reasons—perhaps they are avid hockey players, and stores in the Sunset do not sell hockey gear. With the exception of such exotic merchandise, stores outside the Sunset may not be competitors after all.

◆ ◆ ◆ ◆ ◆ MEASURING MARKET STRUCTURE

Markets are often characterized according to the degree of seller concentration. As we will see, this often permits a quick and reasonably accurate assessment of the likely nature of competition in a market. These characterizations are aided by having measures of *market structure*.

Market structure refers to the number and distribution of firms in a market. A common measure of market structure is the *N*-firm concentration ratio. This gives the combined market share of the *N* largest firms in the market. For example, the four-firm concentration ratio in the soft drink industry is about .90, which indicates that the combined market share of the four largest soft drink manufacturers is about 90 percent. When calculating market share, one usually uses sales revenue, although concentration ratios based on other measures, such as production capacity, may also be used. Table 6.1 shows 4-firm and 20-firm concentration ratios for selected U.S. industries in 2002.

One problem with the *N*-firm ratio is that it is invariant to changes in the sizes of the largest firms in the market. For example, a 4-firm ratio does not change value if the largest firm gains 10 percent share at the expense of the second largest firm. Another commonly used measure of market structure that avoids this problem is the

TABLE 6.1
CONCENTRATION STATISTICS FOR SELECTED U.S. INDUSTRIES, 2002

NAICS Code	Industry	Number of Firms	4-firm CR	20-firm CR
44311	Appliance, television, and other electronics stores	33847	53	65
44312	Computer and software stores	10133	51	65
44711	Gasoline stations with convenience stores	92979	11	29
45121	Book stores and news dealers	12751	62	70
45122	Prerecorded tape, compact disc, and record stores	6894	58	76
45311	Florists	22753	2	4
48111	Scheduled passenger air transportation	1301	34	73
48412	General freight trucking, long distance	37446	13	35
49311	General warehousing and storage	8194	11	25
49312	Refrigerated warehousing and storage	1255	36	62
51211	Motion picture and video production	11106	51	73
51213	Motion picture and video exhibition	5268	40	75
51511	Radio broadcasting	6897	43	65
51512	Television broadcasting	1959	51	76
51521	Cable and other subscription programming	714	63	91
52211	Commercial banking	81076	30	56
52393	Investment advice	14617	25	43
52411	Direct life, health, and medical insurance carriers	13004	14	45
52593	Real estate investment trusts	2729	21	53
61141	Business and secretarial schools	488	14	44
72111	Hotels (except casino hotels) and motels	46163	22	36
72112	Casino hotels	283	44	76
72121	RV parks and recreational camps	7334	5	11
72211	Full service restaurants	195492	9	16

Source: 2002 Economic Census, Various Industry Series Reports; Washington, DC: U.S. Census Bureau.

EXAMPLE 6.2 DEFINING COCA-COLA'S MARKET

In 1986, the Coca-Cola Company sought to acquire the Dr Pepper Company. At the time, Coca-Cola was the nation's largest seller of carbonated soft drinks, and Dr Pepper was the fourth largest. The Federal Trade Commission (FTC) went before federal judge Gerhard Gesell seeking an injunction to block the merger on the grounds that it violated Section 7 of the Clayton Act, which prohibits any acquisition of stock or assets of a company that may substantially lessen competition. Coca-Cola apparently sought the deal to acquire, and more fully exploit, the Dr Pepper trademark. Coca-Cola's marketing skills and research ability were cited as two factors that would allow it to increase the sales of Dr Pepper. Judge Gesell also noted that Coca-Cola was motivated, in part, by a desire to match the expansion of Pepsi-Cola, which had simultaneously been seeking to acquire 7 Up. Although the threat of FTC action caused Pepsi to abandon the 7-Up acquisition, Coca-Cola pressed on.

Judge Gesell granted the injunction, and the Coca-Cola/Dr Pepper deal was never consummated. In his decision, Judge Gesell addressed the question of market definition. He wrote: "Proper market analysis directs attention to the nature of the products that the acquirer and the acquired company principally sell, the channels of distribution they primarily use, the outlets they employ to distribute their products to the ultimate consumer, and the geographic areas they mutually serve." The judge was concerned not only with the end-user market, but also with intermediate markets for distribution and retailing. Reduction of competition in any of these markets could harm consumers.

Depending on how the market in which Coca-Cola and Dr Pepper competed was defined, one might conclude that the merger would have either no effect on competition or a significant effect. The FTC argued that the appropriate "line of commerce" was carbonated soft drinks. It presented data to show that under this definition, the merger of Coca-Cola and Dr Pepper would increase Coca-Cola's market share by 4.6 percent nationwide and by 10 to 20 percent in many geographic submarkets. (Geographic submarkets were considered because of the special characteristics of soft drink distribution channels.) Given Coca-Cola's already high market share of 40 to 50 percent in many of these markets, the merger would significantly reduce competition.

In defending the merger, Coca-Cola attempted to define the relevant market as "all . . . beverages including tap water." Under this definition, the proposed merger would have a negligible effect on competition. Judge Gesell ruled: "Although other beverages could be viewed as within 'the outer boundaries' of a product market . . . determined by the reasonable interchangeability of use or the cross elasticity of demand between carbonated soft drinks and substitutes for them, carbonated soft drinks . . . constitute a product market for antitrust purposes." In reaching this decision, he relied on factors such as the product's distinctive characteristics and uses, distinct consumers, distinct prices, and sensitivity to price changes. Judge Gesell found such indicia to be present in this case, stating that the rival firms "make pricing and marketing decisions based primarily on comparisons with rival carbonated soft drink products, with little if any concern about possible competition from other beverages." In other words, carbonated soft drink makers constrain each others' pricing decisions, but are unconstrained by other beverages. Thus, carbonated soft drinks constitute a well-defined market.

Herfindahl index.[3] The Herfindahl index equals the sum of the squared market shares of all the firms in the market, that is, letting S_i represent the market share of firm i, Herfindahl $= \Sigma_i(S_i)^2$. Thus, in a market with two firms that each have 50 percent market share, the Herfindahl index equals $.5^2 + .5^2 = .5$. The Herfindahl index in a market with N equal-size firms is $1/N$. Because of this property, the reciprocal of the Herfindahl index is referred to as the *numbers-equivalent of firms*. Thus, a market whose Herfindahl is .125 has a numbers-equivalent of 8. When calculating a Herfindahl, it is sufficient to restrict attention to firms with market shares of .01 or larger, since the squared shares of smaller firms are too small to affect the Herfindahl.

The Herfindahl conveys more information than the N-firm concentration ratio. If one believes that the relative size of the largest firms is an important determinant of conduct and performance, as economic theory suggests, then the Herfindahl is likely to be more informative.

◆ ◆ ◆ ◆ ◆ MARKET STRUCTURE AND COMPETITION

The structure of a market can profoundly affect the conduct and financial performance of its firms. The Economics Primer showed that in the extreme case of a perfectly competitive market, firms choose production so that price equals marginal cost. Free entry and exit erode any opportunities for profits, so that price is also driven to minimum average cost. In contrast, the price set by a monopoly exceeds marginal and average cost, often by a substantial amount.

Firms may face a continuum of pricing possibilities, ranging from perfect competition at one extreme to monopoly at the other. Economists have added two additional categories to this continuum, monopolistic competition and oligopoly. These categories are briefly described in Table 6.2. Associated with each category is a range of Herfindahls that is common for each kind of competition. These ranges are *only suggestive*, however. For example, the table suggests that if there are only two competitors in a market, they will not behave competitively. But some markets with only two firms could experience fierce price competition with prices near marginal costs. On the other hand, price competition can be all but nonexistent in some markets that have a half dozen competitors or more. Thus it is essential to assess the circumstances surrounding the competitive interaction of firms to make conclusions about the intensity of price competition, rather than rely solely on the Herfindahl or other measures of concentration.

The ensuing discussion of these competitive conditions highlights some intuitive issues for managers. We begin with brief discussions of perfect competition and monopoly. (More detailed discussions may be found in the Economics Primer and in microeconomics textbooks.) We then provide lengthier discussions of monopolistic competition and oligopoly. Because the theory of oligopoly is especially rich, we will elaborate on it in Chapters 7 and 8.

TABLE 6.2
FOUR CLASSES OF MARKET STRUCTURE AND THE INTENSITY
OF PRICE COMPETITION

Nature of Competition	Range of Herfindahls	Intensity of Price Competition
Perfect competition	Usually below .2	Fierce
Monopolistic competition	Usually below .2	May be fierce or light, depending on product differentiation
Oligopoly	.2 to .6	May be fierce or light, depending on interfirm rivalry
Monopoly	.6 and above	Usually light, unless threatened by entry

Perfect Competition

In the theory of perfect competition, there are many sellers of a homogeneous good and many well-informed consumers who can costlessly shop around for the best price. Under these conditions, there is a single market price that is determined by the interaction of all sellers and buyers, but is beyond the control of any one of them. This implies that if a firm charges even one penny more than the market price it will sell nothing, and if it charges one penny less, it will needlessly sacrifice revenue. (In other words, the firm faces infinitely elastic demand.) The firm's only decision, then, is how much output to produce and sell.

Recall from the Economics Primer that a firm maximizes profit by producing a volume of output at which marginal revenue equals marginal cost. Recall, too, that the percentage contribution margin (PCM) equals $(P - MC)/P$, where P = price and MC = marginal cost. The condition for profit maximization can then be written $PCM = 1/\eta$.[4] In perfect competition, $\eta = \infty$, so the optimal PCM is 0.

Many markets approximate perfect competition, including those for many metals and agricultural commodities. As the model predicts, price competition in these markets is fierce. Sellers set identical prices, and prices are generally driven down to marginal costs. Many other markets, including those for most consumer goods and professional services, do not fit the literal conditions of the model of perfect competition. Even so, some of these markets may experience fierce price competition. Chapter 8 provides a rigorous explanation of why prices in some markets are driven down toward marginal costs. Below, we present some informal explanations.

Market conditions will tend to drive down prices when two or more of the following conditions are met:

1. There are many sellers.
2. Consumers perceive the product to be homogeneous.
3. There is excess capacity.

We discuss how each of these features may contribute to fierce pressure to reduce prices.

Many Sellers

A top airline executive once said that "the industry is led by its dumbest competitor."[5] He made this statement in conjunction with a round of price cutting by two competitors. He probably meant that the airlines could increase their profits if they would stop cutting prices in vain attempts to increase market share. This might help the airlines, but it would harm consumers. The DOJ, the Federal Trade Commission (FTC), and their counterparts worldwide vigorously enforce antitrust laws designed to prevent collusive pricing. In enforcing these laws, the antitrust authorities are seldom concerned about markets with more than a few sellers. Experience, coupled with economic theory, has taught them that it is unusual for more than a handful of sellers to raise prices much above costs for a sustained period. This is true for a number of reasons.

First, when there are many sellers, a diversity of pricing preferences is likely. Even if the industry PCM is high, a particular seller may prefer a low price, for example, if it has low costs. In the airline industry, a low-cost airline such as Southwest will often underprice higher-cost competitors, such as Delta and United, on routes in which they directly compete.

Second, a price increase will result in fewer purchases by consumers, so some sellers will have to reduce production to support the elevated prices. It is difficult to get a lot of sellers to agree on who should cut production. This point is illustrated by the contrast between the historical success of cartels in the potash and nitrogen indus-tries.[6] The potash cartel that existed before World War II was highly concentrated and generally succeeded in restricting production and keeping prices high. By con-trast, the world nitrogen cartel consisted of many firms in the United States, Europe, and South America and was far less successful in its attempts to raise prices above com-petitive levels.[7]

Third, even if sellers appear willing to cut production, some may be tempted to "cheat" by lowering price and increasing production. Among the firms most tempted to lower prices are those with small market shares, of which there will be many when the market is relatively unconcentrated. A small firm may view the collusive bargain among bigger rivals as an opportunity to increase market share. Together with increased market share may come learning benefits and economies of scale that will enhance the firm's long-run competitive position. A small firm may also gamble that its larger rivals will not detect its price reductions. Even if they did, they may be reluctant to slash prices further in retaliation, since they would stand to lose more (in absolute terms) from a price war than does the small firm.[8]

Homogeneous Products

When a firm lowers its price, it expects to increase its sales. The sales increase may come from three different sources:

1. Increased sales to customers who were planning to buy a smaller quantity from the firm
2. Sales to customers who were not planning to purchase from the firm or its competitors
3. Sales to customers who were planning to buy from a competitor but switched to take advantage of the lower price

For many firms that reduce prices, customer switching represents the largest source of sales gain. A good example is on-line retail brokerage. When on-line brokers like Ameritrade undercut the prices of traditional retail brokers, most of the resulting business came from traditional retail customers rather than from new traders who had never previously invested in the market (although there was a a lot of that during the era of the day trading frenzy). Subsequent price cuts by one on-line broker or another were intended mainly to steal business rather than increase business from existing customers.

Customers are more willing to switch from one seller to another when the pro-duct is homogeneous, that is, if the characteristics of the product do not vary across sellers. When products are homogeneous, customers tend to be less loyal because any seller's product will meet their needs. This intensifies price competition because firms that lower prices can expect large increases in sales.

Commodities such as gold and graded wheat are homogeneous. All of the on-line brokerage services offer essentially the same product—near instantaneous buying and selling of publicly traded stocks—and therefore are effectively homogeneous. Some pro-ducts, such as DVD players, are slightly differentiated, and many (but not all) consumers will switch to obtain a lower price. Other products, such as medical services, are highly differentiated, and most consumers are unwilling to switch just to obtain a lower price.

Excess Capacity

To understand the role of capacity in pricing problems, recall the distinction between average costs and marginal costs that we made in the Economics Primer and in

EXAMPLE 6.3 A DOG-EAT-DOG WORLD: THE DEMISE OF THE ON-LINE PET SUPPLY INDUSTRY

At the height of the dot-com boom in 1999, there were roughly 100 web sites on the Internet selling pet supplies. Leading the parade was Pets.com, whose commercials featuring a sock puppet had made it a household name. At one point, Pets.com had a $220 million market capitalization and its IPO raised $88 million. Before too long, Pets.com was in the doghouse. It was put to sleep in November 2000, along with many of its litter-mates.

The overall U.S. pet supply industry is not in the doghouse, what annual sales exceeding $30 billion annually. And the annual growth rate of 9 percent is also something to crow about. In the late 1990s, this seemed like an opportune market in which dot-com investors could go fishing for profits. The first entrants had fine pedigrees with support from prominent venture capitalists. But these investors were barking up the wrong tree. Entrants bred like rabbits, and each one offered essentially the same products from the same brand name suppliers. Even the names of the web sites parroted each other: Pets.com, Petstore.com, Petopia.com. There were soon nearly 100 firms in the on-line market. Julie Wainwright, then CEO of Pets.com, noted, "There is probably enough of a market to support two [players]."

Each company spent millions in advertising, engaging in a marketing dogfight to differentiate themselves from the crowd. Pets.com alone spent $80 million on advertising. But these were millions that the companies did not really have. By 2000, none of these companies had turned a profit. Even worse, many of the companies had been forced to sell their goods below cost just to gain market share. For instance, many suppliers offered free shipping. At one point, Pets.com offered a flat fee of $4.95 for a 40-pound bag of dog food, shipping included. Like most of David Dranove's tropical fish, this strategy would not survive for long, inasmuch as shipping costs exceeded $5.

In the end, few of the pet dot-coms could scratch out an existence. Pets.com, Petstore.com, and Petopia.com have all gone belly-up. Some pet supply web sites still exist. Some like Petsmart.com and Petco.com are simply on-line extensions of already existing bricks-and-mortar businesses. Others, like petfooddirect and drsfosterandsmith, have good prospects for success, but investors' sights are set much lower. Only time will tell whether they will survive or join the pet.com cemetery.

Chapter 2. For production processes that entail high fixed costs, marginal cost can be well below average cost over a wide range of output. Only when production nears capacity—the point at which average cost begins to rise sharply—does marginal cost begin to exceed average cost.

The numerical example in Table 6.3 illustrates the implications of excess capacity for a firm's pricing incentives. The table depicts the situation facing a diesel engine manufacturer, such as Deere & Company, whose plant has capacity of 50,000 engines per year. Because of a recession, suppose that Deere has confirmed orders for only 10,000 engines during the upcoming year. Deere is confident, however, that it can increase sales by another 10,000 engines by stealing a major customer from one of its competitors, Navistar. To do so, Deere has to offer this customer a price of $300 per engine.[9] Should Deere offer this price?

Deere is better off offering this price and stealing the business from Navistar, even though this price is well below the average cost of $700 per engine that it would cost Deere to fill the order. To see this, note that the increase in Deere's revenue is $3 million, whereas the increase in its total cost is only $1 million. It is better off selling

TABLE 6.3
CAPACITY UTILIZATION AND COSTS

Annual Output	Total Variable Cost ($millions/year)	Total Fixed Cost ($millions/year)	Total Cost ($millions/year)	Average Cost per Engine
10,000	$1	$12	$13	$1300
20,000	2	12	14	700
30,000	3	12	15	500
40,000	4	12	16	400
50,000	8	12	20	400

the extra engines at $300 apiece because the sale contributes to fixed costs. Of course, Navistar may not let Deere steal its business, so the result may be a battle that drives the price for this order below $300. But as long as the order carries a price greater than the average variable cost of $100, Deere would be better off filling the order than not filling it.

In the long run, competition like this can drive price below average cost. Firms may choose to exit the industry rather than sustain long-run economic losses. But if firm capacity is industry specific—that is, it can only be used to produce in this industry—firms will have no choice but to remain in the industry until the plant reaches the end of its useful life or until demand recovers. If demand does not recover, the industry may suffer a protracted period of excess capacity, with prices below average costs.

Monopoly

The noted antitrust economist Frank Fisher describes monopoly power as "the ability to act in an unconstrained way," such as increasing price or reducing quality.[10] Constraints come from competing firms. If a firm lacks monopoly power, then when it raises price or reduces quality its customers take their business to competitors. It follows that a firm is a *monopolist* if it faces little or no competition in its output market. Competition, if it exists at all, comes from fringe firms—small firms that collectively account for no more than about 30 to 40 percent market share and do not threaten to erode the monopolist's market share.

A firm is a *monopsonist* if it faces little or no competition in one of its input markets. The analysis of monopoly and monopsony is closely related. Whereas an analysis of monopoly focuses on the ability of the firm to raise output prices, an analysis of monopsony would focus on its ability to reduce input prices. We discuss in this chapter issues concerning monopolists, but all of these issues are equally important to monopsonists.

A monopolist faces downward-sloping demand, implying that as it raises price, it sells fewer units. Having monopoly power is not the same as having a stranglehold on demand. Even monopolists can lose customers. If a monopolist can raise price without losing customers, then profit maximization behooves it to raise price even further, until it does lose some! Perhaps some customers will switch to fringe firms; perhaps others will stop buying the product altogether. What distinguishes a monopolist is not the fact that it faces downward-sloping demand, but rather that it can set price without regard to how other firms will respond. This stands in contrast with oligopolists, described below, who also face downward-sloping demand, but must be very mindful of how competitors react to their strategic decisions.

A monopolist selects price so that the marginal revenue from the last unit sold equals the marginal cost of producing it. For example, suppose that the demand facing a monopolist is given by $P = 100 - Q$ and the constant marginal cost of production is 10 per unit. As a benchmark, note that price in a competitive market would equal marginal cost, or 10, and total output would be 90. It is straightforward to calculate the monopolist's optimal price and quantity.

The monopolist's total revenue is price times quantity, or $100Q - Q^2$. The corresponding marginal revenue is $100 - 2Q$ (see the Economics Primer for further discussion of marginal revenue). Hence, marginal revenue and marginal cost are equal when $Q = 45$. It follows that the profit-maximizing price $P = \$55$, and profits (total revenues minus total costs) equal \$2,025. Note that the monopolist's price is well above its marginal cost, and its output is well below the competitive level. Limiting output to boost price well above marginal cost is an example of what Fisher described as unconstrained action.

Antitrust enforcers are concerned about the high profits many monopolists earn. They argue that these profits come at the expense of consumers, who must pay higher prices for limited output. The economist Harold Demsetz notes that high monopoly profits do not necessarily indicate that consumers are worse off.[11] He argues that most monopolies arise when a firm discovers a more efficient way of manufacturing a product, or creates a new product that fulfills unmet consumer needs. Consumers benefit from such innovations, and monopoly profits may represent only a small percentage of the gains consumers enjoy. Moreover, firms will continue to innovate only if they can expect high profits when their innovations succeed. If Demsetz is correct, then restricting monopoly profits may hurt consumers in the long run, by choking off innovation.

Monopolistic Competition

The term *monopolistic competition* was introduced by Edward Chamberlin in 1933 to characterize markets with two main features that are important to understanding pricing:[12]

1. There are many sellers. Each seller reasonably supposes that its actions will not materially affect others. For example, there are many sellers of retail women's clothing in Chicago (there are three pages of listings in the Chicago *Yellow Pages*). If any one seller were to lower its prices, it is doubtful that other sellers would react. There are simply too many retailers to keep track of. Even if some sellers did notice a small dropoff in sales, they would probably not alter their prices just to respond to a single competitor.
2. Each seller offers a differentiated product. Products A and B are differentiated if there is some price for each product at which some consumers prefer to purchase A and others prefer to purchase B. The notion of product differentiation captures the idea that consumers make choices among competing products on the basis of factors other than just price. Unlike under perfect competition, where products are homogeneous, a differentiated seller that raises its price will not lose all its customers.

Economists distinguish between *vertical differentiation* and *horizontal differentiation*. A product is vertically differentiated when it is unambiguously better or worse than competing products. A producer of a household cleaner, such as Colgate-Palmolive's Ajax brand, engages in vertical differentiation when it enhances

EXAMPLE 6.4 THE OPEC CARTEL

With oil prices hovering near $60 per barrel, many analysts point to rising demand from China and limited refining capacity as the culprits. In real terms, $60 is far from the record high price for oil. That came in 1980, when prices reached nearly $100 (adjusted for inflation.) Back then, no one blamed the forces of supply and demand. Instead, everyone blamed the Organization of Petroleum Exporting Countries (OPEC).

Sellers who agree not to cut prices are said to be in a cartel. OPEC is perhaps the world's best known cartel. OPEC was formed in 1960 by Saudi Arabia, Venezuela, Kuwait, Iraq, and Iran in response to efforts by U.S. oil refiners, led by Standard Oil of New Jersey, to reduce the price they were paying for imported oil. Until the early 1970s, OPEC had little impact on world markets. In 1973, however, OPEC members agreed not to ship oil to any nations that had supported Israel during the six-day war. The resulting oil embargo sent prices soaring to what remain record levels. By the early 1980s, OPEC members were actively cooperating to maintain high oil prices for economic rather than political reasons. (Antitrust laws do not apply to OPEC, which consists of government-controlled businesses.)

To maintain high prices, OPEC members restricted their output, lest they produce more oil than the world demanded at the high price. Each member nation agreed to an output quota. In 1982, OPEC set an overall output limit of 18 million barrels per day, down from 31 million barrels per day in 1979. Prices were to be maintained at $34 per barrel. Each member nation had an individual production quota, except for Saudi Arabia, the largest producer, which adjusted its output as necessary to maintain prices.

Maintaining the cartel proved difficult. Sometimes, such as during the Iran–Iraq War (1980–1988), member nations sought to produce more than their allotment. This glutted the world market with OPEC oil. Despite Saudi Arabia's efforts to reduce output, prices plunged. Further pressure on prices came from companies that elected not to participate in OPEC, such as the British National Oil Company. When this company cut the price of its North Sea oil by $3 per barrel in 1983, the Nigerian oil minister (Nigeria is a member of OPEC) was prompted to say "We are ready for a price war." Before long, OPEC had slashed its price by 15 percent and reduced its output by 3 percent. Throughout most of the 1980s and 1990s, oil prices hovered around $15 to $20 per barrel.

Today, OPEC accounts for less than 30 percent of world oil production and would seem to have lost control over world oil prices. Market forces have taken over, with staggering results. Saudi Arabia remains the world's largest oil exporter and is concerned that current high prices might reduce long-run oil demand. It is pumping oil as fast as it can (profiting handsomely at current prices) and offering verbal assurances that its reservoirs will last another century. Oil speculators are not convinced.

Efforts have been made to cartelize many other international commodities industries, including copper, tin, coffee, tea, and cocoa. A few cartels have had short-term success, such as bauxite and uranium, and one or two, such as the DeBeers diamond cartel, appear to have enjoyed long-term success. In general, however, most international cartels are unable to substantially affect pricing for long.

the cleaning effectiveness of its product (e.g., Colgate-Palmolive might alter the formula for Ajax so that smaller amounts of cleaner need to be mixed with water to clean a given surface). This enhances the product for all prospective consumers, although consumers may disagree about how much they are willing to pay for this enhancement. A product is horizontally differentiated when only some consumers prefer it to competing products (holding price equal). Colgate-Palmolive engages in horizontal differentiation when it adds a lemon scent to Ajax. This makes the cleaner more attractive to consumers who like a lemon scent but perhaps less attractive to those who prefer pine.

An important source of horizontal differentiation is geography, because consumers prefer stores that are convenient to reach. Horizontal differentiation allows firms to raise prices without losing many customers who would rather pay a little more than travel a little further. As an illustration, consider Figure 6.1, which depicts a market in which products are differentiated based on location. The figure shows the town of Linesville. The only road in Linesville—Straight Street—is depicted by the straight line in the figure, and it is exactly 10 miles long. There is a video rental store at each end of Straight Street. Blockbuster Video is at the left end of town (denoted by L in the figure); Hollywood Video is at the right end (denoted by R). Each store carries identical inventory. There are 100 video rental customers in Linesville, and their homes are equally spaced along Straight Street. Thus, 50 consumers live closer to Blockbuster and 50 live closer to Hollywood Video.

When consumers decide which store to visit, they take two factors into account: the prices that each store charges and the cost of traveling to each store, including direct costs, such as gasoline, as well as indirect costs, such as the cost of the time required to get to the store. Let the cost of traveling one mile equal 50 cents for all consumers. Given this information, we can determine the degree to which consumers will switch from one store to another as the stores vary their prices.

Suppose that both stores initially charge $3 per video rental. In this case, each store will have 50 customers. Now suppose that Blockbuster lowers its price per video from $3 to $2, while Hollywood Video keeps its price at $3. How will this affect the sales of both stores? To answer, we need to identify the location on Straight Street at which a consumer would be indifferent between purchasing from Blockbuster versus Hollywood Video. Because travel is costly, all consumers living to the left of that location will visit Blockbuster and all living to the right will visit Hollywood Video.

A consumer will be indifferent between the two stores if purchase costs are identical, where costs include both video rental and transportation costs. Consider a consumer living M miles from Blockbuster (and therefore living $10 - M$ miles from Hollywood Video) who is planning to rent just one video. For this consumer, the total cost of visiting Blockbuster is $2 + .50M$. The total cost of visiting Hollywood Video is $3 + .50(10 - M)$. These costs are equal if $M = 6$; a consumer located at $M = 6$ will have total purchase costs of $5 at both stores. It follows that 60 consumers will visit Blockbuster and 40 will visit Hollywood Video.

FIGURE 6.1
VIDEO RETAILERS IN LINESVILLE

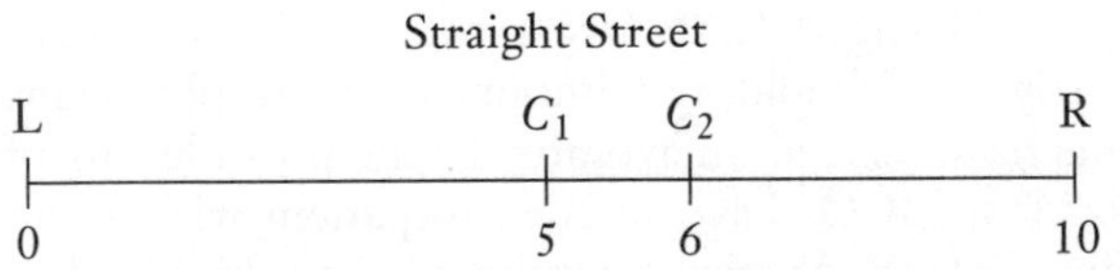

If store L and store R both charge $3 per video, then all consumers living to the left of C_1 shop at store L and all consumers living to the right of C_1 shop at store R. If store L lowers its price to $2 per video, then some customers living to the right of C_1 may wish to travel the extra distance to buy from store L. If travel costs $.50 per mile, then all customers living between C_1 and C_2 will travel the extra distance to save a dollar on the rental.

Because consumers prefer not to travel, Blockbuster gains only 10 customers from Hollywood video even though it charges $1 less per rental. One would intuitively expect that as product differentiation declines in importance—in this case, as the transportation cost decreases—Blockbuster would gain more from its price decrease. The model bears this out. If the transportation cost were only 20 cents per mile rather than 50 cents, the indifferent consumer lives at $M = 7.5$ and Blockbuster gets 75 customers. As transportation costs diminish further, Blockbuster and Hollywood Video become homogeneous—consumers have no strong preference for either store. Indeed, if the transportation cost is 1 cent, then Blockbuster need only lower its price by 10 cents to gain all the business.

This example shows that horizontal differentiation results when consumers have *idiosyncratic preferences*, that is, if tastes differ markedly from one person to the next. Location is an important source of idiosyncratic preferences. Some consumers happen to live near Blockbuster, and others happen to live near Hollywood Video. Location is not the only source of idiosyncratic preferences. Some consumers prefer conservative business suits, whereas others want Italian styling. Some want the biggest sports utility vehicle they can find, whereas others want good mileage. In these and countless other ways, firms can differentiate their products, raise their prices, and yet find that many of their customers remain loyal.

Of course, consumers will not switch from their favorite seller, even if that seller raises price substantially, unless they are aware of a better one. The degree of horizontal differentiation depends on the magnitude of consumer *search costs*, that is, how easy or hard it is for consumers to get information about alternatives. Retailers like Blockbuster Video often rely on advertising to reduce consumer search costs. It is easy to understand why low-price sellers would want to minimize search costs, for this would likely boost their market shares. But low search costs reduce horizontal differentiation, leading to lower prices and lower profits for all firms.

In some markets search costs can be very high. These tend to be markets in which consumers have highly idiosyncratic preferences along "hard-to-describe" dimensions. Physician services are a good example. Patients may not care very much about price, especially if they have insurance. They probably care a lot about a physician's bedside manner, experience, and access to specific specialists and hospitals. It may be difficult (and ethically questionable) for a physician to advertise this information. Instead, patients must rely on their own personal experiences, and those of trusted friends and family, to obtain information about different physicians. As a result, most patients who have had good experiences with their physicians will remain loyal to them, even if that physician raises price or the service deteriorates. It is too difficult to find another good physician.

Because they sell highly differentiated services, physicians practicing in unregulated markets have been able to charge prices well above their incremental costs. Physician prices in the United States are often double those of other nations where governments regulate physician fees. Managed Care Organizations (MCOs) have tried to cut physician prices, primarily by withholding reimbursements to physicians who refuse to discount. But patients have reacted unfavorably to the possible loss of access to their favorite physicians. Most MCOs have acceded to patient wishes and moderated their threats to physicians. As long as patients continue to have highly idiosyncratic preferences, physicians will be able to maintain relatively high prices.

Entry into Monopolistically Competitive Markets

The theory of optimal pricing implies that firms in differentiated product markets will set prices in excess of marginal costs. The resulting high PCMs help to defray the fixed costs of doing business. If prices are high enough to more than cover fixed costs, firms will earn positive economic profits, inviting entry. Entry will reduce prices and erode market shares until economic profits equal zero.

These forces can be understood with a numerical example. Suppose that a market currently has 10 firms, called *incumbents*. Each of the 10 incumbents has a constant marginal cost of $10 per unit and a fixed cost of $120. Each incumbent sells a horizontally differentiated product and faces a price elasticity of demand $\eta = 2$. With this elasticity, the profit-maximizing price for each incumbent firm is $20.[13] Suppose that at this price the total market demand is 240, which is evenly divided among all sellers in the market. Thus, each incumbent sells 24 units. It is straightforward to calculate each incumbent's profits. Each one has revenues of $480 and total costs of $360, so profits equal $120. These facts are summarized in Table 6.4 in the column labeled "Before Entry."

Profits attract entry by other firms. Suppose that entrants' and incumbents' costs are identical, and that each entrant can differentiate its product, so that all sellers have the same market share. Suppose further that differentiation is such that the price elasticity of demand facing all sellers remains constant at 2. Then each entrant will set a price of $20. If enough entrants are interested in pursuing profit opportunities, entry will continue until there are no more profits to be earned. This occurs when there are 20 firms in the market, each with sales of 12. The last column of Table 6.4 summarizes these results.

This example shows that when product differentiation enables sellers to set prices well above marginal costs, new entrants will erode the resulting profits, even if price remains unchanged. Entrants usually steal some market share from incumbents, thereby reducing each incumbent's revenue and making it increasingly difficult for incumbents to cover fixed costs. In our example, entry did not intensify price competition. If prices fall, entry will erode profits even faster.

Entry occurs in monopolistically competitive markets because sellers enjoy customer loyalty and this loyalty allows them to raise price above marginal cost. In Chamberlin's classic model, the amount of entry is thought to be excessive because it drives up fixed costs without a comcomitant reduction in price. But this simple analysis is misleading, for it fails to consider another implication of loyalty. If customers are loyal to different sellers, it follows that customers value variety. If some customers prefer seller A, whereas others prefer B, and B is shut out of the market, its customers are worse off. Entrants increase the variety in the market by staking out new locations, flavors, product styles, and so on. If consumers place a high value on variety, then entry in monopolistically competitive markets will not be excessive.

TABLE 6.4
PROFITS AND NUMBER OF FIRMS UNDER MONOPOLISTIC COMPETITION

	Before Entry	*After Entry*
Number of firms	10	20
Fixed costs per firm	$120	$120
Marginal cost	$10	$10
Price	$20	$20
Market demand	240 units	240 units
Sales per firm	24 units	12 units
Profit per firm	$120	0

EXAMPLE 6.5 PRICING IN THE AIRLINE INDUSTRY

For the first 15 years after deregulation in 1978, the U.S. airline industry was plagued by frequent price wars and large financial losses. The airlines were particularly hard hit by the recession of the early 1990s, and several nearly went bankrupt. U.S. airlines enjoyed soaring profits during the economic recovery of the mid- to late 1990s, only to suffer record losses during the 2001 recession and the aftermath of the terrorist attacks of September 11. Prices are rising once again, owing partly to fuel costs but also in keeping with ongoing economic growth. These trends are partly due to fluctuations in demand but are exacerbated by the industry cost structure and the nature of competition among carriers.

Airline costs fall into three broad categories:

1. *Flight-sensitive costs*, which vary with the number of flights the airline offers. These include the costs associated with crews, aircraft servicing, and fuel. Once the airline sets its schedule, these costs are fixed.
2. *Traffic-sensitive costs*, which vary with the number of passengers. These include the costs associated with items such as ticketing agents and food. Airlines plan their expenditures on these items in anticipation of the level of traffic, but in the short run, these costs are also fixed.
3. *Fixed overhead costs*, which include general and administrative expenses, advertising and marketing, and interest expenses.

Once an airline has set its schedule, flight-sensitive and overhead costs are fixed. Traffic-sensitive costs, which make up only a small percentage of total costs, are the only variable costs. This means that the airline is better off selling a seat at a low price—near marginal cost but well below average total cost—than not selling the seat at all. Thus, if airlines are operating well short of capacity, as they were in the early 1990s and early 2000s, they have tremendous incentives to reduce prices. Because marginal costs are so far below average costs, the airlines lost staggering sums during these price wars. The airlines covered their marginal costs but failed to make appreciable contributions toward fixed costs. On the other hand, if airlines are at or near capacity, as they were during the economic expansion of the mid- to late 1990s, and as they are returning to in the mid-2000s, they can raise prices substantially above average costs without losing customers to competitors. In 2000, American Airlines recognized this close connection between capacity utilization, pricing, and profits. Anticipating the recession, American removed seats from all of its planes. Marketed as a quality enhancement, the strategy was also designed to prevent excess capacity and associated price reductions. Other carriers failed to follow suit, however, and the recession set the industry back on its heels.

Many other factors affect airline pricing. In some cases, such as when a carrier dominates a hub, an airline faces little competition on certain routes and may raise price accordingly. Even when two or three carriers compete on a route, they may be able to price at or near the monopoly level. Chapter 8 discusses how firms that compete over a long time or in many markets often avoid price competition. Finally, although airlines seem to sell homogeneous products, there are a number of sources of differentiation among them. Business travelers prefer carriers that offer frequent service, which gives them flexibility to schedule meetings. Many travelers accumulate frequent-flier miles, which encourages them to use the same carrier for all their flights. Differentiation based on mileage programs appears to be the main competitive lever that gives carriers like United and American a chance to survive against low-cost competitors.

Oligopoly

In perfectly competitive and monopolistically competitive markets, sellers do not believe that their pricing or production strategies will affect rivals' prices or production volumes. This makes sense in markets with many sellers. In a market with only a few sellers, however, it is more reasonable to expect that the pricing and production strategies of any one firm will affect rivals' pricing and output decisions. A market in which the actions of individual firms materially affect the overall market is called an oligopoly.

Economists have produced many models of oligopolistic markets. A central element of many models is the careful consideration of how firms respond to each other and to opportunities in the market. This is illustrated by considering two of the oldest and most important oligopoly models—Cournot quantity competition and Bertrand price competition. We investigate these models below and further elaborate on oligopoly models in the next two chapters.

Cournot Quantity Competition

One of the first models of oligopoly markets was developed by Augustin Cournot in 1835.[14] Cournot initially considered a market in which there were only two firms, firm 1 and firm 2. These might be two producers of DRAM chips, such as Samsung (firm 1) and Micron (firm 2). These firms produce identical goods, so that they are forced to charge the same prices. In Cournot's model, the sole strategic choice of each firm is the amount they choose to produce, Q_1 and Q_2. Once the firms are committed to production, they set whatever price is necessary to "clear the market." This is the price at which consumers are willing to buy the total production, $Q_1 + Q_2$. The intuition behind this assumption is that because both firms are committed to production, their incremental costs are zero. Thus, if either one is unable to sell all its output, it will lower price until it is able to do so. The market price is that which enables both firms to sell all their output.

We will analyze the output decisions of Samsung and Micron facing specific demand and cost functions. Suppose that both Samsung and Micron have the following total costs of production:

$$TC_1 = 10Q_1$$
$$TC_2 = 10Q_2$$

In other words, both firms have constant marginal costs of $10 per unit, just as in the case of monopoly discussed earlier. Thus, if $Q_1 = Q_2 = 10$, then $TC_1 = TC_2 = 100$. As in our monopoly example, let market demand be given by $P = 100 - Q_1 - Q_2$. With this demand curve, the market price falls if either firm tries to increase the amount that it sells. For example, if Samsung and Micron both produce 10 units (i.e., $Q_1 = Q_2 = 10$), then $P = \$80$. If they both produce 20 units (i.e., $Q_1 = Q_2 = 20$), then $P = \$60$.

How much will each firm produce? Each firm cares about the market price when it selects its production level. Because market price depends on the total production of both firms, the amount that, say, Samsung desires to produce depends on how much it expects Micron to produce. Cournot investigated production under a simple set of expectations. Each firm "guesses" how much the other firm will produce and believes that its rival will stick to this level of output. Each firm's optimal level of production is the *best response* to the level it expects its rival to choose. Put another way, Samsung chooses the level of production that maximizes its own profits, given the level of production it guesses Micron will choose, and Micron chooses the level of production that maximizes its profits given the amount of output it guesses Samsung will produce.

A *Cournot equilibrium* is a pair of outputs Q_1^* and Q_2^* and a market price P^* that satisfy three conditions:

(C1) P^* is the price that clears the market given the firms' production levels; that is, $P^* = 100 - Q_1^* - Q_2^*$.

(C2) Q_1^* is Samsung's profit-maximizing output given that it guesses Micron will choose $Q2^*$.

(C3) Q_2^* is Micron's profit-maximizing output given that it guesses Samsung will choose Q_1^*.

Thus, in a Cournot equilibrium, each firm's guess about its rival's production level is "correct,"; that is, it corresponds to the output its rival actually chooses.

To find the market equilibrium choices of Q_1 and Q_2, consider first Samsung's choice of Q_1. According to condition (C2), for Q_1 to be an equilibrium choice it must maximize Samsung's profits, given Micron's choice of Q_2. Suppose that Samsung thinks that Micron is going to produce output Q_{2g}, where the subscript g reminds us that this is a guess rather than the actual value. Then Samsung estimates that if it produces Q_1 units of output, its profits, denoted by π_1, will be

$$\pi_1 = \text{Revenue} - \text{Total cost} = P_1 Q_1 - TC_1 = (100 - Q_1 - Q_{2g})Q_1 - 10Q_1$$

Samsung needs to solve for the value of Q_1 that maximizes its profits. We can use calculus to determine that the profit-maximizing value of Q_1 satisfies:[15]

$$\text{Profit-maximizing value of } Q_1 = 45 - .5Q_{2g}$$

The profit-maximizing value of Q_1 is called Samsung's best response to Micron. According to this equation, Samsung's best response is a decreasing function of Q_{2g}. This implies that if Samsung expects Micron to increase output, it will reduce its own output. This makes sense. If Micron increases output, then condition (C1) states that the market price must decrease. Facing a lower price, Samsung prefers to produce less itself. The line labeled R_1 in Figure 6.2 depicts Samsung's choice of Q_1

FIGURE 6.2
COURNOT REACTION FUNCTIONS

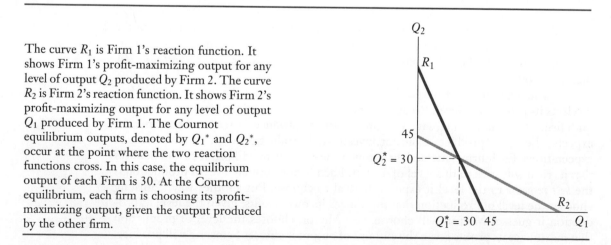

The curve R_1 is Firm 1's reaction function. It shows Firm 1's profit-maximizing output for any level of output Q_2 produced by Firm 2. The curve R_2 is Firm 2's reaction function. It shows Firm 2's profit-maximizing output for any level of output Q_1 produced by Firm 1. The Cournot equilibrium outputs, denoted by Q_1^* and Q_2^*, occur at the point where the two reaction functions cross. In this case, the equilibrium output of each Firm is 30. At the Cournot equilibrium, each firm is choosing its profit-maximizing output, given the output produced by the other firm.

as a function of its conjecture about Q_2. Economists call this line Samsung's *reaction function*.

Similarly, we can use condition (C3) to solve for Micron's best response to Samsung's choice of Q_1:

$$\text{Profit-maximizing value of } Q_2 = 45 - .5Q_{1g}$$

Micron's choice of Q_2 as a function of Samsung's choice of Q_1 is shown as reaction function R_2 in Figure 6.2.

We need one more step before we can solve for the equilibrium choices of Q_1 and Q_2. Recall that in equilibrium, each firm's guess about its rival's output must be correct. If a firm guesses incorrectly, then it would have an incentive to change its output, thereby violating condition (C2) or (C3). For example, suppose that Samsung expects Micron to choose $Q_2 = 50$, and, as a result, Samsung selects $Q_1 - 20$. If it turns out that Micron chooses $Q_2 = 30$, then Samsung's choice would not be optimal, and Samsung would want to adjust its output of chips.

Only one pair of outputs is simultaneously the best response to each other. These outputs, which we denote by Q_1^* and Q_2^*, are found by solving both firms' reaction functions simultaneously. This solution turns out to be $Q_1^* - Q_2^* = 30$. Graphically, this corresponds to the point in Figure 6.2 where the two reaction functions intersect. We can also solve for the equilibrium market price P^* and the profits each firm earns. Recall that $P = 100 - Q_1 - Q_2$. In this case, $P^* = \$40$. Substituting price and quantity into the equation for each firm's profits reveals that each firm makes $900 in profit in equilibrium.

Cournot's assumption that firms will simultaneously select the best response to each other's choices is often hard to accept as an accurate depiction of how real firms behave. It seems to impose unrealistic omniscience on each firm. Each firm somehow expects that its rival will choose its Cournot equilibrium output, and in response, each firm actually chooses its Cournot equilibrium output.[16] As a focal point for analysis, this assumption may not be too bad. It means that in equilibrium, each firm will be content with its decision. This seems more satisfying than assuming that firms are consistently unhappy with their choices. Moreover, neither Samsung nor Micron need be omniscient for the Cournot equilibrium quantities to emerge. Suppose that both firms are "out of equilibrium" in the sense that at least one firm has chosen to produce a quantity other than 30. For example, suppose that $Q_1 = Q_2 = 40$. Neither firm will be happy with its choice of quantity—each is producing more than it would like given its rival's production. As a result, we would expect each firm to adjust to the other firm's choices.

Table 6.5 shows an example of the adjustment process. Suppose that Samsung makes the first adjustment. It examines its profit-maximization equation and determines

TABLE 6.5
THE COURNOT ADJUSTMENT PROCESS

Starting Q_1	Starting Q_2	Firm That Is Adjusting	Ending Q_1	Ending Q_2
40	40	Firm 1	25	40
25	40	Firm 2	25	32.5
25	32.5	Firm 1	28.75	32.5
28.75	32.5	Firm 2	28.75	30.63
28.75	30.63	Firm 1	29.69	30.63

that if $Q_2 = 40$, it should choose $Q_1 = 25$. Suppose now that Samsung reduces its output to 25. Micron will examine its own profit-maximization equation and determine that if Samsung chooses $Q_1 = 25$, then it should choose $Q_2 = 32.5$. Now it is Samsung's turn to adjust its output. If $Q_2 = 32.5$, then Samsung will prefer $Q_1 = 28.75$. Table 6.5 shows that Q_1 and Q_2 continue to converge toward the equilibrium values of $Q_1 = Q_2 = 30$.

The Cournot model implies that the equilibrium industry output does not maximize industry profit. Industry profit is maximized at a total output of 45 and a market price of $55. (This is the monopoly quantity and price computed earlier.) By independently maximizing their own profits, firms produce more output than they would if they collusively maximized industry profits. This is characteristic of oligopolistic industries: The pursuit of individual self-interest does not maximize the well-being of the group as a whole. This occurs under Cournot competition for the following reason. When one firm, say Samsung, expands its output, it reduces the market price and thus lowers the sales revenues of rival chip producers. Samsung does not care about this *revenue destruction effect* because it is maximizing its own profit, not total industry profit. Thus, Samsung expands its production volume more aggressively than it would if its objective had been to maximize industry profit. If all DRAM producers behave this way, the market price must be less than the monopoly price.

The smaller a firm's share of industry sales, the greater the divergence between its private gain and the revenue destruction effect from output expansion. This helps explain why smaller firms may be more willing to "rock the boat" to gain market share. They enjoy the full benefits of each additional unit sold, but they suffer only a small percentage of the revenue destruction effect, which is instead borne mainly by their larger rivals. The revenue destruction effect also explains why the Cournot equilibrium price falls as the number of firms in the market increases. Each firm has, on average, a smaller share of the market and so is less concerned about the revenue destruction effect. Table 6.6 illustrates this point by showing equilibrium prices, profits, and outputs in a Cournot industry with the same demand curve and cost function as in the preceding example. The equilibrium price and profit per firm decline as the number of firms increases. More generally, it can be shown that the average PCM of a firm in a Cournot equilibrium is given by the formula $PCM = H/\eta$, where H denotes the Herfindahl, and η is the price elasticity of market demand. Thus, the less concentrated the industry (the lower the industry's H), the smaller will be PCMs in equilibrium.

Antitrust enforcers often use the Herfindahl index to assess market power. For example, the DOJ and FTC closely scrutinize mergers in markets in which the Herfindahl exceeds .18. Cournot's model provides a direct justification for this approach; in markets where firms behave as Cournot describes, the Herfindahl provides

TABLE 6.6
COURNOT EQUILIBRIA AS THE NUMBER OF FIRMS INCREASES

Number of Firms	Market Price	Market Quantity	Per-Firm Profits	Total Profits
2	$40	60	$900	$1,800
3	$32.5	67.5	$506.25	$1,518.75
5	$25	75	$225	$1,125
10	$18.2	81.8	$66.94	$669.40
100	$10.9	89.1	$0.79	$79

important information about the relationship between market concentration and price. Because many factors besides market concentration may ultimately affect equilibrium output and price, computation of the Herfindahl is usually just the first step in merger analysis. We will discuss additional factors in the next two chapters.

The Cournot model has another practical use. It is very straightforward to alter one or more parameters of the model—the demand curve and firm costs—and recompute equilibria. This makes it possible to forecast how changes in demand and costs will affect profitability in markets in which firms behave strategically. This makes the Cournot model a valuable tool for planning.

Bertrand Price Competition

In Cournot's model, each firm selects a quantity to produce, and the resulting total output determines the market price. Alternatively, one might imagine a market in which each firm selects a price and stands ready to meet all the demand for its product at that price. This model of competition was first analyzed by Joseph Bertrand in 1883.[18] In Bertrand's model, each firm selects a price to maximize its own profits, given the price that it believes the other firm will select. Each firm also believes that its pricing practices will not affect the pricing of its rival; each firm views its rival's price as fixed.

We can use the cost and demand conditions from the Cournot model to explore the Bertrand market equilibrium, again using the (hypothetical) example of rival DRAM producers Samsung and Micron. Recall that when $MC_1 = MC_2 = \$10$, and demand is given by $P = 100 - Q_1 - Q_2$, then the Cournot equilibrium is $Q_1 = Q_2 = 30$ and $P_1 = P_2 = \$40$. This is not, however, a Bertrand equilibrium. Consider, for example, the pricing decision of Samsung. If Samsung believes that Micron will charge a price of \$40, then it would reason that if it were to slightly undercut Micron's price, it would get all of Micron's business. Thus, Samsung believes that if $P_1 = \$39$ and $P_2 = \$40$, then $Q_1 = 61$ and $Q_2 = 0$. In this case Samsung expects to earn profits of \$1,769, well above the profits of \$900 it would earn if it charged a price of \$40.

Of course, $P_1 = \$39$ and $P_2 = \$40$ cannot be an equilibrium either because at these prices, Micron will wish to undercut Samsung's price. As long as both firms set prices that exceed marginal costs, one firm will always have an incentive to corner the market by slightly undercutting its competitor. This implies that the only possible equilibrium is $P_1 = P_2 = $ marginal cost $= \$10$. At these prices, neither firm can do better by changing its price. If either firm lowers price, it will lose money on each unit sold. If either firm raises price, it would sell nothing.

In Bertrand's model, rivalry between two firms results in the perfectly competitive outcome. Price competition is particularly fierce in this setting because the firms' products are perfect substitutes. When firms' products are differentiated (as in monopolistic competition), price competition is less intense. Later in this chapter, we will examine Bertrand price competition when firms produce differentiated products. Bertrand competition can be unstable in markets where firms must make upfront investments in plant and equipment to enter. As firms cut prices to gain market share, they may fail to cover long-run costs. If one firm should exit the market, the remaining firm could try to raise its price. But this might simply attract a new entrant that will wrest away some of the remaining firm's business. Fierce price competition may also end if one or both firms run up against capacity constraints (so that the ability to steal market share is limited), or learn to stop competing on the basis of price. These ideas are covered in greater depth in Chapter 8.

EXAMPLE 6.6 COURNOT EQUILIBRIUM IN THE CORN WET MILLING INDUSTRY

Michael Porter and Michael Spence's case study of the corn wet milling industry is a real-world illustration of the Cournot model.[17] Firms in the corn wet milling industry convert corn into cornstarch and corn syrup. The corn syrup industry was a fairly stable oligopoly until the 1960s, when several firms entered the market, including Archer-Daniels-Midland and Cargill. The new competitors and new capacity disrupted the old equilibrium and drove prices downward. By the early 1970s, however, competitive stability returned to the industry as capacity utilization rates and prices rose.

In 1972, a major development hit the industry: The production of high-fructose corn syrup (HFCS) became commercially viable. HFCS can be used instead of sugar to sweeten products, such as soft drinks. With sugar prices expected to rise, a significant market for HFCS beckoned. Firms in the corn wet milling industry had to decide whether and how to add capacity to accommodate the expected demand.

Porter and Spence studied this capacity expansion process. They did so through a detailed simulation of competitive behavior based on an in-depth study of the 11 major competitors in the industry. Porter and Spence postulated that each firm's expansion decision was based on a conjecture about the overall expansion of industry capacity, as well as expectations about demand and sugar prices. Their model also took into account that capacity choices coupled with demand conditions determined industry prices of cornstarch, corn syrup, and HFCS. The notion that a firm's capacity choice is based on conjectures about the capacity choices of other firms is directly analogous to the idea in the Cournot model that each firm bases its output choice on conjectures of the output choices of other firms. The notion that capacity decisions then determine a market price is also analogous to the Cournot model.

Porter and Spence's simulation of the industry attempted to find an "equilibrium": an industry capacity expansion path that, when each firm made its optimal capacity decision based on the conjecture that this path would prevail, resulted in an actual pattern of capacity expansion that matched the assumed pattern. This is directly analogous to the notion of a Cournot equilibrium, in which each firm's expectations about the behavior of its competitors are confirmed by their actual behavior. Based on their simulation of industry decision making, Porter and Spence determined that an industry equilibrium would result in a moderate amount of additional capacity added to the industry as a result of the commercialization of HFCS. The specific predictions of their model compared with the actual pattern of capacity expansion are shown below.

Though not perfect, Porter and Spence's calculated equilibrium comes quite close to the actual pattern of capacity expansion in the industry, particularly in 1973 and 1974. The discrepancies in 1975 and 1976 mainly reflect timing. Porter and Spence's equilibrium model did not consider capacity additions in the years beyond 1976. In 1976, however, the industry had more than 4 billion pounds of HFCS capacity under construction, and that capacity did not come on line until after 1976. Including this capacity, the total HFCS capacity expansion was 9.2 billion pounds, as compared with the 9.1 billion pounds of predicted equilibrium capacity. Porter and Spence's research suggests that a Cournot-like model, when adapted to the specific conditions of the corn wet milling industry, provided predictions that came remarkably close to the actual pattern of capacity expansion decisions.

	Post-1973	1974	1975	1976	1976	Total
Actual industry capacity	0.6	1.0	1.4	2.2	4	9.2 (billions of lb)
Predicted equilibrium capacity	0.6	1.5	3.5	3.5	0	9.1

Why Are Cournot and Bertrand Different?

The Cournot and Bertrand models make dramatically different predictions about the quantities, prices, and profits that will arise under oligopolistic competition. How can one reconcile these dramatic differences?

One way to reconcile the two models is to recognize that Cournot and Bertrand competition may take place over different time frames. Cournot competitors can be thought of as choosing capacities and then competing as price setters given the capacities chosen earlier. The result of this "two-stage" competition (first choose capacities and then choose prices) can be shown to be identical to the Cournot equilibrium in quantities.[19]

Another way to reconcile the models is to recognize that they make different assumptions about how firms expect their rivals to react to their own competitive moves. The Cournot model applies most naturally to markets in which firms must make production decisions in advance, are committed to selling all of their output, and are therefore unlikely to react to fluctuations in the rivals' output. This might occur if the majority of production costs are sunk, or because it is costly to hold inventories. In such settings, firms will do what it takes to sell their output, even if that means allowing the price to fall. Each firm will also believe that its competitors will keep their sales equal to their planned production volumes. Thus, if a firm lowers its price, it cannot expect to steal customers from its rivals. Because "business stealing" is not an option, Cournot competitors must suffer a substantial revenue destruction effect if they are to expand output. As a result, they set prices less aggressively than Bertrand competitors. Thus, the Cournot equilibrium outcome, while not the monopoly one, nevertheless results in positive profits and a price that exceeds marginal and average cost.

The Bertrand model pertains to markets in which capacity is sufficiently flexible that firms can meet all of the demand that arises at the prices they announce. If firms' products are perfect substitutes, then each Bertrand competitor believes that it can steal massive amounts of business from its competitors through a small cut in price. In fact, firms expect that all increases in sales will come through business stealing. The revenue destruction effect is nil, making growth through price reductions a very attractive option. Of course, all competitors think this way, so each firm in the market attempts to steal market share from competitors through price cutting. In equilibrium, price-cost margins and profits are driven to zero.

These distinctions help to explain the pro-cyclicality of airline industry profits. During business downturns, the airlines have substantial excess capacity on many routes. Because many consumers perceive the airlines as selling undifferentiated products, and search costs are low, each airline can fill empty seats by undercutting rivals' prices and stealing their customers. The resulting competition resembles Bertrand's model and can lead to substantial losses for the industry. During boom times, airlines operate near capacity. Airlines have little incentive to cut prices. Because they have few empty seats, they are unable to steal business even if they wanted to. Competition in each route is based on capacity, not price, resembles Cournot's model, and allows the airlines to reap substantial profits.

Many other issues may be considered when assessing the likely conduct and performance of firms in an oligopoly. Competition may be based on a variety of product parameters, including quality, availability, and advertising. Firms may not know the strategic choices of their competitors. The timing of decision making can profoundly influence profits. We discuss all of these issues in Chapters 7 and 8.

Bertrand Price Competition When Products Are Horizontally Differentiated

In many oligopolistic markets, products are close, but not perfect, substitutes. The Bertrand model of price competition does not fully capture the nature of price competition in these settings. Fortunately, we can adapt the logic of the Bertrand model to deal with horizontally differentiated products.

When products are horizontally differentiated, a firm will not lose all of its business to rival firms that undercut its price. As in the theory of monopolistic competition, this implies that a firm will not lose all of its customers if it were to slightly raise price. Nor will it steal all of its rival's customers if it were to slightly reduce price. To illustrate, consider the U.S. cola market. Farid Gasini, J. J. Lafont, and Quang Vuong (GLV) have used statistical methods to estimate demand curves for Coke (denoted by 1) and Pepsi (denoted by 2):[20]

$$Q_1 = 63.42 - 3.98P_1 + 2.25P_2$$
$$Q_2 = 49.52 - 5.48P_2 + 1.40P_1$$

With these demand functions, as Coke raises its price above that of Pepsi, Coke's demand falls gradually.

GLV estimated that Coca-Cola had a constant marginal cost equal to $4.96, and Pepsi had a constant marginal cost of $3.96. What price should each firm charge? As in the preceding models, an equilibrium occurs when neither firm has an incentive to change its price, given the price the other firm sets. The logic of finding this equilibrium is similar to the logic of the Cournot model. Because firms are choosing prices rather than quantities, however, this is called a *differentiated Bertrand* model. We begin by computing each firm's profit-maximizing price as a function of its guess about its rival's price. Coca-Cola's profit can be written as its price–cost margin times the quantity it sells, which is given by its demand function.[21]

$$\pi_1 = (P_1 - 4.96)(63.49 - 3.98P_1 + 2.25P_{2g})$$

(We again use the subscript g to emphasize that Coca-Cola is making a guess about Pepsi's price.) Using calculus to solve this maximization problem yields a reaction function[22]

$$P_1 = 10.44 + .2826P_{2g}$$

Pepsi's optimal price is derived similarly. It maximizes

$$\pi_2 = (P_2 - 3.94)(49.52 - 5.48P_2 + 1.40P_{1g})$$

which yields a reaction function

$$P_2 = 6.49 + .1277P1g$$

Note that these reaction functions, displayed in Figure 6.3, are upward sloping. Thus, the lower the price the firm expects its rival to charge, the lower the price it should charge. In this sense, "aggressive" behavior by one firm (price cutting) is met by "aggressive" behavior by rivals. Note the contrast with the Cournot model, where "aggressive" behavior by one firm (output expansion) was met by "passive" behavior by rivals (output reduction).

FIGURE 6.3
BERTRAND EQUILIBRIUM WITH HORIZONTALLY DIFFERENTIATED PRODUCTS

Firm 1's reaction function shows its profit-maximizing price for any price charged by Firm 2. Firm 2's reaction function shows its profit-maximizing price for any price charged by Firm 1. The Bertrand equilibrium prices occur at the intersection of these reaction functions. In this example, this is at $P_1 = \$12.72$ and $P_2 = \$8.11$. At this point, each firm is choosing a profit-maximizing price, given the price charged by the other firm.

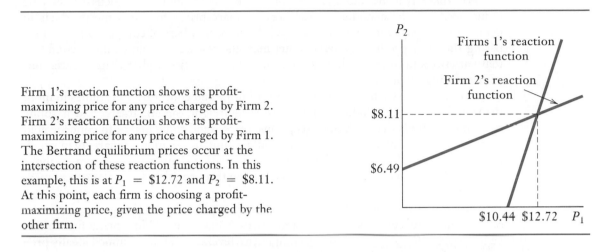

Solving the two reaction functions simultaneously yields the Bertrand equilibrium in prices:

$$P_1 = \$12.72$$
$$P_2 = \$8.11$$

Interestingly, the actual average real prices over the period (1968–1986) to which GLV's analysis pertains were $12.96 for Coca-Cola and $8.16 for Pepsi. The differentiated Bertrand model does an excellent job matching the actual pricing behavior of these two firms in the U.S. market. Note that both Coke and Pepsi's equilibrium prices are well in excess of their marginal production costs. This illustrates that product differentiation softens price competition. This is because when products are differentiated, price cutting is less effective for stealing a rival's business than when products are perfect substitutes.

EVIDENCE ON MARKET STRUCTURE AND PERFORMANCE   ◆ ◆ ◆ ◆ ◆

The theories examined in the previous sections suggest that market structure should be related to the level of prices and profitability that prevail in a market. This is clearly true under Cournot competition, where price is directly related to the Herfindahl. It may also be true under Bertrand competition, because each additional firm reduces the opportunities for differentiation. Many economists have tested whether the predicted link between structure and performance actually exists.

Price and Concentration

The relationship between price and concentration could be studied by comparing differences in price-cost margins and concentration levels across different industries. But price-cost margins may vary across markets for many reasons besides concentration, such as accounting practices, regulation, product differentiation, the nature of sales transactions, and the concentration of buyers.

For these reasons, most studies of concentration and price focus on specific industries.[23] In these studies, researchers compare prices for the same products in geographically separate markets that have different numbers of competitors. By comparing the same products across distinct markets, researchers can be more confident that variations in price are due to variations in competition rather than to variations in accounting or other factors.

Leonard Weiss summarizes the results of price and concentration studies in more than 20 industries, including cement, railroad freight, supermarkets, and gasoline retailing. He finds that with few exceptions, prices tend to be higher in concentrated markets. For example, one study found that gasoline prices in local markets in which the top three gasoline retailers had a 60 percent market share were, on average, about 5 percent higher than in markets in which the top three retailers had a 50 percent market share.

Timothy Bresnahan and Peter Reiss used a novel methodology to study the relationship between concentration and prices. They asked, "How many firms must be in a market for price to approach competitive levels?"[24] They examined locally provided services such as doctors, tire dealers, and plumbers. For each service, they calculated "entry thresholds," defined as the minimum population necessary to support a given number of sellers. Let E_n denote the entry threshold for n sellers. For all services, they found that E_2 was about four times E_1. This could make sense only if prices are lower when there are two sellers than when there is one. When this happens, demand must more than double to make up for the intensified competition. They also found that $E_3 - E_2 > E_2 - E_1$, suggesting further intensification of price competition as the number of sellers increases from two to three. Finally, they found that $E_4 - E_3 = E_3 - E_2$, suggesting that once there are three sellers in a market, price competition is as intense as it will get.

Other Studies of the Determinants of Profitability

Chapter 2 discussed the theoretical link between economies of scale and market structure, while this chapter has discussed the theoretical link among market structure, competition, and profitability. Together, these theories suggest a link between economies of scale and profits. Researchers have used a number of approaches to validate these ideas.

Many studies verify the link between economies of scale and market structure. One consistent finding is that the same industries tend to be highly concentrated in all countries. This suggests that some underlying factor, such as economies of scale, determines market structure in all markets. Studies in which researchers have attempted to measure the magnitude of scale economies are consistent with this conclusion. Industries in which the minimum efficient scale of production is large relative to the size of the market tend to be more concentrated than industries with minimal scale economies.

Researchers have had a more difficult time demonstrating the link between concentration and profitability. Richard Schmalensee has summarized this work as follows: "The relation, if any, between seller concentration and profitability is weak statistically, and the estimated concentration effect is usually small."[25] One explanation may be that different accounting practices across industries hide underlying differences in profitability. Another explanation may be that if an industry were truly profitable, we would expect to observe entry. That an industry has only a few firms may indicate that it is inherently unprofitable for reasons that the researcher cannot identify.

A second line of research copes with this problem by examining the relationship between profits and economies of scale that might limit entry. Some researchers have examined economies of scale in production processes as reflected in large capital-to-sales ratios. Others have examined economies of scale in marketing as reflected in large advertising-to-sales ratios. In most cases, industry profits are higher when production and/or marketing displays economies of scale. This is consistent with the theory that when industries are concentrated because entry is difficult, profits are high.

CHAPTER SUMMARY

◆ The first step in analyzing competition is to identify competitors. Competitors in output markets sell products that are substitutes. Competitors in input markets buy inputs that are substitutes.

◆ Generally, two sellers are competitors in an output market if their products are close substitutes, that is, have similar product-performance characteristics. Price elasticities are useful for determining whether a product has close substitutes.

◆ Once a market is well defined, its structure may be measured using an N-firm concentration ratio or a Herfindahl index.

◆ The structure of a market is often related to the conduct of the firms within it. The spectrum of competitive interaction ranges from competition and monopolistic competition to oligopoly and monopoly.

◆ In competitive markets, consumers are extremely price sensitive, forcing sellers to set prices close to marginal costs. Markets with homogeneous products and many sellers are more likely to feature competitive pricing. Excess capacity exacerbates pricing pressures, often driving prices below average costs.

◆ Monopolists have such a substantial share of their market that they ignore the pricing and production decisions of fringe firms. They may set prices well above marginal cost without losing much business.

◆ Monopolistically competitive markets have many sellers, each with some loyal customers. Prices are set according to the willingness of consumers to switch from one seller to another—if consumers are disloyal and have low search costs, sellers may lower prices to steal business from their competitors. Profits may be eroded further by entrants.

◆ Oligopolies have so few firms that each firm's production and pricing strategy appreciably affects the market price. Market prices can be well above marginal costs, or driven down to marginal costs, depending on the interaction among oligopolists and the degree of product differentiation among them.

◆ Studies confirm that prices are strongly related to industry structure. Price-cost margins tend to be much lower in more competitive markets.

◆ Factors that may deter entry, such as economies of scale and advertising, are associated with higher profits. This is consistent with the theoretical link between market structure and firm profits.

QUESTIONS

1. Why are the concepts of own and cross-price elasticities of demand essential to competitor identification and market definition?

2. In a recent antitrust case, it was necessary to determine whether certain "elite" schools (mainly the Ivy League schools and MIT) constituted a separate market. How would you go about identifying the market served by these schools?

3. How would you characterize the nature of competition in the restaurant industry? Are there submarkets with distinct competitive pressures? Are there important substitutes that constrain pricing? Given these competitive issues, how can a restaurant be profitable?

4. How does industry-level price elasticity of demand shape the opportunities for making profit in an industry? How does the firm-level price elasticity of demand shape the opportunities for making profit in an industry?

5. What is the "revenue destruction effect"? As the number of Cournot competitors in a market increases, the price generally falls. What does this have to do with the revenue destruction effect? Smaller firms often have greater incentive to reduce prices than do larger firms. What does this have to do with the revenue destruction effect?

6. How does the calculation of demand responsiveness in Linesville change if customers rent two videos at a time? What intuition can you draw from this about the magnitude of price competition in various types of markets?

7. Numerous studies have shown that there is usually a systematic relationship between concentration and price. What is this relationship? Offer two brief explanations for this relationship.

8. The relationship described in question 7 does not always appear to hold. What factors, besides the number of firms in the market, might affect margins?

9. The following are the approximate market shares of different brands of soft drinks during the 1980s: Coke—40 percent; Pepsi—30 percent; 7-Up—10 percent; Dr Pepper—10 percent; All other brands—10 percent.

   (a) Compute the Herfindahl for the soft drink market. Suppose that Pepsi acquired 7-Up. Compute the postmerger Herfindahl. What assumptions did you make?

   (b) Federal antitrust agencies would be concerned to see a Herfindahl increase of the magnitude you computed in (a) and might challenge the merger. Pepsi could respond by offering a different market definition. What market definition might it propose? Why would this change the Herfindahl?

10. The dancing machine industry is a duopoly. The two firms, Chuckie B Corporation and Gene Gene Dancing Machines, compete through Cournot quantity setting competition. The demand curve for the industry is $P = 100 - Q$, where Q is the total quantity produced by Chuckie B and Gene Gene. Currently, each firm has marginal cost of $40 and no fixed costs. Show that the equilibrium price is $60, with each firm producing 20 machines and earning profits of $400.

11. Consider a market with two horizontally differentiated firms, X and Y. Each has a constant marginal cost of $20. Demand functions are

$$Q_x = 100 - 2P_x + 1P_y$$
$$Q_y = 100 - 2P_y + 1P_x$$

Calculate the Bertrand equilibrium in prices in this market.

ENDNOTES

[1]Indirect competitors may also include firms that are not currently direct competitors but might become so. This definition forces managers to go beyond current sales data to identify potential competitors.

[2]Capps, C., D. Dranove, D. Greensteins, and M. Satterthwaite use this approach to identify a hospital's substitutes. "The Silent Majority Fallacy of the Elzinga Hogarty Criteria," NBER Working Paper 8216. Cambridge, MA, National Bureau of Economic Research, 2001.

[3]The index is named for Orris Herfindahl, who developed it while writing a Ph.D dissertation at Columbia University on concentration in the steel industry. The index is sometimes referred to as the Herfindahl-Hirschman index and is often abbreviated HHI.

[4]See the Economics Primer.

[5]*Fortune*, October 20, 1980, p. 27.

[6]Potash (potassium oxide) is a compound used to produce products such as fertilizer and soap.

[7]Chapters 5 and 6 of Markham, J., *The Fertilizer Industry*, Nashville, TN, Vanderbilt University Press, 1958.

[8]This point is developed more fully in Chapter 8.

[9]We will assume that this offer does not require Deere to adjust the price at which it sells engines to its other customers.

[10]Fisher, F., Industrial organization, Antitrust, and the Law, Cambridge, MA, MIT Press, 1991.

[11]Demsetz, H., "Two Systems of Belief about Monopoly," in Goldschmidt, H. et al. (eds.), *Industrial Concentration: The New Learning*, Boston, Little, Brown, 1974.

[12]Chamberlin, E. H., *The Theory of Monopolistic Competition*, Cambridge, MA, Harvard University Press, 1933.

[13]Recall that the optimal $PCM = 1/\eta$. Thus, in this case, $PCM = (P - 10)/P = .5$. Solving for P yields $P = \$20$.

[14]Cournot, A., "On the Competition of Producers," Chap. 7 in *Research into the Mathematical Principles of the Theory of Wealth*, translated by N. T. Bacon, New York, Macmillan, 1897. For an excellent review of the Cournot model and other theories of oligopoly behavior, see Shapiro, C., "Theories of Oligopoly Behavior," Chap. 6 in Willig, R. and R. Schmalensee (eds.), *Handbook of Industrial Organization*, Amsterdam, North Holland, 1989.

[15]Profit p_1 can be written as: $90Q_1 - Q_1^2 - Q_{2g}Q_1$. If we treat Q_{2g} as a constant and take the derivative of p_1 with respect to Q_1, we get $\partial p_1/\partial Q_1 = 90 - 2Q_1 - Q_{2g}$. Setting this derivative equal to 0 and solving the resulting equation for Q_1 yields the profit-maximizing value of Q_1.

[16]Cournot's assumption is actually a special case of a modeling assumption known as the Nash equilibrium, which is used to identify likely strategies in a variety of contexts. The Nash equilibrium is discussed in the Economics Primer. We will rely heavily on it in Chapters 7 and 8.

[17]Porter, M. and A. M. Spence, "The Capacity Expansion Decision in a Growing Oligopoly: The Case of Corn Wet Milling," in McCall, J. J. (ed.), *The Economics of Information Uncertainty*, Chicago, University of Chicago Press, 1982, pp. 259–316.

[18]Bertrand, J., "Book Review of Recherche sur Les Principes Mathematiques de la Theorie des Richesses," *Journal des Savants*, 67, 1883, pp. 499–508.

[19]The idea that the Cournot equilibrium can (under some circumstances) emerge as the outcome of a "two-stage game" in which firms first choose capacities and then choose prices is due to Kreps, D. and J. Scheinkman, "Quantity Precommitment and Bertrand Competition Yield Cournot Outcomes," *Bell Journal of Economics*, 14, 1983, pp. 326–337.

[20]Gasini, F., J. J. Lafont, and Q. Vuong, "Econometric Analysis of Collusive Behavior in a Soft-Drink Market," *Journal of Economics and Management Strategy*, Summer 1992, pp. 277–311.

[21]These profits expressions do not deduct fixed production or marketing expenses.

[22]Differentiating total profits π_1 with respect to P_1 (treating P_{2g} as a constant), setting this expression equal to 0, and solving the resulting equation for P_1 yields firm 1's reaction function.

[23]Two excellent surveys are provided by Weiss, L. (ed.), *Concentration and Price*, Cambridge, MA, MIT Press, 1989, and Schmalensee, R., "Interindustry Studies of Structure and Performance," in Schmalensee R. and R. Willig (eds.), *The Handbook of Industrial Organization*, 951–1010.

[24]Bresnahan, T. and P. Reiss, "Entry and Competition in Concentrated Markets," *Journal of Political Economy*, 99, 1991, pp. 997–1009.

[25]Schmalensee, R., "Interindustry Studies of Structure and Performance," in Schmalensee and Willig (eds.), *The Handbook of Industrial Organization*, 951–1010.

STRATEGIC COMMITMENT

7

n 1982, the management of Philips, N.V. of the Netherlands faced a critical choice: Should it build a disc-pressing plant to supply compact discs (CDs) to the American market, or should it delay its decision a year or so, until the commercial appeal of the CD market became more certain?[1] Philips' prototype had emerged as the industry standard for CDs, and within the next year, Philips was preparing to introduce CDs to the American market. By investing in substantial capacity in the American market in 1982, Philips might be able to discourage other firms—including its erstwhile partner Sony, which had allied itself with Philips in 1979 to promote the Philips CD standard—from investing on their own in disk-pressing capacity in the United States, an outcome that might avert overcapacity among firms in the CD market and brutal price competition. Yet in 1982, the commercial viability of the CD was very much unproven. With a cost of $25 million, a minimum efficient scale CD plant was an expensive proposition. If Philips' bet on the commercial success of the CD proved to be wrong, it would be stuck with a costly facility that had practically no alternative uses.

Whether to invest in new capacity or introduce new products are examples of strategic commitments. Strategic commitments are decisions that have long-term impacts and are difficult to reverse. Strategic commitments should be distinguished from tactical decisions—decisions that are easily reversed and whose impact persists only in the short run. What price to charge or how much output to produce in a given quarter are examples of decisions that can be easily altered or reversed. Unlike strategic commitments, tactical decisions can be adapted to whatever situation the firm currently faces. Strategic commitments can significantly influence competition in an industry. A decision by a firm to expand capacity, for example, might deter new firms from entering the market, but it also could intensify pricing rivalry among firms that are already in the market. If firms are farsighted when they make their commitments, however, they will anticipate the effect their decisions will have on market competition. This implies that the details of market rivalry can influence the commitments firms make and the levels of commitment they choose.

Philips' dilemma illustrates the tensions associated with strategic commitments. When these commitments are effective, they can often shape competitors' expectations and change their behavior in ways that benefit the firm making the commitment. But because strategic commitments are hard to reverse, they are inherently risky. Firms facing commitments of the sort Philips faced must balance the benefits that come from preempting or altering competitors' behavior with the loss in flexibility that comes from making competitive moves that may be hard to undo once they have been made. This chapter discusses the economic considerations that underlie this balancing act.

◆ ◆ ◆ ◆ ◆ WHY COMMITMENT IS IMPORTANT

To illustrate the importance of commitment, consider a simple example. Two firms are competing in an oligopolistic industry. Firm 1, the dominant firm, is contemplating its capacity strategy and is considering two options, which we will broadly characterize as "aggressive" and "passive." The aggressive strategy involves a large and rapid increase in capacity aimed at increasing its market share, whereas the passive strategy involves no change in the firm's capacity. Firm 2, a smaller competitor, is also contemplating its capacity expansion strategy; it will also choose between an aggressive strategy or a passive strategy. Table 7.1 shows the net present value of profit associated with each pair of options the two firm can choose.

If we imagine that they choose their strategies simultaneously, there is a unique Nash equilibrium in this game: Firm 1 chooses passive, and Firm 2 chooses aggressive, yielding a net present value of 15 for Firm 1.[2] For Firm 1, this is not the best outcome. For example, Firm 1 is always better off if Firm 2 chooses passive, and it most prefers the outcome in which both firms choose passive. Yet, without the cooperation of Firm 2, Firm 1 could probably not achieve this outcome. Can Firm 1 improve on the equilibrium that both firms actually reach?

The answer is yes, by committing to choose the aggressive strategy no matter what Firm 2 does. One way to pull this off would be for Firm 1 to make a preemptive aggressive move: accelerating its decision and expanding its capacity before Firm 2 decides what to do. Such a move would transform a *simultaneous*-move game into a *sequential* game in which Firm 2 would choose its capacity strategy only after it had seen what Firm 1 had done. Firm 1 could also announce that it planned to "go for share" and that it would reward its manager on the basis of market share rather than profit. It would then be in the interest of Firm 1's managers to select the aggressive strategy, even though it is seemingly less profitable than the passive strategy.

TABLE 7.1
PAYOFFS IN THE SIMPLE STRATEGY SELECTION GAME

		Firm 2	
		Aggressive	Passive
Firm 1	Aggressive	12.5, 4.5	16.5, 5
	Passive	15, 6.5	18, 6

Net present values are in millions of dollars. First payoff listed is Firm 1's; second is Firm 2's.

It may seem odd that Firm 1 would want to commit itself to an irreversible aggressive strategy. After all, for Firm 1 the profit from passive is greater than the profit from aggressive, no matter what strategy Firm 2 chooses. Yet, look what happens when Firm 1 commits itself to aggressive. Firm 2, realizing that Firm 1 has bound itself in this way, finds that it is better off choosing passive rather than aggressive. The resulting equilibrium (Firm 1 chooses aggressive, Firm 2 chooses passive) gives Firm 1 a higher profit (16.5 versus 15) than it would have gotten in the equilibrium that would have resulted if it had not committed itself to aggressive.

This simple example illustrates a profound point. Strategic commitments that seemingly limit options can actually make a firm better off. Inflexibility can have value because a firm's commitments can alter its competitors' expectations about how it will compete. This, in turn, will lead competitors to make decisions that benefit the already committed firm. In this example, by committing itself to choose what seems to be an inferior strategy (aggressive), Firm 1 alters Firm 2's expectations about what Firm 1 will do. Had Firm 1 not made the commitment, Firm 2 would calculate that it would have been in Firm 1's interest to "capitulate" and play passive. This would have led Firm 2 to choose aggressive. Firm 1's commitment makes aggressive an undesirable strategy for Firm 2. With Firm 1 committed to play aggressive, Firm 2 chooses passive, moving the industry to an equilibrium that makes Firm 1 better off.

Generals throughout history have understood the value of inflexibility, as the famous example of Hernán Cortés's conquest of the Aztec Empire in Mexico illustrates. When he landed in Mexico in 1518, Cortés ordered his men to burn all but one of his ships. What appeared to be an act of lunacy was in fact a move that was purposeful and calculated: by eliminating their only method of retreat, Cortés forced his men to fight hard to win. According to Bernal Diaz del Castillo, who chronicled Cortés's conquest of the Aztecs, "Cortés said that we could look for no help or assistance except from God for we now had no ships in which to return to Cuba. Therefore we must rely on our own good swords and stout hearts.[3]

A commitment by one firm will not generate the desired response from its competitors unless it has three characteristics:

1. It must be *visible*.
2. It must be *understandable*.
3. It must be *credible*.

To understand why these characteristics are necessary for successful commitment, consider the example we have been discussing. Firm 2 must understand that Firm 1 has made the commitment to the aggressive strategy. Thus, whatever tangible form the commitment takes, whether it be through preemptive capacity expansion or a change in compensation structure for Firm 1's managers, Firm 2 must observe and understand it. Otherwise, it will not affect Firm 2's decision making. Visibility and understandability are not enough; the commitment must also be credible. Firm 2 must believe that Firm 1 intends to limit its options the way it claims it will. This is important because in our simple example, Firm 1's ideal course of action is to bluff Firm 2 into believing that it intends to choose aggressive, thereby causing Firm 2 to choose passive, but then to actually choose passive itself. For example, Firm 1 might announce that it intends to expand its capacity in the hope that Firm 2 will then abandon its own decision to expand. Once this happens, Firm 1 would then abandon its own decision to expand.[4] If Firm 1 bluffs and forces the outcome (passive, passive), it enjoys a profit of 18, as opposed to the 16.5 it would get if it carried out the

---

EXAMPLE 7.1 LOBLAW VERSUS WAL-MART CANADA[5]

If you have ever gone grocery shopping in Canada, chances are that you have encountered a store owned by Loblaw. With more than 1,050 stores, Loblaw Companies Limited is the largest grocery chain in Canada. Among the stores in its stable of properties are Loblaws, Fortinos, Zehrs Markets, and Your Independent Grocer. In total, Loblaw's various stores account for about 33 percent of Canada's grocery market.

Loblaw's most recent strategic initiative is to construct large superstores that will bear the name "The Real Canadian Superstore" or RCSS. These stores, which will have 135,000 square feet of selling area, will contain a pharmacy-drug store, a home electronics department, an optical department, a dry cleaner store, apparel and shoe departments, a photo studio, a financial services counter, and, of course, groceries, including the 5,000-plus private label items sold under Loblaw's "President's Choice" brand.

The commitment to build RCSS stores was launched in late 2002. Loblaw's management announced that it would cease building large grocery stores under the names Loblaws, Fortinos, and Zehrs, and would instead embark on a plan to build RCSS stores throughout Canada. Loblaw was very clear about its intentions: it wanted to preempt Wal-Mart Canada from building its own megastores, Wal-Mart Supercenters. Wal-Mart had already built five Sam's Clubs stores in Ontario, but as of 2002, it had yet to build any Wal-Mart Supercenters.

Loblaw took a number of steps to enhance the credibility of its strategic commitment. First, starting in early 2003, Loblaw opened talks with the United Food and Commercial Workers (UFCW) union in an attempt to negotiate wage rollbacks for employees transferring to newly opened RCSS stores. The resulting deal was complex, but Loblaw was ultimately successful in achieving a deal for lower wages in RCCS stores. In addition, Loblaw's management was very public about its ambitions to open RCSS stores throughout Canada. For example, at its annual meeting in May 2004, Loblaw's president, John Lederer, announced that the company had set aside a $1.4 billion capital budget to construct new RCSS stores during 2004.

A case can be made that Loblaw's commitment to build multiple RCSS stores has successfully preempted Wal-Mart. The first RCSS store was opened in late 2003; 13 stores were added in 2004, and 7 were slated to be opened in 2005. By contrast, as of mid-2005, Wal-Mart Canada had yet to open any Supercenters and reputedly had no immediate plans to do so. But even if Loblaw ends up merely delaying Wal-Mart's entry into the megastore segment in Canada, Loblaw's preemptive commitment might still be considered a success. For one thing, by moving first, Loblaw may be able to lock up the best locations in high population areas, such as Toronto. For another thing, the high publicity surrounding the opening of RCSS stores, coupled with the enormous selection of grocery and nongrocery items, and an ambience that is reportedly "appealing to all the senses,"[6] may make an RCSS a destination store that shoppers go out of their way to visit despite the presence of lower-priced stores nearby.

---

aggressive strategy. Of course, Firm 2 should understand this and discount as bluster any claims that Firm 1 makes regarding its intention to choose the aggressive strategy unless those claims can be backed up with credible actions.

A key to credibility is *irreversibility*. To be a true commitment, a competitive move must be hard or costly to stop once it is set in motion. For Firm 1 to state publicly, for example, that it intends to expand its capacity may not be enough. "Talk is cheap," and press releases can be repudiated. It may instead have to begin constructing a new plant, which is far more irrevocable than a press release. The degree to which real firms see

EXAMPLE 7.2 STRATEGIC COMMITMENT AND PREEMPTION IN
THE GLOBAL AIRFRAME MARKET: AIRBUS VERSUS BOEING[8]

In 2000, Airbus announced plans to launch the A380, a super jumbo jet capable of carrying 555 passengers. An enormous aircraft, the A380 was designed to have two decks of seating. Its wings are so large that 70 automobiles could be parked on each one. Before Airbus's announcement, Boeing held a virtually unchallenged monopoly on the long-haul high-capacity aircraft market with its hugely successful 747 model. A few months later, Boeing announced that it would scrap its plans to build a higher-capacity version of the 747, dubbed the 747X, to compete with Airbus.

Boeing's management justified the decision to abandon the 747X by articulating a dramatically different view about the future of air travel from that which informed Airbus's decision to proceed with the A380. Traditionally, airlines have utilized a hub system in which airlines fly passengers from city to city through a central "hub," where passengers change planes and fly from the hub to their outbound destinations. Because of current congestion at hub cities, Boeing's management concluded that airline routes will become fragmented—airlines will demand smaller and faster jetliners that can fly passengers directly from city to city, bypassing hubs altogether. Based on this vision, a few months after abandoning the 747X, Boeing's management announced that it planned to develop a 175-to-250-seat aircraft that could fly faster than any commercial aircraft in service other than the supersonic Anglo-French Concorde. The new aircraft would be named the Sonic Cruiser and would be capable of flying at Mach 0.95, just under the speed of sound. The Sonic Cruiser is intended to trim long-range flight times by 20 percent while shuttling passengers from point to point.[9]

Airbus does not dispute that fragmentation will occur. However, Airbus's management believes that airlines will continue to maximize existing hub-and-spoke systems using larger aircraft. A high-capacity aircraft like the A380 will help alleviate growing numbers of passengers and airport slot congestion. Also, Airbus argues that hub systems will continue to gain importance as airline alliances evolve. In addition, Airbus claims that in carrying such a large number of passengers, the A380 can cut direct operating costs by 17 percent versus the existing 747-400.[10]

Despite the rhetoric, it is possible that Boeing abandoned the 747X because it recognized that Airbus had made a credible commitment to the high-capacity aircraft market, a market that is probably large enough to allow only one firm to make a profit (experts have estimated that the total market for super-jumbo jets is about 400 aircraft). Airbus enhanced the credibility of its commitment by securing over 60 early orders for the plane from such high-profile customers as Singapore Airlines, Qantas of Australia, and Virgin Atlantic Airways. In addition, UPS and Federal Express ordered freighter versions of the A380. These orders not only increased the visibility of Airbus's commitment to the high-capacity aircraft market, it also put the company in a situation where it would be both costly and embarrassing to back out of the commitment to the A380 at a later date. Boeing, by contrast, had failed to secure any orders or generate much interest in the 747X before announcing its decision to abandon this program.

Thus, Airbus's high-visibility commitment to the A380 may have preempted Boeing from competing in the super-jumbo jet market. It is telling that Boeing would back out of this market when development costs for the 747X would be significantly lower than for the A380. After all, the 747X is merely a stretched version of an already existing aircraft (the 747), while Airbus has never produced any jet closely resembling the A380.

The maiden flight of the A380 took place at the Paris Air Show in April 2005. Up to that point, Airbus had secured 125 orders (at $252 million each), about half the number that Airbus would need to sell in order to break even on the program. With the first commercial service of the A380 scheduled for 2006 (flown by Singapore Airlines), only time will tell if the A380 ultimately becomes profitable.

EXAMPLE 7.3 COMMITMENT AND IRREVERSIBILITY IN THE
AIRLINE INDUSTRY

Ming-Jer Chen and Ian MacMillan surveyed senior airline executives and industry analysts (e.g., financial analysts and professors) to study irreversibility in competitive moves in the airline business.[11] Mergers and acquisition, investment in the creation of hubs, and feeder alliances with commuter airlines had the highest perceived irreversibility. Hubs required the creation of transaction-specific assets (e.g., maintenance facilities) that could not be redeployed if the hub was abandoned. Mergers and acquisitions required cooperation with the management of other airlines and third parties, such as investment bankers and regulatory authorities. Not only does the negotiation of the merger or acquisition entail significant non-recoverable negotiation costs, it may also entail significant transaction-specific changes in operating procedures or systems.

The reputation of a firm's management would also suffer greatly (e.g., the firm would be seen as capricious or frivolous) if, after negotiating the merger or acquisition, it backed out at the last minute or tried to undo it once it was consummated. Feeder alliances with commuter airlines were seen as hard to reverse because employees and unions would oppose reversing the move. Promotions, decisions to abandon a route, and increases in commission rates for travel agents were considered the easiest moves to reverse. Price cuts, while seen as having a below-average degree of irreversibility, were not considered the easiest competitive move to reverse. Evidently, airline executives and industry analysts believe that once an airline cuts its prices, the inescapable cost of advertising the change is significant enough to make the airline maintain the new prices for some time. However, because price cuts are visible and clearly affect competing airlines' profitability, they are more provocative than other moves, such as temporary ad campaigns, that might be considered more reversible. Indeed, as we show in the next section, a firm's profit-maximizing response to a price cut by a competitor is generally to cut its own price. In addition, in the airline business, prices are instantaneously known through a computerized clearinghouse, so competitors learn them and can quickly match them.

Chen and MacMillan hypothesized that competitors are less likely to match an airline's competitive move when the original move is hard to reverse. Their logic is akin to the simple example we discussed earlier. The more credible a firm's commitment to play aggressive, the more likely it is that its competitors will respond by playing soft. This logic would suggest that a preemptive move by one airline to expand its route system by acquiring another airline is less likely to provoke a matching response than is a decision to engage in a short-term promotional or advertising campaign. Chen and MacMillan tested this hypothesis through an exhaustive study of competitive moves and countermoves reported over a seven-year period (1979–1986) in a leading trade publication of the airline industry, *Aviation Daily*. In general, their findings support their hypothesis: Harder-to-reverse moves are less frequently matched than easier-to-reverse moves. The study also supports the hypothesis that price cuts are especially provocative and thus likely to be matched frequently and quickly. MacMillan and Chen find that rival airlines responded to price cuts more frequently than other moves the authors saw as having a similar, or even higher, degree of irreversibility.

competitive moves as irreversible commitments or reversible tactics is an interesting question.[7] Competitive moves, such as capacity expansion, that require significant upfront expenditures and create relationship-specific assets have a high commitment value. This is because once the assets have been created, the firm's ability to redeploy them outside their intended use is limited. For example, a CD pressing plant of the sort contemplated by Philips had virtually no alternative uses. Once it was built, Philips would have few options other than to run it full out.

Contracts can also facilitate commitment. One example of this that we will discuss in greater detail in Chapter 8 is a contract provision known as a most favored customer clause (MFCC). If a seller includes such a clause in a sales contract with a buyer, the seller is required to extend the same price terms to the buyer that it extends to its other customers. For example, if the seller discounts below its list price to steal a customer from a competitor, the buyer with an MFCC in its contract is entitled to the same discount. The MFCC makes discounting "expensive" and thus can be considered a tool that creates a credible commitment not to compete on price.

Sometimes, even public statements of intentions to act ("We plan to introduce a new and improved version of our existing product six months from now.") can have commitment value. For this to be true, however, the firm's competitors and its customers must understand that the firm or its management are putting something at risk if it fails to match words with actions; otherwise, they will discount the claims, promises, or threats the firm is making. The credibility of public announcements is enhanced when it is clear that the reputation of the firm or its senior management will suffer if the firm fails to do what it has said it will do. In the computer software industry, it is more common for established firms, such as Microsoft, to make promises about new product performance and introduction dates than it is for smaller firms or newcomers to do so. This may, in part, be related to the fact that a newcomer has far more to lose in terms of credibility with consumers and opinion setters in the various personal computer magazines (an important forum for product reviews) than an established firm has. Smaller firms may thus be more reluctant to make exaggerated claims than established firms that have a track record of success. Failure to match actions to words will result in loss of face or reputation for both the firm and its senior management.

STRATEGIC COMMITMENT AND COMPETITION ◆ ◆ ◆ ◆ ◆

In the simple game described in Table 7.1, the link between strategic commitments and tactical decisions was not explicit. To be explicit, we need to introduce some new concepts. *Strategic complements* and *strategic substitutes* are concepts that capture how competitors react when one competitor changes a tactical variable such as price or quantity. *Tough commitments* and *soft commitments* are concepts that capture whether a commitment by one firm places its rivals at a disadvantage.

Strategic Complements and Strategic Substitutes

It is easiest to introduce the concepts of strategic complements and strategic substitutes with an example. Suppose that Honda announces a massive cut in the price of its Accord family sedan. In reaction, Ford would probably conclude that its best response would be to lower the price of the Taurus. In this case, Honda's and Ford's prices are strategic complements. Suppose instead that Honda greatly increases production of the Odyssey minivan, driving down minivan prices to 10 percent below current levels. Observing this capacity increase, Ford might believe that its best response would be to reduce production of Freestar minivans. In this case, Honda and Ford's production volumes are strategic substitutes.

To formalize the concepts of strategic complements and substitutes, we return to the two models of product market competition introduced in Chapter 6: the Cournot model of quantity setting and the Bertrand model of price setting. Recall that in the Cournot model it was convenient to represent the equilibrium using reaction functions. In a two-firm Cournot industry, a firm's reaction function shows its profit-maximizing quantity as a function of the quantity chosen by its competitor. In the Cournot model, reaction functions are downward sloping, as Figure 7.1a shows. Reaction functions in the Bertrand model with horizontally differentiated products are defined analogously.[12] In this case, however, the reaction functions are upward sloping, as in Figure 7.1b.

In general, when reaction functions are upward sloping, the firm's actions (e.g., prices) are strategic complements. When reaction functions are downward sloping, the actions are strategic substitutes.[13] When actions are strategic complements, the more of the action one firm chooses, the more of the action the other firm will also optimally choose. In the Bertrand model, prices are strategic complements because a reduction in price is the profit-maximizing response to a competitor's price cut. When actions are strategic substitutes, the more of the action one firm takes, the less of the action the other firm optimally chooses. In the Cournot model, quantities are strategic substitutes because a quantity increase is the profit-maximizing response to a competitor's quantity reduction. Determining whether actions are strategic complements or substitutes involves careful consideration of the competitive interdependence among the firms. One general rule is that prices are usually strategic complements, whereas quantity and capacity decisions are usually strategic substitutes. We will employ these concepts later in our discussion. But to see why they are important, note that these concepts tell us how a firm expects its rival to react to its tactical maneuvers. When actions are strategic complements, one firm's aggressive behavior leads its competitors to behave more aggressively as well. For example, if Honda lowers its price (an aggressive move) on the Accord, Ford will also lower the price of a Taurus (an aggressive response) because its price reaction function is upward sloping. When actions are strategic substitutes, aggressive behavior by a firm leads its rival to behave

FIGURE 7.1
STRATEGIC SUBSTITUTES AND COMPLEMENTS

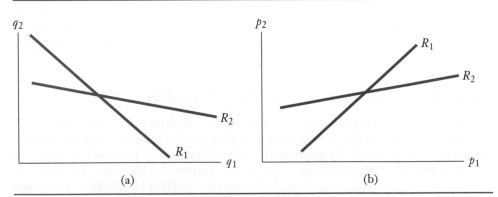

Panel (a) shows the reaction functions in a Cournot market. The reaction functions R_1 and R_2 slope downward, indicating that quantities are strategic substitutes. Panel (b) shows the reaction functions in a Bertrand market with differentiated products. The reaction functions slope upward, indicating that prices are strategic complements.

less aggressively. For example, if Honda increases its output of Odyssey minivans (an aggressive move), Ford will decrease its output of Freestar minivans (a soft response), since its output reaction function is downward sloping.

Strategic Incentives to Make Commitments

Commitments have both a direct and a strategic effect on a firm's profitability. The direct effect of the commitment is its impact on the present value of the firm's profits, assuming that the firm adjusts its own tactical decisions in light of this commitment and that its competitor's behavior does not change. For example, if Nucor invests in a process that reduces the average variable cost of producing sheet steel, the direct effect of the investment is the present value of the increase in Nucor's profit due to the reduction in its average variable costs, less the upfront cost of the investment. The increase in profit would come not only from cost savings on existing units produced, but also from any benefits Nucor gets from lowering its price or increasing its output. The strategic effect takes into account the competitive side effects of the commitment. How does the commitment alter the tactical decisions of rivals and, ultimately, the market equilibrium? For example, the strategic effect of Nucor's investment is the incremental change in the present value of its profits, as compared to the direct effect, owing to the effect of the commitment on the market equilibrium for sheet steel. This strategic effect can be positive or negative; that is, it can benefit or harm the firm making the commitment. As we will show, the direction of the strategic effect depends on whether the choice variables affected by the commitment (e.g., prices) are strategic complements or strategic substitutes. If a firm takes the long view when making its commitment decision, as we believe it should, then it must take into account how the commitment alters the nature of the equilibrium.

Tough versus Soft Commitments

To understand the impact of a commitment on market equilibrium, it is useful to distinguish between *tough* commitments and *soft* commitments. Conceptually, a firm's tough commitment is bad for competitors, whereas a soft commitment is good for its competitors. In Cournot competition, if a firm makes a tough commitment, then no matter what output its rival produces, it is certain to produce more output than it would have done without the commitment. A soft commitment leads the firm to produce less than it otherwise would have. In Bertrand competition, if a firm makes a tough commitment, then no matter what price its rival charges, the firm's price will be lower than it would have been without the commitment. A soft commitment leads the firm to charge more than it otherwise would have.

Tough commitments are easier to visualize than soft commitments because they conform to the conventional view of competition as an effort to outdo one's rivals. For example, we "understand" why firms may commit to be the lowest price seller or the largest volume producer in a market. But firms should not automatically refrain from making soft commitments. A firm may benefit from a soft commitment that produces a sufficiently beneficial strategic effect.

Tough and Soft Commitments in Cournot and Bertrand Equilibria

The strategic effects of tough and soft commitments may be illustrated by considering a market with two firms. Firm 1 (but not Firm 2) is contemplating making a strategic commitment.[14] For example, the commitment might be the decision to adopt a process innovation that lowers variable production costs, such as Nucor's decision in 1987 to pioneer the thin-slab casting process in the steel industry. Or it might be a decision about how to position a new product, such as Quaker's 1994 decision to sell bagged cereals to appeal to price-sensitive customers. Whatever its nature, the decision has two key properties. First, the rival firm must be aware of it. Second, the decision cannot be reversed once the firm makes it. The commitment is thus credible.

The timing of decision making in this market is as follows. Firm 1 first decides whether to make the commitment. Then, the two firms compete with each other. This two-stage game corresponds roughly to the distinction between strategy and tactics: Firm 1 first makes a strategic commitment in stage 1, then both firms maneuver tactically in stage 2. We will focus on two competitive scenarios in stage 2: Cournot quantity competition and Bertrand price competition. In the Cournot model, once Firm 1 decides whether to make the commitment, both firms then simultaneously choose quantities. In the Bertrand model, once Firm 1 decides whether to make the commitment, both firms then simultaneously choose prices.

To keep the analysis simple, we assume that Firm 1 believes that the market will quickly reach the relevant equilibrium once it has made the commitment. For example, in the quantity-setting market, Firm 1 believes that the market will immediately reach a new Cournot equilibrium after it has made its commitment. In the price-setting market, Firm 1 believes that the market will quickly reach a new Bertrand equilibrium. The assumption that Firm 1 is forward looking and anticipates how its commitment will alter the market equilibrium means that we are searching for a subgame perfect Nash equilibrium (SPNE) in a two-stage game in which, at stage 1, Firm 1 makes its commitment decision, and then at stage 2, both firms simultaneously choose quantities (or prices).[15] For Firm 1 to analyze the SPNE in a two-stage game, it should first consider the equilibrium in the second stage as a function of the capacity that it selects in the first stage. This analysis varies according to whether competition in the second stage is Cournot or Bertrand.

Stage 2 Competition Is Cournot

Firm 1 must anticipate how the commitment might alter the Cournot equilibrium between it and Firm 2. This depends on whether the commitment is tough or soft. If Firm 1 makes a tough commitment, then no matter what output level Firm 2 produces, Firm 1 will produce more output than it would have done if it had not made the commitment. This corresponds to a rightward shift in Firm 1's reaction curve R_1, from R_1^{before} to R_1^{after}, as shown in Figure 7.2. For example, Firm 1 would be making a tough commitment if it adopted a process innovation that reduced its marginal cost of production.[16] If Firm 1 makes a soft commitment, then no matter what output level Firm 2 produces, it will produce less output than it would have done if it had not made the commitment. This corresponds to a leftward shift in Firm 1's reaction curve R_1, as shown in Figure 7.3. To illustrate a soft commitment under Cournot competition, suppose that Firm 1, in addition to producing the good it produces in the Cournot market, has the opportunity to sell the same good as a monopolist in a second, geographically distinct, market. Suppose, further, that the marginal cost of production goes up as the firm produces more output overall. That is, the firm's technology is characterized by diseconomies of scope. This might occur because the firm would use the same factory to produce output for both markets, and as a greater volume of output is produced, the managerial resources of the firm become increasingly strained and production becomes less efficient. The decision to enter

FIGURE 7.2

COMMITMENT MAKES FIRM 1 "TOUGH" IN A COURNOT MARKET

For any output produced by Firm 2, Firm 1 wants to produce more output than it would have before it made the commitment. This is represented by a rightward shift in its reaction function from R_1^{before} to R_1^{after}. As a result, the Cournot equilibrium moves to the southeast and involves a higher quantity for Firm 1 and a lower quantity for Firm 2.

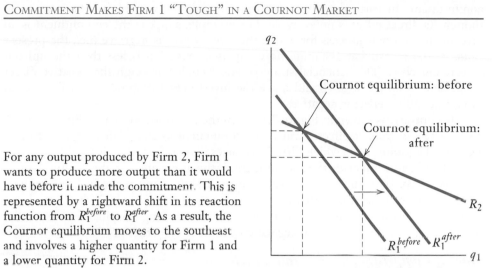

the monopoly market would be a soft commitment. By making that decision, Firm 1 would cause its marginal cost in the Cournot market to go up, and as a result, it would reduce its profit-maximizing output level for any given output expected from Firm 2. This would shift Firm 1's reaction function inward, as shown in Figure 7.3.

Figure 7.2 reveals that Firm 1 gets a beneficial competitive side effect from making the tough commitment: R_1 shifts rightward, which results in a Cournot equilibrium in which Firm 2 produces less output. Because, in the Cournot model, Firm 1 is better off, the less output its rival produces (because the market price will be higher), the Cournot equilibrium in which Firm 1 makes the commitment is better than the Cournot equilibrium in which Firm 1 does not make the commitment. Taking this

FIGURE 7.3

COMMITMENT MAKES FIRM 1 "SOFT" IN A COURNOT MARKET

For any output produced by Firm 2, Firm 1 wants to produce less output than it would have before it made the commitment. This is represented by a leftward shift in its reaction function from R_1^{before} to R_1^{after}. As a result, the Cournot equilibrium moves to the northwest and involves a lower quantity for Firm 1 and a higher quantity for Firm 2.

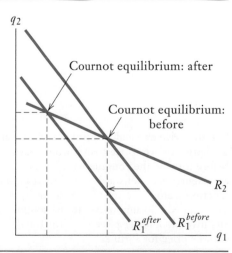

beneficial side effect into account can significantly affect how Firm 1 evaluates the commitment. In particular, the commitment might be valuable in this case, even though its direct effect is unfavorable. For example, suppose the commitment is an investment in a new process for which the direct effect is negative (i.e., the present value of the investment assuming no competitive reaction is less than the upfront investment cost). The beneficial strategic effect could outweigh the negative direct effect, and if so, the firm should make the investment for strategic purposes, even though its direct effect is negative.

By contrast, as shown in Figure 7.3, when the commitment makes Firm 1 soft, it has a negative strategic effect. Firm 1's reaction curve R_1 shifts leftward, resulting in a Cournot equilibrium in which Firm 2 produces more output than it would have produced had Firm 1 not made the commitment. If the direct effect of the commitment is negative, zero, or even slightly positive, Firm 1 should not make it. This analysis would suggest, for example, that entry into a new market in which the firm would be a monopolist may be undesirable if, owing to diminishing marginal returns or diseconomies of scope, the firm's marginal cost in its first market goes up.

Stage 2 Competition Is Bertrand

Incentives for strategic commitment are different when stage 2 competition is Bertrand. As before, we distinguish between tough and soft commitments. If Firm 1 makes a tough commitment, then no matter what price Firm 2 charges, Firm 1 will charge a lower price than it would have if it had not made the commitment. This corresponds to a leftward shift in Firm 1's reaction curve R_1, as shown in Figure 7.4. If Firm 1 makes a soft commitment, then no matter what price Firm 2 charges, Firm 1 will charge a higher price than it would have if it had not made the commitment. This corresponds to a rightward shift in Firm 1's reaction curve R_1, as shown in Figure 7.5.

Consider, now, the competitive side effects of the commitment when it makes Firm 1 tough. As shown in Figure 7.4, Firm 1's reaction curve R_1 shifts leftward, moving the Bertrand equilibrium down to the southwest.[17] Firm 1 charges a lower price in

FIGURE 7.4
COMMITMENT MAKES FIRM 1 "TOUGH" IN A BERTRAND MARKET

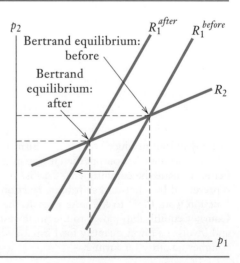

For any price charged by Firm 2, Firm 1 wants to charge a lower price than it would have before it made the commitment. This is represented by a leftward shift in its reaction function from R_1^{before} to R_1^{after}. As a result, the Bertrand equilibrium moves to the southwest and involves a lower price for Firm 1 and a lower price for Firm 2.

FIGURE 7.5
COMMITMENT MAKES FIRM 1 "SOFT" IN A BERTRAND MARKET

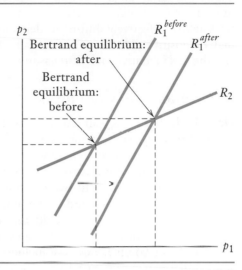

For any price charged by Firm 2, Firm 1 wants to charge a higher price than it would have before it made the commitment. This is represented by a rightward shift in its reaction function from R_1^{before} to R_1^{after}. As a result, the Bertrand equilibrium moves to the northeast and involves a higher price for Firm 1 and a higher price for Firm 2.

equilibrium, but so does Firm 2, although its drop in price is smaller than Firm 1's. Firm 2's drop in price hurts Firm 1; the strategic effect is negative from Firm 1's perspective. If, for example, the strategic commitment is investment in a new process technology, and the direct effect is positive (i.e., the present value of the investment assuming no competitive reactions exceeds the upfront investment cost), it might be optimal for Firm 1 to refrain from this investment if the strategic effect is sufficiently negative.

If the net present value of a cost-reducing commitment is positive, why wouldn't Firm 1 make the investment, but keep its price constant afterward? It would then enjoy the benefits of its commitment (the cost reduction) without the negative competitive side effects. However, Firm 1 could not implement this strategy. Even though it seems appealing before the commitment is made, it runs counter to Firm 1's self-interest after the commitment is made. After Firm 1 makes the commitment, its profit-maximizing price is lower than it was before, and its reaction function shifts inward (see Figure 7.4). Thus, once the commitment has been made, Firm 1 wants to behave more aggressively in the second-stage pricing game. Since Firm 2 observes the commitment, it anticipates that Firm 1 will behave more aggressively, and it does so as well. The result is the Bertrand equilibrium in which both firms charge lower prices than they would have before Firm 1 made its commitment. Firm 1 could attempt to short circuit this dynamic by announcing in advance that it planned to cut its costs but not its price. Such an announcement would not be credible because both parties would understand that it would require Firm 1 to go against its self-interest once the commitment was made.

Finally, let us consider the incentives to make the commitment when it makes Firm 1 soft. In that case, shown in Figure 7.5, the commitment shifts Firm 1's reaction function rightward. This, in turn, moves the Bertrand equilibrium to the northeast. The result is a higher price for both Firm 1 and Firm 2. This competitive side effect benefits Firm 1 and may make the commitment worthwhile, even if its direct effect is negative.

Consider, for example, the direct and strategic effects of repositioning Firm 1's product to appeal to a narrower segment of the market in which consumers have more specialized tastes. This move will make the products of Firm 1 and 2 more horizontally differentiated.[18] Holding the prices of both firms fixed, the direct effect of this move is probably negative because Firm 1's product now appeals to fewer consumers than before, effectively shifting its demand curve inward. However, the strategic effect may be positive. The more horizontally differentiated the products of Firms 1 and 2 are, the less incentive each firm has to cut price to capture each other's customer base.

A Taxonomy of Commitment Strategies

Drew Fudenberg and Jean Tirole argued that two-stage models of commitment can be analyzed by considering the two important dimensions that we discussed earlier—whether commitments are tough or soft and whether the stage 2 tactical variables are strategic substitutes or strategic complements.[19] There are four ways of combining these dimensions. In two combinations, *making* the commitment generates a beneficial strategic effect, and in the other two, *refraining* from making the commitment avoids a harmful strategic effect. Fudenberg and Tirole described and named these four combinations. These are shown in Table 7.2 and are marked by the superscript *FT*. For completeness, we include and name in Table 7.2 those commitment actions that generate harmful strategic effects.

The four combinations described by Fudenberg and Tirole represent different strategic situations. If the stage 2 tactical variables are strategic complements—that is, the reaction curves slope upward—and the commitment makes the firm tough, then the commitment alters the stage 2 equilibrium, so that rival firms behave more aggressively (e.g., set lower prices in the Bertrand model). In this case, the commitment has a harmful strategic effect, and the firm has an incentive either to forsake the commitment altogether or to underinvest in it—to make the commitment at a lower level (e.g., spend less on a new process) than it would have had it not considered the strategic side effects. Fudenberg and Tirole call this the "puppy-dog ploy." By contrast, when the commitment makes the firm soft, it results in an

TABLE 7.2

Nature of Stage 2 Tactical Variable	Commitment Posture	Commitment Action	Strategy	Comments/Role of Actor in Competitive Arena
Strategic substitutes	Tough	Make	Top Dog[FT]	Assert dominance; force rivals to back off
Strategic substitutes	Tough	Refrain	Submissive Underdog	Accept follower role; avoid fighting
Strategic substitutes	Soft	Make	Suicidal Siberian	Invite rivals to exploit you; may indicate exit strategy
Strategic substitutes	Soft	Refrain	Lean and Hungry Look[FT]	Actively submissive; posturing to avoid conflict
Strategic complements	Tough	Make	Mad Dog	Attack to become top dog; invite battle heedless of costs
Strategic complements	Tough	Refrain	Puppy Dog Ploy[FT]	Placate top dog; enjoy available scraps
Strategic complements	Soft	Make	Fat-Cat Effect[FT]	Confidently take care of self; share the wealth with rivals
Strategic complements	Soft	Refrain	Weak Kitten	Accept status quo out of fear; wait to follow the leader

equilibrium in which rivals behave less aggressively (e.g., set higher prices). The commitment thus has a beneficial strategic effect, and the firm has an incentive to overinvest in it—to make the commitment at a higher level than it would have had it not considered the competitive side effects. They call this the "fat-cat effect."

If the stage 2 tactical variables are strategic substitutes—that is, the reaction curves slope downward—and the commitment makes the firm tough, then in the second-stage equilibrium, rival firms become less aggressive (e.g., choose lower quantities). The commitment has a beneficial strategic effect, and the firm has an incentive to overinvest in the commitment. This is the "top-dog" strategy of investing to become a more aggressive competitor. The other possibility is that the commitment makes the firm soft, which has a negative strategic effect because rival firms respond by behaving more aggressively. Here the firm has an incentive to underinvest in the commitment. This is the "lean and hungry" look.

One may occasionally see a firm pursue one of the strategies that Fudenberg and Tirole do not describe, even though they generate harmful strategic effects. For example, a firm may pursue the "mad-dog" strategy of making a tough commitment when the tactical variables are strategic complements. An example is the firm that commits to low prices even though this will invite a price war. Such strategies, though seemingly counterintuitive, can make sense if the firm views price competition as a dynamic competitive process. If so, short-term strategic losses might be offset by long-term gains. Chapter 8 discusses the long-run dynamics of competition in greater detail. A mad-dog strategy can also make sense if the firm is attempting to deter entry. By making a tough commitment, the firm intensifies price competition with existing rivals, but by driving down price–cost margins, it might deter new firms from entering the market. Chapter 9 discusses entry deterrence in more detail.

Making Sense of the Taxonomy

The taxonomy of strategic commitments shown in Table 7.2 has two important implications for strategic decision making and market analysis. First, and most basic, it suggests that when making hard-to-reverse investment decisions, managers ought not to look only at the effects of the investment on their own firm. They should also try to anticipate how the decision to invest or not invest will affect the evolution of market competition in the future. One way to promote this way of thinking is what management consultants often refer to as "war gaming". Elaborate computer simulations allow managers to track the likely competitive implications of pricing and investment decisions over many years.[20] For example, RJR managers used a war game created by the consulting firm Booz Allen to help plot competitive reactions to Philip Morris's decision to cut the price of its Marlboro brand of cigarettes in April 1993.

Second, the details of market rivalry can profoundly influence the willingness of firms to make commitments. For example, the theory developed previously tells us that an investment in a process innovation that reduces marginal costs has a beneficial strategic effect in a Cournot industry but a negative strategic effect in a Bertrand industry. At one level, this implication may not seem to be terribly useful. In practice, it is often difficult to distinguish which model applies in any particular situation. However, one should not take the models of product market competition so literally that they obscure the robust point that comes out of the theoretical discussion above: A commitment that induces competitors or potential entrants to behave less aggressively—for example, to refrain from price cutting, to postpone or abandon capacity expansion plans, or to reduce their advertising or promotion—is likely to have a beneficial strategic effect on the firm making the commitment. By contrast, a commitment that induces competitors or potential entrants to behave more aggressively is likely to have a harmful strategic effect.

Assessing how a commitment will affect the evolution of market competition depends on industry conditions and the characteristics of the firm's competitors. Sometimes the effect of the strategic commitment on a competitor may depend on whether the competitor is currently in the industry or has not yet entered. For example, if a firm adopts a process innovation, it may price more aggressively, disrupting the industry equilibrium and leading to more aggressive pricing by existing competitors as they attempt to preserve their market shares. Yet, as discussed earlier, the expectation of intensified pricing rivalry may deter potential competitors from entering the market at all.

The strategic effects of the commitment might also depend on capacity utilization rates in the industry. For example, when these rates are low, a firm's commitment to a process innovation that lowers its marginal cost may be met by an aggressive price response from rivals who fear further losses in capacity utilization and who have the capacity to take on new business that comes their way if they cut price. In this case, the strategic effect of the commitment is likely to be negative. By contrast, when capacity utilization rates are high, competitors are less well positioned to respond aggressively unless they expand their capacities. But the expectation of more aggressive behavior by the firm making the commitment may deter its competitors from going forward with their plans to expand capacity. If so, the strategic effect is likely to be positive. The strategic effects of the commitment may also depend on the degree of horizontal differentiation among the firm making the commitment and its competitors. For example, Figure 7.6a shows that in a Bertrand market the magnitude of

FIGURE 7.6
STRATEGIC EFFECTS AND PRODUCT DIFFERENTIATION

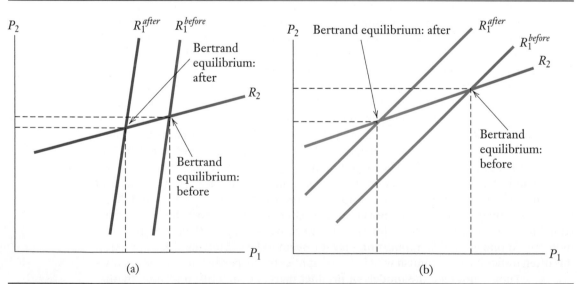

Panel (a) shows a market in which the two firms' products are highly differentiated. Firm 1's commitment to a cost-reducing investment hardly affects Firm 2's pricing decision, so the strategic effect in this case is negligible. Panel (b) shows a market in which the two firms' products are less differentiated. Firm 2's commitment to a cost-reducing investment has a relatively bigger impact on Firm 2's pricing decision, so the strategic effect is more significant than it is in the market in panel (a).

EXAMPLE 7.4 COMMITMENT AT NUCOR AND USX: THE CASE OF THIN-SLAB CASTING[21]

Pankaj Ghemawat's case study of the adoption of thin-slab casting by Nucor and the nonadoption by USX (now renamed U.S. Steel) illustrates the relationship between commitment and product market competition, and how previous commitments can limit a firm's ability to take advantage of new commitment opportunities.

In 1987, Nucor Corporation became the first American steel firm to adopt thin-slab casting, a significant improvement over the standard technology of the day, continuous casting. At that time, Nucor was looking to enter the flat-rolled sheet segment of the steel business, a segment that had been unavailable to the minimills, of which Nucor was the largest. Adoption of this thin-slab casting was a major commitment for Nucor. All told, the upfront investment in developing the process and building a facility to use it was expected to be $340 million, close to 90 percent of Nucor's net worth at the time. Nucor's commitment was successful. By 1992, Nucor's thin-slab casting mill in Crawfordsville, Indiana, had become profitable, and Nucor built a second thin-slab casting plant in Arkansas.

USX, the largest American integrated steel producer, which was 60 times larger than Nucor, also showed an early interest in thin-slab casting, spending over $30 million to perfect a thin-slab casting technology known as the Hazelett process. Yet USX eventually decided not to adopt thin-slab casting. Ghemawat argued that this decision was anomalous in light of extant economic theory on process innovations.

So why did USX not adopt thin-slab casting? Ghemawat argues that the decision stemmed from prior organizational and strategic commitments that constrained USX's opportunity to profit from thin-slab casting. For example, in the mid-1980s, USX had already modernized four of its five integrated steel mills. The fifth plant, located in the Monongahela River Valley in Pennsylvania, was a vast complex in which the steel-making facility and the rolling mill were 10 miles apart. Moreover, the labor cost savings that would accrue to a nonunionized firm like Nucor would not be nearly as significant to unionized USX, which was bound by restrictive work rules. Finally, there was doubt as to whether appliance manufacturers, which were major customers of the sheet steel produced in the Monongahela Valley plant, would purchase sheet steel produced via continuous casting due to the adulteration in the surface quality of the steel that the new process might cause.

Ghemawat argues that XSX's prior commitment to modernize existing facilities—in particular the one at Monongahela Valley—as opposed to building "greenfield" plants, locked USX into a posture in which nonadoption of thin-slab casting was a natural outcome. This conclusion highlights an important strategic point: In forecasting the likely reactions of competitors to major strategic commitments, a firm should recognize that prior commitments made by its competitors can constrain those firms' potential responses. In this case, Nucor's management anticipated USX's behavior. Nucor decided to enter the flat-rolled sheet steel business because it expected that integrated producers, such as USX, would not adopt thin-slab casting.

the strategic effect depends on the degree of horizontal differentiation. When the firms' products are highly differentiated, as in panel (a), the strategic effect from an investment in cost reduction is likely to be relatively unimportant. However, when products are relatively less differentiated, as in panel (b), the strategic effect is relatively larger.

◆ ◆ ◆ ◆ ◆ FLEXIBILITY AND REAL OPTIONS

The strategic effect of a commitment is positive when the commitment alters competitors' behavior in ways that are advantageous to the firm making the commitment. These beneficial strategic effects are often rooted in inflexibility. For example, by preemptively investing in capacity expansion, a firm may have to price aggressively to maintain capacity utilization rates. In doing so, it may force rival firms to scale back their plans to expand capacity.[22]

However, strategic commitments are almost always made under conditions of uncertainty about market conditions, costs, or competitors' goals and resources. For example, in deciding whether to build a CD plant in the United States, Philips had to confront the risk that CDs would appeal only to the most dedicated audiophiles. When competitive moves are hard to reverse and their outcomes are shrouded in uncertainty, the value of preserving flexibility, of keeping one's future options open, must be considered when evaluating the benefits of the commitment.

A firm has a number of ways it can preserve its flexibility when making a strategic commitment. First, a firm can modify the commitment as future conditions change. For example, a firm that sets out to expand its capacity by building a large plant might, if market demand conditions change for the worse, build a smaller plant instead, or maybe even abandon the capacity expansion altogether. Second, a firm can choose to delay making a commitment to some future point in time until it has a better idea of how profitable it is likely to be. For example, a firm launching a new product may delay the rollout date until it receives the results of test marketing studies designed to provide a clue about the potential size of the market for the new product. Finally, because some commitments are linked through time, a firm may decide to undertake an unprofitable commitment today in order to preserve the option of making a follow-on commitment in the future. For example, a software firm may begin selling a new applications software today, even though it is likely to be unprofitable, because by selling the software today, it preserves the option to sell an improved version of the software several years from now. This would make sense if, by not making the commitment to sell the original product today, the firm loses the opportunity to sell the follow-on product and there is some possibility that the follow-on product could be highly profitable.

Flexibility gives rise to what are called *real*[23] *options*.[24] A real option exists when a decision maker has the opportunity to tailor a decision to information that will be received in the future. To illustrate real options analysis, we will consider the value of delaying a commitment to some future date. Specifically, consider a firm that can invest $100 million in a plant to enter a new market. Given the uncertainties about how the market will accept the new product, the firm forecasts two scenarios: a high-acceptance scenario in which the investment will have a present value of $300 million, and a low-acceptance scenario in which the present value of the investment will be $50 million. The firm believes that each scenario is equally likely. If the firm invests today, the expected net present value (NPV) of the investment is $0.5(300) + 0.5(50) - 100 = \$75$ million. But suppose, by waiting a year, the firm can learn for certain which scenario will arise (perhaps by observing the demand for the product in another geographically distinct market). If the firm waits, and the product turns out to have a high level of market acceptance, the firm should invest and obtain a net present value of $200 million. But if the investment has a present value of

$50 million, the firm is better off not investing in this project and putting its money in the next best alternative, which we will assume is a zero NPV investment. Assuming a 10 percent annual discount rate, if the firm waits, its expected NPV is $[0.5(200) + 0.5(0)]/(1.10) = \$91$ million. Because the firm has the flexibility to delay the investment project and gain additional information, the investment project has a higher expected NPV ($91 million versus $75 million) than if the firm were forced to make the investment decision solely on the basis of its current, uncertain assessment of demand. In other words, an investment project that embodies an option to delay is more valuable than one for which the firm faces a "now-or-never" choice of investing or not investing in the project. In this example, the incremental value of the real option is $91 million − $75 million = $16 million. This incremental value arises because, by waiting, the firm can tailor its decision making to the underlying circumstances. In particular, by waiting, the firm avoids a significant investment mistake (i.e., investing in a new plant when demand is low).

Real options arise in a variety of business settings.[25] For example, Airbus and Boeing offer airline customers, such as British Airways and United Airlines, the option of canceling or downsizing orders. Airlines exercise these options when the demand for airline services falls, as it did in the wake of 9/11. Airbus uses the theory of real options to determine the extra value that these options provide to customers and has adjusted the pricing of its jets to reflect this extra value. As another example, Hewlett-Packard (HP) customizes some of its products (e.g., ink-jet printers) to particular foreign markets (e.g., it makes ink-jet printers for France, ink-jet printers for Germany, and so forth). Traditionally, it would customize the product at the factory and ship it in finished form to individual foreign markets. This was a risky strategy because demand in foreign markets was difficult to predict, and HP often guessed wrong and ended up shipping too many or too few printers. To reduce its risk, HP, in effect, created a real option. Rather than shipping finished printers to individual foreign markets, it shipped partially assembled printers to large overseas warehouses and then customized the printers once it had definite orders from particular markets. This increased HP's production costs, but it allowed the company to tailor the quantity of printers to demand conditions in foreign markets once demand became known. HP's management believed that the incremental value of the real option implied by this approach exceeded the increased production cost.

The HP example illustrates two important points. First, firms can often create real options by altering the way in which they configure their internal processes. This implies that a key managerial skill is spotting the potential to create value-enhancing real options. Second, real options often do not come for free; they typically involve tradeoffs. In the case of HP, the company traded higher production costs for the added flexibility that came from delaying the customization of printers until it gained more definitive demand information in its individual markets.

The value of a real option can also be limited by the risk of preemption. An interesting real-life example of the tension between the option value of delay and the risk of preemption has been suggested by Hugh Courtney in his engaging book on the use of real options analysis in the formulation of business strategy.[26] Imagine that two young people are in a serious dating relationship that could eventually result in marriage. Should they continue to date, or should they get married right away? By continuing to date, each party can learn more about the other, leaving open the possibility that they can terminate the relationship if it becomes clear that they are not "right" for each other. This generates option value by reducing the possibility that the parties

EXAMPLE 7.5 COMMITMENT VERSUS FLEXIBILITY IN THE CD MARKET

In the introduction to this chapter and again in this section, we have referred to Philips' decision in 1983 on whether to invest in a new CD pressing plant in the United States. That decision highlights the tension between the strategic effects of commitment and the option value of waiting. By building a plant in 1983, Philips might preempt Sony and other potential competitors from building their own CD plants, an example of the top-dog strategy. But because the investment in a CD plant involved a large, irreversible commitment, there was an option value for Philips to wait and see whether market acceptance of CDs would be strong enough to justify an investment in a U.S. plant.

Anita McGahan studied Philips' decision in detail and derived thresholds on what the probability of market acceptance would have to have been to justify Philips' decision to delay investment.[27] To isolate the pure option effect, McGahan first analyzed what Philips' decision would have been if it had faced no competition in the CD market. She concludes that Philips would have been better off waiting and retaining flexibility if the probability that the popular market would accept the CD was 0.38 or lower, indicating a nontrivial, albeit not overwhelmingly large, option effect. By contrast, if Philips faced competitors that would learn about market demand at the same time it did, Philips would have been better off delaying investment only if the probability of market acceptance was 0.006 or lower. This substantially lower threshold indicates that had Philips faced competitors that were as well informed as it was about market demand, Philips should have almost certainly built a plant immediately, despite the demand uncertainty. This indicates that Philips' incentive to be a top dog was strong, even taking into account the option value of flexibility. But, as McGahan points out, Philips' information about demand was likely to be obtained through its experience with CD operations in Europe. Thus, it would know before the competition whether market acceptance was likely to justify investment in a CD plant in the United States. This informational advantage raises the option value of flexibility; McGahan estimates that Philips would have been better off waiting if the probability of market acceptance were 0.13 or lower.

Philips ultimately decided not to build the U.S. plant in 1983, suggesting that it was fairly pessimistic about the prospects of CDs in the American market. In 1984, Sony became the first CD manufacturer to produce in the United States, opening a plant in Terre Haute, Indiana. Philips initially chose to increase capacity at its pressing plant in Hanover, Germany. It decided to invest in a U.S. plant only after Sony's plant was fully operational.

will rush into a bad marriage. At the same time, by continuing to date, each individual in the relationship runs the risk that the other party will find someone better. In effect, waiting increases the risk that each individual in the relationship will be preempted by an outsider.

An analogous tension exists in business. Returning to our example above, if the firm waits to build its new plant, it avoids the possibility of making an investment mistake (building a new plant when demand is low), but it also runs the risk that the market opportunity might be seized by a competitor, perhaps permanently locking the firm out of the opportunity in the future. In business, as in personal relationships, a complete analysis of the option value of delaying major strategic commitments should consider both the option value of delay and the risk of being preempted.

EXAMPLE 7.6 CORNING'S NUCLEAR WINTER[28]

Corning Inc. is the world's largest producer of fiber-optic cable, accounting for nearly 40 percent of the world's supply in 2001. In the late 1990s, with telecommunications carriers installing millions of kilometers of fiber in the United States each year and with annual growth rates in fiber cable sales expected to exceed 20 percent, Corning developed an ambitious plan to extend its dominance in the fiber-optic cable market, a market it pioneered nearly 20 years ago. In December 2000, Corning announced that it would spend $450 million to expand the capacity of a recently constructed fiber-optic cable plant in Concord, North Carolina, and $400 million to build a new fiber-optics plant in Oklahoma City, Oklahoma. Together, the two projects would have increased Corning's fiber manufacturing capacity at a rate of 25 percent a year from 2002 to 2004, a move intended to enlarge Corning's share of the fiber-optic cable market relative to its two largest competitors, Lucent and Alcatel.

For a time, the market rewarded Corning's aspirations. As late as March 2000, Corning had a market capitalization of $51 billion and a price-earnings ratio of 80. Unfortunately, Corning became a high-profile victim of the bursting of the telecom bubble. In 2001, Corning suffered an after-tax loss of over $5.5 billion, representing a return on invested capital of -76.4 percent. From a high of $112.55 per share on September 29, 2000, Corning's stock price plummeted to $1.10 per share on October 11, 2002. (In Fall 2005, Corning's stock price was about $19 per share.) Corning's fiber-optic business experienced a decline in revenue of over 40 percent, leading a Merrill Lynch analyst to liken Corning's situation to a nuclear winter, referring to the barren landscape and devastating loss of life following a nuclear war. Corning's nuclear winter arose when spending by telecommunications carriers on new fiber lines came to an abrupt halt in 2001. With so much dark fiber (i.e., unused fiber-optic capacity) already in the ground, virtually no one foresaw a return to the growth expectations that underlay Corning's ambitious capacity expansion plans of a year earlier.

As disastrous as Corning's experience was, it could have been worse. This is because of the real option that is inherent in the lead time associated with building new fiber-optic capacity. Even though Corning announced its capacity expansion program in late 2000, work on the two projects had hardly started before the abrupt collapse of the fiber-optic cable market. In light of the new reality, in June 2001, Corning suspended construction work on the new Oklahoma City plant, and slowed its expansion of its Concord, North Carolina plant. In July 2002, Corning announced its intention to cancel both projects altogether, while at the same time shutting down the active portion of the Concord plant. Although Corning had committed a significant amount of capital to both expansion projects, it did not end up spending the nearly $1 billion it had originally planned on spending. The fact that it takes time to add new fiber-optic capacity gave Corning the flexibility to terminate the projects once it became clear that future demand for fiber-optic cable was going to be significantly less than what Corning and other firms expected it would be when the two capacity expansion projects were announced in late 2000.

As of 2005, the market for fiber-optic cable remained depressed. Corning derives just 40 percent of its total revenue from fiber-optic and other telecommunications-related products, as compared to 70 percent just before the bubble burst in 2001. Still, Corning has not foreclosed all of its options in this business. Though its Concord plant remains closed, Corning continues to spend money to maintain it. This can also be interpreted as a real option. By keeping the plant in working order, Corning can ramp up production more quickly to respond to an increase in demand for fiber-optic cable than if it had shut down the plant completely. And, of course, if demand remains depressed, Corning has the option to close the plant permanently.

◆ ◆ ◆ ◆ ◆ A FRAMEWORK FOR ANALYZING COMMITMENTS

Pankaj Ghemawat argues that major strategic decisions usually involve investments in "sticky factors": physical assets, resources, and capabilities that are durable, specialized to the particular strategy that the firm follows, and untradeable (i.e., they cannot be sold on the open market).[29] Once made, investments in such assets cannot be easily transformed or redeployed elsewhere. For example, once Wang Laboratories staked its future on dedicated word processing, it would have been extremely difficult for Wang to move into personal computer manufacturing, which required capabilities that it did not have and could not quickly acquire. Because strategic investments are durable, specialized, and untradeable, after a firm has made them, it is stuck. The firm must continue with its chosen strategy for a considerable time. In this sense, according to Ghemawat, the choice of a strategy is manifested in a few commitment-intensive decisions. The essence of strategy, in his view, is getting these commitments right.

But getting these decisions right is difficult. Commitment-intensive decisions are fraught with risk and require that managers look far into the future to evaluate alternative strategic actions. To help managers make such choices, Ghemawat developed a four-step framework for analyzing commitment-intensive choices:

1. Positioning analysis
2. Sustainability analysis
3. Flexibility analysis
4. Judgment analysis

Positioning analysis can be likened to determining the direct effects of the commitment. It involves analyzing whether the firm's commitment is likely to result in a product market position in which the firm delivers superior benefits to consumers or operates with lower costs than competitors. Chapter 11 develops a set of concepts, frameworks, and tools for conducting positioning analysis.

Sustainability analysis can be likened to determining the strategic effects of the commitment. It involves analyzing potential responses to the commitment by competitors and potential entrants in light of the commitments that they have made and the impact of those responses on competition. It also involves analyzing the market imperfections that make the firm's resources scarce and immobile and the conditions that protect the firm's competitive advantages from imitation by competitors. Chapters 9, 11, and 12 develop frameworks and concepts for conducting sustainability analysis.

The culmination of positioning and sustainability analysis, in Ghemawat's view, should be a formal analysis of the net present value of alternative strategic commitments. Positioning analysis provides the basis for determining the revenues and costs associated with each alternative. Sustainability analysis provides the basis for determining the time horizon beyond which the firm's rate of return on incremental investments is no greater than its cost of capital; that is, its economic profits are zero.[30]

Flexibility analysis incorporates uncertainty into positioning and sustainability analysis. As discussed earlier, flexibility gives the firm option value. Ghemawat points out that a key determinant of option value is the learn-to-burn ratio. This is the ratio of the "learn rate"—the rate at which the firm receives new information that allows it to adjust its strategic choices—and the "burn rate"—the rate at which the firm invests in the sunk assets to support the strategy. A high learn-to-burn ratio implies that a strategic choice has a high degree of flexibility. In this case, the option value of delay is low because the firm can quickly accumulate information about the prospects of its strategic choice before it is too heavily committed. Ghemawat argues that many commitment-intensive choices have the potential for high learn-to-burn ratios, but that realizing this potential requires careful management. Experimentation and pilot programs are ways that a firm can increase its learn-to-burn ratio and increase its flexibility in making commitment-intensive choices.

The final part of Ghemawat's framework is judgment analysis: taking stock of the organizational and managerial factors that might distort the firm's incentive to choose an optimal strategy. Ghemawat notes that firms can make two types of errors in making commitment-intensive choices: (1) Type I errors—rejecting an investment that should have been made and (2) Type II errors—accepting an investment that should have been rejected. Theoretical work by Raaj Kumar Sah and Joseph Stiglitz suggests that decision-making systems inside the organization can influence the likelihood of both types of errors.[31] Specifically, they show that organizations in which the authority to screen and accept investment projects is decentralized will accept more investment opportunities—both good and bad—than an organization in which investment decisions are made hierarchically; that is, they are first screened at lower levels and then sent "upstairs" for final approval. This implies that decentralized decision making results in a relatively higher incidence of Type II errors, whereas hierarchical decision making results in a relatively higher incidence of Type I errors. This analysis suggests that part of the process of making commitment-intensive decisions is a choice of how to make such decisions. In working through the first three parts of this framework, managers must be cognizant of the biases imparted by the incentives of the firm's managers to send accurate information up through the hierarchy, by the structure of the organization, and by its politics and culture. We take up these issues in Chapters 16 and 17.

CHAPTER SUMMARY

♦ Strategic commitments are hard-to-reverse decisions that have long-term impacts. They should be distinguished from tactical decisions that are easy to reverse and have short-term impact.

♦ Strategic commitments that seemingly limit options may make a firm better off. Inflexibility can have value because a firm's commitments can lead competitors to make decisions that are advantageous for the firm making the commitment.

♦ The impact of strategic commitments depends on the nature of product market competition. The concepts of strategic complements and strategic substitutes are useful for characterizing how commitment affects competition. When reaction functions are upward sloping, actions are strategic complements. When reaction functions are downward sloping, actions are strategic substitutes.

♦ The direct effect of a commitment is its impact on the present value of the firm's profits, assuming that competitors' actions remain unchanged after the firm has made its commitment. The strategic effect of a commitment is the impact of competitive side effects of the commitment on the firm's profits.

♦ In a two-stage setting, in which a firm makes a commitment and then the firm and its competitors choose tactical actions, the desirability of the commitment depends on whether the actions are strategic substitutes or complements and whether the commitment makes the firm tough or soft.

◆ Flexibility gives the firm option value. A simple example of option value occurs when the firm can delay an investment and await new information that bears on the investment's profitability.

◆ Strategic choices are commitment-intensive because they involve investments in durable, specialized, and immobile resources and capabilities. Analyzing commitment-intensive choices thus requires careful consideration of the likely sources of competitive advantage (i.e., positioning), the sustainability of the advantage, and the flexibility a firm possesses once it makes a strategic investment. An important determinant of flexibility is the learn-to-burn ratio. Managers must also carefully analyze the biases created by internal organizational factors, such as structure and culture.

QUESTIONS

1. What is the difference between a soft commitment and no commitment?
2. How are commitments related to sunk costs?
3. Explain why prices are usually strategic complements and capacities are usually strategic substitutes.
4. Why did Fuderberg and Tirole identify only four of the eight possible strategic commitment strategies? Of the four that they did not identify, which do you think firms might actually adopt?
5. Use the logic of the Cournot equilibrium to explain why it is more effective for a firm to build capacity ahead of its rival than it is for that firm to merely announce that it is going to build capacity.
6. An established firm is considering expanding its capacity to take advantage of a recent growth in demand. It can do so in one of two ways. It can purchase fungible, general-purpose assets that can be resold at close to their original value if their use in the industry proves to be unprofitable. Or it can invest in highly specialized assets that, once put in place, have no alternative uses and virtually no salvage value. Assuming that each choice results in the same production costs once installed, under what choice is the firm likely to encounter a greater likelihood that its competitors will also expand their capacities?
7. Consider a monopoly producer of a durable good, such as a supercomputer. The good does not depreciate. Once consumers purchase the good from the monopolist, they are free to sell it in the "second-hand" market. Often in markets for new durable goods, one sees the following pricing pattern: The seller starts off charging a high price but then lowers the price over time. Explain why, with a durable good, the monopolist might prefer to commit to keep its selling price constant over time. Can you think of a way that the monopolist might be able to make a credible commitment to do this?
8. Indicate whether the *strategic effects* of the following competitive moves are likely to be positive (beneficial to the firm making them) or negative (harmful to the firm making them).
   (a) Two horizontally differentiated producers of diesel railroad engines—one located in the United States and the other located in Europe—compete in the European market as Bertrand price competitors. The U.S. manufacturer lobbies the U.S. government to give it an export subsidy, the amount of which is directly proportional to the amount of output the firm sells in the European market.
   (b) A Cournot duopolist issues new debt to repurchase shares of its stock. The new debt issue will preclude the firm raising additional debt in the foreseeable future, and is expected to constrain the firm from modernizing existing production facilities.
9. Consider two firms competing in a Cournot industry. One firm—Roomkin Enterprises—is contemplating an investment in a new production technology. This new technology will result in efficiencies that will lower its variable costs of production. Roomkin's competitor, Juris Company, does not have the resources to undertake a similar investment. Roomkin's

corporate financial planning staff has studied the proposed investment and reports that *at current output levels* the present value of the cost savings from the investment is less than the cost of the project but just barely so. Now, suppose that Roomkin Enterprises hires you as a consultant. You point out that a complete analysis would take into account the effect of investment on the market equilibrium between Roomkin Enterprises and Juris Company. What would this more complete analysis say about the desirability of this investment?

10. The chapter discussed a situation in which a Cournot competitor would refrain from entering a geographically distinct market for its product, even though it would have a monopoly in that market. Under what circumstances would this incentive be reversed?

11. This question refers to information in question 10 in Chapter 6. Chuckie B Corporation is considering implementing a proprietary technology it has developed. The one-time sunk cost of implementing this process is $350. Once this investment is made, marginal cost will be reduced to $25. Gene Gene has no access to this, or any other cost-saving technology, and its marginal cost will remain at $40. Chuckie B's financial consultant observes that the investment should not be made because a cost reduction of $15 on each of the 20 machines results in a savings of only $300, which is less than the cost of implementing the technology. Is the consultant's analysis accurate? Why or why not? Compute the strategic effect of the investment.

ENDNOTES

[1] This discussion is based on McGahan, A. M., "The Incentive Not to Invest: Capacity Commitments in Compact Disc Introduction," *Research on Technological Innovation, Management and Policy*, 5, 1993, pp. 177–197.

[2] See the Economics Primer for a formal definition and discussion of the concept of a Nash equilibrium.

[3] This quote comes from Luecke, R., *Scuttle Your Ships Before Advancing and Other Lessons from History on Leadership and Change for Today's Managers*, Oxford, Oxford University Press, 1994, p. 23.

[4] One might wonder whether Firm 2's decision to abandon a capacity expansion decision is irreversible. Why couldn't Firm 2 reverse its decision not to build once it sees that Firm 1 has called off its plans? However, this may be difficult to do. For example, Firm 2 may have an option on the land where the plant is to be built that it may be unable to exercise later. If other sites are distinctly inferior, Firm 2's choice may be "now or never."

[5] This example draws from "Loblaw's Store of the Future Ready," *Business and Industry*, 21(15), September 20, 2004, p. 11; "Loblaw Companies Limited," *Hoovers Guide*, http://premium.hoovers.com.

[6] Loblaw's Store of the Future Ready," *Business and Industry*, 21(15), September 20, 2004, p. 11.

[7] Avinash Dixit and Barry Nalebuff's excellent book, *Thinking Strategically: The Competitive Edge in Business, Politics and Everyday Life*, New York, Norton, 1991, contains a thorough discussion of credibility and the commitment value of various competitive moves.

[8] This example was developed by Jondy Syjuco and Li Liu, Kellogg MBA class of 2002.

[9] Holmes, Stanley, "Diverging Flight Plans at the Paris Air Show," *Business Week*, June 22, 2001.

[10] Sparaco, Pierre, "Airbus Thinks Bigger, Not Faster," *Aviation Week & Space Technology*, June 18, 2001, p. 106.

[11] Chen, M.-J. and I. C. MacMillan, "Nonresponse and Delayed Response to Competitive Moves: The Roles of Competitor Dependence and Action Irreversibility," *Academy of Management Journal*, 35, 1992, pp. 539–570.

[12]Reaction functions in the Bertrand model with undifferentiated products do not concern us because a firm always wants to slightly undercut its rival's price. Hence, throughout this section, we confine our attention to Bertrand industries where firms' products exhibit some degree of horizontal differentiation.

[13]The terms *strategic complements* and *strategic substitutes* were introduced by Bulow, J., J. Geanakopolos, and P. Klemperer, "Multimarket Oligopoly: Strategic Substitutes and Complements," *Journal of Political Economy*, 93, 1985, pp. 488–511.

[14]The case in which both firms make strategic commitments is similar to the one where only one firm makes a commitment. However, the economics of this case are more difficult to describe, so we concentrate on the simpler case of a one-firm commitment to keep the discussion compact.

[15]The Economics Primer contains a full discussion of the SPNE.

[16]Strategic incentives for investments of this kind have been analyzed by Brander, J. and B. Spencer, "Strategic Commitment with R&D: The Symmetric Case," *Bell Journal of Economics*, 14, Spring 1983, pp. 225–235.

[17]Firm 1's commitment could also result in a shift in Firm 2's reaction function. For example, if Firm 1 made its product less differentiated than Firm 2's, then Firm 2's demand function would change, which would alter its profit-maximizing pricing decisions and thus shift its reaction function. However, taking this shift into account would move the Bertrand equilibrium even farther down to the southwest in Figure 7.4.

[18]Chapter 6 discusses horizontal differentiation.

[19]Fudenberg, D. and J. Tirole, "The Fat-Cat Effect, the Puppy-Dog Ploy, and the Lean and Hungry Look, American Economic Review 74(2) (May 1984), pp. 361–366.

[20]See "Business War Games Attract Big Warriors," *Wall Street Journal*, December 22, 1994, pp. B1, B4.

[21]This example is based on Ghemawat, P., "Commitment to a Process Innovation: Nucor, USX, and Thin Slab Casting," *Journal of Economics and Management Strategy*, 2, Spring 1993, pp. 133–161.

[22]This is an example of the top-dog strategy.

[23]The term *real* is used in order to distinguish this general concept of an option from the narrower notion of a financial option. There are many kinds of financial options. An example is a call option on a share of stock. The owner of a call option has the right, but not the obligation, to buy a share of stock at a prespecified price.

[24]See Dixit, A. K. and R. S. Pindyck, *Investment under Uncertainty*, Princeton, NJ: Princeton University Press, 1994, for pioneering work on real options. M. Amaran and N. Kulatilaka, *Real Options: Managing Strategic Investments in an Uncertain World*, Boston, Harvard Business School Press, 1999, present a very accessible applied introduction to the analysis of real options.

[25]The following examples draw from "Exploiting Uncertainty: The Real-Options Revolution in Decision Making," *Business Week*, June 7, 1999, p. 118.

[26]Courtney, Hugh, *20-20 Foresight: Crafting Strategy in an Uncertain World*, Boston, Harvard Business School Press, 2001.

[27]McGahan, A. M., "The Incentive Not to Invest: Capacity Commitment in the Compact Disc Introduction," *Research on Technological Innovation, Management and Policy*, 5 1993, pp. 177–197.

[28]This example draws from a variety of sources including Creswell, J., "The New Old Thing: Corning Invented Fiber Optics But Lacked the Focus to Capture Wall Street's Imagination—Until Now," *Fortune*, March 20, 2000, p. 124; Denton, J., "Optical Fiber Maker Brings Oklahoma City Promise of New Jobs," *Daily Oklahoman*, December 19, 2000; Metha, S., "Can Corning Find Its Optic Nerve? The Giants of Optical Networking May Be Crashing, but the No. 1 Maker of Fiber Is Spinning a Tale of Profits," *Fortune*, March 19, 2001; Denton, J., "Construction Work Halted at Corning's Oklahoma Plant," *Daily Oklahoman*, June 8, 2001;

Colberg, S., "Corning May Never Open Oklahoma City Plant, Experts Say," *Daily Oklahoman*, June 15, 2001; Blumenstein, R., S. Thurm, and G. Ip, "Downed Lines: Telecom Sector's Bust Reverberates Loudly Across the Economy," *Wall Street Journal*, July 25, 2001: "Corning Cancels Plant Expansion," *Dow Jones Newswires*, July 24, 2002; "New Corning Chief Learns Lessons of Past; Firm Is Wary of Relying on One Product," *International Herald Tribune*, September 21, 2005.

[29]Ghemawat, P., *Commitment: The Dynamic of Strategy*, New York, Free Press, 1991.

[30]The concept of a time horizon beyond which the firm's investments yield a rate of return no greater than its cost of capital is a standard part of models used by financial analysts to determine the value of firms. In some models, it is called the forecasting horizon. G. Bennett Stewart refers to this horizon as "big T." See *The Quest for Value: A Guide for Senior Managers*, New York, HarperBusiness, 1991.

[31]Sah, R. K. and J. Stiglitz, "The Architecture of Economic Systems: Hierarchies and Polyarchics," *American Economic Review*, 76, September 1986, pp. 716–727.

8

THE DYNAMICS
OF PRICING RIVALRY

For many years, two companies dominated the morning and afternoon newspaper markets in Sydney, Australia: John Fairfax and Sons, which published the *Sydney Morning Herald* in the morning and the *Sun* in the afternoon; and Rupert Murdoch's News Limited, which published the *Daily Telegraph* in the morning and the *Daily Mirror* in the afternoon.[1] The morning market was clearly segmented; the *Morning Herald* appealed to a more affluent readership than the *Daily Telegraph*. By contrast, the newspapers in the afternoon market competed for the same readers and were close substitutes for one another.

Throughout much of the post–World War II period, prices in the afternoon market moved in lockstep. Seven price increases occurred between 1941 and January 1974. In four of these cases, the price increase was announced by the *Sun* (acknowledged to be the price leader in the afternoon market) and was matched within days by the *Daily Mirror*. In the other three instances, papers gave simultaneous notice of the price increase. In the morning market, by contrast, a price increase by one paper would often go unmatched by the other for 9 or 10 months.

But pricing behavior in the afternoon market changed in July 1975 when Fairfax increased the price of the *Sun* from 10 cents to 12 cents. Breaking with more than 30 years of tradition, Murdoch chose to keep the price of the *Daily Mirror* at 10 cents. The price war waged by Murdoch's paper lasted for three and a half years. During this time, the *Daily Mirror*'s share of the afternoon market rose from 50 to 53 percent, helping it increase its advertising revenues relative to the *Sun*. William Merrilees estimates that by underpricing the *Sun*, the *Daily Mirror* increased its annual profit by nearly $1.6 million, while the *Sun*'s annual profit fell by approximately $1.3 million. In January 1979, Fairfax finally surrendered, dropping its price back down to 10 cents. Henceforth, Murdoch's *Daily Mirror* was the price leader in Sydney's afternoon paper market.

This example raises issues about the dynamics of rivalry within a market. What conditions influence the intensity of price competition in a market? Why do firms in some markets seem to be able to coordinate their pricing behavior to avoid costly price wars, while in other markets intense price competition is the norm? Why do price wars erupt in previously tranquil markets? What is the value, if any, of policies under which the firm commits to matching the prices its competitors charge? When should a firm match its rival's price, and when should it go its own way? These are some of the questions we consider in Chapter 8.

This chapter builds on the analytical frameworks introduced in Chapter 6 to help us understand why firms compete as they do. We are especially interested in price competition as a dynamic process, that is, one that unfolds over time. This implies that a firm's decisions made at one point in time affect how competitors, and indeed the firm itself, will behave in the future. For example, had Murdoch believed that Fairfax would abandon its price increase once he refused to go along, he might have chosen to match the increase. This suggests that Fairfax should have clearly communicated that it would match whatever price Murdoch's paper charged in the previous week, a policy known as tit-for-tat pricing.

This chapter also discusses nonprice competition, focusing in particular on competition with respect to product quality. In this part of the chapter, we explore how market structure influences a firm's incentives to choose its product quality and how consumer information shapes the nature of competition with respect to quality.

DYNAMIC PRICING RIVALRY

Firms that compete with one another do so repeatedly. This implies that competitive moves that might have short-run benefits may, in the longer run, hurt the firm once its competitors have had time to make countermoves. For example, a firm that cuts its price today to steal business from rivals may find that they retaliate with their own price cuts in the future, thus nullifying the business-stealing "benefits" of the original price cut and driving down profits for all. This section develops a theory of long-term, or dynamic, rivalry. The next section uses the theory to illuminate the link between market structure and the intensity of price competition.

Why the Cournot and Bertrand Models Are Not Dynamic

The reader might wonder whether dynamic elements of competition have not already been included within the context of the Cournot and Bertrand models. After all, in Chapter 6, we described the process of attaining a Cournot or Bertrand equilibrium as if it came out of a sequence of firm actions and reactions. For example, in a simple Cournot industry with two firms, Firm 1 and Firm 2, the process of achieving an equilibrium is described as follows: Firm 2 makes an output decision; Firm 1 then reacts to the quantity chosen by Firm 2 by selecting the quantity along its reaction function that is associated with the quantity chosen by Firm 2 (see Figure 8.1). Firm 2 then reacts to the quantity chosen by Firm 1 by choosing the quantity along its reaction function corresponding to Firm 1's choice. This process unfolds until the equilibrium is reached.

This depiction of Cournot competition (and analogous depictions of Bertrand competition) is, strictly speaking, not correct, however. In truth, both models are static rather than dynamic because in each model all firms simultaneously make once-and-for-all quantity or price choices. The reaction–counterreaction story is only a convenient fable that reinforces the notion that a Cournot (or Bertrand) equilibrium

FIGURE 8.1
CONVERGENCE TO A COURNOT EQUILIBRIUM

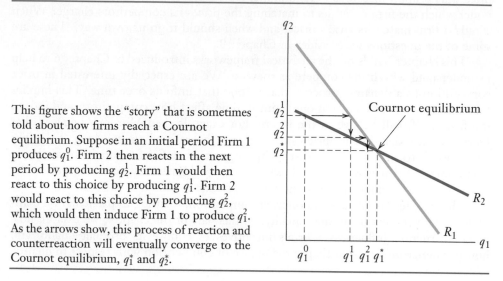

This figure shows the "story" that is sometimes told about how firms reach a Cournot equilibrium. Suppose in an initial period Firm 1 produces q_1^0. Firm 2 then reacts in the next period by producing q_2^1. Firm 1 would then react to this choice by producing q_1^1. Firm 2 would react to this choice by producing q_2^2, which would then induce Firm 1 to produce q_1^2. As the arrows show, this process of reaction and counterreaction will eventually converge to the Cournot equilibrium, q_1^* and q_2^*.

is a point of "stability." To see the inadequacy of the "dynamic" depiction of the Cournot model in Figure 8.1, note that each time a firm chooses its quantity, it bases that decision on what its rival did in its previous move. Moreover, its "reaction" is the choice that maximizes its current (i.e., single-period) profit. But presumably an intelligent firm would take the long view and choose its quantity to maximize the present value of profits over its entire time horizon. To do this, it must anticipate what its rival will do in the future, not just naively react to what it has done in the past. Figure 8.1 reveals the limitations of naively reacting to the rival firm's previous output choice. Unless the two firms are at the equilibrium point, what either firm did in the past is an unreliable guide to what each will do in the future.

This discussion does not imply that the Cournot or Bertrand models are wrong or useless. Both models reduce a complicated phenomenon—industry rivalry—to an analytically convenient form that helps answer such questions as "What impact does the number of firms have on the prevailing level of prices in the market?" or "What would be expected to happen to prices in an oligopolistic market as demand shifts outward?" These models are also useful—as Chapter 7 emphasized—for examining the interplay between strategic commitments of various kinds and tactical maneuvering. However, neither the Cournot nor the Bertrand model can fully explain why in certain highly concentrated oligopolies (e.g., the U.S. steel industry until the late 1960s or the U.S. cigarette industry until the early 1990s) firms can maintain prices above competitive levels without formal collusion and why in other comparably concentrated markets (e.g., regional cement markets) price competition is often fierce. Nor do these models offer guidance to managers assessing their own pricing decisions in rivalrous situations. Dynamic models of price competition are more useful for exploring such questions.

Dynamic Pricing Rivalry: Intuition

The starting point for our analysis is the premise that, all else being equal, firms would prefer prices to be closer to their monopoly levels than to the levels reached under Bertrand or Cournot competition. For example, Figure 8.2 depicts the demand and cost conditions in the world market for a commodity chemical. Imagine that the market consists of two firms, Shell Chemical and Exxon Mobil Chemical. This is a mature business in which demand is neither growing nor shrinking and both firms have access to the same technology and factors of production and thus have equal costs. We assume that marginal cost is constant at $20 per hundred pounds over the entire range of possible output levels. Buyers regard each firm's product as a perfect substitute for the other's, so consumers choose solely on the basis of price.

By colluding, the two competitors could charge the monopoly price, which is $60 per hundred pounds, and together they would produce 40 million pounds of the chemical per year. How they divide this market cannot be deduced from monopoly theory, but given that the firms are identical, we can assume that they will split the market 50:50. If so, the monopoly outcome would give each firm an annual profit of $8 million. By contrast, if the two firms were to compete as Bertrand competitors, they would charge $20, and their annual profit would be zero.[2]

Colluding—formally agreeing to fix prices above the Bertrand/competitive level, is illegal in most developed countries. To emphasize that we are not focusing on formal collusion, we use the term *cooperative pricing* to refer to situations in which firms can sustain prices in excess of those that would arise in a noncooperative single-shot price or quantity-setting game, such as Cournot or Bertrand.

Is cooperative pricing achievable when firms make pricing decisions noncooperatively? Put another way, suppose two firms are unilaterally setting prices that are near the prices they would set if they successfully colluded. Are there conditions under which neither firm would wish to undercut its rival? Under those conditions, cooperative pricing is feasible. Without those conditions, cooperative pricing is difficult to achieve. In the remainder of this section, we describe the benefits and costs confronting a firm that contemplates undercutting the prices of its competitors. In the following section, we identify market conditions that affect these benefits and costs.

FIGURE 8.2

MONOPOLY PRICE AND QUANTITY

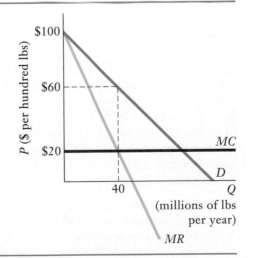

With the market demand curve shown in the figure and a constant marginal cost of $20, the monopoly quantity is 40 million pounds per year, and the monopoly price is $60 per pound.

A firm that contemplates undercutting its rivals confronts a tradeoff. It stands to reap a short-term increase in profits if the price reduction translates into an increase in market share. It might also enjoy a long-term increase in profits if, once pricing stability is restored to the market, it experiences a permanent increase in market share. On the other hand, the firm's rivals might respond by lowering their own prices. Once they do, the firm that initiated the price reduction could end up with no increase in market share, but with lower price–cost margins.

The economist Edward Chamberlin identified these forces when he argued that sellers in concentrated markets would recognize that the profit they gain from cutting price below the monopoly level is likely to be fleeting:

> *If each seeks his maximum profit rationally and intelligently, he will realize that when there are two or only a few sellers his own move has a considerable effect upon his competitors, and that this makes it idle to suppose that they will accept without retaliation the losses he forces upon them. Since the result of a cut by any one is inevitably to decrease his own profits, no one will cut, and although the sellers are entirely independent, the equilibrium result is the same as though there were a monopolistic agreement between them.*[3]

Competitor Responses and Tit-for-Tat Pricing

To understand how Chamberlin's argument works in our example, suppose that Shell and Exxon Mobil are currently charging a price somewhere between the Bertrand price of $20 and the monopoly price of $60, say $40 per hundred pounds. Suppose that Shell has recently suffered setbacks in its other markets and is considering raising its price to the monopoly level of $60.

You might think that it would be foolish for Shell to raise its price to $60 without having enlisted Exxon Mobil's agreement to follow suit. After all, if Shell raises its price, but Exxon Mobil does not, Exxon Mobil will capture 100 percent of the market. At a price of $40, Exxon Mobil's profits will increase to $12 million per year, which exceeds the $8 million annual profit Exxon Mobil would get if it follows Shell's lead and raises its price to the monopoly level. Thus, Shell and Exxon Mobil face a prisoners' dilemma similar to that described in the Economics Primer: although it is in the collective interest of both firms to charge the monopoly price, Exxon Mobil is better off undercutting Shell's price if Shell raises its price to the monopoly level.

But now suppose that prices can be changed every week, so that if Shell can rescind its price increase, it can do so without waiting more than a week. Furthermore, suppose that Shell can observe Exxon Mobil's pricing decision immediately, so Shell will know at once whether Exxon Mobil has followed its price increase.

Under these conditions, Shell's decision to raise price carries little risk. If Exxon Mobil refuses to follow, Shell can drop its price back to $40 after one week. At most, Shell sacrifices one week's profit at current prices (roughly $115,400 or $0.1154 million). Not only is the risk to Shell low from raising its price, but if Shell puts itself in Exxon Mobil's position, it would see that Exxon Mobil has a compelling motive to follow Shell's price increase. To see why, suppose that both firms use a 10 percent annual rate to discount future profits. On a weekly basis, this corresponds roughly to a discount rate of .2 percent (i.e., .002).[4] Shell reasons as follows:

- *If Exxon Mobil sticks with the current price of $40, we will learn this quickly, so Exxon Mobil should anticipate that we will drop our price back down to $40 after the first week if it does not follow. By keeping its price at $40, Exxon Mobil will get a one-week "bump" in profit from $0.1154 million to $0.2307 million per week ($0.2307 = 12/52). However, after we rescind*

EXAMPLE 8.1 THE GENERAL MOTORS EMPLOYEE DISCOUNT PRICE WAR

The U.S. passenger car market has some of the ingredients that, when brewed together, make for cutthroat price competition. The market is not especially concentrated; market leader General Motors realizes no better than a 25 percent share most quarters. The wide variety of makes and models and the secrecy of dealer pricing make it difficult for manufacturers to coordinate on pricing. A few factors contribute to pricing stability. The major players are essentially unchanged from three decades ago. There is some brand loyalty, especially in the minivan, SUV, sports, and luxury segments. The result is that car makers enjoy respectable, if not superlative, margins on most lines, with razor thin margins in the economy car and family sedan segments.

General Motors has been one of the few automakers that have attempted to alter the fundamentals of new car pricing. When GM launched the Saturn nameplate in 1990, it advertised that they would be sold at the sticker price. This simplified pricing policy was very attractive to many buyers, especially first-time car buyers who had no experience negotiating with the dealer for a discount, or simply preferred the no-hassle process.

Despite Saturn's modest success, GM's market share steadily eroded over the past two decades and stood below 25 percent in 2004. On June 1, 2005, GM launched another bold pricing initiative. For a limited time, GM would extend its employee discount (usually about 10 percent off sticker) to all customers. The promotion was an immediate hit. In the first month, GM enjoyed a 41 percent increase in sales and an 8 percentage point increase in market share. Quite a few of the cars were sold to people who were considering buying another brand.

GM was helped by the wait-and-see attitude adopted by the other car makers. But once GM extended its promotion until August 1, Ford and Chrysler felt they could no longer sit idly by while their cars gathered dust on dealer lots. In early July, both Ford and Chrysler extended the same employee discount promotion. A few foreign manufacturers swiftly followed suit.

Some back of the envelope calculations suggest how the price war affected GM's bottom line. Consider a car that costs GM $20,000 to manufacture and suppose that in a normal month, GM sells 100,000 of them. Typically, GM would realize a price of about $25,000 for this car, for a gross profit of $500 million. Under employee discounting, GM sells the car for $24,000 but increases its monthly sales to about 140,000. Its monthly gross profits increase to $560 million. So far, so good, but what happens once Ford and Chrysler match prices?

Continuing the example, we may imagine that in the second month, GM sells 120,000 cars. Its gross profits fall to $480 million. Over the two-month promotion period, GM enjoyed a gross margin of $1.04 billion, versus $1 billion had it kept status quo pricing. Had the price war continued much longer, all three car makers might have been awash in considerable red ink. They allowed the promotion to end on September 30. Unfortunately, the temptation to win market share proved irresistible, and a new round of discounts began in the late fall.

There are two additional considerations not accounted for by these calculations. Some customers who were planning to purchase GM vehicles may have accelerated their purchases to take advantage of the discount. GM sales did slump considerably soon after the promotion ended. The lost profits in the post-sale period—which coincided with the roll-out of higher margin 2006 models—must be weighed against the profits reaped during the sale. The second consideration is whether any of the new GM customers lured away from Ford and Chrysler might become loyal customers willing to purchase additional GM cars in the future at higher margins. Only time will tell if GM enjoys this benefit of having led the way in reducing prices.

our price increase, Exxon Mobil's weekly profit would go back to $0.1154 million. The discounted present value of Exxon Mobil's weekly profit (expressed in millions of dollars) under this scenario would be

$$0.2308 + 0.1154/(1.002) + 0.1154/(1.002)^2 + 0.1154/(1.002)^3 + \ldots,$$

which equals $57.93 million.[5]

- *If Exxon Mobil follows us and raises its price to $60, we each will earn annual profits of $8 million, which translates into a weekly profit of $153,846 or $0.1538 million. By following our price increase, the discounted value of Exxon Mobil's weekly profit is*

$$0.1538 + 0.1538/(1.002) + 0.1538/(1.002)^2 + 0.1538/(1.002)^3 + \ldots,$$

which equals $77.05 million. Clearly, Exxon Mobil is better off following our lead, even though for the first week it would be better off if it refused to raise its price to $60.

Because Exxon Mobil has much to gain by matching Shell's price and Shell loses little if Exxon Mobil does not match, it makes sense for Shell to raise its price to $60. If Exxon Mobil behaves rationally, then it will behave the way Shell expects it to behave (as described by the preceding reasoning), and Exxon Mobil will match Shell's price increase. The outcome thus corresponds to the monopoly outcome even though each firm acts unilaterally. A simple calculation reveals that the monopoly price is sustainable as long as Exxon Mobil's weekly discount rate is less than 50 percent, which corresponds to an annual discount rate of 2,600 percent!

Shell would be even more confident that Exxon Mobil would match its price increase if Shell also announced to Exxon Mobil that starting next week, its price in any given week would match the price that Exxon Mobil charged in the preceding week. This *tit-for-tat strategy* is akin to a commitment by Shell to its customers that "We will not be undersold." If Shell signals to Exxon Mobil that it is following a tit-for-tat strategy, and if Exxon Mobil does not match Shell's increase to $60, then Exxon Mobil knows that Shell will drop its price back down to the original level of $40 after the first week. As it figures out its best reply, Exxon Mobil will thus go through exactly the same reasoning described earlier and will find it worthwhile to match Shell's price of $60.

By following a policy of tit-for-tat, Fairfax & Sons might have avoided the costly price war described in the introduction to this chapter. Once it became clear that Murdoch's *Daily Mirror* was not going to raise its price to 12 cents, Fairfax would have dropped its price back down to 10 cents. Had Murdoch's paper anticipated this behavior by Fairfax, it would have had a powerful incentive to match Fairfax's price increase.

Tit-for-Tat Pricing with Many Firms

It is straightforward to extend the logic of the Shell–Exxon Mobil example to an arbitrary number of firms and to pricing periods of arbitrary lengths (e.g., one month, one quarter, or one year). To do so, let π_0 be the per-period industry profit at the prevailing price P_0, and let π_M be the industry's profit when all firms charge the monopoly price, P_M. The industry as a whole would be better off at the monopoly price than at the prevailing price P_0, so $\pi_0 < \pi_M$. However, as in the Shell–Exxon Mobil example, imagine that each of the N firms in this industry faces a prisoner's dilemma. If an individual firm expects its competitors to raise their prices to the monopoly level, that firm gets a larger profit by sticking at P_0 (thereby undercutting its competitors and capturing the entire market at the prevailing price P_0) than it would get if it matched the price increase and captured $1/N$th of the monopoly profit. A firm's one-period profit gain from refusing to cooperate with an industrywide move to the monopoly price is thus $\pi_0 - (1/N)\pi_M$.

Suppose that the firms compete with each other over an infinite horizon (i.e., period after period, without end) and that each firm discounts future profits using a discount rate of i per period. If each firm believes that its competitors will raise the price from P_0 to P_M in the current period and thereafter will follow a tit-for-tat strategy, then each firm will find it in its self-interest to charge the monopoly price as long as[6]

$$\frac{\frac{1}{N}[\pi_M - \pi_0]}{\pi_0 - \frac{1}{N}\pi_M} \geq i \tag{8.1}$$

If the condition in (8.1) holds, each firm will independently (i.e., without collusion) raise price to the monopoly level. Though formidable looking, this condition has a straightforward interpretation and—as we will discuss later—some powerful implications. The numerator of the left-hand side is the single-period benefit to an individual firm from cooperating; it represents the difference in an individual firm's per-period profit when all firms set the monopoly price as opposed to P_0. The denominator is the extra profit the firm could have earned in the current period if it had refused to cooperate. The inequality in (8.1) states that cooperative pricing will be sustainable when this ratio exceeds the per-period discount rate, i. For example, if $N = 5$, $\pi_M = \$100,000$ per month and $\pi_0 = \$40,000$ per month, then the ratio is

$$\frac{\frac{1}{5}[100,000 - 40,000]}{40,000 - \frac{1}{5}(100,000)} = \frac{12,000}{20,000} = 0.60$$

If the pricing period is one month long, this calculation implies that as long as the monthly discount rate is below 60 percent (or an annual rate below 720 percent), each firm has an incentive to independently raise price to the monopoly level.

The "Folk Theorem"

The benefit–cost condition in (8.1) implies that if each firm is reasonably patient (i.e., if the discount rate i is not too large), then the cooperative outcome will be sustainable. This result is a special case of what game theorists have referred to as the *folk theorem* for infinitely repeated prisoner dilemma games.[9] The folk theorem says that for sufficiently low discount rates, any price between the monopoly price P_M and marginal cost can be sustained as an equilibrium in the infinitely repeated prisoners' dilemma game being studied here. Of course, strategies other than tit-for-tat would be necessary to generate these other equilibria. For example, one equilibrium would be for each firm to set a price equal to marginal cost in each period. Given that it expects its competitors to behave this way, a firm can do no better than to behave this way as well.

Coordination

The folk theorem implies that cooperative pricing behavior is a possible outcome in an oligopolistic industry, even if all firms act unilaterally. There can be many other

EXAMPLE 8.2 WHAT HAPPENS WHEN A FIRM RETALIATES QUICKLY TO A PRICE CUT: PHILIP MORRIS VERSUS B.A.T IN COSTA RICA[7]

An excellent illustration of what can happen when one firm cuts its price and its competitor immediately matches the cut occurred in the cigarette industry in Costa Rica in 1993. The most famous cigarette price war of 1993 occurred in the United States, when Philip Morris initiated its "Marlboro Friday" price cuts.[8] The lesser-known Costa Rican price war, also initiated by Philip Morris, began several months before and lasted one year longer than the Marlboro Friday price war.

At the beginning of the 1990s, two firms dominated the Costa Rican cigarette market: Philip Morris, with 30 percent of the market, and B.A.T, with 70 percent of the market. The market consisted of three segments: premium, midpriced, and value-for-money (VFM). Philip Morris had the leading brands in the premium and midpriced segments (Marlboro and Derby, respectively). B.A.T, by contrast, dominated the VFM segment with its Delta brand.

Throughout the 1980s, a prosperous Costa Rican economy fueled steady growth in the demand for cigarettes. As a result, both B.A.T and Philip Morris were able to sustain price increases that exceeded the rate of inflation. By 1989, industry price–cost margins exceeded 50 percent. However, in the late 1980s, the market began to change. Health concerns slowed the demand for cigarettes in Costa Rica, a trend that hit the premium and midpriced segments much harder than it did the VFM segment. In 1992, B.A.T gained market share from Philip Morris for the first time since the early 1980s. Philip Morris faced the prospect of slow demand growth and a declining market share.

On Saturday, January 16, 1993, Philip Morris reduced the prices of Marlboro and Derby cigarettes by 40 percent. The timing of the price reduction was not by chance. Philip Morris reasoned that B.A.T's inventories would be low following the year-end holidays, and that B.A.T would not have sufficient product to satisfy an immediate increase in demand should it match or undercut Philip Morris's price cut. Philip Morris also initiated its price cut on a Saturday morning, expecting that B.A.T's local management would be unable to respond without first undertaking lengthy consultations with the home office in London.

But, B.A.T surprised Philip Morris with the speed of its response. B.A.T cut the price of its Delta brand by 50 percent, a price that industry observers estimated barely exceeded Delta's marginal cost. Having been alerted to Morris's move on Saturday morning, B.A.T had salespeople out selling at the new price by Saturday afternoon. The ensuing price war lasted two years. Cigarette sales increased 17 percent as a result of the lower prices, but market shares did not change much. By the time the war ended in 1994, Philip Morris's share of the Costa Rican market was unchanged, and it was U.S. $8 million worse off than it was before the war had started. B.A.T lost even more—U.S. $20 million—but it had preserved the market share of its Delta brand and was able to maintain the same price gaps that had prevailed across segments before the war. Why did Philip Morris act as it did? In the early 1990s, Philip Morris had increased Marlboro's market share at B.A.T's expense in other Central American countries, such as Guatemala. Perhaps it expected that it could replicate that success in Costa Rica. Still, had it anticipated B.A.T's quick response, Philip Morris should have realized that its price cut would not gain it market share. Whatever the motivation for Philip Morris's actions, this example highlights how quick retaliation by competitors can nullify the advantages of a price cut. If firms understand that and take the long view, the anticipated punishment meted out by a tit-for-tat pricing strategy can deter using price as a competitive weapon.

outcomes, however, and thus there is no guarantee that cooperative pricing will emerge. Achieving cooperative pricing when other, less attractive outcomes are possible is a *coordination problem*. To attain the cooperative outcome, firms in the industry must coordinate on a strategy, such as tit-for-tat, that makes it in each firm's self-interest to refrain from aggressive price cutting.

An obvious—and in most countries, illegal—way to solve this coordination problem is through a collusive agreement. Achieving coordination without an agreement or overt communication is far more difficult. Somehow, each firm in the industry must adopt a strategy, such as tit-for-tat, that moves the industry toward cooperative pricing. To succeed, this cooperation-inducing strategy must be a *focal point*—a strategy so compelling that a firm would expect all other firms to adopt it.

Theories of how focal points emerge in economic or social interactions are not well-developed.[10] Focal points are highly context- or situation-specific. For example, consider a game called "Divide the Cities" concocted by David Kreps, a professor at the Stanford Graduate School of Business.[11]

> *The following is a list of eleven cities in the United States: Atlanta, Boston, Chicago, Dallas, Denver, Houston, Los Angeles, New York, Philadelphia, San Francisco, and Seattle. I have assigned to each city a point value from 1 to 100 according to the city's importance and its "quality of life." You will not be told this scale until the game is over, except that I tell you now that New York has the highest score, 100, and Seattle has the least, 1. I do think you will find my scale is fair. I am going to have you play the following game against a randomly selected student of the Harvard Graduate School of Business. Each of you will be asked to list, simultaneously and without consultation, some subset of these eleven cities. Your list must contain San Francisco and your opponent's must contain Boston. Then, I will give you $100 simply for playing the game. And I will add to/subtract from that amount as follows: For every city that appears on one list but not the other, the person who lists the city will get as many dollars as that city has points on my scale. For every city that appears on both lists, I will take from each of you twice as many dollars as the city has points. Finally, if the two of you manage to partition the cities, I will triple your winnings. Which cities will you list?*

There are hundreds of possible outcomes to this game. Yet, when the game is played by American students, the outcome is nearly always the same: The Stanford student's list is Dallas, Denver, Houston, Los Angeles, Seattle, and San Francisco. The focal point is an East–West division of the United States, coupled with some elementary equity considerations to deal with the fact that there is an odd number (11) of cities to be divided. (Since Seattle is the lowest-valued city, students generally let the western list contain the extra city.) Kreps notes that the focal point of East–West geography becomes less focal when one of the students playing the game is from outside the United States. The U.S. student then often has concerns about the non-U.S. student's knowledge of geography. The game also loses its focal point when the list of cities has a less natural division, for example, if it contains eight western cities and only three eastern ones.

This example offers several insights for firms attempting to coordinate on price or other decisions. Firms are likely to settle on round number price points (e.g., $300 for digital music players, or perhaps cost plus $100) and round number price increases (e.g., 10 percent annual increases, or perhaps cost plus 5 percent). Even splits of market share are likely to outlast other, less obvious divisions. Status quo market shares are also sustainable. Coordination is likely to be easier when competitors sell products that are nearly identical. Coordination is likely to be difficult in competitive environments that are turbulent and rapidly changing.

Firms can facilitate coordination through traditions and conventions that stabilize the competitive environment, making competitors' moves easier to follow and their intentions easier to interpret. For example, in the turbine generator industry in the United States in the 1960s, the two sellers, GE and Westinghouse, employed a single multiplier to determine discounts off the list price. This reduced a complicated pricing decision to a single, easy-to-understand number. Many industries have standard cycles for adjusting prices. Until the early 1990s, in the U.S. cigarette industry, June and December were the traditional dates for Philip Morris and RJR to announce price changes. The tacit understanding that prices will not be changed except on the traditional dates reduces suspicions that competitors may be trying to disrupt the status quo, making it easier for firms to coordinate on prices at or close to the monopoly level.

Why Is Tit-for-Tat So Compelling?

Tit-for-tat is not the only strategy that allows firms to sustain monopoly pricing as a noncooperative equilibrium. Another strategy that, like tit-for-tat, results in the monopoly price for sufficiently low discount rates is the "grim trigger" strategy:

> Starting this period, we will charge the monopoly price P_M. In each subsequent period, if any firm deviates from P_M we will drop our price to marginal cost in the next period and keep it there forever.

The grim trigger strategy relies on the threat of an infinite price war to keep firms from undercutting their competitors' prices. In light of other potentially effective strategies, such as grim trigger, why would we necessarily expect firms to adopt a tit-for-tat strategy? One reason is that tit-for-tat is a simple, easy to describe, and easy to understand strategy. Through announcements such as "We will not be undersold" or "We will match our competitors' prices, no matter how low," a firm can easily signal to its rivals that it is following tit-for-tat.

Another reason for firms to choose a tit-for-tat strategy is that they probably do well over the long run against a variety of different strategies. A compelling illustration of this is discussed by Robert Axelrod in his book *The Evolution of Cooperation*.[12] Axelrod conducted a computer tournament in which entrants were invited to submit strategies for playing a (finitely) repeated prisoners' dilemma game. Each of the submitted strategies was pitted against every other, and the winner was the strategy that accumulated the highest overall score in all of its "matches." Even though tit-for-tat can never beat another strategy in one-on-one competition (at best it can tie another strategy), it accumulated the highest overall score. It was able to do so, according to Axelrod, because it combines the properties of "niceness," "provocability," and "forgiveness." It is nice in that it is never the first to defect from the cooperative outcome. It is provocable in that it immediately punishes a rival that defects from the cooperative outcome by matching the rival's defection in the next period. It is forgiving in that if the rival returns to the cooperative strategy, tit-for-tat will too.

Misreads

In Axelrod's strategy games, each player was fully informed about its rival's prices. In the real world, firms sometimes *misread* their rivals. By "misread," we mean that either (1) a firm mistakenly believes a competitor is charging one price when it is really charging another or (2) a firm misunderstands the reasons for a competitor's pricing decision. Although tit-for-tat is successful against a wide range of strategies, it may

EXAMPLE 8.3 FORGIVENESS AND PROVOCABILITY:
DOW CHEMICALS AND THE MARKET FOR REVERSE
OSMOSIS MEMBRANE[16]

Achieving the right balance between provocability and forgiveness is important, but it can be difficult to do. Dow Chemicals learned this lesson in the mid-1990s in the market for reverse osmosis membranes, an expensive component used in environmental systems for waste water treatment and water purification. Dow sells this product to large industrial distributors that, in turn, resell it to end users.

Until 1989, Dow held a patent on its FilmTec membrane and had the U.S. market entirely to itself. In 1989, however, the U.S. government made Dow's patent public property on the grounds that the government had co-funded the development of the technology. Shortly thereafter, a Japanese firm entered the market with a "clone" of Dow's FilmTec membrane.

In 1989, Dow's price was $1,400 per membrane. Over the next seven years, the Japanese competitor reduced its price to about $385 per unit. Over this period, Dow also reduced its price. With slight differentiation based on superior service support and perceived quality, Dow's price bottomed out at about $405 per unit.

During the downward price spiral, Dow alternated back and forth between forgiving and aggressive responses to its competitor's pricing moves as Dow sought to ascertain its rival's motives and persuade it to keep industry prices high. On three different occasions, Dow raised the price of its membrane. Its competitor never followed Dow's increases, and (consistent with tit-for-tat pricing) Dow ultimately rescinded its price increase each time.

During this period, Dow also attempted several strategic moves (in the spirit of Chapter 7) to insulate itself from price competition and soften the pricing behavior of its competitor. For example, Dow invested in product quality to improve the performance of its membranes. It also tried to remove distributors' focus on price by heavily advertising its membrane's superior performance features. These moves were only moderately successful, however, and Dow was unable to gain a price premium greater than 13 percent.

Eventually, Dow learned that its competitor manufactured its product in Mexico, giving it a cost advantage based on low-cost labor. It also learned that in 1991 the competitor had built a large plant and that its aggressive pricing moves were, in part, prompted by a desire to keep that plant operating at full capacity. Based on this information, Dow abandoned its efforts to soften price competition, either through forgiving pricing moves or strategic commitments aimed at changing the equilibrium in the pricing game. Dow's current strategy is to bypass industrial distributors and sell its product directly to end users. This move was motivated by Dow's discovery that, despite the decreases in manufacturers' prices, distributors' prices to end users remained fairly constant. It is not clear that this strategy would help insulate Dow from price competition. Dow's competitor can presumably imitate this strategy and deal directly with end users as well. It is hard to imagine pricing rivalry in this industry becoming less aggressive.

not be forgiving enough that a firm can misread its competitors' pricing moves and still make a wise pricing decision.

Consider what might happen when two firms are playing tit-for-tat and a cooperative move is misread as an uncooperative one. The firm that misreads the cooperative move as an uncooperative one responds by making an uncooperative move. That firm's competitor then responds in kind. A single misread leads to a pattern in which firms alternate between cooperative and uncooperative moves. If, in the midst of this dynamic, another cooperative move is misread as an uncooperative one, the resulting pattern becomes even worse: Firms become stuck in a cycle of choosing uncooperative moves each period.

Avinash Dixit and Barry Nalebuff have argued that when misreads are possible, pricing strategies that are less provocable and more forgiving than tit-for-tat are desirable.[13] It may be desirable to ignore what appears to be an uncooperative move by one's competitor if the competitor then reverts to cooperative behavior in the next period.

McKinsey consultants Robert Garda and Michael Marn suggest that some real-world price wars are not prompted by deliberate attempts by one firm to steal business from its competitors.[14] Instead, they stem from misreads. To illustrate their point, Garda and Marn cite the example of a tire manufacturer that sold a particular tire at an invoice price of $35, but with an end-of-year volume bonus of $2 and a marketing allowance of $1.50, the manufacturer's net price was really $31.50.[15] This company received reports from its regional sales personnel that a rival firm was selling a competing tire at an invoice price of $32. In response, the manufacturer lowered its invoice price by $3, reducing its net price to $28.50. The manufacturer later learned that its competitor was not offering marketing allowances or volume discounts. By misreading its competitor's price and reacting immediately, the tire manufacturer precipitated a vicious price war that hurt both firms. Garda and Marn emphasize that to avoid overreacting to apparent price cuts by competitors, companies should carefully ascertain the details of the competitive initiative and figure out what is driving it before responding.

◆ ◆ ◆ ◆ ◆ How Market Structure Affects the Sustainability of Cooperative Pricing

Pricing cooperation is harder to achieve under some market structures than others, partly because under certain conditions, firms cannot coordinate on a focal equilibrium and partly because market structure conditions systematically influence the benefit–cost ratio in equation (8.1). This section discusses market structure conditions that may facilitate or complicate the attainment of cooperative pricing and competitive stability. We already described one facilitating practice used by GE in the large turbine industry: standardizing pricing so as to make it easier for rivals to announce and match prices. We now focus on four additional conditions:

• Market concentration

• Structural conditions that affect reaction speeds and detection lags

• Asymmetries among firms

• Price sensitivity of buyers

Market Concentration and the Sustainability of Cooperative Pricing

The benefit–cost ratio in equation (8.1) goes up as the number of firms goes down. This implies that cooperative pricing is more likely to be achieved in a concentrated market (few firms) than in a fragmented market (many firms). The insight that market concentration facilitates the sustainability of cooperative pricing is important for anti-trust policy in the United States and the European Community. For example, in the United States, the Department of Justice and the Federal Trade Commission are unlikely to challenge mergers between two competitors unless the postmerger market concentration exceeds certain thresholds.[17]

The intuition behind the relationship between concentration and the sustainability of cooperative pricing is straightforward. When considering a price reduction, firms must always balance the potential gain against any costs. What is telling is the revenue destruction effect described in Chapter 6: if a firm lowers price to gain market share, it usually must lower its price to all its customers, not just the ones it steals from its rivals. In other words, the price-cutting firm must lose revenue on its existing customers in order to gain revenue from new ones. In a concentrated market, a typical firm's market share is larger than it would be in a fragmented market. Thus, the revenue destruction effect from a price decrease is larger in more concentrated markets. At the same time, the pool of potential new customers is smaller, reducing the potential gains from price cutting in more concentrated markets. This tilts the price-cutting equation in favor of maintaining high prices rather than attempting to steal market share.

To be more specific, consider a firm considering a 20 percent price reduction intended to steal 10 percent of its rivals' business. If that firm is in a symmetric duopoly, it will suffer a 10 percent revenue destruction effect (20 percent price reduction on half the market) to gain 5 percent market share (10 percent of half the market.) If the firm is 1 of 10 equal-size competitors, then it will suffer just a 2 percent revenue destruction effect to gain 9 percent share.

This logic fails when firms can target price reductions at the consumers of rival products. For example, thanks to UPC codes and scanners, firms can identify consumers of rival products at the time of purchase and offer them coupons for their next visit to the store. This is common practice at grocery stores. Other firms may obtain shopping lists from retailers and mail out coupons and other promotional materials. While targeted discounts offer a way to steal customers without suffering from the revenue destruction effect, they also enable rivals to execute a "surgical" retaliation to price discounts and may facilitate higher prices across the board.

There is another sense in which high concentration facilitates cooperative pricing. As we discussed, for firms to coordinate on tit-for-tat as a focal strategy, competitors must think alike. Although it is difficult to formalize this aspect theoretically, intuitively one expects that coordinating on a particular focal strategy is likely to be more difficult the more firms there are in the market. Established department stores have experienced this firsthand during the past two decades. For nearly a century, until the 1970s, they used simple rule-of-thumb pricing, such as setting prices for clothing equal to 200 percent of costs. As a result, they rarely worried about price competition. Entry by newcomers, such as TJ Maxx and Filene's Basement, disrupted the cooperative pricing equilibrium, and the dramatic expansion of Wal-Mart and Target has further intensified competition. These entrants have gained market share by undercutting big department stores, which in turn have resorted to more frequent sales to compete effectively with these newcomers. Thanks to their superior inventory management capabilities, Wal-Mart and Target have managed to turn a profit even at the low prices that traditional retailers offer as "sale" prices.

Reaction Speed, Detection Lags, and the Sustainability of Cooperative Pricing

The speed with which firms can react to their rivals' pricing moves also affects the sustainability of cooperative pricing. To see why, let's return to the benefit–cost condition in equation (8.1) and imagine initially that a "period" corresponds to one year. The profits in equation (8.1) would then be annual profit, and the discount rate i would be an annual rate. If, by contrast, the pricing period were a quarter and sales were distributed uniformly through the year, all profits that go into the benefit–cost ratio would be divided by 4, but the ratio itself would not change.[18] However, the threshold on the right-hand side of equation (8.1) becomes a quarterly discount rate, which is the annual rate divided by 4. Thus, the benefit–cost condition becomes:

$$\frac{\frac{1}{N}[\pi_M - \pi_0]}{\pi_0 - \frac{1}{N}\pi_M} \geq \frac{i}{4} \tag{8.2}$$

The key difference between equations (8.1) and (8.2) is that the threshold above which it is optimal for a firm to follow the tit-for-tat strategy and raise its price to the monopoly level is now smaller. Holding the discount rate fixed, it then follows that an increase in the speed of reaction from one year to one quarter widens the set of circumstances in which the cooperative outcome is sustainable. If price cuts can be matched instantly, the effective discount rate goes to zero, and cooperative pricing will always be sustainable.

A firm may be unable to react quickly to its competitors' pricing moves because of (1) lags in detecting competitors' prices; (2) infrequent interactions with competitors (e.g., the firm competes against its rivals for business only a few times in a year); (3) ambiguities in identifying which firm among a group of firms in a market is cutting price; and (4) difficulties distinguishing drops in volume due to price cutting by rivals from drops in volume due to unanticipated decreases in market demand. All of these factors reduce the speed with which firms can respond to defections from cooperative pricing and thus also reduce the effectiveness of retaliatory price cuts aimed at punishing price-cutting firms.

Several structural conditions affect the importance of these factors:

- Lumpiness of orders

- Information about sales transactions

- The number of buyers

- Volatility of demand and cost conditions

Lumpiness of Orders

Orders are lumpy when sales occur relatively infrequently in large batches as opposed to being smoothly distributed over the year. Lumpiness of orders is an important characteristic in such industries as airframe manufacturing, shipbuilding, and supercomputers. Lumpy orders reduce the frequency of competitive interactions between firms. This makes price a more attractive competitive weapon for individual firms and intensifies price competition throughout the industry.

To illustrate the implications of lumpy orders, consider the problem faced by two manufacturers of automobile seats—Johnson Controls and Lear—that are competing to supply seats for the new model of the Honda Accord. The contract will apply for the life of the model, which is expected to be six years. Johnson Controls and Lear also compete for the seat contracts for other automobile models, but these are also multiyear contracts. Thus, at any one time, neither company is likely to have more than 30 contracts. This means that after competing for the Accord contract, these companies may not face off against one another for the rest of the year. Orders in this industry are very lumpy.

Could Johnson Controls and Lear sustain cooperative pricing in this business? It would be difficult. Think about the problem from Johnson Control's perspective. The Accord contract probably represents an important portion of its automotive seating business for the next half-decade, so securing the order is attractive. Moreover, even if Johnson Controls expected a tit-for-tat response from Lear on the next contract to come along, the relatively long lag between this contract and the next diminishes the perceived cost to Johnson Controls of such retaliation. From Johnson Control's perspective, the gain from undercutting Lear is likely to exceed the future costs. Lear is likely to think in much the same way, and if so, both companies will bid aggressively for the Accord contract, and probably for most other contracts as well. This happens even though both companies would be collectively better off if they did not compete so aggressively on price. Although we have left out details, this account describes how firms in the automobile seating business have actually competed for years.

Information about the Sales Transaction

When sales transactions are "public," deviations from cooperative pricing are easier to detect than when prices are secret. For example, a gasoline station can easily learn that a rival has cut its price because prices are publicly posted. By contrast, in many industrial goods markets, prices are privately negotiated between buyers and sellers, so it may be difficult for a firm to learn whether a competitor has cut its price. Because retaliation can occur more quickly when prices are public than when they are secret, price cutting to steal market share from competitors is likely to be less attractive, enhancing the chances that cooperative pricing can be sustained.

Secrecy is a significant problem when transactions involve other dimensions besides a list or an invoice price, as they often do in business-to-business marketing settings. For example, a manufacturer of cookies, such as Keebler, that wants to steal business from a competitor, say Nabisco, can cut its "net price" by increasing trade allowances to retailers or by extending more favorable trade credit terms. Because it is often more difficult to monitor trade allowance deals or credit terms than list prices, competitors may find it difficult to detect business-stealing behavior, hindering their ability to retaliate. Business practices that facilitate secret price cutting create a prisoners' dilemma. Each firm individually prefers to use them, but the industry is collectively worse off when all firms do so.

Deviations from cooperative pricing are also difficult to detect when product attributes are customized to individual buyers, as in airframe manufacturing or the production of diesel locomotives, for example. When products are tailor-made to individual buyers, a seller may be able to increase its market share by altering the design of the product or by throwing in "extras," such as spare parts or a service agreement. These are typically more difficult to observe than the list price, complicating the ability of firms to monitor competitors' behavior.

Secret or complex transaction terms can intensify price competition not only because price matching becomes a less effective deterrent to price-cutting behavior, but also because misreadings become more likely. Firms are more likely to misinterpret a competitive move, such as a reduction in list prices, as an aggressive attempt to steal business, when they cannot fully observe all the other terms competitors are offering. When this happens, the odds of accidental price wars breaking out rise, as discussed earlier. To the extent that a firm's pricing behavior is forgiving, the effects of misreadings may be containable. Still, with secret and complex sales terms, even forgiving strategies may not work in environments where misreadings can occur.

The Number of Buyers

When firms normally set prices in secret, it is easier to detect deviations from cooperative pricing when each firm sells to many small buyers than when each sells to a few large buyers. The reason is that a buyer that receives a price concession from one seller will often have an incentive to report the price cut to other sellers in an attempt to receive even more favorable concessions. This frequently occurs, for example, in the wholesale market for natural gas as industrial customers and buying groups shop around for supply contracts from various gas marketers, such as Duke Energy, that sell natural gas in bulk.

The number of buyers can dramatically affect the likelihood that secret price cuts will be detected. Consider an industry in which buyers generally keep news of price cuts to themselves, so that if a seller offers a discount to a particular customer, there is only a 1 percent probability that rival sellers will learn about it. Suppose, now, that your firm, as part of an initiative to build its market share, offers "secret" discounts to attract 300 customers away from their current supplier. What is the probability that your competitors will learn about at least one of these price cuts? It equals one minus the probability that your rivals do not learn of *any* of the 300 price cuts, or $1 - (0.99)^{300} = 0.951$, a surprisingly large probability. Thus, if there are enough buyers, chances are that your rivals will learn that you have cut your price to at least one of them, even when they have difficulty detecting that you have offered a price cut to any particular buyer. By contrast, if the number of buyers in your industry is small, and you offer discounts to just 10 customers, the probability that at least one of these discounts will get detected is just $1 - (0.99)^{10} = 0.096$. Thus, price cuts are more difficult to detect in industries, such as automobile seats, in which buyers are few. In such industries, the ability to make secret price cuts to which competitors cannot react makes price more attractive as a competitive weapon and can increase price competition.

Volatility of Demand Conditions

Price cutting is harder to detect when market demand conditions are volatile. Demand volatility is a particularly thorny problem when a firm can observe only its own price and volume and not those of its rival. If a firm's sales unexpectedly fall, is it because market demand has fallen or because one of its competitors has cut price and is taking business from it?

Demand volatility is an especially serious problem when much of a firm's costs are fixed. Then, marginal costs decline rapidly at output levels below capacity, and fluctuations in demand will ordinarily cause the monopoly price to fluctuate, too. By contrast, when costs are mainly variable, the marginal cost function will be nearly flat, and the monopoly price will not change as demand shifts back and forth. With high fixed costs and variable demand, the problem of coordinating on the monopoly equilibrium is severe because firms are chasing a moving target (the monopoly price).

Moreover, at output levels even a little below capacity, marginal costs are likely to be low. Thus, during times of excess capacity, the temptation to cut price to steal business can be high.

Asymmetries among Firms and the Sustainability of Cooperative Prices

The theory on which equations (8.1) and (8.2) are based assumes that firms were identical. When firms are not identical, either because they have different costs or are vertically differentiated, achieving cooperative pricing becomes more difficult. For one thing, when firms differ, the price a firm would charge if it were the monopolist depends on its marginal cost or product quality. When firms are identical, a single monopoly price can be a focal point. However, when firms differ, there is no single focal price, and it thus becomes more difficult for firms to coordinate their pricing strategies toward common objectives. Figure 8.3 depicts two firms with different marginal costs and shows that the firm with the lower marginal cost prefers a monopoly price lower than the one with the higher marginal cost.

Differences in costs, capacities, or product qualities also create asymmetric incentives for firms to agree to cooperative pricing, even when all firms can agree on the cooperative price. For example, small firms within a given industry often have more incentive to defect from cooperative pricing than larger firms. There are two related reasons for this. First, because industry profit rises when firms move toward the monopoly price and a large firm typically captures a larger share of industry profit than a smaller firm, a larger firm benefits more from the move toward cooperative pricing than does a smaller firm.

FIGURE 8.3
MONOPOLY PRICES WITH ASYMMETRICAL FIRMS

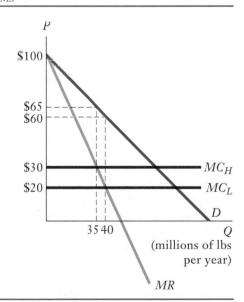

The low-cost firm's marginal cost curve is MC_L, while the high-cost firm's marginal cost curve is MC_H. If the low-cost firm was a monopolist, it would set a price of $60. If the high-cost firm was a monopolist, it would set a price of $65.

Second, small firms may also anticipate that large firms have weak incentives to punish a small firm that undercuts its price. (This is related to the revenue destruction effect.) To illustrate this point, consider the market for dot matrix printers in South Africa, a market that Epson dominated in the early 1990s but Panasonic entered in 1992.[19] Suppose that Panasonic offered a price 5 percent below that of Epson for printers of comparable quality. If Epson matches Panasonic's price cut, it regains its original demand. If not, Epson expects to lose a fraction α of its market share.

Should Epson match? Suppose that Epson's price is Rand 1000 (the rand is the South African unit of currency) per printer, its marginal cost is Rand 500, and its original level of demand is 1,000 printers. If it matches Panasonic's price of Rand 950, Epson's profit is

$$(950 - 500) \cdot 1,000 = 450,000$$

If it does not match, Epson's profit is

$$(1,000 - 500) \cdot 1,000 \cdot (1 - \alpha) = 500,000 \cdot (1 - \alpha)$$

Not matching is optimal if the second expression is bigger than the first, which occurs if $\alpha < 0.10$ or if Epson expects to lose less than 10 percent of its business to Panasonic.

By allowing Panasonic to sell printers at a lower price than it charges, Epson would be extending a *price umbrella* to Panasonic. When should a firm do that, and when should it match a price cut by a competitor or new entrant? If β represents the percentage price cut, and $PCM = (P - C)/P$ is the percentage contribution margin of the large firm, then a price umbrella is optimal when

$$\alpha < \frac{\beta}{PCM}$$

This inequality implies that a price umbrella strategy is desirable when

- β is large compared to α; that is, the price cut is relatively large, but the price cutter does not steal much market share from the larger firm.

- PCM is small: that is, margins in the industry are relatively small to begin with.

In the South African dot matrix printer market, neither of these conditions held. Margins for Epson's dot matrix printers were initially high. Moreover, the principal buyers of printers (wholesale distributors) were price sensitive, so the effect of Panasonic's price cuts on the demand for Epson printers was probably significant. Consistent with the predictions of theory, Epson refused to extend a price umbrella to Panasonic. However, as it turned out, Epson may have overreacted. It didn't just match Panasonic's price; it undercut it, which in turn prompted Panasonic to cut its price even more. Between 1992 and 1995, prices for dot matrix printers in South Africa spiraled downward, until they reached a point (about Rand 600) at which both companies were barely breaking even.

Smaller firms have an additional incentive to lower price on products for which buyers make repeat purchases. For such products, which include most consumer goods, consumers often purchase the same brand again and again. A small firm might lower price to induce some consumers to try its product. Once prices are

EXAMPLE 8.4 PRICING DISCIPLINE IN THE U.S. CIGARETTE
INDUSTRY[20]

Throughout most of the twentieth century, the cigarette industry displayed remarkable pricing cooperation. Twice a year the dominant firms (which since the 1970s have been Philip Morris or RJR) would announce their intention to raise the list prices of their cigarettes, and within days the other cigarette manufacturers followed suit. Such pricing discipline helped the industry raise prices by 14 percent per year from 1980 through 1985. The result was one of the most profitable businesses in the American economy, with operating profit margins averaging close to 40 percent.

Liggett and Myers did not benefit much from the industry's success in keeping prices high. Having misjudged the potential for filter cigarettes in the 1950s, Liggett saw its share of the cigarette market decline from 21 percent to just over 2 percent by the late 1970s. As a result, Liggett had the least to gain from raising prices in lockstep with its rivals, and it had the most to gain by undercutting prices. When the grocery store cooperative Topco approached Liggett in 1980 with a plan to market and sell discount cigarettes at prices 30 percent below branded cigarettes, Liggett was receptive. By 1984, its share of overall cigarette sales had tripled, largely by virtue of its success in the discount cigarette business.

Liggett gambled that the discount market was a niche that its competitors would ignore. However, Liggett failed to anticipate how discounting would affect the demand for premium brands. For example, Brown and Williamson (B&W), the third largest domestic cigarette producer, estimated that discount cigarettes cost it $50 million in revenues in 1983. In 1984, B&W introduced its own line of discount cigarettes called Filter Lights. B&W offered its line at the same list price as Liggett's cigarettes, but it effectively undercut Liggett's price by giving trade allowances to wholesalers. During the mid-1980s, other manufacturers introduced their own discount brands, and by 1989, Liggett's share of the discount cigarette market had fallen from nearly 90 percent to under 15 percent.

In the early 1990s, Liggett introduced "deep-discount" cigarettes that sold for prices 30 percent below those of the discount brands. Other manufacturers also began selling their own deep-discount brands, and by 1992, RJR and Philip Morris had over 60 percent of this segment of the market. By 1992, the domestic business could be divided into three clearly defined segments: premium, discount, and deep-discount.

The emergence of a segmented market complicated pricing coordination. Competitors had to coordinate an entire structure of prices. With declining consumer demand, much of the growth in the discount and deep-discount segments came at the expense of the premium brands. A profit-maximizing pricing structure had to take this into account.

This consideration explains Philip Morris's decision to cut the price of its flagship brand Marlboro by 20 percent on Friday, April 3, 1993. Low prices in the discount and deep-discount segments had eroded Marlboro's market share from 30 percent of the entire cigarette market in 1988 to 21 percent in 1993. Philip Morris's decision to cut the price of Marlboro was quickly matched by RJR and other competitors, which lowered prices on their premium brands by the same amount.

In the aftermath of "Marlboro Friday," pricing discipline returned to the cigarette business. Both Philip Morris and RJR led the industry to price increases in all segments in 1994, 1995, 1996, and 1997. As the great cigarette price war of 1993 ended, prices in the premium segment had fallen by 25 percent, but prices in the discount and deep-discount segments had risen by 8 percent and 48 percent, respectively. Marlboro's share of the market, which was 21 percent in April 1993, had risen to 30 percent by mid-1995.

restored to their initial levels, the small firm hopes that some of the consumers who sampled its product will become permanent customers. This strategy will succeed only if there is a lag between the small firm's price reduction and any response by its larger rivals. Otherwise, few if any new consumers will sample the small firm's product, and its market share will not increase.

Price Sensitivity of Buyers and the Sustainability of Cooperative Pricing

A final factor affecting the sustainability of cooperative pricing is the price sensitivity of buyers. When buyers are price sensitive, a firm that undercuts its rivals' prices by even a small amount may be able to achieve a significant boost in its volume. Under these circumstances, a firm may be tempted to cut price even if it expects that competitors will eventually match the price cut. This is because, when buyers are price sensitive, even a temporary cut in price below that of a firm's rivals may result in a significant and profitable boost in market share for the firm. (In other words, the revenue destruction effect is small relative to the additional revenue generated from new sales.)

A key factor shaping buyers' price sensitivity is the extent to which competing firms' products are horizontally differentiated. Recall from Chapter 6 that two products are horizontally differentiated if, at equal prices, some consumers prefer one product while others prefer the other. Moreover, if the price of either product were to increase modestly, some customers would continue to purchase it. When products are horizontally differentiated, consumer purchase decisions are driven by more than just the relative prices of competing firms. The strong horizontal differentiation that exists between competing brands of ready-to-eat cereal is one reason why, historically, price competition in this market tends to be rather soft. By contrast, in heavy capital goods industries such as turbine generators in which the buyers are firms rather than households (in the case of turbines, the buyers are electric power companies), buyers tend to give significant weight to price differences among sellers.

In practice, markets typically contain different segments of consumers, some of whom are highly sensitive to differences in price, while others are less price sensitive. This is especially so in consumer goods markets. For example, in a study of the catsup market of the mid-1980s, David Besanko, J-P Dube, and Sachin Gupta found evidence of three different market segments, one of which was especially price sensitive and the other two of which were less so due to loyalties to particular brands.[21] But even within capital goods markets, segmentation can exist. For example, in the turbine generator market, some power companies historically sourced their turbines from only one supplier (e.g., General Electric), and one would expect that these buyers were probably less sensitive to price than buyers that routinely solicited bids from multiple suppliers. In markets that exhibit segmentation according to buyer sensitivity, the likelihood that cooperative pricing is sustainable depends on the relative size of the price-sensitive and less-price-sensitive segments of consumers.

Market Structure and the Sustainability of Cooperative Pricing: Summary

This section has discussed how market structure affects the sustainability of cooperative pricing. Table 8.1 summarizes the impact of the market structure characteristics discussed in this section.

EXAMPLE 8.5 HOW MARKET STRUCTURE CONDITIONS
CONSPIRE TO LIMIT PROFITABILITY IN THE HEAVY-DUTY
TRUCK ENGINE INDUSTRY[22]

As its name suggests, the heavy-duty truck engine (HDTE) industry consists of firms that supply large diesel engines to companies that produce heavy-duty trucks capable of carrying loads in excess of 33,000 pounds. Four firms account for nearly 100 percent of HDTE sales: Caterpillar (with roughly 32 percent of the market in 2002), Detroit Diesel Corporation (26 percent market share), Cummins Engine (23 percent market share), and Volvo/Mack (19 percent market share). One might expect that firms in a highly concentrated industry such as this one would be routinely able to earn positive economic profits. However, this is not the case. Even the most successful HDTE firms struggle to earn returns in excess of their costs of capital. This is not because this industry faces significant threats of entry, nor is it because suppliers exert significant monopoly power in the market for inputs. Rather, the low profitability of this industry can be explained by a set of market structure conditions that make it virtually impossible for firms in the industry to avoid price competition and sustain cooperative prices.

About 70 percent of all truck purchases in the United States are accounted for by approximately 300 large fleet owners of trucks (i.e., companies that are engaged in the business of hauling freight by truck). These large fleet owners are key decision makers in the selling process for engines. The truck manufacturers (or original equipment manufacturers) such as Paccar or Navistar will customize the design of trucks to individual fleet buyers. A fleet buyer would select the truck manufacturer (e.g., Navistar) and then would specify certain key components that are to be engineered into the design of the truck. The most expensive of these components is the diesel engine. Because they operate in the highly competitive, low-margin trucking industry, fleet buyers are extremely price sensitive. As long as engines comply with EPA regulations and meet minimum standards for performance and drivability, fleet owners choose among engine vendors on the basis of price. This creates a strong temptation for engine manufacturers to rely on price as their primary competitive weapon when they compete for fleet owners' business.

The remaining 30 percent of trucking sales are made to independent owner-operators who typically purchase trucks from the inventories of truck dealers. Independent owner-operators are also price sensitive, although on average somewhat less so than fleet operators because some independents develop loyalties to particular manufacturers. Trucks sold to dealers are usually equipped with a standard engine that is engineered by the original equipment manufacturer (OEM) into the design of the truck. Engine manufacturers compete vigorously to become the standard engine for an OEM's product line, and this competition usually takes the form of aggressive pricing.

Price competition is also exacerbated by the lumpiness of truck engine orders. The cost to produce a typical engine ranges between $14,000 and $17,000. Buyers (whether fleet owners or OEMs) typically place orders for hundreds of engines at a time. Moreover, a typical heavy-duty engine will last 8 to 10 years, and each engine sold provides the manufacturer with a stream of profits worth close to $4,000 in present-value terms. As a result of these factors, any individual engine order will constitute a nontrivial fraction of an engine maker's business, and engine makers will thus fight tenaciously for that chunk of business through aggressive pricing. Put another way, the lumpiness of orders in this business works to increase the numerator in equation (8.1)— the benefit from undercutting one's competitors on the current order—relative to the denominator in (8.1)—the forgone profit that results when, as a result of aggressive pricing on the current order, a firm makes it difficult or impossible for the industry to sustain cooperative pricing on future orders.

Further intensifying price competition are the secrecy and complexity of sales terms. While a manufacturer's price book is public and firms inevitably learn the list prices of their competitors, engine-makers negotiate the actual terms of sales with each buyer individually and secretively. For fleet purchases, engine specifications are customized to individual buyers. In addition, engines are sold in multiunit bundles, and so the price of the engine depends on how many units the buyer orders. Finally, a deal for a bundle of engines will typically also include other products or features, such as a warranty and service plan. Overall, given the secrecy and customization of sales terms, it is very difficult for a firm's competitors to know whether it has discounted below its list price. This creates a strong temptation to deviate from the list price, and because of that, the standing assumption in the industry is that competitors will, in fact, routinely discount below their list prices. All of this fosters a climate of paranoia that works to make this assumption a self-fulfilling prophecy.

All in all, these market structure conditions make it extremely difficult for cooperation-inducing strategies such as tit-for-tat to work effectively, and they induce truck engine manufacturers to engage in brutal profit-destroying price cutting to win business. As a result, engine manufacturers compete away a significant amount of the value they create.

TABLE 8.1

MARKET STRUCTURE CONDITIONS AFFECTING THE SUSTAINABILITY OF COOPERATIVE PRICING

Market Structure Condition	How Does It Affect Cooperative Pricing?	Reasons
High market concentration	Facilitates	• Coordinating on the cooperative equilibrium is easier with few firms • Increases the benefit–cost ratio from adhering to cooperative pricing
Firm asymmetries	Harms	• Disagreement over cooperative price • Coordinating on cooperative price is more difficult • Possible incentive of large firms to extend price umbrella to small firms increases small firms' incentives to cut price • Small firms may prefer to deviate from monopoly prices even if larger firms match
High buyer concentration	Harms	• Reduces probability that a defector will be discovered
Lumpy orders	Harms	• Decreases the frequency of interaction between competitors, increasing the lag between defection and retaliation
Secret price terms	Harms	• Increases detection lags because prices of competitors are more difficult to monitor • Increases the probability of misreads
Volatility of demand and cost conditions	Harms	• Increases the lag between defection and retaliation (perhaps even precluding retaliation) by increasing uncertainty about whether defections have occurred and about identity of defectors
Price-sensitive buyers	Harms	• Increases the temptation to cut price, even if competitors are expected to match

FACILITATING PRACTICES ◆ ◆ ◆ ◆ ◆

As the discussion in the previous section suggests, market structure can affect firms' ability to sustain cooperative pricing. Firms themselves can also facilitate cooperative pricing by

- Price leadership
- Advance announcement of price changes
- Most favored customer clauses
- Uniform delivered prices

These practices either facilitate coordination among firms or diminish their incentives to cut price.

Price Leadership

Under price leadership, one firm in an industry (the price leader) announces its price changes before all other firms, which then match the leader's price. Examples of well-known price leaders include Kellogg in breakfast cereals, Philip Morris in tobacco, and (until the mid-1960s) U.S. Steel in steel.

Price leadership is a way to overcome the problem of coordinating on a focal equilibrium. In price leadership, each firm gives up its pricing autonomy and cedes control over industry pricing to a single firm. Firms thus need not worry that rivals will secretly shade price to steal market share. Of course, as the Sydney newspaper market illustrates, systems of price leadership can break down if the price leader does not retaliate against defectors.

The kind of oligopolistic price leadership we discuss here should be distinguished from the barometric price leadership that sometimes occurs in competitive markets, such as that for prime rate loans. Under barometric price leadership, the price leader merely acts as a barometer of changes in market conditions by adjusting prices to shifts in demand or input prices. Under barometric leadership, different firms are often price leaders, while under oligopolistic leadership the same firm is the leader for years. Recent federal and state antitrust inquiries into the pricing policies of infant-formula makers centered on whether the price-matching strategies of Abbott Labs and Bristol Myers represented oligopolistic or barometric price leadership. The two firms alternated as price leaders during the 1980s, but the follower always matched the leader, as did a third firm, Wyeth. The firms settled these inquiries out of court without admitting wrongdoing.

Advance Announcement of Price Changes

In some markets, firms will publicly announce the prices they intend to charge in the future. For example, in chemicals markets firms often announce their intention to raise prices 30 or 60 days before the price change is to take effect. These preannouncements can benefit consumers, such as when cement makers announce prices weeks ahead of the spring construction season, enabling contractors to more intelligently bid on projects. But advance announcements can also facilitate price increases, much to the harm of consumers. Advance announcements of price changes reduce the uncertainty that firms' rivals will undercut them. The practice also allows firms to harmlessly rescind or roll back proposed price increases that competitors refuse to follow. In the early 1990s, the U.S. Department of Justice challenged the airline industry's common practice of announcing fare increases for travel commencing weeks later. The DOJ argued that these preannouncements could not possibly benefit consumers and therefore served only the purpose of facilitating price increases. The airlines consented to abandon the practice, though in recent years, the DOJ has charged that some airlines have violated the agreement.

Most Favored Customer Clauses

A most favored customer clause is a provision in a sales contract that promises a buyer that it will pay the lowest price the seller charges. There are two basic types of most favored customer clauses: contemporaneous and retroactive.

To illustrate these two types, consider a simple example. Xerxes Chemical manufactures a chemical additive used to enhance the performance of jet fuel. Great Lakes Refining Company, a manufacturer of jet fuel, signs a contract with Xerxes calling for delivery of 100,000 tons of the chemical over the next three months at the "open order" price of $.50 per ton.[23] Under a contemporaneous most favored customer policy, Xerxes agrees that while this contract is in effect, if it sells the chemical at a lower price to any other buyer (perhaps to undercut a competitor), it will also lower the price to this level for Great Lakes. Under a retroactive most favored customer clause, Xerxes agrees to pay a rebate to Great Lakes if during a certain period after the contract has expired (e.g., two years) it sells the chemical additive for a lower price than Great Lakes paid. For example, suppose Great Lakes' contract expired on December 31, 2005, but its contract contained a two-year retroactive most favored customer clause. If sometime in 2006 Xerxes announces a general reduction in price from $.50 per ton to $.40 per ton, it would have to pay Great Lakes a rebate equal to ($.50 − $.40) · 100,000 or $10,000, the difference between what Great Lakes actually paid and what it would have paid under the new lower price.

Most favored customer clauses appear to benefit buyers. For Great Lakes, the "price protection" offered by the most favored customer clause may help keep its production costs in line with those of competitors. However, most favored customer clauses can inhibit price competition. Retroactive most favored customer clauses make it expensive for Xerxes to cut prices in the future, either selectively or across the board. Contemporaneous most favored customer clauses do not penalize the firm for making across-the-board price reductions (e.g., if Xerxes cuts prices to all its customers, it does not have to pay rebates to past customers), but they discourage firms from using selective price cutting to compete for customers with highly price-elastic demands.

Why would firms ever adopt most favored customer policies if their customers do not demand them? After all, the ideal situation from a given manufacturer's perspective arises when its competitors tie their hands in the competition for customers by adopting most favored customer policies, leaving the manufacturer free to selectively or generally cut price. However, Thomas Cooper has shown that because adopting a retroactive most favored customer clause softens price competition in the future, oligopolists may have an incentive to adopt the policy unilaterally, even if rival manufacturers do not.[24]

Uniform Delivered Prices

In many industries, such as cement, steel, or soybean products, buyers and sellers are geographically separated, and transportation costs are significant. In such contexts, the pricing method can affect competitive interactions. Broadly speaking, two different kinds of pricing policies can be identified. Under uniform FOB pricing, the seller quotes a price for pickup at the seller's loading dock, and the buyer absorbs the freight charges for shipping from the seller's plant to the buyer's plant.[25] Under uniform delivered pricing, the firm quotes a single delivered price for all buyers and absorbs any freight charges itself.[26]

Uniform delivered pricing facilitates cooperative pricing by allowing firms to make a more "surgical" response to price cutting by rivals. Consider, for example, two brick producers, one located in Mumbai and the other in Ahmadabad, India. These firms have been trying to maintain prices at the monopoly level, but the Mumbai producer cuts its price to increase its share of the market in Surat, a city between Mumbai and Ahmadabad. Under FOB pricing, the Ahmadabad producer must retaliate by cutting its mill price, which effectively reduces its price to all its customers (see Figure 8.4). On the other hand, if the firms were using uniform delivered pricing, the Ahmadabad firm could cut its price selectively; it could cut the delivered price to its customers in Surat, keeping delivered prices of other customers at their original level (see Figure 8.5). Like targeted couponing, uniform delivered pricing reduces the "cost" that the "victim" incurs by retaliating. This makes retaliation more likely and enhances the credibility of policies, such as tit-for-tat, that can sustain cooperative pricing.

Facilitating Practices and Antitrust

Antitrust enforcers generally frown on facilitating practices and try to stop egregious practices that do not appear to offer any consumer benefit. Managers who are seeking pricing stability should heed the following advice:[27]

1. All pricing decisions should be made unilaterally. Avoid all direct contacts with competitors about price.

FIGURE 8.4
FOB PRICING

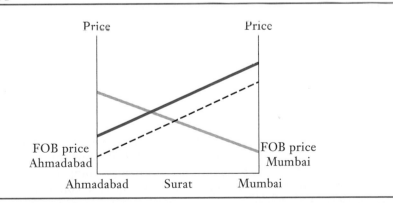

When both firms use FOB pricing, the delivered price that a customer actually pays depends on its location. The delivered price schedules are shown by the solid lines in the figure. If the brick producer in Ahmadabad lowers its FOB price to match that of the Bombay producer, then it effectively shifts its delivered price schedule downward. (It now becomes the dashed line.) Even though the Ahmadabad firm is retaliating against the Bombay firm's stealing business in Surat, the Ahmadabad firm ends up reducing its delivered prices to all of its customers.

FIGURE 8.5
DELIVERED PRICING

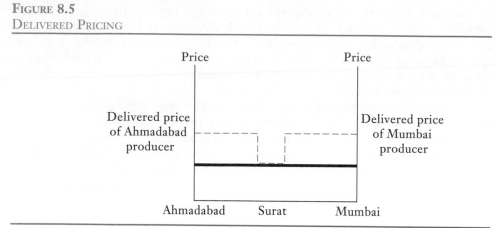

When both firms use delivered pricing, a firm's customer pays the same delivered price, no matter what its location. If the Mumbai firm cuts its delivered price to steal business in Surat, the Ahmadabad producer need only cut its delivered price in Surat to retaliate.

2. It is okay to match a competitor's price reduction, but do not overretaliate. Setting a very low price may be perceived as an attempt to instill pricing discipline.
3. Carefully handle public pricing communications.
4. Have a legitimate justification for price increases, most favored customer clauses, and pricing audits.
5. By the same token, have a legitimate justification for price cuts. "Meeting the competition" is a legitimate justification. Pricing below-average variable costs is often deemed to be anticompetitive.
6. Do not preannounce price increases without a legitimate business justification.
7. Limit the audience. Generally it is better to tell customers directly whenever feasible.
8. Monitor the content. Announce price changes; do not lecture competitors about the need to raise prices, or the consequences of reducing them.
9. Keep analyses of probable competitive reactions private. It is okay to perform such analyses, but it is not okay to share them.
10. Clear your pricing tactics with an attorney well-versed in antitrust law.

◆ ◆ ◆ ◆ ◆ QUALITY COMPETITION

Although we have focused on price competition, price is obviously not the only factor that drives consumer decisions and firm strategies. Product attributes such as performance and durability also matter, and firms may compete just as fiercely on these dimensions as they do on price. Even so, quality competition may be less destructive of profits than price competition. As quality increases, firms can increase price to cover the costs. Their ability to do so is limited only by the willingness of consumers to abandon the product category altogether. Firms engaged in a price war could also maintain their profit margins, but only if they could reduce costs to keep pace with price reductions. This is impractical for many goods and services for which the demand of production requires a certain minimum expenditure.

The industry price elasticity of demand provides a good measure of whether consumers would be driven away by industrywide price increases. The industry elasticity is usually much smaller in magnitude than the elasticity of demand facing a single firm (see the Primer for details), especially when the good is highly valued and has few substitutes. Thus, the pharmaceutical industry could successfully raise prices to cover the cost of research and development without driving away customers, because the industry price elasticity of demand is low. But efforts by the breakfast cereal industry to boost prices to cover the costs of marketing failed in the 1990s when consumers turned to other breakfast foods as well as unbranded cereals.

In the remainder of this chapter, we focus on how market structure and competition influence the firm's choice of quality. To simplify the discussion, we will lump all nonprice attributes into a single dimension called quality—any attribute that increases the demand for the product at a fixed price.

Quality Choice in Competitive Markets

In a competitive market, either all goods are identical, or they exhibit pure vertical differentiation. Recall from Chapter 6 that when products are vertically differentiated, for any set of prices, all consumers will agree about which products they most prefer. Firms may offer different levels of quality at different prices, but the market will force all firms to charge the same price per unit of quality. This conclusion depends on a critical unstated assumption. In particular, consumers must be able to perfectly evaluate the quality of each seller. If consumers cannot perfectly judge quality, then sellers who charge more than the going price per unit of quality may still have customers. This might encourage them to raise their price above the competitive level.

To explore how consumer information affects quality, consider a market in which some consumers have information about product quality and others do not. Suppose that it is costly to be an informed consumer—one must invest time and effort to identify good-quality sellers. In this market, uninformed consumers may be able to infer the quality of sellers merely by observing the behavior of informed consumers. For example, a prospective car buyer may be considering the purchase of a recently introduced model. If she learns sales of that model are low (e.g., she never sees anyone driving that model), she might well question the quality of the automobile even if she has no direct information about it. If no one else likes it, the car must not be very good. The car buyer can thus make an informed judgment about the quality of the car without knowing anything about cars except how many people appear to drive different models.

If there are enough well-informed buyers in a market, most buyers will be satisfied with the quality of what they buy, even if they are themselves uninformed about quality at the time they make their purchase (other than being informed about what other buyers are purchasing). But if uninformed consumers cannot gauge quality by observing informed consumers, then a lemons market can emerge. The term *lemons market* is derived from the used car market, in which owners are more anxious to sell low-quality cars ("lemons") than high-quality cars.[28] A lemons market requires two ingredients: uninformed consumers and the fact that low-quality products are cheaper to make than high-quality products.

If consumers cannot determine the quality of what they are buying, then some sellers might skimp on quality and sell only low-quality products but still charge the going price. Of course, consumers may realize that their ignorance of quality makes them susceptible to buying lemons. They may even insist on paying less for

EXAMPLE 8.6 QUALITY COMPETITION AMONG U.S. HEALTH PLANS

Until the 1980s, most U.S. health insurance companies sold "indemnity" insurance. To the naked eye, all indemnity insurance looked the same. Insurers paid all provider claims, no questions asked. They covered a similar range of services that always included hospitalizations and physician care. Most competitors—including the large Blue Cross and Blue Shield plans as well as plans offered by diversified such as Aetna, Connecticut General, and Prudential—had unblemished reputations.

Not surprisingly, competition among indemnity insurers was largely driven by price. The main point of differentiation was customer service—mainly processing claims on time. There were a few other points of differentiation. A potentially important switching cost was based on claims experience. A firm's current insurer had information about employee health care costs that enabled it to more accurately underwrite future policies. This gave the incumbent insurer only a modest advantage, however.

Modern health insurers scarcely resemble their indemnity ancestors. Today's insurers assemble networks of providers based on costs and quality. They actively review the appropriateness of care. Some insurers have instituted aggressive pay for performance programs that give bonuses to physicians who meet a variety of quality of care standards.

Just as the health insurance product has become considerably more complex, so too have the methods used by employers to evaluate insurers. In 1990, a consortium of large employers helped form the National Consortium for Quality Assurance (NCQA). NCQA offers two important tools for evaluating health plan quality. The first is the Health Plan Data and Information Set (HEDIS). HEDIS measures health plan performance on several dimensions, including preventive care, access to services, and member satisfaction. The second tool is a formal accreditation process. While most employees remain unaware of either HEDIS or NCQA accreditation, research shows that when employers aggressively publicize HEDIS scores, employees do pay attention. Accreditation has been more successful—many employers will not offer a nonaccredited plan.

Despite these changes, many insurers remain concerned about their ability to differentiate themselves on the basis of quality. Most insurers use virtually identical provider networks. Most of the work done to evaluate the appropriateness of care is outsourced to one of two companies that perform "utilization review," again eliminating a possible point of differentiation. The plans also use similar educational programs, which are of questionable value anyway. Many plans believe they can eventually differentiate themselves in their ability to identify and reward high-quality care, but this will require clinical information systems that remain years away.

Plans are also having a difficult time differentiating themselves on NCQA measures. Many HEDIS scores depend on the quality of the provider network—similar networks make for similar scores. Many other NCQA objectives are met through accurate recordkeeping and other straightforward activities. Some of the HEDIS scores that do vary, such as use of preventive services, depend as much or more on the actions of enrollees than they do on the actions of the plans. This limits the usefulness of these scores as accurate indicators of plan quality.

In a recent meeting of health plan executives hosted by David Dranove, many participants suggested that despite all the changes that have occurred, customer service remains the key point of differentiation. Although consumer concerns have raised the quality bar, they are all able to clear it. The result is that price competition will remain the norm for many years to come.

a product, anticipating that its quality is likely to be low. This poses a problem for sellers of high-quality products who cannot get their money's worth from suspicious consumers. High-quality sellers may refuse to sell their product, figuring that they cannot get a price to cover their opportunity cost. If they want to get a price commensurate with quality, they may have to rely on money-back guarantees, reviews in independent consumer magazines, and a reputation for quality to convince buyers that their products are not lemons.

Sanford Grossman and Joseph Stiglitz point out one further problem that may arise in markets where some individuals are well-informed and others are not.[29] They consider a market in which consumers of information compete against each other, for example, the market for corporate control discussed in Chapter 5. Some consumers might spend resources gathering information, but if uninformed consumers can infer what that information is, all consumers may end up on an even footing. As a result, those who gathered the information may be worse off than those who did not, having borne the expense without realizing extra benefits. This implies that there will be underinvestment in information gathering. In the market for corporate control, for example, an investor may devote considerable effort to identifying an underperforming firm. As soon as that investor tenders an offer for control of the firm, however, other investors will learn the identity of the undervalued firm because tender offers are public information. In the ensuing competition between investors to gain control of the underperforming target, profits may be bid away. This helps explain why takeover artists, such as T. Boone Pickens and the late Sir James Goldsmith, are extremely secretive in their dealings and why there is a need for speed in effecting takeovers.

Quality Choices of Sellers with Market Power

Sellers with market power view quality as critical to the demand for their product. Figure 8.6 depicts the demand facing a seller at two levels of quality. We have defined quality to include anything that increases demand, and this is reflected in the figure. When quality is high, demand is higher than when it is low. The vertical difference between the high- and low-quality demand curves represents the additional amount

FIGURE 8.6
DEMAND CURVES ASSOCIATED WITH DIFFERENT QUALITY LEVELS

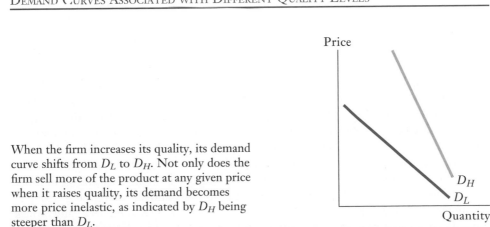

When the firm increases its quality, its demand curve shifts from D_L to D_H. Not only does the firm sell more of the product at any given price when it raises quality, its demand becomes more price inelastic, as indicated by D_H being steeper than D_L.

that consumers are willing to pay for quality. As shown in the figure, the demand curve gets steeper as quality increases. This would occur if consumers who are willing to pay the most for a product will also pay the most to improve quality.

Suppose that a seller with market power had to select a single level of quality for all its products. This could be an appliance maker selecting a level of reliability that will be consistent across its product line, or a car maker selecting a level of safety that will be consistent across its fleet. What level of quality should the seller choose? As with other economic tradeoffs, it should choose quality so that the marginal cost of the quality increase equals the marginal revenue that results when consumers demand more of the product.[30]

The Marginal Cost of Increasing Quality

The idea that it is costly to improve quality contrasts with the literature on continuous quality improvement (CQI).[31] According to the principles of CQI, improvements in the production process can simultaneously reduce costs and increase quality. But once firms address inefficiencies in production, they must eventually confront tradeoffs between lowering costs and boosting quality. For example, improving the fit of air-frame components can simultaneously boost safety and reduce costs (by eliminating rejected parts.) Beyond this, further improvements in safety can be achieved by installing costly backup features, such as additional engines and brakes.

A popular concept in CQI is that of 6-sigma—trying to achieve quality levels that are six standard deviations above the mean. We will not comment on the motivational aspects of striving for perfection, but we should mention a pragmatic problem that arises in some systems. Consider a university that is trying to minimize the chance of losing data in a mainframe computer crash. The university can minimize its losses by running a program to back up the system. Each run of the program is costly, in terms of both staffing and computer downtime. If the university wants to limit losses to a maximum of one week's work, it must run the backup program 52 times annually. Limiting the loss to three days' work requires running the backup program 122 times per year. Limiting the loss to one day's work requires 365 runs. It requires incrementally more and more computer runs to provide incrementally less and less additional protection. Achieving perfection would be infinitely costly.

The Marginal Benefit of Improving Quality

When a firm improves the quality of its product, more consumers will want to buy it. How much revenue this brings in depends on two factors:

1. The increase in demand caused by the increase in quality.
2. The incremental profit earned on each additional unit sold.

Michael Spence has pointed out that when contemplating an increase in quality, the firm should ignore its "inframarginal" customers—those loyal to it. These customers will continue to buy the product whether or not the firm makes marginal improvements to quality.[32] Instead, the firm should focus on its "marginal consumers," those who are indifferent to the idea of buying from that firm and buying elsewhere. These are the customers who will be swayed by a change in quality.

Firms raise quality to attract these marginal customers. But how can a firm determine how many more customers it will get? An increase in quality will bring in more new customers if (a) there are more marginal customers and (b) marginal customers can determine that quality has, in fact, increased. David Dranove and Mark Satterthwaite show that these factors are determined, in turn, by (1) the degree of horizontal differentiation in the market and (2) the precision with which consumers observe quality.[33]

Recall from Chapter 6 that in a horizontally differentiated market, consumers will strongly prefer sellers who offer a good idiosyncratic match between the product's differentiated attributes and the consumer's tastes and preferences. For example, consumers traveling along a superhighway will have strong preferences for restaurants located near interchanges. At the same time, these restaurants have little incentive to boost quality, since it is unlikely to significantly affect demand. In recent years, most states have replaced independent highway restaurants with national chains, such as Wendy's, which are concerned about brand image and thus generally maintain higher quality than the independents did.

Sellers that offer high-quality products will benefit only if consumers know it. High-quality firms are, of course, eager to advertise their quality. There are many examples of this, such as when a film advertisement cites "two thumbs up" or when a car maker boasts of being ranked number one in a J. D. Powers survey. Another way to do this is to allow consumers to sample the product, such as when food makers distribute free samples in supermarkets. Massive advertising may also help to convince consumers to sample a new product, as consumers may reason that only a high-quality seller could afford to advertise so lavishly.

Conveying quality information is especially critical for goods and services whose quality is difficult to evaluate before purchase, such as stereo equipment, restaurant food, and medical services. Sellers use various techniques to enable consumers to evaluate such products. For example, manufacturers of high-end stereo equipment, such as Avalon Acoustics, Ayre Electronics, and Theta Digital, rely on specialized dealers to demonstrate the quality of their products. Dealers often build customized audition rooms, attend seminars on sound technology, and learn which recordings best enhance the features of each stereo component. They even provide in-home consultation and setup. These costly investments often convince consumers to spend thousands of dollars on stereo components that would likely go unsold if offered at a Best Buy or Wal-Mart.

Sometimes, consumers can judge with precision the quality of only some attributes of a product. Naturally, they tend to focus on those attributes that they can easily observe and evaluate. This helps explain why retailers are so concerned about the external appearance of their shops, and why doctors and lawyers who graduated from prestigious schools prominently display their diplomas (but do not display data on their patient survival rates or success rates at trial). Of course, this emphasis on observable attributes may mean that consumers may be shortchanged on the hard-to-measure attributes that really matter.

Suppose that two sellers face equally responsive consumers—a given investment in improving quality will lead to the same increase in sales. Which seller has a stronger incentive to boost quality? All else being equal, the seller with the higher price–cost margin will make more money from the increase in sales and thus has a stronger incentive to boost quality. (A similar result applies to investments in advertising; all else being equal, advertise more for the higher margin products.)

Sometimes, market structure creates conflicting incentives to boost quality. A monopolist may have a higher price–cost margin than a competitive firm, but may face few marginal consumers. In contrast, every consumer in a competitive market is a marginal consumer, but a firm contemplating a quality improvement may have razor thin margins. Horizontal differentiation has similar offsetting implications for incentives to boost quality. On the one hand, horizontal differentiation creates loyal customers, which allows sellers to boost price–cost margins, raising the gains from attracting more customers by boosting quality. On the other hand, loyal customers are less likely to switch sellers when quality differences are low, implying that each seller faces fewer marginal customers.

CHAPTER SUMMARY

◆ If firms are sufficiently patient (i.e., they do not discount the future too much), cooperative pricing (i.e., the monopoly price) may be sustainable as an equilibrium outcome, even though firms are making decisions noncooperatively. This is a specific application of the folk theorem from game theory, which says that any outcome between marginal cost and the monopoly price is sustainable as a subgame perfect Nash equilibrium in the infinitely repeated prisoners' dilemma game.

◆ Market structure affects the sustainability of cooperative pricing. High market concentration facilitates cooperative pricing. Asymmetries among firms, lumpy orders, high buyer concentration, secret sales transactions, volatile demand, and price-sensitive buyers make pricing cooperation more difficult.

◆ Practices that can facilitate cooperative pricing include price leadership, advance announcements of price changes, most favored customer clauses, and uniform delivered pricing.

◆ In competitive markets, firms will provide acceptable quality as long as there are enough informed consumers. If consumers are generally uninformed, lemons markets can develop in which owners or producers of high-quality goods may refuse to sell altogether.

◆ The quality provided by sellers with market power depends on the marginal cost and the marginal benefit of increasing quality. The marginal benefit of increasing quality depends on the increase in demand brought on by the increase in quality and the incremental profit earned on each additional unit sold. This implies that a firm's price–cost margin is an important determinant of its incentives to raise quality.

QUESTIONS

1. Explain why Cournot and Bertrand models are not dynamic.
2. An article on price wars by two McKinsey consultants makes the following argument.[34]

   That the [tit-for-tat] strategy is fraught with risk cannot be overemphasized. Your competitor may take an inordinately long time to realize that its actions can do it nothing but harm; rivalry across the entire industry may escalate precipitously; and as the "tit-for-tat" game plays itself out, all of a price war's detrimental effects on customers will make themselves felt.

   How would you reconcile the views expressed in this quote with the advantages of tit-for-tat claimed in this chapter?
3. How does the revenue destruction effect (see Chapter 6) affect the ability of firms to coordinate on a pricing equilibrium?
4. Why do misreads encourage firms to lower prices?
5. Firms operating at or near capacity are unlikely to instigate price wars. Briefly explain.
6. "Pricing cooperation is more likely to emerge in markets where one firm raises a price and competitors follow suit and market shares remain unchanged. It is less likely to work well in markets where price matching may not leave market shares constant." Evaluate this statement. Can you think of circumstances under which price-matching behavior could alter market shares?

7. Suppose that you were an industry analyst trying to determine whether the leading firms in the automobile manufacturing industry are playing a tit-for-tat pricing game. What real-world data would you want to examine? What would you consider to be evidence of tit-for-tat pricing?

8. Studies of pricing in the airline industry show that carriers that dominate hub airports (Delta in Atlanta, USAir in Pittsburgh, American in Dallas) tend to charge higher fares on average for flights into and out of the hub airport than other, nondominant carriers flying in and out of the hub. What might explain this pattern of prices?

9. It is often argued that price wars may be more likely to occur during low-demand periods than high-demand periods. (This chapter makes that argument.) Are there factors that might reverse this implication? That is, can you think of reasons why the attractiveness of deviating from cooperative pricing might actually be greater during booms (high demand) than during busts (low demand)?

10. Consider a duopoly consisting of two firms, Amalgamated Electric (AE) and Carnegie-Manheim (C-M), which sell products that are somewhat differentiated. Each firm sells to customers with different price elasticities of demand and, as a result, occasionally discounts below list price for the most price elastic customers. Suppose, now, that AE adopts a contemporaneous most favored customer policy, but C-M does not. What will happen to AE's average equilibrium price? What will happen to C-M's average equilibrium price?

11. Firms often complain that their competitors are setting prices that are too low. Can you give any recommendations to the firm regarding how they should handle such public complaints?

12. How might an increase in the number of competitors in a market affect overall product quality? Under what circumstances might a high-quality firm prosper by entering a competitive market?

ENDNOTES

[1] This example is based on Merrilees, W., "Anatomy of a Price Leadership Challenge: An Evaluation of Pricing Strategies in the Australian Newspaper Industry," *Journal of Industrial Economics*, 31, March 1983, pp 291–311.

[2] If the firms competed as Cournot competitors, prices and profits would be $46.67 and $711.11 million, respectively.

[3] Chamberlin, E. H., *Monopolistic Competition*, Cambridge, MA: Harvard University Press, 1933, p. 48.

[4] The weekly discount rate is the annual discount rate divided by 52. Thus, $.10/52 = .002$.

[5] This calculation easily follows by using the formula for the present value of an annuity, which is discussed in the appendix to the Economics Primer. Specifically, for any amount C and discount rate i, $C/(1 + i) + C/(1 + i)^2 + \ldots = C/i$. Thus, the preceding calculation simplifies to $0.2308 + 0.1154/0.002 = 57.93$.

[6] To derive equation (8.1), we first derived the present value of a firm's profit if, like its competitors, it raised its price to the monopoly level. In this case, the firm gets a per-period profit of $(1/N)\pi_M$ in all periods, and the present value of that profit stream is $(1/N)(\pi_M + \pi_M/i)$. We then derived the present value of the firm's profit if it kept its price at the current level. Under this scenario, the firm enjoys a one-period increase in its profit to π_0, but in all periods thereafter, its profit equals $(1/N)\pi_0$, as the firm's competitors follow their tit-for-tat strategies and match the firm's first-period price P_0. The present value of the profit stream in this latter scenario is thus $\pi_0 + (1/N)\pi_0/i$. We subtracted the two present value expressions, used algebra, and rearranged terms to get the resulting equation.

[7]Former Kellogg student Andrew Cherry developed this example.

[8]See Example 8.5 for a description of events leading up to Marlboro Friday.

[9]The term *folk theorem* is used because, like a folk song, it existed in the oral tradition of economics long before anyone got credit for proving it formally.

[10]Perhaps the best work on this subject remains Thomas Schelling's *The Strategy of Conflict*, Cambridge, MA, Harvard University Press, 1960.

[11]Kreps, D. M., *A Course in Microeconomic Theory*, Princeton, NJ, Princeton University Press, 1990, pp. 392–393.

[12]Axelrod, R., *The Evolution of Cooperation*, New York, Basic Books, 1984.

[13]Dixit, A. and B. Nalebuff, *Thinking Strategically: The Competitive Edge in Business, Politics, and Everyday Life*, New York, Norton, 1991.

[14]Garda, R. A. and M. V. Marn, "Price Wars," *McKinsey Quarterly*, 3, 1993, pp. 87–100.

[15]A marketing allowance is a discount offered by a manufacturer in return for the retailer's agreement to feature the manufacturer's product in some way.

[16]Kellogg students Sanjay Malkani, David Pereira, Robert Kennedy, Katarzyna Pitula, and Mitsunari Okamoto developed this example.

[17]The thresholds are expressed in terms of changes in the Herfindahl index. See Chapter 6 for a discussion of this measure of market concentration.

[18]For example, if $N = 5$, $\pi_M = 100,000$ per year and $\pi_0 = 40,000$ per year, the benefit–cost ratio with a period length of one year is $(1/5)(100,000 - 40,000)/(40,000 - (1/5)(100,000)) = 0.60$. If the period length is one quarter, then quarterly monopoly and current profit are 25,000 and 10,000, respectively. The benefit–cost ratio is then $(1/5)(25,000 - 10,000)/(10,000 - (1/5)(25,000))$, which also equals 0.60.

[19]We would like to thank Fuminori Takemura, Edward Arnstein, Tod Salzman, Rory Altman, and Masahiro Murakami for suggesting this example to us.

[20]This example is adapted from a paper by Kellogg students Diane Kitiyama, Jon Passman, Todd Reichmann, Craig Safir, and Philip Yau. It also draws from "Tobacco Suit Exposes Ways Cigarette Firms Keep the Profits Fat," *Wall Street Journal*, March 5, 1990, pp. A1–A8.

[21]Besanko, D., J. P. Dube, and S. Gupta, "Retail-Level Strategies for Price Discrimination," working paper, June 2002.

[22]This example is adapted from a paper by Kellogg students Megan Ainsworth, David Baker, Christopher Brown, Chip Craw, Shoba Narayanan, and Catherine Vaughn.

[23]An open order price is the price the manufacturer charges any buyer who orders the additive.

[24]Cooper, T. E., "Most Favored Customer Clauses and Tacit Collusion," *RAND Journal of Economics*, 17, Autumn 1986, pp. 377–388. David Besanko and Thomas Lyon prove a similar result for contemporaneous most favored customer clauses, but show that voluntary adoption is most likely in concentrated industries where a given firm internalizes much of the "competition-softening" effect of most favored customer policies. Both the Cooper model and the Besanko-Lyon model are examples of two-stage commitment models, discussed in Chapter 7.

[25]FOB stands for "free on board," so the FOB price is the seller quotes for loading the product on the delivery vehicle. If the seller pays the transport charges, they are added to the buyer's bill, and the net price the seller receives is known as the uniform net mill price.

[26]A third type of pricing is basing point pricing in which the seller designates one or more base locations and quotes FOB prices from them. The customer chooses a basing point and absorbs the freight costs between the basing point and its plant.

[27]Some of these suggestions are from Kessler, J. and R. Wheeler. "An Old Theory Gets New Life: How to Price Without Being a 'Price signaler,'" 1993, *Antitrust* (Summer), pp. 26–29.

[28]For a formal treatment of the lemons problem and an interesting discussion of its applications, see Akerlof, G., "The Market for Lemons: Qualitative Uncertainty and the Market Mechanism," *Quarterly Journal of Economics*, 84, 1970, pp. 488–500.

[29]Grossman, S. and J. Stiglitz, "On the Impossibility of Informationally Efficient Markets," *American Economic Review*, 70, June 1980, pp. 393–408.

[30]To highlight the key tradeoffs, we ignore what in Chapter 7 we called strategic effects. Thus, we focus on the quality choice of a single firm in isolation and ignore the side effects of its quality choice on the intensity of price competition.

[31]See, for example, Crosby, P. B., *Quality Is Free: The Art of Making Quality Certain*, New York, McGraw-Hill, 1979.

[32]Spence, A. M., "Monopoly, Quality, and Regulation," *Bell Journal of Economics*, 1975, pp. 417–429.

[33]Dranove, D. and M. Satterthwaite, "Monopolistic Competition When Price and Quality Are Not Perfectly Observable," *RAND Journal of Economics*, Winter 1992, pp. 518–534.

[34]Garda, R. A. and M. V. Marn, "Price Wars," *McKinsey Quarterly*, 3, 1993, pp. 87–100. Quote from pp. 98–99.

9

ENTRY AND EXIT

*I*n early 1997, a consortium of electronics firms led by Toshiba, Sony, Matsushita, and Philips introduced a new digital video format called DVD. This format offered video resolution and sound quality that was superior to conventional videocassettes. In the first months, several major studios, including Warner, MGM, and Columbia, released a few movies in DVD format. The DVD hardware consortium expected "early adopters"—individuals willing to pay a premium price for new technology—to purchase DVD players at high prices, despite the shortage of movies to play on them. This would encourage the release of more movies and generate additional hardware sales. The consortium hoped to have a large installed base of DVD players in consumers' homes by Christmas 1997. Studios would then rush to release their movies on DVD, and consumers would replace their videotape players with DVD players, just as they had replaced their record players with CD players a decade earlier.

Sales of DVD players exceeded expectations through the summer of 1997, but the Christmas season was a disappointment. Partly to blame was a surprise announcement in the fall of 1997 by electronics retailer Circuit City. Circuit City announced the impending release of a digital video format called DIVX that was partially incompatible with DVD. Consumers, wary of previous format wars such as the one between VHS and Beta videotape, stayed on the sidelines that Christmas season, as did several major studios, including Paramount and Fox.

Circuit City eventually released DIVX hardware and software in two test markets in early summer 1998. It offered only a few brands of DIVX players and sold only a handful of exclusive DIVX movie titles. Circuit City was unable to persuade most other electronics retailers to sell DIVX hardware and software, and video rental outlets refused to carry DIVX software. Early adopters witnessed these delays and setbacks to DIVX and decided that DVD was the real deal. Hardware sales increased steadily through 1998, all the major studios climbed on board, on-line DVD retailers aggressively discounted software, and video rental stores heavily promoted DVD rentals. It was a good Christmas for DVD—sales of DVD hardware in the Christmas season of 1998 topped sales in all of 1997. It was a bad Christmas for DIVX—Circuit City promoted DVD alongside its promotions of DIVX and repositioned DIVX as a DVD product feature rather than an alternative format. Circuit City's entry strategy had failed.

This chapter is about *entry* and *exit*. Entry is the beginning of production and sales by a new firm in a market, and exit occurs when a firm ceases to produce in a market. The experience of the DVD consortium demonstrates that *incumbent* firms—firms that are already operating—should take entry into account when making their strategic decisions. *Entrants*—firms that are new to a market—threaten incumbents in two ways. First, *they take market share away from incumbent firms*, in effect reducing an incumbent's share of the "profit pie." Second, entry often *intensifies competition*. This is a natural consequence of oligopoly theory (more firms mean lower prices) and of entrants often reducing prices to establish a foothold in the market. In this way, entry reduces the size of the profit pie. When entry creates a format war, it can further reduce the size of the pie. (We say a lot more about format wars in Chapter 12.) Exit has the opposite effect on competitors: surviving firms increase their share and competition diminishes.

Entry by specialty hospitals illustrates both of these effects. Beginning in the late 1990s, hospitals specializing in narrow clinical areas such as cardiovascular disease or cancer began opening in many metropolitan areas. Specialist physicians are often partners in these hospitals and have begun referring their patients away from traditional community hospitals. The physician-owners often "cherry pick" their referrals to the specialty hospitals while continuing to admit their least profitable patients (such as those with limited insurance coverage) to the community hospitals. To make matters worse for community hospitals, the specialty hospitals often negotiate with insurers to obtain special "carve-out" prices for their narrow range of services, placing downward pressure on the prices enjoyed by community hospitals.

In this chapter we demonstrate the importance of entry and exit. We then describe structural factors (i.e., factors beyond the control of the firms in the market) that affect entry and exit decisions. We also address strategies that incumbents may employ to reduce the threat of entry and/or encourage exit by rivals.

SOME FACTS ABOUT ENTRY AND EXIT   ◆ ◆ ◆ ◆ ◆

Entry is pervasive in many industries and may take many forms. An entrant may be a new firm, that is, one that did not exist before it entered a market. An entrant may also be a firm that is active in product or geographic market but has chosen to diversify into others. The distinction between new and diversifying firms is often important, as it may affect the costs of entry and the appropriate strategic response. Recent new entrants in various markets include Dreamworks SKG (a motion picture studio founded by Stephen Spielberg, Jeffrey Katzenberg, and David Geffin), British Midlands (which provides airline service to the British Isles and several European destinations), and AcousticSounds.com (which sells audiophile recordings over the Internet). Recent diversifying entrants include the San Francisco Symphony (which is recording and distributing its own symphonic performances), International Truck and Engine Corporation (which sells a sports utility vehicle that dwarfs the Hummer), and Corona Beer (which has entered new geographic markets in Australia and Europe).

Exit is the reverse of entry—the withdrawal of a product from a market, either by a firm that shuts down completely or by a firm that continues to operate in other markets. In the last two decades, Rhino Records exited the music recording industry, Renault and Peugeot exited the U.S. automobile market, and Sega exited the video game hardware market.

The best systematic analysis of entry and exit rates across industries is by Timothy Dunne, Marc Roberts, and Larry Samuelson (henceforth DRS).[1] They examined entry and exit in over 250,000 U.S. manufacturing firms through 1982. Though dated, their findings are valuable because they emphasize the importance of entry and exit in many industries, and offer insights about patterns of growth and decline.

To summarize the main findings of DRS, imagine an average industry in 2007. This industry has 100 firms, with combined annual sales of $100 million. Here is what that industry can expect in the next 5 to 10 years:

1. *Entry and exit will be pervasive.* By 2012, between 30 and 40 new firms will enter, with combined annual sales of $12 to $20 million. At the same time, 30 to 40 incumbent firms will exit. About half of the entrants will be diversified firms and half will be new firms. About 40 percent of the exiters will be diversified firms that may still operate in other markets.
2. *Entrants and exiters tend to be smaller than established firms.* A typical greenfield entrant will be only one-third the size of a typical incumbent. Diversifying entrants tend to be about the same size as the average incumbent. In 2007, firms that will leave the industry by 2012 will be only about one-third the size of the average firm.
3. *Most entrants do not survive 10 years, but those that do grow precipitously.* Of the 30 to 40 firms that enter the market between 2007 and 2012, roughly 60 percent will exit by 2017. The survivors will nearly double their size by 2017.
4. *Entry and exit rates vary by industry.* Not surprisingly, entry and exit are more common in some industries than in others. Some industries in which entrants are successful include apparel, lumber, furniture, and fabricated metals. Industries with high exit rates include apparel, lumber, furniture, and leather. Industries with little entry include food processing, tobacco, paper, chemicals, and primary metals. Industries with little exit include tobacco, paper, chemicals, petroleum and coal, and primary metals. Entry and exit are highly related: Conditions that encourage entry also foster exit.

The facts about entry and exit have four important implications for strategy:

1. When planning for the future, the manager must account for an unknown competitor—the entrant.
2. Not many diversifying competitors will build new plants but the size of their plants can make them a serious threat.
3. Managers should expect most new ventures to fail quickly. However, survival and growth usually go hand in hand, so managers of new firms will have to find the capital to support expansion.
4. Managers should know the entry and exit conditions of their industry. Entry and exit are powerful forces in some industries but relatively unimportant in others.

◆ ◆ ◆ ◆ ◆ ENTRY AND EXIT DECISIONS: BASIC CONCEPTS

Entry is like an investment. The entrant must sink some capital and hope that post-entry profits exceed the sunk costs.[2] There are many potential sunk costs to enter a market, ranging from the costs of specialized capital equipment to government licenses. Later in this chapter we elaborate on these and other entry costs.

Postentry profits will vary according to demand and cost conditions, as well as the nature of *postentry competition*. Postentry competition represents the conduct and performance of firms in the market after entry has occurred. The potential entrant may use many different types of information about incumbents, including historical pricing practices, costs, and capacity, to assess what postentry competition may be like. The sum total of this analysis determines whether there are *barriers to entry*.

Barriers to Entry

Barriers to entry are those factors that allow incumbent firms to earn positive economic profits, while making it unprofitable for newcomers to enter the industry.[3] Barriers to entry may be *structural* or *strategic*. Structural entry barriers result when the incumbent has natural cost or marketing advantages, or benefits from favorable regulations. Strategic entry barriers result when the incumbent aggressively deters entry. *Entry-deterring strategies* may include limit pricing, predatory pricing, and capacity expansion, all of which we discuss later in this chapter.

Bain's Typology of Entry Conditions

In his seminal work on entry, Joe Bain argued that markets may be characterized according to whether entry barriers are structural or strategic, and whether incumbents can profit from using entry deterring strategies.[4] Bain described three entry conditions:

Blockaded Entry Entry is blockaded if structural barriers are so high that the incumbent need do nothing to deter entry. For example, production may require large fixed investments, or the entrant may sell an undifferentiated product for which it cannot raise price above marginal cost.

Accommodated Entry Entry is accommodated if structural entry barriers are low, and either (a) entry deterring strategies will be ineffective or (b) the cost to the incumbent of trying to deter entry exceeds the benefits it could gain from keeping the entrant out. Accommodated entry is typical in markets with growing demand or rapid technological improvements. Entry is so attractive in such markets that the incumbent(s) should not waste resources trying to prevent it.

Deterred Entry Entry is deterred, if not blockaded, if (a) the incumbent can keep the entrant out by employing an entry-deterring strategy and (b) employing the entry-deterring strategy boosts the incumbent's profits. Frank Fisher calls such entry-deterring strategies *predatory acts*.[5] We describe several predatory acts later in this chapter.

Bain argued that an incumbent firm should analyze the entry conditions in its market and choose an entry-deterring strategy based on these conditions. If entry is blockaded or accommodated, the firm need do nothing more to deter entry. If entry is deterred, the firm should engage in a predatory act.

Analyzing Entry Conditions: The Asymmetry Requirement

Bain's typology has great intuitive appeal, and his discussion of entry-deterring strategies has guided strategists for several decades. However, economists have recently

EXAMPLE 9.1 HYUNDAI'S ENTRY INTO THE STEEL INDUSTRY

In December 1997, Hyundai announced that it would enter the steel business. Its plan was to build a fully integrated blast furnace–type steel mill in Korea by 2005. The mill would have a production capacity of 6 million tons per year. Hyundai's steel mill business plan has been one of the nation's hottest economic issues. Hyundai's announcement was a surprise to many Koreans because the government had opposed the plan.

Hyundai, Korea's largest firm, started as a construction business and expanded into engineering, automobile, shipbuilding, and other heavy equipment manufacturing. Although most of the Korean conglomerates overlap in many industries, Hyundai has a greater focus on heavy industrial sectors. Samsung, the next largest Korean conglomerate, is regarded as more of a consumer products company.

Hyundai has long been eager to participate in the steel industry. The dominant firm, POSCO, was once owned by the government. The government still owns a major portion of the shares of POSCO and appoints its CEO. POSCO has two big steel mills with combined production capacity of about 26 million tons. No other company in Korea has a mill approaching even 6 million tons, which is generally regarded to be the minimum efficient scale. (It should be noted that some of the new production technologies have narrowed the cost disadvantage of smaller mills.) Given its cost advantage, POSCO can easily outcompete its rivals and has been one of the most profitable companies in Korea. Although POSCO priced below the competition, it did not have enough capacity to meet industry demand. Experts in the Korean steel business noted that POSCO's supply was critical; without POSCO, its customers would have to turn to imports. Hyundai felt that demand for steel would continue to grow, far outstripping POSCO's production capabilities. Without a new plant, Korea would have to import steel.

Hyundai had many good reasons to enter the steel market. With demand forecast to grow, the market was ripe for entry. Hyundai, a private company, felt it could be more efficient than POSCO, which is thought to have much redundancy and bureaucracy. Moreover, Hyundai consumes so much steel itself that it could achieve minimum efficient scale without selling to the market. Thus, Hyundai stood to lower its steel costs through backward integration. By assuring capacity, Hyundai might also be better able to plan its other operations (such as car or ship production) more flexibly and easily. Finally, Hyundai's growth orientation might have led it to conclude that the steel mill would be the most cost-effective way to pull far ahead of Samsung in the battle to be Korea's top firm.

The Korean government discouraged Hyundai from building the plant, claiming that demand was likely to slacken. Hyundai suspected that POSCO had been influencing the government's opinion. Not only would a new plant threaten POSCO's profits, but Hyundai would no longer need to purchase steel from POSCO. In the end, the government failed to dissuade Hyundai from building the plant. As it turned out, the worldwide economic downturn of the early 2000s sharply reduced steel demand. The Korean government's forecast turned out to be correct after all!

challenged the most fundamental element of Bain's analysis—the distinction between entrants and incumbents. At first blush the distinction seems simple enough—incumbents are already in the market and entrants are not. But this alone does not explain why we often consider predatory pricing by an incumbent but rarely consider that an entrant might slash prices to drive out the incumbent! The same logic applies to virtually all entry-deterring strategies—most of the strategies available to incumbents are also available to entrants.

So what distinguishes incumbents from entrants? In general, the asymmetry between incumbent firms and entrants is due to sunk costs that the incumbent has incurred but the entrant has not. For example, Boeing and Airbus are protected from entry by other potential manufacturers of large commercial aviation airframes because they have already made hundreds of millions of dollars of sunk investments in construction facilities, tools, and training. To a newcomer these would represent incremental costs rather than sunk costs.

Asymmetries also arise from relationships with customers and suppliers that can take years to build. United Airlines spent many years establishing good working relationships with its Mileage Plus travelers, employees, government agencies, and Star Alliance partners. These relationships are somewhat specific to Chicago, Denver, and its other hub cities. An upstart carrier could establish the same relationships, but this would take time, during which it would suffer significant losses. It is these "adjustment costs" associated with trying to match United's relationships, rather than any fixed costs of operating an airline, that protect incumbents like United. From United's point of view, these costs are sunk. But a new carrier has yet to incur them, creating the asymmetry that deters entry. Of course, United can easily destroy these relationships—this is a major challenge as it emerges from bankruptcy. If it does so, it will lose any advantage it may have over upstart firms and might be better off selling its assets to another carrier, even a newcomer.

Asymmetries can also arise when incumbents move down the learning curve or when it is costly for a consumer to switch from one seller to another. Prior to 2004, cellular phone users in the United States could not keep their phone numbers when switching to a new provider. This served as a barrier to newcomers trying to sign up customers of incumbent firms. Thus, the switching costs that can soften competition among incumbent rivals (recall Chapter 7) can also protect them from entry.

Structural Entry Barriers

To assess entry conditions, the incumbent firm must understand the magnitude of structural entry barriers and consider the likely consequences of strategic entry barriers. We discuss the former in this section and the latter in the next section.

There are three main types of structural entry barriers:

- Control of essential resources

- Economies of scale and scope

- Marketing advantages of incumbency

Control of Essential Resources An incumbent is protected from entry if it controls a resource necessary for production and can use that resource more effectively than newcomers. DeBeers in diamonds, Alcoa in aluminum, and Ocean Spray in cranberries all maintained monopolies or cartels by controlling essential inputs. Their accumulated knowledge, investments in technology, trade relationships, and brand identities all create asymmetries that make it pointless to sell these inputs to newcomers. The success of these firms may suggest that firms should acquire key inputs to gain monopoly status. However, this approach poses several risks, some of which we discussed in Chapter 3, in the context of make-or-buy decisions. First, just when the firm thinks that it has tied up existing supplies, new input sources may emerge. A recent diamond find in northwestern Canada has loosened DeBeers's grip on the worldwide diamond market, for example. Second, owners of scarce resources may hold out for high prices before selling to the would-be monopolist. DeBeers tried to buy out much of the Canadian diamonds, but the high price cut into the cartel's profits.

There is also a regulatory risk associated with attaining monopoly status through acquisition. Antitrust laws in many nations forbid incumbents with dominant market shares from preventing competitors from obtaining key inputs. Under what has become known as the *essential facilities doctrine*, the U.S. Supreme Court in 1912 ordered the Terminal Railroad Association to permit competing railroads to use a bridge that Terminal owned. The bridge provided the only access into St. Louis from the east, and the Court feared that Terminal might use its control of the bridge to exclude rival railroads.[6] In 1985, the Supreme Court used similar reasoning to force the Aspen Skiing Company, which controlled three of the principal skiing mountains in Aspen, Colorado, to include in its six-day lift ticket access to a fourth facility controlled by another company.[7]

Incumbents can legally erect entry barriers by obtaining a patent to a novel and nonobvious product or production process. Patent laws vary by country, and in some countries, such as China and Brazil, they are extremely weak. An individual or firm that develops a marketable new product or process usually applies for a patent in its home country. In Europe and Japan, the patent rights go to the first person to apply for the patent. In the United States the first person to invent the idea gets the patent. As might be expected, firms seeking U.S. patents often go to considerable expense to document precedence of discovery. Once the patent is approved (it usually takes one to two years, and the invention is protected from imitation during the waiting period), anyone who wishes to use the process or make the product must obtain permission from the patent holder. Patent lives are currently 20 years in most developed nations.

Patents are not always effective entry barriers because they can often be "invented around," in part because a government patent office sometimes cannot distinguish between a new product and an imitation of a protected product. As a result, some innovations, such as rollerblades and the personal computer, seem to have had no patent protection whatsoever. Conversely, incumbents may file patent-infringement lawsuits against entrants whose products are seemingly different from the incumbent's. Some observers claim that Intel used this strategy to protect its microprocessors from entry by Advanced Micro Devices. It took a pair of U.S. Supreme Court decisions in the late 1990s to loosen Intel's grip on this market.

Incumbents may not need patents to protect specialized know-how. Coca-Cola has zealously guarded its cola syrup formula for a century, and no one has learned how to duplicate the sound of a Steinway piano or the beauty of Daum crystal. Firms may turn to the legally and ethically questionable practice of industrial espionage to steal such information.

Economies of Scale and Scope   When economies of scale are significant, established firms operating at or beyond the minimum efficient scale (MES) will have a substantial cost advantage over smaller entrants. The average cost curve in Figure 9.1 illustrates the problem facing a potential entrant in an industry where the MES is 1,000 units and total industry sales are 10,000 units. An incumbent with a market share of 10 percent or higher reaches the MES and has an average cost of AC_{MES}. If the entrant only achieves a market share of, say, 2 percent, it will have a much higher average cost of AC_E. The market price would have to be at least as high as AC_E for entry to be profitable.

EXAMPLE 9.2 EMIRATES AIR[8]

Most major airlines earn a disproportionate share of their profits on international routes, where competition is limited and fares are high. Even frequent price wars on domestic routes have failed to put much of a dent in the profits of transoceanic travel. A recent upheaval in a relatively small corner of the industry may subvert this status quo.

Emirates Group is a government-owned enterprise that operates international flights out of its hub in Dubai. Emirates has grown rapidly in recent years, with low prices that remind analysts of the no-frills carriers that shook up the U.S. airline industry in the 1980s. Smaller state-owned carriers in Abu Dhabi and Qatar are also slashing prices by as much as a third while expanding capacity by buying dozens of brand new super-jumbo jets including the Airbus A380.

The growth of these Arab-flag carriers is taking a toll on established carriers to the Middle East such as Air France and Qantas, which rely on high margins from international travel for the bulk of their profits. The incumbents have complained that carriers like Emirates are taking advantage of an unfair "home field advantage" whereby the United Arab Emirates (UAE) not only subsidizes Emirates but also owns and subsidizes the hub in Dubai. Among other benefits, the UAE does not ban late-night flights, as is customary at other hubs where there is concern about noise pollution. This has allowed Emirates to make fuller use of its planes as well as to offer flight schedules that are especially attractive to travelers from the Pacific Rim. Emirates and other Arab flag carriers point out that British Airways, Qantas, and other carriers that are complaining are themselves subsidized by their governments and enjoy similar home field advantages in their own nations. The Arab flag carriers also benefit from being able to pay lower wages.

Thus far, none of the Arab carriers competes directly with U.S. carriers—there are no overlapping origin/destination pairs. But the U.S. carriers are feeling the impact nonetheless. As Emirates and others expand, there is less room in the market for incumbents. The result is that incumbents are reducing flights to the area and shifting planes to other routes, including transoceanic flights to the United States. Such mobility is commonplace in the airline industry, because there are few sunk costs associated with expanding capacity on established routes. Unless global demand along traditional transoceanic routes keeps pace, there could be a glut of capacity, triggering a global price war and killing the goose that has laid the airline's golden egg.

The entrant might try to overcome the incumbent's cost advantage by spending to boost its market share. For example, it could advertise heavily or form a large sales force. Although this strategy may allow the entrant to achieve a market share greater than 2 percent and average production costs below AC_E in Figure 9.1, it involves two important costs. The first is the direct cost of advertising and creating the sales force. Once again, asymmetries are important. If the incumbent has already established its brand, then it can retain its share without the same level of advertising. In addition, the incumbent may be committed to a certain level of production owing to existing contracts with workers and other suppliers. The incremental cost required to achieve a market share of 2 percent or more is therefore much lower for the incumbent.

This poses a second problem for the entrant. If it does manage to expand its share, the incumbent is not likely to quickly back out, as many of the incumbent's costs are sunk. With an increase in industry output, price will necessarily fall. The entrant thus faces a dilemma: To overcome its cost disadvantage, it must increase its market share. But if its share increases, price competition may intensify. Such fierce price competition

FIGURE 9.1
ECONOMIES OF SCALE MAY BE A BARRIER TO ENTRY

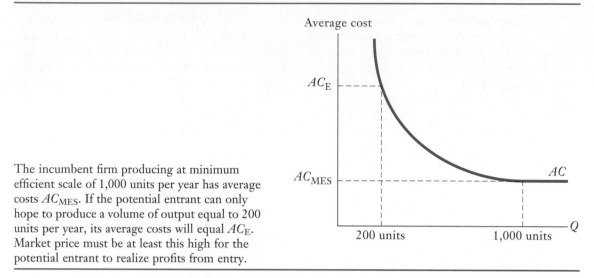

The incumbent firm producing at minimum efficient scale of 1,000 units per year has average costs AC_{MES}. If the potential entrant can only hope to produce a volume of output equal to 200 units per year, its average costs will equal AC_E. Market price must be at least this high for the potential entrant to realize profits from entry.

frequently results from large-scale entry into capital-intensive industries where capital costs are largely sunk. The U.S. gunpowder industry in the nineteenth century offers an example of intense postentry rivalry. In 1889, eight firms, including the industry leader DuPont, formed a "gunpowder pool" to fix price and output. In the early 1890s, three new firms entered the industry. Their growth challenged the continued success of the pool. DuPont's response to one entrant was to "put the Chattanooga Powder Company out of business by selling at lower prices."[9] In this way, the gunpowder pool survived until antitrust enforcers broke it up. More recently, rapid entry by fiber-optic telecom providers intensified price competition, saddling market leader WorldCom with over $20 billion in debt and driving them into bankruptcy.

Incumbents may also derive a cost advantage from economies of scope. The ready-to-eat breakfast cereal industry provides a good example.[10] For several decades, the industry has been dominated by a few firms, including Kellogg, General Mills, General Foods, and Quaker Oats, and there has been virtually no new entry since World War II. There are significant economies of scope in producing cereal, stemming from the flexibility in materials handling and scheduling that arises from having multiple production lines within the same plant. Economies of scope in marketing are due to substantial upfront expenditures on advertising that are needed for a new entrant to establish a minimum acceptable level of brand awareness. It has been estimated that for entry to be worthwhile, a newcomer would need to introduce 6 to 12 successful brands.[11] Thus, capital requirements for entry are substantial, making entry a risky proposition.

An incumbent launching a new cereal would not face the same incremental costs as an entrant. Incumbents have brand awareness and may be able to use existing facilities to manufacture new cereals. Indeed, despite the near total absence of entry by outsiders, incumbents increased the number of cereals offered for sale from 88 in 1980 to over 200 in 2005. High profit margins eventually invited limited entry by private-label manufacturers Malt-O-Meal and Ralston Purina. Even so, most of the successful newcomers have chosen niche markets, such as granola-based cereals, in which they may try to offset their cost disadvantage by charging premium prices.

Marketing Advantages of Incumbency   Chapter 2 discussed umbrella branding, whereby a firm sells different products under the same brand name. This is a special case of economies of scope but an extremely important one in many consumer product markets. An incumbent can exploit the umbrella effect to offset uncertainty about the quality of a new product that it is introducing. The brand umbrella makes the incumbent's sunk cost of introducing a new product less than that of a new entrant because the entrant must spend additional amounts of money on advertising and product promotion to develop credibility in the eyes of consumers, retailers, and distributors.

The umbrella effect may also help the incumbent negotiate the vertical chain. If an incumbent's other products have sold well in the past, distributors and retailers are more likely to devote scarce warehousing and shelf space to its new products. When Coke or Pepsi launches a new product, for example, grocery retailers are confident that there is solid market research behind the launch and are willing to allocate scarce shelf space to them. At the same time, suppliers and distributors may be more willing to make relationship-specific investments in or sell on credit to successful incumbents.

A brand umbrella may increase the expected profits of an incumbent's new product launch, but it might also increase the risk. If the new product fails, consumers may become disenchanted with the entire brand and competitors may view the incumbent as less formidable. Thus, although the brand umbrella can give incumbents an advantage over entrants, the exploitation of brand name credibility or reputation is not risk free.

Barriers to Exit

To exit a market, a firm stops production and either redeploys or sells off its assets. (A change in ownership that does not entail stopping production is not considered an exit.) When deciding whether to exit a market, the firm must compare the value of its assets if deployed in their best alternative use against the present value from remaining in the market. *Exit barriers* can keep a firm in the market even when the prevailing conditions are such that the firm, had it known with certainty that these conditions would prevail, would not have entered in the first place. Figure 9.2 illustrates why this is so. The price P_{entry} is the *entry price*—the price at which the firm is indifferent between entering the industry and staying out. The price P_{exit} is the price below which the firm would either liquidate its assets or redeploy them to another market. Exit barriers drive a wedge between P_{exit} and P_{entry}. Because $P_{\text{exit}} < P_{\text{entry}}$, firms may remain in a market even though price is below long-run average cost. For this reason, high exit barriers are viewed negatively in an analysis of industry rivalry.

FIGURE 9.2
THE PRICES THAT INDUCE ENTRY AND EXIT MAY DIFFER

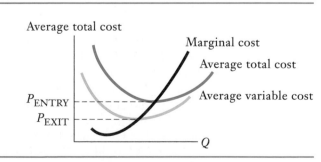

Firms will enter the industry as long as the market price exceeds P_{ENTRY}, the minimum level of average total costs. Firms will exit the industry only if price falls below P_{EXIT}, the minimum level of average variable costs.

Exit barriers often stem from sunk costs. For example, firms have obligations that they must meet whether or not they cease operations. These obligations represent sunk costs. Examples of such obligations include labor agreements and commitments to purchase raw materials. Because these costs are effectively sunk, the marginal cost of remaining in operation is low and exit is less attractive. Obligations to input suppliers are a more significant exit barrier for diversified firms contemplating exit from a single market, since the suppliers to a faltering division are assured payment out of the resources of the rest of the firm. Relationship-specific productive assets will have a low resale value and are thus a second exit barrier. Government restrictions are often a third exit barrier. For example, some states forbid hospitals to close without regulatory approval.

♦ ♦ ♦ ♦ ♦ ENTRY-DETERRING STRATEGIES

Under what conditions does it pay for incumbent firms to raise the barriers to entry into their market? At the most general level, entry-deterring strategies are worthwhile only if two conditions are met:

1. The incumbent earns higher profits as a monopolist than it does as a duopolist.
2. The strategy changes entrants' expectations about the nature of postentry competition.

The need for the first condition is obvious. The second condition is necessary because the entrant will ignore any strategy that does not change its expectations about postentry competition, rendering the strategy useless.

It seems that a firm is always better off as a monopolist, because it can set prices well above average costs. But this may not always be the case. If a monopolist cannot raise price above long-run average cost, the market is said to be *perfectly contestable*, a concept developed by William Baumol, John Panzar, and Robert Willig.[12] The key requirement for contestability is hit-and-run entry. When a monopolist raises price in a contestable market, a hit-and-run entrant rapidly enters the market, undercuts the price, reaps short-term profits, and exits the market just as rapidly if the incumbent retaliates. The hit-and-run entrant prospers as long as it can set a price high enough, and for a long enough time, to recover its sunk entry costs. If its sunk entry costs are zero, then hit-and-run entry will always be profitable. In that case, the market price can never be higher than average cost, even if only one firm is currently producing. If the incumbent raised price above average cost, there would be immediate entry, and price would fall. The incumbent has to charge a price that yields zero profits, even when it is an apparent monopolist.

Contestability theory shows how the mere threat of entry can keep monopolists from raising prices. However, finding contestable markets has proven difficult. When the theory was first developed, it was felt that it might apply to the airline industry. Entry into the industry is fairly easy, especially by established carriers entering new routes. A carrier can redeploy aircraft almost overnight, and can secure gates and ground personnel almost as quickly (provided the airports involved are not at capacity). To test contestability theory, Severin Borenstein examined airline pricing.[13] Borenstein found that monopoly routes have higher fares than duopoly routes of comparable lengths. He concluded that airline markets are not perfectly contestable; otherwise, fares would be independent of concentration. He also found that fares on monopoly routes are reduced when another carrier is already operating at one or both ends of the route. Apparently, monopolists in these situations fear that high fares will invite competition. Borenstein concluded that the threat of potential competition causes the monopolist carrier to moderate its prices but not to competitive levels.

Assuming that the incumbent monopolist's market is not perfectly contestable, it may expect to reap additional profits if it can keep out entrants. We now discuss three ways in which it might do so:

1. Limit pricing
2. Predatory pricing
3. Capacity expansion

Limit Pricing

Limit pricing refers to the practice whereby an incumbent firm discourages entry by charging a low price before entry occurs.[14] Limit pricing can take two forms. The first, which we call *contestable limit pricing*, occurs when the incumbent has excess capacity and a marginal cost advantage over entrants. As in a contestable market, the incumbent sets a price just below the entrants' marginal costs and meets all market demand at that price. Example 9.3 describes such limit pricing in the Brazilian cement industry.

If the incumbent with increasing marginal costs or limited capacity sets a price just below the entrants' marginal costs, it may be unable to meet all market demand, or it may have to sacrifice profits to do so. Although contestable limit pricing will not succeed, the incumbent may still be able to use a low price as an entry deterrent. We call this *strategic limit pricing*. The entrant observes the low price and infers that the postentry price would be as low or even lower. This may be enough to keep it out of the market, as we now show.

Consider a market that will last for two years. Demand in each year is given by $P = 100 - Q$, where P denotes price and Q denotes quantity. The production technology has nonrecoverable fixed costs of $800 per year, and constant marginal costs of $10. (We ignore discounting.) In the first year, there is a single firm with the technological know-how to compete in this market. We call this firm N. Another firm that we call E has developed the technology to enter the market in year 2. Table 9.1 summarizes useful pricing and profit information about this market. This information can be confirmed by solving for the appropriate profit-maximizing prices and quantities.

If there were no danger of entry, N would select the monopoly price of $55 in each year, earning two-year total profits of $2,450. Unfortunately for firm N, Firm E might enter in year 2. To determine if it should enter, E must anticipate the nature of postentry competition. Suppose that when E observes N charging $55 in the first year, it concludes that N will not be an aggressive competitor. Specifically, it expects the Cournot equilibrium to prevail in the second year, with both firms sharing the market equally. Based on this expectation, E calculates that it will earn profits of

TABLE 9.1
PRICE AND PROFITS UNDER DIFFERENT COMPETITIVE CONDITIONS

Market Structure	Price	Annual Profit per Firm
Monopoly	$55	$1,225
Cournot duopoly	$40	$100

EXAMPLE 9.3 LIMIT PRICING BY BRAZILIAN CEMENT MANUFACTURERS

Like many developing nations, Brazil produces and uses a lot of cement. The 57 plants operated by Brazil's 12 cement producing firms output over 40 million tons per annum, making Brazil the world's sixth leading cement maker. Each of the 57 plants dominates its local market and makes virtually no shipments to adjacent markets. This could be explained by a combination of competitive pricing and high shipping costs. After all, if cement was priced near cost, then only local producers could afford to sell it. But Brazilian cement is priced well above costs—price-cost margins often exceed 50%. This is more than enough to cover transportation costs.

Despite the lure of high profit margins, few firms attempt to ship cement across regions. The main exception is when a firm ships cement from a plant in one region into another region dominated by one of its own plants. This provides compelling evidence that it is economically feasible to transport cement across regions. Yet aside from these "friendly" shipments, cross-region shipping almost never occurs. The absence of substantial cross-region shipping is strong evidence that the Brazilian cement makers are tacitly dividing the market.

There is one group of cement makers that may not be willing to go along with this tacit

agreement—foreign producers. Thanks to reductions in shipping costs, cement makers in Asia have successfully increased their exports to the Americas—the foreign share of cement in the United States is nearly 20%. But in Brazil, that share is at most 2%. Part of the difference between the United States and Brazil may be due to shipping costs—shipments to Brazil must pass through the Panama Canal. But economist Alberto Salvo believes that the main reason for the near complete absence of exports to Brazil is that the Brazilian cement makers are limit pricing.[15]

Salvo argues that Brazil's firms have successfully colluded in two ways. The first is by dividing the market. The second is by setting a monopoly price that deters entry by firms with higher costs. This argument is consistent with the facts about market shares. Salvo offers even more confirming evidence. He observes during periods of high demand for cement in Brazil, that the price does not rise. A cartel that is not worried about entry would normally increase price during such boom times. But a cartel determined to deter entry by higher cost rivals would hold the line on price. This is exactly what Brazilian firms have been doing.

$100 if it enters. If N shares E's belief that competition will be Cournot, then conditional on entry, firm N would also expect to earn $100 in the second year. This would give it a combined two-year profit of $1,325, which is far below its two-year monopoly profit of $2,450.

Firm N may wonder if it can deter entry. It could reason as follows:

If we set a first-year price of, say, $30, then E will surely expect the postentry price to be as low or lower. This will keep E out of the market, allowing us to earn monopoly profits in the second year.

From Firm N's point of view, the thought process might go as follows:

If Firm N charges a price of $30 when it is a monopolist, then surely its price in the face of competition will be even lower. Suppose we enter and, optimistically, the price remains at $30, so that total market demand is 70. If we can achieve a 50 percent market share, we will sell 35 units and realize profits of $\{(30 - 10) \times 35\} - 800 = -\$100$. If the price is below $30, we will fare even worse. We should not enter.

If both firms follow this logic, then N should set a limit price of $30. By doing so, it will earn $\{(30 - 10) \times 70\} - 800 = \$600$ in the first year and full monopoly profits of $1,225 in the second year, for total profits of $1,825. This exceeds the profits it would have earned had it set the monopoly price of $55 in the first period and then shared the market in the second year.

Is Strategic Limit Pricing Rational?

A closer look at the preceding argument pricing reveals some potential problems with strategic limit pricing. One problem is that the potential entrant may hang around for a while, forcing the incumbent to set the limit price indefinitely. Depending on costs and demand, the incumbent might be better off as a Cournot duopolist than as a perpetual monopoly limit pricer.

The second problem is that we must accept the assumption that the incumbent is able to influence the entrant's expectations about the nature of postentry competition. To see why this is critical to the argument, we will examine how limit pricing might play itself out were the entrant to be less easily manipulated. We depict the limit pricing game in game tree form in Figure 9.3 (See the Primer for more on game trees.) The payoffs to N and E are calculated by using the demand and cost data from the previous example. Figure 9.3 shows that in year 1, the incumbent's strategic choices are (P_m, P_l) where P_m refers to the monopoly price of $55 and P_l refers to the limit price of $30. The entrant observes N's selection and then chooses from (In, Out). If E selects "Out," then N selects P_m in year 2. If E selects "In," then competition is played out in year 2. We suppose that N can control the nature of year 2 competition. In particular, N can maintain the price at $P_l = 30$, or it can "acquiesce" and permit Cournot competition, in which case the price will be $P_c = 40$. Two-year payoffs are reported at the end node for each branch of the game tree.

The limit-pricing outcome is shown by the dashed line in Figure 9.3. Under this outcome, Firm N earns total profits of $1,825 and Firm E earns $0. However, firm

FIGURE 9.3
LIMIT PRICING: EXTENSIVE FORM GAME

The limit-pricing equilibrium is shown by the dashed line. The incumbent selects P_b, and the potential entrant stays out. This is not a subgame perfect Nash equilibrium because if the potential entrant goes in, the incumbent will select the accommodating price P_c in the second period. The subgame perfect Nash equlibrium is depicted by the heavy line. The incumbent knows that it cannot credibly prevent entry, so it sets P_m in the first period.

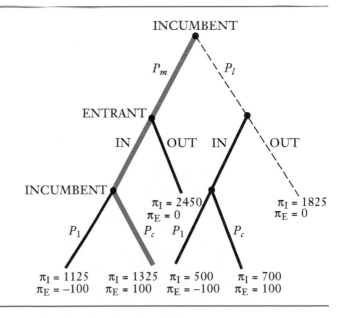

EXAMPLE 9.4 ENTRY BARRIERS AND PROFITABILITY
IN THE JAPANESE BREWING INDUSTRY

The Japanese market for beer is enormous, with per-capita consumption approaching 16 gallons per year. Four firms—Kirin, Asahi, Sapporo, and Suntory—dominate the market. The industry after-tax return on assets ranges from 3 to 4 percent, which is good in Japan where inflation is low. Moreover, these firms have been profitable for decades.

Normally, a profitable industry attracts entrants seeking to share the pie. Even so, Suntory is the only brewery to gain significant market share in Japan in the last 20 years, and its market share is only about 10 percent. Profitable incumbents combined with minimal entry usually indicate the presence of entry barriers. In the United States, profitable breweries are protected by strong brand identities. Japanese brewers also enjoy brand identity, and brands like Kirin's Ichibanshibori, and Asahi's Super Dry have loyal followings. But Japanese brewers also enjoy two entry barriers not shared by U.S. firms. Entry has historically been restricted by the Japanese government, and the dominance of "Ma-and-Pa" retail stores complicates access to distribution channels.

Breweries in Japan must have a license from the Ministry of Finance (MOF). Before 1994, the MOF would not issue a license to any brewery producing fewer than 2 million liters annually. Although this is a relatively small percentage of the total market of 7 billion liters, it represents an imposing hurdle to a start-up firm without an established brand name. As part of an overall liberalization of marketplace restrictions, the MOF has reduced the license threshold to 60,000 liters. In the wake of this change, existing small brewers formed the Japan Craft Beer Association and many microbreweries opened. Today, the Association has over 100 members.

The four incumbents responded by offering their own "gourmet" brews. This has earned them the continued loyalty of restaurant and bar owners, who are responsible for 50 percent of all retail beer sales in Japan. By combining clever marketing strategies with the cost advantages of well-established distribution channels, the major breweries have maintained their stranglehold on the beer market.

Changes in Japanese retailing practices have caused the major breweries to offer entirely new styles of beer to fend off entry. After restaurants and bars, the second largest category of beer retailers is Ma- and-Pa liquor stores. In recent years, however, Japanese consumers have begun to turn to discount liquor stores offering savings of 25 percent or more on the same beers sold at family-run stores. At the same time, the Japanese government liberalized laws permitting the development of discount stores. These discount stores (and, to a lesser extent, the supermarkets that are replacing neighborhood groceries) are willing to sell imported beers costing one-third less than domestic beers. To meet the challenge, the Japanese breweries introduced new low-malt Happoshu beers. Benefitting from lower taxes, Happoshu beers sold for 30 percent less than regular beer, and quickly captured 40 percent of the overall beer market. When the Japanese government hiked taxes on Happoshu in 2003, the major breweries responded by introducing "third-sector" beers made from peas and beans instead of hops and thereby subject a 50-yen lower tax rate per bottle. Within two years, these somewhat odd-tasting brews had captured 10 percent market share.

Ironically, though protected from entry in their home country, the big Japanese breweries have aggressively expanded overseas. Asahi began producing beer in China in 1994, and now has at least six plants. It also has a joint venture with Chinese brewer Tsingtao to produce and sell beer in third-world nations. At the same time, Kirin and Suntory have either acquired or entered into joint ventures with foreign distillers and now sell hard liquor worldwide.

behavior in the limit-pricing outcome is not rational. (In the parlance of game theory developed in the Primer, the outcome is not a "subgame perfect Nash equilibrium.") To see why not, we must analyze the game using the "fold-back" method.[16] First consider the branch of the game tree in which E ignores the limit price and chooses to enter. According to the limit-pricing argument, E stays out because it expects that *after entry has occurred*, N will select P_l. But examination of the game tree shows that it is not rational for N to select P_l. Conditional on entry having already occurred, N should select P_c. N would earn total profits of $700, which exceeds the profits of $500 it earns if it selects P_l. Thus, E's expectation of N's postentry behavior is flawed.

E should anticipate that if it enters, N will select P_c. E should calculate its profits from entry to be $100, which exceeds the profits of 0 that it earns if it stays out. Thus, E will choose to enter, even if N has selected P_l in the first stage of the game. Continuing to work backward, N should anticipate that it cannot prevent entry even if it selects P_l. It should calculate that if it does select P_l, it will earn profits of $700. By selecting P_m in the first stage and P_c in the second stage, N could earn $1,325.

Our analysis of the game tree is now complete. N will select P_m in the first stage. E will select "In." Second-year competition will be Cournot. This outcome is shown by the heavy solid line in Figure 9.3.

According to this analysis, limit pricing fails because the incumbent's preentry pricing does not influence the entrant's expectations about postentry competition. It seems that the intuitive appeal of limit pricing has run up against the cold hard logic of the game tree. It turns out that there is one additional ingredient that bolsters the intuitive justification but is not captured by the game tree. That ingredient is asymmetric knowledge about industry conditions. To understand the importance of such asymmetries, it is helpful to first discuss another entry-deterring strategy for which simplified economic models and intuition sometimes diverge.

Predatory Pricing

When a large incumbent sets a low price to drive smaller rivals from the market, this is known as *predatory pricing*. Predatory pricing may not only drive out current rivals, the low prices might deter future rivals from entering. In this way, it is similar to limit pricing. The predatory firm expects that whatever losses it incurs while driving competitors from the market can be made up later through future monopoly profits.[17]

The Chain-Store Paradox

The idea that an incumbent can slash prices to drive out rivals and deter entry is highly intuitive. Yet a relatively simple example shows that this strategy might not make sense. Imagine that a rational incumbent firm operates in 12 markets and faces entry in each. In January, it faces entry in market 1; in February, it faces entry in market 2; and so on. Should the incumbent slash prices in January so as to deter entry later in the year?

We can answer this question by working backward from December to see how earlier pricing decisions affect later entry. The most important thing to note is that regardless of what has occurred in prior months, the incumbent will not benefit from predatory pricing in December. By this time, there is no further entry to deter and therefore no reason for the incumbent to continue slashing prices. *The entrant in the twelfth market knows this* and should enter regardless of previous price cuts. Backing up to November, the forward-looking incumbent knows that it cannot deter entry in December. Thus, the incumbent cannot benefit from slashing prices in November—this can have no deterrent effect on December entry. The potential November entrant can figure this out too and so enters without fear of retaliation. In this way, the problem completely unravels, so that the incumbent realizes that it has nothing to gain from predatory pricing in January! The striking conclusion: In a world in which entrants can accurately predict the future course of pricing, we should not observe predatory pricing. This idea is astonishing but does have some empirical support, as we describe in Example 9.5.

This result that predation is seemingly irrational is associated with a puzzle in economics known as the *chain-store paradox*.[18] The paradox is that, despite the conclusion that predatory pricing to deter entry appears irrational, many firms are commonly perceived as slashing prices to deter entry. The gunpowder pool cited earlier is one example. Standard Oil, whose pricing policies in the nineteeth century drove rivals into bankruptcy, is another.

Rescuing Limit Pricing and Predation: The Importance of Uncertainty and Reputation

The economic models presented above suggest that limit pricing and predatory pricing are irrational strategies. Yet anecdotal examples and a few systematic analyses indicate that firms do pursue them. One possible explanation is that firms set prices irrationally. If this is correct (and we doubt that it often is), then this analysis should warn firms that set low prices to deter entry: Don't do it! Another explanation is that firms are rational but that the analysis thus far fails to capture important elements of their strategies.

Game theorists have shown that predatory actions may be profitable if incumbent firms have information about their own costs or market demand that entrants lack. Hence, uncertainty and asymmetry make predation rational. Reexamination of the limit-pricing game shows why this is so. The incumbent wants the entrant to believe that postentry prices will be low. If the entrant is certain about what determines postentry pricing, the entrant can analyze all possible postentry pricing scenarios and correctly forecast the postentry price. If the incumbent is best off selecting a high postentry price, the entrant will know this and will not be deterred from entering.

If the entrant is uncertain about the postentry price, however, then the incumbent's pricing strategy could affect the entrant's expectations. In a paper that explored the rationality of limit pricing, Paul Milgrom and John Roberts argued that an entrant is likely to know less about the incumbent's costs than the incumbent itself does.[20] If so, by engaging in limit pricing, the incumbent makes it appear that it has low costs. This will lower the entrant's expectations of postentry profitability and potentially deter it from entering.

Garth Saloner has pointed out that for limit pricing to deter entry, the entrant must be unable to perfectly infer the incumbent's cost from its limit price.[21] Saloner showed that this could occur if the entrant was uncertain about the level of demand as well as the incumbent's cost. These two types of uncertainty firmly support a limit-pricing strategy. The limit price signals to the entrant that the incumbent's costs may be low and/or market demand may be low. Either signal may deter entry.

Similar arguments explain why firms would want slash prices today to deter future entrants. Such predatory pricing appears to be irrational because potential entrants can *perfectly* predict incumbent behavior in every market. Most critically, the entrant in the last model is confident that the incumbent would not slash price because there is no further entry to deter. But suppose that the last entrant is uncertain about whether the incumbent would slash prices. Perhaps an "easy" incumbent would not slash

EXAMPLE 9.5 PREDATORY PRICING IN THE LABORATORY

Predatory pricing is a violation of antitrust laws in most developed nations. Yet there have been very few successful prosecutions for predatory pricing, and most antitrust economists doubt that it happens very often in practice. One reason is that it is difficult, in practice, to distinguish between low prices designed to boost the market shares of efficient firms from abnormally low prices designed to drive rivals from the market. The former is an acceptable business practice that no court would want to outlaw. The rival seems unacceptable but may have no practical impact on consumers if new rivals emerge. Thus, the courts may be hesitant to block any price reductions, regardless of apparent intent.

Economists have wondered whether it is possible to generate true predatory pricing even under laboratory conditions. The relatively new field of experimental economics provides an opportunity to find out. Experimental economists conduct small-scale simulations of business situations, frequently enlisting the participation of undergraduate and graduate students. One of the first important simulations involves participants who "play" a repeated prisoner's dilemma with cash awards determined by which game cell is played. In the past two decades, the experiments have become more sophisticated, with several experiments exploring predatory pricing.

Mark Isaac and Vernon Smith published the results of the first predatory pricing experiment in 1985.[19] Here was the setup. Two participants competed in a market where they would sell up to a total of 10 units. Each player was "endowed" by Isaac and Smith with a cost function displaying increasing marginal costs. The players named their own prices and the maximum amount they were willing to sell at that price. A player who sold one or more units at a price that exceeded the cost got to keep the profits. Lastly, players had to sell at least one unit in a period to earn the right to play the game again.

Isaac and Smith made sure that one player had lower costs than the other. The low cost player could drive the rival from the market by offering to sell all 10 units at a price that was below its own marginal cost of selling its last unit, but also below the rival's cost of selling its first unit. This would be an prime example of predatory pricing. Isaac and Smith repeated this experiment with dozens of participants. The lower-cost player never set a predatory price. This explains the title of Isaac and Smith's paper, "In Search of Predatory Pricing."

Other experimental economists pointed out that the high-cost rival in Isaac and Smith's experiment had no opportunity to make money if it exited the market. This might give the rival a strong incentive to match the low-cost player's predatory pricing, even if it meant losing money in the short run. This, in turn, might have discouraged the low-cost player from preying. Economists modified Isaac and Smith's setup to allow high-cost rivals to make money in other markets. In these experiments, low-cost players often did set predatory prices. Other economists have modified Isaac and Smith's experiment by allowing for a series of potential entrants, so that even if the low-cost player drives one rival from the market, it will face future potential rivals. Once again, this seems to encourage low cost players to set predatory prices.

It is now commonly accepted that predatory pricing occurs in laboratory settings. Does this imply that predation occurs in the real world? It certainly suggests that relative novices can figure out the potential benefits of predation and are willing to take short-run losses provided they are playing with someone else's money. As with the entire field of experimental economics and similar studies of tit-for-tat strategies, price discrimination, commitment, and other game theoretic situations, there is considerable debate as to what this implies for experienced strategists making real-world decisions that involve millions of their own dollars.

prices, but a "tough" incumbent would. We can envision the types of firms that might be "tough." They might have very low costs, or they might simply dislike competition, even to the point of sacrificing profits to remain a monopolist. Or perhaps they face additional competition that the entrant is unaware of. In any event, if the last entrant believes that the incumbent is easy, then it may enter the last market. If the incumbent has not slashed prices in prior months, this would reinforce the view that it is easy. If entrants are unsure of the incumbent's costs, motives, or future plans, then an easy incumbent may want to slash prices beginning in January, thereby establishing a *reputation for toughness*. In an experiment, Yun Joo Jung, John Kagel, and Dan Levin found that when students playing a predation game were unsure about the incumbent's tendencies, incumbents did slash prices to deter entry.[22]

Some well-known firms, including Wal-Mart and American Airlines, enjoy a reputation for toughness earned after fierce price competition led to the demise of rivals. Aggressiveness is also a natural outgrowth of strategies to increase market share. Some firms may announce a mission to achieve dominant market shares, such as Black and Decker and McCormick Spices. These announcements may effectively signal to rivals that these firms will do whatever is necessary, even sustain price wars, to secure their share of the market. Along these lines, firms may promote toughness by rewarding workers for aggressiveness in the market. Chaim Fershtman and Kenneth Judd suggest that a firm might want to reward managers based on market share rather than profits.[23] This will encourage them to price aggressively, thereby enhancing the firm's reputation for toughness, and could ultimately lead to higher profits than if managers were focusing on the bottom line.

The chain-store paradox not only sheds light on the role of uncertainty; it also reveals the importance of asymmetry. In our analyses, the terms *incumbent* and *entrant* are arbitrary. It is reputation, not incumbency per se, that matters. An entrant might come into the market and slash prices. If the incumbent is uncertain about the entrant's costs, motives, or future plans, then it may elect to exit, rather than try to ride out the price war.

Capacity Expansion

Many firms carry excess capacity. To measure capacity utilization, every year the U.S. Census of Manufacturers asks plant managers to state the levels of current and desired production. The resulting ratio, called *capacity use*, is typically about 80 percent. Firms hold more capacity than they use for several reasons. In some industries, it is economical to add capacity only in large increments. If firms build capacity ahead of demand, then such industries may be characterized by periods in which firms carry excess capacity. Downturns in the general economic business cycle, or a decline in demand for a single firm can also create excess capacity. Firms in imperfectly competitive industries may be profitable when operating at capacity. Other firms may then enter seeking a share of those profits, creating excess capacity. In these examples, excess capacity results from market forces.

Firms may also hold excess capacity for strategic purposes. By holding excess capacity, an incumbent may affect how potential entrants view postentry competition and thereby blockade entry. Because the incumbent's excess capacity is sunk, this creates a natural asymmetry (and if it is not sunk, the strategy will not work). Unlike predatory pricing and limit pricing, excess capacity may deter entry even when the entrant possesses complete information about the incumbent's strategic intentions. The reason is that when an incumbent builds excess capacity, it can expand output at a relatively low cost. Facing competition, the incumbent may find it desirable to expand its output considerably, regardless of the impact on the entrant's profits. This will have the effect, intended or not, of substantially reducing the entrant's postentry profits. If postentry profits are less than the sunk costs of entry, the entrant will stay out. The monopolist incumbent may even decide not to utilize all of its capacity, with the idle capacity serving as a *credible commitment* that the incumbent will expand output should entry occur.

Marvin Lieberman has detailed the conditions under which an incumbent firm can successfully deter entry by holding excess capacity:[24]

- The incumbent should have a sustainable cost advantage. This gives it an advantage in the event of entry and a subsequent price war.

- Market demand growth is slow. Otherwise, demand will quickly outstrip capacity.

- The investment in excess capacity must be sunk prior to entry. Otherwise, the entrant might force the incumbent to back off in the event of a price war.

- The potential entrant should not itself be attempting to establish a reputation for toughness.

"Judo Economics" and the "Puppy-Dog Ploy"

In this chapter, we have provided examples in which an incumbent firm has used its size and reputation to put smaller rivals at a disadvantage. Sometimes, however, smaller firms and potential entrants can use the incumbent's size to their own advantage. This is known as "judo economics."[25] Consider that when an incumbent slashes prices to drive an entrant from the market, it sacrifices its own short-run profits. With its higher volume, the incumbent probably loses more than the entrant. If an entrant does not appear to pose a significant long-term threat, the incumbent might think twice about incurring large losses to drive the entrant from the market. This logic is closely related to the "puppy-dog ploy" described in Chapter 8.

An example is provided by Braniff Airlines. Restaurateur and doll company owner Jeffrey Chodorow and real estate developer Arthur Cohen purchased a struggling Braniff in 1988. Braniff went bankrupt the next year. In settling the Braniff assets, Chodorow and Cohen bought the rights to the Braniff trademark for $313,000, took over bankrupt Emerald Airlines, and combined the two into a new Braniff. Braniff publicly announced in the spring of 1991 that it intended to limit its flights from Dallas to Los Angeles, New York, Florida, and the Caribbean. Braniff started flying scheduled trips in June 1991. It had some immediate setbacks, including flying a banned Boeing 727 into Los Angeles International Airport (the plane violated local noise-pollution ordinances). But Braniff's fate was sealed even before its first scheduled flight took off. In a move that many believe was prompted by Braniff's reentry into its home market of Dallas, American Airlines introduced "value pricing" on May 27, 1991, triggering a price war that drove Braniff from the market for good two months later.

If it had stayed true to its word, Braniff's market share would have been one-thirtieth that of American. So why did American respond aggressively to Braniff's puppy-dog ploy? Perhaps American slashed prices to deter potential future entry by other carriers. Even if American was unconcerned about future entry, it might not have believed Braniff's promise to stay small. In general, there are few ways that a firm can credibly commit not to grow.

A more successful example is provided by Amazon's entry into the online book retail market. Many observers wondered why Barnes & Noble did not immediately respond with their own web site, potentially driving Amazon from the market. Because of its dominant presence in the bricks-and-mortar market, Barnes & Noble had much to lose by entering the online segment. This would quickly legitimize online sales and would probably trigger an online price war, thereby cannibalizing Barnes & Noble's bricks-and-mortar sales. As it turned out, Amazon succeeded beyond the expectations of most market analysts, legitimizing the sector without any help from Barnes & Noble.

◆ ◆ ◆ ◆ ◆ EXIT-PROMOTING STRATEGIES

Firms occasionally complain about predatory pricing by larger rivals. They even argue that consumers should object to the resulting low prices, because the price slasher will eventually dominate the market and set monopoly prices. Oil refiners advanced these arguments when they attempted to break up the Standard Oil Trust 100 years ago. In 1993, three drugstores in Conway, Arkansas, made a similar claim about the local Wal-Mart store. They sued Wal-Mart under state antitrust statutes and won a $300,000 award, plus a court order forcing Wal-Mart to increase its drug prices. (Similar antitrust challenges to Wal-Mart have failed.)

Complaints about unfair low prices are common during trade disputes. In 1991, the U.S. Department of Commerce ruled that Toyota and Mazda were *dumping* mini-vans into the U.S. market by pricing below cost. The International Trade Commission (ITC) ruled a year later that American automakers were not harmed by such practices and were not entitled to compensation (ignoring the question of why Toyota and Mazda would sell below cost in the first place). In a seeming replay of this dispute in 2000, the Commerce Department ruled that Japanese manufacturers were dumping seamless stainless steel and set import tariffs as high as 150 percent. Two years later, the ITC found no evidence of harm against U.S. manufacturers, opening the door to ending the tariffs. The European Commission has leveled dumping charges against Czech steel makers, and Thailand has accused 14 nations of dumping steel. The international General Agreement on Tariffs and Trade (GATT) is frequently renegotiated to deal with complex dumping issues.

Wars of Attrition

The purpose of predatory pricing is to eliminate competition and create monopoly. For the strategy to work, the rival firm must exit before the aggressor pulls back. It is not obvious why this should happen. A price war harms all firms in the market regardless of who started it and hurts large firms the most. Price wars are examples of *wars of attrition*. In a war of attrition, two or more parties expend resources battling with each other. Eventually, the survivor claims its reward, while the loser gets nothing and regrets ever participating in the war. If the war lasts long enough, even the winner may be worse off than when the war began because the resources it expended to win the war may exceed its ultimate reward. Besides price wars, many other types of interactions are wars of attrition. The U.S./Soviet nuclear arms buildup between 1945 and the late 1980s is a classic example. Both countries spent huge sums to increase their nuclear arsenals, each hoping that the other country would be the first to make concessions. Eventually, the Soviet Union fell apart, and Russia acknowledged that it could not afford to carry on the buildup.

EXAMPLE 9.6 SYMBIAN: KEEPING MICROSOFT OUT OF THE
MOBILE PHONE BUSINESS[27]

The mobile phone industry continues to grow rapidly, with sales of phone hardware increasing 20 percent annually. Originally, cellular phones were just that—telephones. Today's third-generation ("3G") technology is much more than a telephone. "Smartphones," as they are sometimes called, can perform many of the same functions as a personal computer, including e-mail, web browsing, electronic messaging, and digital photography.

The capabilities of a smartphone depend on its software, and this has captured the attention of Microsoft. From word processing to web browsing to video gaming, Microsoft has been an aggressive second mover in software markets. Microsoft has had great success entering markets where software operates on a personal computer. But its second-place status in video gaming (after Sony) demonstrates that Microsoft's entry can be successfully thwarted when other hardware is involved.

In 1998, the leading manufacturers of cellular phones, including Nokia, Ericsson, Sony, Panasonic, and Samsung, formed Symbian. Symbian is a software licensing company that develops and supplies an open, standard operating system—Symbian OS—for data-enabled mobile phones. A total of 14 manufacturers currently use Symbian, including all of the consortium members. The attractiveness for Symbian licensees and software developers is that they are able to examine and modify the operating system's innards, or the user interface. Just like car makers who use a same platform (chassis) to develop entirely different models, the Symbian software is flexible enough to allow handset makers to develop different designs without having to start from scratch every time. This is not an available feature under Microsoft's software, and it is one of the main reasons why the handset makers refused to license its software.

Having failed to agree with the large handset makers, Microsoft entered this market by teaming up with contract manufacturers or original design manufacturers (ODMs; manufacture and design) to produce operator-specific handsets, bypassing the established handset-maker. Microsoft hopes that the industry will develop as the computer industry did: away from a vertically integrated model, in which the same companies make hardware and software, and toward a horizontally layered model in which software is supplied by Microsoft and hardware becomes a commodity made by firms such as the ODMs. Thus far, Symbian has tied up virtually the entire market. However, the "3G era" is in its infant state. Two decades ago, IBM learned that consumers would purchase just about any personal computer so long as it ran the Windows operating system. Time will tell if the cellular market moves in the same direction.

Virtually all firms are worse off during a prolonged price war. If the price war drives some firms from the market, however, the survivors can raise prices above the prewar levels. Thus, every firm must ask if it has a chance to survive; if so, it might be worth the suffering. If a firm were certain that it would lose a price war, it should exit immediately. If no firms exit in the early stages of a price war, the war may last so long that all firms, including the survivors, lose in the end. This may have occurred in the price wars among "warehouse club" stores during the early to mid-1990s.[26] Although some competitors exited the market, the losses incurred during the war were so large that the survivors could not recoup them. All firms would have been better off if the price war had never begun.

The more that a firm believes it can outlast its rivals, the more willing it will be to enter and sustain a price war. Firms may even try to convince their rivals that they are better positioned to survive the price war. They might claim that they are actually making money during the price war, or that they care more about winning the war than they do about profits. Such messages may cause rivals to think twice about their own changes of survival and encourage early exit. (An analogy in the arms race is Ronald Reagan's pronouncement that the United States could survive and win a nuclear war.)

We are again reminded of the importance of sunk costs. If two firms face an impending price war and one has made sunk commitments to workers and other input suppliers, its rival may as well give up. A firm that has made sunk commitments has low incremental costs of remaining in the market. Any rivals who persist in fighting the price war should expect a long battle.

◆◆◆◆◆ EVIDENCE ON ENTRY-DETERRING BEHAVIOR

Although theorists have devoted considerable attention to entry deterrence, there is little systematic evidence regarding whether firms pursue entry-deterring strategies and, if they do, whether those strategies are successful. Most of our evidence comes from antitrust cases, where discovery requirements often provide researchers with detailed cost, market, and strategic information.

There may be little evidence on entry deterrence from sources other than antitrust cases for several reasons. First, firms are naturally reluctant to report that they deter entry, because this may be sensitive, competitive information and might also violate antitrust statutes. Second, many entry-deterring strategies involve pricing below the short-term monopoly price. To assess whether a firm was engaging in such a practice, the researcher would need to know the firm's marginal costs, its demand curve, the degree of industry competition, and the availability of substitutes. Outside of antitrust cases, such information is difficult for researchers to obtain. Finally, to measure the success of an entry-deterring strategy, a researcher would need to determine what the rate of entry would have been without the predatory act. This, too, is a difficult question to answer.

Survey Data on Entry Deterrence

Despite concerns about the willingness of firms to provide frank responses, Robert Smiley asked major consumer product makers if they pursued a variety of entry-deterring strategies.[28] Smiley surveyed product managers at nearly 300 firms. He asked them whether they used several strategies discussed in this chapter, including:

1. Aggressive price reductions to move down the learning curve, giving the firm a cost advantage that later entrants could only match by investing in learning themselves
2. Intensive advertising to create brand loyalty
3. Acquiring patents for all variants of a product
4. Enhancing firm's reputation for predation through announcements or some other vehicle
5. Limit pricing
6. Holding excess capacity

The first three strategies create high entry costs. The last three change the entrant's expectations of postentry competition.

TABLE 9.2
REPORTED USE OF ENTRY-DETERRING STRATEGIES

	Learning Curve	Advertising	R&D Patents	Reputation	Limit Pricing	Excess Capacity
New Products						
Frequently	26%	62%	56%	27%	8%	22%
Occasionally	29	16	15	27	19	20
Seldom	45	22	29	47	73	48
Existing Products						
Frequently		52%	31%	27%	21%	21%
Occasionally		26	16	22	21	17
Seldom		21	54	52	58	62

Table 9.2 reveals the percentage of product managers who report that their firms frequently, occasionally, or seldom use each of the preceding strategies for new products and existing products. Note that managers were asked about exploiting the learning curve for new products only. More than half of all product managers surveyed report frequent use of at least one entry-deterring strategy, and virtually all report occasional use of one or more entry-deterring strategies. Product managers report that they rely much more extensively on strategies that increase entry costs rather than on strategies that affect the entrant's perception about postentry competition.

CHAPTER SUMMARY

◆ Entry and exit are pervasive. In a typical industry, one-third of the firms are less than five years old, and one third of firms will exit within the next five years.

◆ A firm will enter a market if it expects postentry profits to exceed the sunk costs of entry. Factors that reduce the likelihood of entry are called entry barriers.

◆ A firm will exit a market if it expects future losses to exceed the sunk costs of exit.

◆ Entry barriers result from asymmetries between incumbent firms and entrants.

◆ Exogenous market forces can create structural entry barriers. Low demand, high capital requirements, and limited access to resources are all examples of structural entry barriers. Exit barriers arise when firms must meet obligations whether or not they produce.

◆ An incumbent firm can use predatory acts to deter entry or hasten exit by competitors. Limit pricing, predatory pricing, and capacity expansion change entrants' forecasts of the profitability of postentry competition.

◆ Limit pricing and predatory pricing can succeed only if the entrant is uncertain about the nature of postentry competition.

◆ Firms may hold excess capacity to credibly signal their intent to lower prices in the event of entry.

◆ Firms can engage in predatory practices to promote exit by rivals. Once a firm realizes that it cannot survive a price war, it exits, permitting the survivors to raise price and increase share. A firm may try to convince its rivals that it is more likely to survive a price war to hasten the rival's exit.

◆ Managers report that they frequently engage in entry-deterring strategies, especially to protect new products.

QUESTIONS

1. Dunne, Roberts, and Samuelson found that industries with high entry rates tended also to have high exit rates. Can you explain this finding? What does this imply for pricing strategies of incumbent firms?

2. Dunne, Roberts, and Samuelson examined manufacturing industries in the 1960s to 1980s. Do you think that entry and exit rates have changed in the past two decades? Do you think that entry and exit rates are systematically different for service and retail industries?

3. "All else equal, an incumbent would prefer blockaded entry to deterrable entry." Comment.

4. Under what conditions do economies of scale serve as an entry barrier? Do the same conditions apply to learning curves?

5. How a firm behaves toward existing competitors is a major determinant of whether it will face entry by new competitors. Explain.

6. Why is uncertainty key to the success of entry deterrence?

7. An incumbent firm is considering expanding its capacity. It can do so in one of two ways. It can purchase fungible, general-purpose equipment and machinery that can be resold at close to its original value. Or it can invest in highly specialized machinery which, once it is put in place, has virtually no salvage value. Assuming that each choice results in the same production costs once installed, under which choice is the incumbent likely to encounter a greater likelihood of entry and why?

8. In most models of entry deterrence, the incumbent engages in predatory practices that harm a potential entrant. Can these models be reversed, so that the entrant engages in predatory practices? Why do you think incumbents are more likely to set predatory pricing than are entrants?

9. Recall the discussion of monopolistic competition in Chapter 6. Suppose that an entrepreneur considered opening a video store along Straight Street in Linesville. Where should the entrepreneur position the store? Does your answer depend on whether further entry is expected?

10. Consider a firm selling two products, A and B, that substitute for each other. Suppose that an entrant introduces a product that is identical to product A. What factors do you think will affect (a) whether a price war is initiated and (b) who wins the price war?

ENDNOTES

[1]Dunne, T., M. J. Roberts, and L. Samuelson, "Patterns of Firm Entry and Exit in U.S. Manufacturing Industries," *RAND Journal of Economics*, Winter 1988, pp. 495–515.

[2]The theory of real options described in Chapter 7 discusses many of the issues affecting the timing of the entry and exit decisions. We will not revisit these issues here.

[3]This definition is a synthesis of the definitions of entry barriers of Joe Bain in *Barriers to New Competition: Their Character and Consequences in Manufacturing Industries*, Cambridge, MA, Harvard University Press, 1956, and C. C. Von Weizsäcker in *Barriers to Entry: A Theoretical Treatment*, Berlin, Springer-Verlag, 1980.

[4]Bain, *Barriers to New Competition*.

[5]Fisher, F., *Industrial Organization, Economics, and the Law*, Cambridge, MA, MIT Press, 1991.

[6]*United States v. Terminal R. R. Assn.*, 224 U.S. 383 (1912).

[7]*Aspen Skiing Co. v. Aspen Highlands Skiing Corp.*, 472 U.S. 585 (1985).

[8]Much of the information for this example was taken from Michaels, D., 2005 "From Tiny Dubai, an Airline with Global Ambition Takes Off," *Wall Street Journal*, January 11, 2005, p. 1.

[9]Fligstein, N., *The Transformation of Corporate Control*, Cambridge, MA, Harvard University Press, 1990.

[10]For a detailed discussion see Schmalensee, R., "Entry Deterrence in the Ready-to-Eat Breakfast Cereal Industry," *Bell Journal of Economics*, 9 (2), 1978, pp. 305–327.

[11]Scherer, F. M., "The Breakfast Cereal Industry," in Adams, W. (ed.), *The Structure of American Industry*, 7th ed., New York, Macmillan, 1986.

[12]Baumol, W., J. Panzar, and R. Willig, *Contestable Markets and the Theory of Industrial Structure*, New York, Harcourt Brace Jovanovich, 1982.

[13]Borenstein, S., "Hubs and High Fares: Dominance and Market Power in the U.S. Airline Industry," *RAND Journal of Economics*, 20, 1989, pp. 344–365.

[14]Bain, J. S., "A Note on Pricing in Monopoly and Oligopoly," *American Economic Review*, 39, March 1949, pp. 448–464.

[15]Salvo, A. (2005) "Inferring Conduct under the Threat of Entry: The Case of the Brazilian Cement Industry" London School of Economics, Mimeo.

[16]See the Economics Primer for a discussion of the use of the "fold-back" method to determine subgame perfect equilibria.

[17]See Martin, S., *Industrial Economics*, New York, Macmillan, 1988, for a good review of the various legal tests for predatory pricing that have been proposed.

[18]This term was coined by the game theorist Reinhard Selten in his article, "The Chain Store Paradox," *Theory and Decision*, 9, 1978, pp. 127–159.

[19]Isaac, R. M. and V. Smith, "In Search of Predatory Pricing," *Journal of Political Economy*, 93, 1985, pp. 320–345.

[20]Milgrom, P. and J. Roberts, "Limit Pricing and Entry Under Incomplete Information," *Econometrica*, 50, 1982, pp. 443–460.

[21]Saloner, G., "Dynamic Equilibrium Limit Pricing in an Uncertain Environment," mimeo, Graduate School of Business, Stanford University. See also Matthews, S. and L. Mirman, "Equilibrium Limit Pricing: The Effects of Stochastic Demand," *Econometrica*, 51, 1983, pp. 981–996.

[22]Jung, Y. J., J. Kagel, and D. Levin, "On the Existence of Predatory Pricing: An Experimental Study of Reputation and Entry Deterrence in the Chain-store Game," *Rand Journal of Economics*, 25(1), 1994, pp. 72–93.

[23]Fershtman, C. and K. Judd, "Equilibrium Incentives in Oligopoly," *American Economic Review*, 77, 1984, pp. 927–940.

[24]Based on Lieberman, Marvin B., "Strategies for Capacity Expansion," *Sloan Management Review*, Summer 1987, pp. 19–25.

[25]Gelman, J. and S. Salop, "Judo Economics: Capacity Limitation and Coupon Competition," *Bell Journal of Economics*, 14, 1983, pp. 315–325.

[26]Warehouse clubs are less luxurious versions of mass merchandisers such as Target and Wal-Mart. They offer substantial savings on bulk purchases. They are called clubs because shoppers must pay a nominal fee to become members.

[27]This example was prepared by Kellogg student Guillermo Fretes.

[28]Smiley, R., "Empirical Evidence on Strategic Entry Deterrence," *International Journal of Industrial Organization*, 6, 1988, pp. 167–180.

10

INDUSTRY ANALYSIS

*I*n Part One of this text, we explored the economics of the firm's relationships with its upstream and downstream trading partners. We saw how factors such as incomplete contracts, asset specificity, and long-term market interactions can affect the ability of firms to prosper in these relationships. In Part Two, we have examined the economics of competition and seen how market and product characteristics such as concentration, entry barriers, and differentiation can affect the profits of individual firms and entire industries. Because these chapters introduce so many important concepts, the student could lose track of the key insights. *Industry analysis* frameworks, such as Michael Porter's *Five Forces* and Adam Brandenberger and Barry Nalebuff's *Value Net*, provide a structure that enables us to systematically work through these wide-ranging and often complex economic issues. An industry analysis based on such frameworks facilitates the following important tasks:

- Assessment of industry and firm performance.

- Identification of key factors affecting performance in vertical trading relationships and horizontal competitive relationships.

- Determination of how changes in the business environment may affect performance.

- Identifying opportunities and threats in the business landscape. In this regard, industry analysis is essential to performing "SWOT" analysis, a "bread-and-butter" tool in strategic planning. (SWOT stands for strengths, weaknesses, opportunities, and threats. Chapter 11 will offer insights into identifying firm strengths and weaknesses.)

In addition, industry analysis is invaluable for assessing the generic business strategies that we introduce in Part Three.

Parts One and Two are grounded in microeconomics, particularly the economics of the firm and the economics of industrial organization. Although the roots of these fields can be traced back a century or more, they had little impact on business strategy until Michael Porter published a series of articles in the 1970s that culminated in his pathbreaking book *Competitive Strategy*. Porter presents a convenient framework for exploring the economic factors that affect the profits of an industry. Porter's main innovation is to classify these factors into five major forces that encompass the vertical chain and market competition.

In their book *Coopetition*, Brandenberger and Nalebuff make a significant addition to the five-forces framework. They describe the firm's "Value Net," which includes suppliers, distributors, and competitors. Whereas Porter describes how suppliers, distributors, and competitors might destroy a firm's profits, Brandenberger and Nalebuff's key insight is that these firms often *enhance* firm profits. In otherwords, strategic analysis must account for both cooperation and competition. (Hence the title of their book.)

This chapter shows how to perform a five-forces industry analysis that accounts for the economic principles in Parts One and Two. It also shows how to accommodate the Value Net principles introduced by Brandenberger and Nalebuff. We illustrate these ideas by examining three very different markets: hospitals, professional sports, and airframe manufacturing. We selected these markets both because they present a diversity of competitive forces and because we have a strong institutional understanding of each. Indeed, solid industry analysis is not possible without such understanding. Economic knowledge that is devoid of institutional knowledge can be dangerous!

The five-forces framework has several limitations. First, it pays little attention to factors that might affect demand. It accounts for the availability and prices of substitute and complementary products but ignores changes in consumer income, tastes, and firm strategies for boosting demand, such as advertising. Second, it focuses on a whole industry rather than on that industry's individual firms. Firms may occupy unique positions in their markets that insulate them from some competitive forces. Third, the framework does not explicitly account for the role of the government, except when the government is a supplier or buyer. The government as a regulator can profoundly affect industry profitability and could be considered a sixth force. Fourth, the five-forces analysis is qualitative. For example, an analysis of industry structure may suggest that the threat of entry is high, but the framework does not show how to estimate the probability of entry. Because it is qualitative, the framework is especially useful for assessing trends—that is, identifying changes in market conditions that might cause industry profitability to increase or decrease.

PERFORMING A FIVE-FORCES ANALYSIS   ◆ ◆ ◆ ◆ ◆

The five-forces framework is not a set of principles per se. The relevant principles have been developed in the preceding chapters. Instead, the five-forces framework is a tool for ensuring that you systematically use these principles to assess the current status and likely evolution of an industry.

The five forces, as represented in Figure 10.1, are internal rivalry, entry, substitute and complementary products, supplier power, and buyer power. Internal rivalry is in the center because it may be affected by each of the other forces. One assesses each force by asking "Is it sufficiently strong to reduce or eliminate industry profits?" To answer this question, it is essential to refer to the economic principles that apply for each force. For example, when assessing the power of suppliers to affect industry and firm performance, you should determine whether firms in the industry have made

FIGURE 10.1
THE FIVE-FORCES FRAMEWORK

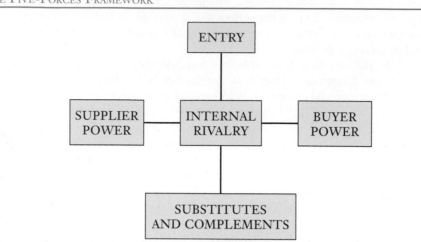

relationship-specific investments with their suppliers (or vice versa) and whether they are protected from potential holdup either by contracts or market forces. In the following discussion, we will identify those principles that are most relevant to each force.

The appendix offers a "five-forces scorecard" for doing industry analysis. The template includes specific questions about each force. Your responses should indicate whether this force poses a major threat to profits today, as well as identify trends.

Internal Rivalry

Internal rivalry refers to the jockeying for share by firms within a market. Thus, an analysis of internal rivalry must begin by defining the market. Be sure to include all firms that constrain each other's strategic decision making, as described in Chapter 6, and pay attention to both the product market and geographic market definitions. For example, if you are analyzing internal rivalry among hotels, note that most consumers have specific geographic preferences when selecting a hotel. Consumers may also have strong preferences for particular categories of hotels, such as business hotels or family-style resorts. This implies that competition is local and may differ by hotel category, and your analysis should reflect this difference. If you are unsure whether to include a firm in the relevant market, remember that you can always exclude it from your consideration of internal rivalry and still consider it when you assess substitutes and complements.

As we discussed in Chapters 6 through 8, firms may compete on a number of price and nonprice dimensions. Price competition erodes profits by driving down price-cost margins. Nonprice competition erodes profits by driving up fixed costs (e.g., new product development) and marginal costs (e.g., adding product features). To the extent that firms can pass cost increases along to consumers in the form of higher prices (i.e., the industry price elasticity of demand is not too large), nonprice competition is less likely to erode profits than is price competition. In fact, firms in many industries are engaged in vigorous nonprice competition, yet have been able to enjoy solid profits over an extended period of time. Good examples include couture fashion, where competition is based on style and image; cola, where advertising and new product varieties drive market share; and pharmaceuticals, driven by R&D "patent races."

Price competition is far more likely to erode industry profits, in part because it is difficult to reduce costs by enough to maintain price-cost margins. Industry prices do not fall by themselves—one or more firms must reduce prices. A firm reduces prices if it believes it can gain market share by doing so. Hence, the incentives for a firm to reduce price are related to the degree to which it expects its market share to increase. Each of the following conditions therefore tends to heat up price competition:

- *There are many sellers in the market.* The structure/conduct/performance paradigm introduced in Chapter 6 predicts that prices are lower when there are more firms in the market. There are several reasons for this condition. When there are many competitors, there is a good chance that at least one is dissatisfied with the status quo and will want to lower price to improve its market position. At the same time, it will shoulder a smaller portion of the revenue-destruction effect. Thinking long term, a firm with a low market share might conclude that its rivals will not respond if it lowers price.

- *The industry is stagnant or declining.* Firms cannot easily expand their own output without stealing from competitors. This often elicits a competitive response that tends to intensify competition.

- *Firms have different costs.* Low-cost firms may be unhappy with a high price, reasoning that if price falls, their high-cost rivals may exit.

- *Some firms have excess capacity.* Firms with excess capacity may be under pressure to boost sales and often can rapidly expand output to steal business from rivals.

- *Products are undifferentiated/buyers have low switching costs.* When products are undifferentiated and switching costs are low, firms are tempted to undercut their rivals' prices because this can generate a substantial increase in market share.

- *Prices and terms of sales are unobservable/prices cannot be adjusted quickly.* This condition increases the response time of rivals, enabling the price cutter to potentially gain substantial market share before its rivals match the price cut. This also increases the chances of misreads/misjudgments and makes it more difficult for firms to develop "facilitating practices" (see below).

- *There are large/infrequent sales orders.* A firm may be tempted to undercut its rivals to secure a particularly large order, believing that the substantial gains may more than offset any losses from future rounds of price cutting. This is especially true if different managers are responsible for different bids, and each is rewarded on the basis of his or her own sales.

- *Industry does not use "facilitating practices" or have a history of cooperative pricing.* In the absence of price leadership, price announcements, or other facilitating practices, firms may be unable to "agree" on a suitable industry price, and some may lower price to gain an advantage. A history of cooperative pricing may assure industry participants that each is striving to find a price that works to everyone's collective benefit.

- *There are strong exit barriers.* This condition can prolong price wars as firms struggle to survive instead of exiting.

- *There is high industry price elasticity of demand.* This condition can cut into sales and profits when nonprice competition heats up.

Entry

Entry erodes incumbents' profits in two ways. First, entrants divide market demand among more sellers. (Entrants rarely grow the market enough so that even the incumbents are better off.) Second, entrants decrease market concentration and heat up internal rivalry. Some entry barriers are exogenous (i.e., they result from the technological requirements for successful competition), whereas others are endogenous (i.e., they result from strategic choices made by incumbents). Each of the following tends to affect the threat of entry:

- *Production entails significant economies of sales—minimum efficient scale is large relative to the size of the market.* The entrant must achieve a substantial market share to reach minimum efficient scale, and if it does not, it may be at a significant cost disadvantage.

- *Government protection of incumbents.* Laws may favor some firms over others.

- *Consumers highly value reputation/consumers are brand loyal.* Entrants must invest heavily to establish a strong reputation and brand awareness. Diversifying entrants using a brand umbrella may be more successful than entirely new entrants. Third-party report cards (e.g., *Consumer Reports*) can facilitate quality shopping and reduce the advantage of incumbency.

- *Access of entrants to key inputs, including technological know-how, raw materials, distribution, and locations.* Patents, unique locations, and so forth can all be barriers to entry. Incumbent must avoid overpaying to tie up unique inputs and may find it more profitable to sell its patent, location, and the like, to a would-be entrant.

- *Experience curve.* A steep experience curve puts entrants at a cost disadvantage.

- *Network externalities.* This gives an advantage to incumbents with a large installed base. If incumbents are slow to establish an installed base, an entrant may do so through a large-scale product launch.

- *Expectations about postentry competition.* Historical evidence is invaluable to predicting postentry competition. Does the incumbent have a reputation for predatory pricing in the face of entry? Do incumbents have a history of persevering through price wars? Do incumbents have sufficient excess capacity to flood the market, and if necessary, to drive the entrant from the market?

Substitutes and Complements

Although the five-forces analysis does not directly consider demand, it does consider two important factors that influence demand—substitutes and complements. Substitutes erode profits in the same way as entrants by stealing business and intensifying internal rivalry. (Think of low-priced cellular communications competing with land-lines and the Internet.) Complements boost the demand for the product in question, thereby enhancing profit opportunities for the industry. (Think of innovations in big-screen televisions boosting the demand for home theater loudspeakers.) Bear in mind, however, that changes in demand can affect internal rivalry, entry, and exit. Be sure to consider these indirect effects of substitutes and complements. Factors to consider when assessing substitutes and complements include:

- *Availability of close substitutes and/or complements.* Consider product performance characteristics when identifying substitutes and complements.

- *Price-value characteristics of substitutes/complements.* Seemingly close substitutes may pose little threat if they are priced too high. Similarly, complements may fail to boost demand if priced too high. Many new products may be weak substitutes or complements, but may gain strength as manufacturers move down the learning curve and prices fall.

- *Price elasticity of industry demand.* This is a useful measure of the pressure substitutes place on an industry. When the industry-level price elasticity is large, rising industry prices tend to drive consumers to purchase substitutes' products.[1]

Supplier Power and Buyer Power

An assessment of supplier power takes the point of view of a downstream industry and examines the ability of that industry's upstream input suppliers to negotiate prices that extract industry profits. Sometimes, the upstream market is competitive. We say that suppliers in a competitive upstream market have "indirect power" because they can sell their services to the highest bidder. The price they charge depends on supply and demand in the upstream market. For example, fuel suppliers have indirect power relative to the airline industry. When supply and demand conditions cause fuel prices to increase, airline profits suffer.

Recall from Chapters 3 and 4 that upstream suppliers can also erode industry profits if (a) they are concentrated or (b) their customers are locked into relationships with them because of relationship-specific investments. In these situations, we say that suppliers have "direct power." An input supplier with direct power can raise prices when its target market is faring well, thereby extracting a share of its customers' profits. The converse also applies—a powerful supplier may lower prices when its target market is doing poorly. Consistent application of both pricing strategies will permit the supplier to extract much of its target market's profits without destroying that market. Historically, unions have used this strategy to increase workers' wages. Similarly, an input supplier with a relationship-specific investment in an industry can squeeze profits from a successful industry and ease the burden on an industry in trouble.

Buyer power is analogous to supplier power. It refers to the ability of individual customers to negotiate purchase prices that extract profits from sellers. Buyers have indirect power in competitive markets, and the price they pay will depend on the forces of supply and demand. The willingness of consumers to shop for the best price could instead be considered a source of internal rivalry, not indirect buyer power. When buyers are concentrated, or suppliers have made relationship-specific investments, buyers may wield direct power.

The following factors must be considered when assessing supplier power and buyer power. We state each in terms of supplier power relative to the downstream industry that it sells to. An analogous factor must be assessed when considering buyer power:

- *Competitiveness of the input market.* If inputs are purchased in competitive markets, then input prices will be determined by the forces of supply and demand.

- *The relative concentration of the industry in question, its upstream, and its downstream industries.* Firms in the more concentrated industry may have greater bargaining power and may be able to achieve a cooperative price that puts firms in the less concentrated industry (due to internal rivalry in that industry) at a disadvantage.

- *Purchase volume of downstream firms.* Suppliers may give better service and lower prices to larger purchasers.

- *Availability of substitute inputs.* The availability of substitutes limits the price that suppliers can charge.

- *Relationship-specific investments by the industry and its suppliers.* The threat of holdup may determine the allocation of rents between the industry and its suppliers.

- *Threat of forward integration by suppliers.* If credible, firms in an industry may be forced to accept the high supply price or risk direct competition from suppliers.

- *Ability of suppliers to price discriminate.* If suppliers can price discriminate, they can raise the prices they charge more profitable firms.

Strategies for Coping with the Five Forces

A five-forces analysis identifies the threats to the profits of all firms in an industry. Firms may pursue several strategies to cope with these threats. First, firms may position themselves to outperform their rivals by developing a cost or differentiation advantage that somewhat insulates them from the five forces. Chapter 11 discusses positioning strategies in detail. Second, firms may identify an industry segment in which the five forces are less severe. For example, in the 1970s, Crown, Cork and Seal served manufacturers of "hard-to-hold" liquids, a niche market that was far less competitive than the metal-can segments served by industry leaders American Can and Continental Can. Through this and similar strategies, Crown earned significantly higher rates of return. Third, a firm may try to change the five forces, although this is difficult to do. Firms may try to reduce internal rivalry by establishing facilitating practices or creating switching costs. Firms may reduce the threat of entry by pursuing entry-deterring strategies. Firms may try to reduce buyer or supplier power by tapered integration. In the extended examples presented later in this chapter, we will see how firms in a variety of industries have attempted to cope, with varying degrees of success, with the five forces.

◆ ◆ ◆ ◆ ◆ COOPETITION AND THE VALUE NET

Porter's five forces is an enduring framework that remains widely used for industry analysis. In their book *Coopetition*, Adam Brandenberger and Barry Nalebuff identify an important weakness of the framework. From the viewpoint of any one firm, Porter tends to view all other firms, be they competitors, suppliers, or buyers, as threats to profitability. Brandenberger and Nalebuff point out that interactions among firms can sometimes enhance profits and emphasize the many positive interactions that Porter generally ignores. Examples of positive interactions include the following.

- Efforts by competitors to set technology standards that facilitate industry growth, such as when consumer electronics firms cooperated to establish a single format for high-definition television, or when Sony and Toshiba formed an alliance to establish a compatible standard for digital video discs.

- Efforts by competitors to promote favorable regulations or legislation, such as when domestic U.S. automakers worked together to get the U.S. Department of

Energy to endorse a proposal to develop fuel cells rather than tighten gasoline fuel economy standards.

- Cooperation among firms and their suppliers to improve product quality to boost demand, such as when Nintendo priced its Nintendo Entertainment System (NES) video games so that software developers earned a higher profit per cartridge than did Nintendo. This encouraged developers to invest heavily in developing high-quality games, which in turn boosted overall demand for the NES system.

- Cooperation among firms and their suppliers to improve productive efficiency, such as when Edward Hospital in Naperville, Illinois worked closely with its cardiovascular surgeons to develop a handheld computer system to allow the two to rapidly exchange clinical information.

In support of these ideas, Brandenberger and Nalebuff introduce the concept of the *Value Net* as a counterpart to Porter's five forces. The Value Net, which consists of suppliers, customers, competitors, and complementors (firms producing complementary goods and services), is similar to the five forces. Brandenberger and Nalebuff's admonition to perform a comprehensive analysis of the Value Net to prevent blind spots is also reminiscent of Porter. But whereas a five-forces analysis mainly assesses threats to profits, a Value Net analysis assesses opportunities. This important change does not nullify the five-forces approach so much as complement it. A complete five-forces analysis should, therefore, consider both the threats and opportunities each force poses. To illustrate this point, contrast a traditional five-forces industry analysis of the DVD hardware market in 1997–1998 (the first two years of introduction) with an analysis that accounts for the Value Net. Here are some conclusions that might have emerged from a traditional analysis.

- *Internal rivalry.* The main source of differentiation was brand—the players were otherwise fairly homogeneous. Unless firms could establish loyalty based on brand, intense price competition could result.

- *Entry.* There were modest technological and physical capital requirements limiting entry. A dozen or more consumer electronics firms had the know-how and access to channels to successfully enter the market.

- *Substitutes and complements.* Satellite TV posed a clear threat as a substitute. Digital video streaming over the Internet was another potential threat.

- *Supplier power and buyer power.* Powerful studios such as Disney and producers such as George Lucas and Stephen Spielberg could have demanded substantial payments to supply their movies in DVD format, especially given the threat from the alternative DIVX format that Circuit City was poised to launch. Powerful distributors such as Best Buy and Circuit City might demand high margins in exchange for clearing the shelf space needed to promote the new format.

Given this five-forces analysis, DVD hardware makers would have had every reason to be pessimistic about the format.

But this analysis fails to account for the Value Net and, as a result, fails to identify opportunities for industry growth and profitability. The participants in the Value Net—manufacturers, studios, and retailers—recognized that their fortunes were intertwined. If they could generate sufficient interest in DVD, then demand would grow fast enough to make everyone profitable while thwarting DIVX.

Manufacturers had many options for boosting demand. The most obvious would be to set low prices. This would encourage hardware sales that would, in turn, encourage studios to release more movies in DVD, thereby further boosting demand for hardware. Manufacturers could also heavily promote DVD so as to boost product awareness while blunting the threat from DIVX. In the first year, hardware makers did none of this. They kept prices high so as to profit from early adopters (players sold for $500 to $1,000) rather than to stimulate mass-market acceptance. They ran few advertisements or promotions. As a result, manufacturers sold only about 300,000 players in the United States and a comparable number in Europe in Japan, well within expectations, but hardly enough to guarantee the success of the format. In the second year, manufacturers lowered prices on some players to less than $300 and spent heavily on advertising and promotions. Other participants in the Value Net also pitched in. MGM released special editions of classic films such as *Gone With the Wind*. Warner slashed prices on dozens of popular titles. Columbia and Universal studios accelerated the release of popular action titles such as *Godzilla*. Meanwhile, electronics retailers, especially Best Buy, heavily promoted DVD hardware and software, including a much publicized half-price software sale for Internet purchases.

DVD succeeded when all the players in the Value Net did their part to promote the overall success of the product. Some members of the Value Net, such as Warner and Best Buy, took a temporary loss (by setting prices below costs) so as to contribute to the future success of the format. The DVD market finally took off when firms worked to increase the size of the DVD "pie," rather than fight for their share of a fixed pie. Through their complementary actions, the participants in the DVD Value Net secured its future and reaped the benefits.

◆ ◆ ◆ ◆ ◆ APPLYING THE FIVE FORCES: SOME INDUSTRY ANALYSES

The best way to illustrate the five-forces framework is by example. In this section we perform three detailed industry analyses. For each industry, we present background information, proceed with market definition, and identify the most salient economic principles from each of the five forces.

Chicago Hospital Markets Then and Now

It has been a turbulent two decades for American hospitals. For 30 years up until the mid-1980s, hospitals thrived. Yet between 1985 and 2000, an average of 75 hospitals a year went bankrupt (about 1.5 percent of the nation's total each year), and many others struggled to stay solvent. In the last few years, most hospitals have enjoyed a measure of prosperity, with returns on sales in 2005 nearing historically high levels. Even so, storm clouds are on the horizon. This dynamic has been repeated throughout the nation, including the Chicago market, which is the focus of this analysis. An industry analysis conducted at various points in time demonstrates the problems that hospitals have grown accustomed to and identifies profit opportunities that some hospitals have exploited.

Market Definition

Market definition requires identifying both product and geographic markets. We consider the product market to be acute medical services such as maternity care, surgery, and complex diagnostic services. While other providers besides hospitals offer many of these services—outpatient surgery centers are a good example—we will treat their offerings as substitutes. This decision is not essential to our conclusions and illustrates the flexibility of the five-forces framework. (We would be remiss, of course, if we did not consider outpatient surgery at all.)

The geographic scope of hospital competition is subject to considerable debate; federal courts are grappling with this issue as they review the antitrust implications of recent hospital mergers. Research shows that patients strongly prefer to visit nearby hospitals. The geographic market in which Chicago hospitals compete is certainly no larger than the metropolitan area, and in one recently decided antitrust case, a federal judge ruled that there are distinct submarkets (e.g., suburban regions) that have their own unique competitive dynamics. We will assess internal rivalry in the Chicago metropolitan area and, when appropriate, discuss the importance of submarkets.

Internal Rivalry

There are about 70 community hospitals in the Chicago market.[1] Virtually all of them were independent in 1980, when the Herfindahl index for the entire metropolitan area was below 0.05. Today, many hospitals belong to systems. There is no dominant system, however, and if we treat each system as a single entity to compute market shares, the regional Herfindahl index is roughly 0.20. If we instead examine geographic submarkets, such as the North Shore suburbs, the Herfindahl increases to 0.25 or higher.

The relatively large number of hospitals is just one factor that could intensify internal rivalry. Another factor to consider is the considerable variation in production costs, based on differences in productive efficiency and the fact that Chicago has several large teaching hospitals that must bear the cost of training young, inefficient doctors. There is also excess capacity, though not so much as in years past; occupancy rates at many hospitals remain below 70 percent, though some suburban hospitals operate at 85 percent or higher. Finally, demand for admissions had been stagnant or declining for a long time. This trend has now reversed itself, thanks to aging baby boomers and their many ailments.

Despite these factors, internal rivalry in 1980 was benign. The reason had to do mainly with how patients shopped for hospital services. When choosing a hospital, patients deferred to their physicians, who tended to concentrate their practices at one or two hospitals. This created a kind of seller loyalty that greatly lessened the importance of prices. Patients also enjoyed staying close to home, creating additional product differentiation, especially in suburban markets. (Downtown Chicago was home to over a dozen hospitals within a few miles of each other.) Another important factor was that most patients had insurance that paid their bills no matter which hospital they chose. For patients with the most generous insurance, price was a complete nonissue. The combination of price-insensitive patients and physician-dominated admission decisions limited the incentives of hospitals to use price as a strategic weapon. As a result, internal rivalry in 1980 was low, and most hospitals in Chicago enjoyed healthy price–cost margins from their privately insured patients.

During the 1980s, managed-care organizations (MCOs) entered the Chicago market and began selectively contracting with those hospitals that offered the best value. MCOs offered enrollees financial inducements (in the form of lower copayments) to encourage them to select the contracting hospitals. By steering patients to the "preferred" hospitals, insurers effectively increased price elasticities of demand. Three additional factors intensified internal rivalry. First, MCOs treated all hospitals as nearly identical, seemingly ignoring patient loyalties. Second, price negotiations between insurers and hospitals were secret, encouraging hospitals to lower prices to win contracts. Finally, sales were infrequent (i.e., a contract lasts one to three years) and lumpy (i.e., one insurer may have represented over 5 percent of a hospital's business). This intensified the pressure on hospitals to lower prices to win each individual contract without considering the impact on future price rivalry. It also limited opportunities for hospitals to develop facilitating practices.

Price rivalry intensified. Hospitals lowered prices by 20 percent or more to stay competitive in the managed-care marketplace. Profit margins declined through the early 1990s, and many Chicago-area hospitals closed. During the late 1990s, hospitals fought back. Some, like Northwestern Memorial Hospital, established a strong brand identity. Others diversified into related products, such as skilled nursing services (for which insurers provided generous reimbursements). Some sought to differentiate their services by developing "centers of excellence" in clinical areas such as cancer care and heart surgery. These strategies had varying degrees of success. Diversification helped boost revenues but did nothing to soften competition in the inpatient market. Branding helped those hospitals that already enjoyed strong reputations, but it did little for the average community hospital. And patients saw most centers of excellence for what they were—existing facilities were renamed without demonstrably improving quality.

Two recent trends have done much more to soften competition. First, patients have spoken out against MCOs with "narrow" networks. They want free choice of hospital and distrust MCOs that claim that their network hospitals offer the greatest value. The result is that MCOs must include nearly all hospitals in their networks. Hospitals know this and hold out for higher prices. Second, there has been considerable consolidation in regional submarkets, including the city of Chicago and the important North Shore suburbs. Mergers among hospitals in these submarkets have further strengthened the hands of hospitals in their contract negotiations with MCOs. Several merging hospitals raised their prices by 20 percent or more.

Entry

No new hospitals have been built in Chicago in over two decades. State regulation provides an important barrier to entry. Potential entrants in Illinois must demonstrate that the projected utilization at the new hospital could not be met by existing hospitals. (This would be like requiring Samsung's cellular phone division to show that Motorola could not meet demand before allowing Samsung to enter.) The entry barrier has been nearly absolute, and instead the region has witnessed major expansion and remodeling of existing hospitals.

Under political pressure, state regulators have relaxed their intrepretations of rules in recent years and have begun approving a few applications to build new hospitals. Even if this barrier breaks down and hospitals continue to prosper, incumbents might be protected by additional entry barriers. Hospitals are capital intensive. A new modest-sized 150-bed hospital can cost $200 million to build. A *de novo* entrant (i.e., an entrant with no current hospital in Chicago) would also have to establish a brand identity, since patients may be reluctant to trust their health to an unknown entity. By the same token, a *de novo* entrant would also need access to distribution "channels"—the medical staff that admits patients. These factors may help explain why nearly all proposals to build new hospitals in Chicago have been floated by existing hospitals.

The barriers to entry are large but not overwhelming. The Chicago area continues to grow, with suburbs stretching 50 miles from downtown. "Outsider" hospital corporations such as Tenet have considerable experience entering new markets and recruiting physicians and could view Chicago's "exurbs" as fertile ground for growth. Technological change may further lower entry barriers. Innovations in medicine might make it possible to open smaller, cost-competitive inpatient facilities that focus on specific treatments, such as heart surgery. This will reduce the capital and number of physicians required for successful entry. If the regulatory barrier breaks down and Chicago hospitals remain profitable, *de novo* entry is sure to follow.

Substitutes and Complements

In 1980, a patient who needed surgery or a complex diagnostic procedure went to the hospital. Outpatient facilities and physicians in their private offices provided routine therapy and diagnostic services but were poor substitutes for inpatient care. Over the past 25 years, there have been dramatic improvements in surgical technique, anesthetics, and antibiotics, so that many types of surgeries can be safely performed outside the hospital. Changes in insurance payments have spurred a shift toward outpatient diagnostic imaging facilities. Home health care has also boomed, allowing providers to monitor the recoveries of surgical patients and care for chronically ill patients in the patients' homes.

Hospitals have turned out to be the dominant sellers of outpatient services in many markets, including Chicago. They already possessed the technology, personnel, and brand appeal to offer outpatient care and were often first to do so. Some of the bigger Chicago hospital systems, including Evanston Northwestern and Advocate, have opened their own technologically advanced outpatient treatment centers. Economies of scope have enabled these systems to thrive even as their core inpatient business shrinks.

New medical technologies will continue to emerge. Some, such as laparoscopic surgery, will facilitate even more outpatient treatment. But some technologies, such as advances in respiratory medicines that sustain the lives of low-birthweight babies, complement and boost the demand for inpatient care. An important generation of new technologies will emerge from genetic research, and it is difficult to predict whether these will be substitutes or complements to inpatient care.

Supplier Power

The main suppliers to hospitals include labor (nurses, technicians, etc.), medical equipment companies, and drug houses. Hospital-based physicians, such as radiologists, anesthesiologists, and pathologists (RAP physicians), are also suppliers. (We consider admitting physicians to be buyers because they often determine which hospitals patients will purchase services from.) All these suppliers have indirect power. Supply and demand forces in the market for nurses have been especially tight in recent years, forcing up nurse wages. The prices of drugs and other medical supplies have also risen precipitously.

Hospitals and their suppliers make few relationship-specific investments. Personnel learn to work in teams but seem to adjust rapidly to new settings. Hospitals can usually replace them at the market wage, and some hospitals routinely use "nursing pools" to handle short-term needs. A national recruiting market usually makes RAP physicians easy to replace, although hospital bylaws and staffing policies can pose obstacles. Medical suppliers without monopoly power cannot credibly threaten to hold up hospitals to obtain higher prices. Suppliers whose innovations are protected by patents can command very high prices if their products make the difference between life and death.

The magnitude of supplier power has not changed much over time. A much-discussed national physician's union movement could greatly increase the power of RAP physicians.

Buyer Power

Buyers include patients, physicians, and insurers who decide which hospitals will get business and how they will be paid. Patients and their physicians in 1980 did little to discipline high price hospitals. Insurers in 1980 were also passive, usually reimbursing hospitals for whatever they charged rather than shopping around for the best value. State regulations actually prevented such price shopping by insurers, though large state Blue Cross plans did obtain discounts because of their size. The two major government insurers, Medicaid and Medicare, also paid generously. Buyer power in 1980 was low.

Selective contracting has enabled insurers to wield buyer power. At the same time, government payers have used their regulatory powers to command discounts. Medicare, which insures the elderly and disabled, pays a fixed price per hospital stay—adjusted for the diagnosis—forcing hospitals to swallow excessive treatment costs. Owing to federal budget cuts, Medicare payments are declining. Medicaid, the joint federal/state program that covers treatments for the medically indigent, may be the toughest payer of all. Medicaid in Illinois pays hospitals 25 to 50 percent less than the amount paid by other insurers for comparable services. Medicaid knows each hospital's cost position and can use this information to minimize what it offers to pay.

Physicians may also wield significant power, especially those charismatic and highly skilled physicians who can attract patients regardless of where they practice. The University of Chicago Hospital recently lured a pair of lung transplant specialists from Loyola Medical Center, offering them high pay, state of the art facilities, and top-notch staffing. Loyola is upping the ante in its search to replace them. This is only the latest salvo in a wide-ranging and long-run battle to tie up the physician market. During the 1990s, hospitals paid as much as $500,000 to purchase the practices of "run of the mill" physician practices, anticipating an increase in referrals. The strategy has largely failed, however, with many hospitals reporting massive losses. The careful student should be able to use the lessons from Chapters 3 and 4 to diagnose the risks of such an integration strategy.

Table 10.1 summarizes the five-forces analysis of the Chicago hospital market in 1980, 2000, and today. Virtually every factor that affects industry profitability changed for the worse between 1980 and 2000, but many have since softened. As hospitals look to the future, they should be concerned about a few possible trends:

- The Federal Trade Commission recently won an antitrust case that forced Evanston Hospital to sell nearby Highland Park hospital. (The decision has been appealed to an appellate court.) That merger had enabled the two nearby competitors to sharply raise prices.

TABLE 10.1
FIVE-FORCES ANALYSIS OF THE CHICAGO HOSPITAL MARKET

Force	Threat to Profits		
	1980	*2000*	*Today*
Internal rivalry	Low	Medium	Medium but declining
Entry	Low	Low	Low but growing
Substitutes and complements	Medium	High	High
Supplier power	Medium	Medium	Medium
Buyer power	Low	Medium	Medium but declining

- Concerned about rising health insurance premiums, employers are asking employees to bear more of their health care costs. This could make patients more price sensitive. At the same time, some employers are reconsidering the decision to opt for wide, but costly, MCO networks.

- If regulatory barriers fall, entry by specialty hospitals in wealthier communities could skim off some of the areas' most profitable patients.

- Employers, payers, regulators, and patients are demanding and getting more information about hospital quality. This could allow the best hospitals to command premium prices but could also increase the willingness of patients and their doctors to switch from hospitals whose quality is merely satisfactory.

Commercial Airframe Manufacturing

The firms that build airplanes are called airframe manufacturers. Airbus Industries and the Boeing Company have been in an effective duopoly since Lockheed pulled out in 1986 and Boeing acquired McDonnell Douglas in 1997. Despite limited competition, Airbus and Boeing still face threats from each other, as well as from some key fringe players.

Market Definition

We confine our analysis to companies that make airplanes for commercial aviation. Business jets, such as Citations and Gulfstreams, are not considered relevant since their prices have no bearing on the market for big jet airplanes. Two other companies, Montreal-based Bombardier and Brazil-based Embraer manufacture small-capacity (50 seats) and medium-capacity (50 to 100 seats) turboprop and jet aircraft for commercial use. Taken together, these fringe players have a combined market share of 25 percent by aircraft and a much lower share by revenue. If we restrict attention to planes with more than 100 seats, then Boeing and Airbus have the entire market to themselves. Thus, we will largely pay attention to the competitive battle between Boeing and Airbus. Boeing and Airbus compete globally; there are no meaningful geographic submarkets in which other companies compete.

Internal Rivalry

Boeing was established in 1917 and built military aircraft for the better part of 40 years. It delivered its first commercial aircraft in 1958. Airbus was established in 1967 by a consortium representing the governments of Great Britain, France, and Germany. Airbus did not deliver its first plane until 1974. In part because it is an older company, Boeing has produced many more airplanes than has Airbus—15,000 compared to 4,000. Airplanes are built to last—25 years or longer—and most of the planes that Boeing has built are still flying. Boeing's market dominance seems to be waning, however. In the past few years, both Boeing and Airbus have delivered about 300 new planes annually, with Airbus slightly in the lead most years.

It has always been Airbus's stated intention to have a 50 percent market share. In pursuit of this objective, Airbus has priced aggressively and expanded productive capacity. European governments heavily subsidized Airbus, especially during its early years. These subsidies enabled Airbus to undercut Boeing's prices and build market share. For example, in 2001 Britain gave over £530 million toward the development of Airbus's latest plane, the A380. Airbus also continues to receive low-interest loans from its government sponsors to subsidize research and development. Boeing receives tax breaks for its R&D efforts, but these are much smaller than the subsidies enjoyed by Airbus. Boeing has been able to remain price competitive, in part, because it enjoys scope economies from its military aircraft division. (Airbus often accuses the U.S. government of indirectly subsidizing Boeing by paying well in excess of costs for military planes.)

Several factors have tempered Airbus's incentives to reduce prices. Demand for air travel grew steadily throughout the 1990s. Although air travel declined during the 2001 recession (and particularly after the September 11 attacks), it quickly recovered and now exceeds pre-2001 levels. New carriers, such as Emirates Air, have placed large orders for jumbo jets while established carriers are replacing older planes. Lucrative transcontinental carriers are finding that passengers have strong preferences for new planes with amenities such as personal DVD screens. The upshot is that Airbus can continue to grow rapidly without cutting prices. But nothing is guaranteed. Airline profits tend to be pro-cyclical; airlines can suffer multibillion-dollar losses during economic downturns. Many airlines cancel orders when economic conditions deteriorate; in the wake of September 11, orders fell by 10 to 20 percent. This in turn severely damaged the profits of the airframe manufacturers.

Another factor affecting internal rivalry is the high fixed costs associated with airframe manufacturing. During good times, Airbus and Boeing run at capacity, maintaining backlogs that can take years to complete. This helps reduce rivalry to some extent, as neither firm can rapidly expand market share at the other's expense. However, backlogs decline or even disappear during downturns. Neither Boeing nor Airbus has seemed willing to shed productive capacity (through large-scale layoffs and plant closings) in the face of falling backlogs. The result is that marginal costs decline dramatically during downturns. Not surprisingly, Boeing and Airbus are both willing to renegotiate deals at these times. The fact that a single deal with an American or United Airlines can account for nearly 15 percent of Boeing or Airbus's business only intensifies the willingness to shave prices in downtimes.

Historically, Boeing and Airbus enjoyed little product differentiation. Flag carriers British Airways and Air France preferred Airbus, for obvious reasons. Otherwise, the airlines feel that the two manufacturers offer virtually identical products. For example, the Boeing 737 and Airbus A320 have similar seating capacities, performance, and flying range. Even so, airlines have developed loyalties. After witnessing the astonishing success of Southwest, which flies only Boeing 737s, the airlines recognized that they could economize on parts and maintenance if they reduced the variety of planes they flew. Boeing and Airbus have exploited this trend by making parts interchangeable across different models. The result is that some carriers buy exclusively from Airbus while others rely on Boeing. This may limit incentives to reduce prices on airplanes in the future, for it will be increasingly difficult for Airbus and Boeing to steal each other's customers.

There is even some differentiation in the products themselves. Airbus has developed the A380, a double-decker plane capable of seating over 550 passengers (but likely to be configured for fewer passengers with more amenities.) Sales thus far are sluggish, in part because airports need to reconfigure arrival gates to accommodate the jumbo planes. Boeing abandoned its plans to build the Sonic Cruiser, capable of flying 20 percent faster than the A380. It is instead focusing its development efforts on the 350-passenger 787 dreamliner, which is said to be more fuel efficient than other planes.

Barriers to Entry

High development costs and the experience-based advantages of the incumbents combine to make entry into the commercial airframe manufacturing industry extremely difficult. It cost Airbus an estimated $13 billion to develop the A380. Airbus hopes to make about $50 million in profit per aircraft. With discounting, Airbus will need to sell over 350 planes to break even. A start-up manufacturer would likely face higher development costs owing to experience effects. It could also expect smaller margins, both because airlines are reluctant to purchase from start-ups (Airbus discovered this 20 years ago) and because entry would likely engender a price response by Airbus and Boeing. Entry by a newcomer in the jumbo segment would therefore be very risky.

Incumbents are also protected by the learning curve in production. Stanford University economist Lanier Benkard used detailed data on the production of the Lockheed L1011 to estimate the learning curve for producing that plane.[2] He found that with a doubling of experience, the number of personnel required to produce a plane would fall by 35 to 40 percent. However, this effect is mitigated by "forgetting" (i.e., past experience is less valuable as time goes by). In fact, the economic downturn of the early 1970s, which caused a decline in demand for the L1011, helps explain why Lockheed failed to achieve the anticipated learning benefits. Even so, learning effects are usually substantial and help further insulate incumbents from competition by newcomers.

We have already noted that airlines prefer to purchase from the same manufacturer. This poses yet another barrier to entry. One positive note for entrants—access to raw materials and labor is not a significant barrier.

Substitutes and Complements

From the perspective of the airlines, the only substitute for an airplane made by Boeing or Airbus would be an airplane made by someone else. Historically, Boeing and Airbus made the only planes that met airlines' needs for medium- and large-capacity planes capable of flying thousands of miles. But this is no longer the case.

Passengers are weary of hub-and-spoke travel and the associated delays and lost baggage. Even so, it has not always been economically viable for airlines to replace medium- to long-haul hub-and-spoke flights with nonstop point-to-point travel. Simply put, demand for these routes has been too small to fill the smaller Boeing and Airbus jets. Around 1990, Canadian manufacturer Bombardier and Brazilian manufacturer Embraer filled this important void. The Bombardier CRJ series and Embraer ERJ series "regional jets" seat 50 to 90 passengers and are capable of flying over 2,000 miles. These planes immediately increased the number of economically viable point-to-point routes. They also enabled airlines to increase the frequency of flights on existing viable routes, for example, flying four round trips daily from Chicago to Syracuse on a small jet, instead of just twice daily on a larger plane. (This proved to be especially appealing in the lucrative business segment.)

The market response was overwhelming, with more than 2,000 regional jets sold to date. There is no doubt that much of this came at the expense of Boeing 737s and Airbus 320s, the traditional workhorses of the major carriers. As demand for air travel rises, some carriers are finding it profitable to switch back to 737s and 320s; the cost per passenger mile is lower on a full 120-seat plane than on a full 50-seater. In 2005, Bombardier put a temporary halt on construction of CRJ regional jets.

Substitution also comes indirectly from other forms of transportation. High-speed rail may be a particularly important substitute, for it matches or exceeds the airline's "product performance characteristic" of high-speed transport. High-speed rail is currently operational in Japan. The Maglev (a high-speed train) is a levitating train able to reach speeds of up to 500 kilometers per hour. Although this may affect regional aircraft in certain routes, it is unlikely to affect commercial aircraft owing to the high development costs, the long time horizon for development, and their physical constraints.

Supplier Power

Boeing and Airbus can obtain raw materials and components from competitive supplier markets. However, most parts suppliers do more business selling replacement parts to airlines than selling original equipment to Boeing and Airbus, so the airframe makers do not have an iron grip on their suppliers. Boeing has started a program that may further enhance its leverage with suppliers. Its Global Airlines Inventory Network (GAIN) enables airlines to directly order spare parts from suppliers. Suppliers like it too, even though it further ties them to Boeing, because they can more accurately plan production and inventories, and they are thus willing to tie themselves even more closely to Boeing. There are a few suppliers with whom Boeing and Airbus do not hold the upper hand. General Electric competes primarily with Pratt & Whitney and Rolls Royce in the manufacturing of jet engines. When Boeing and Airbus do well, these three firms can negotiate more favorable supplier contracts for themselves.

Unionized labor has substantial supplier power. Currently, nearly half of Boeing's workforce is unionized. The unions have cooperated in developing work rules to encourage and protect specific investments by workers. But unions have threatened to strike (and actually have gone on strike) over wages and can extract a substantial fraction of Boeing profits.

It is unclear what percentage of Airbus's workforce is unionized. European labor regulations are stricter than regulations in the United States, providing greater protection of unionized employees. However, about 40 percent of work on Airbus planes is done by subcontractors, and about 40 percent of this work is on short-term agreements that can be canceled within a year. This fact serves to mitigate the effects of regulations.

Buyer Power

There are two categories of buyers, each of which has limited power. Many airlines own their own fleets, but many also lease aircraft from aircraft-leasing companies. These companies purchase airframes directly from the manufacturer and then lease the planes to the airlines, keeping the assets off the airlines' books. The major airlines and the largest leasing companies often place orders for dozens of planes at a time. One company's order can make up approximately 15 percent of all of Boeing's or Airbus's commercial airframe orders in a single year.

The fact that there are few substitutes works to the advantage of the manufacturers, but only to the point where it begins to compete with its rival manufacturer to maintain a minimum level of backlog orders. In addition, in times of economic downturns, buyers have the ability to cancel deliveries of aircraft, directly affecting the profitability of manufacturers.

Table 10.2 summarizes the five forces of the commercial aviation industry. As long as market conditions are favorable, Airbus and Boeing will prosper, threatened only by Bombardier and Embraer, and then only in a segment of their market.

Professional Sports

Our last example of industry analysis explores the popular world of professional sports. We focus on the four major U.S. sports leagues—Major League Baseball

TABLE 10.2
FIVE-FORCES ANALYSIS OF THE CHICAGO HOSPITAL MARKET

Force	Threat to Profits
Internal rivalry	Low to Medium
Entry	Low
Substitutes/complements	Medium
Supplier power	Medium
Buyer power	Medium

(MLB), the National Basketball Association (NBA), the National Football League (NFL), and the National Hockey League (NHL). Most of this analysis would apply equally well to sports leagues in other nations, such as European club football (i.e., soccer.)

Market Definition

It is difficult to define the markets in which professional sports teams compete. Each league competes for labor in a single national (or international) labor market, yet individual teams may be monopolists in the output of say, "professional football entertainment" in their home cities. We will bear in mind these distinctions as we address how each of the five forces affects firm and industry profits in the major professional sports.

Internal Rivalry

Competition on the playing field does not equate to competition in the business world. Exciting athletic competition that will attract fans requires considerable collusion among the teams. Teams must agree on rules and schedules; they employ the same pool of referees and share national broadcast revenues. A sports league also requires some degree of "competitive balance" to attract fan interest. This has given rise to rules and other arrangements (most notably "rookie drafts" that are discussed in more detail below) that are jointly designed and agreed-upon by all teams in the league. Teams *do not* collude on ticket prices, but they do not have to. When it comes to competition in output markets, most sports teams have substantial market power.

Most sports teams generate the lion's share of revenues from ticket sales. (The exception is the NFL, whose 32 teams split over $2 billion in annual payments from a consortium of television networks.) In a broad sense, teams compete for local entertainment dollars. For example, the Chicago Bulls professional basketball team vies for customers who might instead consider attending local blues, jazz and classical music concerts, theater, movies, restaurants, the DePaul Blue Demons college basketball games, and the Chicago Blackhawks professional hockey games. But the Bulls are monopolists in the market for Chicago professional basketball, and the elasticity of substitution between Bulls tickets and other entertainment events is modest.[3] Even teams that face direct competition in their local markets—for example, the Chicago White Sox and Chicago Cubs in major league baseball—have fiercely loyal fans who would hardly think of buying tickets to their cross-town rival's games just to save a few dollars. When it comes to selling tickets to see a major sport, nearly every team in the National Football League (NFL), National Basketball Association (NBA), Major League Baseball (MLB), and National Hockey League (NHL) has considerable market power.

When sports teams do compete against each other in the traditional business sense, the "playing field" is the market for labor. The market to employ athletes hardly fits the "textbook" model of competition. Athletes in all four major sports are unionized, so the market for their labor is subject to labor laws. These laws are particularly important when it comes to employment of new ballplayers (i.e., rookies). Labor laws permit managers and unionized workers in any U.S. industry, including professional sports, to set conditions for employment of new workers through their collective bargaining agreements. While this sounds unfair to rookies, this rule serves to facilitate competitive balance on the playing field by enabling weaker teams to hire the best rookies. Courts have routinely blocked attempts by rookies to undo these rules.

All sports fans know how the rookie market works. Each major sports league conducts a "rookie draft" at the conclusion of its season. Only players meeting certain criteria based on age and/or educational attainment are eligible to be drafted. Teams pick in inverse order of their past performance, so that the worst teams get to choose the best players, and all teams have one year exclusive rights to contract with their chosen players.[4] Depending on the league, rookies are afforded some latitude in negotiating their initial contract terms, including length and salary. Rookies have few alternatives if they do not wish to sign with the team that drafted them; mainly, they can refuse to play for one year (and lose one year's compensation), or they can sign with another league. Because these alternatives are generally very unattractive, sports teams have tremendous bargaining power over rookies. Some baseball teams, such as the Pittsburgh Pirates and Tampa Bay Devil Rays, have managed to remain reasonably prosperous, though they have not been especially successful on the playing field, by relying on low-priced young players. By contrast, some basketball teams, such as the Indiana Pacers, have shied away from drafting very young rookies, feeling that by the time these athletes develop into stars, their contracts will have expired and they will be free agents, able to sell themselves to the highest bidders.

Until about 25 years ago, all the major sports leagues had rules limiting the mobility of veterans. The NFL had the "Rozelle Rule," named for its famous commissioner Pete Rozelle, which required any team that signed a player from another team to pay compensation, often in the form of a future draft pick. The NBA and NHL had similar rules. By the early 1980s, these rules had been eliminated as part of collective bargaining agreements.

Baseball's route toward a free labor market was more circuitous. For years, professional baseball contracts contained a provision known as the reserve clause. If a player refused to sign the contract offered by his team, the reserve clause gave the team the right to automatically renew his expiring contract for the next year. The traditional interpretation of the reserve clause was that if a player continued to remain unsigned, a team could renew the old contract year after year in perpetuity. As a result, baseball players had virtually no bargaining power vis-à-vis their teams. The reserve clause explains why the immortal Babe Ruth never earned more than $100,000 per season—roughly $1 million today in inflation-adjusted dollars—far less than major league stars earn today.

In 1970, St. Louis Cardinals outfielder Curt Flood (who balked at being traded to the Philadelphia Phillies) filed an antitrust challenge to the reserve clause. In a confusing 1972 ruling, the Supreme Court cited Justice Learned Hand's old ruling that baseball was the "national pastime" and was therefore exempt from antitrust laws. For a time it appeared as if the reserve clause had dodged a bullet and would remain intact.

However, in 1975, two major league baseball pitchers, Andy Messersmith and Dave McNally, challenged the interpretation of the reserve clause, contending that the right to re-sign a player who refuses to sign a contract extended, not indefinitely as baseball owners had always contended, but for just one year. Arbitrator Peter Seitz agreed with the Messersmith–McNally interpretation, ruling that a ball club could renew an unsigned player's contract for just one year, after which the player would become a "free agent" who would be able to sell his services to the highest bidder. Seitz, who had been retained by Major League Baseball, was promptly fired, and baseball owners went to court to challenge his decision. In February 1976, a federal judge upheld Seitz's ruling, ushering in baseball's free agency era.

For many reasons, competition in the input market for free agents can be intense. There are numerous competitors—in principle every team in the league is a potential buyer. There is little differentiation—most players can be equally productive on any team and have little hometown loyalty. To make matters worse, whereas some owners run their teams to make money, others are in it to win a championship and are willing to lose some money to do it. There is nothing wrong with this—owning a sports team is a fine billionaire's hobby—but it makes it difficult for other owners to hold the line on payroll.

A few factors soften wage competition, however. Very few athletes can make a major impact on a team's chances of winning a championship; as a result, salaries for midlevel athletes fall well short of the salaries of superstars. Moreover, the number of serious competitors for a star athlete is limited. When superstar pitcher Pedro Martinez became a free agent after leading the Boston Red Sox to the 2004 World Series championship, only two or three teams entered the bidding war. (He signed with the New York Mets for $53 million over four years.) Martinez had the advantage that every team could benefit from another pitcher, yet he still aroused little interest. The situation is worse for position players. Slugging first baseman and World Series hero Paul Konerko of the Chicago White Sox was of interest only to those teams that did not already have a solid player at that position. Three teams ultimately made him offers, and he re-signed with the White Sox for $60 million over five years.

Ask any professional sports team owner and he or she will probably say that unchecked competition in the labor market makes it almost impossible to make a profit. This is why owners have been so adamant in seeking "salary caps" that limit the total amount teams can pay their players. The NHL owners went so far as to cancel the entire 2004–2005 season to force players to accept a salary cap. Through the salary cap, teams and players share the profits they enjoy from their monopoly status in the output market. The most important issue in contract negotiations between the NBA and NFL and their respective unions is the magnitude of the cap; this is what determines who gets the largest piece of the monopoly pie. Instead of a salary cap, baseball has a "luxury tax" that kicks in when a team's aggregate salaries exceed roughly $120 million. Thus far, only George Steinbrenner's New York Yankees have substantially exceeded this limit. In fact, many teams spend nowhere near this limit and, like the Pirates and Devil Rays, make little effort to field a team that has a legitimate chance to win the World Series.

Entry

Sports team owners are a motley group—there include media companies like Cablevision (owner of the NBA New York Knicks and NHL New York Rangers), Time Warner (MLB's Atlanta Braves), and the Tribune Corporation (MLB's Chicago Cubs), who view their sports holdings as integral parts of their entertainment empires.

The Green Bay Packers are owned by over 100,000 stockholders, mostly fans residing in Wisconsin. (Don't bother trying to become a part owner—the Packers are not issuing new shares, and existing shares may not be resold.)

Most owners are wealthy businessmen for whom owning a sports team is the ultimate high-priced hobby. They include Micky Aronson (heir to the Carnival Cruise empire and owner of the Miami Heat basketball team), real estate tycoon Malcolm Glazer (owner of the NFL Tampa Bay Buccaneers and, much to the chagrin of their fans, English Soccer League powerhouse Manchester United), and Microsoft co-founder Paul Allen (owner of the NFL Seattle Seahawks and NBA Portland Trailblazers). Perhaps the most famous billionaire owners are George Steinbrenner, shipping magnate turned infamous owner of the New York Yankees, and dot-com mogul Marc Cuban, who sits on the bench and prowls the locker room of his NBA Dallas Mavericks franchise.

There is no shortage of rich men (and the occasional rich woman) who want to enjoy the limelight of sports team ownership. But it is not so easy—the barriers to entry are very high. Each league has rules governing the addition of new franchises. Potential new owners must pay current owners hundreds of millions of dollars. Most potential owners also offer to build new stadiums, knowing that visiting team owners will share ticket revenues (and therefore might be more inclined to vote in favor of league expansion). Incumbent team owners usually have the right to veto new franchises in their own geographic markets, further hindering entry. Unable to start sports teams from scratch, billionaires looking to join a league are usually forced to purchase an existing team. Because the number of billionaires has increased faster than the supply of teams, the purchase prices have risen dramatically; a few teams like the NFL Dallas Cowboys and MLB New York Yankees would reportedly sell for over $1 billion. So even though many sports teams post operating losses, their owners are enjoying huge capital gains.

Short of buying an existing team, the only other way for a would-be sports entrepreneur to enter the professional sports market is to form an entire new league. This raises the stakes for entry considerably—most of the new teams must succeed or the entire league is likely to fail. Though the risks are high, the rewards can be even higher, and a number of leagues have come and gone over the years, including the World Football League, the United States Football League (USFL), the XFL, and the Arena Football League (the NFL is *very* profitable), the American Basketball Association (ABA), and the World Hockey League.

Entry barriers are so severe that new leagues feel the need to differentiate their product in order to survive: The ABA introduced the 3-point shot; the USFL played its games in late winter and spring, after the NFL's Super Bowl; the XFL presented a more violent game. The Arena Football League plays indoors on a field the size of a hockey rink.

Not every new league fails. The Arena Football League is nearly 20 years old, though few fans feel it is an adequate substitute for the NFL. The older American Football League (AFL) and, to a lesser extent, the ABA, can be considered success stories, and the paths to their success were very similar. The AFL began in 1960, just as the NFL's popularity was on the rise. The AFL took advantage of three problems with the NFL: the NFL had teams in just 13 cities, the NFL style downplayed the exciting passing game, and NFL players had yet to earn the rights to free agency and the high salaries that would result. The AFL attacked these weaknesses. The league began with eight teams, six of which were located in cities that did not have NFL franchises.[5] AFL teams emphasized passing, and the resulting high scoring games proved appealing to many fans. Even so, AFL teams lost money year after year. Following the dictum that you have to spend money to make money, in 1965 the AFL launched its most brazen attack on the NFL.

In the previous year, 1964, the AFL signed a $34 million television contract with NBC. (CBS had exclusive rights to NFL games.) AFL teams used the money to outbid the NFL for superstar players. New York Jets owner Sonny Werblin moved first by signing University of Alabama star quarterback Joe Namath to a deal paying an unprecedented $427,000 for the first year. When the AFL's Denver Broncos made a big offer to University of Illinois star Dick Butkus, the NFL assured the future Hall-of-Famer that he would receive "wheelbarrows" full of money if he signed with them. (He chose the NFL's Chicago Bears.) Soon, both leagues were giving wheelbarrows of money to stars like Roman Gabriel, John Brodie, and Pete Gogolak. After Oakland Raider head coach Al Davis became the AFL's commissioner in April 1966, the bidding wars intensified. The AFL, which was never profitable, took big losses, but it did not matter. The NFL was losing money for the first time in over a decade and sued for peace. In June 1966, the two leagues merged. The owners of AFL teams got what they wanted—the same fan base enjoyed by the NFL. In today's NFL, the American Football Conference still consists largely of former AFL teams.

The American Basketball Association (ABA) started in 1967. Like the AFL, most of the original 11 teams were located in non-NBA cities. Like the AFL, the ABA emphasized scoring, with a wide-open "up and down the court game" and the innovative 3-point shot. Like the AFL, the ABA paid big dollars to sign budding superstars such as "Dr. J" Julius Erving and scoring phenom Rick Barry. All of these strategies helped the ABA enjoy a loyal fan base. But playing in secondary markets like Pittsburgh, Louisville, and New Orleans, the national fan base was never large enough to generate a big television contract, and the league was unprofitable. The ABA did have one thing going for it that the AFL did not: Basketball fans had become disenchanted with the NBA, and attendance was falling. In 1977, when the NBA agreed to absorb four ABA teams, it hoped that the infusion of the upbeat style embodied by Dr. J would change the league's fortunes. Indeed, Dr. J's popularity heralded a new era for basketball, based on stars rather than teams. The later success of the NBA and superstars like Magic Johnson, Larry Bird, Michael Jordan, and Kobe Bryant can be traced to the product differentiation strategy that embodied the short-lived ABA.

It is hard to fathom how a new sports league today could match even the modest success of the ABA. All the major sports leagues have blanketed the nation with teams. The NFL even has "minor league" teams in Europe. Free agency means that star players are sure to make at least as much money signing with major leagues as they could with any upstart league. And except for MLB, the leagues are constantly changing rules to assure a pleasing style of play. As a result, opportunities for favorable geographic or product differentiation by a new league are virtually nonexistent. Leagues have attempted to differentiate by time of year—notably the USFL and the XFL—but either because the product was poor or fans had already moved on to other sports, these efforts failed.

Substitutes and Complements

Professional sports teams compete for entertainment dollars. Owners worry not only about the product on the field, but also the overall entertainment experience. One of the first owners to fully realize sports as entertainment was Tex Schramm, the legendary general manager of the Dallas Cowboys. In the early 1970s, Schramm hired

334 • Chapter 10 • Industry Analysis

professional models to cheer from the sidelines. The models were unaccustomed to the Dallas heat, however, and were quickly exhausted. In 1972, Schramm decided to create a squad of professional dancers. The Dallas Cowboy Cheerleaders first appeared in 1973, and the rest is history—there is even a movie about these athletic beauties. Today's professional sporting events feature skilled cheerleaders, musical performances, costumed mascots (most famously, the San Diego Chicken), and fan participation events during game breaks. Off the court entertainment is so important that during the depths of the post–Michael Jordan basketball era, the Chicago Bulls still sold out most games, thanks, in part, to the circus-like atmosphere at the United Center.

There are many complements to professional sports. The most successful sports league in the United States, the NFL, is helped by two important complements. One is television. The Super Bowl is the top-rated television show every year, and playoff games and Monday Night Football also enjoy huge ratings. But football would not enjoy its phenomenal success without one other complement—gambling. Over $2 billion is bet legally on sports every year, mostly on the NFL and mostly through Las Vegas "sports books." This is just the tip of the iceberg; estimates of illegal sports betting (including gray market gambling through offshore Internet sites) exceed $100 billion, again mostly on the NFL. Millions of bets may be placed on each regular season NFL game and probably ten times that many for the Super Bowl.[6] With this many people betting so much money, it is no wonder that NFL games get huge television audiences, even when the home team is not playing.

Gambling poses a dilemma for professional sports. While gambling boosts fan interest, league management perpetually fears that players will come under the influence of bookmakers and intentionally throw a game in exchange for a big payday. If fans thought that the outcomes of games were determined by bribes, rather than the play on the field, the foundation of sports would crumble. The 1919 "Black Sox" scandal, which resulted when eight Chicago White Sox baseball players were accused of taking bribes (seven of whom admitted to the fact), nearly took down the sport. It took the charismatic Babe Ruth and his prodigious bat to revive MLB's fortunes. More recently, Pete Rose, arguably one of the best ballplayers of all time, was banned from the Hall of Fame for gambling on baseball.

Gambling may pose an even bigger dilemma for college sports. Most professional athletes are paid well enough to have little cause to take money from bookmakers. (This was not true in 1919, when professional gambler "Sport Sullivan" offered White Sox players at least $10,000 apiece to throw the World Series, at a time when team owner Charlie Comiskey paid his best player, "Shoeless" Joe Jackson, only $6000 annually.[7]) But college players have little guarantee of reaching the pros, and the temptation of a big payday is large. In the late 1990s, two starters on the Northwestern University basketball team were charged with "point shaving," intentionally losing games by large margins in exchange for cash payments from bettors.[8]

Supplier Power

We have discussed the most powerful suppliers, the players' unions, at length. Most players are trained in college, making undergraduates sports teams a critical supplier to professional sports. The National Collegiate Athletic Association (NCAA), which governs all undergraduate athletics, has been a benign supplier. At worst, it has pressured major league sports not to draft underclassmen, but it has never broached the topic of direct financial support from the major leagues.

Cities are another major supplier to sports teams. Most local politicians believe that local sports teams add significantly to their economies, despite research suggesting that the economic benefits are vastly overstated, and are willing to use taxpayer dollars to subsidize new sports stadiums.[9] Such payments have precedent in American business—witness the millions of dollars in subsidies or tax breaks given to companies to build factories or relocate headquarters. But the amounts spent on sports stadiums are staggering, often reaching several hundred million dollars. This may change. Municipal finances have gone south in the past decade, owing to rising spending on health and education and ongoing resistance to tax increases. At the same time, local politicians are gradually learning that the benefits of new stadiums are largely illusory. The result is that sports owners can no longer count on local governments to build their stadiums and must increasingly rely on corporate sponsorships or their own personal wealth.

Buyer Power

There are four major television networks and three major sports cable systems (ESPN, Comcast, and FoxSportsNet). They often compete head-to-head to obtain the national broadcast rights for major sports. Most networks view professional sports as a loss leader and are willing to pay huge sums to get sports fans to associate the network's name with specific sports. ABC's Monday Night Football is the best example, but the "NFL on CBS" and other associations also come to mind. Given that at any time of the year there are more networks than there are leagues in action, the upper hand in these negotiations will belong to the sports leagues. The same applies to negotiations over the right to broadcast games locally on television and radio.

Conclusion

Loyal fans and league bylaws give sports teams the kind of product market differentiation and entry barriers that sellers of other goods and services envy. Teams can set prices well above marginal costs year after year, only to have the resulting profits bargained away by powerful unions. But such buyer power cannot explain why so many sports teams report operating losses year after year. To explain this, we have to remember that many owners are not in the business to make money. Owner-hobbyists are in it to win, and spending an additional $10 million on a top free agent will not deter them. As long as the supply of billionaires keeps up, sports owners should continue to expect operating losses and capital gains.

Table 10.3 summarizes the five-forces analysis.

TABLE 10.3
FIVE-FORCES ANALYSIS OF PROFESSIONAL SPORTS LEAGUES

Force	Threat to Profits
Internal rivalry	Low (output markets); High (input markets)
Entry	Low
Substitutes/complements	Low
Buyer power	Low
Supplier power	Low (except for players' unions)

CHAPTER SUMMARY

◆ An industry analysis provides an overview of the potential profitability of the average firm in an industry.

◆ A comprehensive analysis examines the five forces: internal rivalry, entry, substitutes, buyer power, and supplier power. The latter four operate independently and may also intensify internal rivalry.

◆ Internal rivalry is fierce if competition drives prices toward costs. This is more likely when there are many firms, products are perceived to be homogeneous, consumers are motivated and able to shop around, prices may be set secretly, sales orders are large and received infrequently, and the industry has excess capacity.

◆ The threat of entry is high if firms can easily enter an industry and capture market share from profitable incumbents while intensifying price competition.

◆ Substitutes also capture sales and intensify price rivalry.

◆ Buyers and suppliers exert power directly by renegotiating the terms of contracts to extract profits from profitable industries, and indirectly by shopping around for the best prices.

◆ The government can affect profitability and should be considered either as part of the five forces or as a separate force.

◆ Profits may be threatened by any or all of the five forces. Although it is useful to construct a "five-forces scorecard" on which the forces can be rated, the exercise of assessing the five forces is more important than the actual scores. Through this exercise, the analyst develops deep knowledge of key strategic issues affecting the industry in question.

◆ A sound five-forces analysis should be based on economic principles. The tools for analyzing internal rivalry, entry, and substitutes are derived from industrial organization and game theory, which are discussed in Chapters 6 through 9. The tools for analyzing buyer and supplier power are derived from the economics of vertical relationships, which were discussed in Chapters 3 and 4.

QUESTIONS

1. It has been said that Porter's five-forces analysis turns antitrust law on its head. What do you think this means?

2. Comment on the following: All of wisdom contained in the five-forces framework is reflected in the economic identity:

$$\text{Profit} = (\text{Price} - \text{Average Cost}) \times \text{Quantity}$$

3. How does the magnitude of scale economies affect the intensity of each of the five forces?

4. How does capacity utilization affect the intensity of internal rivalry? the extent of entry barriers?

5. How does the magnitude of consumer switching costs affect the intensity of internal rivalry? of entry?

6. How do exit barriers affect internal rivalry? entry?

7. Consider an industry whose demand fluctuates over time. Suppose that this industry faces high supplier power. Briefly state how this high supplier power will affect the variability of profits over time.

8. What does the concept of "coopetition" add to the five-forces approach to industry analysis?

9. Coopetition often requires firms to communicate openly. How is this different from collusion? How can antitrust enforcers distinguish between coopetition and collusion?

10. The following listing reports the approximate distribution of profits (on a per disc basis) for different steps in the vertical chain for music compact discs:

Artist: $.60
Record company: $1.80
Retailer: $.60

Use the five forces to explain this pattern. (*Note*: There are about half a dozen major record companies. They are responsible for signing up artists, handling technical aspects of recording, securing distribution, and promoting the recordings.)

APPENDIX
TEMPLATE FOR DOING A FIVE-FORCES ANALYSIS

FACTORS AFFECTING RIVALRY AMONG EXISTING COMPETITORS

To what extent does pricing rivalry or nonprice competition (e.g., advertising) erode the profitability of a typical firm in this industry?

	Characterization (Current)	Future Trend
Degree of seller concentration?		
Rate of industry growth?		
Significant cost differences among firms?		
Excess capacity?		
Cost structure of firms: sensitivity of costs to capacity utilization?		
Degree of product differentiation among sellers? Brand loyalty to existing sellers? Cross-price elasticities of demand among competitors in industry?		
Buyers' costs of switching from one competitor to another?		
Are prices and terms of sales transactions observable?		
Can firms adjust prices quickly?		
Large and/or infrequent sales orders?		
Use of "facilitating practices" (price leadership, advance announcement of price changes)?		
History of "cooperative" pricing?		
Strength of exit barriers?		
High industry price elasticity of demand?		

FACTORS AFFECTING THE THREAT OF ENTRY

To what extent does the threat or incidence of entry work to erode the profitability of a typical firm in this industry?

	Characterization (Current)	Future Trend
Significant economies of scale?		
Importance of reputation or established brand loyalties in purchase decision?		
Entrants' access to distribution channels?		
Entrants' access to raw materials?		
Entrants' access to technology/know-how?		
Entrants' access to favorable locations?		
Experience-based advantages of incumbents?		
Network externalities: demand-side advantages to incumbents from large installed base?		
Government protection of incumbents?		
Perceptions of entrants about expected retaliation of incumbents/reputations of incumbents for "toughness"?		

FACTORS AFFECTING OR REFLECTING PRESSURE FROM SUBSTITUTE PRODUCTS AND SUPPORT FROM COMPLEMENTS

To what extent does competition from substitute products outside the industry erode the profitability of a typical firm in the industry?

	Characterization (Current)	Future Trend
Availability of close substitutes?		
Price-value characteristics of substitutes?		
Price elasticity of industry demand?		
Availability of close complements?		
Price-value characteristics of complements?		

FACTORS AFFECTING OR REFLECTING POWER OF INPUT SUPPLIERS

To what extent do individual suppliers have the ability to negotiate high input prices with typical firms in this industry? To what extent do input prices deviate from those that would prevail in a perfectly competitive input market in which input suppliers act as price takers?

	Characterization (Current)	Future Trend
Is supplier industry more concentrated than industry it sells to?		
Do firms in industry purchase relatively small volumes relative to other customers of supplier? Is typical firm's purchase volume small relative to sales of typical supplier?		
Few substitutes for suppliers' input?		
Do firms in industry make relationship-specific investments to support transactions with specific suppliers?		
Do suppliers pose credible threat of forward integration into the product market?		
Are suppliers able to price-discriminate among prospective customers according to ability/willingness to pay for input?		

FACTORS AFFECTING OR REFLECTING POWER OF BUYERS

To what extent do individual buyers have the ability to negotiate low purchase prices with typical firms in this industry? To what extent do purchase prices differ from those that would prevail in a market with a large number of fragmented buyers in which buyers act as price takers?

	Characterization (Current)	Future Trend
Is buyers' industry more concentrated than the industry it purchases from?		
Do buyers purchase in large volumes? Does a buyer's purchase volume represent a large fraction of the typical seller's sales revenue?		
Can buyers find substitutes for industry's product?		
Do firms in industry make relationship-specific investments to support transactions with specific buyers?		
Is price elasticity of demand of buyer's product high or low?		
Do buyers pose credible threat of backward integration?		
Does product represent significant fraction of cost in buyer's business?		
Are prices in the market negotiated between buyers and sellers on each individual transaction, or do sellers post a "take-it-or-leave-it" price that applies to all transactions?		

ENDNOTES

[1] Community hospitals treat a variety of patients on a short-term basis. Another type of hospital not considered here is the psychiatric hospital.

[2] Benkard, L. "Learning and Forgetting: The Dynamics of Airplane Production," *American Economic Review*, September 2000.

[3] The Chicago Sky, a new team in the Women's NBA, does not play during the same time of the year.

[4] There are nuances in some sports, as in basketball where the worst teams participate in a "lottery" to decide which one gets the top pick. The Cleveland Cavaliers won the lottery in 2003 and selected LeBron James with the top pick, immediately rejuvenating a struggling franchise.

[5] The cities with overlapping franchises were New York and Los Angeles. By 1962, the Los Angeles franchise had moved to San Diego. In 1960, the NFL added a new franchise in Dallas, one of the original AFL cities. In 1963, the AFL Dallas franchise moved to Kansas City.

[6] Just one web site, http://BETonSPORTS.com, totaled over 500,000 wagers for the 2005 Super Bowl.

[7] As it turned out, Sullivan initially paid a total of $10,000 to eight players. Most of the Sox involved in the scandal still went along with the plan, except apparently for Jackson. Sullivan eventually came up with more money, and Cincinnati won the series five games to three.

[8] In both cases, bettors gambled that Northwestern would lose by more than 14 points. By intentionally missing shots or turning the ball over to the other team, the players involved made sure that Northwestern lost by more than 14 points. Two other nonstarters on the basketball team were also implicated. In an unrelated matter, a former Northwestern football player was charged with betting against his own team in the early 1990s and taking actions (such as deliberately fumbling the football) aimed at increasing the odds that his team would lose. We are obliged to point out that Northwestern is not the only school where such scandals have occurred.

[9] The typical argument by politicians is that sports stadiums generate millions of dollars in ticket sales for the local economy. This ignores the fact that virtually all ticket buyers live in the community and would have spent their entertainment dollars on some other local activity had there been no sports. Moreover, many, if not most, athletes do not live in the community, so much of the ticket revenues flow out of the local market. This would not be the case for money spent on, say, restaurants or local theater.

PART THREE

STRATEGIC POSITION AND DYNAMICS

STRATEGIC POSITIONING FOR COMPETITIVE ADVANTAGE

11

*U*ntil the U.S. airline industry was deregulated in 1978, most major domestic airlines competed in the same way. With entry and prices controlled by the Civil Aeronautics Board (a regulatory agency that no longer exists), airlines competed by scheduling more frequent and convenient departures and by enhancing amenities, such as meals and movies. Deregulation of the industry led to new entry and new ways of doing business. Consider, for example, the variety of competitive strategies airlines have pursued since deregulation:

- American Airlines (currently the largest domestic carrier with a market share of about 18 percent) developed a nationwide route structure organized around the hub-and-spoke concept. It built traveler loyalty through its frequent-flier program, and it attempted to maximize revenue through its sophisticated computerized reservation system (known as SABRE) and its state-of-the-art yield management capabilities.

- Southwest, an intrastate carrier operating only in Texas before deregulation, expanded incrementally to selected cities in the Midwest and Southwest by flying into little-used airports such as Chicago's Midway Airport. Eschewing the hub-and-spoke concept, Southwest flies passengers from one city to another in one or two short hops. With less restrictive work rules than other major airlines, a highly motivated workforce, and a fleet that consists only of Boeing 737s to economize on maintenance and training, Southwest has average operating costs that are among the lowest in the industry. (See Figure 11.1 which shows yield, unit costs, and market shares for major U.S. airlines in the first quarter of 2004.) Its flights offer few amenities other than drinks and cheerful attendants, and rather than attempting to capture traveler loyalty with frequent-flier programs, Southwest emphasizes low fares and reliable on-time service.

FIGURE 11.1

UNIT COSTS, YIELDS, AND MARKET SHARES IN THE U.S. AIRLINE INDUSTRY, 2004

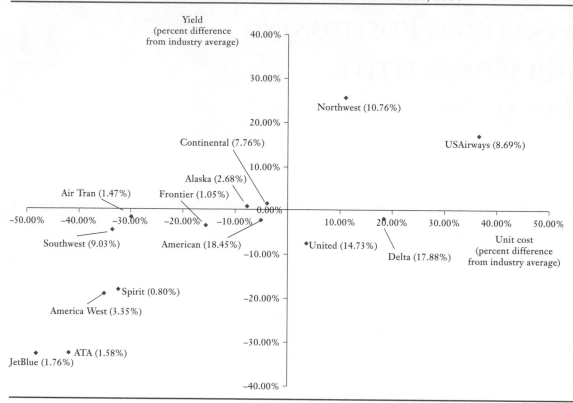

This graph shows unit costs and yields for major U.S. airlines for the first quarter of 2004. Unit costs and yields are expressed as a percentage difference from the industry average. Each airline is represented by a print in the graph. The market share of the airline is shown in parentheses next to each airline's name.

Source: Bureau of Transporation Statistics, U.S. Department of Transportation.

- Prior to deregulation, Northwest (then known as Northwest Orient) was primarily an international carrier with a relatively small number of domestic routes that fed into its routes between Asia and cities in the Pacific Northwest. After deregulation, Northwest grew through acquistions of domestic carriers (e.g., Republic Airlines) and developed a domestic route network with hubs in Minneapolis and Detroit. Still, the size of that network lagged behind those of the "Big Three"—American, United, and Delta—so throughout the 1980s and 1990s, Northwest was considered to be among the second tier of trunk airlines (along with USAir and Continental) that sought to offer transcontinental service based on a hub-and-spoke system. More recently, Northwest has changed its strategy, and rather than emphasizing transcontinental service, it now attempts to avoid competition with other large carriers by emphasizing point-to-point service between cities in the upper Midwest of the United States that are underserved by other airlines.[1]

- JetBlue Airways, a well-financed start-up airline launched in February 2000, has outfitted its airplanes (brand-new Airbus A320s) with leather seats and free satellite-television programming from DIRECTV. JetBlue serves a limited set of cities (18 cities in 9 states), and with much of its traffic originating from New

York's JFK Airport, JetBlue has tried to a convey an "edgy" urban "attitude" to appeal to tough, jaded New Yorkers. Within six months of its founding, JetBlue had turned a profit, and despite the events of September 11, JetBlue ended 2001 in the black. In 2004, JetBlue was among the most profitable U.S airlines. (See Figure 11.2 for sales revenues and profitability of selected U.S. airlines.)

This example illustrates several fundamentally different ways in which firms can position themselves to compete within the same industry. With its extensive route network and its emphasis on loyalty-inducing devices, American attempts to differentiate its services from those of its competitors by offering an attractive frequent-flier program (a program whose benefits are dramatically enhanced by American's vast domestic and international network) and by providing a level of comfort (more leg room, better food) that makes the experience of flying tolerable. Ordinarily, these characteristics would enable American to offer seats at a price premium relative to other airlines. However, during the recession that the airline industry has experienced since 2000, American has aggressively cut fares in order to keep its planes full so that it can realize the economies of scale inherent in the hub and-spoke system. As a result, American's yield, which historically has been above the industry average, was slightly below average in 2004.

In contrast to American, Northwest has a narrower geographic scope, and with its smaller, shorter-distance markets and deemphasis on transcontinental service, it tends

FIGURE 11.2
REVENUE AND PROFITABILITY IN THE U.S. AIRLINE INDUSTRY, 2004

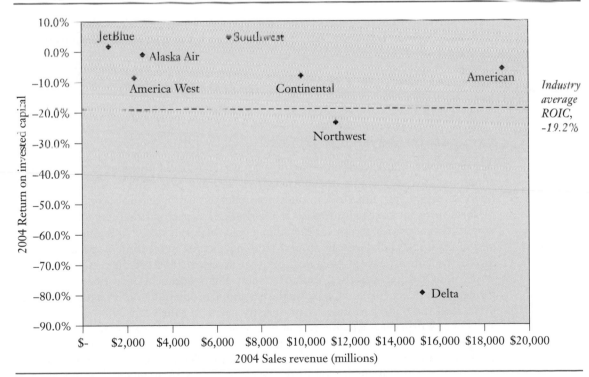

This graph shows sales revenue and profitability (as measured by return on assets) for major U.S. airlines for 2004.

Source: Hoovers Guide, www.hoovers.com

to have relatively more business travelers among its fliers. As a result, Northwest currently has the highest yield of all U.S. airlines. Unfortunately, it also has one of the highest unit costs.

Southwest's geographic scope is also narrower than American's, and like Northwest, it has attempted to serve markets that its larger competitors have bypassed. Unlike Northwest, however, the basis of Southwest's success has been a cost advantage that allows it to offer low fares and still make a profit. JetBlue is even more sharply focused than Northwest and Southwest, and it explicitly positions itself to appeal to the tastes of fliers originating in its New York market.

Of course, not all of these positions have been equally profitable. Throughout the 1990s, Southwest Airlines and American enjoyed rates of profitability that exceeded industry averages, whereas Northwest's profit performance lagged behind that of the rest of the industry. During the post–2000 industry recession, Southwest and JetBlue have been profitable (see Figure 11.2), while Northwest has incurred losses that exceed the industry average. American has also been unprofitable (a reflection of just how hard the recession has hit the large network airlines); however, its losses have been somewhat less than the industry average.

This chapter develops a conceptual framework for characterizing and analyzing a firm's strategic position within an industry. This framework employs simple economic concepts to identify conditions necessary for competitive advantage in a market. The chapter is organized in three sections. The first defines the concept of competitive advantage and argues that to achieve it a firm must create more value than its rivals. The ability to create value is shaped by how firms position themselves to compete in an industry. The second section discusses the economic and organizational logic of two broad alternative approaches to positioning: cost leadership and benefit leadership. The third section explores broad coverage versus focus strategies. An appendix to this chapter presents specific tools for diagnosing a firm's cost and benefit position in its market.

◆ ◆ ◆ ◆ ◆ COMPETITIVE ADVANTAGE

Competitive Advantage Defined

The five-forces framework presented in Chapter 10 is based on the idea that industry conditions are an important determinant of a firm's profitability. This premise is undoubtedly correct: firms in some industries, such as pharmaceuticals, consistently outperform firms in other industries, such as airlines. However, profitability does not only vary across industries; it also varies within a particular industry. For example, over the period 2000–2004, Safeway in grocery retailing, Amgen in biotechnology, and Merck in pharmaceuticals earned rates of profit that exceeded those of their industry peers, while in these same industries A&P, Millenium Pharmaceuticals, and Pfizer underperformed their peers. Table 11.1 shows the economic profitability of firms that have outperformed and underperformed their industry peers over the years 2000–2004.[2]

When a firm earns a higher rate of economic profit than the average rate of economic profit of other firms competing within the same market, the firm has a *competitive advantage* in that market. Careful application of this definition, of course, requires an economically sensible definition of the firm's market, a topic taken up in Chapter 6. For example, to assess whether Sun has a competitive advantage in its core business of designing and selling high-end enterprise servers, we would compare Sun's

TABLE 11.1
ECONOMIC PROFITABILITY WITHIN AND ACROSS INDUSTRIES, 2000–2004

Industry	High Performers		Low Performers	
	Firm	Return on invested capital minus cost of capital (percent) 2000–2004	Firm	Return on invested capital minus cost of capital (percent) 2000–2004
Tobacco Products	UST	23.26	Altria Group	6.67
Computers	Dell	21.57	Apple Computer	−14.41
Computer Software	Microsoft	20.25	Siebel Systems	−22.78
Soft Drinks	Coca-Cola	13.70	Pepsico	4.02
Pharmaceuticals	Merck	13.30	Pfizer	−0.78
Credit Card Issuers	MBNA	10.77	Providian Financial	2.73
Beer	Anheuser-Busch	9.36	Molson Coors	1.84
Steel	Nucor	7.75	United States Steel	−1.58
Household Products	Colgate-Palmolive	7.29	Clorox	0.48
Aerospace and Defense	General Dynamics	7.26	Lockheed Martin	−1.95
Health Care Equipment and Supplies	Guidant	7.25	Boston Scientific	−0.14
Building Supplies Superstores	Home Depot	6.90	Lowe's	3.78
Integrated Oil Producers	Marathon Oil Corporation	6.74	Exxon Mobil	2.60
Biotechnology	Amgen	5.54	Millenium Pharmaceuticals	−23.28
Automobile Components	Magna International	5.07	Lear Corporation	1.72
Mass Merchandising	Wal-Mart	5.02	Target	1.54
Discount Department Stores	Kohls	4.11	J.C. Penney	−3.56
Dollar Stores	Family Dollar Stores	3.96	Dollar General	2.85
Copper Mining	Freeport-McMoRan	3.87	Phelps Dodge	−1.30
Pharmacy and Drug Retailing	Walgreens	3.65	Rite Aid	−2.81
Chemicals	Lubrizol	2.68	Dow Chemical	−2.89
Personal Care Products	The Estee-Lauder Companies	2.53	Revlon	−6.27
Department Stores	Neiman-Marcus	2.30	Federated Department Stores	−2.47
Grocery Retailing	Safeway	2.17	Great Atlantic & Pacific Tea Company	−3.26
Newspapers	New York Times	2.12	Dow Jones & Co.	−3.12
Electrical Equipment	Emerson Electric	1.96	Rockwell Automation	−5.22
Containers	Ball Corp.	1.61	Crown Holdings	−1.97

(continued)

TABLE 11.1
CONTINUED

Industry	High Performers		Low Performers	
	Firm	Return on invested capital minus cost of capital (percent) 2000–2004	Firm	Return on invested capital minus cost of capital (percent) 2000–2004
Appliances	Whirlpool	1.22	Maytag	0.93
Trucking	J.B. Hunt	1.10	Swift Transportation	− 0.41
Semiconductors	Intel	0.95	Advanced Micro Devices	− 12.72
Office Supply Superstores	Staples	0.16	OfficeMax	− 3.04
Paper and Forest Products	Louisiana-Pacific	− 0.23	Georgia-Pacific	− 1.51
Railroads	Burlington Northern Santa Fe	− 0.68	CSX	− 2.30
Aluminum	Alcoa	− 1.40	Kaiser Aluminum	− 5.13
Book Retailing	Borders Group	− 1.94	Amazon.com	− 14.26
Airlines	Southwest	− 2.23	UAL Corp.	− 7.26
Automobiles	Ford Motor Co.	− 2.31	Daimler-Chrysler	− 4.63
Toys	Mattel	− 3.31	Hasbro	− 3.86
Network Equipment	Cisco Systems	− 7.66	Nortel Networks	− 16.98
Satellite Radio	XM Satellite Radio	− 26.54	Sirius Satellite Radio	− 28.88

profitability in this business to the profitability of the business units within firms such as IBM and Hewlett-Packard that also sell enterprise servers and whose fortunes are materially affected by Sun's pricing and marketing decisions.

Figure 11.3 summarizes the framework that we develop in this chapter. According to this framework, a firm's economic profitability within a particular market depends on the economic attractiveness or unattractiveness of the market in which it competes (as summarized by a five-forces analysis) and on its competitive position in that market (i.e., whether it has a competitive advantage or disadvantage). Whether a firm has a competitive advantage or disadvantage depends on whether it is more or less successful than rivals at creating and delivering economic value. As we will see, a firm that can create and deliver more economic value than its competitors can simultaneously earn higher profits and offer higher net benefits to consumers than its competitors can.

What Matters More for Profitability: The Market or the Firm?

The framework in Figure 11.3 implies that the economics of the firm's market and the firm's position in that market jointly determine the firm's profitability. But how would we determine which is more important?

FIGURE 11.3
FRAMEWORK FOR COMPETITIVE ADVANTAGE

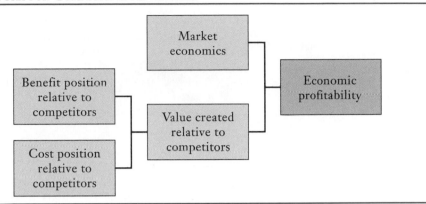

A firm's profitability depends jointly on the economics of its market and its success in creating more value than its competitors. The amount of value the firm creates compared to competitors depends on its cost and benefits position relative to competitors.

To answer this question, imagine taking a broad sample of different firms over many years and calculating their profitability (e.g., using standard accounting measures, such as return on assets, or more sophisticated tools, such as Economic Value Added, aimed at measuring profitability). Would we see considerable variation in profitability of business units *within industries* but little variation in profitability *across industries?* If so, the effect of the market environment on profitability (the market effect) is unimportant, but the effect of a firm's competitive position in the industry (the positioning effect) is important. Or would we see little variation in profitability of firms within industries but lots of variation in profitability across industries? If so, the market effect is paramount, and the positioning effect is unimportant.

In fact, both market and positioning effects can explain profitability. The profitability of business units varies within the same industry and across industries. Research by Anita McGahan and Michael Porter, summarized in Figure 11.4, suggests that the industry is responsible for about 18 percent of the variation in profit across firms, while competitive position accounts for about 32 percent of the variation in profit.[3] Other potential systematic influences on profitability, such as year-to-year variation in profit due to changes in macroeconomic conditions, or the firm's corporate parentage (e.g., does it make a difference for Post Cereal's profit whether it is owned by Kraft or some other corporation), have a relatively small impact. Note that a large component (almost 43 percent) of the variation in profitability across firms is unsystematic. This component represents variation that cannot be accounted for by any systematic influence. For example, Kraft's Post Cereal unit might earn a high profit in 2005 but a lower profit in 2006, not because of a change in its competitive position within the ready-to-eat cereal market or poor macroeconomic circumstances, but simply because of "bad luck."

The fact that both the market and positioning effects are important drivers of profitability reinforces the need to flesh out the framework in Figure 11.3. We now proceed to do this.

FIGURE 11.4
INDUSTRY AND BUSINESS UNIT EFFECTS IN EXPLAINING PROFITABILITY

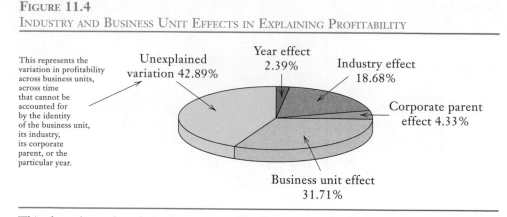

This chart shows the relative importance of business unit and industry effects in explaining variations in profitability across firms. The industry accounts for about 19 percent of profit variation across a large sample of firms and business units, while the competitive position of the business unit accounts for about 32 percent of the variation in profit.

◆ ◆ ◆ ◆ ◆ COMPETITIVE ADVANTAGE AND VALUE CREATION: CONCEPTUAL FOUNDATIONS

The purpose of a business, Peter Drucker writes, is to create a customer.[4] Businesses do this by creating and delivering economic value. They survive and prosper when they capture a portion of this value in the form of profits. As Figure 11.3 suggests, businesses that are successful in creating more value than competitors will attain an advantaged position relative to competitors in the marketplace. To illustrate why, we need to define *value creation* and show how it relates to competitive advantage. To do this, we must first discuss maximum willingness-to-pay and consumer surplus.

Maximum Willingness-to-Pay and Consumer Surplus

A particular software package is worth $150 to you. If its market price was $80, you would buy it. The purchase makes you better off because you have given up $80 to receive something more valuable—a software package worth $150 to you. The extent by which you are better off—in this case $150 − $80, or $70—is your *consumer surplus*.

More formally, let B denote a dollar measure of what one unit of the product is worth to a particular consumer, or equivalently, the consumer's maximum willingness-to-pay for the product. To understand what maximum willingness-to-pay means, let's see how we might assess a consumer's maximum willingness-to-pay for a Honda Accord. Our consumer starts off with no automobile of any kind and is then given, free of charge, a Honda Accord. She is certainly better off than before. Now, let's successively take money away from her. At some point, perhaps after we've taken away $30,500, she deems her situation (owning a Honda but with $30,500 less wealth) completely equivalent to her original situation (no Honda but with her wealth intact). That dollar amount—$30,500—represents our consumer's maximum willingness-to-pay for a Honda Accord and would be her assessment of the Accord's B.

Let's explore another example of maximum willingness-to-pay—and a somewhat different way to arrive at a numerical estimate of it—but now for an intermediate good that is used as an input in the production of a finished product. Consider, for example, a producer of soft drinks—say Cadbury Schweppes, the producer of 7-Up and Dr Pepper—that uses corn syrup sold by Archer Daniel's Midland (ADM) as a sweetener for its products. What is the maximum amount that Cadbury Schweppes would be willing to pay for ADM's corn syrup before switching from corn syrup to an alternative sweetener? Suppose that Cadbury Schweppes's best available alternative to using corn syrup is to use sugar. Let's further suppose that as far as the end consumer of soft drinks is concerned, Cadbury Schweppes's choice of sugar or corn syrup is immaterial; the final product—for example, 7-Up or Dr Pepper—tastes exactly the same. Given this, the Cadbury Schweppes's maximum willingness-to-pay for ADM's corn syrup (i.e., the B for ADM's corn syrup) depends on the cost economics of corn syrup versus the cost economics of sugar.

Figure 11.5 shows how. Suppose Cadbury Schweppes's best available alternative to corn syrup is sugar. The left-hand side of Figure 11.5 shows the economics of production when Cadbury Schweppes uses sugar to manufacture its soft drinks. In particular, when the cost of sugar is 3 euros per hundredweight, the "all-in" production cost using sugar (the sum of the costs of sugar, other materials, processing, and packaging) is 17 euros per hundredweight of soft drink. The right-hand side shows that by using corn syrup, Cadbury Schweppes incurs a somewhat higher processing cost and a somewhat higher cost of other materials. What is the most that Cadbury Schweppes

FIGURE 11.5
A SOFT DRINK PRODUCER'S MAXIMUM WILLINGNESS-TO-PAY FOR CORN SYRUP

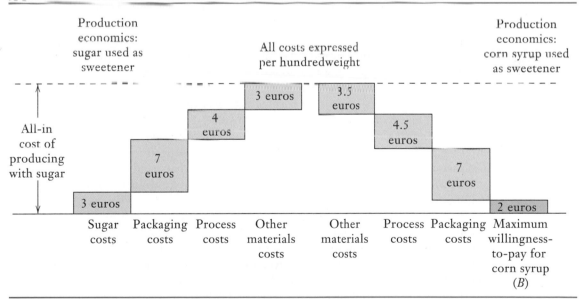

A cola maker's maximum willingness-to-pay for corn syrup (i.e., its B) is represented by the height of the shaded bar at the far right. At this price of corn syrup, the cola producer is just indifferent between producing cola with corn syrup and producing cola with the best available substitute for corn syrup, namely sugar. If the price of corn syrup were any higher, the cola maker would not purchase corn syrup and would use sugar instead.

would be willing to pay for ADM's corn syrup? Figure 11.5 shows that it would be willing to pay at most 2 euros per hundredweight, that is, $B = 2$. This is the price of corn syrup at which Cadbury Schweppes's "all-in" production cost using ADM's corn syrup is the same as its "all-in" production cost using sugar. If the price of ADM's corn syrup was any higher than 2 euros per hundredweight, Cadbury Schweppes would save money by switching to sugar as its sweetener.

The unifying feature of both the Honda Accord and corn syrup examples is that the maximum willingness-to-pay for a firm's product is the answer to the question: "At what price is the consumer just indifferent between buying the product and going without it?" As the corn syrup example shows, developing an explicit answer to that question will often require that we explore, from a buyer's perspective, the economics of the best available substitute to the product whose maximum willingness-to-pay we are seeking to determine. As those economics change, a buyer's maximum willingness-to-pay for the product will change as well. For instance, a change in the price of sugar will change the maximum willingness-to-pay for ADM's corn syrup.

From Maximum Willingness-to-Pay to Consumer Surplus

If we let P denote the product's monetary price, consumer surplus is the difference $B - P$. For example, if the price of the Honda Accord is $21,000, the consumer surplus of our hypothetical consumer would be $30,500 - $21,000 = $9,500. This example suggests a simple model of consumer behavior: a consumer will purchase a product only if the product's consumer surplus is positive. Moreover, given a choice between two or more competing products, the consumer will purchase the one for which consumer surplus, $B - P$, is largest.

Whether its customers are firms or individuals, a seller must deliver consumer surplus to compete successfully. The value map in Figure 11.6 illustrates the competitive implications of consumer surplus. The vertical axis shows the monetary price P of the product. Each point in the value map corresponds to a particular price–quality combination. The solid upward-sloping line in Figure 11.6 is called an *indifference curve*. For a given consumer, any price–quality combination along the indifference curve yields the same consumer surplus (i.e., has the same $B - P$). In Figure 11.6, products A and B offer the same $B - P$. A consumer choosing among products located along the indifference curve would thus be indifferent among the offerings. A product offering a price–quality combination located below a given indifference curve (e.g., product C) yields a higher consumer surplus than that yielded by products along the indifference curve. From the consumer's perspective, product C provides superior value to products A and B (and, as we will soon see, product D as well). A product offering a price–quality combination located above a given indifference curve (e.g., product D) yields a consumer surplus lower than that yielded by products along the indifference curve. From the consumer's perspective, such products provide inferior value. From the consumer's perspective, product D provides inferior value to products A and B (and also C).

Competition among firms in a market can be thought of as a process whereby firms, through their prices and product attributes, submit consumer surplus "bids" to consumers. Consumers then choose the firm that offers the greatest amount of consumer surplus. A firm that offers a consumer less surplus than its rivals (e.g., the firm producing product D) will lose the fight for that consumer's business. When firms' price–quality positions line up along the same indifference curve—that is, when firms are offering a

FIGURE 11.6
THE VALUE MAP

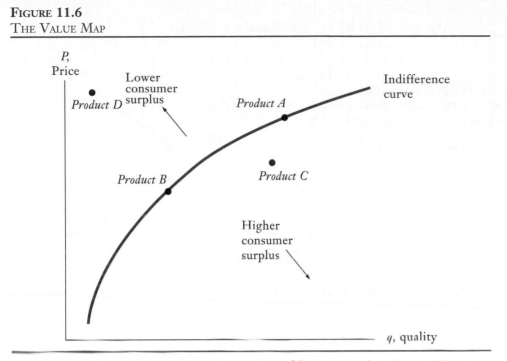

The value map illustrates the price-quality positions of firms in a market. The solid line is an indifference curve. It illustrates price-quality combinations that yield the same consumer surplus. Price-quality positions located below a given indifference curve yield a consumer surplus that is higher than that yielded by positions along the indifference curve. Price-quality positions located above an indifference curve yield consumer surplus that is lower than that yielded by positions along the indifference curve. When some products are positioned on a given indifference curve while others are positioned off the curve, consumers will flock to the firms providing the higher consumer surplus.

consumer the same amount of consumer surplus—we say that the firms have achieved consumer surplus parity. (In Figure 11.6, the firms selling products A and B have attained consumer surplus parity.) If firms achieve consumer surplus parity in a market in which consumers have identical preferences (i.e., the same indifference curves), no consumer within that market has an incentive to switch from one seller to another, and market shares will thus be stable. If all firms in the market have the same quality, then consumer surplus parity means that each firm charges the same price.

When a firm moves from a position of consumer surplus parity or consumer surplus advantage to one in which its consumer surplus is less than that of its competitors, its sales will slip and its market share will fall. This happened to Sun in the market for high-end servers in the late 1990s and the early 2000s. Sun dominated this market in the late 1990s, but by 2002 IBM and HP had developed high-end servers that were considered to be superior to Sun's offerings. Not surprisingly, IBM and HP gained market share at Sun's expense.

The steepness (i.e., the slope) of an indifference curve indicates the tradeoff between price and quality a consumer is willing to make. Indeed, as shown in Figure 11.7, the increase in the price along a given indifference curve corresponds exactly to the incremental benefit ΔB caused by an increase Δq in the quality delivered by the product.[5] A steeply sloped indifference curve indicates that a consumer is

The steepness of an indifference curve indicates the tradeoff between price and quality consumers are willing to make. The increase in price from P_E to P_F along the indifference curve is equal to the change in perceived benefit, ΔB, that results from an increase, Δq, in quality from q_E to q_F. We couch our discussion in terms of the tradeoff between price and quality. More generally, however, the same discussion applies to the tradeoff between price and any benefit-enhancing or cost-reducing attribute.

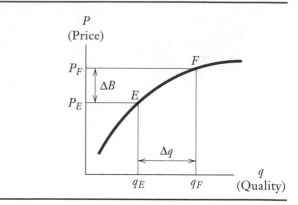

willing to pay considerably more for additional quality, while a shallow indifference curve indicates that extra quality is not worth much to the customer.

Firms that overestimate the willingness of consumers to trade off price for quality risk overpricing their products and either losing market share to competitors or never becoming a viable competitor. Such was the fate of *The National*, an all-sports daily newspaper launched with great fanfare in January 1990. Without question, its longer features, color photographs, detailed statistics, and columns and bylines by big-name sportswriters, such as Mike Lupica and John Feinstein, made it superior to the sports coverage provided by local newspapers. However, at a price of 75 cents per issue, most potential readers did not find it to be a good value compared to the available alternatives. *The National*'s circulation remained far below projections, and the advertising revenue needed to support the highly paid staff of reporters and columnists never materialized. *The National* folded in June 1991.

Value-Created

Economic value is created when a producer combines inputs such as labor, capital, raw materials, and purchased components to make a product whose perceived benefit B exceeds the cost C incurred in making the product. The economic value created (or value-created, for short) is thus the difference between the perceived benefit and cost, or $B - C$, where B and C are expressed per unit of the final product.

Value-created must be divided between consumers and producers. Consumer surplus, $B - P$, represents the portion of the value-created that the consumer "captures." The seller receives the price P and uses it to pay for the inputs that are needed to manufacture the finished product. The producer's profit margin, $P - C$, represents the portion of the value-created that it captures. Adding together consumer surplus and the producer's profit gives us the value-created expressed as the sum of consumer surplus and profit:

$$\text{Value Created} = \text{Consumer Surplus} + \text{Producer Surplus}$$
$$= (B - P) + (P - C)$$
$$= B - C$$

Figure 11.8 depicts value-created for a hypothetical producer of aluminum cans (e.g., a firm such as Crown, Cork and Seal). The cost of producing 1,000 aluminum cans is $30 (i.e., $C = \$30$). The maximum willingness-to-pay for a buyer of aluminum cans, for example, a soft-drink bottler such as Coca-Cola Enterprises, is $100 per thousand (i.e., $B = \$100$). This represents the highest price the buyer is willing to pay for aluminum cans before switching to the best available alternative product, perhaps plastic containers. The difference between maximum willingness-to-pay and cost is the value-created, which in this case equals $70 (i.e., $B - C = \$70$). Working our way down the right side of the diagram, we see that value-created equals the sum of consumer surplus and producer profit. If the seller of aluminum cans charges a price of $55 (i.e., $P = \$55$), consumer surplus is $45 per thousand cans (i.e., $B - P = \$45$), while producer profit margin is $25 per thousand (i.e., $P - C = \$25$). The price P thus determines how much of the value-created sellers capture as profit and how much buyers capture as consumer surplus.

FIGURE 11.8

THE COMPONENTS OF VALUE-CREATED IN THE MARKET FOR ALUMINUM CANS

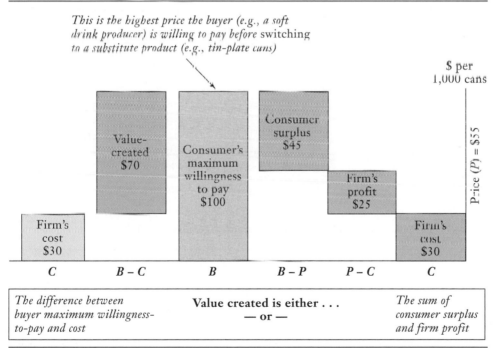

Start on the left side of the figure. The cost of producing 1,000 aluminum cans is $30. The maximum willingness-to-pay for a buyer of aluminum cans (e.g., a soft-drink bottler such as Coca-Cola Enterprises) is $100 per thousand. This represents the highest price the buyer is willing to pay for aluminum cans before switching to the best available alternative product, perhaps plastic containers or tin-plate steel cans. The difference between maximum willingness-to-pay and cost is the value-created, which in this case equals $70. Working our way down the right side of the diagram, value-created can be seen to equal the sum of consumer surplus and producer profit. If the seller of aluminum cans charges a price of $55, consumer surplus is $45 per thousand cans, while producer profit is $25 per thousand.

EXAMPLE 11.1 THE DIVISION OF THE VALUE-CREATED IN THE SALE OF BEER AT A BASEBALL GAME

Assigning numbers to the areas in Figure 11.8 is usually difficult because B is hard to measure. But when the product is sold under conditions of monopoly and no reasonable substitutes are available, B can be approximated by making some simplifying assumptions about the nature of the demand curve for the product. An example of a product sold under these circumstances is beer at a baseball game. Because a purchaser of beer would probably not regard soft drinks as a close substitute and because patrons are not allowed to bring in their own beer, the stadium concessionaire has as tight a monopoly on the market as one could imagine.

Here are some basic data on beer sold at Cincinnati Reds baseball games in the late 1980s. The price of a 20-ounce cup of beer was $2.50. The stadium concessionaire, Cincinnati Sports Service, paid the distributor $0.20 per cup for this beer; paid royalties to the city of Cincinnati of $0.24 per cup; paid royalties to the Cincinnati Reds baseball team of $0.54 per

cup; and paid an excise tax of $0.14 per cup. Its total costs were thus $1.12.[6]

If we assume that the demand curve for beer is linear, then a plausible estimate of consumer surplus that is consistent with the data above is $0.69 per 20-ounce cup of beer.[7] Table 11.2 shows the division of value in the sale of the beer using $0.69 per cup as an estimate of consumer surplus.

The brewer clearly captures only a small fraction of the value that is created.[8] By contrast, by controlling the access of the concessionaire to the stadium and to the event, the city of Cincinnati and the Cincinnati Reds are able to capture a significant fraction of the value that is created. They can capture value because prospective concessionaires are willing to compete for the right to monopolize this market. As a result, the city and the Reds can extract a significant portion of the monopoly profit that would otherwise flow to the concessionaire.

TABLE 11.2
DIVISION OF VALUE IN THE SALE OF BEER AT RIVERFRONT STADIUM

Consumer Surplus $.69
Profit to Sports Service ?
· $1.38
Sports Service's Costs (labor, materials, insurance, etc.) ?
Profit to Cincinnati Reds $.54
Profit to City of Cincinnati $.20
Taxes $.14
Distributor's Profit ?
· $.10
Distributor's Costs (excl. price paid to brewer) ?
Brewer's Profit $.03
Brewer's Costs $.07

Value Creation and "Win–Win" Business Opportunities

No product can be viable without creating positive economic value. If $B - C$ was negative, there would be no price that consumers would be willing to pay for the product that would cover the cost of the resources that are sacrificed to make the product. Manufacturers of the product, along with their input suppliers, would be unable to make a profit. Vacuum tubes, rotary-dial telephones, and dedicated word processing units are products that at one time created positive value, but because of changes in tastes and technology, they no longer create enough benefits to consumers to justify their production. Many of the businesses created during the dot-com frenzy of the late 1990s were doomed because they had no prospect of creating positive $B - C$.

By contrast, when $B - C$ is positive, a firm can profitably purchase inputs from suppliers, convert them into a finished product, and sell it to consumers. When $B > C$, it will always be possible for an entrepreneur to strike win–win deals with input suppliers and consumers, that is, deals that leave *all* parties better off than they would be if they did not deal with each other. In economics, win–win trade opportunities are called *gains from trade*. When $B > C$, clever entrepreneurs can exploit potential gains from trade.

Value Creation and Competitive Advantage

Although a positive $B - C$ is *necessary* for a product to be economically viable, just because a firm sells a product whose $B - C$ is positive is no guarantee that it will make a positive profit. In a market in which entry is easy and all firms create essentially the same economic value, competition between firms will dissipate profitability. Existing firms and new entrants will compete for consumers by bidding down their prices to the point at which all producers earn zero profit. In such markets, consumers capture all the economic value that the product creates.

It follows, then, that in order for a firm to earn positive profit in an industry in which competition would otherwise drive profitability to zero, the firm must create more economic value than its rivals. That is, the firm must generate a level of $B - C$ that its competitors cannot replicate. This simple but powerful insight follows from our earlier discussion of the competitive implications of consumer surplus. To see why, imagine that two sellers are competing for your business. The seller whose product characteristics and price provides you the greatest amount of consumer surplus will win your business. The most aggressive consumer surplus "bid" that either seller would be prepared to offer is the one at which its profit is equal to zero, which occurs when it offers a price P that equals its cost C. At such a bid, a firm would hand over all of the value it creates to you in the form of consumer surplus. The firm with the advantage in this competition is the one that has the highest $B - C$. This is because that firm will be able to win your patronage by offering you a slightly more favorable consumer surplus "bid" than the most aggressive bid its rival is prepared to offer, while retaining the extra value it creates in the form of profit. That is, it can outbid the rival for your business and still end up with a positive profit on the sale.[9]

Superior creation of economic value never takes place in the abstract; it always occurs in the context of particular customers. Because different customers will typically make different tradeoffs between price and the attributes that drive B, in any particular market, it is possible that one firm might create a higher $B - C$ among one segment of consumers, while another firm may create a higher $B - C$ among other segments. We saw this, for example, in the personal computer industry in the late 1990s in which Gateway probably created more economic value in the SOHO (small office/home

FIGURE 11.9
ECONOMIC PROFITABILITY OF PERSONAL COMPUTER MAKERS

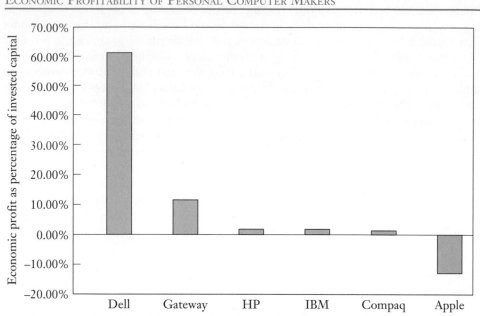

This figure shows average economic profits (expressed as a percentage of invested capital) of selected personal computer makers over the period 1995–1999.

Source: 2000 Stern Stewart Performance 1000 database.

office) segment of the market, while Dell created more economic value in most of the rest of the market. As Figure 11.9 shows, both Dell and Gateway consistently outperformed industry peers during the latter half of the 1990s.

Analyzing Value Creation

Understanding how a firm's product creates economic value and whether it can continue to do so is a necessary first step in diagnosing a firm's potential for achieving a competitive advantage in its market. Diagnosing the sources of value creation requires an understanding of why the firm's business exists and what its underlying economics are. This, in turn, involves understanding what drives consumer benefits (e.g., how the firm's products serve consumer needs better than potential substitutes) and what drives costs (e.g., which costs are sensitive to production volume, or how costs change with cumulative experience).

Projecting the firm's prospects for creating value also involves critically evaluating how the fundamental economic foundations of the business are likely to evolve, an exercise that Richard Rumelt calls consonance analysis.[11] Perhaps the most basic of all is the question of whether changes in market demand or the conditions of technology are likely to threaten how the firm creates value. Although this point seems transparent, firms can easily overlook it when they are in the throes of month-to-month battles for market share with their immediate rivals. Evaluating future prospects is also difficult due to the sheer complexity of predicting the future and the risks involved in acting on such predictions.

EXAMPLE 11.2 KMART VERSUS WAL-MART

Kmart's battle with Wal-Mart in the early 2000s provides a good illustration of a firm's disadvantage when it has a lower $B - C$ than its rivals. During 2001, Kmart attempted to copy Wal-Mart's "Everyday Low Prices" strategy by cutting prices on 38,000 items while at the same time cutting back on weekly newspaper circulars that touted promotion of selected items at sale prices. But because Wal-Mart's unit costs were generally lower than Kmart's, Wal-Mart could (and did!) match Kmart's prices and still remain profitable. In most of the markets in which a Kmart was located, there was a Wal-Mart within five miles of the Kmart store. As a result, Kmart's strategy merely succeeded in lowering margins without materially affecting its market share. The failure of this strategy contributed to a deterioration in Kmart's performance in 2001 that eventually led to Kmart's declaration of bankruptcy in early 2002.

Kmart emerged from bankruptcy in 2003 after undertaking substantial layoffs and store closings, as well as backing away from its attempt to mimic Wal-Mart's strategy. In 2005, Kmart acquired Sears Robuck, with both retailers operating under the corporate umbrella, Sears Holdings. In the wake of the merger, Kmart announced plans to convert more than one-third of its stores in the United States and Canada to Sears outlets.

Kmart's current strategy is to position itself as the "store of the neighborhood." This strategy is aimed primarily at racial or ethnic communities in urban areas, most especially African Americans and Hispanics. It will be interesting to see if this strategy succeeds. The goal of the strategy seems to be to differentiate Kmart from its traditional rivals, Wal-Mart and Target, by further exaggerating the income differential between Kmart shoppers and shoppers at Wal-Mart and Target.[10] However, this strategy runs the risk of bringing Kmart into more direct competition with the deep discount "dollar retailers," such as Dollar General and Family Dollar, that have been targeting lower income urban communities for many years.

The history of an industry may also dull managers to the prospects for change. Threats to a firm's ability to create value often come from outside its immediate group of rivals and may threaten not just the firm, but the whole industry. Honda's foray into motorcycles in the early 1960s occurred within segments that the dominant producers at the time—Harley-Davidson and British Triumph—had concluded were unprofitable. IBM's initial dominance in the personal computer (PC) market may well have diverted its attention from the serious threat that the PC and related products, such as workstations, held for its core business of mainframes. The revolution in mass merchandising created by Wal-Mart occurred in out-of-the-way locations that companies such as Kmart and Sears had rejected as viable locations for large discount stores.

Value Creation and the Value Chain

Value is created as goods move along the vertical chain. The vertical chain is therefore sometimes referred to as the *value chain*.[12] The value chain depicts the firm as a collection of value-creating activities, such as production operations, marketing and sales, and logistics, as Figure 11.10 shows. Each activity in the value chain can potentially add to the benefit B that consumers get from the firm's product, and each can add to the cost C that the firm incurs to produce and sell the product. Of course, the forces that influence the benefits created and cost incurred vary significantly across activities.

In practice, it is often difficult to isolate the impact that an activity has on the value that the firm creates. To do so requires estimating the incremental perceived benefit

FIGURE 11.10
THE VALUE CHAIN

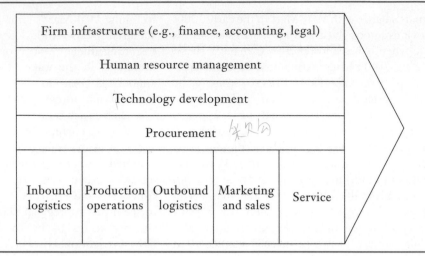

The value chain depicts the firm as a collection of value-creating activities. Porter distinguishes between five primary activities (inbound logistics, production operations, outbound logistics, marketing, and sales and service) and four support activities (firm infrastructure activities, such as finance and accounting, human resources management, technology development, and procurement).

that an activity creates and the incremental cost associated with it. However, when different stages produce finished or semifinished goods that can be valued using market prices, we can estimate the incremental value that distinctive parts of the value chain create. This is called *value-added analysis*. The appendix to this chapter presents a fuller explanation and an example of value-added analysis.

Value Creation, Resources, and Capabilities

Broadly speaking, there are two ways in which a firm can create more economic value than the other firms in its industry. First, it can configure its value chain differently from competitors. For example, in the car-rental market in the United States, Enterprise's focus on the replacement-car segment has led it to operate with a fundamentally different value chain from the "Airport 7" (Hertz, Avis, National, Alamo, Budget, Dollar, and Thrifty), which are focused on the part of the market whose business originates at airports (primarily business and vacation travelers).[13] By optimizing its activities to serve renters seeking to replace their vehicles for possibly prolonged periods of time, Enterprise creates more economic value for this segment of customers than do the Airport 7 (see Example 11.3).

Alternatively, a firm can create superior economic value by configuring its value chain in essentially the same way as its rivals, but within that value chain, performing activities more effectively than rivals do. To do this, the firm must possess resources and capabilities that its competitors lack; otherwise, the competitors could immediately copy any strategy for creating superior value.

Resources are firm-specific assets, such as patents and trademarks, brand-name reputation, installed base, organizational culture, and workers with firm-specific expertise or know-how. The brand recognition that Coca-Cola enjoys worldwide is

EXAMPLE 11.3 CREATING VALUE AT ENTERPRISE
RENT-A-CAR[14]

Can you name the largest rental car corporation in the United States? Hertz? Avis? You might be surprised to learn that it is Enterprise Rent-a-Car, a company founded in 1957 by a St. Louis-based Cadillac dealer, Jack Taylor, who named the company for the USS *Enterprise*, the ship on which he served as a Navy pilot. Enterprise boasts the largest fleet size and number of locations in the United States.

Enterprise is widely believed to be the most profitable rental car firm in the United States. During the 1990s and early 2000s, it grew at a rapid rate, averaging nearly 13 percent annual revenue growth between 1995 and 2004. How has Enterprise maintained such profitability and growth in an industry widely believed to be very unattractive? The answer: Enterprise has carved out a unique position in the rental car industry by serving a market segment that historically was ignored by the airport-based rental car companies and optimizing its value-chain activities to serve this segment.

Traditional car rental companies cater primarily to the business traveler. The Airport 7 companies generally charge higher prices than Enterprise and are present mainly at airport locations. They rent cars for short periods of time, rely on travel agents for bookings, and employ reward programs to garner loyalty with end customers. Among these companies, Hertz owns the largest share of the airport market at approximately 30 percent.

By contrast, Enterprise targets not business travelers but drivers who need a replacement car because of repairs or body work. While the Airport 7 firms operate out of large, fully stocked parking lots at airports, Enterprise maintains smaller-sized lots in towns and cities across America, which are more accessible to the general population. Moreover, Enterprise will pick customers up at home. The company saves money by not relying on travel agents. Instead, it cultivates relationships with body shops, insurance agents, and auto dealers who, in turn, direct business toward Enterprise. To this end, Enterprise benefited from a legal ruling in 1969 that required insurance companies to pay for loss of transportation. Enterprise has extended its reach to weekend users, for whom it provides extremely low weekend rates. While almost nonexistent when Enterprise was founded, the replacement-car market now comprises 40 percent of the rental car market, of which Enterprise has, by far, the largest share.[15]

In 1999, Enterprise expanded into the airport market. However, it did so not to cater to the business traveler but to another relatively underserved segment—the infrequent leisure traveler. It offers inexpensive rates while providing value-added services that an infrequent leisure traveler could appreciate, such as providing directions, restaurant recommendations, and help with luggage. A trend toward remote parking lots for rental car companies at congested airports benefited Enterprise's foray into the airport market. When rental car parking lots were located near the terminal, Enterprise would be at a disadvantage because its own lots would not be located at the airport. Now that virtually all rental car companies have to shuttle customers to remote lots at major airports, Enterprise no longer faces such a severe disadvantage in competing against the Airport 7.

Despite Enterprise's expansion into the airport market, as of 2002 it still derived 95 percent of its revenue from the replacement-car market. Enterprise developed and sustained its competitive advantage in this market by tightly optimizing its value-chain activities to the replacement-car segment. For example, unlike airport-based rental car companies, which traditionally relied almost exclusively on television and print advertising to market their service to potential customers, Enterprise augments its television advertising by marketing to key intermediaries such as auto dealerships, body shops, and insurance companies, with whom a potential customer would interact when he or she needed a replacement vehicle. Enterprise can sustain its competitive advantage because it is difficult for its airport-based rivals, operating with very different business models, to replicate Enterprise's unique mix of activities. Its strong presence in the replacement-car market also makes Enterprise less susceptible to downturns in business travel such as occurred in the wake of 9/11.

EXAMPLE 11.4 MEASURING CAPABILITIES
IN THE PHARMACEUTICAL INDUSTRY

Drawing on detailed quantitative and qualitative data from 10 major firms, Rebecca Henderson and Iain Cockburn attempted to measure resources and capabilities associated with new drug research in the pharmaceutical industry.[20] Although drug discovery is not the only skill that pharmaceutical firms must possess to compete effectively, it is extremely important. Henderson and Cockburn hypothesize that research productivity (measured as the number of patents obtained per research dollar invested) depends on three classes of factors: the composition of a firm's research portfolio; firm-specific scientific and medical know-how; and a firm's distinctive capabilities. The composition of the research portfolio is important because it is easier to achieve patentable discoveries in some areas than in others. For example, in the 20 years prior to Henderson and Cockburn's study, investments in cardiovascular drug discovery were consistently more productive than investments in cancer research. Firm-specific know-how is critical because modern drug research requires highly skilled scientists from disciplines such as biology, biochemistry, and physiology. Henderson and Cockburn use measures such as the firm's existing stock of patents as proxies for idiosyncratic firm know-how.

Henderson and Cockburn also hypothesize that two capabilities are likely to be especially significant in new drug research. The first is skill at encouraging and maintaining an extensive flow of scientific information from the external environment to the firm. In pharmaceuticals, much of the fundamental science that lays the groundwork for new discoveries is created outside the firm. A firm's ability to take advantage of this information is important for its success in making new drug discoveries. Henderson and Cockburn measure the extent of this capability through variables such as the firm's reliance on publication records in making promotion decisions, its proximity to major research universities, and its involvement in joint research projects with major universities.

The second capability they focus on is skill at encouraging and maintaining flow of information across disciplinary boundaries inside the firm. Successful new drug discoveries require this type of integration. For example, the commercial development of HMG CoA reductase inhibitors (drugs that inhibit cholesterol synthesis in the liver) depended on pathbreaking work at Merck on three disciplinary fronts: pharmacology, physiology, and biostatistics. Henderson and Cockburn measure this capability with variables such as the extent to which the research in the firm was coordinated through cross-disciplinary teams and giving one person authority to allocate resources for research. The former would facilitate the flow of information across disciplines; the latter would inhibit it.

Henderson and Cockburn's study indicates that differences in firms' capabilities explain much variability in firms' research productivity. For example, a firm that rewards research publications is about 40 percent more productive than one that does not. A firm that organizes by cross-disciplinary research teams is about 25 percent more productive than one that does not. Does this mean that a firm that switches to a team-based research organization will immediately increase its output of patents per dollar by 40 percent? Probably not. This and other measures Henderson and Cockburn used were proxies for deeper resource-creation or integrative capabilities. For example, a firm that rewards publications may have an advantage at recruiting the brightest scientists. A firm that organizes by teams may have a collegial atmosphere that encourages team-based organizations. A team-based organization inside a firm that lacks in collegiality may generate far less research productivity. These observations go back to our earlier point. It is often far easier to identify distinctive capabilities once they exist than for management to create them.

an example of an economically powerful resource. As a testament to the power of Coke's brand, the marketing consultancy InterBrand estimated that two-thirds of Coca-Cola's market capitalization at the end of 2004 was due to the value of the Coke brand name alone.[16] Unlike nonspecialized assets or factors of production, such as buildings, raw materials, or unskilled labor, resources cannot easily be duplicated or acquired by other firms in well-functioning markets. Resources can directly affect the ability of a firm to create more value than other firms. For example, a large installed base or an established reputation for quality may make the firm's B higher than its rivals. Resources also indirectly impact value creation because they are the basis of the firm's capabilities.

Capabilities are activities that a firm does especially well compared with other firms.[17] You might think of resources as "nouns" (they are things that firms "have") and capabilities as "verbs" (they are things that firms "do"). Capabilities might reside within particular business functions (e.g., Procter & Gamble's skills in brand promotion, American Airlines' capabilities in yield management, or Nine West's ability to manage its sourcing and procurement functions in the fashion shoe business). Alternatively, they may be linked to particular technologies or product designs (e.g., DuPont's proficiencies in nylon, Nan Ya Plastics' skills in working with polyester, or Honda's legendary skill in working with small internal-combustion engines and power trains).[18] Or they might reside in the firm's ability to manage linkages between elements of the value chain or coordinate activities across it (e.g., an important element in Dell's cost advantage in the personal computer industry relative to other comparable broad based competitors such as Hewlett-Packard is its ability to tightly integrate order-taking, procurement of components, manufacturing, and outbound logistics in a way that minimizes the costs of carrying component and finished-goods inventories).

Whatever their basis, capabilities have several key common characteristics:

1. They are typically valuable across multiple products or markets.
2. They are embedded in what Richard Nelson and Sidney Winter call organizational routines—well-honed patterns of performing activities inside an organization.[19] This implies that capabilities can persist even though individuals leave the organization.
3. They are tacit; that is, they are difficult to reduce to simple algorithms or procedure guides.

Chapters 2 and 3 discussed the implication of point 1 for the horizontal and vertical boundaries of the firm. Points 2 and 3 have important implications for the sustainability of competitive advantages built on organizational capabilities and will be discussed more fully in the next chapter.

STRATEGIC POSITIONING: COST ADVANTAGE AND BENEFIT ADVANTAGE

Generic Strategies

Competitive advantage cannot be reduced to a formula or an algorithm. Even if such formulas or algorithms could be concocted, describing them in a textbook such as this would make them valueless because they would be accessible to everyone. But although there is no single formula for success, we can discern broad commonalities across industries in the different ways that firms position themselves to compete. For example, in the desktop computer business, Dell is a broad-based competitor serving a wide array of customers, including business of all sizes, government and educational institutions, and individual buyers. Gateway, by contrast, focuses on selling desktop computers to SOHO customers whose needs and preferences are somewhat unique from the rest of the market.

In the language of strategic management, Dell and Gateway each represent a different example of a generic strategy, a concept first introduced by Michael Porter.[21] A firm's generic strategy describes, in broad terms, how it positions itself to compete in the market it serves. Figure 11.11 illustrates Porter's generic strategies—benefit leadership, cost leadership, and focus—and briefly describes their economic logic.[22] As Figure 11.12 illustrates, in the personal computer industry, Dell is an example of a broad-coverage cost leader, while Gateway follows a focus strategy.

In the remainder of this chapter, we explore the economic logic of these generic strategies. We do so by first exploring the logic of positions based on cost leadership and benefit leadership. We then discuss the logic of focus strategies.

The Strategic Logic of Cost Leadership

A firm that follows a strategy of cost leadership creates more value (i.e., $B - C$) than its competitors by offering products that have a lower C than its rivals. This can happen

FIGURE 11.11
PORTER'S GENERIC STRATEGIES

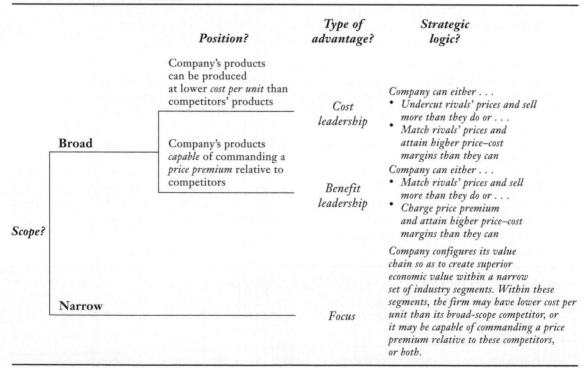

This figure depicts Michael Porter's generic strategies: benefit leadership, cost leadership, and focus. These strategies are distinguished by the breadth of a firm's product or customer scope and by whether the firm seeks competitive advantage by having the lowest costs in its industry or by offering products/services that deliver superior customer benefits.

FIGURE 11.12
GENERIC STRATEGIES IN THE U.S. PERSONAL COMPUTER INDUSTRY

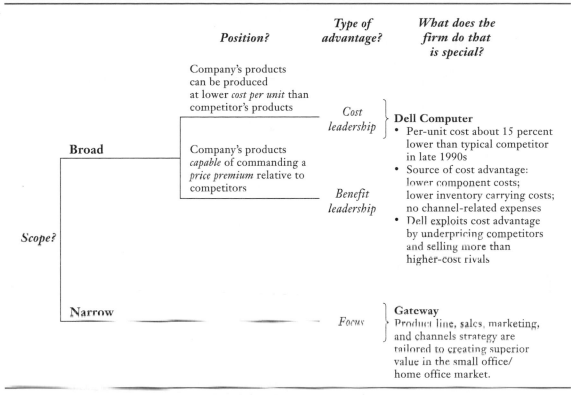

In the U.S. personal computer industry, Dell is an example of a cost leader, while Gateway is an example of a firm following a focus strategy.

in three qualitatively different ways. First, the cost leader can achieve *benefit parity* by making products with the same *B* but at a lower *C* than its rivals. The competitive advantage achieved by low-cost producers in commodity markets (e.g., Mittal Steel in the global steel industry) is an example of this. Second, the cost leader can achieve *benefit proximity*, which involves offering a *B* that is not much less than competitors. This could occur if the low-cost firm automates processes that are better performed by hand, hires fewer skilled workers, purchases less expensive components, or maintains lower standards of quality control. Yamaha's cost advantage over traditional piano producers, such as Steinway, is a good example of this. Finally, a cost leader may *offer a product that is qualitatively different from that of its rivals.* Firms can sometimes build a competitive advantage by redefining the product to yield substantial differences in benefits or costs relative to how the product is traditionally defined. For example, a formerly high-margin product may be redefined to allow for economies of scale in production and distribution while still providing benefits to consumers. The Timex watch or the 19-cent Bic crystal pen are well-known historical examples.

Figure 11.13 illustrates the economic logic of cost leadership using a value map. For simplicity, let's consider an industry in which all firms except the cost leader offer a product with a cost C_E and price-quality position at point *E*. Through a combination of automation and cheaper components, suppose that the cost leader offers a

FIGURE 11.13
THE ECONOMIC LOGIC OF COST LEADERSHIP

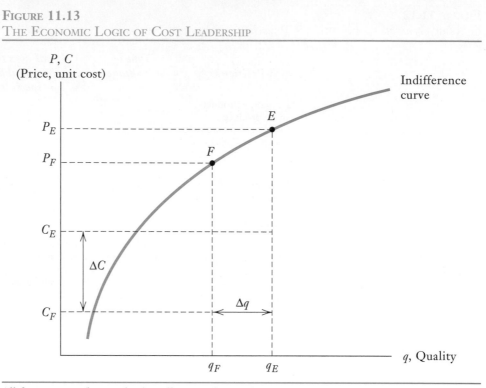

All firms except the cost leader offer a product with a cost C_E and price-quality position at point E. The cost leader offers a product with a lower quality level, q_F, but a substantially lower cost, C_F, resulting in a cost advantage of ΔC. Consumer surplus parity is achieved when the cost leader operates at point F by charging a price P_F. At point F, $P_E - P_F < C_E - C_F$, or rearranging terms, $P_F - C_F > P_E - C_E$. This tells us that despite its quality disadvantage, the cost leader achieves a higher profit margin than its higher-cost competitors.

product with a lower quality level, q_F, but a substantially lower cost, C_F, resulting in a cost advantage of ΔC. Market shares in the industry will be stable when the cost leader and its higher-cost competitors attain consumer surplus parity. Consumer surplus parity is achieved when the cost leader operates at point F by charging a price P_F. From the figure, notice that $P_E - P_F < C_E - C_F$, or rearranging terms, $P_F - C_F > P_E - C_E$. Given consumer surplus parity between the cost leader and its higher-cost competitors, the cost leader achieves a higher profit margin. In essence, the leader's cost advantage gives it the ability to charge a price that is lower than that of its higher-cost, higher quality rivals, while at the same time allowing it to "bank" some of its cost advantage in the form of a higher price-cost margin.

The Strategic Logic of Benefit Leadership

A firm that follows a strategy of benefit leadership creates more value (i.e., $B - C$) than its competitors by offering products that have a higher B than its rivals. This can happen in three qualitatively different ways. First, the benefit leader can achieve benefit parity by making products with the same C but at a higher B than its rivals. A good example is the Japanese automakers in the 1980s, whose family sedans (e.g., Honda Accord) were no more costly to produce than American-made models but offered

EXAMPLE 11.5 COST LEADERSHIP BY CEMEX[23]

Mexican cement manufacturer Cemex is the third largest cement producer in the world and the largest producer of ready-mix cement, the cement that is used to manufacture concrete. Cemex not only dominates its home market of Mexico (where it earns above-average profit margins and has delivered attractive returns on invested capital), but it also is a significant force in cement markets in Egypt, Spain, the Philippines, and a number of Latin American markets, including Colombia, Venezuela, and Costa Rica. Cemex even sells cement in the United States, where it has a market share of 15 percent. Widely admired as an "excellent" company, Cemex has won numerous awards and accolades from publications ranging from the *Industry Standard* to *Red Herring* to *Latin Finance*.

Cemex has achieved this acclaim by following a strategy that explicitly aims to achieve cost leadership in the various cement markets in which it competes. The cornerstone of this strategy is a corporate philosophy known as the "Cemex Way," a shorthand for a relentless focus on achieving cost advantage throughout Cemex's global organization. The Cemex Way emphasizes the use of information technology, automation, and the integration of key business processes to attain cost efficiencies. But perhaps even more important is its attempt to explicitly manage the sharing of best practices so that all of Cemex's cement plants around the world can benefit from the know-how developed at any one plant. The Cemex Way seems to have worked: Cemex appears to have attained cost efficiencies that other cement producers have

been unable to match. For example, because of a combination of automation and savings in energy consumption, the cement manufactured at Cemex's flagship plant in Tepeaca, Mexico, cost $10 per ton less than the industry average of $35 per ton in the 1990s.[24]

The Cemex Way explains some of Cemex's cost advantage, but it is probably not the entire story. Part of Cemex's cost advantage is also due to the nature of Cemex's global growth strategy and its implications for capacity utilization and economies of scale. Cemex does not randomly choose the countries into which it expands. Rather, it expands in such a way that allows it to diversify away some of the risk of regional economic downturns, which, in turn, increases the odds that its cement plants consistently operate at full capacity. The enhanced odds of full-capacity utilization, in turn, make it worthwhile for Cemex to build some of the largest plants in the world and not have to worry that they will be idled due to recession. For example, much of the cement that Cemex supplies in Latin and North America comes from Cemex's Tepeaca plant, which is the largest cement production unit in the Americas. When operated at full capacity, a larger cement plant typically results in lower unit costs than a smaller cement plant (provided that other drivers of cost, such as input prices are the same across the two plants). By expanding into Latin America and the United States, Cemex is able to operate its Tepeaca plant at or near full capacity, allowing it to achieve low unit costs through the realization of economies of scale.

superior performance and reliability. Second, the benefit leader might achieve cost proximity, which entails a *C* that is not too much higher than competitors. Nordstrom, whose employees earn above-average wages but provide superior service, is a good example of this strategic position. Finally, a firm could offer substantially higher *B* and *C*, which occurred when Eli Lilly introduced the first cephalosporin, a "magic bullet" antibiotic. Cephalosporins cost much more to produce than available substitutes, such as penicillin, but had fewer side effects and attached a broader spectrum of bacteria.

Figure 11.14 illustrates the economic logic of benefit leadership using a value map. For simplicity, let's consider an industry in which all firms except the benefit

FIGURE 11.14
THE ECONOMIC LOGIC OF BENEFIT LEADERSHIP

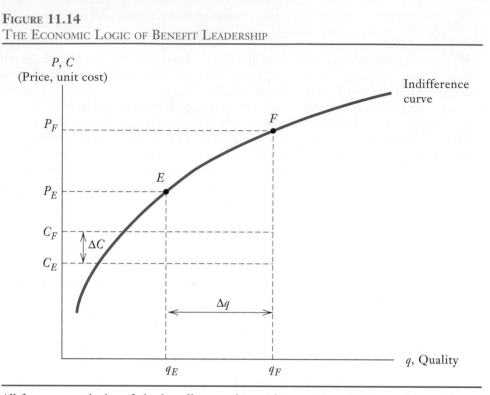

All firms except the benefit leader offer a product with a cost C_E and price-quality position at point E. The benefit leader offers a product with a higher quality level, q_F, and in so doing, incurs a higher cost C_F, resulting in a cost disadvantage of ΔC. Consumer surplus parity is achieved when the cost leader operates at point F by charging a price P_F. At point F, $P_F - P_E > C_F - C_E$, or rearranging terms, $P_F - C_F > P_E - C_E$. This tells us that despite its cost disadvantage, the benefit leader achieves a higher profit margin than its lower-benefit competitors.

leader offer a product with a cost C_E and price-quality position at point E. Suppose the benefit leader offers a product with a higher quality level, q_F, and in so doing, incurs a somewhat higher cost C_F, resulting in a cost disadvantage of ΔC. Market shares in the industry will be stable when the benefit leader and its lower-quality competitors attain consumer surplus parity. Consumer surplus parity is achieved when the benefit leader operates at point F by charging a price P_F. From the figure, notice that $P_F - P_E > C_F - C_E$, or rearranging terms, $P_F - C_F > P_E - C_E$. Given consumer surplus parity between the benefit leader and its lower-quality competitors, the benefit leader achieves a higher profit margin. In essence, the leader's benefit advantage gives it the "wiggle room" to charge a price premium relative to its lower-benefit, lower cost rivals without sacrificing market share.

Extracting Profits from Cost and Benefit Advantage: The Importance of the Price Elasticity of Demand

A firm that creates more value than its competitors would like to capture as much as possible of that value for itself in the form of profits. However, competition limits the

EXAMPLE 11.6 BENEFIT LEADERSHIP BY SUPERQUINN

"A visit to a Superquinn," wrote Fred Crawford and Ryan Matthews in 2001, "is a life altering experience, not in the metaphysical or theological sense, but rather in how one views the way a retail operation—grocery or otherwise—should be run."[25] Superquinn, the subject of this enthusiastic praise, is a 4,500-employee, 19-store chain of grocery stores in Ireland. Superquinn's historical success in the Irish grocery retailing business has been grounded in its willingness to make the tradeoffs necessary to stake out a position of benefit leadership in the markets in which it competes. Its merchandise is second to none in quality and freshness (e.g., each Superquinn grocery has a bakery on premises and guarantees that its bread is no more than four hours old), and it offers an almost-unbelievable level of customer service (e.g., Superquinn personnel stock special items at the request of individual customers and followup by phone, or even pay personal visits to customers, to resolve customer complaints).

Achieving a position of benefit leadership requires that Superquinn operate with higher unit costs than rival grocery chains in Ireland. For example, Superquinn's high level of customer service results in higher staffing costs (e.g., a typical Superquinn store would staff more personnel than would be employed at a comparable supermarket with the same square footage). Similarly, Superquinn's commitment to ensure fresh, high quality merchandise also results in higher costs (e.g., by deliberately maintaining small cooling rooms, Superquinn is forced to discard still-fresh products that other grocers would keep on the shelves or in the dairy or meat cases, a practice that increases Superquinn's merchandise costs relative to those of its rivals).

Though smaller in scope than its British rivals such as Tesco, Superquinn historically had been the market leader in the local markets in which it competed (most notably in areas around Dublin). However, in the early 2000s, Superquinn's market position began to erode.[26] The reasons for this reflect the economic logic of benefit advantage discussed where: Superquinn's benefit advantage vis-à-vis rivals was weakened, and its cost disadvantage became more pronounced. Superquinn's benefit advantage grew smaller as all grocery chains began investing in modern supply chain management systems that enabled it to quickly restock sold-out merchandise. Unfortunately, Superquinn's investments in these systems came on stream more slowly and proved to be more expensive than expected. Superquinn's cost disadvantage grew when several low-cost German grocery chains (Aldi and Lidl) entered the Irish market in the early 2000s. For brand-name merchandise that could be purchased in large package sizes, some shoppers were willing to forego the superior benefits offered by a Superquinn and shop instead at one of the discount stores.

In the midst of these trends, the Quinn family sold nearly all of its interest in the Superquinn chain to a large retail consortium, Select Retail Holdings, in early 2005. Whether Superquinn stores continue to stake out the benefit leadership position in the Irish grocery market is an interesting question. Feargal Quinn, the founder of Superquinn, was known in Ireland as the "pope of customer service," and though he and other Quinn family members continue to have a 20 percent stake in the company, he will no longer be involved in the management of the business. Furthermore, if the discount grocers continue to be an attractive alternative in the Irish market, Superquinn may feel the need to take actions that reduce costs and enable them to compete more aggressively on price with the discount outlets. This may have already begun happening even before the sale to Select Retail Holdings. In 2004, Superquinn announced the layoff of nearly 300 workers. It also introduced a range of fresh products that were priced lower than its standard fare. If not managed carefully, such steps could affect Superquinn's customer service, confuse consumers, and thus compromise its benefit leadership.

firm's ability to capture profits. If consumers have identical preferences (i.e., the same value map applies to all consumers in the market), competition would take an especially stark form. When consumers have identical preferences, if a firm provides the highest consumer surplus to one consumer, it also provides the highest consumer surplus to all consumers in the market. Competition then would resemble a "winner-take-all" auction: When a firm increases its consumer surplus "bid" slightly above competitors, it captures the entire market. The auction will end only when no firm can submit a profitable consumer surplus bid that tops the bids rivals submit. This leads to two clear recipes for retaining profits for a firm that creates more value than its competitors:

1. A cost leader that has benefit parity with its rivals can lower its price just below the unit cost of the firm with the next lowest unit cost. This makes it unprofitable for higher-cost competitors to respond with price cuts of their own and thus allows the firm to capture the entire market.
2. A benefit leader that has cost parity with its rivals can raise its price just below its unit cost plus the *additional benefit* ΔB it creates relative to the competitor with the next highest B. To top this consumer surplus bid, a competitor would have to cut price below its unit cost, which would be unprofitable. At this price, then, the firm with the benefit advantage captures the entire market.

These unrealistic recipes result because when consumers have identical preferences, an infinitesimally small decrease in price or increase in quality leads to a large shift in market share. This would not happen in a market characterized by horizontal differentiation. As we discussed in Chapter 6, horizontal differentiation arises when products possess attributes that increase B for some consumers but decrease it for others, and firms differ according to these attributes. For example, a brand's external packaging may appeal to some consumers but not to others. A retailer's location may be very convenient for some shoppers but quite inconvenient for others. Some consumers may have an intense loyalty to one brand of cola that other consumers would never consider purchasing, even at very low prices.

Horizontal differentiation is likely to be strong when there are many product attributes that consumers weigh in assessing overall benefit B, and consumers disagree about the desirability of those attributes. Ready-to-eat breakfast cereals and soft drinks are businesses in which horizontal differentiation is significant. Horizontal differentiation is likely to be weak when the product is simple, and only a few easily ranked attributes matter to potential consumers. Light bulbs and copying paper are products for which horizontal differentiation is likely to be weak. Horizontal differentiation also tends to be weak when business buyers rather than households purchase the good. Business buyers are often more knowledgeable and sophisticated than households because business-to-business transactions are often conducted by professional purchasing agents who specialize in the items they buy and often have financial incentives to seek the "best deal." Business buyers are also less likely to pay attention to a product's image.

In markets where there is horizontal differentiation, a firm's price elasticity or quality elasticity of demand will no longer be infinite. Lowering price or boosting quality will attract some consumers, but others will not switch unless the differential in price or quality is large enough. When there is horizontal differentiation, the price elasticity of demand an individual firm faces becomes a key determinant of a seller's ability to extract profits from its competitive advantage. Table 11.3 summarizes how the price

TABLE 11.3
EXPLOITING A COMPETITIVE ADVANTAGE THROUGH PRICING

		Type of Advantage	
		Cost Advantage (lower C than competitors)	Benefit Advantage (higher B than competitors)
Firm's Price Elasticity of Demand	High price elasticity of demand (weak horizontal differentiation)	• Modest *price cuts* gain lots of market share. • Exploit advantage through higher market share than competitors. • *Share Strategy*: Underprice competitors to gain share.	• Modest *price hikes* lose lots of market share. • Exploit advantage through higher market share than competitors. • *Share Strategy*: Maintain price parity with *competitors* (let benefit advantage drive share increases).
	Low price elasticity of demand (strong horizontal differentiation)	• Big *price cuts* gain little share. • Exploit advantage through higher profit margins. • *Margin Strategy*: Maintain price parity with competitors (let lower costs drive higher margins).	• Big *price hikes* lose little share. • Exploit advantage through higher profit margins. • *Margin Strategy*: Charge price premium relative to competitors.

elasticity of demand facing a firm influences the choice between two polar strategies for exploiting competitive advantage: a margin strategy and a share strategy.

Consider, first, a firm that has a cost advantage. When the firm's product has a low price elasticity of demand (i.e., when consumers are not very price-sensitive because of strong horizontal differentiation among competitors' products), even deep price cuts will not increase the firm's market share much. In this case, the optimal way for a firm to exploit its cost advantage is through a *margin strategy*: the firm maintains price parity with its competitors and profits from its cost advantage primarily through high price–cost margins rather than through higher market shares. In the health care industry, this practice is known as shadow pricing and is especially common in health insurance, where low-cost HMOs often set prices that are comparable to more costly forms of insurance. By contrast, when the firm's product has a high price elasticity of demand (i.e., when consumers are price-sensitive because horizontal differentiation is weak), modest price cuts can lead to significant increases in market share. In this case, the firm should exploit its cost advantage through a *share strategy*: the firm underprices its competitors to gain market share at their expense.

In practice, the distinction between a margin strategy and a share strategy is one of degree, not kind, and firms with cost advantages will often pursue mixed strategies: cutting price to gain share but also "banking" some of the cost advantage through higher margins. For example, using the sample of firms in the PIMS database, we found that, for the typical firm in a noncommodity industry, a 10 percent reduction in unit cost relative to that of competitors translates into a 3.4 percent reduction in the firm's price relative to the prices of competitors.[27] In market environments in which the price elasticity of demand is extremely high, a firm might also be able to follow a share strategy with virtually no price cuts. When horizontal differentiation is weak, small cuts in price can achieve large increases in market share. In this case, a firm with a cost advantage can have the best of both worlds: it can significantly increase its market share while offering prices that are barely below those of its higher-cost rivals.

Table 11.3 illustrates the notion that the logic governing the exploitation of a benefit advantage is analogous to that governing the exploitation of a cost advantage. When a firm has a benefit advantage in a market in which consumers are price sensitive, even a modest price hike could offset the firm's benefit advantage and nullify the increase in market share that the benefit advantage would otherwise lead to. In this case, the best way for the firm to exploit its benefit advantage is through a share strategy. A share strategy involves charging the same price as competitors and exploiting the firm's benefit advantage by capturing a higher market share than competitors. (The increase in market share is driven by the firm's benefit advantage.) By contrast, when consumers are not price-sensitive, because horizontal differentiation is strong, large price hikes will not completely erode the market share gains that the firm's benefit advantage creates. The best way for the firm to exploit its benefit advantage is through a margin strategy: it charges a price premium relative to competitors (sacrificing some market share in the process), and it exploits its advantage mainly through higher profit margins. This is the strategy Apple Computer followed before 1991. This strategy was eventually undermined when the release of Windows 3.0 in 1990 reduced the degree of horizontal differentiation between Apple PCs and IBM-compatible PCs.

Of course, other factors besides horizontal differentiation affect the relative profitability of alternative pricing strategies for exploiting a competitive advantage. For example, as Chapter 8 points out, a firm should consider the reactions of competitors before making any major pricing move. The prospect of competitor reactions can alter the broad recommendations in Table 11.3. For instance, in markets with price-sensitive consumers, a share strategy of cutting price to exploit a cost advantage would be attractive if competitors' prices remained unchanged. However, it would probably be unattractive if the firm's competitors quickly matched the price cut because the net result will be lower margins with little or no net gain in the firm's market share. In this case, a margin strategy might well be a more attractive option. One way to incorporate competitor reactions into the framework in Table 11.3 is to think in terms of a firm's *perceived* price elasticity of demand: the rate of percentage change in the quantity demanded for the firm's product for every 1 percent change in price, *taking into account likely pricing reactions by competitors*. For example, the prospect of quick price matching by competitors will negate the market share increases that would otherwise result when the firm cuts its price and thus would tend to reduce a firm's perceived price elasticity of demand. The logic of Table 11.3 would then suggest that a margin strategy would better exploit a cost advantage than a share strategy.

Comparing Cost and Benefit Advantages

Under what circumstances is one source of advantage likely to be more profitable than the other? Though no definitive rules can be formulated, the underlying economics of the firm's product market and the current positions of firms in the industry can sometimes create conditions that are more hospitable to one kind of advantage versus another.

An advantage based on lower cost is likely to be more profitable than an advantage built on superior benefits when:

- The nature of the product limits opportunities for enhancing its perceived benefit B. This might be the case for commodity products, such as chemicals and paper. If so, then, more opportunities for creating additional value may come from lowering C rather than from increasing B. Still, we must bear in mind that the drivers of differentiation include far more than just the physical attributes of the product and that opportunities may exist for differentiation through better postsale service, superior location, or more rapid delivery than competitors offer.

- Consumers are relatively price-sensitive and will not pay much of a premium for enhanced product quality, performance, or image. This would occur when most consumers are much more price-sensitive than quality-sensitive. Graphically, this corresponds to the case in which consumer indifference curves are relatively flat, indicating that a consumer will not pay much more for enhanced quality. Opportunities for additional value creation are much more likely to arise through cost reductions than through benefit enhancements.

- The product is a search good rather than an experience good. A *search good* is one whose objective quality attributes the typical buyer can assess prior to the point of purchase. Examples include apparel and office furniture. An *experience good* is a product whose quality can be assessed only after the consumer has purchased it and used it for a while. Examples include automobiles, appliances, and consumer packaged goods. With search goods, the potential for differentiation lies largely in enhancing the product's observable features. But if buyers can discern among different offerings, so can competitors, which raises the risk that the enhancements will be imitated. When this is so, a firm can best create a lasting competitive advantage by keeping its costs lower than those of its competitors, while matching their initiatives in product enhancement.

An advantage based on superior benefits is likely to be relatively more profitable than an advantage based on cost efficiency when:

- The typical consumer will pay a significant price premium for attributes that enhance B. This corresponds to the case in which the typical consumer's indifference curve is relatively steep. A firm that can differentiate its product by offering even a few additional features may command a significant price premium. Gillette counted on this effect when it launched its Mach 3 razor system in 1998. It concluded that many men would pay a premium price for blades that gave a better shave than existing cartridge or disposable razors. As a result, Gillette priced the Mach 3 blades 15 percent above its Sensor Excel blades, the highest-priced blades in the market at the time.

- Economies of scale or learning are significant, and firms are already exploiting them. In this case, opportunities for achieving a cost advantage over these larger firms are limited, and the best route toward value creation would be to offer a product that is especially well-tailored to a particular niche of the market. Microbreweries, such as the Boston Beer Company, have attempted to build a competitive advantage in this way.

- The product is an experience good rather than a search good. In this case, a benefit advantage could be based on image, reputation, or credibility, which are more

374 • **Chapter 11** • **Strategic Positioning for Competitive Advantage**

difficult to imitate or neutralize than objective product features or performance characteristics. Bose made major inroads in stereophonic equipment by exploiting its reputation developed through product innovations that originally appealed to a few stereophiles willing to pay $1,000 or more for high-end speakers.

- The points above should not be taken to imply that in any given industry there is one ideal strategic position toward which all firms should strive. More than anything else, a firm's ability to outperform its competitors arises from its ability to create and deliver a distinctive bundle of economic value. In markets in which consumers differ in their maximum willingness to pay or differ in how expensive it is for firms to access and serve them, a variety of powerful strategic positions can flourish at the same time. The U.S. mass-merchandising industry exhibits this point: Wal-Mart has thrived as the cost leader, while Target has successfully pursued a strategy of benefit leadership built on trendy merchandise and a bright, user-friendly shopping environment. In this and other industries, there is almost never one ideal strategic position.

"Stuck in the Middle"

Michael Porter has coined the phrase *stuck in the middle* to describe a firm that pursues elements of cost leadership and benefit leadership at the same time and in the process fails to achieve neither a cost advantage nor a benefit advantage.[28] According to Porter, a firm that does not clearly choose between an emphasis on building a cost advantage or building a benefit advantage will typically be much less profitable than competitors that have clearly pursued a generic strategy of cost leadership or benefit leadership.

Firms end up stuck in the middle because they fail to make choices about how to compete, and as a result, their strategies lack clarity and coherence. Clear choices about how to compete are critical because economically powerful strategic positions typically require tradeoffs.[29] In particular, a firm that configures its activities to deliver superior customer benefits must typically incur higher costs in order to do so. In the department store business, for example, shoppers at Neiman-Marcus expect fashionable, superior-quality merchandise, along with an upscale-shopping experience; to deliver this, Neiman-Marcus must incur levels of merchandising, labor, and location rental costs that other department store retailers are not prepared to incur. Similarly, a firm that seeks a low-cost position in its market will typically compromise its ability to deliver abundant levels of customer benefit. For example, the furniture retailer Ikea has made the conscious choice to sacrifice some elements of customer service (e.g., customers pick up and deliver Ikea furniture themselves) in order to keep its costs low.

Can a firm outperform its competitors by pursuing both benefit leadership and cost leadership at the same time? The results of empirical studies on the tradeoff between cost and benefit strategies suggest that benefit-based advantages and cost-based advantages might not be incompatible. For example, Danny Miller and Peter Friesen found that in consumer durables industries, firms that appeared to have achieved benefit advantages in their industries also tended to operate newer plants, had significantly better-than-average capacity utilization, and had direct costs per unit that were significantly lower than the industry average. Firms that appeared to have achieved cost advantages also scored highly on measures related to benefit superiority, such as product quality, and advertising and promotion expenses.[30]

EXAMPLE 11.7 STRATEGIC POSITIONING IN THE AIRLINE INDUSTRY: FOUR DECADES OF CHANGE

As we have just discussed, the profitability of a firm's strategic position depends on underlying economic conditions. When these conditions change, a strategic position that, at one time, led to competitive advantage may no longer do so. The strategy followed by the "Big Three" U.S. airlines—American, United, and Delta—is an excellent illustration of this point.

For all the talk of upheaval in the airline industry, one remarkable fact is that of the seven largest domestic carriers (ranked by enplanements), six—American, Continental, Delta, Northwest, United, and USAir—have been flying since the 1960s, either in their present incarnations or under an older name. (The seventh largest domestic carrier is Southwest Airlines.) Prior to deregulation of the airline industry in 1978, each of these trunk carriers was given a protected route corridor by the U.S. Civil Aeronautics Board (CAB). For example, United had protected transcontinental routes across the northern third of the nation, while American had protected routes across the southern east-west corridor. In exchange for obtaining monopoly power over their routes, the airlines ceded pricing authority to the CAB. The CAB kept prices very high, and while the airlines did engage in some forms of nonprice competition on the routes served by more than one airline (most notably, competition over scheduling frequency and amenities), the airlines prospered under CAB regulation. The key threat to profitability came from powerful unions, which extracted handsome salary and work rule concessions in exchange for labor peace. This was not unusual—many protected monopolies "share the spoils" with strong unions. Even after deregulation, these costly labor agreements continued to bind, embedding costs into an airline's cost structure that were extremely difficult to reduce.

In a deregulated environment, an existing airline could no longer depend on protected monopoly status to assure profits. The Big Three responded by adopting a strategy built around large hub-and-spoke systems. Delta

had actually begun to build such a system with a hub in Atlanta prior to deregulation, while American and United quickly built systems based on multiple hub airports (Chicago and Dallas for American and Chicago and Denver for United).

Organizing a schedule around a hub-and-spoke system had clear advantages for a large airline. As described in Example 2.1, the hub-and-spoke model allowed a carrier to fill planes flying from feeder airports into a hub and refill them by flying from the hubs to destination cities. Full planes meant lower operating costs per revenue passenger mile, and it protected the incumbent airlines from direct competition from new entrants (e.g., Peoples Express) with a point-to-point route structure. This advantage was especially strong in the battle for lucrative transcontinental traffic because point-to-point entrants typically lacked the jumbo jets required for nonstop transcontinental flights and did not have the hubs to facilitate one-stop flights.

Of course, hub-and-spoke operations involve significant tradeoffs. A hub-and-spoke carrier requires a diverse fleet so that it can fly full airplanes over both short and long hauls between big and small cities. A diverse fleet means higher maintenance costs and less flexibility in utilizing airport gates. Flying through hubs also can result in lost baggage, delays that can cascade throughout the system, and missed connections. These disadvantages came on top of the already high labor costs that were a legacy of CAB regulation. Still, a large airline could shoulder these disadvantages as long as it kept its planes full. Under these circumstances, the economies of scale achievable under a hub-and-spoke system more than offset the impact of higher labor and maintenance costs, and they created barriers to new entry that made it possible for the Big Three to charge premium prices for service in and out of their hub cities despite mediocre levels of service. These barriers to entry were reinforced by the customer loyalty that was "bought" through attractive frequent-flier programs. This was the strategic position of American, United, and Delta (and to a lesser extent, Continental, Northwest, and USAir as well). It made sense for a long time.

Southwest was the first airline to have great success using the point-to-point model. Owing to its legacy as an unregulated airline, Southwest enjoyed lower labor costs than the major carriers. With a fleet consisting entirely of Boeing 737s, it also enjoyed lower maintenance costs. It achieved consistent on-time performance by avoiding congested hub airports. And it carefully selected the markets it entered, restricting itself to city pairs that were underserved by the major carriers (thus avoiding destructive head-to-head competition with them), while at the same time having sufficient demand to enable Southwest to fill its planes.

Over time, the advantages offered by the hub-and-spoke model over the point-to-point model have nearly fully eroded, while the disadvantages (higher maintenance costs, poor service resulting from delays, and sensitivity to weather conditions) continue to be significant. Simple population growth makes more city pairs large enough to support point-to-point flights. This takes money directly out of the big carriers' pockets and also makes it harder for them to keep the flights full with traffic from the remaining spokes. "Fringe"

airframe manufacturers Bombardier and Embraer have introduced small planes capable of nonstop transcontinental flight, removing yet another source of the major carriers' positioning advantage.

Given their inherent cost disadvantages, the "Big Three" have learned that business as usual is not acceptable, and they have taken similar steps to respond to the changes that have undermined the economic power of their traditional competitive position. American, United, and Delta increasingly rely on international service, effectively exploiting the same benefits of hub-and-spoke operations that used to provide scale-based advantages in domestic service. In addition, they are working with their unions to eliminate cost and operational disadvantages, though some airlines (American) have been more effective at doing this than others (United). Even with all of these changes, however, the future of the major hub-and-spoke carriers in domestic air travel appears bleak.[28] Every year, more and more passengers fly point-to-point via low-cost airlines built on the Southwest model. Unless one of the "points" is a hub, the hub-and-spoke carriers have no advantage serving that market. With these airlines lacking any surefire way to position themselves, the future of the U.S. domestic aviation industry appears less settled than ever before.

From a theoretical perspective, several factors might weaken the observed tradeoff between benefit and cost positions in an industry:

• A firm that offers high-quality products increases its market share, which then reduces average cost because of economies of scale or the experience curve. As a result, a firm might achieve both a high-quality and a low-cost position in the industry. Figure 11.15 illustrates how. By pursuing benefit leadership, the firm raises its average cost at each level of output, represented by an upward shift in its average costs, from AC_0 to AC_1. But owing to its benefit advantage, the firm's demand curve shifts rightward, from D_0 to D_1. Even if the firm raises its price, the movement to the new demand curve coupled with the fact that average cost is a decreasing function of output (reflecting economies of scale) implies that the firm's realized average cost actually goes down, from $AC_0(Q_0)$ to $AC_1(Q_1)$. Charles River Breeding Labs typified this situation in the 1970s with its germ-free technology for raising laboratory animals. The first to adopt germ-free barrier breeding technologies, Charles River Breeders became the quality leader, moved

FIGURE 11.15

ACHIEVING BENEFIT AND COST ADVANTAGE SIMULTANEOUSLY

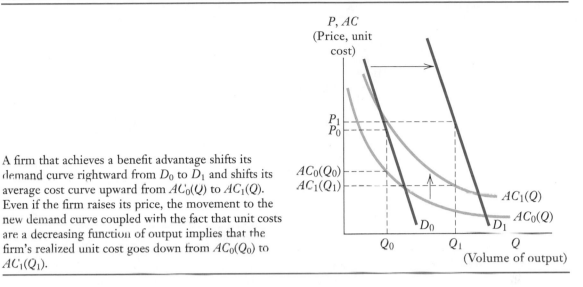

A firm that achieves a benefit advantage shifts its demand curve rightward from D_0 to D_1 and shifts its average cost curve upward from $AC_0(Q)$ to $AC_1(Q)$. Even if the firm raises its price, the movement to the new demand curve coupled with the fact that unit costs are a decreasing function of output implies that the firm's realized unit cost goes down from $AC_0(Q_0)$ to $AC_1(Q_1)$.

down the experience curve, and established a superior cost position relative to its nearest competitors.

- The rate at which accumulated experience reduces costs is often greater for higher-quality products than for lower-quality products. The reason is that production workers must exercise more care to produce a higher-quality product, which often leads to the discovery of bugs and defects that might be overlooked in a lower-quality product.

- Inefficiencies muddy the relationship between cost position and benefit position. The argument that high quality is correlated with high costs ignores the possibility that firms may be producing inefficiently—that is, that their C is higher than it needs to be given their B. If so, then at any point in time, in most industries one might observe firms that create less B and have higher C than their more efficient counterparts. Figure 11.16, which depicts cost and quality positions in the U.S. heavy-duty truck industry in the late 1970s, illustrates how inefficiencies complicate the relationship between cost and benefit positions.[32] If all firms were producing as efficiently as possible, but were pursuing competitive advantages that emphasized different degrees of cost and benefit, then firms' positions would line up along the upward-sloping line that we label the efficiency frontier. The efficiency frontier shows the lowest level of cost that is attainable to achieve a given level of product quality, given the available technology and know-how. Based on previous arguments, one might expect that the efficiency frontier would be upward sloping. Some firms, such as White Motors and International Harvester, however, operated above the efficiency frontier. These firms delivered less quality and incurred higher costs than competitors, such as Ford and Paccar. Not surprisingly, these firms were consistently less profitable than their more efficient rivals.

What, then, can we conclude about the notion of "stuck in the middle"? Although we can find examples of firms that simultaneously attain both a benefit advantage and a cost advantage (e.g., Frito-Lay in the salty snack food market), the admonition to avoid

FIGURE 11.16

QUALITY AND COST POSITIONS IN THE U.S. HEAVY-DUTY
TRUCK MANUFACTURING INDUSTRY IN THE LATE 1970S

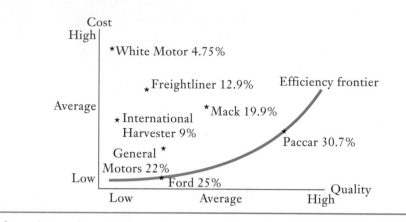

The figure depicts the quality and cost positions of various competitors in the heavy truck manufacturing industry in the United States, as well as each firm's return on assets for the period 1975–1979. If all firms were producing as efficiently as possible, their positions would line up along an upward-sloping efficiency frontier. The efficiency frontier indicates the lowest level of cost that is attainable to achieve a given level of quality, given the available technology and know-how. Firms that are closer to the frontier are generally more profitable than those that are farther away.

Source: Exhibit VII in Hall, W. K., "Survival Strategies in a Hostile Environment," *Harvard Business Review*, September–October 1980, pp. 75–85.

being stuck in the middle is nevertheless extremely important. It reminds us that trade-offs are fundamental in business decisions and that firms can rarely be excellent at everything. A belief that excellence can be attained on all dimensions can often lead to unfocused decision making and the pursuit of inconsistent actions that either have a limited impact in terms of lowering C or increasing B or cancel each other out entirely. It can also lead to uninspired imitation of rival firms' "best practices," a posture that, at best, leads to competitive parity and, at worst, intensifies competition among a group of firms that end up looking alike. Kmart is a telling example of these points. During the 1990s and early 2000s, Kmart careened back and forth, at some points seeking to emulate Target's fashionability and trendiness (e.g., offering the Martha Stewart line on some merchandise), while at other points seeking to compete on price with Wal-Mart (e.g., its move to Every Day Low Pricing in 2001). But over no prolonged period of time did Kmart sustain a deep, consistent focus on achieving *either* superior customer benefits or superior cost efficiency relative to its key competitors. As a result, Kmart was unable to attain either. In effect, by trying to emulate the apparent strengths of each of its rivals, Kmart ended up a pale and unsuccessful imitation of both.

◆ ◆ ◆ ◆ ◆ STRATEGIC POSITIONING: BROAD COVERAGE
VERSUS FOCUS STRATEGIES

The pursuit of cost leadership or benefit leadership relates to the broad issue of *how* the firm will create economic value. A second key positioning issue is *where* the firm will seek to create value. In particular, will a firm seek to create value across a broad scope of market segments, or will it focus on a narrow set of segments?

Segmenting an Industry

Nearly every industry can be broken down into smaller pieces known as segments. Figure 11.17 illustrates what Michael Porter terms an *industry segmentation matrix*.[33] The industry segmentation matrix shows that any industry can be characterized by two dimensions: the varieties of products offered by firms that compete in the industry and the different types of customers that purchase those products. Each point of intersection between a particular buyer group and a particular product variety represents a potential segment. Differences among segments arise because of differences in customer economics (e.g., differences in willingness-to-pay or differences in willingness to trade off quality for price), supply conditions (e.g., costs of producing different product varieties), and segment size. Figure 11.18 shows an industry segmentation matrix for the injection molding equipment industry. This is the industry that makes the machines, molds, and ancillary equipment that are needed to produce molded plastic products such as polyethylene tetraphthalate (PET) containers.[34]

As a result of differences in customer economics, supply conditions, and size within a given industry, the structural attractiveness of segments—as characterized by a segment-level five-forces analysis—can differ greatly across segments. For

FIGURE 11.17
INDUSTRY SEGMENTATION MATRIX

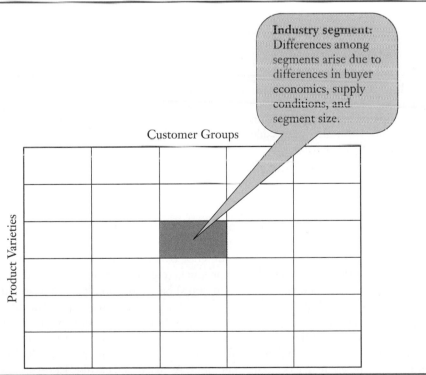

An industry segmentation matrix characterizes the industry along two dimensions: the variety of products that industry participants offer for sale and the different types of buyers that purchase those products.

FIGURE 11.18
INDUSTRY SEGMENTATION MATRIX FOR THE INJECTION MOLDING
EQUIPMENT INDUSTRY

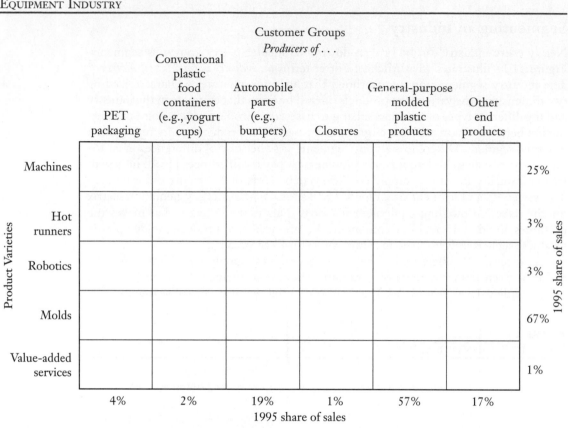

The figure shows an industry segmentation matrix for the injection molding equipment industry. Firms in this industry sell to producers of a variety of end products including PET containers, conventional plastic containers, and automobile parts. Industry participants manufacture a variety of different products including machines and molds. Some firms also offer value-added services related to the design of manufacturing facilities in which the equipment will be deployed.

Source: The data in this figure draws from "Husky Injection Molding Systems," Harvard Business School, Case 9-799-157.

example, in the steel fabrication industry, the fabrication of structural steel members (the cutting and welding of girders, beams, and so forth for use in construction projects) is a relatively unattractive segment since barriers to entry are relatively low. By contrast, the fabrication of metal plate products (e.g., the cutting and bending of steel pieces that are used to construct vats and tanks) has traditionally been more attractive because engineering know-how and product quality are more important differentiators of firm success than in structural steel fabrication, which tends to raise the barriers to entry. In addition, differences in buyer economics, supply conditions, and segment size give rise to opportunities for crafting value chains that are specifically tailored to create economic value in a particular segment. As discussed earlier, Enterprise Rent-a-Car has optimized its value chain to provide superior economic value to replacement renters.

Buyer types can be categorized in a variety of different ways. For example, buyers can be differentiated according to demographic factors (e.g., age group, income class), geography, and the primary channel through which they purchase the product (e.g., physical retailer, catalog, Internet). Buyers can also be distinguished according to how frequently or intensively they use the product (e.g., heavy users versus infrequent users of a product); their depth of knowledge about the product (consumers who are knowledgeable versus consumers who are less well-informed); their occasion of purchase; and their willingness to trade off quality for price. In industrial goods markets, segmentation variables include the buyer's industry; the size of the purchasing firm; the consumer segments the buyer serves; the size of a buyer's order; or the buyer's willingness to trade off price for performance, speed of delivery, and other dimensions of quality.

However buyers are grouped, the classification should be done so that buyers within a particular class have similar tastes, product needs, or responses to marketing mix variables, such as price or advertising, whereas buyers across different classes should have different tastes, needs, or marketing responses.

Broad Coverage Strategies

A broad coverage strategy seeks to serve all customer groups in the market by offering a full line of related products. Gillette follows this strategy in shaving products.[35] It offers a full line of razors (both cartridge and disposable) for both men and women, as well as complementary products, such as shaving cream and after-shave lotions. Frito-Lay follows this strategy in snack foods, offering a full line of high-caloric and "light" snacks, such as potato chips, corn chips, tortilla chips, and pretzels, as well as condiments, such as salsa, that can be eaten with those snacks. The economic logic behind a broad coverage strategy is the existence of economies of scope across product classes. These economies of scope might come from production if the products share common production facilities or components. They might also come from distribution, as Frito-Lay has done through the breadth of its product line, which other manufacturers of salty snack foods, such as Lance, Inc. (which makes Cape Cod Potato Chips), have been unable to match. Or they might come from marketing, the way Gillette has attempted to use its brand name to convey a strong image of quality and tradition not only for its razors, but also for its shaving cream and after-shave lotion. This has allowed Gillette to establish the basis for a benefit advantage in these latter markets at a lower cost than it would have had to incur had it not already established brand equity in razor blades.

Both Gillette and Frito-Lay are examples of broad coverage strategies that depend on products being tailored to different market segments. (Gillette sells razors to men and women; Frito-Lay offers both regular and light versions of its best-selling snacks.) However, broad coverage strategies might be either more or less customized to the firm's target customers than is true of Gillette or Frito-Lay. For example, some firms follow a one-size-fits-all strategy whereby a common product line is marketed to different market segments. In computer software, Microsoft's major software products—Word, Excel, and PowerPoint—appeal to many kinds of users but are not tailor-made to any particular customer group. A one-size-fits-all strategy exploits economies of scale in production to achieve a cost advantage over competitors. The opposite case would be a firm that seeks to appeal to many classes of buyers but attempts to customize its product line to each of them. The economic logic of this variant of a broad-based design is to create a benefit advantage in each of the segments the firm competes in by offering bundles of attributes to fit the needs of consumers in those segments. The large management consulting companies, such as McKinsey, BCG, and Booz Allen, are examples of this kind of strategy.

Focus Strategies

Under a focus strategy, a firm either offers a narrow set of product varieties, serves a narrow set of customers, or does both. Figure 11.19 uses industry segmentation matrices to illustrate a number of common focus strategies.

FIGURE 11.19
COMMON FOCUS STRATEGIES

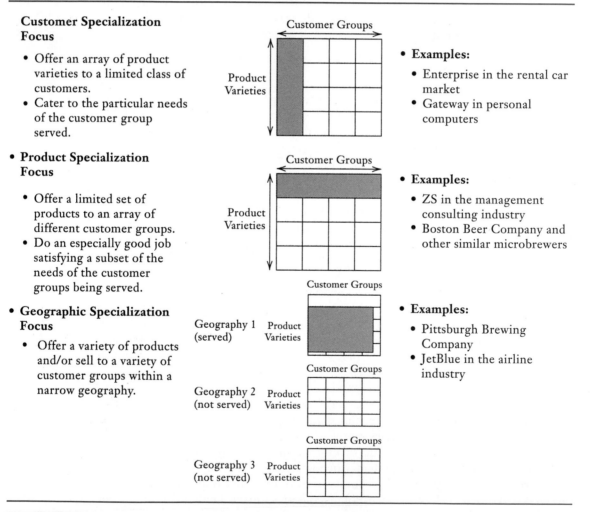

Customer Specialization Focus

• Offer an array of product varieties to a limited class of customers.
• Cater to the particular needs of the customer group served.

• **Product Specialization Focus**

• Offer a limited set of products to an array of different customer groups.
• Do an especially good job satisfying a subset of the needs of the customer groups being served.

• **Geographic Specialization Focus**

• Offer a variety of products and/or sell to a variety of customer groups within a narrow geography.

• **Examples:**
  • Enterprise in the rental car market
  • Gateway in personal computers

• **Examples:**
  • ZS in the management consulting industry
  • Boston Beer Company and other similar microbrewers

• **Examples:**
  • Pittsburgh Brewing Company
  • JetBlue in the airline industry

This figure illustrates three common focus strategies: customer specialization, product specialization, and geographic specialization. Under customer specialization, the firm offers an array of related products to a limited class of customers. Under product specialization, the firm produces a limited set of product varieties for a potentially wide class of customers. Under geographic specialization, the firm offers a variety of related products within a narrowly defined geographic market.

One common basis for a focus strategy is *customer specialization*. Here the firm offers an array of related products to a limited class of customers, with the goal of catering to the particular needs of customers in this class. An example would be a firm that produces and sells industrial process control systems and related devices, such as valves, flowmeters, and recording instruments, to a particular class of buyers such as petroleum refiners. In this case, the focuser's goal is to meet all the process control needs of its target customers (e.g., oil refiners). Enterprise Rent-a-Car is another example of a focus strategy based on customer specialization. Enterprise targets a particular type of car renter—those who seek a replacement vehicle for a prolonged period of time—and offers a wide variety of vehicle types (including trucks) in order to cater to the potentially diverse needs of the customers in this class.

The ability of a customer-specialized focuser to create extra economic value relative to a broad-coverage competitor rests on the extent to which broad-coverage competitors underserve or overserve the focuser's target customer group. A broad coverage competitor *underserves* a customer group when it offers insufficient levels of product attributes that customers in the target set especially value. For example, Microsoft's popular word processing software underserves the needs of authors who prepare technical manuscripts that include lots of mathematical symbols and expressions. These underserved customers created an opportunity for a focused software competitor, TCI Software Research, to offer a word processing product (Scientific Word) that is tailored to the needs of academic researchers who write technical manuscripts. A broad-coverage competitor *overserves* a customer group when it offers costly product attributes that customers in that group do not especially value. Traditional rental car companies with their lucrative rewards programs and airport locations overserve the infrequent renters that Enterprise Rent-a-Car targets, renters who do not value accumulated frequent-renter miles or the proximity of the rental car company to the airport.

A second common basis of a focus strategy is *product specialization*. Here the firm produces a limited set of product varieties for a potentially wide set of customer groups. The product specializer's goal is to do an especially good job satisfying a *subset* of the needs of the customer groups to whom it sells. A good example of a company with this sort of focus is the consulting firm ZS Associates. ZS serves an array of clients in a variety of different industries; however, its consulting work focuses primarily on sales force and marketing-related issues. This contrasts with the broad-based management consultancies with whom ZS competes (e.g., McKinsey and BCG), which consult on a broad range of operational and strategic issues faced by firms. The economic logic of product specialization focus rests on the ability of the focuser to exploit economies of scale or learning economies within the service or the product in which the focuser specializes. ZS's focus over the years on sales force management issues gives it an expertise in these kinds of issues that broad-coverage management consultancies would find difficult to replicate.

A third common basis of a focus strategy is *geographic specialization*. Here the firm offers a variety of related products within a narrowly defined geographic market. Pittsburgh Brewing Company (PBC) illustrates this kind of focus. PBC, located in Pittsburgh, Pennsylvania, offers a number of different lines of beer, with its flagship brands being Iron City and I.C. Light. Even though it sells these beers in a variety of geographies outside of Pittsburgh, its greatest focus of attention is on its home market of Pittsburgh. A focus strategy based on geographic specialization can often enable a firm to achieve economies of scale that it could not achieve if it expanded beyond the geography in which it was concentrating. For example, the strong local image of

PBC's I.C. Light brand ensures it a large market share in the Pittsburgh area, which in turn allows it to benefit from economies of scale in local marketing. Outside of Pittsburgh, however, PBC is unable to match the economies of scale of national marketing that the large brewers such as Anheuser-Busch can attain. Geographic-based focus strategies can also exploit unique conditions in the geography that result in broad-based competitors overserving or underserving the geography. JetBlue illustrates this point in the U.S. airline industry. With its sassy, hip attitude, JetBlue arguably offers service that is better attuned to the unique tastes and predispositions of New Yorkers than broad-based competitors such as American and United. As such, it can survive (and maybe even thrive) despite the obvious disadvantage that comes from competing against airlines with such valuable strategic assets as established reputations and lucrative frequent-flier programs.

In addition to exploiting economies of scale or better serving underserved or overserved customers, focus strategies have another significant potential advantage: they can insulate the focusing firm from competition. In some segments, customer demand may only be large enough to allow just two firms or even one to operate profitably. This implies that a firm may be far more profitable as a focused seller in a low-demand segment than as one of several competitors in high-demand segments. For example, Southwest Airlines and Columbia/HCA (a for-profit hospital chain) have prospered by establishing monopoly or near-monopoly positions in small markets, while their competitive counterparts in larger markets have been less profitable. Indeed, Southwest Airlines avoids markets that would bring it into head-to-head competition with major trunk airlines. Similarly, in Japan, Kubota has dominated the agricultural machinery market. It produces lightweight, compact tractors that are especially well-suited to small Japanese farms, and because that market is limited, it faces little competition. By contrast, the U.S. tractor market is much larger and has many more competitors, including Deere & Company, Case, and Caterpillar.

CHAPTER SUMMARY

◆ A firm achieves a competitive advantage if it can earn higher rates of profitability than rival firms. A firm's profitability depends jointly on industry conditions and the amount of value the firm can create relative to its rivals.

◆ Consumer surplus is the difference between the perceived benefit B of a product and its monetary price P. A consumer will purchase a product only if its consumer surplus is positive. A consumer will purchase the product from a particular seller only if that seller offers a higher consumer surplus than rival sellers offer.

◆ A value map illustrates the competitive implications of consumer surplus. An indifference curve shows the price-quality combinations that yield the same level of consumer surplus.

◆ Value-created is the difference between the perceived benefit B and the unit cost C of the product. Equivalently, it is equal to the sum of consumer surplus and economic profit.

◆ To achieve a competitive advantage, a firm must not only create positive value, it must also create more value than rival firms. If it does so, it can outcompete other firms by offering a higher consumer surplus than rivals.

◆ The bases of competitive advantage are superior resources and organizational capabilities. Resources are firm-specific assets that other firms cannot easily acquire. Organizational capabilities refer to clusters of activities that the firm does especially well compared to rivals.

◆ There are three generic strategies: cost leadership, benefit leadership, and focus.

◆ A firm that follows a strategy of cost leadership seeks to achieve a cost advantage over rival firms by offering a product with a lower C for the same, or perhaps lower, B.

◆ A firm that follows a strategy of benefit leadership seeks to achieve a benefit advantage over rivals by offering products with a higher B for the same, or perhaps higher C.

◆ When firms are horizontally differentiated, the price elasticity of demand strongly affects how a firm profits from a cost advantage. With a low price elasticity of demand, the firm best profits from its cost advantage through higher margins, rather than through higher market share (a margin strategy). With a high price elasticity of demand, it will underprice its competitors and will profit through higher volume (a share strategy).

◆ The price elasticity of demand also determines the profitability of a benefit advantage. With a low price elasticity of demand, the firm should charge a significant price premium relative to competitors (a margin strategy). With a high price elasticity of demand, the firm should maintain price parity with competitors and use its advantage to gain a higher market share (a share strategy).

◆ Building a competitive advantage based on superior cost position is likely to be attractive when there are unexploited opportunities for achieving scale, scope, or learning economies; the product's nature limits opportunities for enhancing its perceived benefit; consumers are relatively price sensitive and are unwilling to pay a premium for enhanced quality or performance; and the product is a search good rather than an experience good.

◆ Building a competitive advantage based on a superior benefit position is likely to be attractive when the typical consumer is willing to pay a significant price premium for attributes that enhance B; existing firms are already exploiting significant economies of scale or learning; and the product is an experience good rather than a search good.

◆ A firm is "stuck in the middle" when it pursues elements of a cost leadership strategy and a benefit leadership strategy at the same time, and in the process, fails to achieve either a cost advantage or a benefit advantage.

◆ Under a broad-coverage strategy, a firm offers a full line of related products to most or all customer groups in the market. Under a focus strategy, a firm either offers a narrow set of product varieties or serves a narrow set of customers, or does both.

◆ A focus strategy based on customer specialization exploits situations in which broad-based competitors are underserving or overserving customers whom the focuser is targeting.

◆ A focus strategy based on product specialization takes advantage of situations in which the focuser can achieve economies of scale or learning economies that broad-based competitors are unable to attain.

◆ A focus strategy based on geographic specialization can allow the focuser to attain economies of scale within the geography that broad-based competitors may be unable to attain.

◆ Focus strategies can often insulate a firm from competition. If the focuser's industry segment is small, it may face little competition and earn substantial returns.

Questions

1. How can the value chain help a firm identify its strategic position?
2. Analysts sometimes suggest that firms should outsource low value-added activities. Do you agree or disagree?
3. Two firms, Alpha and Beta, are competing in a market in which consumer preferences are identical. Alpha offers a product whose benefit B is equal to $75 per unit. Alpha's average cost C is equal to $60 per unit, while Beta's average cost is equal to $50 per unit.

      a. Which firm's product provides the greatest value-created?

      b. In an industry equilibrium in which the firms achieve consumer surplus parity, by what dollar amount will the profit margin, $P - C$, of the firm that creates the greatest amount of value exceed the profit margin of the firm that creates the smaller amount of value? Compare this amount to the difference between the value-created of each firm. What explains the relationship between the difference in profit margins and the difference in value-created between the two firms?

4. Consider a market in which consumer indifference curves are relatively steep. Firms in the industry are pursuing two positioning strategies: some firms are producing a "basic" product that provides satisfactory performance; others are producing an enhanced product that provides performance superior to that of the basic product. Consumer surplus parity currently exists in the industry. Are the prices of the basic and the enhanced product likely to be significantly different or about the same? Why? How would the answer change if consumer indifference curves were relatively flat?

5. Why would the role of the marketing department in capital-intensive industries (e.g., steel) differ from that in labor-intensive industries (e.g., athletic footwear)? How does this relate to positioning?

6. In the value-creation model presented in this chapter, it is implicitly assumed that all consumers get the identical value (e.g., identical B) from a given product. Do the main conclusions in this chapter change if consumer tastes differ, so that some get more value than others?

7. Identify one or more experience goods. Identify one or more search goods. How does the retailing of experience goods differ from the retailing of search goods? Do these differences help consumers?

8. Recall from Chapter 2 Adam Smith's dictum, "The division of labor is limited by the extent of the market." How does market growth affect the viability of a focus strategy?

9. "Firms that seek a cost advantage should adopt a learning curve strategy; firms that seek to differentiate their products should not." Comment on both of these statements.

10. Consumers often identify brand names with quality. Do you think branded products usually are of higher quality than generic products and therefore justify their higher prices? If so, why don't all generic product makers invest to establish a brand identity, thereby enabling them to raise price?

11. Industry 1 consists of four firms that sell a product that is identical in every respect except for production cost and price. Firm A's unit production costs are 10 percent less than the others, and it charges a price that is 1 percent less than the others. Industry 2 consists of four firms that sell a product that is identical in every respect except for production cost and price. Firm X's unit production costs are 10 percent less than the others, and it charges a price that is 8 percent less than the others. Both industries are characterized by stable demand and comparable entry barriers. The preceding situations have prevailed for years. The managers of these firms are very smart and are surely acting in the best interest of their owners, whose only goal is to maximize profits. Based on this information only, can you determine which industry has the higher price–cost margin (i.e., [price–unit production cost] as a percentage of price) and why?

◆ ◆ ◆ ◆ ◆ **APPENDIX**

Cost Drivers

Cost and consumer benefit drive value-creation. Understanding how a firm creates value and why it creates more or less value than its competitors often requires a diagnosis of cost and benefit drivers.

Cost drivers explain why costs vary across firms. We discuss cost drivers in terms of average costs, rather than total costs, because a larger firm's total costs would be higher than a smaller firm's simply because it is larger. We can classify cost drivers into four broad categories, each of which has several subcategories:

- Cost drivers related to firm size or scope
  - Economies of scale
  - Economies of scope
  - Capacity utilization
- Cost drivers related to cumulative experience
  - Learning curve
- Cost drivers independent of firm size, scope, or cumulative experience
  - Input prices
  - Location
  - Economies of density
  - Complexity/focus
  - Process efficiency
  - Discretionary policies
  - Government policies
  - Cost drivers related to the organization of transactions
  - Organization of the vertical chain
  - Agency efficiency

Cost Drivers Related to Firm Size, Scope, and Cumulative Experience

Chapter 2 contains an extensive discussion of economies of scale, scope, and cumulative experience, so here we will just review the key ideas. Economies of scale exist when average costs go down as the scale of operation increases. Economies of scope exist when average costs go down as the firm produces a greater variety of goods. A paramount source of economies of scale and scope is indivisible inputs. Indivisible inputs cannot be scaled down below a certain minimum size and thus give rise to fixed costs. As the volume or variety of output increases, these fixed costs get spread out, leading to lower per-unit costs of production. In the short run, fixed costs are often spread because of greater capacity utilization. In the long run, fixed costs are spread when it becomes economical for a firm to substitute a technology with high fixed costs but low variable costs for one with low fixed costs but high variable costs. Other important sources of economies of scale are: (1) the physical properties of processing units (i.e., the cube-square rule); (2) increases in the productivity of variable inputs as volume increases (e.g., because of greater specialization of labor); (3) economies of inventory management.

Cumulative experience can reduce average costs as firms move down the learning curve. Learning economies should not, however, be confused with economies of scale that arise when the firm spreads out nonrecurring fixed costs over the volume of output it produces over time. To illustrate this distinction, consider a small producer of a specialty valve. The upfront costs of designing the valve are incurred only once. The dies and jigs used to fabricate the valve can be reused from one year to the next, so these costs are also nonrecurring. Even though the firm's annual rate of production may be small, its average cost per unit might still be low because it has produced the same model year after year, a phenomenon sometimes known as *economies of model volume*. Spreading nonrecurring fixed costs causes unit production costs to decrease with volume, even if the firm does not become more proficient in manufacturing the good as it accumulates experience.

Cost Drivers Independent of Firm Size, Scope, or Cumulative Experience

These factors make one firm's unit costs different from a competitor's even if their sizes and cumulative experience are the same. An important cost driver independent of scale is input prices (e.g., wage rates, energy prices, and prices of components and raw materials). When firms in the same industry purchase their inputs in national markets, their input prices will be the same. But firms in the same industry often pay different prices for inputs. Differences in wage rates may be due to differences in the degree of unionization (e.g., large airlines, such as United and American, are unionized, but many new entrants are not). Differences in wages, the price of energy, or the price of delivered materials can also be attributed to location differences among firms.

Location can also influence costs in other ways. For example, because of weak local infrastructure and coordination problems that arose due to the distance between corporate headquarters and its production facility, in the 1980s the Lionel Corporation found it more expensive to produce toy trains in Tijuana, Mexico, than in Michigan, despite the large wage-rate advantage of the Mexican location.

Economies of density refer to cost savings that arise with greater geographic density of customers. Economies of density can arise when a transportation network within a given geographic territory is utilized more intensively (e.g., when an airline's unit costs decline as more passengers are flown over a given route). They also arise when a geographically smaller territory generates the same volume of business as a geographically larger territory (e.g., when a beer distributor that operates in a densely populated urban area has lower unit costs than a distributor selling the same amount of beer in more sparsely populated suburbs). In both cases, the cost savings are due to an increase in density (e.g., passengers per mile, customers per square mile) rather than an increase in scope (e.g., number of routes served) or scale (e.g., volume of beer sold).

One firm may achieve lower average costs than its competitors because its production environment is less complex or more focused. A firm that uses the same factory to produce many different products may incur large costs associated with changing over machines and production lines to produce batches of the different products. It may also incur high administrative costs to track different work orders. A good example of the impact of complexity on production costs is the railroad industry. Historically, the Pennsylvania and New York Central railroads had some of the highest costs in the business because they carried a much higher proportion of less-than-carload freight than railroads such as the Norfolk and Western and the Southern. The Pennsylvania and the New York Central needed more classification yards, more freight terminals, and more personnel per ton of freight than their more focused counterparts, which specialized in bulk traffic, such as coal and lumber. After the two railroads merged to form the Penn Central in 1968, they were spending 15 cents for every dollar of sales revenue on yard expenses, as compared with an average of less than 10 cents per dollar of sales for all other railroads.[36]

A firm may have lower average costs than its rivals because it has been able to realize production process efficiencies that its rivals have not achieved; that is, the firm uses fewer inputs than its competitors to produce a given amount of output, or its production technology uses lower-priced inputs than those utilized by rivals. This effect is often difficult to disentangle from the learning curve, because the achievement of process efficiencies through learning-by-doing is at the heart of the learning curve. An example of a process efficiency not based on experience is the Chicago and Northwestern Railroad's (CNW) decision in the mid-1980s to reduce the crew size on its freight trains from four to three by eliminating one of the brakemen. This move allowed the CNW to become one of the lowest-cost competitors in the railroad business.

One firm may also have lower average costs than its competitors because it avoids expenses that its rivals are incurring. Its costs are lower because of discretionary factors that, at least to some extent, are within the firm's control. For example, in the tire business, Cooper Tire and Rubber generally refrains from national advertising. This results in sales and administrative expenses that are significantly lower than those of competitors such as Goodyear.

Finally, a firm may have lower average costs than those of its rivals because of the effects of government policies. For obvious reasons, this factor affects international markets. For example, Japanese truck producers have long been at a disadvantage in selling trucks in the United States because of the steep import duty the U.S. government levies on foreign trucks.

Cost Drivers Related to the Organization of the Transaction

Chapters 3 and 4 discussed how the vertical chain can influence production costs. For transactions in which the threat of holdup is significant, in which private information can be leaked, or coordination is complicated, a firm that organizes the exchange through the market may have higher administrative and production expenses than a firm in which the same exchange is vertically integrated. In the production of men's underwear, for example, vertical integration of sewing and textile conversion operations in the same plant reduces coordination costs by improving scheduling of production runs. One firm's costs may be higher than another's because of differential degrees of agency efficiency. A firm's internal administrative systems, organizational structure, or compensation system may make it more vulnerable to agency or influence costs than its competitors are. For example, prior to the 1990s, IBM had what was known as a "contention system" under which executives within one business unit or functional area were empowered to critique ideas that came from outside their primary areas of responsibility. According to one account, this system made IBM slow to recognize the opportunities and threats associated with the rise of personal computers in the 1980s and early 1990s.[37]

Agency costs often increase as the firm expands and gains more activities to coordinate internally or grows more diverse and thus creates greater conflicts in achieving coordination. The firm's agency efficiency relative to other firms can also deteriorate as its competitors adopt new and innovative internal organization that solves the same coordination problems at lower cost.

Cost Drivers, Activity-Cost Analysis, and Cost Advantage

In general, the cost of each activity in the firm's vertical chain may be influenced by a different set of cost drivers. For example, in the production of men's underwear, cumulative experience is an important cost driver in sewing but not in the more capital-intensive processes of yarn production and textile conversion. Economies of scale, by contrast, are an important cost driver in yarn production and textile conversion but not in sewing.

Viewing firms as a collection of activities, each influenced by its own set of cost drivers, suggests that there are two major routes to achieving a cost advantage. The first is to exploit or control the key cost drivers within various activities better than competitors. The second is to fundamentally alter activities in the vertical chain. Changes in the vertical chain may be necessary owing to changes in technology, which will alter the tradeoffs between outsourcing activities or performing them internally. They may also stem from changes in market conditions, which alter the prevailing costs of using the market rather than the internal organization to coordinate transactions. Altering the vertical chain is at the heart of what has come to be known as *process reengineering*, a management philosophy that urges firms not to take the existing configuration of activities and processes for granted, but rather to redesign the chain of activities to maximize the value that it can deliver. Classic examples include Federal Express, which dramatically changed the economics of small-package delivery in the 1970s by using the hub-and-spoke network; Dell, which ignored conventional wisdom in the computer business by selling personal computers directly to consumers, thereby avoiding sales force and distribution expenses; and Wal-Mart, which pioneered the use of electronic computerized inventory control systems and hub-and-spoke-based logistics systems, fundamentally changing the economics of mass merchandising.

Benefit Drivers

A firm creates a benefit advantage by offering a product that delivers larger perceived benefits to prospective buyers than competitors' products, that is, by offering a higher B. The perceived benefit, in turn, depends on the attributes that consumers value, as well as on those that lower the user and the transactions costs of the product. These attributes, or what we call benefit drivers, form the basis on which a firm can differentiate itself. Benefit drivers can include many things, and analyzing them in any particular case involves identifying who the firm's prospective buyers are, understanding how they might use the firm's product or service, and discovering which of their needs the firm's product satisfies.

Benefit drivers can be classified along five dimensions:

1. *Physical characteristics of the product itself.* These drivers include factors such as product performance, quality, features, aesthetics, durability, and ease of installation and operation.
2. *The quantity and characteristics of the services or complementary goods the firm or its dealers offer for sale.* Key drivers here include postsale services, such as customer training or consulting, complementary products (e.g., spare parts) that the seller bundles with the product, product warranties or maintenance contracts, and the quality of repair or service capabilities.
3. *Characteristics associated with the sale or delivery of the good.* Specific benefit drivers include speed and timeliness of delivery, availability and favorability of credit terms, location of the seller, and the quality of presale technical advice.
4. *Characteristics that shape consumers' perceptions or expectations of the product's performance or its cost to use.* Specific drivers include the product's reputation for performance, the seller's perceived staying power or financial stability (this would be important for industrial transactions in which the buyer anticipates an ongoing

relationship with the seller), and the product's installed base (i.e., the number of consumers currently using the product; a large installed base would lead us to expect that the costs of developing product know-how will be low).

5. *The subjective image of the product.* Image is a convenient way of referring to the constellation of psychological rewards that the consumer receives from purchasing, owning, and consuming the product. Image is driven by the impact of advertising messages, packaging, or labeling, and by the prestige of the distributors or outlets that carry the products.

Methods for Estimating and Characterizing Perceived Benefits

Unlike a firm's costs, which (at least in principle) can be tracked through its accounting system or estimated with statistical techniques, a product's perceived benefit is more difficult to estimate. Any approach for estimating and characterizing benefits has four components. First, the firm must measure the benefits provided to the consumer. Second, it must identify the relevant benefit drivers. Third, it must estimate the magnitude of the benefit. Fourth, it must identify the willingness of consumers to trade off one driver for another. A full analysis of the techniques for estimating benefits falls within the domain of demand estimation in economics and marketing research. Four approaches might be used to estimate a firm's benefit position relative to its competitors and the importance of benefit drivers.

1. Reservation price method
2. Attribute-rating method
3. Hedonic pricing analysis
4. Conjoint analysis

Reservation Price Method

Because a consumer purchases a product if and only if $B - P > 0$, it follows that the perceived benefit B represents a consumer's reservation price—the maximum monetary price the consumer will pay for a unit of the product or service. Since such an overall measure of consumer benefit is rarely available, it must be estimated from survey data or else imputed from database information on consumer choices. One approach to estimating B, then, is simply to ask consumers the highest price they would pay. Marketing survey research that precedes the introduction of new products often includes such a question. Once reservation prices have been identified, the analysis of benefit drivers can follow using the techniques discussed below.

Attribute-Rating Method

Attribute rating is a technique for estimating benefit drivers directly from survey responses and then calculating overall benefits on the basis of attribute scores. Target consumers are asked to rate products in terms of attributes. For example, for each attribute consumers might be given a fixed number of points to allocate among each product. Each attribute is then assigned an "importance weight," and relative perceived benefits are determined by calculating the weighted average of the product ratings. Weighted scores can be divided by costs to construct "B/C ratios." Recall that a firm's strategic position is determined by the amount of $B - C$ it generates versus its competitors. As long as products have cost and/or benefit proximity, the ranking of B/C ratios across firms will be similar (though not necessarily equal) to the rankings of $B - C$ differences. Thus, products with high B/C ratios will generally enjoy a superior strategic position to their lower B/C rivals.

Hedonic Pricing Analysis

Hedonic pricing uses data about actual consumer purchases to determine the value of particular product attributes. (The term *hedonic* comes from *hedonism* and is meant to convey the idea that the pleasure or happiness a consumer derives from a good depends on the attributes that the good embodies.) For example, consumers purchase automobiles according to a variety of attributes, including horsepower, interior room, and braking capabilities. By examining how automobile prices vary with different combinations of attributes, analysts can determine how much consumers are willing to pay for each individual attribute. Hedonic pricing has been used to identify the value of innovations in automobiles and computerized axial tomography, the value of spreadsheet compatibility, and the benefits of improving job safety.

Hedonic pricing requires multiple regression analysis to estimate the impact of product attributes on a product's price. The dependent variable in the regression is the product's price. The predictors are variables measuring the presence and extent of different product attributes. If you were studying the automobile market, hedonic pricing analysis could identify the extent to which a 1 percent increase in horsepower or chassis length, or the addition of side-impact air bags, translates into automobile prices. This analysis generates implicit "hedonic prices" for individual product attributes.

Hedonic pricing can be an extremely powerful tool in evaluating the economic tradeoffs involved in enhancing a product. In effect, this analysis can help a firm determine the slope of the consumer indifference curves that were discussed previously. A firm considering adding extra features to a basic product or enhancing the product's performance would compare the hedonic price of the enhancement to its incremental cost. If, in the target market, the hedonic price exceeds the incremental cost, the enhancement will be worthwhile.

Conjoint Analysis

Hedonic pricing analysis uses market prices for existing combinations of product attributes. This is inadequate for studying the value of new features. To do this, market researchers use conjoint analysis. Like hedonic pricing, conjoint analysis estimates the relative benefits of different product attributes. Its principal value is in estimating these benefits for hypothetical combinations of attributes. Although conjoint analysis can take several different forms, consumers are usually asked to rank a product with different features at different prices. For example, they might be asked to rank the following four "bundles": (1) a CD player without a shuffle-play feature at a price of $200; (2) the same CD player without a shuffle-play feature at a price of $300; (3) the same CD player with a shuffle-play feature, at a price of $200; and (4) the CD player with a shuffle-play feature at a price of $300. Consumers would almost certainly rank (1) over (2) and (3) over (4). However, the choice between (1) and (4) is less clear. The proportion of consumers that ranks (4) over (1) provides information about consumers' willingness to pay for a shuffle-play feature. In a typical conjoint analysis, consumers are asked to rank many different bundles, and researchers then use regression analysis to estimate the impact of price and product features on the rankings. From this, researchers can estimate the market value of different features.

Alternatively, consumers may be asked to state how much they are willing to pay for different combinations of features. Researchers then treat the responses as if they were actual market prices and use regression techniques to estimate the value of each attribute. This approach closely mirrors hedonic pricing, except that the prices and products are hypothetical.

Value-Added Analysis

Value-added analysis is a tool for understanding where economic value is created within a firm's value chain. Consider the example of a firm that produces blue jeans. The firm sells its product to three different types of customers. It sells unlabeled jeans to manufacturers that attach their own labels and sell the jeans as house brands. It also sells jeans under its own brand name label (which it supports through extensive advertising and product promotion) to independent wholesalers, which then distribute them to retailers. Finally, it uses in-house distribution capabilities to sell and distribute its labeled blue jeans directly to retailers. For simplicity, then, we can think of the firm's value chain as consisting of three major activities: manufacturing; brand management, which includes the marketing undertaken to support the brand; and distribution. Manufacturing creates value by transforming raw materials into finished jeans. Brand management creates value by transforming what would otherwise be no-name jeans into branded jeans with a superior image. Distribution creates value by distributing jeans that would otherwise be sold to wholesalers. Value-added analysis determines the incremental profit each of these activities creates.

Consider the information shown in Table A11.1. Note that the profit contribution is:

$$25,000(4 - 2.50) + 70,000(14 - 2.55) + 15,000(18 - 2.55 - 1.80) - 800,000$$
$$= \$243,750.$$

The value-added analysis proceeds as follows:

- *Value added in manufacturing* = profit that would have been made if all jeans are sold unlabeled to private labelers:

$$= 110,000(4 - 2.50) = \$165,000, \text{ or } \$1.50 \text{ per pair.}$$

- *Value added in brand management* = incremental profit made by selling all labeled jeans to wholesalers as opposed to selling them as unlabeled jeans to private labelers:

$$= 85,000[(14 - 2.55) - (4 - 2.50)] - \$800,000 = \$45,750, \text{ or } \$0.54 \text{ per pair.}$$

TABLE A11.1
VOLUMES, PRICES, AND COSTS FOR A BLUE JEANS FIRM

Total quantity of blue jeans manufactured	110,000 pairs per year
Unlabeled jeans sold to private labelers	25,000 pairs per year
Labeled jeans sold to wholesalers	70,000 pairs per year
Labeled jeans, self-distributed	15,000 pairs per year
Selling price, unlabeled jeans	$4.00 per pair
Selling price, labeled jeans sold to wholesalers	$14.00 per pair
Selling price, labeled jeans, self-distributed	$18.00 per pair
Production cost per unit, unlabeled jeans	$2.50 per pair
Production cost per unit, labeled jeans	$2.55 per pair
Distribution cost per unit	$1.80 per pair
Total brand promotion and advertising expenses	$800,000 per year

- *Value added in distribution* = incremental profit made by self-distributing labeled jeans to retailers as opposed to selling them to wholesalers:

$$= 15,000[(18 - 2.55 - 1.80) - (14 - 2.55)] = \$33,000, \text{ or } \$2.20 \text{ per pair.}$$

Note that the sum of the value added across the three activities is equal to the total profit contribution. This is not coincidental. It happens because value-added analysis carefully counts only the incremental profit an activity generates. Perhaps surprisingly, the analysis reveals that the highest total value added comes from manufacturing, not from branding the jeans, and the highest value added per unit comes from distribution. Although branding the product and supporting it with advertising and promotion are important activities in this company, they do not contribute much to profit because they are costly compared with the benefits they generate.

ENDNOTES

[1]See "Northwest Airlines Bets on Hinterlands for Its Survival," *Wall Street Journal*, June 15, 2005, p. B1.

[2]The data reported in Table 11.1 were obtained for the companies listed in the 2004 Performance 1000 universe collected by Stern Stewart & Company. A positive spread between return on invested capital and cost of capital in a particular year indicates positive economic profitability, while a negative spread indicates negative economic profitability.

[3]McGahan, A. M. and M. E. Porter, "How Much Does Industry Matter Really?" *Strategic Management Journal*, 18, Summer 1997, pp. 15–30. See also Rumelt, R. P., "How Much Does Industry Matter?" *Strategic Management Journal*, 12, 1991, pp. 167–185.

[4]Drucker, P. F., *Management: Tasks, Responsibilities, Practices*, New York, HarperBusiness, 1973, p. 61.

[5]The logic is straightforward. Each point (*A* and *B* in Figure 11.6) yields the same consumer surplus, so $B_A - P_A = B_B - P_B$. Rearranging yields: $\Delta B = B_A - B_B = P_A - P_B$.

[6]The data for this example comes from "Sports and Suds: The Beer Business and the Sports World Have Brewed Up a Potent Partnership," *Sports Illustrated*, August 8, 1988, pp. 68–82.

[7]For interested readers, here is how this number was derived. Total (as opposed to per-unit) consumer surplus can be shown to equal the area under the demand curve above the price. For a linear demand curve given by the formula $P = a - bQ$ (where Q is total demand), this area is given by $0.5bQ^2$. Consumer surplus per unit is thus given by $0.5bQ^2 \div Q = 0.5bQ = 0.5P(bQ/P)$. But the term in parentheses is the reciprocal of the price elasticity of demand (i.e., $\eta = P/bQ$). Thus, per-unit consumer surplus is given by $.5P/\eta$. To estimate η, we proceed as follows. The stadium concessionaire, Cincinnati Sports Service, pays the distributor $0.20 per 20-ounce cup of beer, pays royalties to the city of Cincinnati of $0.24 per cup, pays royalties to the Cincinnati Reds of $0.54 per cup, and an excise tax of $0.14 per cup. The concessionaire's marginal cost is thus at least $1.12 per cup of beer. If we assume that $2.50 is the profit-maximizing monopoly price, then the price elasticity of demand η at $2.50 must be at least 1.8 (we'll see why in just a moment). Using the preceding formula for per-unit consumer surplus, we conclude that the average consumer surplus for a 20-ounce cup of beer is no greater than $0.69. The reason that the price elasticity of demand must be at least 1.8 is as follows: from the Economics Primer, the optimal monopoly price is given by $(P - MC)/P = 1/\eta$. Thus, if $2.50 is the monopoly price, $(2.50 - MC)/2.50 = 1/\eta$. Since $MC = \$1.12$, straightforward algebra implies $\eta = 1.8$.

[8]Without knowing the production costs of Sports Service or the distributor, we cannot pin down the actual amount of value that is created through the vertical chain. Whatever it is, however, the brewer captures only a small portion of it.

[9]Here is the math. Suppose Firm 1 creates more value than Firm 2, so that $B_1 - C_1 > B_2 - C_2$. The most aggressive bid Firm 2 can offer is $P_1^* = C_2$, leaving you with consumer surplus of $B_2 - C_2$. Firm 1 can offer you a slightly more favorable bid than this by offering a price slightly lower than $P_1^* = C_2 + (B_1 - B_2)$. At this price, Firm 1's profit is slightly less than $P_1^* - C_1$ which equals $C_2 + (B_1 - B_2) - C_1$. After rearranging terms, we can write this as $(B_1 - C_1) - (B_2 - C_2)$, which is positive. Thus, Firm 1 can always profitably outbid Firm 2 for your business.

[10]In 2002, the average household income of the Kmart shopper was $35,000, while the average household incomes for the Wal-Mart and Target shoppers were $37,000 and $45,000, respectively. "Wal-Mart Discount King, Eyes the BMW Crowd," *New York Times*, February 24, 2002, pp. A1, A24.

[11]Rumelt, R., "The Evaluation of Business Strategy," in Glueck, W. F., *Business Policy and Strategic Management*, 3rd ed., New York, McGraw-Hill, 1980.

[12]The concept of the value chain was developed by Michael Porter. See Chapter 2 of *Competitive Advantage*, New York, Free Press, 1985.

[13]The term *Airport 7* was coined by Andrew Taylor, the current CEO of Enterprise, to describe the seven airport-based rental car firms. Actually, three pairs of the "Airport 7" operate under common ownership: Vanguard Rental owns both National and Alamo; Cendant Corporation owns both Avis and Budget, and Dollar Thrifty Automotive Group owns both Dollar and Thrifty.

[14]This example was developed by Jesus Syjuco and Li Liu, Kellogg School of Management, MBA class of 2002.

[15]Suhr, Jim, "Rent-a-Car Companies Expand into Rivals' Turf," *Associated Press State and Local Wire*, October 1, 2004.

[16]"Cult Brands: The Business Week/InterBrand Annual Ranking of the World's Most Valuable Brands Shows the Power of Passionate Customers," *Business Week* (August 2, 2004), pp. 64–67.

[17]Other terms for this concept include distinctive competencies and core competencies.

[18]C. K. Prahalad and Gary Hamel emphasize this type of capability in their notion of "core competence." See "The Core Competence of the Corporation," *Harvard Business Review*, May–June 1990, pp. 79–91.

[19]Nelson, R. R., and S. G. Winter, *An Evolutionary Theory of Economic Change*, Cambridge, MA, Belknap, 1982.

[20]Henderson, R. and I. Cockburn, "Measuring Competence? Exploring Firm Effects in Pharmaceutical Research," *Strategic Management Journal*, 15, Winter 1994, pp. 63–84.

[21]Porter, Michael, *Competitive Strategy*, New York, Free Press, 1980.

[22]Porter uses the term *differentiation* to describe what we have called benefit leadership.

[23]This example has been adapted from an earlier example developed by Jesus Syjuco and Li Liu, Kellogg School of Management, MBA class of 2002.

[24]Dombey, Daniel, "Well-Built Success," *Industry Week*, May 5, 1997.

[25]Crawford, Fred and Ryan Matthews, *The Myth of Excellence: Why Great Companies Never Try to Be the Best at Everything*, New York, Crown Business, 2001. This example draws from Crawford and Matthew's account of Superquinn, as well as from business press articles on Superquinn.

[26]This section draws from the article, O'Kane, Paul, "All to Play for as Superquinn Changes Hands; Serious Challenges Face Premium Retailer's New Owners," *The Sunday Tribune* (January 16, 2005).

[27]Besanko, D., D. Dranove, and M. Shanley, "Exploiting a Cost Advantage and Coping with a Cost Disadvantage," *Management Science*, 47(2), February 2001, pp. 221–235.

[28]See Chapter 2 of Porter, *Competitive Strategy*.

[29]Michael Porter makes this point most forcefully in his article, "What Is Strategy," *Harvard Business Review*, November–December, 1996, pp. 61–78.

[30]Miller, D. and P. H. Friesen, "Porter's (1980) Generic Strategies and Quality: An Empirical Examination with American Data—Part I: Testing Porter," *Organization Studies*, 7, 1986, pp. 37–55.

[31]As we write this in the first quarter 2006, United had been in bankruptcy since late 2002, while Delta and American have teetered on the brink of insolvency over the same period.

[32]This figure is adapted from Hall, W. K., "Survival Strategies in a Hostile Environment," *Harvard Business Review*, September–October 1980, pp. 75–85.

[33]See Chapter 7 of Porter, *Competitive Advantage*.

[34]The data in this figure are drawn from "Husky Injection Molding Systems," Harvard Business School, Case 9-799-157.

[35]In January 2005, Procter & Gamble acquired Gillette. P&G plans to organize Gillette's core businesses (most notably its shaving business) into a new business unit named Global Gillette Business.

[36]Daughen, J. R., and P. Binzen, *The Wreck of the Penn Central*, Boston, Little, Brown, 1971, pp. 210–212.

[37]Carroll, P., *Big Blue: The Unmaking of IBM*, New York, Crown, 1993.

SUSTAINING COMPETITIVE ADVANTAGE

12

*F*ederal Express created the overnight package delivery service in 1973, when it began service in 25 U.S. cities. For the better part of a decade, FedEx nearly monopolized the business, and the company's name became synonymous with overnight delivery. The success of FedEx caught the attention of UPS, the nation's leading "longer-than-overnight" package delivery service. In the early 1980s, UPS launched its own overnight delivery service. Unfamiliar with what it took to deliver parcels overnight, UPS decided to learn from the market leader. UPS studied FedEx procedures for taking orders, scheduling, and delivering shipments. UPS even had its drivers follow FedEx trucks to learn their methods. By 1985, UPS was able to match FedEx's nationwide overnight service offerings and within a few years was also matching FedEx for reliability. UPS gradually won business from FedEx, and by 2004 UPS had captured 40 percent of the total express-mail market, compared with 45 percent for FedEx. Moreover, by taking advantage of the scale economies afforded by their existing fleet of delivery trucks, UPS could deliver overnight parcels at a lower cost than FedEx and enjoyed a substantially higher profit margin.

What happened to Federal Express has also happened to many other companies: Competitive advantages that have taken years to build up are suddenly and quickly eroded by imitators who copy or improve the firm's formula for success or by innovators who neutralize the firm's advantage through new technologies, products, or ways of doing business. All this, combined with a dose of bad luck, can destroy even the top firms. Yet, while competitive advantages for many firms are fleeting, other firms seem to sustain competitive advantages year after year. Coca-Cola in soft drinks, Walgreens in pharmacy and drug retailing, and Nucor in steel have consistently outperformed their competitors.

Chapter 11 asked: Why do some firms outperform their industries? This chapter asks: Why do some firms persistently outperform their competitors, despite the efforts of other firms to imitate or neutralize their advantage? What, in short, makes a competitive advantage sustainable, and why?

◆ ◆ ◆ ◆ ◆ How Hard Is It to Sustain Profits?

Regardless of the competitive environment the firm is in, it is often difficult to sustain profits. Some enemies of sustainability, such as imitability and entry, are threats in all market structures. Others, such as price competition, may be greater threats in competitive markets.

Threats to Sustainability in Competitive and Monopolistically Competitive Markets

The theory of perfect competition is a logical starting point for our discussion of sustainability of competitive advantage. That theory—discussed in detail in the Economics Primer—has a fundamentally important implication: opportunities for earning profit based on favorable market conditions will quickly evaporate as new entrants flow into the market, increase the supply of output, and drive price down to the point where economic profits are zero (see Figure 12.1). But just how relevant is this theory? After all, it seems to be cast in the context of special industry structure: firms produce a homogeneous good, face identical technologies and input costs, and are so small relative to the size of the market that they act as price takers. Few industries outside of agriculture and fishing seem to be characterized by these stark conditions.

But the dynamic of competition can operate under seemingly more complex conditions than the standard theory assumes. Even in industries where firms offer differentiated products, potential profits can be dissipated through entry and imitation. Consider monopolistically competitive markets, in which sellers are differentiated in distinct niches (i.e., they cater to consumers with different preferences over key product attributes). Unlike perfect competition, a monopolistically competitive seller can raise its price without losing all its customers. As pointed out in Chapter 6, it is optimal for it to set a price above marginal cost.

FIGURE 12.1
THE PERFECTLY COMPETITIVE DYNAMIC

This figure depicts a market in which consumers have identical tastes, which are reflected by indifference curves, such as I_1, I_2, and I_3. The upward-sloping line is the efficiency frontier for this market. A price-quality position, such as (P_A, q_A), could not be sustained when there is free entry and costless imitation. An entrant could offer a lower price and higher quality (e.g., P_B, q_B) and steal the market from incumbent firms. The perfectly competitive equilibrium occurs at price-quality combination (P_z, q_z). At this point, economic profits are zero, and no other price-quality position simultaneously results in greater consumer surplus and higher profit.

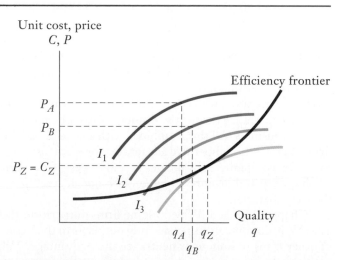

EXAMPLE 12.1 "VON-A-BEES"[1]

By now, most readers have probably heard of—and maybe even have subscribed to—Internet-based phone service. This service allows a user to make telephone calls that are routed over the Internet rather than traditional phone lines. The key advantage of Internet-based phone service is its cost: telephone service with quality comparable to land-line phones can be offered at a fraction of the cost of conventional telephone service.

In 2002, a firm by the name of Vonage was an early entrant into the Internet-based market. Vonage was a start-up company with just 50 employees when it began offering service. Armed with over $400 million raised from venture capital funds, Vonage grew quickly, acquiring 800,000 subscribers on its way toward becoming a dominant player in the Internet-based phone market. Along the way, Vonage's success helped reinforce the perception that Internet-based phone service was ripe for growth.

Vonage's CEO, Jeffrey Citron, talked as if the company's success was assured. In early 2005 he gave an interview in which he talked about driving conventional phone companies out of business. But as is discussed in the text, opportunities for earning economic profits attract new entrants. As it became clear that there was a meaningful market for Internet-based phone service, new entrants came into the industry to challenge Vonage's dominance. The first large company to enter the market was AT&T in March 2004. Seven months later came Verizon, which launched a service called VoiceWing. In addition to these large telecom companies, several cable companies and numerous small start-ups have also entered the market.

Vonage derisively dismissed its new competitors as "Von-a-bees." However, their presence could not be ignored. In May 2004, shortly after AT&T's entry, Vonage lowered its monthly rate from $35 to $30. When Verizon entered in October 2004, both Vonage and AT&T responded by dropping their rates to $30 per month. By late 2004, Vonage's rates had dropped to $25 per month.

To deflect the impact of the intense price competition in the U.S. market, Vonage is attempting to position itself as the high-quality, high-reliability player in the market. According to Jeffrey Citron, "It's not our desire to be the cheapest operator." Whether Vonage's attempt to position itself as a premium player will ultimately succeed is an interesting question since, up to now, the value proposition of Internet-based phone service has been its low cost. Vonage is also seeking growth outside the United States. For example, it has started service in the United Kingdom and the Netherlands. Unfortunately for Vonage, the competitive dynamic that is playing out in the U.S. market is also playing out in European markets, once again underscoring a fundamental law of economics: where profit opportunities exist, new entrants will arise in order to exploit those opportunities.

Even though a monopolistically competitive seller sets price above marginal cost, there is no guarantee that it will earn profits. The seller may be covering incremental costs, but it must also have sufficient sales volume to cover its fixed costs. If incumbent sellers are making profits, and there is free entry into the market, new firms will enter. By slightly differentiating themselves from incumbents, these entrants will find their own niches but will inevitably take some business from incumbents. As discussed in Chapter 6, entry will continue in this way until incremental profits just cover fixed costs. The fast-food market shows how entry by differentiated sellers (e.g., Taco Bell) led to the decline of the successful incumbent (McDonald's). Other examples include household appliances, luxury cars, and mass-market retailing.

Successful incumbents in both competitive and monopolistically competitive markets can do little to preserve profits unless they can deter entry. We discussed strategies for doing this in Chapter 9.

Threats to Sustainability under All Market Structures

Even in oligopolistic or monopolistic markets, where entry might be blockaded or deterred, a successful incumbent may not stay successful for long. One reason is that success may be due to factors that the incumbent cannot control, such as the weather or general business conditions. A March blizzard in Colorado that delays shipments of Coors beer to the West Coast will hurt Coors sales for the month and will boost sales of competing brands, such as Budweiser and Miller. But one would not expect Coors' April sales to stay down, nor would one expect Budweiser and Miller to sustain the one-month sales increase. If, as expected, April sales revert to historical levels, we would say that profits showed *regression to the mean*. The general point about regression to the mean is as follows. Whenever a firm does exceedingly well, one must consider whether it benefited from unusually good luck. Conversely, an underperforming firm might have had bad luck. Since good luck is unlikely to persist (or it would not have been luck), one might expect the successful firm to be less successful and the underperforming firm to improve. The possibility of regression toward the mean means that one should not expect firms to repeat extreme performances, whether good or bad, for long.

Extremely good or bad performance may not always be the result of luck. (If it was, there would be little point in pursuing a business education!) As we discuss later in this chapter, firms may develop genuine advantages that are difficult for others to duplicate. Even this does not guarantee a sustainable flow of profits, however. Although the advantage may be inimitable, so that the firm is protected from the forces of rivalry and entry, the firm may not be protected from powerful buyers and suppliers. As discussed in Chapter 10, powerful buyers and suppliers can use their bargaining leverage to extract profits from a thriving firm. By the same token, they will often give back some of their gains when the firm is struggling. This tends to even out the peaks and valleys in profits that might be experienced by firms that lack powerful buyers and suppliers.

A good example of where supplier power has threatened sustainability is Major League Baseball in the United States. Thanks in part to economies of scale and an exemption from the U.S. antitrust laws, Major League Baseball has been a monopoly throughout the twentieth century. Even so, many team owners cannot turn a profit. One reason is the powerful Major League Baseball Players' Association which, through litigation and a series of successful job actions in the 1970s and 1980s, has elevated the average salary of their players to more than $1 million a year. Fearful that they could no longer sustain profits in the face of ever-escalating salaries, the owners took a tough bargaining stance in 1994, which eventually led to a players' strike and the cancellation of the 1994 World Series. The home runs of Mark McGwire and Sammy Sosa and the longevity of Cal Ripken Jr. helped baseball get back on its feet. But these accomplishments were not enough to prevent an unprecedented effort in 2001 to eliminate two teams; this was the first proposed contraction in the history of major American team sports.

Evidence: The Persistence of Profitability

If the forces threatening sustainability are pervasive, economic profits in most industries should quickly converge to zero. By contrast, if there are impediments to the

EXAMPLE 12.2 APEX DIGITAL

Apex Digital was founded in 1999 by David Ji and Ancle Hsu. The offspring of a company that exported scrap metal to China, Apex seized on an opportunity in the DVD market. The DVD hardware market was dominated by major brands such as Sony and Panasonic whose retail prices included healthy profit margins. The conventional wisdom was that the typical consumer at that time was an early adopter who demanded high quality; there was no room in the market for a low-cost competitor. Apex intended to defy that logic.

From the outset, Apex outsourced production of DVD players to China. Chinese manufacturers were eager to build expertise and develop channels to other electronics companies. They offered to sell to Apex at or near their costs. Apex was also willing to take small margins in order to establish a toehold in retail channels. There have also been accusations that Apex failed to pay up to $25 per unit in licensing fees for the use of DVD technology. In any event, Apex had a clear cost advantage over its rivals and priced its DVD players accordingly. When the first Apex players hit U.S. store shelves in 2000, they were priced at $179 per unit, about half of competitors' entry-level DVD players. Quality was suspect, but only when compared with the DVD players of other brands, not with the VCRs that Apex units were replacing. Few consumers complained.

By 2000, DVDs and DVD players were becoming mainstream products, and many consumers found Apex's low price irresistible. An initial shipment of 5,000 units to Circuit City flew off the shelves. By 2001, Apex DVD players were priced below $100 and Apex machines were available at Wal-Mart, Target, and other large retailers. Some drug stores and grocery stores even stocked Apex players next to canned goods! On the day after Thanksgiving 2001, several retailers sold Apex DVD players for under $70; Apex claims it sold over 1 million units that day, making it the top-selling brand. In 2002, Apex began selling budget televisions, pushing its annual revenues over $1 billion.

But this is not a success story. In the first week of January, 2005, David Ji traveled to China to meet with a supplier of televisions, Sichuan Changhong. Instead of ironing out a production agreement, Ji found himself detained by Chinese authorities; some reports had him under arrest. Changhong claimed that Apex owed it over $300 million and that checks issued by Ji had failed to clear. A Taiwanese DVD supplier claims that Apex owes it $4.3 million.

Apex has tried to pull off one of the most difficult tasks in the business world—establishing a sustainable position as a low-cost leader without any obvious resources or capabilities. Apex's only possible advantage was its established business relationships in China. But its knowledge about the scrap metal trade had little use in the world of consumer electronics (though it may have helped Apex deal with Chinese government officials.)

Anyone can contract with a Chinese company to make a cheap DVD player. If anything, the success of Apex made it easier to convince retailers to carry other no-name products. Today there are several budget brands; for example, Mintek DVD players sell for around $20. Stung by the success of Apex, the big brands also outsourced production of low-end units to China. Pioneer even built its own Chinese factory. Major brands offer DVD players at $60 that have modern styling and more features than discount products. This has proven to be a low enough price to attract many budget buyers. Apex has also struggled because of rapid changes in DVD technology. Keeping design changes to a minimum to hold down costs, Apex players have failed to keep pace in video decoding (progressive scan) and digital video connections (HDMI).

Everyone knows the old joke about the firm that lost money on every sale but hoped to make it up with volume. For a short time, Apex enjoyed remarkable volume growth. But the absence of any unique resources or capabilities has made it difficult for it to enjoy any sustained period of profits. Whether Apex climbs out of its $300 million hole remains to be seen.

competitive dynamic (e.g., entry barriers as discussed in Chapter 9 or barriers to imitation as we discuss later in this chapter), then profits should persist: Firms that earn above-average profits today should continue to do so in the future; low-profit firms today should remain low-profit firms in the future. What pattern of profit persistence do we actually observe?

The economist Dennis Mueller has done the most comprehensive study of profit persistence.[2] For a sample of 600 U.S. manufacturing firms for the years 1950–1972, Mueller used statistical techniques to measure profit persistence. Perhaps the easiest way to summarize Mueller's results is to imagine two groups of U.S. manufacturing firms. One group (the "high-profit" group) has an after-tax accounting return on assets (ROA)—that is, on average, 100 percent greater than the accounting ROA of the typical manufacturing firm. If the typical manufacturing firm has an ROA of 6 percent in 2006 (which is roughly the average ROA for U.S. manufacturing firms over the last 20 years), the average ROA of the high-profit group would be 12 percent. The other group (the "low-profit" group) has an average ROA of 0 percent. If profit follows the pattern in Mueller's sample, by 2009 (three years later), the high-profit group's average ROA would be about 8.6 percent, and by 2016 its average ROA would stabilize at about 7.8 percent, a level 35 percent greater than that of the average manufacturing firm. Similarly, by 2009 the low-profit group's average ROA would be about 4.4 percent, and by 2016 its average ROA would stabilize at about 4.9 percent, or about 19 percent less than the average manufacturing firm. Figure 12.2 shows these patterns.[3]

FIGURE 12.2
THE PERSISTENCE OF PROFITABILITY IN MUELLER'S SAMPLE

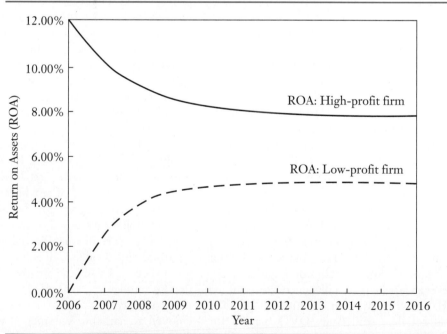

The high-profit group's average ROA starts out at 12 percent in 2006 and decreases over time, converging to slightly less than 8 percent. The low-profit group's average ROA starts at 0 percent in 2006 and increases over time, converging to about 4.9 percent. The profits of the two groups get closer over time but do not converge toward a common mean, as the theory of perfect competition would predict.

Mueller's results suggest that firms with abnormally high levels of profitability tend, on average, to decrease in profitability over time, while firms with abnormally low levels of profitability tend, on average, to experience increases in profitability over time. However, as Figure 12.2 illustrates, the profit rates of these two groups of firms do not converge to a common mean. Firms that start out with high profits converge, in the long run, to rates of profitability that are higher than the rates of profitability of firms that start out with low profits.[4]

Mueller's work implies that market forces are a threat to profits, but only up to a point. Other forces appear to protect profitable firms. Michael Porter's five forces, summarized in Chapter 10, are an important class of such forces. Many factors, such as high entry barriers or other structural conditions that soften price competition, protect the profitability of an entire industry. Here, however, we are concerned with a different class of forces: those that protect the competitive advantage of an individual firm and allow it to persistently outperform its industry. These forces are, at least in principle, distinct from Porter's five forces. A firm may prosper indefinitely in an industry with intense pricing rivalry and low entry barriers. The sources of its competitive advantage may be so difficult to understand or to imitate that its advantage over its competitors is secure for a long time. By contrast, structural conditions in an industry may facilitate pricing coordination among firms in that industry, allowing higher-than-competitive returns, but the barriers to imitation within the industry may be so low that no firm can be more profitable than any other.

SUSTAINABLE COMPETITIVE ADVANTAGE ◆ ◆ ◆ ◆ ◆

This section discusses the economic foundations of sustainable competitive advantage. We begin by linking sustainable advantage to the concepts of resources and capabilities in Chapter 11. We then introduce the concept of an isolating mechanism and discuss its importance for sustainable advantage.

The Resource-Based Theory of the Firm

Chapter 11 defined competitive advantage as the ability of a firm to outperform its industry, that is, to earn a higher rate of profit than the industry norm. To achieve a competitive advantage, a firm must create more value than its competitors. A firm's ability to create superior value, in turn, depends on its stock of resources (i.e., firm-specific assets and factors of production, such as patents, brand-name reputation, installed base, and human assets) and its distinctive capabilities (i.e., activities that the firm does better than competitors) that arise from using those resources.

Resources and capabilities alone do not ensure that a firm can sustain its advantage. A competitive advantage is sustainable when it persists despite efforts by competitors or potential entrants to duplicate or neutralize it.[7] For this to occur, there must be persistent asymmetries among the firms. Firms must possess different resources and capabilities, and it must be difficult for underperforming firms to obtain the resources and capabilities of the top performers. Resource heterogeneity is the cornerstone of an important framework in strategy: the *resource-based theory of the firm*.[8] That theory points out that if all firms in a market have the same stocks of resources and capabilities, no strategy for value-creation is available to one firm that would not also be available to all other firms in the market. Any other firm could immediately

EXAMPLE 12.3 EXPLOITING RESOURCES: THE MATTEL STORY

In the early 1980s, toy manufacturer Mattel neared bankruptcy. At the time, the maker of the Barbie and Hot Wheels brands faced annual profit shortfalls while heading off competition from rival Hasbro. Within a few years, however, Mattel would rule triumphant over the rest of the toy industry. Between 1988 and 1998, Mattel would grow by an astonishing 33 percent compounded annually.[5] Mattel's turnaround can be attributed to a change in strategy that maximized the value of its key strategic resources: its brands.

Founded in 1945, Mattel produced some of the most successful toy brands in history. Launched in 1959, Mattel's Barbie doll would become an American icon. Other brands like Hot Wheels (launched in 1968) proved to be similarly popular. By the 1970s, however, Mattel began to focus less on developing its brands. It adopted a "World of the Young" strategy and diversified into many non–toy businesses including Golden Books and the Ringling Brothers Circus. This strategy ultimately dispersed resources that could have been used to develop "core" brands. Furthermore, Mattel failed to maximize value from its brands. Earnings of the company's once-proud Barbie brand suffered during this period. Within each brand that it sold, Mattel offered a narrow array of product lines. The company missed revenue opportunities by selling only a few variations of its basic Barbie doll. It also sold a limited number of Barbie friend dolls (like Ken, Barbie's male friend). Barbie's accessories were limited only to clothing. Moreover, Mattel aimed to sell only one Barbie per child, while opting to make money on accessories sold after the sole doll's purchase. Barbie was available at only one price point. Indeed, Mattel continued to place limitation upon limitation on the income it could generate from a Barbie franchise, lacking variety in product offerings.

There were other problems. Mattel failed to capitalize on licensing deals for its brands. Nor did the company exercise significant oversight on inventories, receivables, and overall costs. Perhaps not surprisingly, the company faced bankruptcy by the early 1980s.

In the mid 1980s, Mattel changed course and adopted a "core brands" strategy that allowed Barbie and Hot Wheels to rediscover their original luster. Mattel expanded product lines and proliferated accessories. Under the leadership of then-brand-manager Jill Barad, Mattel tried to sell multiple Barbie's per child rather than just one. Each Barbie had a different story, theme, or occupation. For Barbie, accessories now included collectibles, play sets, and electronic items rather than just clothing. Varied Barbie and Hot Wheels products were now available at several price points. Mattel aggressively pursued licensing agreements involving its Barbie and Hot Wheels lines. Indeed, the new strategy allowed Mattel to extract as much value as possible from its brands. At the same time, Mattel cut costs and improved financial controls.

Ultimately, Mattel's profitability and improved fiscal management enabled the firm to acquire complementary assets. Mattel soon acquired other toy corporations with which it hoped to find synergies. These companies included, most notably, Fisher-Price, which made toys for young children, and Tyco Toys, then America's third largest toy company and maker of Tickle Me Elmo and Matchbox cars. (The merger of Matchbox and Hot Wheels also helped reduce competition in the metal car submarket.)

In adopting the "core brands" strategy, Mattel recognized that its brands were superior resources that could be aggressively exploited. At the time it adopted this strategy, Barbie was one of the most recognizable brands in the world. In the mid- to late 1990s, Barbie regularly appeared in Interbrand's list of the top 100 global brands. The value of the Barbie brand stemmed from her popularity with young girls. This popularity—as well as the corresponding popularity of Hot Wheels with young boys—is difficult for other toy makers to replicate.

Mattel's decision to divest other holdings and focus on initiatives involving its flagship brands allowed the company to reap great rewards.

While it experienced great success in the 1990s, Mattel was plagued by earnings shortfalls in the late 1990s, which led to the demise of CEO Jill Barad (who served as CEO from 1997 to 2000). These difficulties can be partially attributed to Mattel's ill-advised foray into software in 1998. Many criticized Mattel for paying too much for the Learning Company, an educational software firm that it acquired for $3.8 billion in 1998. "The brands at the Learning Center are ancient in software years and feature fairly generic characters," noted one reporter.[6] With its purchase of the Learning Company, Mattel had ventured too far away from its core capabilities. In the end, it was hard-pressed to find synergies between itself and a software firm with inherently weaker brands. Ironically, Mattel had gotten away from the focused strategy that made it so successful in the first place, and, ultimately, it paid the price.

As it attempted to recover from the ill-fated purchase of the Learning Company, Mattel returned to a strategy built around the aggressive exploitation of its core brands. A key part of this strategy involves licensing arrangements with a variety of different companies, such as glasses-maker REM Eyewear, which sells a line of Barbie eyewear for young girls, the Cartoon Network, which airs the Hot Wheels AcceleRacers made-for-TV movies, and Sony, which produces a Hot Wheels AcceleRacers CD that includes a mix of rock and roll, rap, and punk rock music from the movies and DVDs. Still, Mattel has continued to struggle. Between the end of 2003 and the summer of 2005, sales of Barbie dolls declined in seven consecutive quarters, including a 15 percent decline in the first quarter of 2005. Part of this decline reflects the impact of a new source of competition for Barbie: an appealing line of dolls known as Bratz, introduced in June 2001 by MGA Entertainment. Part of it also reflects an acceleration in the time it takes young girls to outgrow dolls. Whether Barbie can rebound is a critical question for Mattel: Barbie and her accessories remain the biggest selling item in Mattel's portfolio of toys, accounting for one-third of the company's sales in 2005.

replicate a strategy that confers advantage. To be sustainable, a competitive advantage must be underpinned by resources and capabilities that are *scarce* and *imperfectly mobile*.

It should be readily apparent why resources must be scarce to sustain a competitive advantage. But scarcity is not itself a guarantee of sustainability. When value creating resources are scarce, firms will bid against one another to acquire them. The additional economic profit that would have resulted from the competitive advantage would then be transferred to the owner of the resources. For example, where key resources are talented employees, such as superstars in creating specialized financial derivatives, the extra-value-created would be captured by the superstar employees as higher salaries, rather than by the firm as higher profit.

A firm that possesses a scarce resource can sustain its advantage if that resource is *imperfectly mobile*. This means that the resource cannot "sell itself" to the highest bidder. Retailer Kmart may have sold millions of dollars' worth of housewares under a licensing deal with homemaker/media star/businesswoman Martha Stewart, but it was Ms. Stewart's company that reaped all the profits. Indeed, had any profits been left on the table for Kmart, Ms. Stewart could have sold her housewares through a different retailer under more favorable terms. Talented employees who can sell their labor services to the highest bidders are also mobile resources—just think of the lucrative contracts paid to free-agent baseball and basketball players. Firms can limit mobility through long-term labor contracts or "noncompete clauses." Highly productive workers are usually aware of the value they bring to organizations, however, and can negotiate higher wages in advance of signing such contracts.

Fortunately for firms, many resources are imperfectly mobile. Some resources are inherently nontradable. These include the know-how an organization has acquired through cumulative experience, or a firm's reputation for toughness in its competition with rivals. Other resources may be tradable, but because they are relationship specific, they may be far more valuable inside one organization than another. This limits the incentive for parties outside the organization to bid them away. Some resources may be *cospecialized*—that is, they are more valuable when used together than when separated. For example, Delta Airlines' gates and landing slots at Atlanta's Hartsfield Airport are probably far more valuable to it than they are to a potential bidder for those slots because of the strong "brand identification" Delta has in Atlanta and because prospective fliers out of Atlanta have built up large stocks of frequent-flier miles on Delta. As a result, Delta can obtain gates and slots at a price that allows it to earn a profit. No other airline is willing to bid higher. Employees in productive work teams are also cospecialized. Although the team of workers could conceivably agree to sell their services to another firm, such coordination is in practice rather difficult, especially if some of the workers have personal ties to the local market.

Imperfectly mobile assets are so valuable that firms may compete away the profits in an attempt to acquire them. An example would be where the key resource is a potentially valuable location that can support only one retail outlet. Retailers can bid away the rents by offering to pay extravagant prices for the land. A forward-looking retailer might even prematurely build a store before the location is ready to yield its maximal profit to preempt potential competitors from acquiring the location. This would dissipate the profitability of the location.

Isolating Mechanisms

Scarcity and immobility of critical resources and capabilities are necessary for a competitive advantage to be sustainable, but they are not sufficient. A firm that has built a competitive advantage from a set of scarce and immobile resources may find that advantage undermined if other firms can develop their own stocks of resources and capabilities that duplicate or neutralize the source of the firm's advantage. For example, Xerox's advantage in the plain-paper copier market in the 1970s was built, in part, on superior servicing capabilities backed by a network of dealers who provided on-site service calls. Canon successfully challenged Xerox in the small-copier market by building highly reliable machines that rarely broke down and did not have to be serviced as often as Xerox's. Canon's superior product neutralized Xerox's advantage and reduced the value of Xerox's servicing capabilities and its dealer network.

Richard Rumelt coined the term *isolating mechanisms* to refer to the economic forces that limit the extent to which a competitive advantage can be duplicated or neutralized through the resource-creation activities of other firms.[11] Isolating mechanisms thus protect the competitive advantages of firms that are lucky enough or foresightful enough to have acquired them. Isolating mechanisms are to a firm what an entry barrier is to an industry: Just as an entry barrier impedes new entrants from coming into an industry and competing away profits from incumbent firms, isolating mechanisms prevent other firms from competing away the extra profit that a firm earns from its competitive advantage.

There are different kinds of isolating mechanisms, and different authors classify them in different ways.[12] We divide them into two distinct groups:

1. *Impediments to imitation.* These isolating mechanisms impede existing firms and potential entrants from duplicating the resources and capabilities that form the

EXAMPLE 12.4 AMERICAN VERSUS NORTHWEST IN YIELD MANAGEMENT

An example of resource mobility arose in a lawsuit involving American Airlines and Northwest Airlines.[9] The case centered on an allegation that Northwest Airlines stole valuable information related to American's yield management capabilities.

Yield management refers to a set of practices designed to maximize an airline's yield—the dollars of revenue it collects per seat-mile it flies. Yield management techniques combine mathematical optimization models with forecasting techniques to help an airline determine fares, fix the number of seats it should sell in various fare categories, and adjust its inventory of seats in response to the changes in demand conditions. American Airlines has the most sophisticated yield management capabilities in the airline industry. At the time of the lawsuit in the early 1990s, American's system was thought to have added $300 million to American's annual revenues.

By contrast, Northwest's yield management capabilities were below average. In the late 1980s, it hired a consultant to devise a mathematical model to underpin a new system. But management soon became skeptical of the consultant's efforts. The system the consultant devised was estimated to cost $30 million, but its success was uncertain. In 1990, Northwest fired the consultant.

Northwest then tried to purchase a yield management system from American. However, in return for the system, American demanded Northwest's operating right to fly between Chicago and Tokyo, a route whose market value was estimated at between $300 million and $500 million. Northwest refused to trade.

Instead, in the fall of 1990, Northwest hired John Garel, the chief of the yield management department at American. Garel then tried to lure American's best yield managers to Northwest. Out of the 38 new yield management employees hired by Northwest in 1990, 17 came from American, often with generous raises of 50 to 100 percent.

Along with hiring many of American's yield managers, Northwest also managed to acquire a diskette containing American's "spill" tables, which are a key part of mathematical models used to plan the acquisition of new aircraft. Northwest had tried to purchase the spill tables along with American's yield management system in 1990. American alleged that one of its former employees recruited by Northwest copied the diskette. Northwest also obtained internal American documents on how to improve a yield management system. One of the documents was entitled "Seminar on Demand Forecasting," which Northwest used to vastly improve its system called AIMS. American alleged that its system contains five critical techniques, all of which Northwest copied. One Northwest yield manager characterized the revision as "a heart transplant of the AIMS system."

In 1993, American sued Northwest in federal court. It sought to bar Northwest from using its revised yield management system and $50 million in damages. American also brought a suit against KLM, the Dutch airline that is Northwest's international marketing partner. According to American, Northwest passed along the internal American documents to KLM.[10]

This example illustrates that the resources that are the basis of competitive advantage can be highly mobile. This is especially true when those resources are talented individuals, but is also true when the resource is information, a technique, or a formula that can be written down and copied. It is also noteworthy that Northwest was unable to capture all of the extra value that it hoped to obtain by hiring the American yield managers. Some of it had to be shared with these individuals by paying them higher salaries. This highlights a general point about competitive markets. When a scarce resource is fully mobile and is as valuable to one firm as to another, the extra profit that the firms can earn from the resource will be competed away as they bid against one another to acquire it.

basis of the firm's advantage. For example, many firms compete in the golf equipment market, but few have been able to match Callaway's distinctive capabilities in designing innovative golf clubs and golf balls. Clearly, impediments prevent competitors from copying the strengths of this successful firm. One tangible indicator of how hard it is to imitate Callaway's capabilities in golf club design is that some firms have resorted to making counterfeit versions of Callaway clubs. In March 2004, for example, Callaway seized 27,000 club heads from a company, Newport Golf, that was accused of counterfeiting Callaway clubs.

2. *Early-mover advantages.* Once a firm acquires a competitive advantage, these isolating mechanisms increase the economic power of that advantage over time. Cisco Systems, for example, dominates the market for products such as routers and switches, which link together LANs (local area networks). Its success in this business helped establish its Cisco Internetwork Operating System (Cisco IOS) software as an industry standard. This, in turn, had a feedback effect that benefited Cisco's entire line of networking products. Perhaps not surprisingly, during the 1990s, a period of significant growth in the network equipment business, Cisco Systems earned rates of return that vastly exceeded its cost of capital. For example, between 1992 and 1996, Cisco earned a 40.36 percentage-point average "spread" between its annual return on capital and its cost of capital, a performance that exceeded those of Intel, Coca-Cola, and Microsoft.[13] Even after the crash of network equipment business in the wake of the technology meltdown in 2000–2001, Cisco continued to outperform its industry peers (although its absolute profitability was considerably worse than the profitability it enjoyed throughout the 1990s).

Figure 12.3 illustrates the distinction between these two classes of isolating mechanisms. In Figure 12.3a, all firms in an industry initially occupy the same competitive position. A "shock" then propels firm G into a position of competitive advantage over

FIGURE 12.3
IMPEDIMENTS TO IMITATION AND EARLY-MOVER ADVANTAGES

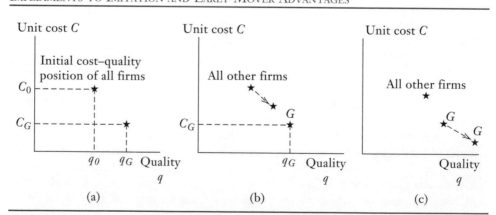

(a) The initial cost-quality position of all firms in the markets is (C_0, q_0). Following a shock, firm G achieves a competitive advantage based on higher quality and lower cost.
(b) Impediments to imitation: As time passes, G's competitors may be able to reduce costs and increase quality, but they cannot duplicate G's superior cost-quality position. (c) The dynamics of an early-mover advantage: As time passes, G's cost and quality advantage over competing firms grows more pronounced.

other firms in the market. "Shock" here refers to fundamental changes that lead to major shifts of competitive positions in a market. Examples of shocks are proprietary process or product innovations, discoveries of new sources of consumer value or market segments, shifts in demand or tastes, or changes in regulatory policy that enable firms to significantly shift their strategic position in a business. Isolating mechanisms that impede imitation prevent other firms from fully replicating G's advantage. This is shown in Figure 12.3b as the inability of other firms to match G's. Early-mover advantages work somewhat differently. Because G was the first firm to benefit from a shock, it can eventually widen its competitive advantage over other firms in the market. This is shown in Figure 12.3c.

If shocks are infrequent and isolating mechanisms are powerful, a firm's competitive advantage will be long-lived. Firms whose competitive advantages are protected by isolating mechanisms, Rumelt argues, may be able to take their strategies as given for a long time, while still earning higher returns than existing competitors (or new entrants that might come into the business). The companion insight is that consistently high profitability does not necessarily mean that a firm is well managed. As Rumelt notes, "even fools can churn out good results (for a while)."[14]

In the next two sections, we discuss impediments to imitation and early-mover advantages in greater detail.

Impediments to Imitation

In this section, we discuss four impediments to imitation:

1. Legal restrictions
2. Superior access to inputs or customers
3. Market size and scale economies
4. Intangible barriers to imitating a firm's distinctive capabilities: causal ambiguity, dependence on historical circumstances, and social complexity

Legal Restrictions

Legal restrictions, such as patents, copyrights, and trademarks, as well as governmental control over entry into markets, through licensing, certification, or quotas on operating rights, can be powerful impediments to imitation.[15] Jeffrey Williams points out that between 1985 and 1990, patent-protected products as a group yielded higher returns on investment than any single industry in the United States.[16]

Patents, copyrights, trademarks, and operating rights can be bought and sold. For example, Ted Turner has bought copyrights to old movies, such as *Gone With the Wind*, and re-released them to theaters or showed them on his television stations. Thus, though scarce, these resources may also be highly mobile. This mobility implies that a firm that tries to secure a competitive advantage by purchase of a patent or an operating right may have to pay a competitive price to get it. If so, the purchase of the asset will be a breakeven proposition unless the buyer can deploy it in ways that other prospective purchasers cannot. This requires superior information about how to best utilize the asset or the possession of scarce complementary resources to enhance the value of the asset.

We encountered this issue in Chapter 5 in our discussion of acquisition programs by diversifying firms. Target firms are mobile assets—their owners may sell them to the highest bidder. The evidence shows that acquirers generally lose money unless there are complementarities between the business units of the acquiring and target firms. (In Chapter 5, we used the term *relatedness* to describe such complementarities.) Otherwise, the owners of the target firm reap all the profits from the acquisition.

Asset mobility also implies that the owner of the patent or operating right may be better off selling it to another firm. For example, many universities have offices that sell the patents obtained by members of their faculties. Universities realize that it makes more sense for other firms to develop marketable products. This illustrates the key point about patents and other operating rights: once a patent or operating right is secured, its exclusivity gives it sustainable value. Whoever holds the asset holds that value. But maximizing that value is ultimately a make-or-buy decision, whose resolution rests on the principles developed in Part One of this book.

Superior Access to Inputs or Customers

A firm that can obtain high-quality or high-productivity inputs, such as raw materials or information, on more favorable terms than its competitors will be able to sustain cost and quality advantages that competitors cannot imitate. Firms often achieve favorable access to inputs by controlling the sources of supply through ownership or long-term exclusive contracts. For example, International Nickel dominated the nickel industry for three-quarters of a century by controlling the highest-grade deposits of nickel, which were concentrated in western Canada. Topps monopolized the market for baseball cards in the United States by signing every professional baseball player to a long-term contract giving Topps the exclusive right to market the player's picture on baseball cards sold with gum or candy. This network of long-term contracts, which was declared illegal in the early 1980s, blocked access by other firms to an essential input in card production—the player's picture.

The flip side of superior access to inputs is superior access to customers. A firm that secures access to the best distribution channels or the most productive retail locations will outcompete its rivals for customers. A manufacturer could prevent access to retail distribution channels by insisting on exclusive dealing clauses, whereby a retailer agrees to sell only the products that manufacturer makes. Before World War II, most American automobile producers had exclusive dealing arrangements with their franchised dealers, and according to Lawrence White, this raised the barriers to entering the automobile business.[17] Most of these clauses were voluntarily dropped in the early 1950s, following antitrust decisions that seemed to threaten the Big Three's ability to maintain their exclusive dealing arrangements. Some observers speculate that the termination of these exclusive dealing requirements made it easier for Japanese manufacturers to penetrate the American market in the 1970s and 1980s.[18]

Many firms that pursue sustained advantage by securing superior access to inputs and customers fall victim to a variant of the make-or-buy fallacies described in Chapter 3. Just as patents and trademarks can be bought and sold, so too can locations or contracts that give the firm control of scarce inputs or distribution channels. Thus, superior access to inputs or customers can confer sustained competitive advantage only if the firm can secure access at "below-market" prices. If, for example, a certain site is widely known to contain a high-quality supply of uranium, the price of that land would be bid up until the economic profits were transferred to the original owner, and the profitability of the firm that purchases the land would be no higher than the profitability of the losing bidders. Similarly, baseball teams, recognizing the extra revenues that result from signing a superstar, such as Luis Pujols or Chris Carpenter, will compete against one another to acquire these players, so that the original owners (Pujols or Carpenter) capture the economic profit associated with their rare and valuable skills.

The corollary of this logic is that control of scarce inputs or distribution channels allows a firm to earn economic profits in excess of its competitors only if it acquired control of the input supply when other firms or individuals failed to recognize its value or could not exploit it. But this exposes firms to the possibility of a "winner's curse." The firm that wins the bidding war for an input may be overly optimistic about its value. Unless it accounts for the possibility of overoptimism, the winning bidder may end up overpaying for the asset.

Market Size and Scale Economies

Imitation may also be deterred when minimum efficient scale is large relative to market demand and one firm has secured a large share of the market. We have already discussed this situation in Chapters 2 and 10 in connection with the idea that economies of scale can limit the number of firms that can "fit" in a market and thus represent a barrier to entry. Scale economies can also discourage a smaller firm already in the market from seeking to grow larger to replicate the scale-based cost advantage of a firm that has obtained a large market share.

Figure 12.4 illustrates the logic of this isolating mechanism. Two firms, one large and one small, produce a homogeneous product and face the same long-run average cost function. The large firm's volume of 5,000 units per year exceeds minimum

FIGURE 12.4

ECONOMIES OF SCALE AND MARKET SIZE AS AN IMPEDIMENT TO IMITATION

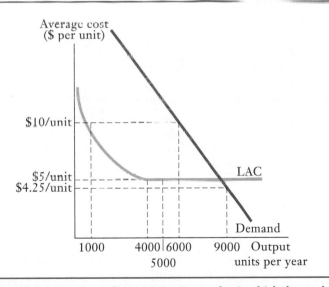

A large firm and a small firm are currently competing in a market in which the product cannot be effectively differentiated. The downward-sloping straight line is the market demand curve. Production technology is characterized by economies of scale, with the long-run average cost function (*LAC*) declining until the minimum efficient scale of 4,000 units per year is reached. The large firm currently has a capacity of 5,000 units per year, while the small firm has a capacity of 1,000 per year. If the small firm attempted to expand capacity to 4,000 units, and both firms produced at full capacity, the market price would fall to $4.25. At this price the small firm would be unable to cover the costs of its investment in the new plant. Thus, although the small firm could theoretically imitate the source of the large firm's cost advantage, it would be undesirable to do so.

EXAMPLE 12.5 COLA WARS: SLUGGING IT OUT IN VENEZUELA

The long-standing international success of Coca-Cola and Pepsi shows that a powerful brand name can confer a sustainable advantage. In recent years, there have been few credible challengers to the two leading cola makers. The reason has only partly to do with taste—many consumers believe that other colas, such as RC Cola, taste just as good as Coke or Pepsi. Competitors lack Coke and Pepsi's brand images and would need to spend huge sums in advertisements to achieve it. The owner of one potential competitor even risked his life to boost his cola's brand image. Richard Branson has twice attempted to fly around the world in a hot-air balloon emblazoned with the Virgin Cola logo. Branson crashed shortly after the beginning of each flight (both crashes occurred in remote regions) and has failed to generate the publicity necessary for Virgin Cola to take off.

While Coca-Cola and Pepsi have remarkable international brand recognition, they do not share international markets equally. For example, Coca-Cola has long been the dominant cola throughout South America. The lone exception has been Venezuela, where Pepsi held an 80 percent share of the $400 million cola market until August 1996. That is when Coca-Cola struck a deal to buy half of Venezuela's largest soft drink bottler, Hit de Venezuela, from the Cisneros Group. The bottler, which changed its name to Coca-Cola y Hit, immediately switched operations to Coca-Cola, and 4,000 Pepsi trucks became Coke trucks. In a scene that could have been lifted from the movie *The Coca-Cola Kid*, Coke trucks began rolling across Venezuela, and Coke replaced Pepsi as Venezuela's dominant cola. Coca-Cola secured its dominant market share by tying up the distribution channel. As might be expected, Coke had to pay dearly for it—an estimated $500 million for a 50 percent stake. Economic theory suggests that Coca-Cola should not have profited from this deal. After all, the source of monopoly power in this market belonged to the Cisneros Group rather than cola makers. Coca-Cola officials claimed that the benefits from the Venezuelan acquisition would accrue in the long run. A Venezuelan director stated, "We'll do whatever we have to win this market. We don't think about today. We think about ten years from now.[19] Coca-Cola's dominance of the Venezuelan market will undoubtedly increase its cash flows over the long run. The important question was whether the present value of the cash flows from having a dominant share of the Venezuelan market exceeded what Coca-Cola paid to obtain that market share. If so, the deal created wealth for Coca-Cola's shareholders. If not, it destroyed wealth.

Whether Coca-Cola overpaid to gain market share became moot in May 1997 when Panamco, an independent Coke bottler headquartered in Mexico, paid $1.1 billion to acquire Coca-Cola y Hit. Coca-Cola appears to have made out handsomely from these deals: it profited from the purchase and subsequent sale of Hit de Venezuela, and it still has a dominant market share in Venezuela.

Coca-Cola might have wrested control of the Venezuelan market from Pepsi, but Pepsi still possessed valuable assets in Venezuela: Pepsi's brand image and taste. (Many Venezuelans apparently prefer Pepsi's sweeter taste.) Months after Coca-Cola's takeover of the market, Venezuelans continued to express a decided preference for Pepsi—if they could find it in the stores. To exploit its assets, Pepsi formed a joint venture—known as Sorpresa—with Polar, Venezuela's largest brewer. The joint venture had fewer bottling plants in Venezuela than Coca-Cola had, but its plants were larger and were believed to be more efficient than Coke's. This enabled Pepsi to compete aggressively on price with Coke, and by the end of the 1990s, it was able to rebuild its market share to 38 percent.

Cisneros Group, Polar, and Coke are the clear winners of this competitive battle. Although Pepsi has been able to recover partially from its drastic drop in market share in 1996, on balance, it has probably been a loser. One other loser: any other soft drink maker contemplating entry into the Venezuelan market. As a combined force, Coke and Pepsi are stronger today than before August 1996. As always seems to happen, Coca-Cola and Pepsi might bloody themselves in the cola wars, but in doing so they gain protection from outside threats.

efficient scale (MES), which is 4,000 units in the figure; the small firm's volume—1,000 units per year—is less than MES. If the small firm invested in additional capacity and expanded output to MES to lower its average cost, the market price would fall below the minimum of long-run average cost ($5 in the figure). The small firm would thus be unable to earn an adequate rate of return on its investment in its new plant. Thus, although a small firm may theoretically imitate the source of a larger firm's competitive advantage, it may nevertheless be unprofitable for it to do so.

Scale-based barriers to imitation and entry are likely to be especially powerful in markets for specialized products or services where demand is just large enough to support one large firm. This has been the case, for example, in the market for hot sauce, which has been monopolized by McIlhenny (producer of Tabasco sauce) for over a century. But a scale-based advantage can be sustainable only if demand does not grow too large; otherwise, the growth in demand will attract additional entry or induce smaller competitors to expand, allowing them to benefit from economies of scale. This happened in the market for personal computers, as Dell and Gateway expanded in a growing market in the late 1990s and virtually matched the scale advantages held by industry leader Compaq and Hewlett-Packard. This led to intensified price competition, so that Compaq and Hewlett-Packard profits from personal computers failed to keep pace with the growth of the market.

Intangible Barriers to Imitation

Legal restrictions and superior access to customers or scarce inputs are tangible barriers to imitation. But barriers to imitation may also be intangible, especially when the basis of the firm's advantage is distinctive organizational capabilities. We can identify these conceptually distinct intangible barriers to imitation:

* Causal ambiguity
* Dependence on historical circumstances
* Social complexity

Causal Ambiguity Richard Rumelt uses the term *causal ambiguity* for situations in which the causes of a firm's ability to create more value than its competitors are obscure and only imperfectly understood.[20] Causal ambiguity is a consequence of the fact that a firm's distinctive capabilities typically involve tacit knowledge. That is, capabilities are difficult to articulate as an algorithm, formula, or set of rules. Swinging a golf club in a way to hit the ball with long-range accuracy is an example of tacit knowledge: one could conceivably learn how to do it with enough practice, but it would be difficult to describe how a person should do it. Much of the know-how and collective wisdom inside an organization is of this sort. Tacit capabilities are typically developed through trial and error and refined through practice and experience; rarely are they written down or codified in procedures manuals. As a result, the firm's managers may not even be able to describe persuasively what they do better than their rivals.[21] For this reason, causal ambiguity not only may be a powerful impediment to imitation by other firms, but it also may be an important source of diseconomies of scale. For example, David Teece has pointed out that causal ambiguity might prevent the firm from translating the operational success it achieves in one of its plants to another.[22]

Just as superior firms may be unable to describe what they do especially well, ordinary firms may mistakenly believe they have superior skills. Their inability to articulate their strengths may be chalked up to causal ambiguity. Absent evidence of superior skills (e.g., cost data, market research, competitive benchmarks relative to other firms, financial measures, or comments of knowledgeable observers, such as securities analysts), managers should never assume that they are more capable than competitors.

Dependence on Historical Circumstances   Competitors might also be unable to replicate the distinctive capabilities underlying a firm's competitive advantage because the distinctiveness of these capabilities is partly bound up with the history of the firm. A firm's history of strategic action comprises its unique experiences in adapting to the business environment. These experiences can make the firm uniquely capable of pursuing its own strategy and incapable of imitating the strategies of competitors. For example, in the 1960s and 1970s, Southwest Airlines was constrained by U.S. regulatory policy to operate out of secondary airports in the unregulated (and thus highly price competitive) intrastate market in Texas. The operational efficiencies and the pattern of labor relations it developed in response to these conditions may be difficult for other airlines, such as American and United, to imitate. Neither of these large carriers would be comfortable with Southwest's smaller scale of operation and historically constrained route structure.

Historical dependence implies that a firm's strategy may be viable for only a limited time. To use another airlines example, People's Express prospered in the period

EXAMPLE 12.6 SWITCHING COSTS FOR THE NEWBORN SET: GARANIMALS

Readers who were children during the 1970s or early 1980s may remember Garanimals. Introduced by Garan Inc. in 1972, this line of children's clothes was designed to enable children to dress themselves. The problem that most children have is that they do not know how to match tops and bottoms. Children may pair up a blue striped top with an orange plaid bottom—they may even like the combination—but their parents would be horrified by it. Garanimals provided a simple solution to this problem. Each separate article of clothing had a hangtag depicting a different animal. Put a zebra top with a zebra bottom and, *voila*, the clothes are sure to match.

Garanimals was a clever gimmick that quickly caught on. By the mid-1970s, Garanimals were as popular as Carters, OshKosh B'Gosh, and other leading names in children's apparel. But the Garanimals gimmick assured Garan Inc. of greater consumer loyalty than was enjoyed by Carters et al. Parents of Garanimals kids knew that they could easily expand

their children's wardrobes by purchasing more outfits with the same animal hangtags. If little Suzie loved her crocodile top and bottom, another pair of crocodiles would give her four mix-and-match possibilities. In this subtle way, Garanimals created switching costs for parents. No other brand could afford such wardrobe flexibility.

Unfortunately, by the mid-1980s, Garanimals had lost their appeal. Perhaps parents grew tired of the cute designs and merely acceptable product quality. Or perhaps kids preferred to mix crocodiles with zebras, defeating the purpose of the hangtag system. Garan continues to make Garanimals today, but it ranks behind a number of popular brands. A survey of mothers of toddlers ranked Garanimals sixth in popularity—behind OshKosh B'Gosh, Gap Kids, and Disney—while mothers of 3- to 5-year-olds ranked Garanimals seventh. Still, there are web sites devoted to sharing memories of wearing Garanimals, a possible indication of the cleverness of the concept and the loyalty it inspired.

immediately after deregulation through a low-price strategy based on lower labor costs. This strategy was viable, however, only as long as the major carriers were burdened by high labor costs from their union contracts. In time, these costs were reduced as more labor contracts were renegotiated. This, in turn, made it difficult for People's Express to sustain its advantage.

Social Complexity   Jay Barney has pointed out that a firm's advantage may also be imperfectly imitable because it stems from socially complex processes. Socially complex phenomena include the interpersonal relations of managers in a firm and the relationship between the firm's managers and those of its suppliers and customers. Social complexity is distinct from causal ambiguity. For example, every one of Toyota's competitors may understand that an important contributor to Toyota's success is the trust that exists between it and its component suppliers. But it is difficult to create such trust, however desirable it may be.

The dependence of competitive advantage on causal ambiguity, history, and social complexity implies that major organizational change runs the risk of neglecting these factors and thus harming the firm's position. If the sources of advantage are complex and difficult to articulate, they will also be hard to consciously redesign. This may be why organizational changes, such as reengineering, are often more successful in new or "greenfield" plants than in existing ones.

Early-Mover Advantages

This section discusses four distinctive isolating mechanisms that fall under the heading of early-mover advantages:

1. Learning curve
2. Reputation and buyer uncertainty
3. Buyer switching costs
4. Network effects

Learning Curve

We discuss the economies of the learning curve at length in Chapter 2. A firm that has sold higher volumes of output than its competitors in earlier periods will move farther down the learning curve and achieve lower unit costs than its rivals. Firms with the greatest cumulative experience can thus profitably "underbid" rivals for business, further increasing their cumulative volume and enhancing their cost advantage.

Reputation and Buyer Uncertainty

In the sale of experience goods—goods whose quality cannot be assessed before they are purchased and used—a firm's reputation for quality can give it a significant early mover advantage.[23] Consumers who have had a positive experience with a firm's brand will be reluctant to switch to competing brands if there is a chance that the competing products will not work. Buyer uncertainty coupled with reputational effects can make a firm's brand name a powerful isolating mechanism. Once the firm's reputation has been created, the firm will have an advantage competing for new customers, increasing the number of customers who have had successful trials and thus further strengthening its reputation.

The nature of a later mover's disadvantage can be illustrated with a simple example.[24] Consider a new brand of analgesic that is competing with the brand that pioneered this product category. The pioneer entered the market at a price of $2.50, and at that price a certain number of consumers tried its product. Suppose that the pioneer's product works, that is, that it treats sinus headaches more effectively and with fewer side effects than aspirin. What price should the new brand charge? It would almost certainly have to charge less than $2.50. Why? Those consumers who purchased the analgesic from the pioneer and liked it will not switch to the newcomer if the prices are similar. Those who did not purchase it from the pioneer because they felt the price was too high would presumably be unwilling to buy it from the newcomer at the same price. And those who had not previously considered the product would presumably be drawn by the reputation of the pioneer. It follows, then, that the later mover can penetrate the market only by selling at a price below the pioneer's, even if both products are indistinguishable. If later movers fail to penetrate the market, the reputation of the early mover becomes stronger over time, as more and more consumers purchase the brand and are satisfied with it.

IBM's competitive advantage in the market for mainframes was, for years, sustained by considerations such as these. The saying, "You'll never get fired for buying an IBM," captures this point. In the 1970s, one industry expert said that it would take at least a 30 percent difference in the price-performance ratio to induce a customer to choose a competing brand over IBM.[25] IBM's reputational advantage also extended to peripheral equipment, such as tape drives. For example, Gerald Brock reports the results of an internal IBM study which revealed that 46 percent of IBM's customers would pass up a 20 percent discount from a competitor and continue to purchase equipment from IBM.[26]

Of course, the new entrant could try to overcome a pioneering brand's reputational advantage by advertising to persuade consumers that its product's benefits are superior to those of the early mover. However, this is easier said than done. Research suggests that pioneering brands profoundly influence the formation of consumer preferences.[27] If a pioneer can persuade enough consumers to try its product, consumers will consider its attributes the ideal for that type of product. To persuade consumers to switch to a new brand, they must perceive the new brand as significantly better than the pioneer brand. A good example of the perceptual advantage a pioneering brand enjoys is Chrysler's position in the minivan market. Chrysler introduced the first minivan in 1983. Even though Chrysler's Dodge minivan is not significantly superior or lower priced than those of other car makers, it leads the minivan market with a 20 percent share. The resilience of the Tylenol brand against competitors following its 1984 tampering crisis is another example of the advantage pioneering brands enjoy.

Buyer Switching Costs

For some products, buyers incur substantial costs when they switch to another supplier. Switching costs can arise when buyers develop brand-specific know-how that is not fully transferable to substitute brands. For example, a consumer who develops extensive knowledge in using Microsoft Word would have to reinvest in the development of new know-how if he or she switched to Word Perfect. Switching costs also arise when the seller develops specific know-how about the buyer that other sellers cannot quickly replicate or provides customized after-sale services to buyers. For example, a client of a commercial bank whose managers have developed extensive knowledge of the client's business would face a switching cost if it changed banks.

Sellers can design their products and services to increase switching costs in several ways. Sellers can offer coupons or "frequent-customer" points that tie discounts or special offerings to the completion of a series of transactions with customers. Everyone is familiar with airline frequent-flier programs. Restaurants, car washes, and even law firms are among many other businesses that use similar programs to encourage customer loyalty. Manufacturers can offer warranties that become void if the product is serviced at a nonauthorized dealer. Consumers will thereby tend to patronize authorized dealers, who usually charge higher fees and share the resulting profits with the manufacturer. Automakers and consumer electronics firms have imposed such requirements. However, in the late 1990s the U.S. Supreme Court overturned certain provisions of warranties for Kodak cameras, and as a result, the future of such warranty-related switching costs is up in the air. Finally, sellers can offer a bundle of complementary products that fit together in a product line. Once customers have purchased one product, they will naturally seek out others in the same line. Parents who have purchased a Lego Castle playset for their children are likely to buy other Lego Castle products because the parts are interchangeable and share the same look and feel. Example 12.6 describes Garanimals, an ill-fated attempt to create switching costs in children's clothes.

Switching costs can be a powerful advantage to an early mover. Suppose an established firm faces competition from a new entrant whose product provides the same quality as the established firm but requires a cost of S dollars (per unit output) to learn to use. To steal business from the early mover, the new entrant must charge a price that is at least S dollars less than the price the established brand charges.

Still, the early-mover advantage of switching costs has its limits. Frequent customer rewards are costly, and their value must steadily increase to maintain the loyalty of customers who have achieved early milestones. Conditional warranties may antagonize customers who anticipate the resulting high service costs. Designing complementary products may lock a seller into a particular niche. If tastes change, consumers may abandon the entire product line *en masse*.

Firms that have created switching costs for established customers may be at a disadvantage competing for new customers. As economists have shown, however, an established firm might be less willing to compete on price to win new customers.[28] If the established firm cuts price to attract new customers, it reduces its profit margin on sales to its existing customers. The new entrant, which has no loyal customers, incurs no such sacrifice. The established firm's installed base of loyal customers acts like a "soft" commitment, of the kind we discussed in Chapter 8, which induces it to compete less aggressively on price than the entrant does. When this occurs, new entrants will be able to capture a disproportionate share of market demand growth over time, while the established firm's share would erode. This dynamic might explain the tremendous recent growth of the statistical software package STATA, which sells for less and enjoys higher growth than traditional market leaders, such as SAS and SPSS.

Network Effects

Consumers often place higher value on a product if other consumers also use it. When this occurs, the product is said to display *network effects* or *network externalities*. In some networks, such as telephone and e-mail networks, consumers are physically linked. The network effect arises because consumers can communicate with other users in the network. These are known as *actual networks*. The more users in the actual network, the greater the opportunities for communication, and the greater the value of the network.

In *virtual networks*, consumers are not physically linked. The network effect arises from the use of complementary goods. Computer operating systems, video gaming (e.g., Sony Playstation), and DVD players are all examples of virtual networks. As the number of consumers in a virtual network increases, the demand for complementary goods increases. This increases the supply of the complementary goods, which in turn enhances the value of the network. This is evidenced by the vast selection of software to run on Windows-based PCs, video games for the Playstation, and movies to enjoy on DVD. Notice that consumers in virtual networks never need to communicate with each other to enjoy the network effects. As long as their collective purchasing power encourages the supply of complementary products, each individual consumer benefits from the network.

eBay, the on-line trading community, is an example of a company that has created a sustainable advantage through network effects. Early on, eBay attracted people interested in buying and selling all kinds of collectibles. Today, one can buy almost anything at eBay, including expensive jewelry, stereo equipment, baseball trading cards, and even the occasional Lexus or Ferrari (the real things, not toys!). Buyers like eBay because there are so many items for sale and because there are often several sellers of the same items. (In a recent search, we found nine different sellers offering the 1960s 3M horse-racing game Win, Place, and Show.) In addition, eBay offers buyers information about the credibility of sellers. Sellers like eBay because there are so many buyers. Thus, the sheer volume of transactions on eBay brings buyers and sellers back for more. eBay makes a small commission (2 to 5 percent on most transactions), but with over one million items for sale every week, this is more than enough to make eBay one of the most profitable Internet companies.

In markets with network effects, the first firm that establishes a large installed base of customers has a decided advantage. New customers will observe the size of the network and gravitate toward the same firm. Thus, network effects offer a prime opportunity for first-mover advantage, provided the first mover can develop an installed base.

Networks and Standards Many networks evolve around standards. In the late nineteenth century, the American railroad industry suffered from needless inefficiencies owing to incompatible tracking. The rails in one state might be 4 feet 7 inches apart; in a neighboring state, they might be 5 feet apart! Railroad crews had to stop their trains at the state line, unload, and reload on a new train. (This problem still exists in other parts of the world.) Eventually, the industry coalesced around the Northern Standard gauge of track, with a width of 4 feet 8.5 inches. With all rails conforming to this standard, the efficiency of the nation's rail network improved immeasurably. In the modern economy, the list of products and services that depend on standards seems endless: cellular communications, personal computing, the Internet, video gaming, high-definition television, and surround-sound processing for home theater, just to name a few.

Once a standard is established, it can be very difficult to replace. For example, the QWERTY standard for keyboards emerged in the 1860s and remains dominant, despite having lost its original technological advantage. The persistence of standards makes standard-setting a potentially powerful source of sustainable competitive advantage. The world's most valuable company, Microsoft, provides ample evidence of the power of network effects.

The importance of standards raises two key issues. First, should firms in fledgling markets attempt to establish a standard, thereby competing "for the market," or should they share in a common standard, thereby competing "in the market"? Second, what does it take to topple a standard?

EXAMPLE 12.7 THE MICROSOFT CASE

In the late 1990s, the U.S. Department of Justice (DOJ) launched an antitrust investigation against Microsoft. Several states joined in the probe, and a European antitrust challenge is ongoing. A federal district court judge found Microsoft to be in violation of antitrust laws. An appellate court upheld that opinion and the U.S. Supreme Court refused to rehear the case. It was without question that Microsoft had violated U.S. antitrust laws. In 2001, the DOJ and most of the states reached a settlement on remedies to the antitrust violations. The settlement was controversial, in part because professional staffers at the DOJ did not approve it; to many, the settlement was a political rather than an economic decision.

Tim Bresnahan, who served as the chief economist for the DOJ during the Microsoft investigation, was especially troubled by the settlement. Bresnahan argued that incumbent standards are very difficult to replace, even if they represent inferior technology. Under some circumstances, however, enough consumers may gravitate toward another standard so as to threaten the incumbent. To make this happen, the market needs to demonstrate *divided technical leadership* (DTL). When there is DTL, different firms excel in different layers of the vertical chain of complementary products. In the PC market in the mid- to late 1990s, Microsoft excelled in operating systems, but Netscape excelled in web browsing. In Bresnahan's opinion, DTL provides a competitive threat in each layer of the vertical chain. If a firm that dominates one layer does not deliver value to consumers, the firm that dominates the other layer may take steps to oust it. In the case of Microsoft, the success of Netscape created an unprecedented opportunity for a competitive alternative to Windows.

This view was apparently shared by many at Microsoft. In numerous internal e-mails that were presented at trial, Microsoft executives noted that consumers who bought computers to surf the Internet did not need the Windows operating system. Not only did Netscape's browser run on a variety of operating systems, including Windows and Linux, but it had its own applications programming interface (API)

enabling developers to write software that runs on top of the browser without any other operating system. Moreover, this software could be compatible across platforms, thereby eliminating a key source of network externalities. Microsoft's fear was that millions of consumers who bought low-priced websurfing computers would discover that they did not need Windows for surfing the web, e-mail, and instant messaging. In time, they might also find software for text editing, spreadsheet analysis, and other traditional uses of the PC. Through a variety of practices held to be illegal by the courts, Microsoft attempted to drive Netscape from the market. AOL's acquisition of Netscape in 1999 was an attempt to prevent Netscape from total collapse. Unfortunately, in the years since, Netscape continued to lose market share, and by 2005 its share of the browser market had dwindled to less than 1 percent.

Given the demise of Netscape, is it likely that another company will emerge to provide Microsoft with competitive discipline? Some have argued that Google represents a potential competitive threat to Microsoft. While it is true that certain of Google's products are competing with comparable products offered by Microsoft (e.g., G-mail versus Hotmail), at this point Google does not offer products that compete with Microsoft's core products (i.e., operating systems and office applications software). Still, this has not stopped Microsoft's management from highlighting Google as a significant competitive threat. One early sign of the battle: in summer 2005 Microsoft went to court to contest the issue of whether Kai-Fu Lee, a senior executive who left Microsoft to join Google in 2005, violated the terms of his noncompete clause by accepting the position at Google. Lee was one of several Microsoft employees who jumped to Google in the mid-2000s. The fact that Microsoft was willing to fight a court battle to enforce a noncompete clause could be interpreted as a willingness by Microsoft to "take the gloves off" and fight against Google before Google has the opportunity to emerge as a significant threat to Microsoft's valuable core businesses.

Competing "For the Market" versus "In the Market" A firm must consider several factors when deciding whether to compete "for the market" or "in the market."

- The oligopoly theory presented in Chapter 6 shows that, on average, it is better to be a monopolist half the time than a duopolist all the time. This means that if all other factors are equal, a firm will earn higher expected profits by trying to achieve monopoly status for its own standard (competing for the market) than by settling for a share of the market with a common standard (competing in the market).

- When two or more firms compete for the market, the winner is often the firm that establishes the largest installed base of customers, thereby enhancing the value of the network and attracting even more customers. Competition to grow the installed base can be very costly, however, as firms invest heavily in advertising, pay steep fees to encourage production by complementary product manufacturers, and offer deep discounts to lure early adopters. When the prospects for a costly standards battle loom large, the firms might be better off agreeing to a common standard.

- To win a standards war, it is critical to attract early adopters. Sellers need to tailor their products to the tastes of early adopters while hoping that mainstream consumers will be sufficiently attracted by these products to jump into the market themselves.

- When complementary products are extremely important, a standards war may deter manufacturers of the complements from entering the market until a standard has emerged. This can destroy the value of all the competing standards and stifle the growth of the entire industry.

- By the same token, the manufacturers of the complementary products will favor the standard that provides them with the greatest share of the value added. Thus, to win a standards battle, a firm must take care of the other firms in its value net.

All of these factors came into play in the battle between DIVX and DVD described in Chapter 10. Circuit City introduced DIVX with the hope of establishing a proprietary industry standard. Had they succeeded, they would have enjoyed huge profits. Circuit City invested heavily to promote DIVX, including payments of about $100 million to encourage studios like Disney to release movies in the DIVX format. Unless Circuit City won its gamble, it would suffer heavy losses. The DIVX format did not appeal to early adopters, however. To keep the costs low enough to justify the "one-time use" feature of DIVX discs, Circuit City did not include many special features favored by early adopters, including widescreen format and director commentaries. Circuit City was probably correct that mainstream users would be less interested in these features, but it did not matter. Mainstream users noticed that early adopters had shunned DIVX players, and surmised that the future of DIVX was in doubt. As mainstream users trickled into the market, they stuck with the DVD format. To make matters worse for Circuit City, firms throughout the value chain, from studios to video retailers, favored the DVD format. Circuit City was unable to convince any other firm to be a meaningful partner in its efforts to promote DIVX.

It is clear that Circuit City's decision to compete for the market was a high-stakes gamble with little chance of success. To make matters worse, the decision had a chilling effect on the entire industry. Throughout 1998, there was considerable doubt as to whether either format would survive. The overwhelming majority of mainstream consumers postponed purchases of hardware, and movie studios held off production of software. In 1999, Circuit City finally abandoned DIVX. The DVD market took off, but the fallout for Circuit City would last for years. By 2000, Best Buy had replaced Circuit City as the United States' leading electronics retailer, with sales of DVD hardware and software leading the way.

Knocking off a Dominant Standard Dominant standards do not last forever. Nintendo once held nearly 100 percent of the video game market but now has just half the market share enjoyed by Sony's PlayStation. (Nindendo does, however, dominate the portable video game market.) IBM dominated computing for 30 years before giving way to "Wintel" computers. But it is not easy to knock off a dominant standard. The installed base of the incumbent gives it a decided advantage in any battle. The rival standard can succeed, however, especially in markets with virtual networks. There are two keys to success. First, the rival must offer superior quality, or new options for using the product. Second, the rival must be able to tap into complementary goods markets.

Both keys to success were available to Sega when it took on Nintendo in the early 1990s. The Sega "Genesis" system offered twice the computing power as Nintendo's NES system. At the same time, Nintendo had achieved only about 30 percent market penetration, with even lower penetration among households with older children. (One reason is that it had virtually no sports games.) When Sega came to the market, there was no shortage of programmers. A few were disgruntled suppliers to Nintendo. Other programmers were new to the market, attracted by the growth of computing. The combination of new characters like Sonic the Hedgehog and sports games from programmers like Entertainment Arts enabled Sega to dramatically cut into Nintendo's dominance.

Even a seemingly invincible monopolist like Microsoft faces significant threats from time to time. Example 12.6 describes the threat that was at the heart of the famous antitrust inquiry.

Early-Mover Disadvantages

Some firms pioneer a new technology or product but fail to become the market leader. Royal Crown in diet cola and EMI with computerized axial tomography (the CAT scanner) are notable examples. This suggests that it is not inevitable that early movers will achieve sustainable competitive advantage in their industries.

Early movers may fail to achieve a competitive advantage because they lack the complementary assets needed to commercialize the product.[29] This happened to EMI Ltd., a British music and electronics company perhaps best known for signing the Beatles to a record contract in the early 1960s. EMI lacked the production and marketing know-how to successfully commercialize the CAT scanner developed in its R&D laboratory, and it sold this business to GE in the late 1970s. The importance of complementary assets goes back to our discussion of the evolution of the hierarchical firm in Chapter 1. In the nineteenth century, firms that became successful early movers in their industries, such as Swift, International Harvester, and BASF, not only invested in the physical assets needed to produce their products, but also developed organizational capabilities and administrative hierarchies needed to market the product and coordinate the flow of product through the vertical chain.

Early movers may also fail to establish a competitive advantage because they bet on the wrong technologies or products. Thus, Wang Laboratories bet that the "office of the future" would be organized around networks of dedicated word processors.

Given the uncertainty about demand or technology that exists when an early mover enters a market, these bets may be good ones; that is, the expected present value of profits exceeds the cost of entering the market. But an inherent property of decision making under uncertainty is that good decisions do not always translate into good outcomes. In the 1970s, Wang could not have known that the personal computer would destroy the market for dedicated word processors. Of course, early movers can sometimes influence how the uncertainty is resolved, as when the early mover can establish a technology standard when there are network externalities. If so, being a pioneer can be attractive, even in the face of considerable uncertainty.

But even when network externalities or learning effects are present, luck or trivial circumstances can still be important. The technology or product design that becomes the industry standard is sometimes determined by factors unrelated to the relative superiority of competing designs. For example, in the 1950s, when nuclear reactors were beginning to be built in the United States, various nuclear technologies seemed feasible: reactors cooled by light water, heavy water, gas, and liquid sodium.[30] But following the Russians' launch of Sputnik in 1957, the priority for the U.S. government became not technological virtuosity, but quick construction of land-based reactors to preserve the United States' lead over the Soviets in nonmilitary applications of nuclear power. Because the Navy had been using light-water designs in nuclear submarines, light-water reactors became the early favorites as the government encouraged private utilities to embark on crash programs to construct reactors. Once development began, firms moved down the learning curve for this particular technology, and by the 1960s it had become the industry standard. This was so despite research that suggested that gas-cooled reactors might have been technologically superior.

◆ ◆ ◆ ◆ ◆ IMPERFECT IMITABILITY AND INDUSTRY EQUILIBRIUM

In the previous section, we argued that imperfect imitation and early-mover advantages prevent the perfectly competitive dynamic from running full course. But how, specifically, would an industry equilibrium depart from the perfectly competitive model when these isolating mechanisms are at work?

Richard Rumelt and Steven Lippman point out that when there is imperfect imitability, firms in an otherwise perfectly competitive market may be able to sustain positive economic profits over long periods, but some firms will earn below-average profits and indeed may appear to be making negative economic profits.[31] These arguments can be illustrated with a simple numerical example. Consider an industry in which firms produce undifferentiated products but have different production costs. Average variable cost (AVC) and marginal cost (MC) are constant up to a capacity of 1 million units per year. We assume that this level of capacity is small relative to the overall size of the market, so the industry can accommodate many firms producing at capacity. The most efficient firms in this industry can achieve an AVC of $1 per unit. There are many potential entrants into this market, but because imitation is imperfect, not all of them can emulate those that achieve the low-cost position in the market. (See Figure 12.5.)

The problem that each entrant faces is that before entry, it does not know what its costs will be. Accordingly, before entering the market, a prospective competitor believes that there is a 20 percent probability that its AVC will take on each of five values: $1, $3, $5, $7, $9. A potential entrant thus realizes that although it may be

FIGURE 12.5
AVERAGE VARIABLE AND MARGINAL COST FUNCTIONS
WITH IMPERFECT IMITABILITY

The figure shows the different average variable cost functions (*AVC*) that a firm might have if it enters this market. Since *AVC* is constant up to the capacity of 1 million units per year, the *AVC* function coincides with the marginal cost (*MC*) function. The firm's *AVC* can take on one of five values, $1, $3, $5, $7, or $9, each with equal (i.e., 20 percent) probability. The equilibrium price in this market is $6 per unit. At this price, each firm's expected economic profit is zero.

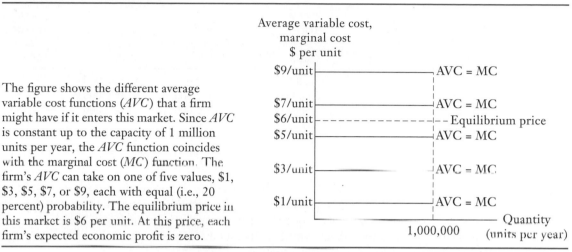

able to imitate the most efficient firms, its costs may also be higher than theirs. Suppose, finally, that a firm must incur the cost of building a factory if it comes into the industry. This factory costs $36 million to build and (for simplicity) never depreciates. Investors expect a return of 5 percent on their capital, so the annualized cost of the factory is .05 × $36,000,000 = $1,800,000, or $1.8 per unit of capacity. If we suppose further that the factory represents specialized capital that can be used only in this industry, and therefore has zero scrap value, the $1.8 represents the per unit cost of entry.

What will the equilibrium price be? Because there are many potential entrants, entry will occur as long as expected economic profit is positive, or equivalently, as long as the firm's expected operating profit (i.e., revenues minus variable costs) exceeds the costs of entry. In equilibrium, price will fall to the level at which entry is no longer attractive. Thus, at the equilibrium price, a firm's expected operating profit just equals the cost of entry. This seems straightforward, but there is one complication: not all entrants will survive. Some will find that their *AVC* is greater than the price and will drop out of the market. The expected profit calculation must consider this possibility.

In this example, the price that makes a prospective entrant just indifferent between entering and not entering is $6.[32] Why? At that price, firms that learn that their *AVC* is $7 or $9 exit the industry because they would lose money on each unit of output they produced. These firms, in effect, earn zero operating profits, but because they have incurred the upfront entry cost, they end up net losers. A firm with an *AVC* of $1, $3, or $5 will produce up to its capacity, and at a price of $6, will earn a per-unit operating profit of $5, $3, and $1, respectively. A potential entrant's expected operating profit per unit of capacity, when the price is $6, is thus:

$$(0.2 \times 5) + (0.2 \times 3) + (0.2 \times 1) + (0.2 \times 0) = \$1.8$$

Since this expected operating profit equals the entry costs of $1.8 per unit, a price of $6 leaves potential entrants just indifferent between entering or not. Put another way, at a price of $6, each firm's expected rate of return on its invested capital (ROIC) is equal to its cost of capital of 5 percent. This is illustrated in Table 12.1.

TABLE 12.1
SUMMARY STATISTICS FOR IMPERFECT IMITABILITY EXAMPLE

AVC	Annual Revenue @ $6/unit	Annual Total Variable Costs	Annual Operating Profit	Annual Operating Profit	ROIC (annual operating profit/$36 million)
$1/unit	0.2	$6,000,000	$1,000,000	$5,000,000	13.89%
$3/unit	0.2	$6,000,000	$3,000,000	$3,000,000	8.3%
$5/unit	0.2	$6,000,000	$5,000,000	$1,000,000	2.78%
$7/unit	0.2	$0	$0	$0	0%
$9/unit	0.2	$0	$0	$0	0%

At the equilibrium price of $6, some firms in the industry (those with *AVC* of $1 or $3) earn positive economic profits, that is, their ROIC exceeds their cost of capital. Other firms (those with *AVC* of $5) fail to recover their entry cost; their return on investment is less than their cost of capital. They remain in the industry even though they cannot fully cover the entry cost because the entry cost is sunk.

The example illustrates the distinction between *ex ante* and *ex post* economic profitability. Before entering (i.e., *ex ante*), each firm's expected economic profit is zero, that is, each firm expects to earn its 5 percent cost of capital (see Table 12.1). After entering (i.e., *ex post*), a firm's economic profit may be positive or negative; that is, a firm may earn more or less than the competitive return of 5 percent. This yields a fundamental insight: to assess the profit opportunities available in a particular business, managers should not just focus on the performance of the most successful firms. For example, the fact that some biotechnology firms (e.g., Amgen) earn annual returns on capital in excess of 20 percent does not mean a typical entrant can expect to earn this return. The average return of active firms can also be a misleading statistic of expected *ex ante* profitability. In the preceding example, the average ROIC of active producers is (13.89 + 8.33 + 2.78)/3 = 8.33 percent, which overstates *ex ante* profitability. The reason for this is that a simple average of the profitability of active firms ignores unsuccessful firms that have lost money and exited the industry.

CHAPTER SUMMARY

◆ Under the dynamic of perfect competition, no competitive advantage will be sustainable, and the persistence of profitability over time should be weak, because most firm's profits will converge to the competitive level.

◆ Evidence suggests that the profits of high-profit firms decline over time, while those of low-profit firms rise over time. However, the profits of these groups do not converge to a common mean. This lack of convergence cannot be ascribed to differences in risk between high-profit and low-profit firms. More likely, it reflects impediments to the operation of the dynamic of perfect competition.

◆ The resource-based theory of the firm emphasizes asymmetries in the resources and capabilities of firms in the same business as the basis for sustainable competitive advantage. Resources and capabilities must be scarce and immobile—not tradable on well-functioning markets—to serve as the basis of sustainable advantage.

◆ Competitive advantages must also be protected by isolating mechanisms to be sustainable. An isolating mechanism prevents competitors from duplicating or neutralizing the source of the firm's competitive advantage. Isolating mechanisms fall into two broad classes: barriers to imitation and early-mover advantages.

◆ Specific barriers to imitation are: legal restrictions, such as patents or copyrights, that impede imitation; superior access to scarce inputs or customers; economies of scale coupled with limited market size; and intangible barriers to imitation, including causal ambiguity, dependence on historical circumstances, and social complexity.

◆ Sources of early-mover advantages include: the learning curve, brand-name reputation when buyers are uncertain about product quality, and consumer switching costs.

◆ Early-mover advantages are also possible in markets with network effects. Firms entering such markets must decide whether to compete "for the market," thereby establishing dominance, or "in the market," thereby sharing a common standard with its competitors.

◆ It is difficult, but not impossible, to topple a firm that has established a dominant standard. The competitor must have highly attractive complementary products.

◆ When there are barriers to imitation, an equilibrium in a competitive market occurs at a price at which *ex ante* expected economic profits are zero. However, some firms may earn *ex post* positive economic profits. The conjunction of sunk costs and uncertainty protects these profits. No firm can be certain that it can imitate the most successful firms in the market, but a firm must incur nonrecoverable entry costs before it can learn how close it is likely to come to the efficiency of the best firms in the market.

QUESTIONS

1. "An analysis of sustainability is similar to a five-forces analysis." Comment.
2. Mueller's evidence on profit persistence is 30 years old. Do you think that profits are more or less persistent today than 30 years ago? Justify your answer.
3. Coke and Pepsi have sustained their market dominance for nearly a century. General Motors and Ford have been hard hit by competition. What is different about the product/market situations in these two cases that affects sustainability?
4. Provide an example of a firm that has co-specialized assets. Has the firm prospered from them? Why or why not?
5. "Often, the achievement of a sustainable competitive advantage requires an investment and should be evaluated as such. In some cases, the benefits from the investment may not be worth the cost. Rather than trying to build a sustainable position, the firm should "cash out," for example, by exiting the industry, selling the assets to another firm, or refraining from investing additional capital in the business for future growth." Evaluate this statement, keeping a focus on two questions: **(a)** In light of the factors that help a firm sustain a competitive advantage, explain in what sense achieving a sustainable advantage requires an "investment." **(b)** Can you envision circumstances under such an investment that would not be beneficial to the shareholders of the firm?
6. Do you agree or disagree with the following statements about sustaining advantage?
   a. In a market with network externalities, the product that would potentially offer consumers the highest "$B - C$" inevitably comes to dominate.
   b. Unusually high-performing firms may get that way either by outpositioning their competitors, belonging to high-performing industries, or both.
   c. If the sunk costs of entering industry A exceed the sunk costs of entering industry B, then there will certainly be fewer firms in industry A than in industry B.
   d. The Kronos Quartet (a popular classical string quartet) provides an example of co-specialized assets.

7. Which of the following circumstances are likely to create first-mover advantages?
   a. Maxwell House introduces the first freeze-dried coffee.
   b. A consortium of U.S. firms introduce the first high-definition television.
   c. SmithKline introduces Tagamet, the first effective medical treatment for ulcers.
   d. Wal-Mart opens a store in Nome, Alaska.

8. Each of the following parts describes a firm that was an early mover in its market. In light of the information provided, indicate whether the firm's position as an early mover is likely to be the basis of a sustainable competitive advantage.
   a. An early mover has the greatest cumulative experience in a business in which the slope of the learning curve is 1.
   b. A bank has issued the largest number of automated teller machine cards in a large urban area. Banks view their ability to offer ATM cards as an important part of their battle for depositors, and a customer's ATM card for one bank does not work on the ATM systems of competing banks.
   c. A firm has a 60 percent share of T3MP, a commodity chemical used to make industrial solvents. Minimum efficient scale is thought to be 50 percent of current market demand. Recently, a change in environmental regulation has dramatically raised the price of a substitute chemical that indirectly competes with T3MP. This change undermines the market for the substitute, which is about twice the size of the market for T3MP.

9. In defending his company against allegations of anticompetitive practices, Bill Gates claimed that if someone developed an operating system for personal computers that was superior to Microsoft's Windows 95 operating system, it would quickly become the market leader, just as Gates' DOS System became the market leader in the early 1980s. Opponents countered that the market situation in the early 2000s was different from the early 1980s, so that even a markedly superior operating system might fail to capture significant market share. Comment.

10. Two high-resolution audio formats, Super Audio CD (SACD) and DVD Audio (DVDA), were introduced in 2000. Both offer surround-sound music at a quality that approaches the original studio master recordings from which they are made. (Standard compact discs and MP3 recordings degrade sound quality due to format limitations.) Both formats can be added to new DVD players for an additional $25 to $250 per format, depending on the quality. SACD was originally supported by Sony and has since won support from many smaller classical music and jazz labels that sell in small numbers to "audiophiles." DVDA was backed by the DVD consortium. However, few recording studios embraced the DVDA format, and few popular music recordings have been released in either format. Unlike DVD video, most consumers remain disinterested in high-resolution audio. Why do you think high-resolution audio has remained a niche product?

ENDNOTES

[1]This example draws from "Market for Internet Calling Once Tiny, Gets Crowded Fast," *Wall Street Journal*, August 26, 2005, p. A1.

[2]Mueller, D. C., "The Persistence of Profits Above the Norm," *Economica*, 44, 1997, pp. 369–380. See also Mueller, D. C., *Profits in the Long Run*, Cambridge, Cambridge University Press, 1986.

[3]Our characterization of these patterns of profit persistence is based on the results in Table 2.2 in Mueller's book. Mueller's study is far more elaborate than we have described here. He uses regression analysis to estimate equations that give persistence patterns for each of the 600 firms in his sample. Our grouping of firms into two groups is done to illustrate the main results.

[4]This lack of convergence may be due to different risk characteristics of the two groups. Perhaps the firms in the high-profit group are riskier on average than the firms in the low-profit

group, and the capital markets require a higher rate of return from them. In his study, Mueller tests whether a systematic relationship exists between the riskiness of firms and the level to which their profits converge in the long run. Using a variety of measures of risk, Mueller concludes that differences in risk among the firms in his sample do not account for the lack of convergence to a common mean.

[5]Morris, Kathleen, "The Rise of Jill Barad," *Business Week*, May 25, 1998, pp. 112–119.

[6]"Is Barad in over Her Head at Mattel?" *Business Week*, September 27, 1999, p. 12.

[7]This definition is adapted from Barney, J., "Firm Resources and Sustained Competitive Advantage," *Journal of Management*, 17, 1991, pp. 99–120.

[8]Presentations of this theory can be found in Barney, J., "Firm Resources and Sustained Competitive Advantage," *Journal of Management*, 17, 1991, pp. 99–120; Peteraf, M. A., "The Cornerstones of Competitive Advantage: A Resource-Based View," *Strategic Management Journal*, 14, 1993, pp. 179–191; Dierickx, I. and K. Cool, "Asset Stock Accumulation and Sustainability of Competitive Advantage," *Management Science*, 35, 1989, pp. 1504–1511; Grant, R. M., "The Resource-Based Theory of Competitive Advantage: Implications for Strategy Formulation," *California Management Review*, Spring 1991, pp. 119–145; Wernerfelt, B., "A Resource-based View of the Firm," *Strategic Management Journal*, 5, 1984, pp. 171–180. The pioneering work underlying the resource-based theory is Penrose, E. T., *The Theory of the Growth of the Firm*, Oxford, Blackwell, 1959.

[9]This example is based on the article, "Fare Game: Did Northwest Steal American's Systems? The Court Will Decide," *Wall Street Journal*, July 7, 1994, pp. A1, A8.

[10]American's case against KLM was dismissed in 1997. Since then, American and Northwest have settled their case.

[11]Rumelt, R. P., "Towards a Strategic Theory of the Firm," in Lamb, R. (ed.), *Competitive Strategic Management*, Englewood Cliffs, NJ, Prentice-Hall, 1984, pp. 556–570.

[12]See, for example, Chapter 5 of Ghemawat, P., *Commitment: The Dynamic of Strategy*, New York, Free Press, 1991, or Yao, D., "Beyond the Reach of the Invisible Hand," *Strategic Management Journal*, 9, 1988, pp. 59–70.

[13]Between 1992 and 1996, Intel averaged a return on capital in excess of its cost of capital of 16.83 percentage points, while Coca-Cola and Microsoft averaged 21.52 and 33.54 percentage points, respectively. These data come from Stern Stewart's 1997 Performance 1000 universe.

[14]Quotation from p. 359 in Rumelt, R. P., "Towards a Strategic Theory of the Firm," in Lamb, R. (ed.), *Competitive Strategic Management*, Engelwood Cliffs, NJ, Prentice-Hall, 1984, pp. 566–570.

[15]We discuss patents, copyrights, and trademarks more fully in Chapter 11.

[16]Williams, J., "How Sustainable Is Your Advantage?" *California Management Review*, 34, 1992, pp. 1–23.

[17]White, L., "The Automobile Industry," in Adams, W. (ed.), *The Structure of American Industry*, 6th ed., New York, Macmillan, 1982.

[18]See, for example, Scherer, F. M. and D. Ross, *Industrial Market Structure and Economic Performance*, 3d ed., Boston, Houghton Mifflin, 1990, pp. 563–564.

[19]Quoted in Beard, D., "The Champ Returns," *Fort Lauderdale Sun Sentinal*, December 1, 1996, p. 1G.

[20]Rumelt, R. P., "Towards a Strategic Theory of the Firm," in Lamb, R. (ed.), *Competitive Strategic Management*, Englewood Cliffs, NJ, Prentice-Hall, 1984, pp. 556–570. See also Reed, R. and R. J. DeFillipi, "Causal Ambiguity, Barriers to Imitation and Sustainable Competitive Advantage," *Academy of Management Review*, 15, 1990, pp. 88–102.

[21]This point has been made by Polanyi, M., *The Tacit Dimension*, Garden City, NY, Anchor, 1967, and by Nelson, R. and S. Winter, *An Evolutionary Theory of Economic Change*, Cambridge, MA, Harvard University Press, 1982.

[22]Teece, D., "Applying Concepts of Economic Analysis to Strategic Management," in Harold Pennings and Associates (eds.), *Organizational Strategy and Change*, San Francisco, Jossey-Bass, 1985.

[23]In Chapter 11 we discuss the distinction between experience goods and search goods and the implications of that distinction for competitive positioning.

[24]The analysis in this section is based on Richard Schmalensee's paper, "Product Differentiation Advantages of Pioneering Brands," *American Economic Review*, 72, June 1982, pp. 349–365.

[25]Greer, D. F., *Industrial Organization and Public Policy*, 3d ed., New York, Macmillan, 1992, p. 141.

[26]Brock, G. W., *The U.S. Computer Industry: A Study of Market Power*, Cambridge, MA, Ballinger, 1975.

[27]See, for example, Carpenter, G. S. and K. Nakamoto, "Consumer Preference Formation and Pioneering Advantage," *Journal of Marketing Research*, August 1989, pp. 285–298.

[28]See Klemperer, P., "Markets with Consumer Switching Costs," *Quarterly Journal of Economics*, 102, 1987, pp. 375–394, and Farrell, J. and C. Shapiro, "Dynamic Competition with Switching Costs," *RAND Journal of Economics*, 19, Spring 1988, pp. 123–137.

[29]Teece, D., "Profiting from Technological Innovation: Implications for Integration, Collaboration, Licensing, and Public Policy," *Research Policy*, 15, 1986, pp. 285–305.

[30]This example comes from Arthur, M. B., "Positive Feedbacks in the Economy," *Scientific American*, 262, February 1990, pp. 92–99.

[31]Lippman, S. A. and R. P. Rumelt, "Uncertain Imitability: An Analysis of Interfirm Differences in Efficiency under Competition," *Bell Journal of Economics*, 13, Autumn 1982, pp. 418–438.

[32]We calculated the equilibrium price through trial and error. A systematic method exists for calculating the equilibrium price in this market, but its discussion would add little to the economic insights that this example generates.

THE ORIGINS OF COMPETITIVE ADVANTAGE: INNOVATION, EVOLUTION, AND THE ENVIRONMENT

13

*P*erhaps no product so epitomizes the emergence of Japanese technological and marketing muscle on a global scale than the videocassette recorder (VCR). The battle to shape the future of the video recording industry began 50 years ago, when the American-based Ampex Corporation invented videotape and a video recording and playback machine. Ampex translated its innovative success into a dominant position in the market for high-performance video recording systems for commercial users. Throughout the 1960s, Ampex sought to develop a cartridge-based video player and an associated video camera for the household market, and in 1970 it introduced a system known as Instavision. But Instavision was a commercial flop: it cost more than $1,500 for a cumbersome-looking video player and $500 for the camera. Two years later, Ampex abandoned the project, concentrating instead on commercial applications of video recording technology.

Two other American entrants into the VCR-race, Cartridge Television Inc. (CTI) and RCA, also failed. CTI developed a video recording and playback machine that was included as a feature on high-end television sets manufactured by Admiral and Packard Bell. However, the product was plagued by technological glitches, and despite an agreement with Columbia and United Artists to provide films on videotape, there were not enough films to maintain consumer interest.[1] RCA, which pioneered the color television set, sought to develop a commercially viable VCR in the early 1970s. But in 1977 it, too, abandoned its efforts, because it could not develop an economical process for manufacturing its VCR designs and because it believed that the videodisc would become the preferred design for playing back recorded images.

While the Americans were faltering, foreign firms were succeeding. By the mid-1970s, JVC, Matsushita, Sony of Japan, and Philips of the Netherlands had all mastered the daunting technological challenges of manufacturing video recorders for a commercial market (e.g., figuring out how to compress two to four hours of videotape into a cartridge the size of a small paperback). Sony's Betamax system got an early head start after Matsushita decided to delay the production of its system, which it believed was technologically inferior to the Video Home System (VHS) being developed by JVC. Betamax developed a strong following in the high-end professional market. However, JVC set the stage for overtaking Sony in the far larger household market when it introduced a VHS machine that could record for two hours, as compared with just one hour for the Sony machines. Soon after, JVC and Matsushita convinced other consumer electronics firms, such as Thorn-EMI in the U.K., Thompson in France, and AEG-Telefunken in West Germany, to adopt the VHS model in their machines, giving VHS an edge in the race to become the technology standard. Philips, whose V2000 format was incompatible with both Sony and JVC, introduced its product a year and a half after JVC introduced VHS. Although it had managed to keep pace with its Japanese rivals in the race to develop the technology, Philips' late introduction put it at a disadvantage in the competition to accumulate an installed base of users. Eventually, Philips also began to manufacture VCRs in the VHS format.

This example shows that the origins of a firm's marketplace success often stretch far back in time. JVC-Matsushita's success in the VCR business was shaped by decisions and commitments that those firms made 15 to 20 years before VCRs became commercially viable. This suggests that developing a competitive advantage involves looking deep into the future to anticipate unmet or even unarticulated consumer needs, betting on alternative technologies, investing in the development of new products and new capabilities to produce and deliver those products to market, and then being the first to introduce those products to the marketplace to benefit from early-mover advantages, such as network externalities or the learning curve that we discussed in Chapter 12.

This chapter studies the origins of competitive advantage. In Chapter 12 we argued that competitive advantage arises from a firm's ability to exploit market shocks and opportunities. Early-mover advantages and various barriers to imitation by other firms then protect the firm's advantage. But we did not discuss why some firms are better or luckier than others at exploiting shocks or taking advantage of opportunities. Why, for example, did Nickelodeon, and not Disney, develop the most successful kids' television network? Why was Honda, and not Harley-Davidson or British Triumph, able to tap into what turned out to be a large U.S. market for light- and middle-weight motorcycles? Why did JVC succeed where Ampex failed in the market for VCRs?

We divide this chapter into seven main parts. The first part discusses the role of innovation and entrepreneurship in a market economy, emphasizing economist Joseph Schumpeter's notion of creative destruction and highlighting its importance for business strategy. The next part examines firms' incentives to innovate. The third part examines the "market for ideas" in which the innovative process begins. We then look at competition among innovators. The fourth part explores innovation from the perspective of evolutionary economics. We focus on how a firm's history and internal resources and capabilities affect its ability to innovate and develop new capabilities. The fifth part examines the relationship between the firm's local environment and its ability to gain competitive advantage. We are particularly concerned with how demand and factor market conditions, as well as the economic infrastructure in the firm's domestic market, determine competitive advantage. In the last part, we discuss the process of managing innovation inside the firm.

◆ ◆ ◆ ◆ ◆ CREATIVE DESTRUCTION

A short answer to the question, "What are the origins of competitive advantage?" is that some firms exploit opportunities for creating profitable competitive positions that other firms either ignore or cannot exploit. Seizing such opportunities is the essence of entrepreneurship. Entrepreneurship is often seen as synonymous with discovery and innovation. But, as Joseph Schumpeter has stated, entrepreneurship is also the ability to act on the opportunity that innovations and discoveries create:

> To undertake such new things is difficult and constitutes a distinct economic function, first, because they lie outside the routine tasks that everybody understands and secondly because the environment resists in many ways that vary, according to social conditions, from simple refusal either to finance or to buy a new thing, to physical attack on the person who tries to produce it. To act with confidence beyond the range of familiar beacons and to overcome that resistance requires aptitudes that are present in only a small fraction of the population and define the entrepreneurial type as well as the entrepreneurial function. This function does not essentially consist in either inventing anything or otherwise creating the conditions which the enterprise exploits. It consists in getting things done.[2]

Schumpeter believed that innovation causes most markets to evolve in a characteristic pattern. Any market has periods of comparative quiet, when firms that have developed superior products, technologies, or organizational capabilities earn positive economic profits. These quiet periods are punctuated by fundamental "shocks" or "discontinuities" that destroy old sources of advantage and replace them with new ones. The entrepreneurs who exploit the opportunities these shocks create achieve positive profits during the next period of comparative quiet. Schumpeter called this evolutionary process *creative destruction*.

Schumpeter's research was largely concerned about the long-run performance of the economy. According to Schumpeter, the process of creative destruction meant that static efficiency—the optimal allocation of society's resources at a given point in time—was less important than dynamic efficiency—the achievement of long-term growth and technological improvement. Schumpeter criticized economists who focused exclusively on the outcomes of price competition when promoting the benefits of free markets. What really counted was not price competition, but competition between new products, new technologies, and new sources of organization.

> This kind of competition is as much more effective than the other as a bombardment is in comparison with forcing a door, and so much more important that it becomes a matter of comparative indifference whether [price] competition in the ordinary sense functions more or less properly; the powerful lever that in the long run expands output and brings down prices is in any case made of other stuff.[3]

From a policy perspective, Schumpeter's ideas have been used to defend monopoly, on the grounds that the concentration of wealth and power leads to greater investments in innovation and higher rates of long-term growth. We will address this claim later on in the chapter.

Schumpeter's ideas have powerful managerial implications as well. If he is correct, then the isolating mechanisms described in Chapter 12 may not be sufficient to assure sustained advantage. Competitive advantages based on inimitable resources or capabilities or early-mover advantages can eventually become obsolete as new technologies arise, tastes change, or government policy evolves. Firms must therefore be able to bridge the discontinuities that characterize creative destruction. This process is depicted in Figure 13.1, which shows the hypothetical time path for profits for a firm that has achieved a sustainable advantage.

Disruptive Technologies

There is no end to the list of new technologies that "creatively destroyed" established markets and their dominant firms—quartz watches, cellular communication, and

FIGURE 13.1
HYPERCOMPETITION AND COMPETITIVE ADVANTAGE

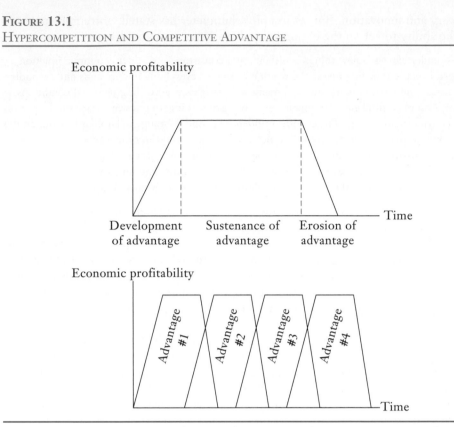

The upper diagram illustrates the dynamic of competitive advantage. Economic profits rise as the advantage is developed. They then plateau while the advantage is sustainable. Eventually, the advantage is eroded, and economic profitability declines. Richard D'Aveni argues that in many markets, the period during which advantages are sustainable is shrinking. In such environments, a firm can sustain positive economic profits only by continually developing new sources of advantage, as shown in the bottom diagram.

Source: Figures 1-1 and 1-2 in D'Aveni, R. A., *Hypercompetition: Managing the Dynamics of Strategic Maneuvering*, New York, Free Press, 1994, pp. 8, 12.

computer flash memory are just a few examples. In the parlance of Chapter 11, these technologies succeeded because they had higher B and lower C than did their predecessors. It was no surprise that they replaced older technologies. Nor was it a surprise that they wreaked havoc on old and established businesses, given Schumpeter's observations about the difficulties that established firms have in bridging technological change. In the popular book, *The Innovator's Dilemma*, Clay Christensen identified a special class of novel technologies that offer much higher $B - C$ than their predecessors, but do so through a combination of lower B and drastically lower C (in terms of both production costs and convenience).[4] In the spirit of Schumpeter, Christensen calls these *disruptive technologies*. Examples include computer workstations (replacing more powerful mainframes), ink jet printers (replacing higher visual resolution laser printers), electronic mail (replacing more personal "snail mail" and the telephone), and downloadable MP3 recordings (replacing higher audio resolution compact discs). Not all low B/low C technologies are disruptive. Backers of the Segway human transporter thought for a brief moment that it would replace the automobile for urban commuting. Most commuters thought the B was too low and so the Segway was relegated to niche status.

The success of disruptive technologies is not surprising—new technologies offering higher $B - C$ should replace older technologies. But disruptive technologies are different from other breakthrough technologies owing to the emphasis on costs. Technologies such as the personal computer and MP3 provide lower B than the technologies that they replaced. But they succeeded because consumers did not put a high value on the extra quality and features of the older technologies. In other words, they did not perceive the difference in B to be very large. Thus, they flocked toward the technologies offering substantially lower C. Established firms could try to forestall the success of disruptive technologies by doing a better job of marketing their products' benefits. By raising perceived B, incumbent technologies will appear to offer higher $B - C$ and will continue to succeed despite their higher costs. This is easier said than done. For example, the music recording industry may be able to withstand the growth of MP3 by educating consumers about the format's inferior audio reproduction. Sony tried very hard to do exactly this around 2000–2001, when it launched the ultra-high-resolution Super Audio CD format well in advance of the Ipod revolution. Unfortunately for Sony, its arguments fell on deaf ears. Having bet on high B when consumers wanted low C, Sony is now far behind in the MP3 marketplace.

Sustainability and Creative Destruction

Scholars have recently identified a number of factors that may enable firms to ride the wave of creative destruction. For example, Jeho Lee studied the success of pharmaceutical companies during the last century.[5] He noted that during the first third of the twentieth century, drug makers were not much different from each other in terms of their commitments to innovation, inasmuch as there was little scientific basis to their work. But during the 1940s, a few firms built on their early success in developing antibiotics to hire additional scientists, putting them in a better position to exploit new research findings. Most of these companies, including Abbott, Eli Lilly, Merck, and Pfizer, have continued to exploit their scientific expertise during the latest wave of creative destruction brought about by the biotech revolution. This example suggests that long-run success is often based on historical accidents (which firms made initial scientific breakthroughs) and that ongoing scientific expertise is essential to adapting to major shifts in technology.

Rebecca Henderson and Ian Cockburn have identified proactive steps that pharmaceutical firms can take to stay ahead of technological changes.[6] Drug makers have found it essential to be located near centers of academic excellence, as well as close to each other. This permits the rapid exchange of new ideas among the academic and applied research communities. In the United States, pharmaceutical companies have disproportionately located in the New York/New Jersey area, amid the largest concentration of medical schools in the world, while biotech companies have located in the San Francisco area and southern California, amid leading research universities (and eager venture capitalists). These companies have also found it important to reward scientists for focusing more on generating general scientific knowledge and less on developing products in hand. The result is a remarkable history of technological change that has benefited established firms, start-ups, and consumers.

Gary Hamel and C. K. Prahalad have promoted related strategies for firms in many industries.[7] They argue that companies such as CNN, Honda, NEC, and Sony succeeded because of their sustained obsession with achieving global dominance in their industries. Prahalad and Hamel call this obsession *strategic intent*. The strategic intent of these companies was out of proportion to their existing resources and capabilities. Prahalad and Hamel refer to this gap between ambition and resources as *strategic stretch*. These companies had to expand and adapt their current stock of resources and create new ones. As we discussed in Chapter 2, firms can achieve lower costs or superior quality through the economies of scope associated with leveraging resources. However, there are limits to the extent that firms can achieve economies of scope. Indeed, as Peter Kontes and Michael Mankins report in "The Dangers of Strategic Intent," most of the firms Hamel and Prahalad hold up as exemplars actually generated below-average shareholder returns.[8]

Richard D'Aveni argues that in industries ranging from consumer electronics to airlines and computer software to snack goods, the sources of competitive advantage are being created and eroded at an increasingly rapid rate.[9] In effect, he argues that the length of the plateau in Figure 13.1 is shrinking. D'Aveni calls this phenomenon *hypercompetition* and argues that a firm's chief strategic goal should be to disrupt existing sources of advantage in its industry (including its own) and create new ones.

The ideas of D'Aveni and Prahalad and Hamel remind us that in environments characterized by rapid technological development and fickle tastes, a firm that rests on its laurels, seeking only to harvest existing sources of advantage, can be quickly displaced by more innovative rivals. Moreover, firms may be able to create their own shocks, rather than waiting for the environment to change or for other firms to disrupt existing sources of advantage in the industry.

◆ ◆ ◆ ◆ ◆ THE INCENTIVE TO INNOVATE

Business history contains many instances of companies with a wealth of assets—innovative products, strong reputations, deep financial resources, and powerful distribution channels—whose market position was eroded or overtaken by companies with seemingly much smaller resource bases. Nokia versus Motorola in cellular phones, Sony versus RCA in television, and CNN versus the networks in news programming come to mind. A frequent explanation for this is that small firms are more "nimble" and less bureaucratic than large firms, and thus are more willing to innovate and break with established practices. This explanation is often expressed in familiar clichés contrasting large and small companies. The managers of large firms are "myopic" and ignore firms that come out of nowhere to challenge their dominance. Small companies are "hungry" and have the courage to pursue innovative approaches that their larger rivals lack.

Though superficially appealing, these arguments are not profound. They fail to answer a fundamental question: Assuming that their managers are rational, why would established firms be systematically less able to innovate or less willing to break with established practice than new entrants or marginal firms in an industry? One reason may be that large established firms fall victim to the kinds of incentive and influence problems we described in Chapter 3. In this section we explore another possibility—namely, under certain economic circumstances it may be rational for firms not to innovate. Two forces may make it rational for firms to refrain from innovating: (1) the sunk cost effect and (2) the replacement effect. We also discuss a force called the efficiency effect, which offsets the sunk cost and replacement effects and strengthens an established firm's incentive to innovate.

EXAMPLE 13.1 THE SUNK COST EFFECT IN STEEL: THE ADOPTION OF THE BASIC OXYGEN FURNACE

In the early 1950s, a new steel-making technology became commercially viable: the basic oxygen furnace (BOF). The BOF reduced milling time to 40 minutes as compared with the 6 to 8 hours in the open hearth (OH) technology that had long been the industry standard. Despite the apparent superiority of BOF, few American steelmakers adopted it. Throughout the 1950s, U.S. steelmakers added nearly 50 million additional tons of OH capacity, but they did not begin to replace their OH furnaces with BOFs until the late 1960s. Meanwhile, foreign steelmakers built new plants incorporating state-of-the-art BOF technology. The cost advantage afforded by this new technology was a key reason why Japanese and Korean steelmakers penetrated the American domestic market.

Why did American steelmakers continue to invest in a seemingly inefficient technology? The standard explanation has been bad management. For example, two knowledgeable observers of the steel industry, Walter Adams and Hans Mueller, wrote:

> The most likely explanation of the hesitant adoption of the Austrian converter [i.e., the BOF] by the large American firms is that their managements were still imbued with Andrew Carnegie's motto "invention don't pay." In other words, let others assume the cost and risk of research and development, and of breaking in a new process, then we'll decide. The result was that during the 1950s, the American steel industry installed 40 million tons of melting capacity that, as *Fortune* observed, "was obsolete when it was built."[10]

Without denying the possibility of managerial myopia, there is another explanation. American steel firms throughout the first half of the twentieth century had developed a considerable amount of specific know-how related to the OH technology. Their investment in this know-how was sunk: it could not be recovered if they switched to the BOF technology. This sunk investment created an asymmetry between established American firms and new Japanese firms that made it cost effective for American firms to stick with the older OH technology.

The findings of Sharon Oster's study of technology adoption in the steel industry is consistent with the hypothesis that American steel firms chose between alternative technologies based on profit-maximization criteria.[11] For example, because the BOF technology used relatively more pig iron, as opposed to scrap iron, than the OH technology, a steel plant that was located closer to sources of pig iron would save more operating costs by adopting the BOF technology. Oster found that firms that produced their own pig iron were more likely to adopt BOF than were firms that had to buy it from outside suppliers. More generally, Oster found that the magnitude of the savings in operating costs, ΔVC, from adopting the BOF varied considerably among firms and that firms with larger cost savings were more likely to adopt BOF.

This is not to argue that there was not poor management in the steel industry. There almost certainly was, at least in some firms. However, we cannot attribute the lack of innovation entirely to poor management. Large sunk investments in know-how and capabilities are hard for a firm to ignore when choosing a technology. The presence of these sunk investments distinguished American producers from producers in Japan, Korea, and elsewhere who were investing in "greenfield" plants (i.e., new steel-making facilities). Unfortunately, these differences may have planted the seeds for the competitive decline of the U.S. integrated steel sector in the 1970s and 1980s.

The Sunk Cost Effect

The *sunk cost effect* has to do with the asymmetry between a firm that has already made a commitment to a particular technology or product concept and one that is planning such a commitment. The sunk cost effect arises because a firm that has already committed to a particular technology has invested in resources and organizational capabilities that are likely to be specific to that technology and are thus less valuable if the firm switches to another technology. For an established firm, the costs associated with these investments are sunk and thus should be ignored when the firm considers whether to switch to a new technology. Ignoring these sunk costs creates an inertia that favors sticking with the current technology. By contrast, a firm that has not yet committed to a technology can compare the costs of all of the alternative technologies under consideration and is thus not biased in favor of one technology over another.

The Replacement Effect

Does a profit-maximizing monopolist have a stronger or weaker incentive to innovate than a new entrant? The Nobel Prize–winning economist Kenneth Arrow pondered this question more than 30 years ago.[12] He considered the incentives for adopting a process innovation that would lower the average variable costs of production. The innovation is drastic: once it is adopted, producers using the older technology will not be viable competitors. Arrow compared two different scenarios: (1) the opportunity to develop the innovation is available to a firm that currently monopolizes the market using the old technology, and (2) the opportunity to develop the innovation is available to a potential entrant who, if it adopts the innovation, will become the monopolist. Under which scenario, Arrow asked, is the willingness-to-pay to develop the innovation greatest?

Arrow concluded that assuming equal innovative capabilities, an entrant would be willing to spend more than the monopolist to develop the innovation. The intuition behind Arrow's insight is this: a successful innovation for a new entrant leads to monopoly; a successful innovation by the established firm also leads to a monopoly, but since it already had a monopoly, its gain from innovation is less than that for the potential entrant. Through innovation an entrant can replace the monopolist, but the monopolist can only replace itself. For this reason, this phenomenon is called the *replacement effect*.[13]

Arrow's insight explains why an established firm would be less willing to "stretch" itself to innovate or develop new sources of advantage than a potential entrant or a marginal firm in an industry. Arrow's argument also shows that innovative entrants may overtake established firms, not because established firms are poorly managed or suffer disproportionately from agency costs, but because of a natural market dynamic. An established firm's success can sow the seeds of its (potential) destruction.

The Efficiency Effect

Arrow's analysis applies when the innovation opportunity is not available to competitors or potential entrants. If an incumbent monopolist anticipates that potential entrants may also have an opportunity to develop the innovation, then the efficiency effect comes into play. To understand the *efficiency effect*, compare the following: (1) the loss in profits when a monopolist becomes one of two competitors in a duopoly, and (2) the profits of a duopolist. Most oligopoly models, including the Cournot model discussed in Chapter 6, suggest that (1) is larger than (2). In other words, a monopolist usually has more to lose from another firm's entry than that firm has to gain from entering the market. The reason is that the entrant not only takes business from the monopolist, but also tends to drive down prices. The efficiency effect makes an incumbent monopolist's incentive to innovate stronger than that of a potential entrant.

In the competition between established firms and potential entrants to develop new innovations, the sunk cost effect, replacement effect, and efficiency effect will operate simultaneously. Which effect dominates depends on the specific conditions of the innovation competition. For example, the replacement and sunk cost effects may dominate if the chance that smaller competitors or potential entrants will develop the innovation is low. Then, the main effect of the innovation for the established firm will be to cannibalize current profits and reduce the value of established resources and organizational capabilities associated with the current technology. By contrast, the efficiency effect may dominate when the monopolist's failure to develop the innovation means that new entrants almost certainly will. In this case, a key benefit of the innovation to the established firm is to stave off the deterioration of profit that comes from additional competition from firms that may develop a cost or benefit advantage over it if they successfully innovate.

INNOVATION AND THE MARKET FOR IDEAS ◆ ◆ ◆ ◆ ◆

Several scholars have built on Arrow's ideas to further our understanding of the incentives to innovate. Joshua Gans and Scott Stern have explored a variant of the efficiency effect that applies whenever the incumbent firm has the potential to acquire the technology of the entrant (either through license of the technology or outright acquisition of the firm).[14] This is a natural possibility, as acquisition could lead to monopoly, which is generally more profitable than duopoly. Under these conditions, the incumbent has a strong incentive to invest in R&D—even if it is purely imitative—so as to boost its bargaining power in the event that the entrant innovates first. On the other hand, the incumbent may elect to back off on R&D, viewing the entrant's efforts as a substitute. After all, why duplicate the entrant's efforts if it will soon be acquired?

David Teece has observed that a new firm's ability to prosper from its inventions depends on the presence of a "market for ideas"—a place in which the firm can sell its ideas for full value.[15] Teece identifies two elements of the commercialization environment that affect the market for ideas: (1) the technology is not easily expropriated by others, and (2) the presence of specialized assets, such as manufacturing or marketing capabilities, that must be used in conjunction with the innovative product. The first point is obvious: if a technology is not well protected by patents, the innovator can hardly expect to enjoy significant returns. Consider the fate of Robert Kearns, who invented the intermittent windshield wiper in the early 1960s. He showed the technology to Ford, which rejected a licensing agreement with Kearns, only to introduce its own intermittent wiper soon thereafter. It was not until the 1990s that Kearns was able to uphold his patent in court. An important takeaway is that secrecy is not enough to protect innovators—at some point they must divulge some of their ideas to trading partners. Absent good patent protection, they are immediately at risk for expropriation. Another important takeaway is that by expropriating Kearns's idea, Ford was less likely to be offered new ideas by other innovators. Firms like Ford that face competition in the market to acquire ideas should expropriate with caution.

EXAMPLE 13.2 R&D SPENDING AND FIRM SIZE IN THE BIOTECHNOLOGY SECTOR: THE ROLE OF MANAGEMENT

Before approving prescription drugs for sale in the United States, the Food and Drug Administration requires three "phases" of clinical trials. In Phase I testing of an investigational new drug (IND), the drug maker performs small-scale testing on healthy subjects to learn about safety and dose/response ratios. Phase II involves medium-scale clinical trials to test for efficacy. The large Phase III trials are the final step before the drug company can submit its application for FDA approval. There is a strong chance in each phase that an IND will fail. Sometimes, the FDA informs the drug maker that it will not approve its product for the next phase. Other times, the drug maker voluntarily withdraws its drug from the testing process if test data reveal that it is unlikely to pass the next phase.

Historically, most of the investigational new drugs undergoing FDA review have been shepherded by large, established firms with expansive research portfolios. Thanks to the revolution in biotechnology, it is no longer uncommon for an "early-stage" biotech firm with only one or two drugs to its name to attempt to bring a drug through the FDA review process. In a recent study, Ilan Guedj and David Scharfstein compare the drug development strategies of mature biotech companies versus smaller, early-stage firms.[16] They study 235 cancer drugs that have begun Phase I trials and find that early-stage firms are more likely than mature firms to advance their drugs to Phase II. This is especially true for early-stage firms with large cash reserves. It turns out that this does not reflect superior Phase I results for early-stage firms. In fact, once they make it to Phase II, the drugs of the early-stage firms have less promising clinical results and are less likely to make it to Phase III.

Guedj and Scharfstein conclude from their findings that the managers of early-stage firms are reluctant to acknowledge their failures. Instead, these managers exploit asymmetric information (they know that their drugs are problematic, but their investors do not) by pushing their drugs to Phase II on the slim chance that they will reverse poor Phase I results. The alternative—abandoning their R&D efforts—would likely mean they would have to close down their companies and return any excess cash reserves to their investors. In contrast, managers of larger firms have a broader portfolio of drugs and can take one drug's failure in stride and reallocate funding to other projects. Thus, they are quicker to pull the trigger on failing drugs.

Teece's second point is more subtle. Innovative products must be produced and marketed. If many firms have the required expertise in production and marketing, they will compete for the rights to the innovation, leaving most of the profits for the innovator. But if the required expertise is scarce, the innovator can no longer sell to the highest bidder. The balance of power shifts away from the innovator and toward the established firm that will produce and market the product. Consider that when Nintendo dominated the video game market, game developers had no choice but to accept Nintendo's terms for new software. With the success of Sony and Microsoft, developers of popular software, such as Entertainment Arts and UbiSoft, are no longer beholden to one firm and have gained the upper hand in negotiating rights fees. To take another example, the California biotech firm Celtrix held valuable patents on a cell-regulating protein it hoped would heal damaged cells. Although Celtrix developed the protein, Genentech won the patent for the process for producing the protein. Celtrix had to enter a joint venture arrangement on terms favorable to Genentech to get the rights to use the patented process.

Allocating Innovative Capital

In Chapter 2, we described the Boston Consulting Group's Growth/Share Matrix. According to the BCG paradigm, one advantage of a diversified firm was its ability to allocate profits earned on established products to the development of rising stars. We observed that with the development of capital markets, start-up firms with good ideas are able to attract investor capital, offsetting the benefits of the diversified firm's internal capital markets.

Jeremy Stein has pointed out that managers who allocate research dollars may face very different incentives in large and small firms, so that investors in small firms end up paying for unpromising research programs.[17] Stein observes that investors in R&D firms often have little direct understanding of the underlying science and cannot easily evaluate research progress. The managers of small R&D firms are usually also their founders. They might overstate the success of ongoing research rather than see the plug pulled on their projects and, therefore, on their firms. Allocation of R&D in large firms is conducted by scientists (often with the title of vice president for research). They oversee the funding of numerous projects. If one project is faltering, they can reallocate funds to another without fear of losing their jobs. Example 13.3 discusses an empirical study showing that these forces are at work in the biotechnology industry.

INNOVATION COMPETITION ◆ ◆ ◆ ◆ ◆

Chapters 6 through 10 of this book emphasize the importance of thinking about how competitors will respond when a firm develops products and chooses prices for them. It is equally critical to anticipate rivals' responses when selecting a level of investment in R&D. When several firms are competing to develop the same product, the firm that does so first can gain significant advantage. The most obvious advantage is that the first innovator may be able to protect its ideas with patents and trademarks. Consider, for example, the race to develop the modern telephone. Alexander Graham Bell filed his patent application for the modern phone just two hours before Elisha Gray filed his application. Despite (or perhaps because of) many similarities in the two designs, Bell was able to protect his patent rights in the courts. (Thomas Edison developed his own prototype at about the same time, but had to wait 17 years, until the expiration of Bell's patent, to compete in the market.) Bell's patent has proved to be worth hundreds of billions of dollars while Elisha Gray remains a footnote to history.[18]

Even without the legal protection of patents and trademarks, the first innovator may gain significant early-mover advantages.[19] Given a big enough head start, Bell's technology would have been assured success by virtue of the associated network externalities, regardless of its patent status. The first innovator may also benefit from consumer perceptions. Consumers often view the attributes of pioneering brands as embodying the ideal configuration against which all other brands are benchmarked—witness the ongoing success of the Palm Pilot personal digital assistant.

Patent Races

The term *patent race* describes the race between firms to innovate first. To develop a better understanding of the forces that drive innovation, economists have studied different models of patent races. In these models, the first firm to complete the project

EXAMPLE 13.3 PATENT RACING AND THE INVENTION OF THE INTEGRATED CIRCUIT[20]

The race to develop the first integrated circuit (IC) had two key protagonists: Jack Kilby of Texas Instruments (TI) and Bob Noyce of Fairchild Semiconductor. Kilby began his career in electrical engineering at Centrilab. During World War II, Centrilab scientists discovered how to build electronic parts directly onto circuit boards through a technique that resembled silk screening of fabrics. But Centrilab mainly made low-cost products such as batteries. While at Centrilab, Kilby experimented with miniaturization but paid careful attention to two ongoing developments—the invention of the transistor by William Shockley and his colleagues at Bell Labs and the construction of the first computer, the ENIAC.

Like most good engineers, Kilby recognized that the power of the computer was inextricably tied to the ability to miniaturize the electronics within it. Transistors replaced vacuum tubes. They required virtually no "wire" (the electrical path was carved out of metal bonded to the transistor) and ran much cooler and longer than tubes. The transistor was an important start, but true miniaturization and the elimination of the wires that restricted computing speed would require combining transistors, resistors, and capacitors in a single unit. By 1958, Kilby was convinced that advances in miniaturization would require larger investments than Centrilab was willing to make. He sent out his resume and landed at Texas Instruments. The match was fortuitous—just a few years earlier, TI had invented a process for making transistors out of silicon. The combination of Centrilab's silk screening technique and TI's expertise with silicon would prove to be an inspiration to Kilby.

Robert Noyce had recently received his doctorate in electrical engineering when he went to work with Shockley at Bell Labs. One year later, in 1957, Noyce and seven others left Shockley (partly in reaction to Shockley's shortcomings as a supervisor, partly due to Shockley's decision to change research priorities) to form Fairchild

Semiconductor. Fairchild's first important invention was a planar transistor that placed all the important parts of the transistor on the surface of the silicon, with one part nested within another. The unique design proved an inspiration to Noyce. The race between Noyce and Kilby to integrate the circuit was on.

What happened next is well known. Both Kilby and Noyce found ways to combine transistors, resistors, and capacitors in a single unit with essentially no wires. Kilby proposed to borrow from the silk-screening technique he had learned at Centrilab; Noyce's device borrowed the nesting techniques developed at Fairchild. In 1959, both men filed patents for the designs of their semiconductors. After a 10-year battle, the courts upheld Noyce's patents. Although Kilby was the first to propose his idea for interconnection, his patent's description of how to actually create the integrated circuit was vague. Noyce's planar approach proved to be far more practical.

As a practical matter, the outcome of the patent race was not too important. Both Fairchild and TI continued to refine their integrated circuits while the court case lingered, and the two agreed to share royalties from any use of either design. Today, both Kilby and Noyce share credit for inventing the integrated circuit. Kilby went on to invent the handheld calculator for TI, while Noyce founded Intel.

This example illustrates many key ideas about patent racing. Texas Instruments and Fairchild were not the only firms attempting to create ICs, and they succeeded for different reasons. Path dependence was partly behind each firm's success and each firm's unique approach. Both firms made relatively large investments in research talent. (Though Fairchild was small in comparison with TI, its eight founders were among the top electrical engineers in the world.) Lastly, both firms understood that it is easier to create partnerships before becoming product market competitors, when antitrust laws might stand in the way.

"wins" the patent race and obtains exclusive rights to develop and market the product. The losing firms get nothing. Although this is an extreme characterization, it does highlight the often critical advantage that goes to the first innovator, and it gives insight into how the magnitude of that advantage affects the incentives to innovate. These models also emphasize an important strategic point: firms in a patent race must anticipate the R&D investments of competitors. Failure to do so can be costly.

Models of patent races examine the importance of uncertainty in the R&D process, the timing of R&D investments, and entry. These studies suggest that when a firm that is engaged in a patent race determines whether to increase its investment in innovation, it must account for the following factors:

- How much does the investment increase its R&D productivity and thereby also increase its chances of winning the patent race? If there are diminishing returns to productivity, then increasing R&D outlays may not greatly improve the firm's chances of winning the race. If there are increasing returns, additional expenditures are usually warranted, unless they provoke competitors to increase their expenditures.

- Will other firms increase their R&D expenditures in response, thereby decreasing the firm's chances of winning the patent race? This competitive response will reduce the profitability of R&D whether it demonstrates increasing or decreasing returns.

- How many competitors are there? If there are diminishing returns to R&D, then several small R&D firms may be a bigger threat to successful innovation than a single competitor that spends the same amount of money as do all the small firms put together. If there are increasing returns, then one large firm conducting extensive R&D may be a more formidable competitor. In this case, large investments in R&D by a single firm may crowd out investments by other firms.

Note also that antitrust laws are much more forgiving toward independent firms that agree to join forces in R&D before bringing a product to market than they are willing to allow the same firms to combine after each has made its own invention. Sometimes, the best way to win a patent race is to share the profits no matter who finishes first.

Choosing the Technology

Patent race models often assume that firms have a single R&D methodology, and may choose only how much to spend on it. In reality, firms may be able to select from a variety of methodologies. For example, while some supercomputer makers pursued vector technology that emphasized improvements in hardware, others pursued massively parallel processing that utilized improvements in software. When choosing a research methodology, firms must consider the methods their rivals are pursuing. Two dimensions of interest when choosing a methodology are (1) the riskiness of the methodology; and (2) the degree to which the success of one methodology is correlated with the success of another.

Riskiness of R&D

Research methodologies may have different completion dates. When one methodology is demonstrably faster than another, the choice is clear. The choice is cloudier when two methods have the same expected completion date, but the date for one is less

EXAMPLE 13.4 ORGANIZATIONAL ADAPTATION IN THE
PHOTOLITHOGRAPHIC ALIGNMENT EQUIPMENT INDUSTRY[22]

Photolithographic aligners are an important input in the production of solid-state semiconductor devices. To produce a semiconductor, small intricate patterns must be transferred to a thin wafer of material, such as silicon. This transfer process is known as lithography. The pattern that is transferred is drawn onto a mask, which is used to block light as it falls onto a light-sensitive chemical coating placed on the wafer. A constant stream of seemingly incremental innovations in the industry has dramatically improved the performance of aligners. The industry has moved from so-called contact aligners to proximity aligners and from scanning projection to what are called "steppers." In nearly every case, new technology displaced an established firm that had invested in state-of-the-art equipment and know-how.

Kasper Instruments illustrates this dynamic. It was founded in 1968 and by 1973 had emerged as the leading supplier of contact aligners. But in the mid-1970s, the proximity alignment technique was pioneered. Unlike in contact aligning, in proximity aligning the mask and the wafer are separated during exposure. Although this distinction seems relatively minor, the two techniques involved subtle differences in design. In particular, to design a proximity aligner, one must acquire the latest techniques for designing and producing the gap-setting mechanism—which determines how far apart the mask and

the wafer are held during the lithography process. Incorporating the gap-setting mechanism necessitated subtle changes in integrating components of the aligner. Moving from contact aligners to proximity aligners thus entailed a significant shift in product design and production know-how.

Kasper failed to develop successful proximity aligners, mainly because of its previous success in designing contact aligners. Kasper conceived of the proximity aligner as a modified contact aligner and saw the move into contact aligners as a routine extension of its product line. A gap-setting mechanism that had been used in its contact aligners was slightly modified for use in its proximity aligners. But Kasper's proximity aligner did not work well because the gap-setting mechanism was not accurate enough. In response to customer complaints, Kasper attributed the problems to customers' own errors, which were the main source of malfunctions with its successful contact aligners. When Canon introduced a successful proximity aligner in the mid-1970s, Kasper failed to understand why it worked so well, and dismissed it as a mere copy of the Kasper aligner. The Kasper engineers did not consider the redesigned gap mechanism that made the Canon aligner such a significant advance to be particularly important. From 1974 on, Kasper aligners were rarely used in proximity mode, and by 1981 it had left the industry.

certain than that for the other. To see how competition affects the choice of methods, consider a firm that is choosing between two approaches to developing a new product. If the firm is the first to develop the product, it can obtain a patent or achieve some other early-mover advantage. Approach A follows time-honored methods for R&D and is certain to be successful within two or three years. In contrast, the time frame for Approach B is relatively unproved. Although it is sure eventually to bear fruit, success may come within one to four years. Both approaches distribute the time to innovation uniformly, meaning that it is equally likely to be anytime in the interval.

A monopolist will generally be indifferent between the two approaches because both have identical expected times to development. If several firms are competing to develop the same product, however, each will wish to choose Approach B. To see why, suppose that there are four firms, and each chooses Approach A. Each firm has a .25 chance of being the first to innovate. Now suppose that one firm switches to Approach B. It has a .25 chance of innovating within one year, in which case it is sure to be the first. Even if it innovates after one year, it could still be the first to innovate. Thus, its chances of being first are greater than .25, which is its chance of being first when all firms choose Approach A. Thus, the firm will prefer Approach B. A similar argument may be used to show that all firms will prefer Approach B, no matter what their competitors do.[21]

Correlated Research Strategies

The previous example assumed that Approaches A and B were independent of each other, implying that the success or failure of one approach was unrelated to the success or failure of the other. In fact, research methods may be correlated, so that if one is successful, the other is also more likely to be successful. In general, society benefits more when firms pursue uncorrelated approaches than when they pursue correlated approaches, even when some of the uncorrelated approaches have a low probability of success. The reason is that when firms take uncorrelated approaches, they increase the probability that at least one approach will be successful. But will a firm be willing to undertake a research strategy that has a low probability of success? If many firms are performing research, the answer is yes. If all the firms pursue the same strategy, then each firm has an equal chance of success. The more firms there are, the lower the chance that any particular firm will win the patent race. A firm that pursues a strategy that is uncorrelated with the one pursued by everyone else stands to win the race if the popular approach fails. Thus, a "niche" R&D strategy can be profitable even if it has a low probability of producing an innovation, as long as the outcome is uncorrelated with the outcomes of the other firms.

EVOLUTIONARY ECONOMICS AND DYNAMIC CAPABILITIES ♦ ♦ ♦ ♦ ♦

The theories of innovation we discussed in the previous section are rooted in the tradition of neoclassical microeconomics. In these theories, firms choose the level of innovative activity that maximizes profits. Evolutionary economics, most commonly identified with Richard Nelson and Sidney Winter, offers a perspective on innovative activity that differs from the microeconomic perspective.[23] According to evolutionary economics, firms do not directly choose innovative activities to maximize profits. Instead, key decisions concerning innovation result from organizational routines: well-practiced patterns of activity inside the firm. To understand innovation, it is necessary to understand how routines develop and evolve.

A firm's routines include methods of production, hiring procedures, and policies for determining advertising expenditure. Firms do not change their routines often because getting members of an organization to alter what has worked well in the past is an "unnatural" act. As Schumpeter stressed, however, firms that stick to producing a given set of products in a particular way may not survive. A firm needs to search continuously to improve its routines. The ability of a firm to maintain and adapt the capabilities that are the basis of its competitive advantage is what David Teece, Gary Pisano, and Amy Shuen have referred to as its *dynamic capabilities*.[24] Firms with limited dynamic capabilities fail to nurture and adapt the sources of their advantage over time, and other firms eventually supplant them. Firms with strong dynamic capabilities

EXAMPLE 13.5 THE RISE OF THE SWISS WATCH INDUSTRY[25]

In the eighteenth century, Britain was the largest producer of watches in the world. British master craftsmen produced nearly 200,000 watches per year by 1800, or roughly half the world's supply. Britain's dominance was the result of several factors. First, watchmakers employed laborers in the British countryside, at a considerably lower wage than laborers in London would demand. Second, the watchmakers benefited from the division of labor. In an eight-mile stretch from Prescot to Liverpool in northwest England, one could find cottages of springmakers, wheel cutters, dialmakers, and other specialists. Large local demand helped make this specialization possible. During the 1700s, Britain accounted for half the worldwide demand for watches. Finally, a key raw material, crucible steel, was manufactured by a British monopoly. Foreign manufacturers elsewhere did not learn how to make crucible steel until 1800.

The confluence of specialized, low-cost workers, high local demand, and access to a crucial input gave the British advantages that no other watchmakers could match. In the mid- to late 1700s, British watches were considered the finest in the world and commanded a premium price. But British watchmakers could not keep up with world demand. They began importing watches made elsewhere and reselling them as their own. Watchmakers in Geneva benefited from this policy.

Geneva had been a center of watchmaking ever since Protestant refugees arrived from France in the mid-1500s. By the mid-1700s, Geneva was second only to Britain in watchmaking. Many of today's most prestigious brands, including Constantin Vacheron (formerly Abraham Vacheron) and Patek Philippe (formerly Czapek and Philippe), began during this period.

The Geneva watchmakers differed from their British counterparts in one key respect. The British did not have to market their product—they made high-quality watches and waited for customers to come to them. Geneva watchmakers could not match the reputations of their British counterparts and so had to become merchants as well as artisans. To keep costs down, they outsourced much of the production to workers in the nearby French and Italian Alps, at labor costs well below those in England. They also developed new markets for watches. They marketed themselves in areas such as Italy, where few people wore watches. Some watchmakers devoted themselves to niche markets, such as that for extremely thin watches. Others targeted cost-conscious buyers. As David Landes has written, "The Swiss made watches to please their customers. The British made watches to please themselves."

In the nineteenth century, British watchmakers suffered. Wars drained the British economy and dried up local demand for watches. Ill equipped to market their watches overseas, domestic watch producers in Britain nearly disappeared. At the same time, the Swiss enjoyed growing sales and the benefits of the division of labor. The Swiss also gained access to crucible steel, which by then was available outside of Britain. In addition, desperate British watchmakers exported uncased movements and parts, helping the Swiss match British quality. By the middle of the nineteenth century, Swiss watchmakers were dominant. They made watches at all levels of quality, at costs below those achievable anywhere else. They tailored new product to consumer tastes. The Swiss dominated the watch industry until the mid-twentieth century, when the Japanese used cheap quartz movements to achieve unprecedented accuracy at remarkably low costs.

adapt their resources and capabilities over time and take advantage of new market opportunities to create new sources of competitive advantage.

For several reasons, a firm's dynamic capabilities are inherently limited. First, learning is typically incremental rather than pathbreaking. That is, when a firm searches to improve its operations, it is nearly impossible for the firm to ignore what it has done in the past, and it is difficult for the firm to conceptualize new routines that are fundamentally different from its old ones. Thus, the search for new sources of competitive advantage is *path dependent*—it depends on the path the firm has taken in the past to get where it is now. Even small path dependencies can have important competitive consequences. A firm that has developed significant commitments to a particular way of doing business may find it hard to adapt to seemingly minor changes in technology. This is underscored in Rebecca Henderson and Kim Clark's study of the photolithographic alignment equipment industry described in Example 13.4.

The presence of complementary assets—firm-specific assets that are valuable only in connection with a particular product, technology, or way of doing business—can enhance or impede a firm's dynamic capabilities. The development of new products or capabilities or the opening of new markets can either enhance or destroy the value of complementary assets. Microsoft's installed base in the old MS-DOS ("Microsoft disk operating system") was a valuable complementary asset when it developed Windows in the late 1980s. By contrast, as we discussed in Example 13.1, the development of the basic oxygen furnace in the steel industry reduced the value of American steel firms' existing capabilities in the open hearth process. A proposed change in an organizational routine that undermines the value of a complementary asset can give rise to the sunk cost effect discussed earlier, thereby reducing the likelihood that a firm will adopt the change.

"Windows of opportunity" can also impede the development of dynamic capabilities. Early in a product's development, its design is typically fluid, manufacturing routines have not been developed, and capital is generally nonproduct specific. Firms can still experiment with competing product designs or ways of organizing production. However, as time passes, a narrow set of designs or product specifications often emerge as dominant. At this point, network externalities and learning curve effects take over, and it no longer becomes attractive for firms to compete with established market leaders. This variant of the sunk cost effect implies that firms that do not adapt their existing capabilities or commit themselves to new markets when these uncertain windows of opportunity exist may find themselves eventually locked out from the market or competing at a significant disadvantage with early movers.

THE ENVIRONMENT ◆ ◆ ◆ ◆ ◆

In *The Competitive Advantage of Nations*, Michael Porter argues that competitive advantage originates in the local environment in which the firm is based.[26] Despite the ability of modern firms to transcend local markets, competitive advantage in particular industries is often strongly concentrated in one or two locations: the world's most successful producers of high-voltage electrical distribution equipment are in Sweden; the best producers of equipment for tunneling are Swiss; the most successful producers of large diesel trucks are American; and the leading microwave firms are Japanese.

Porter views competition as an evolutionary process. Firms initially gain competitive advantages by altering the basis of competition. They win not just by recognizing new markets or technologies but by moving aggressively to exploit them. They sustain their advantages by investing to improve existing sources of advantage and to create new ones. A firm's home nation plays a critical role in shaping managers' perceptions about the opportunities that can be exploited; in supporting the accumulation of valuable resources and capabilities; and in creating pressures on the firm to innovate, invest, and improve.

Porter identifies four attributes in a firm's home market, which he collectively refers to as the "diamond," that promote or impede a firm's ability to achieve competitive advantage in global markets (see Figure 13.2):

1. Factor conditions
2. Demand conditions
3. Related supplier or support industries
4. Strategy, structure, and rivalry

Factor Conditions Factor conditions describe a nation's position with regard to factors of production (e.g., human resources, infrastructure) that are necessary to compete in a particular industry. Because general-purpose factors of production are often available locally or can be purchased in global markets, the most important factors of production are highly specialized to the needs of particular industries. For example, since the 1950s, Japan has had one of the highest numbers of engineering graduates per capita. This, according to Porter, has had much more to do with its success in such industries as automobiles and consumer electronics than the low wages of its production workers.

Demand Conditions These conditions include the size, growth, and character of home demand for the firm's product. Sophisticated home customers or unique local conditions stimulate firms to enhance the quality of their products and to innovate. For example, in air conditioners, Japanese firms such as Panasonic are known for producing small, quiet, energy-efficient window units. These product characteristics are critical in Japan, where air conditioning is important (summers are hot and humid),

FIGURE 13.2
THE ENVIRONMENT AND THE ORIGINS OF COMPETITIVE ADVANTAGE

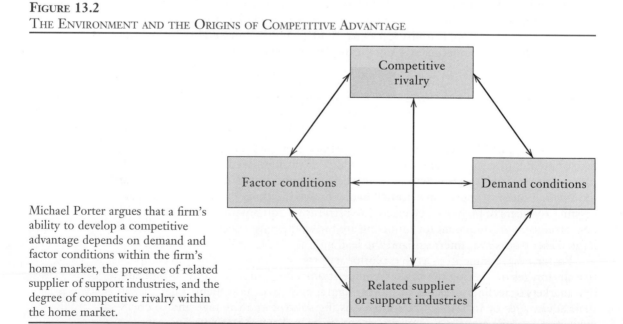

Michael Porter argues that a firm's ability to develop a competitive advantage depends on demand and factor conditions within the firm's home market, the presence of related supplier of support industries, and the degree of competitive rivalry within the home market.

Source: This diagram is based on Figure 3.1 in Porter, M., *The Competitive Advantage of Nations*, New York, Free Press, 1990, p. 72.

EXAMPLE 13.6 COMPETENCE, HISTORY, AND GEOGRAPHY:
THE NOKIA STORY

The Nokia name is synonymous with cellular phones. Yet the Finnish company began nearly 150 years ago as a paper manufacturer. Since then, the company has entered a wide array of businesses. In the early 1900s, it spun off the Finnish Rubber Works, followed in 1912 by the Finnish Cable Works. The latter, which manufactured cables for telegraphs and telephones, was the firm's first foray into telecommunications. In 1967, the three businesses combined to form Nokia.

Throughout the 1960s and 1970s, Nokia struggled to find its identity. On the one hand, it continued to manufacture high-design rubber products such as brightly colored rubber boots. On the other hand, it was one of the first companies to develop radiotelephones and data modems. Eventually, Nokia would put its expertise in design and technology to good effect.

In addition to its unusual history, Nokia benefited from its Scandinavian location. Finns have been called "early adopters" of technologies by sociologists.[27] They were the first to embrace the fax machine in the 1970s and the Internet in the 1980s. The first international cellular communication network, NMT (Nordic Mobile Telephone), was launched in Scandinavia in 1981, and a combination of expertise and "home field advantage" enabled Nokia to land the first contract to manufacture car phones. Throughout the decade, Nokia continued to innovate in the cellular phone market.

Nokia's next big break occurred in 1987, when the European Economic Community agreed on a common standard for cellular communications. Even though most of the United States was adopting analog technology (and Motorola was leading the way in analog sales), European nations adopted the GSM digital standard. Nokia elected to focus on its home markets and concentrated on the new digital technology. In 1991, Finland entered the digital cellular age, thanks to Nokia technology. Two years later, a Finnish engineering student used Nokia technology to broadcast the first GSM text message. By that time, Nokia had made a strategic bet to focus on the mobile phone industry and shed its extraneous businesses.

Even so, Nokia's history in design-driven businesses proved valuable. It segmented the cellular phone market into two demographic groups: younger users and business users. For the younger demographic group, it developed colorful, interchangeable handset covers and customized ring tones. At the same time, Nokia developed an elliptically shaped phone to eliminate the sharp corners that often pierced users and their clothing. With these innovations, Nokia's phones developed a universal appeal.

Nokia's success in the cellular phone market is due to more than good fortune and historical circumstance. Nokia's ability to innovate is rooted in its flat organizational structure. Nokia's lack of hierarchy allows for effective cross-functional cooperation (for instance, between marketing, product design, and manufacturing) and cross-breeding of ideas.[28] These collaborations have yielded many of Nokia's great advances in telecommunications technology and marketing.

but large, noisy units would be unacceptable because houses are small and packed closely together, and electricity is expensive.

Related and Supporting Industries Firms that operate in a home market that has a strong base of internationally competitive supplier or support industries will be favorably positioned to achieve competitive advantage in global markets. Although many inputs are mobile, and thus firms do not need geographic proximity to make exchanges, exchanging key inputs, such as scarce production know-how, does require geographic proximity. Companies with skillful home-based suppliers can be early beneficiaries of newly generated production know-how and may be able to shape innovation in supplying firms. For example, Italian shoe manufacturers have established close working relationships with leather producers that allow the shoe manufacturers to learn quickly about new textures and colors. Leather producers, in turn, learn about emerging fashion trends from the shoe manufacturers, which helps leather producers to plan new products.

Strategy, Structure, and Rivalry The final environmental determinant of competitive advantage, according to Porter, is the context for competition in the firm's home market. This includes local management practices, organizational structure, corporate governance, and the nature of local capital markets. For example, in Germany and Switzerland, most shares in publicly traded firms are held by institutional investors who do not trade frequently, and capital gains are exempt from taxation. As a result, day-to-day movements in share price are not significant, which, according to Porter, creates a stronger propensity for companies in these industries to invest in research and innovation than is true of their counterparts in the United States and Britain.

Rivalry in the home market is another important part of the competitive context. According to Porter, local rivalry affects the rate of innovation in a market far more than foreign rivalry does. Although local rivalry may hold down profitability in local markets, firms that survive vigorous local competition are often more efficient and innovative than are international rivals that emerge from softer local conditions. The airline industry is a good example. The U.S. domestic airline industry is far more price competitive than the international industry, where entry is restricted and many flag carriers receive state subsidies. Coming out of the intensely competitive U.S. industry, U.S. airlines (such as American and United) that fly international routes are far more cost efficient than many of the international airlines they compete with and rely on profits from international routes to offset losses domestically.

◆ ◆ ◆ ◆ ◆ MANAGING INNOVATION

Since large firms are complex organizations whose single-minded actions cannot be taken for granted, we must consider them as vehicles for innovation and not just as inventors and users of it. How innovation occurs within firms is often as important as its results in understanding how firms create value for their customers. As Rosabeth Kanter argues, this involves seeing innovation as the process of bringing any new problem-solving idea into use.[29] This idea of organizational innovation is also developed in research on innovative cultures and internal or corporate entrepreneurship.

Corporate research and development programs have often been inflexible and unresponsive to market opportunities. This has prompted some firms to consider alternative ways of managing their innovative processes. For example, the creation of corporate venture departments since the 1970s reflects the growing sensitivity of larger corporations to their need for mechanisms to identify and exploit opportunities for innovation beyond current products, processes, and services. Innovation outside of formal organizational mechanisms has also received attention in recent years. This work has focused on corporate entrepreneurs who push new projects forward in the face of bureaucratic obstacles.[30]

The innovation strategies of large firms need not focus solely on internal development, however. Other approaches, such as spinoffs, joint ventures, and strategic alliances, can also facilitate entry into new business areas or the development of new capabilities. One example of an interorganizational alternative to firm-based research and development is the public-private research consortium.[31] In these formal alliances, member firms pool their resources and coordinate their research activities with those of academic institutions in explicit collaboration in large-scale high-tech projects. Governments also fund these ventures as well as exempt their activities from antitrust prohibitions. Whereas the Japanese pioneered these consortia in computer technology in the 1970s, American and European counterparts developed in the early 1980s. Perhaps the best known American consortium, MCC (Microelectronics and Computer Technology Corporation), was founded in 1982 by 16 computer and semiconductor firms. By 1993, MCC included more than 100 member firms.

In general, a firm faces a dilemma in managing its innovative activities. On the one hand, formal structure and controls are necessary to coordinate innovative activities. On the other hand, looseness and flexibility may foster innovation, creativity, and adaptiveness to changing circumstances. These competing requirements create ongoing tensions for managing innovation.

CHAPTER SUMMARY

♦ Creative destruction is the process whereby old sources of competitive advantage are destroyed and replaced with new ones. Economist Joseph Schumpeter wrote that the essence of entrepreneurship is the exploitation of the "shocks" or "discontinuities" that destroy existing sources of advantage.

♦ A dominant established firm's incentive to innovate may be weaker than that of a smaller firm or a potential entrant. The sunk cost and the replacement effect weaken the established firm's incentive to innovate. The efficiency effect, by contrast, strengthens the dominant firm's incentive to innovate as compared with a potential entrant's incentive.

♦ The sunk cost effect describes asymmetry between a firm that has already made a commitment to a particular technology and one that is planning such a commitment. It is the phenomenon whereby a profit-maximizing firm sticks with its current technology, even though the profit-maximizing decision for a firm starting from scratch would be to choose a different technology.

♦ When an innovation offers the prospect of the adopter becoming a monopolist, a potential entrant has a stronger incentive to develop the innovation than an incumbent monopolist. Because it already has a monopoly, the monopolist gains less from the innovation than does the potential entrant. This phenomenon is called the replacement effect.

♦ The efficiency effect makes an incumbent monopolist's incentive to innovate stronger than a potential entrant's incentive. The reason is that the incumbent can lose its monopoly if it does not innovate, whereas the entrant will become (at best) a duopolist if it successfully innovates.

♦ "Patent race" describes the battle between firms to innovate first. Patent race models imply that when a firm is determining whether to increase its investment in innovation, it must account for the following factors: (1) By how much must the investment increase its R&D productivity and thereby also increase its chances of winning the patent race? (2) Will other firms increase their R&D expenditures in response, thereby decreasing the firm's chances of winning the patent race? (3) How many competitors are there?

◆ Evolutionary economics sees the firm decisions as determined by routines—well-practiced patterns of activity inside the firm—rather than profit maximization. Firms seldom change their routines because getting their staffs to alter what has worked well in the past is an "unnatural" act. But firms that stick to producing a given set of products in a particular way may not survive. Thus, a firm typically needs to engage in a continuous search for ways to improve its existing routines. Dynamic capabilities are a firm's ability to maintain the bases of its competitive advantage.

◆ Michael Porter argues that competitive advantage originates in a firm's local environment. He identifies four attributes in a firm's home market that promote or impede its ability to achieve competitive advantage in global markets: factor conditions; demand conditions; related supplier or support industries; and strategy, structure, and rivalry.

◆ In general, managing innovation creates a dilemma. On the one hand, formal structure and controls are needed to coordinate innovation. On the other hand, looseness and flexibility can foster innovation, creativity, and adaptiveness to changing circumstances.

QUESTIONS

1. Is the extent of creative destruction likely to differ across industries? Can the risk of creative destruction be incorporated into a five-forces analysis of an industry?

2. In many industries, such as pharmaceuticals, firms are geographically clustered. In others, such as automobile production, clustering has become less common. What factors contribute to clustering? Will the Internet and improvements in telecommunication ultimately eliminate clustering?

3. What is the difference between the efficiency effect and the replacement effect? Could both effects operate at the same time? If so, under what conditions would the efficiency effect be likely to dominate? Under what conditions would the replacement effect be likely to dominate?

4. In their article "Strategy as Stretch and Leverage," Gary Hamel and C. K. Prahalad argue that industry newcomers have a stronger incentive to supplant established firms from their leadership positions than established firms have to maintain their leadership positions. The reason, they argue, is that a greater gap exists between a newcomer's resources and aspirations as compared to a market leader.[32] Is Hamel and Prahalad's argument consistent with profit-maximizing behavior by both the leader and the newcomer? Is their argument consistent with ideas from evolutionary economics?

5. Is patent racing a zero-sum game? a negative sum-game? Explain.

6. What are a firm's dynamic capabilities? To what extent can managers create or "manage into existence" a firm's dynamic capabilities?

7. What is meant by the concept of path dependence? What implications does path dependence have for a firm's ability to create new sources of competitive advantage over time?

8. How does the extent of competition in a firm's domestic market shape its ability to compete globally? Why would local rivalry have a stronger effect on the rate of innovation than foreign competition?

9. "Industrial or antitrust policies that result in the creation of domestic monopolies rarely result in global competitive advantage." Comment.

10. IQ Inc. currently monopolizes the market for a certain type of microprocessor, the 666. The present value of the stream of monopoly profits from this design is thought to be $500 million. Enginola (which is currently in a completely different segment of the microprocessor market from this one) and IQ are contemplating spending money to develop a superior design that will make the 666 completely obsolete. Whoever develops the design first gets the entire market. The present value of the stream of monopoly profit from the

superior design is expected to be $150 million greater than the present value of the profit from the 666.

Success in developing the design is not certain, but the probability of a firm's success is directly linked to the amount of money it spends on the project (more spending on this project, greater probability of success). Moreover, the productivity of Enginola's spending on this project and IQ's spending is exactly the same: Starting from any given level of spending, an additional $1 spent by Enginola has exactly the same impact on its probability of winning. The following table illustrates this point. It shows the probability of winning the race if each firm's spending equals 0, $100 million, and $200 million. The first number represents Enginola's probability of winning the race, the second is IQ's probability of winning, and the third is the probability that neither succeeds. *Note*: This is not a payoff table.

IQ's SPENDING

Enginola's Spending	0	$100 million	$200 million
0	(0,0,1)	(0,.6,.4)	(0,.8,.2)
$100 million	(6,0,.4)	(4,.4,.2)	(3,.6,.1)
$200 million	(8,0,.2)	(6,.3,.1)	(5,.5,0)

Assuming that

(i) each firm makes its spending decision simultaneously and noncooperatively;

(ii) each seeks to maximize its expected profit;

(iii) neither firm faces any financial constraints,

which company, if any, has the greater incentive to spend money to win this "R&D race"? Of the effects discussed in the chapter (sunk cost effect, replacement effect, efficiency effect), which are shaping the incentives to innovate in this example?

ENDNOTES

[1]CTI eventually went bankrupt.

[2]Schumpeter, J., *Capitalism, Socialism, and Democracy*, New York, Harper & Row, 1942, p. 132.

[3]Ibid., pp. 84–85.

[4]Christensen, C., *The Innovator's Dilemma*, New York, Harper Business, 2000.

[5]Lee, J., "Emergence of Large Firms and Innovation in the U.S. Pharmaceutical Industry," *Management Science*, 2002.

[6]For example, see Henderson, R. and I. Cockburn, "Measuring Competence? Exploring Firm Effects in Pharmaceutical Research," *Strategic Management Journal*, 15, 1994, 63–84.

[7]Hamel, G. and C. K. Prahalad, *Competing for the Future*, Cambridge, MA, Harvard Business School Press, 1994. See also Hamel, G., and C. K. Prahalad, "Strategic Intent," *Harvard Business Review*, May–June 1989, pp. 63–76, and "Strategy as Stretch and Leverage," *Harvard Business Review*, March–April 1993, pp. 75–84.

[8]Kontes, P. and M. Mankins, "The Dangers of Strategic Intent," *Marakon Associates*, April 1992.

[9]D'Aveni, R., *Hypercompetition: Managing the Dynamics of Strategic Maneuvering*, New York, Free Press, 1994.

[10]Adams, W. and H. Mueller, "The Steel Industry," in Adams, W. (ed.), *The Structure of American Industry*, 7th ed., New York, Macmillan, 1986, p. 102.

[11]Oster, S., "The Diffusion of Innovation among Steel Firms: The Basic Oxygen Furnace," *Bell Journal of Economics*, 13, Spring 1982, pp. 45–68.

[12]Arrow, K., "Economics Welfare and the Allocation of Resources for Inventions," in Nelson, R. (ed.), *The Rate and Direction of Inventive Activity*, Princeton, NJ, Princeton University Press, 1962.

[13]This term was coined by Jean Tirole. Tirole discusses the replacement effect in his book, *The Theory of Industrial Organization*, Cambridge, MA, MIT Press, 1988.

[14]Gans, J. and S. Stern, 2000, "Incumbency and R&D Incentives: Licensing the Gale of Creative Destruction," *Journal of Economics and Management Strategy*, 9(4), pp. 485–511.

[15]Teece, D., 1986, "Profiting from Technological Innovation: Implications for Integration, Collaboration, Licensing, and Public Policy," *Research Policy*, 15, pp. 285–305.

[16]Guedj, I. and D. Scharfstein, "Organizational Scope and Investment: Evidence from the Drug Development Strategies and Performance of Biopharmaceutical Firms," MIT Working Paper; November 2004.

[17]Stein, J., "Internal Capital Markets and the Competition for Corporate Resources," *Journal of Finance*, 52 (1997), pp. 111–133.

[18]Smith, G. S., *The Anatomy of a Business Strategy: Bell, Western Electric, and the Origins of the American Telephone Industry*, Baltimore, MD, Johns Hopkins University Press, 1985, pp. 35–38, 99.

[19]In Chapter 12 we discuss early-mover advantages in detail.

[20]Much of the information for this example was drawn from Zygmont, J., 2003, *Microchip*, Cambridge, MA, Perseus Publishing.

[21]Firms will generally prefer the risky approach even if there are only two competitors, with the gains from this choice becoming more transparent as the number of firms increases. See Tirole, *The Theory of Industrial Organization*.

[22]This example is based on Henderson, R. and K. B. Clark, "Architectural Innovation: The Reconfiguration of Existing Product Technologies and the Failure of Established Firms," *Administrative Science Quarterly*, 35, March 1990, pp. 9–30.

[23]Nelson, R. R. and S. G. Winter, *An Evolutionary Theory of Economic Change*, Cambridge, MA, Belknap Press, 1982.

[24]Teece, D. J., G. Pisano, and A. Shuen, "Dynamic Capabilities and Strategic Management," University of California at Berkeley, *Strategic Management Journal*, 18, August 1997, pp. 509–534. See also Teece, D. J., R. Rumelt, G. Dosi, and S. Winter, "Understanding Corporate Coherence: Theory and Evidence," *Journal of Economic Behavior and Organization*, 23, 1994, pp. 1–30 for related ideas.

[25]This example is drawn from Landes, David, *Revolution in Time*, Cambridge, MA, Belknap Press, 1983.

[26]Porter, M., *The Competitive Advantage of Nations*, New York, Free Press, 1998.

[27]Behr, Rafael, "Finland: Nation's Hopes Resting on the Next Generation," *Financial Times*, July 7, 2001.

[28]Brown-Humes, Christopher and Michael Skapinaker, "A Symphony of Diverse Ring Tones: Nokia Part 2," *Financial Times*, July 7, 2001.

[29]Kanter, R. M., *The Change Masters*, New York, Simon & Schuster, 1983.

[30]Burgelman, R. A., "A Process Model of Internal Corporate Venturing in the Diversified Major Firm," *Administrative Science Quarterly*, 28, 1983, pp. 223–244; Peterson, R. A., "Entrepreneurship and Organization," in Nystrom, P. C. and W. R. Starbuck (eds.), *Handbook of Organizational Design*, vol. I, New York, Oxford University Press, 1981, pp. 65–83.

[31]Gibson, D. V. and E. M. Rodgers, *R & D Collaboration on Trial*, Cambridge, MA, Harvard Business School Press, 1994; Browning, L. D., J. M. Beyer, and J. C. Shetler, "Building Cooperation in a Competitive Industry: SEMATECH and the Semiconductor Industry," *Academy of Management Journal*, 38, 1995, pp. 113–151.

[32]Hamel, G. and C. K. Prahalad, *Competing for the Future*, Cambridge, MA, Harvard Business School Press, 1994. See also Hamel, G. and C. K. Prahalad, "Strategic Intent," *Harvard Business Review*, May–June 1989, pp. 63–76, and "Strategy as Stretch and Leverage," *Harvard Business Review*, March–April 1993, pp. 75–84.

PART FOUR

INTERNAL ORGANIZATIONS

14

AGENCY AND PERFORMANCE MEASUREMENT

*3*M Corporation is widely known and admired as an innovator. The firm, which spends $1 billion annually on research and development and gives its researchers tremendous latitude to pursue their own inventions, has developed a wide range of successful consumer products, including Scotch tape, Scotchgard fabric protector, Thinsulate thermal insulation, and Post-It Notes. In 2001, the firm earned revenues of $16 billion from more than 50,000 different products in six business areas: health care, transportation and graphics, consumer and office, industrial, electronics and communications, and specialty materials.

In recent years 3M's innovation engine has been driven by the *requirement* that its divisions strive to innovate. The performance of division managers was measured in part by what fraction of the division's sales came from products that had been introduced within the past four years. The firm set an across-the-board target of 30 percent. Although its rapid pace of product innovation continued unabated throughout the late 1990s (with one-third of its sales in 2001 coming from new products), 3M's financial performance over the period was somewhat less stellar. Between 1995 and 2000 yearly earnings per share increased just 8.8 percent on average, and the price of the firm's stock lagged the average for the S&P 500.

In 2001, James McNerney left General Electric to become the first outside chief executive officer in 3M's 99-year history. After just over a year on the job, the new CEO dropped the 30 percent rule as a standard for divisional performance, citing examples of managers devising "new products" simply by changing the color of existing products; pink Post-It Notes, he said, came about as a result of this rule. "It became a game: What could you do to get a new SKU (number)?"[1] McNerney's decision was also driven by concern over the allocation of internal resources. As part of a plan to reduce overhead and improve financial performance, he wants to reduce the total number of products the firm has under development at any one time and focus resources on only the most promising ideas. Managers operating under the 30 percent rule had little incentive to filter out marginal innovations. Internal and external observers appear to agree on the main dilemma facing the firm: how to motivate employees to place greater emphasis on product development efficiency while maintaining their legendary innovative mindset.

This episode illustrates an important question faced by all firms: how can the firm motivate employees to take actions that advance the firm's strategy and increase its profits? In this chapter we address this question in detail. We begin by presenting the principal/agent framework, which is the basic model used by economists in thinking about how firms provide incentives to employees. Our discussion highlights the benefits and costs associated with tying employee rewards to specific measures of on-the-job performance. The primary benefit of tying pay to performance is that employees will work harder to pursue activities that are rewarded. If the firm can devise performance measures that allow it to reward exactly the activities it wants its employees to pursue, linking pay to performance can lead to increased profits. As 3M's dilemma illustrates, however, it can be difficult to devise good measures of an employee's job performance, and firms must be aware of the costs associated with tying pay to less-than-ideal measures of performance.

THE PRINCIPAL/AGENT FRAMEWORK

◆ ◆ ◆ ◆ ◆

The relationship between 3M and its division managers offers an example of the relationship between a *principal* and an *agent*. The principal/agent framework applies whenever one party (the agent) is hired by another (the principal) to take actions or make decisions that affect the payoff to the principal. In the example just presented, the principal is 3M (and its shareholders), and the agents are the firm's division managers. The managers' actions create value in the form of product innovations, but the revenues associated with new products accrue directly to the firm, not to the division managers. The principal/agent framework is broadly applicable: the relationships between a firm's shareholders and the CEO, between a litigant and a lawyer, and even between a town's citizens and its mayor can be analyzed using this paradigm.

Difficulties in principal/agent relationships (referred to as *agency problems* or *agency conflicts*) arise because the two parties' interests typically differ in some way. The principal's objective is to maximize the difference between the value it receives as a result of the agent's actions and any payment it makes to the agent. In the absence of some mechanism to align the interests of the two parties, the agent likely does not care about the value generated for the principal. Instead, the agent is concerned with the value he or she receives from participating in the relationship, minus any costs incurred by doing so. Benefits and costs to an agent can come from a number of sources. The agent values any direct payments from the principal and may receive other indirect benefits, such as opportunities for career advancement, from the actions he or she undertakes on the job. An agent may perceive less value in an agency relationship if the task the principal asks him or her to undertake is difficult, or if the payments the agent is to receive from the principal are risky.

As an example of the differences in interests that characterize an agency relationship, consider the situation faced by 3M. The firm's objective is to maximize its profit. This requires that division managers work to identify the innovations that are potentially profitable and exert their best efforts toward developing and marketing them. In the absence of some incentive, however, the managers receive no direct benefit if the firm's profits increase. Some managers might enjoy the process of innovating and would prefer to pursue all innovations whether or not they appear to be potentially profitable. If it is difficult to identify profitable innovations, other managers may shirk this responsibility and simply approve further research based on hunch or whim.

There are countless other examples of problems in agency relationships. In the case of a firm's shareholders and its CEO, the shareholders' objective is to earn a high return on their investment. As we discussed in Chapter 5, however, a CEO may enjoy undertaking acquisitions (whether or not they are profitable for the firm) in order to boost his or her reputation in the business community. Alternatively, a CEO may like spending the firm's money on perquisites for the top management team, such as fancy offices, country club memberships, or corporate jets. A litigant would like a lawyer to work to achieve a favorable outcome in court. The lawyer may receive some value simply from the act of helping the litigant but may also prefer to spend time on more prominent or remunerative cases, or to engage in leisure activities. A town's citizens may want the mayor to work to identify the lowest-cost bidder for an airport expansion project. The mayor may prefer to direct city funds to construction firms controlled by political allies.

Firms (and other principals) use an astonishing variety of means to align employees' (and other agents) interests with their own. Any mechanism in which current and future benefits received by an employee depend on job performance can be viewed as an attempt to provide incentives and resolve problems in agency relationships. Bonuses, raises, profit sharing, stock options, the promise of future promotions, and the threat of firing *all* serve to make the employee's monetary compensation depend in some way on job performance and thus may help resolve agency problems. Furthermore, the notion of "benefits received by an employee" can be construed quite broadly. Employees value money, but they certainly value other things as well. For example, employees may value peer recognition, vacation time, flexible working schedules, access to training, or the ability to purchase the firm's product at a discount. Firms may attempt to resolve agency problems by making these (and other) forms of rewards contingent on job performance as well. In Chapter 15 we discuss many of the specific ways in which firms link pay and performance.

Using Contracts to Provide Incentives

Agency problems are easily solved if it is feasible to write a *complete contract*. Recall the definition from Chapter 3: a complete contract stipulates each party's responsibilities and rights for each and every contingency that could conceivably arise during the transaction. A complete agency contract could specify a wage payment to be made by the principal to the agent that depends on both the information received by the agent and the action taken by the agent. Using such a contract, the principal can resolve agency problems by directly rewarding the agent when the action that the principal prefers is undertaken.

As an example of such a contract, consider the principal/agent relationship between Ford Motor Company and an assembly-line worker at Ford's Highland Park, Michigan, plant just after the plant opened in 1913. This revolutionary facility was the first to incorporate a moving assembly-line, an innovation that allowed Ford to fully realize the specialization economies it had been seeking since 1903. Jobs held by assembly-line workers at Highland Park were extremely simple. James P. Womack, Daniel T. Jones, and Daniel Roos write that the typical worker "had only one task—to put two nuts on two bolts, or perhaps to attach one wheel to each car."[2] The simplicity of these tasks allowed foremen to detect any malfeasance immediately. The contract offered by Ford to its employees was very simple as well: workers who performed their assigned tasks were allowed to keep their jobs and continue to earn wages, while those who did not were fired.

As discussed in Chapter 3, however, very often complete contracts are not feasible. Our discussion of the principal/agent relationship between 3M and its division managers makes clear why we should expect complete agency contracts to be difficult to write. Suppose the firm determines that its profits are maximized if the division manager (1) identifies the innovations that are potentially profitable and (2) exerts his or her best efforts toward developing and marketing them. How could a contract be written to induce a division manager to pursue precisely this course of action?

Here, the principal's desired action—that the division manager exert his or her "best effort"—is clearly all but impossible to measure. Even if 3M could directly observe the manager's speech and physical actions (as Ford Motor Company could with its assembly-line workers in 1913), it is hard for anyone to say with certainty whether the manager is putting forth his or her best effort. How can one tell whether a manager is using his or her full intellectual capacity to develop a half-formed product idea? The task here is considerably more complex than putting two nuts on two bolts, and it likely requires application of the manager's analytical and creative skills. Situations like this—in which aspects of the agent's action that are important to the principal cannot be observed—are said to suffer from *hidden action*. In agency relationships with hidden action, any contract that is contingent on all important aspects of the agent's action (e.g., "best effort") will not be enforceable, since neither the principal nor a court could verify whether the agent's action fulfilled the terms of the contract.

Similarly, information about which innovations are potentially profitable and which ones are not is likely unavailable to the principal, since the division manager knows considerably more about both the innovation itself and the potential market. Unless the firm has access to all forms of communication among the division manager, the division's research scientists, and potential customers, it will not be able to determine as easily as the division manager which innovations hold the most potential for profit. Here, the firm would like to direct the manager to follow up only on potentially profitable innovations, but no enforceable contract could be based on this piece of information. Situations like this—in which aspects of the productive environment that are important to the principal cannot be observed—are said to suffer from *hidden information*.

When hidden action or hidden information is present, important aspects of the agent's action or the agent's information cannot be used as the basis for an incentive contract. A principal must instead attempt to provide incentives using information that *can* be incorporated into a contract. As discussed in Chapter 3, one way of doing this is to write an *explicit incentive contract*, that is, an incentive contract that can be enforced by an outside third party such as a judge or an arbitrator. Explicit incentive contracts must be based on information that can be observed and verified by this external enforcement mechanism. Under some circumstances, it is possible to base contracts on information that cannot be observed by the courts or arbitrators. *Implicit incentive contracts* must rely on the value of future cooperation to provide an enforcement mechanism. In this chapter, we focus primarily on explicit incentive contracts. Properties of implicit incentive contracts are discussed in Chapter 15.

We refer to a piece of information on which an incentive contract (explicit or implicit) can be based as a *performance measure*. In the case of 3M's division managers, one performance measure used by the firm is the fraction of sales coming from new products; the incentive contract stipulates that the employee's compensation depends, at least in part, on this measure. Fraction of sales coming from new products may, in this case, be a good measure because a manager who applies his or her "best efforts" at all times is likely to develop many innovations. Similarly, a manager who works to make efficient use of hidden information about which innovations are most promising will find it easier to achieve this target.

Performance measures can take many forms. Sales from new products is an example of a performance measure that is directly related to the gross payoff to the principal coming about as a result of the agent's action. This can be thought of as an *output-based* performance measure. *Input-based* performance measures can be devised as well. Consider, for example, the performance measure used for physicians by Montefiore Ambulatory Care Network, a New York-based primary-care medical practice. In 1999, the firm began offering bonuses to physicians based on the number of patient visits they handle. Since the revenue to the firm varies considerably across patient visits, this measure is not directly related to the payoff to the principal. Instead, it is a measure of the actions undertaken by the agent. Such a measure can be useful for resolving agency problems if it is observable and if it motivates the agent to take actions that the principal prefers. In this case, the firm is attempting to motivate physicians to make efficient use of their limited time.[3]

How Employees Respond to Performance Measures in Incentive Contracts

To understand the tradeoffs facing firms in choosing performance measures for incentive contracts, we start by examining how employees respond to performance measures. Consider a firm that hires an employee to perform a sales function. Let the employee's effort level be represented by e, and suppose that every additional unit of effort increases sales by $100. It may be useful to think of units of effort as "hours during which the employee puts forth high effort." Note that while the number of *hours* the employee works may be observable by the principal, the number of hours *during which the employee puts forth high effort* may not.

The output from the salesperson's effort accrues directly to the firm. We assume that, in the absence of some means of providing incentives, the employee would prefer not to exert "extra effort" on the job. That is, the employee is willing to put in some amount of effort without being compensated for doing so but is willing to put in extra effort (by, for example, following up with potential clients, doing extra research on customers' needs, etc.) only if the employee earns extra compensation associated with these actions.

Specifically, we assume the employee's cost of exerting effort level e can be written in monetary terms. Suppose the cost of exerting effort level e is given by an increasing and convex function, as shown in Figure 14.1. We assume the cost of effort function, $c(e)$, is given by

$$c(e) = \begin{cases} 0 & \text{if } e \leq 40 \\ \frac{1}{2}(e-40)^2 & \text{if } e > 40 \end{cases}$$

The interpretation of this function is as follows. The employee is willing to increase his effort level from e_0 to e_1 if and only if the additional value he receives from doing so (whether monetary of nonmonetary) is worth at least $c(e_1) - c(e_0)$. The flat region on the curve (between 0 and 40 units of effort) indicates that the employee is willing to put in some amount of effort for no extra compensation. However, the employee is willing to put in additional effort beyond 40 units only if he or she is compensated for doing so.

FIGURE 14.1
A CONVEX COST OF EFFORT FUNCTION

This employee is willing to exert up to 40 units of effort without being compensated for doing so. The employee is willing to increase effort from e_0 to e_1 only if compensation will increase by $c(e_1) - c(e_0)$ as a result. The marginal cost of effort increases as the employee works harder.

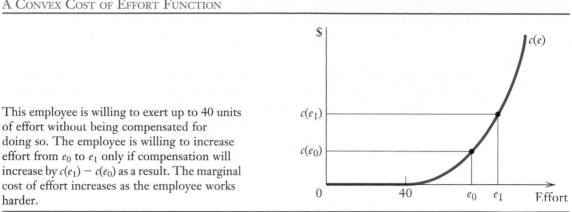

To illustrate the ramifications of the difference in objective between principal and agent here, consider an employee who puts in 40 units of effort and is considering putting in one additional unit of effort. This additional unit of effort would generate $100 in extra sales to the principal. The employee would be willing to exert this one extra unit of effort if compensated

$$c(41) - c(40) = \$0.50$$

for doing so. Hence, one additional unit of effort generates a net surplus of $99.50 for the two parties. However, the $100 in extra sales is captured by the principal, while the $0.50 in effort costs is borne by the employee. If effort were observable, this surplus could be realized through the use of a complete contract: The firm could simply offer to pay the employee an additional $0.50 if the employee puts in 41 units of effort rather than 40.

As noted earlier, however, there are many settings in which it is not possible to observe whether the employee is putting in effort. We therefore consider the effects of two compensation plans that do not involve contracting directly on effort. The first is a straight salary that simply matches the market wage. We assume that the market rate for a sales job that requires no extra effort is $1,000 per week. The second plan also offers a salary of $1,000 per week, but it incorporates a performance measure by paying a 10 percent commission on sales. That is, the employee receives 10 percent of the sales amount on top of this salary.

Since the firm's objective is to select a compensation plan that will maximize its profits, we proceed by comparing profits under each plan. To do this, we must first consider how the employee's effort choice will vary according to which plan is selected, in as much as it is the employee's effort choice that determines the firm's revenue. Note that in making this decision the employee is guided by his or her *own* interests, not those of the firm; hence, the employee's objective is to maximize the difference between pay received and effort costs expended. If the firm offers the salary-only job, the employee's payoff net of effort costs is $1,000 - c(e)$. Given that pay does not depend on sales, the employee in this case is unwilling to put in more than 40 units of effort. The firm's profit from having hired this employee is the difference between the employee's production and his or her wage. The employee's 40 units of effort result in $4,000 in sales, while the wage paid is $1,000. The firm earns $3,000 in profits.

If, on the other hand, the firm offers the salary-plus-commission plan, the employee's compensation is $1,000 plus 10 percent of sales. Given that each unit of effort produces an extra $100 of sales, we can write the employee's payoff as

$$\$1,000 + 0.10(100e) - c(e)$$

The employee increases his or her effort until the marginal benefit of effort is equal to the marginal cost. Given the assumptions shown in Figure 14.1 regarding the employee's cost of effort, we can solve for the effort level that maximizes the employee's payoff. As shown in Figure 14.2, the marginal benefit of effort to the employee is always 10 percent of $100, or $10. For every additional unit of effort he or she puts in, the employee's pay goes up by $10. The marginal cost of effort is the slope of the effort curve. The convex shape of this curve implies that it becomes more and more costly for the employee to exert additional effort. The effort choice that maximizes the employee's payoff is $e = 50$.[4]

How does the employee's total compensation compare to the fixed-salary-only case? Here, the employee exerts 50 units of effort, which results in sales of $5,000. The employee receives a 10 percent commission, or $500, which, added to the salary of $1,000, results in total pay of $1,500. How do the firm's profits compare? In the commission-based job, the employee earns higher wages but is also more productive. The employee makes sales of $5,000, leaving profits of $3,500. Here, the increase in wages paid by the firm is more than offset by the increase in the employee's productivity.

Note, however, that the firm may be able to achieve even higher profits by adjusting this plan slightly. Adding commissions to the salary-only job has two effects: (1) it increases the employee's pay by $500, and (2) it causes the employee to increase his or her effort by 10 units. The employee is willing to exert these 10 additional units of effort if he or she is compensated for it with at least $50. However, the addition

FIGURE 14.2

THE EMPLOYEE INCREASES EFFORT UNTIL THE MARGINAL BENEFIT
OF EFFORT IS EQUAL TO THE MARGINAL COST

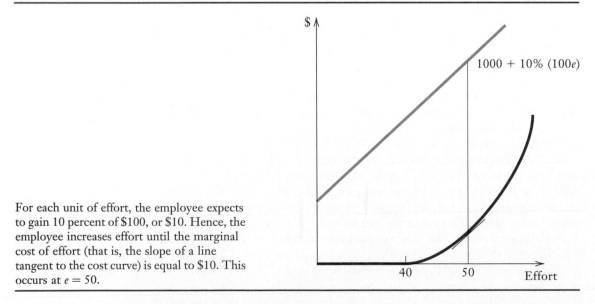

For each unit of effort, the employee expects to gain 10 percent of $100, or $10. Hence, the employee increases effort until the marginal cost of effort (that is, the slope of a line tangent to the cost curve) is equal to $10. This occurs at $e = 50$.

of the commission increases the employee's pay by $500, leaving the employee better off than under the salary-only contract. The firm can reduce the employee's salary and still keep the employee's overall pay well above the $1,000 market wage.

Suppose, for example, that the firm offers a salary of $900 per week with a 10 percent commission. The employee's payoff is now given by

$$\$900 + 0.10(100e) - c(e)$$

The employee again makes a cost–benefit tradeoff, as depicted in Figure 14.3. Note that the marginal benefit from effort is still $10; compared to Figure 14.2, the benefit curve has shifted down, but the slope has remained the same. The marginal cost of effort is still given by the slope of the cost curve. Hence, the employee again maximizes his or her payoff by exerting 50 units of effort. The firm earns revenues of $5,000, pays wages of $1,400, and makes profits of $3,600. It is important to note that despite the reduction in salary, the employee still prefers the salary-plus-commission job to the salary-only job. In the salary-only job, the employee exerts no extra effort and earns $1,000. The employee does exert extra effort in the commission-based job, but the pay received is higher by $400. Given that the employee is willing to exert this extra effort as long as his or her pay is higher by $50 as a result, this employee prefers the commission-based job to the salary only job.

How far can the firm reduce the employee's salary? Could the firm drop the employee's salary to $500, leaving wages of $1,000 and profits of $4,000? The answer is no. The employee prefers a no-extra-effort job paying $1,000 to a job that requires extra effort in order to reach this pay level. Hence, the smallest salary the firm could offer this employee and still make him or her willing to take the job is $550. This employee is indifferent between taking a no-extra-effort job paying $1,000 and a job requiring 10 units of extra effort but paying $1,050.

FIGURE 14.3
THE FIRM CAN OFFER A LOWER SALARY WITHOUT CHANGING
INCENTIVES FOR EFFORT

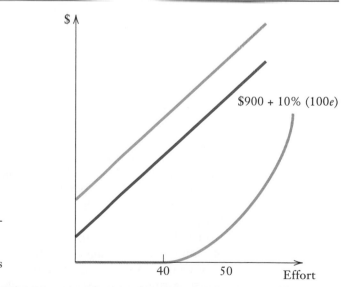

$900 + 10% (100e)

If the firm offers a salary of $900, the employee still selects effort by making a cost-benefit comparison. Since neither the marginal benefit of effort nor the marginal cost is affected, the employee's effort choice is unchanged.

We can make a number of key observations based on this example:

1. It is the *slope* of the relationship between pay and performance that provides incentives for effort, not the *level* of pay. Since employees' actions are guided by a comparison of the marginal benefit and the marginal cost of effort, changing just the level of pay does not affect employees' effort choices. As Figures 14.2 and 14.3 illustrate, raising the employee's salary (say, from $900 to $1,000) does not change the cost–benefit tradeoff determining the employee's effort choice. Although the employee is made better off by this change (as the difference between pay and effort costs increases), the employee's effort choices (and hence his or her productivity) are not affected by this change because the marginal benefit and marginal cost of effort are not affected.

2. Although the firm's profit is higher when it offers the salary-plus-commission job compared to the salary-only job, the firm can do even better if it sets a higher commission rate. In fact, the firm's profit-maximizing commission rate here is 100 percent! Why? The overall value-maximizing effort level—that is, the effort level that maximizes the difference between the total value created and the total effort cost incurred—sets the total marginal benefit from effort equal to the total marginal cost. However, the employee chooses the effort level such that the *personal* marginal benefit to effort is equal to the *personal* marginal cost. As long as the personal marginal benefit of effort is not equal to the total marginal benefit, the employee will not select the effort level that maximizes overall value. With a commission rate of 100 percent, the employee's personal marginal benefit of effort is equal to the total marginal benefit of effort. This means that the employee has full ownership over the extra value he or she creates and will therefore make the decision that maximizes overall value. The firm can capture this extra value by reducing the employee's salary or even making the salary negative. In the example developed earlier, if the firm offers a 100 percent commission, the employee will exert 140 units of effort, yielding sales of $14,000. Since this sales amount is paid directly to the employee in commissions, the firm can require an upfront payment *from* the employee of $8,000 and still make the employee's total payoff (wages less effort costs) equal $1,000.[5] Agency contracts with commission rates approaching 100 percent and "negative" salaries are observed in practice; see the discussion of business format franchise contracts in Example 14.1. Later we discuss the costs of using incentive compensation and offer an explanation for why most agency relationships do not grant the agent the full marginal benefit of his or her actions.

3. Performance-based pay can help resolve hidden information problems as well. Suppose, for example, that the salesperson receives better information than the firm regarding the prospects for a sale to any individual client. Clearly, it is in the firm's interest to have the salesperson spend relatively more time with clients who are somewhat likely to buy, and less time with those who are unlikely to buy. When paid a fixed salary, the employee has little reason to quickly move on from clients who are unlikely to buy. An employee whose pay depends on sales, however, will have an incentive to make effective use of any information he or she receives about the likelihood of making a sale.

4. Performance-based pay is also likely to affect the selection of employees who are attracted to the firm. Suppose there is variation in sales ability among the set of employees who might be attracted to this job. If the firm offers a salary-only compensation plan, the job is equally attractive to high-performing and low-performing salespeople. However, if pay depends in part on sales, the job

EXAMPLE 14.1 AGENCY CONTRACTS IN FRANCHISING

A business format franchise agreement allows one firm (referred to as the franchisee) to use the trade name and business plan of another firm (the franchisor) for a specified period.[6] While such franchising is widely used in the fast-food industry (with chains like McDonald's and Burger King among the best-known franchisors), it is a common form of organization in other sectors of the economy as well. Auto repair, hotels, convenience stores, and business services are among the industries in which this practice is widespread.

Like entrepreneurs, franchisees are known to work long hours to build their individual businesses. While many franchisees own and operate a single outlet, others have parlayed their success into substantial business empires. Indian-born Zubair Kazi bought his first Kentucky Fried Chicken (KFC) outlet in California in 1976. Kazi recalls working with his wife from 8 A.M. to 10 P.M. every day to make the store profitable.[7] As of July 2002, Kazi Foods Inc. operated 165 KFC restaurants as a franchisee, employed over 5,000 people, and was completing the acquisition of 20 Burger King restaurants in Hawaii.[8]

Such entrepreneurial zeal is driven in part by the strong incentives provided by franchise contracts. Business format franchise contracts typically consist of two parts. At the very beginning of the franchisee/franchisor relationship, the franchisee makes a one-time payment of a franchise fee. After that, the franchisee pays the franchisor a royalty, usually a fixed fraction of the franchisee's sales. Francine Lafontaine and Kathryn Shaw collected and analyzed a sample of franchise contracts from a broad range of industries, and found that the average franchise fee is $23,300, while the average royalty rate is 6.4 percent. Hence, the typical franchisee keeps 94 cents of every additional dollar of revenue generated, and 100 percent of any dollar in cost savings.

Franchisors appear to benefit from these relationships as well. Consider, as an alternative to franchising, the possibility that franchisors could own and operate these outlets themselves. Rather than selling the stores to franchisees, who then operate them, the franchisor could simply hire managers. Entrepreneur David Kiger, founder of the overnight shipping firm Worldwide Express Inc., faced this decision in 1994. As part of an ambitious expansion plan, Kiger decided to try business format franchising rather than opening up company-owned outlets. According to the *Wall Street Journal*, because Kiger's franchisees "own the outlets, [they] give him a level of commitment he would never receive from far-flung corporate employees. Worldwide Express's customers, in turn, get better service."[9] Kiger believes that this higher level of service has been crucial to the growth of his business.

Franchising is growing rapidly around the world. According to FranchiseChina.com, more than 20,000 potential franchisees attended franchising trade shows in Beijing, Guangzhou, and Shanghai in 2004. Although some European and American firms are actively seeking franchisees in China—US-based Subway Restaurants and the U.K.'s Amphora Aromatics Beauty Spa, among them—many of the most successful Chinese franchisors are based in Asia. Tsai Yen Ping opened her first Natural Beauty Salon in Taipei, Taiwan, in 1972. She offered business format franchising in Taiwan in 1984 and expanded into mainland China six years later. By 2004, Natural Beauty Salons were the leading retailer of cosmetics in China, with company-wide sales growing more than 12 percent in 2004. The firm and its franchisees operated over 1,500 salons in China, including 300 franchised outlets in Beijing alone.[10]

EXAMPLE 14.2 PAY, PERFORMANCE, AND SELECTION AT SAFELITE GLASS

Safelite Glass Corporation is the largest installer of automobile glass in the United States. Over a 19-month period beginning in January 1994, CEO Garen Staglin and President John Barlow implemented a new compensation system for auto glass installers. Dubbed the Performance Pay Plan (PPP), the new system shifted all installers from hourly pay to piece rates. Piece-rate compensation systems offer employees a fixed payment for each unit of output they produce. Safelite's piece rates varied somewhat in different locations, but on average the PPP system offered employees $20 for every windshield they installed. Like many workers under piece-rate systems, Safelite's installers were given a guaranteed minimum compensation amount; if a worker's weekly compensation from piece rates ended up below this minimum, the worker was paid the guaranteed amount.[11]

Safelite implemented PPP in an attempt to boost worker productivity. According to a study by Edward Lazear, it seems that this objective has been achieved. Analyzing detailed information on individual-level production within the firm, Lazear finds that Safelite's workers installed, on average, 2.70 windshields per eight-hour day prior to the implementation of PPP. After the switch to piece rates, this figure jumped 20 percent, to 3.24 windshields per day.

This increase in workers' productivity may stem from two possible sources. First, the piece rates may provide stronger incentives for effort, leading to increases in individual productivity. Second, the piece rates may lead to a change in the firm's workforce—since piece-rate-based compensation is more remunerative for productive workers, the firm may be better able to attract and retain more productive employees.

Lazear finds evidence suggesting that *both* effects were present at Safelite. Limiting his analysis to only those workers who were present both before and after the implementation of PPP, he shows that about half of the firm's productivity improvement is attributable to increases in the production of workers who were present prior to the implementation of PPP. Lazear also finds that employees who were hired after the implementation of PPP were significantly more productive than those who were hired before.

One perhaps unexpected benefit of the PPP system has been ongoing productivity improvements even after implementation of the system. Although one might expect incentive effects to lead to immediate increases in output, it turns out that individual workers' productivity continued to increase slowly even after an initial jump. Lazear attributes this to the fact that piece rates reward innovation; an employee can increase his or her pay by discovering a faster way to install windshields.

An often-stated concern about piece-rate-based compensation systems has to do with product quality. If the firm rewards output directly, what is to stop workers from cutting corners in order to increase production? Safelite solves this problem by tracking which installers work on which windshields and requiring workers to repair defective installations on their own time.

Did PPP increase profits at Safelite? Lazear finds that PPP did lead to an increase in the firm's wage bill; however, the percentage increase in wages was only about half as large as the percentage increase in productivity. Hence, it appears that Safelite Glass did benefit from implementation of a piece-rate-based compensation system.

is more attractive to high performers. In fact, through careful choice of salary level the firm can effectively screen employees on ability. Setting below-market salary levels will make low performers elect to work elsewhere, while high commission rates will allow top performers to earn market rates. See the discussion of Safelite's piece-rate-based system in Example 14.2.

COSTS OF TYING PAY TO PERFORMANCE ◆ ◆ ◆ ◆ ◆

To this point, we have focused on the benefits of tying employees' pay to measures of performance. We have shown that linking pay to performance measures can help solve agency problems arising from hidden action and hidden information, and can also serve to screen employees on the basis of productivity.

We next discuss the two main costs of tying pay to performance. Both arise directly from difficulties in measuring an employee's performance. The first potential cost arises if the performance measure is affected by random factors that are beyond the employee's control. As we will see, when firms use performance measures that are affected by random factors, tying pay to performance subjects the employee to risk. The second potential cost arises if the measure fails to capture all aspects of desired performance. For example, an employer may want the employee to work on both sales and customer service. If, however, the firm uses sales commissions to provide incentives, the measure of performance reflects only one of the activities the firm deems to be important. By placing greater reliance on such a measure, the firm causes the employee to direct more attention toward sales and less toward customer service.

Risk Aversion and Risk Sharing

To understand how random factors in performance measures affect the cost of providing incentives to employees, we start by taking a short detour to examine individuals' preferences over risky outcomes.

Preferences over Risky Outcomes

Consider a freshly minted MBA graduate who is presented with two job opportunities. The jobs are identical in every way *except* the means of payment. At the first job, the employer will pay the graduate $100,000 at the end of the first year of employment. At the second job, the employer will flip a coin at the end of the first year. If the coin comes up heads (which happens with probability one-half), the employer will pay $40,000. If it comes up tails, the employer will pay $160,000. Note here that the expected value of the risky job is $100,000, which is the same as the certain payment associated with the safe job.[12] Putting yourself in the shoes of this graduate, which job would you prefer?

Most people, when presented with such a choice, prefer the safe job—that is, most people are *risk averse*.[13] A risk-averse person prefers a safe outcome to a risky outcome with the same expected value. A *risk-neutral* decision maker is indifferent between a safe outcome and a risky outcome with the same expected value. A *risk-seeking* decision maker prefers a risky outcome to a safe outcome with the same expected value. Most people are risk averse with respect to large risks.

Why are people risk averse? To answer this question, let us first pose it in a somewhat different way. If the graduate takes the risky job and the coin comes up tails, his wealth will be $60,000 greater than it would have been had he or she taken the safe job. This is good, for the graduate can now consume more goods and services. If the graduate takes the risky job and is unlucky, the resulting wealth is $60,000 lower than it would have been had he or she taken the safe job. This is, of course, bad, as the graduate's level of consumption will fall. But why is the bad prospect of being "down" $60,000 not fully offset by the accompanying good prospect of being "up" 60,000?

Let's consider the set of goods the graduate will consume under each of the possible scenarios. If the graduate takes the risky job and is unlucky, he will be able to consume only goods and services that he values very highly. If the graduate takes the safe job, he or she will be somewhat less constrained. Our graduate can expand his or her range of purchases and consume goods and services that he or she values moderately highly. If he or she takes the risky job and is lucky, the range of purchases can be expanded even further, and the graduate can consume goods that are valued less highly than the goods purchased if he or she had only $100,000 in income (or else the graduate would have bought those goods first). Hence, the graduate places a higher value on the increase in consumption coming when wealth increases from $40,000 to $100,000 than on the increase in consumption coming when wealth increases from $100,000 to $160,000. This means that the loss from being down $60,000 is greater than the gain from being up that same amount; therefore, the grad strictly prefers the safe job to the risky job. As long as the decision maker places a lower value on the consumption associated with each additional dollar of wealth, he or she will be risk averse.

We next extend our example to assess how costly it is for a given individual to bear a given risk. Recall that, by definition, a risk-averse decision maker prefers the safe job paying $100,000 to the risky job. However, that same decision maker would presumably prefer the risky job if, instead of paying $100,000, the safe job paid only $40,000. Hence, there must be a cutoff point between $40,000 and $100,000 at which a decision maker's preference switches—a payment from the safe job at which the decision maker is just indifferent between the safe job and the risky job.

To locate this indifference point, let's consider reducing the payment associated with the safe job in $1,000 increments, and repeatedly asking our recent graduate which job he or she prefers. As shown in the first row of Table 14.1, the graduate's risk aversion means that the safe job is preferred to the risky job when the safe job offers the same expected value. Unless our graduate is extremely risk tolerant, he or she will still prefer the safe job when it pays just a little less, or $99,000. Let's suppose that the grad would prefer to take the risky job when offered a certain payment of $70,000, but prefers a certain $90,000 to the risk. Suppose that the indifference point between the safe job and the risky job occurs when the safe job pays $80,000.

TABLE 14.1
AN MBA GRADUATE'S PREFERENCES OVER JOBS

Safe Job Pays	Risky Job Pays	Graduate's Preference
$100,000	$40,000 with probability $1/2$ $160,000 with probability $1/2$	Safe job
$99,000	$40,000 with probability $1/2$ $160,000 with probability $1/2$	Safe job
$90,000	$40,000 with probability $1/2$ $160,000 with probability $1/2$	Safe job
$80,000	$40,000 with probability $1/2$ $160,000 with probability $1/2$	Indifferent
$70,000	$40,000 with probability $1/2$ $160,000 with probability $1/2$	Risky job

We define $80,000 to be this decision maker's *certainty equivalent* for this risk. It is the certain amount that makes the decision maker indifferent between taking the risk and taking the certain payment. We can think of the certainty equivalent as the smallest certain amount the decision maker would be willing to accept in exchange for the risky payoff. We define the difference between the expected value of a risk and the decision maker's certainty equivalent as the decision maker's *risk premium*. In this case, the expected value of the risk is $100,000, while the graduate's certainty equivalent is $80,000. Hence, his risk premium is $20,000. The risk premium can be thought of as the amount by which the decision maker discounts the risky payoff because of the risk.

The notions of certainty equivalent and risk premium have three key properties:

1. Different decision makers will apply different certainty equivalents to the same risk. If you ask *yourself* what safe wage makes you indifferent between the safe job and the risky job, you may reach a different conclusion than did our hypothetical graduate. People vary in terms of their risk preferences, with some being more risk tolerant than others. If you reached a higher certainty equivalent than did our graduate (that is, you prefer the gamble when the save job pays $80,000), you are less risk averse than our graduate. If you reached a smaller certainty equivalent, you are more risk averse.

2. For a given decision maker, the certainty equivalent is lower (and the risk premium higher) when the *spread* or *variability* in payments is greater. Consider an increase in the upper payment of the risky job to $180,000 and a reduction in the lower payment to $20,000. Because the graduate places a higher value on incremental consumption when he is poor compared to when he is rich, this change makes him strictly worse off if he takes the risky job. Hence, his certainty equivalent for the risky job falls and his risk premium rises.

3. For a given decision maker, we can use the notion of certainty equivalent to compare different risks. Since (a) a decision maker is indifferent between taking the risky outcome and taking a certain outcome offering the certainty equivalent, and (b) a decision maker will always prefer a higher certain amount to a lower certain amount, a decision maker will prefer a risk with a higher certainty equivalent to one with a lower certainty equivalent. In choosing between two risky outcomes, a decision maker will select the one with the higher certainty equivalent.

Risk Sharing

If people are risk averse, they can often make themselves better off by *sharing* their risks. To illustrate this principle, consider two risk-averse homeowners. Each owns a wooden frame house worth $200,000, and each faces the possibility that the house may be destroyed by fire. Suppose the probability that a house burns down in a given year is 10 percent. If, during the upcoming year, a homeowner's house does not burn down, that homeowner will not incur any costs associated with rebuilding. If the house does burn down, the entire value is lost, and the homeowner will have to pay $200,000 to rebuild. Hence, a homeowner's rebuilding costs will be

$$\$200,000 \quad \text{with probability } {}^1\!/_{10}$$

$$\$0 \quad \text{with probability } {}^9\!/_{10}$$

A homeowner's expected rebuilding cost is $20,000. Note, however, that there is a substantial amount of variability in rebuilding costs. The possibility of fire makes the house a risky asset for the homeowner to hold.

Suppose that the first homeowner approaches the second and makes the following contract offer: the first homeowner will pay one-half of the second's rebuilding costs in the event that the second homeowner's home is destroyed, while the second agrees to the same deal if the first's home is destroyed. Note that if the events that the houses burn down are independent, the probability that *both* burn down is $(1/10)^2 = 1/100$. In this case, each homeowner pays half the other's cost, meaning that each pays $200,000. The probability that neither house burns is $(9/10)^2 = 81/100$. In this case, neither homeowner incurs any costs. With probability $2(1/10)(9/10) = 18/100$, exactly one of the two houses burns. In this case, the unlucky homeowner receives half the rebuilding costs ($100,000) from the other; each incurs costs of $100,000.

Why might the second homeowner be interested in accepting this offer? If she accepts, her rebuilding cost (including any payments to or from the first homeowner) will be

$$\$200,000 \quad \text{with probability } {}^{1}\!/_{100}$$

$$\$100,000 \quad \text{with probability } {}^{18}\!/_{100}$$

$$\$0 \quad \text{with probability } {}^{81}\!/_{100}$$

The second homeowner's expected rebuilding cost is therefore

$$\frac{1}{100}\$200,000 + \frac{18}{100}\$100,000 = \$20,000$$

the same as it would be if she did not accept the offer. Note, however, that the probability of the *worst* outcome (that is, incurring rebuilding costs of $200,000) has fallen from 1 in 10 to 1 in 100. Similarly, the probability of the best outcome (incurring $0 costs) has fallen from 9/10 to 81/100. While this contract doesn't change the second homeowner's expected rebuilding costs, it does reduce the *variability* in these costs by making the extreme worst and best outcomes less likely. Since the second homeowner is risk averse, the reduction in variability makes her better off. By sharing their risks, the two homeowners reduce the variability in their payoffs and both are made better off.

Some of the earliest insurance companies were organized on precisely this principle. The great Fire of London in 1666 destroyed property worth £10 million, a figure estimated to be around one-quarter of the total gross domestic product of England at the time. In its aftermath, Londoners searched for ways to protect their wealth against these risks. In 1696, a total of 100 subscribers joined together to form the Amicable Contributorship, a mutual insurance organization whose subscribers pledged their personal wealth to rebuild the homes of other subscribers in the event of damage by fire.

Writer Daniel Defoe, who later authored *Robinson Crusoe*, foresaw the development of the modern insurance industry in 1697, writing that "All the Contingencies of Life might be fenc'd against...(as Fire is already) as Thieves, Floods by Land, Storms by Sea, Losses of all Sorts, and Death itself, in a manner, by making it up to the Survivor."[14] Although most modern insurance firms do not rely on the personal wealth of a group of subscribers to pay claims (with Lloyd's of London being a notable exception), the principle of risk sharing nonetheless continues to underlie the demand for insurance of all forms. Furthermore, the insurance industry is only one of a number of modern institutions that facilitate the sharing of risks. Financial markets serve a similar purpose. In an initial public offering, an entrepreneur sells ownership shares, which are an uncertain claim on the firm's future cash flows, to investors in exchange for a certain, upfront payment. This transaction shifts risk from the entrepreneur to the investor.

An immediate corollary to the logic of risk sharing is the following. If one party is risk averse and another is risk neutral, the efficient allocation of risk places *all* risk with the risk-neutral party and gives a certain payoff to the risk-averse party. The least the risk-averse party is willing to accept in order to sell this risky payoff is his or her certainty equivalent, which is less than the expected value. In contrast, the risk-neutral party values the risky payoff at the expected value. Therefore, the two parties could each benefit from trading; the risk-neutral party can offer the risk-averse party an amount of money somewhere between the expected value and the risk-averse party's certainty equivalent, and both will be better off by accepting this transaction.

Risk and Incentives

We are now ready to incorporate our discussions of risk aversion and risk sharing into the theory of incentives. As noted earlier, the main costs of basing pay on measures of performance stem directly from difficulties in measuring performance. One such problem is that an agent's actions typically do not translate perfectly into measured performance. That is, measured performance depends *in part* on the agent's actions, but it also depends on random factors that are beyond the agent's control. Tying pay more closely to observed performance therefore links the agent's pay to these random factors. If the agent is risk averse, the agent dislikes having his or her pay vary randomly, and the principal must compensate the agent for the cost of bearing this risk.

To illustrate, we adapt an agency model developed by Bengt Holstrom and Paul Milgrom.[15] We consider a risk-neutral firm that selects a commission rate α for a risk-averse salesperson working in a retail store. Why is it reasonable to assume that our firm is risk neutral but the employee is risk averse? A firm has many salespeople and is likely not greatly concerned about variation coming from the sales of any one salesperson. Also, if the firm's stock is publicly traded, its shareholders can easily diversify any risk that is idiosyncratic to the firm. Hence, it is reasonable to assume that the firm is at least significantly less averse than the employee to holding the risk associated with variation in the employee's sales.

For many reasons, the dollar value of the salesperson's sales in a given week depends in part on the actions of that salesperson. A salesperson who works hard to handle customer requests quickly may be able to serve more customers. A salesperson who has worked to learn the store's merchandise offerings will be able to suggest exactly the right product to meet the customer's needs. A personable salesperson who strives to make each customer feel welcome will have high sales from repeat business. Ruth Lazar, a clothing saleswoman at Bergdorf Goodman on Fifth Avenue in New York City, is one example. For 10 years Lazar has kept a Rolodex full of the names of past and potential customers, and she frequently contacts potential buyers when new merchandise comes in. According to Bergdorf's chief executive, Ronald L. Frasch, skilled salespeople like Lazar can earn $200,000 or more per year in commissions on top of their base salaries.[16]

The dollar value of goods sold by a salesperson will also depend on a number of random factors that are beyond the salesperson's control. For example, if the local economy suffers a downturn, it is likely that fewer customers will come into the store. The store's buyers may do a poor job forecasting customer tastes, leaving the salesperson with the difficult job of selling merchandise that no one wants. In a given week, the salesperson may also be unlucky; perhaps an unexpectedly large fraction of

EXAMPLE 14.3 MARKET EFFECTS IN EXECUTIVE COMPENSATION

One of the clearest examples of how random factors can affect measured performance comes from the very top of most organizations. Pay for top executives like chief executive officers, chief operating officers, and chief financial officers is frequently tied directly to the price of the firm's stock through grants of equity or equity-based instruments such as stock options.

The theory of financial markets suggests that the price of a firm's stock will move up or down for a variety of reasons. Share prices are clearly affected by any news bearing directly on the firm's future cash flow, but they are also affected by overall movements in the market. For example, during the late 1990s a major bull market pulled all U.S. share prices up by 25 percent or more annually. Even mediocre firms saw great gains in their share prices over this period. Similarly, the declining stock market during 2001 to 2002 saw nearly all firms' share prices fall—even those of firms with good operating performance over the period.

As a result, some analysts believe that a better measure of management's actions is the firm's performance *relative* to market indices. One tech company that has tried this approach is Level 3 Communications. Level 3 is a diversified communications and information services company, with over $1.6 billion in revenues in 2004. Like other high-tech companies, Level 3 has sought to recruit and reward talented senior employees. To do so, it implemented its Outperform Stock Option (OSO) program in April 1998.[21]

Through the OSO program, the company awarded stock options to senior executives. Like other firms' option grants, Level 3's OSO options did not vest immediately upon being granted. However, unlike traditional options, the exercise price of an OSO option was based on Level 3's stock market performance relative to the performance of the S&P 500 index. Thus, executives could profit even if Level 3's share price fell, as long as the firm's price fell less (on a percentage basis)

than did the S&P 500. Conversely, executives would not automatically profit just because the firm's share price rose—the firm's stock return had to beat that of the market index. The plan also included a built-in "success multiplier"—if the firm's return exceeded that of the S&P 500 by 11 percent or more, the executives' gain from exercising OSO options would be multiplied by eight!

The OSO program was announced with considerable fanfare, and the firm took great pride in the plan. As stated in the firm's 2001 annual report: "The company believes that the qualified candidates it seeks place particular emphasis on equity-based long term incentive programs. . . . The Company believes that [traditional] programs reward employees when company stock price performance is inferior to investments of similar risks, dilute public stockholders in a manner not directly proportional to performance, and fail to provide a preferred return on stockholders' invested capital . . . the OSO program is superior with respect to these issues."

Under the initial OSO plan, executives could benefit only if the firm's stock return exceeded that of the market index, and this clearly had the effect of filtering out market risk. Subsequent adjustments to the plan have weakened this connection somewhat. In 2000, the firm began making "convertible" OSO grants. These options can be converted into one share of Level 3 common stock in the event that the firm's share price lags the S&P index. Thus, executives can earn a payoff from the new convertible grants, even if the firm's share price does not outperform the market. Unfortunately for the firm's shareholders, the firm's share price did indeed lag the market index over the 2001 to 2005 period, so most OSO payouts came in the form of conversions to common stock.

Despite the theoretical appeal of OSO plans, few other companies have adopted them. Rajesh Aggarwal and Andrew Samwick offer a possible answer to this puzzle.[22] They argue that relative performance evaluation for chief executive officers motivates these managers to take actions aimed at reducing competitors' profits. Such actions improve the firm's relative performance (and hence raises the CEO's pay), but they do not create value for the firm's shareholders. These authors show that relative performance evaluation is less prevalent in industries in which competitors have greater potential to affect one another. While this argument explains why firms may not tie executive pay to performance relative to a small group of competitors, it is less clear that it offers a reason not to link pay to a broad index like the S&P 500.

the customers are "just looking." As an example, demand for luxury goods in New York dipped markedly in the aftermath of the September 11 terrorist attacks and during the recession that followed. Lazar reports that her sales in 2001 were likely to be down at least 5 percent from those in the previous year.

Building on our model, we now assume that sales depend on both effort, e, and a random variable, $\tilde{\epsilon}$

$$\text{Sales} - \$100e + \tilde{\epsilon}$$

Let $\tilde{\epsilon}$ be a random variable with expected value zero and variance σ^2.[17] A positive realization of $\tilde{\epsilon}$ causes the employee's sales to be higher than they otherwise would have been. This can be interpreted as resulting from a good local economy, a favorable selection of merchandise, or just good luck. Conversely, a negative realization of $\tilde{\epsilon}$ means that, for reasons beyond the employee's control, sales are unexpectedly low. This may be due to a poor local economy, subpar merchandise, or bad luck.

Suppose that our salesperson is risk averse and has certainty equivalent for an uncertain wage outcome of

$$E(\text{Wage}) - \frac{1}{2}\rho \, \text{Var}(\text{Wage})$$

where E(Wage) is the expected value of the wage payment and Var(Wage) is the variance of the wage payment. The parameter ρ, known as the coefficient of absolute risk aversion, is indicative of how risk averse the employee is.[18] Larger values of ρ imply greater risk aversion, since as ρ increases the employee applies a greater discount to the uncertain wage due to its variability.

Suppose that the employee's cost of effort is 0 up to 40 units of effort and $(1/2)(e - 40)^2$ thereafter. Assume also that the employee's next-best job opportunity offers a certainty equivalent of $1,000, net of effort costs. This means that the employee will take the sales job only if the certainty equivalent minus the cost of effort at the sales job is greater than or equal to $1,000. Suppose that the firm considers pay plans that take the form of a fixed salary F per week and a commission of α on sales. For an effort level e and random variable realization $\tilde{\epsilon}$, the employee's actual pay will therefore be $F + \alpha(100e + \tilde{\epsilon})$. Given that the random variable $\tilde{\epsilon}$ has an expected value of zero, the employee's expected pay is $F + \alpha(100e)$, while the variance of his pay is $\alpha^2 \sigma^2$. Hence, the employee's certainty equivalent minus effort costs is

$$F + \alpha(100e) - \frac{1}{2}(e - 40)^2 - \frac{1}{2}\rho\alpha^2\sigma^2$$

This expression consists of the employee's base salary (F), plus his expected commission ($\alpha100e$), less his costs from effort ($(1/2)(e - 40)^2$), less his cost of bearing risk

$(-(1/2)\rho\alpha^2\sigma^2)$. If the firm hopes to attract the employee to this job and away from the next-best job opportunity, this amount must be greater than \$1,000. Note here that if the firm asks the employee to bear more risk or exert more effort, this reduces the value the employee receives from the job, and it will be harder for the firm to attract the employee. This corresponds to the intuitive notion that people are willing to take jobs that are risky or difficult only if they are well compensated for doing so.

As in the example just given, the employee will choose his effort level to maximize the value he receives from the job. That is, he will increase his effort until the personal marginal benefit of additional effort is just equal to the personal marginal cost. For a commission rate of α, the employee increases his pay by 100α for each unit of effort he exerts. The marginal cost of exerting additional effort is equal to $(e - 40)$, so our employee will exert $40 + 100\alpha$ units of effort.[19] Note that the employee's effort increases with the commission rate, as in our earlier example. Note further that any increase in α intended to increase effort will also increase the employee's cost of bearing risk.

The key tradeoff facing the firm in choosing α is as follows. As the firm ties pay more closely to performance, it provides stronger incentives. This leads to more effort and, hence, more revenue. However, since the performance measure is subject to random factors, tying pay more closely to measured performance also increases the variability of the employee's compensation. This makes the job less attractive to the employee and means that the firm has to pay higher overall wages in order to attract the employee. This leads to higher costs for the firm. The optimal strength of incentives is determined by a balancing of these two forces.

To illustrate this tradeoff, we compare the firm's profit when offering various compensation plans. For concreteness, we assume that the employee's coefficient of absolute risk aversion, ρ, is equal to 3 and that the variance of sales, σ^2, is 10,000.[20] Suppose first that the firm offers a job without commissions. Since this job motivates no extra effort and places no risk on the employee, the firm can pay a salary of \$1,000. As shown in Table 14.2, the employee will put in 40 units of effort, and the firm's expected profit will be \$3,000.

The firm may also elect to offer a commission rate of $\alpha = 10$ percent. The employee will put in 50 units of effort (leading to effort costs of \$50) and earn expected commissions of \$500. Because the pay now depends on output, which, in turn, is affected by random factors beyond the employee's control, the employee is subject to risk. The employee discounts the value of the job because of this risk, applying a risk premium of \$150.

In order to attract the employee, the firm still needs to ensure that the certainty equivalent minus effort costs is greater than or equal to \$1,000. Thus, in order to overcome the increased risk and effort costs, the firm must offer a fixed salary F of \$700. The firm's total expected wage bill goes up to \$1,200, which is just enough to compensate for

TABLE 14.2
THE TRADEOFF BETWEEN RISK AND INCENTIVES

Commission Rate	Effort Level	Effort Costs	Risk Premium	Expected Commission	Salary	Revenue	Profit
0%	40	0	0	0	\$1,000	\$4,000	\$3,000
10%	50	50	150	500	700	5,000	3,800
20%	60	200	600	1,200	600	6,000	4,200
25%	65	312.5	937.5	1,625	625	6,500	4,250
30%	70	450	1,350	2,100	700	7,000	4,200

the increased risk and effort costs associated with the commission-based job. Here, the increase in expected productivity ($5,000, compared to $4,000 for the salary-only job) more than compensates for the increase in expected wages. Thus, the firm's expected profit is higher if it offers the commission-based job than if it offers the salary-only job.

Filling in the remaining rows of Table 14.2, we see that further increases in the commission rate have similar effects. As the firm increases α, the employee exerts more effort but bears more risk. The extra effort leads to additional revenue for the firm, but the extra risk leads to a larger risk premium and thus to higher expected wages. The optimal commission rate is determined by a tradeoff between these benefits and costs. In our example, the firm's profit-maximizing choice of α is 25 percent. If the firm chooses a *higher* α (say, 30 percent), the increase in revenue is smaller than the increase in risk and effort costs. Since the employee's expected compensation must go up by the amount of these costs, the firm's expected profit falls if it raises commissions to 30 percent.

To summarize this analysis, we have shown that if a firm wants to tie pay to a performance measure that is affected by random factors, the firm must compensate employees for the resulting increase in the variability of their pay. In determining how closely to tie pay to performance, the firm must weigh the costs of imposing risk onto risk-averse employees against the benefits of providing additional incentives. There is, therefore, a tradeoff between risk and incentives.

To put this another way, recall that our discussion of how employees respond to incentives concluded that the firm's profit-maximizing commission rate was 100 percent. When the employee captures all the value associated with extra effort, he or she chooses the effort level that equates the total marginal benefit of effort to the total marginal cost. Our discussion of risk sharing, however, suggests that a risk neutral firm can benefit by removing all risk from the pay of a risk-averse employee. Optimizing on just the *incentive* dimension leads us to expect a 100 percent commission, while optimizing on just the *risk* dimension leads us to expect a 0 percent commission. When both risk and incentives are present, the optimal commission rate will reflect a tradeoff among these forces and will be somewhere between 0 percent and 100 percent.

Although the model we have developed here is closely tailored to the problem of selecting an optimal commission rate, the reasoning applies broadly to any way in which rewards to employees are linked to measured performance. Consider, for example, a setting in which an employee is promoted to a higher-paying job if and only if she achieves the best performance from among a group of employees. If the performance measure is affected by random factors, the promotion depends both on effort and on the random factors affecting performance. This form of incentive introduces variability into the employee's compensation and thus places risk onto her. Similarly, many firms tie employee pay to firm performance through the use of profit-sharing or grants of stock options. Clearly, many factors other than the actions of an individual employee affect profits and stock prices, and the use of such pay instruments exposes employees to risk.

Actual firms rarely have detailed information regarding employees' risk preferences ρ and effort costs c, and therefore they cannot solve precisely for an optimal commission rate as we have done here. However, our model does yield a number of insights into the factors that favor the use of incentives. Stronger incentives are called for if

- The employee is less risk averse.

- The variance of measured performance is lower.

- The employee's marginal cost of effort is lower.

- The marginal return to effort is higher.

Consider, for example, the effect on the strength of incentives if the variance of measured performance is lower. The risk premium applied by the employee to any wage offer made by the firm is still given by $\frac{1}{2}\rho\alpha^2\sigma^2$; however, if σ^2 is smaller, any *increase* in α results in a smaller *increase* in the employee's risk premium. When there is less randomness in measured performance, any increase in the strength of incentives results in a smaller increase in the risk on a risk-averse employee. Thus, it is optimal for the firm to offer stronger incentives. Similarly, if the marginal return to effort is higher, an increase in α results in a greater increase in the payoff to the firm. This makes the firm willing to incur higher risk costs in order to motivate effort, as effort is now more valuable.

What tools do firms have to mitigate the costs arising from the presence of randomness in performance measures? The foregoing discussion indicates that a firm's profits are higher when there is less random variability in measured performance. When there is less variability, the firm can reduce its wage costs by paying a smaller risk premium for a given strength of incentives; it can also increase its revenues by using stronger incentives. Firms can reduce the risk that employees are exposed to by selecting performance measures that are subject to as little randomness as possible and investing in reducing the randomness in available measures.

Performance Measures That Fail to Reflect All Desired Actions

Another cost of tying pay to measured performance arises when the performance measure does not capture all aspects of desired performance. In the retail sales model developed earlier, the performance measure (sales) is a reasonably complete summary indicator of the various aspects of job performance. Although a salesperson needs to perform a number of separate "tasks" (such as learning about the store's selection of merchandise, helping customers find items, etc.), each positively affects the salesperson's measured performance and, hence, compensation.[23] In other jobs, however, the available measures of performance may not cover all aspects of job performance. Use of pay-for-performance incentives in this case will cause employees to focus on aspects of performance that are reflected in the measure and to neglect aspects that are not reflected in the measure.

As an example, consider the problem of providing effort incentives for teachers in primary schools.[24] Let's think about dividing the various activities of teachers into two types: (1) activities that develop students' test-taking skills and (2) activities that enhance students' higher-order thinking skills. For skills like multiplication, reading comprehension, and spelling, it is easy to devise a standardized test to measure students' progress. However, it is considerably more difficult to design a tool that assesses whether a student can reason effectively or think creatively. Hence, while both of these teaching activities build students' ability to think, only the first can be measured effectively.

Consider, then, the effect of changing compensation plans for teachers. Suppose that under the initial system, teachers are paid a fixed salary that is unrelated to student performance. One disadvantage of such a plan is that the personal marginal return to effort is zero. Thus, teachers are not motivated to put in extra effort; if teachers' cost of effort function is as drawn earlier in Figure 14.1, they will put in 40 units of effort. Suppose that a school board seeks to reward teachers who put in extra effort, and considers paying bonuses of amount b to teachers whose students show substantial improvement on standardized tests. An advantage of such a plan might be to raise the personal marginal return to effort, thus increasing teachers' effort levels and, presumably, student learning.

EXAMPLE 14.4 CARDIOVASCULAR SURGERY REPORT CARDS

One of the most thoroughly studied agency relationships is that between the patient/principal and the physician/agent. Patients usually trust their physicians to provide high-quality medical care. But research regularly shows that there are wide discrepancies in quality from one provider to another. Many policy analysts believe that patients would benefit substantially if they could obtain valid information about the quality of various providers. What they have in mind is a kind of *Consumer Reports* for hospitals and doctors.

In response to this concern, in 1984 the U.S. government began publishing hospital "report cards" listing each hospital's mortality rates. Perhaps surprisingly, some of the nation's most respected hospitals, such as the Mayo Clinic, showed very high mortality rates—but this, of course, was because these hospitals treated the most difficult cases. To make the reports more useful, the government used data on patient case-mix to calculate a "predicted mortality rate" for each hospital—the mortality rate that would be expected given the hospital's mix of cases. If this measure is computed correctly, the nation's best hospitals should have actual mortality rates well below the predicted rates. Medical providers complained that the federal government did a poor job of computing predicted mortality, so that some very good hospitals had very poor rankings. At the same time, the general public seemed to ignore the rankings when choosing their providers. By the early 1990s, the federal government stopped issuing hospital report cards.

Several states, including New York and Pennsylvania, filled the void, issuing report cards specifically for cardiovascular surgery. Cardiovascular surgery has two features that make it especially appropriate for report cards. First, the mortality risk is relatively high, so that patients stand to gain a lot by finding the best providers. Second, the statistical models for computing predicted mortality are rather sophisticated. Given a good measure of predicted mortality, hospitals offering the best care should rank near the top. Launched in the early 1990s, the report cards have generated considerable fanfare. High-ranking hospitals have publicized their success and enjoyed small increases in market share. Some low-ranking hospitals have invested considerable time and effort into attempts to boost their grade.

Research by David Dranove, Dan Kessler, Mark McClellan, and Mark Satterthwaite has uncovered a disturbing side effect of the report cards.[28] They point out that the models for predicting mortality are not perfect. Providers have information about their patients' health that is not captured by statistical models. Physicians can manipulate their report card rankings by operating less often on patients who are sicker than indicated by the statistical models, and more often on patients who are healthier than indicated.

Dranove and colleagues show that some providers did behave in this unsettling way. Focusing on heart attack patients, they found that the publication of report cards in New York and Pennsylvania caused a small but statistically significant shift in the incidence of cardiovascular surgery toward relatively healthier patients. The result was that the *overall* mortality rate for heart attack patients went up slightly even as the *surgical* mortality rate declined. (Recall that it is only the surgical mortality rate, not the overall mortality rate from heart attacks, that is factored into the report cards.) Total medical costs rose as well. The authors point out, however, that their study examined only the first few years after the report cards were introduced. Concerted efforts on the part of most hospitals to boost quality may have generated substantial long-run benefits.

Teachers, however, have a somewhat richer job than the salesperson in our earlier example. The salesperson had a one-dimensional choice; the only decision was over how much effort to exert. Teachers choose how hard to work, but they also choose how to allocate their efforts *across* the two tasks. Thus, a teacher will equate the personal marginal benefit from effort in a given task to the personal marginal cost. Under the initial compensation plan, the marginal return to effort toward either task is zero. Hence, there is no reason for teachers to allocate their 40 units of effort in any particular way, and they will presumably be willing to select the allocation that maximizes the benefit to students.

By using pay-for-performance incentives tied to test scores, the school district increases the personal marginal benefit of effort directed toward activity (1) but leaves the marginal benefit of effort toward activity (2) unchanged. Let teachers' effort choices toward activities (1) and (2) be denoted by e_1 and e_2, and let the teacher's total cost of exerting effort levels e_1 and e_2 be equal to $\frac{1}{2}(e_1 + e_2 - 40)^2$. Suppose that higher levels of e_1 increase the probability that students score well enough for the teacher to earn the bonus. We let $p(e_1)$ be the probability that a teacher earns the bonus as a function of her effort choice. The teacher will select e_1 and e_2 to maximize the probability that she will earn the bonus minus effort costs:

$$p(e_1) = \frac{1}{2}(e_1 + e_2 - 40)^2$$

Given this situation, the teacher is clearly best off allocating no effort toward teaching higher-order thinking skills; that is, she should set $e_2 = 0$. To verify this, note that if the teacher had elected to set $e_2 > 0$, she could always increase her likelihood of earning the bonus without increasing her effort costs by shifting that effort away from task 2 and toward task 1. To maximize the probability of earning this bonus, the teacher should "teach to the test" and ignore other educational goals. This reasoning is an application of the *multitask principle*, which states that when allocating effort among a variety of tasks, employees will tend to exert more effort toward the tasks that are rewarded.

Our conclusion—that in the presence of test-based incentives teachers will allocate *all* effort toward test-taking skills—is clearly subject to a number of caveats.[25] Most seriously, perhaps, we have ignored the fact that teachers self-select into their profession. A person who becomes a teacher is likely one who cares directly about student achievement. Such nonpecuniary benefits from student progress offer a counterweight to the pecuniary incentives derived from bonuses. Nevertheless, it is clear that the use of such test-based incentives will shift teachers' effort choices in the direction of activity (1) at the potential expense of activity (2).

This discussion indicates that a second major cost of using pay-for-performance incentives is that employees will tend to focus their efforts in the direction of the activities that are rewarded. This presents two main problems. First, as we saw in the example of the teachers, sometimes the performance measure will not capture all the activities that the firm wants the employee to undertake. In this case, stronger incentives will result in less attention being paid to activities that are not rewarded. Second, sometimes the performance measure will reward activities that the firm *does not* want the employee to undertake. In this case, stronger incentives will result in more effort being directed toward activities that the firm does not want the employee to undertake.

As an example, consider the case of Lantech, a small manufacturer of packaging equipment based in Louisville, Kentucky.[26] Hoping to increase productivity, the firm implemented employee bonuses based on the profits recorded by each of the firm's five manufacturing divisions. The employees quickly discovered, however, that there is more than one way to increase a division's profits. Increasing productivity is one, but fighting to have overhead charges allocated to other divisions is another. Disagreements over such charges grew heated, and much of top management's time was consumed in mediating these disputes. Some divisions also began engaging in "channel stuffing"—a practice in which orders from other parts of the company were rushed to be filled at the end of each month. This allowed the division filling the order to recognize the revenue from this sale (and thus increase profits), but it led to problems with excess inventory. Internal strife became so severe that the firm eventually elected to discontinue the division-based bonuses and instead make profit-sharing payments based on the performance of the entire firm. This example illustrates that if performance measures reward activities that the firm does not want employees to pursue, stronger incentives will lead employees to undertake even more of the counterproductive activities.

As a manager designing pay plans, therefore, it is useful to identify precisely what activities an employee can undertake to improve measured performance. Then ask how well this set of activities overlaps with the set of activities the firm would ideally like the employee to pursue. Are there activities that are important to the firm that are not reflected in measured performance? Are there activities that improve the performance measure but that the firm does not want employees to pursue? The larger these sets of activities, the lower the efficacy of pay-for-performance based on the measure in question.

Organizations may respond to this problem in a number of ways. First, they may simply elect not to use pay-for-performance incentives at all. If the performance measures are of poor quality, the firm may be better off paying fixed salaries and instructing employees in how to allocate their efforts toward various activities. While this approach does not motivate employees to exert extra effort on the job, it has the virtue of not motivating them to ignore tasks that are important but difficult to measure. At most U.S. public schools, there is no association (or, at best, a very weak one) between teacher pay and performance. Here, the problems of identifying good performance measures may be so severe that the best outcome may be to rely on teachers' inherent concern for students' educational progress.[27]

A second potential response operates through job design. An important insight from the multitask principle is that providing pay-for-performance incentives for an easy-to-measure activity can be counterproductive if the employee is also expected to undertake a hard-to-measure activity. Grouping tasks according to ease of measurement can mitigate this problem. Suppose, for example, that activities A and C are easy to measure but activities B and D are hard to measure. If tasks A and B are assigned to one employee and C and D are assigned to another, the firm faces the multitask problems identified earlier. The firm will need to choose between offering incentives for tasks A and C (and thus detracting from performance on B and D) or offering no incentives at all (thus reducing employees' total effort). If, on the other hand, the firm assigns tasks A and C to one employee and B and D to the other, it can provide strong incentives for tasks A and C without pulling focus away from B and D.

Third, firms can augment explicit incentive contracts with direct monitoring and subjective performance evaluation. Recalling the Lantech example, it may be difficult indeed to base an explicit contract on whether a manager is fighting "too hard" to allocate overhead to another division. It may, on the other hand, be relatively easy for a CEO or other top manager to subjectively assess whether this is going on. If such assessments can be incorporated into the determination of overall compensation through use of an implicit incentive contract, subjective evaluations of performance can mitigate the problems we have described. One key to using subjective measures of performance effectively, therefore, is for the evaluators to be able to observe both the activities that the firm wants to encourage but that do not improve measured performance, and the activities that the firm wants to discourage but that do improve measured performance. We expand this discussion of subjective performance evaluation and implicit incentive contracts in Chapter 15.

◆ ◆ ◆ ◆ ◆ SELECTING PERFORMANCE MEASURES: MANAGING TRADEOFFS BETWEEN COSTS

The foregoing discussion suggests three factors that make for a good measure of an employee's performance. First, a performance measure that is less affected by random factors will allow the firm to tie pay closely to performance without introducing much variability into the employee's pay. Second, a measure that reflects all the activities the firm wants undertaken will allow the firm to use strong incentives without pulling the employee's attention away from important tasks. Third, a performance measure that cannot be improved by actions the firm *does not* want undertaken will allow the firm to offer strong incentives without also motivating counterproductive actions. Unfortunately, for many jobs, performance measures meeting all three of these criteria are rare. In Table 14.3, we highlight a selection of jobs for which performance is relatively easy to measure, and compare this to another selection for which performance is relatively more difficult to measure. In Table 14.4, we list performance measures that might be used for various jobs, and identify some problems associated with each.

Often performance measures that rate highly on one cost dimension rate poorly on another. Hence, a firm's search for the best performance measure involves identifying tradeoffs among the costs identified earlier. As an example of these tradeoffs, consider the question of whether to use "absolute" or "relative" measures of an employee's performance. A relative measure is constructed by comparing one employee's performance to another's. If the sources of randomness affecting the two employees' individual performance exhibit a positive correlation, basing each employee's pay on the *difference* between the individual performance measures will shield employees from risk.[29] Hence, a firm using relative performance measures may be able to pay a smaller risk premium and therefore use stronger incentives.

Although relative measures may reduce risk costs, they have the potential to exacerbate multitask problems. Consider the possibility that one employee might be able to take actions that *reduce* the productivity of another employee. Clearly, the firm does not want to encourage this activity; however, relative performance evaluation directly rewards it. By reducing the performance of another employee to whom she is compared, an employee can increase her compensation. Note that such activities are not rewarded if performance measures are absolute. Hence, in determining whether to use relative rather than absolute performance measures, firms must weigh the possible reductions in risk against potential increases in the incentive to undertake counterproductive actions.

TABLE 14.3
JOBS WITH VARYING EASE OF PERFORMANCE MEASUREMENT

Job for Which Performance Is Relatively Easy to Measure	Job for Which Performance Is Relatively Difficult to Measure
Harvesting grapes	Vintner
Bicycle messenger	Flight attendant
Pharmaceutical sales representative	Pharmaceutical research scientist
Manager of advertising campaign	Manager of customer service center

TABLE 14.4
PERFORMANCE MEASURES OF VARYING QUALITY FOR DIFFERENT JOBS

Job Description	Performance Measure	Discussion
Baseball pitcher	Number of games won	Depends on how team's batters perform when pitcher is pitching; this measure is therefore affected by random factors beyond the pitcher's control.
	Opponents' batting average	May motivate pitcher to pitch too cautiously. Pitcher would rather issue a walk (which does not count against batting average) than possibly surrender a hit.
	Earned run average	Less noisy than number of wins, and motivates pitcher to take any action that will prevent other team from scoring runs.
Police officer	Crime rate on beat	Crime rates vary considerably by neighborhood; this measure therefore depends on factors beyond the police officer's control.
	Number of arrests	Officer can make an arrest only if a crime has been committed; this measure therefore limits incentive to prevent crimes from being committed.
	Change in crime rate	Less noisy than the level of crime, and motivates officer to take actions that reduce crime even if no arrest results.
Local TV news producer	Profits of station	Profits depend crucially on the quality of network programming shown on the station; this measure may therefore be noisy.
	Number of journalism awards won	May motivate producer to overspend on high-profile stories
	Share of viewing audience retained when news comes on	Motivates actions that retain the potential audience; less noisy than profits.

In a well-known application of this idea, the fictional real estate salesmen in the play *Glengarry Glen Ross* were compensated based on relative performance. The salesmen competed to see who could be among the top three in sales; the rest would be fired. This scheme rewards hard work and ability, and has the advantage of shielding the salesmen from risk associated with economic fluctuations and the quality of the real estate development they were selling. If the economy sours or if the development is unattractive, the sales of all will suffer, but the best salesmen will still be rewarded by being allowed to keep their jobs. The drama centers on one struggling salesman's efforts to steal client lists from others; clearly, a compensation scheme such as this does not reward teamwork.

Similar considerations enter into the choice between narrow or broad performance measures. An example of a narrow measure might be the number of pieces of output produced by an individual employee. A broad measure might be the accounting profits of the plant where the employee works. The broad measure has the advantage of rewarding the employee for helping coworkers or for making suggestions that improve the plant's overall efficiency. However, the broad measure is also likely to be subject to more random factors. The broad measure depends on the actions of many workers and many sources of randomness; hence, linking an individual employee's pay to this measure exposes that employee to considerable risk. A firm may therefore find it very costly (in terms of employee risk premiums) to use high-powered incentives based on broad measures. In determining whether to use the broad measure or the narrow one, the firm must weigh the benefit associated with "help" activities and extra suggestions against the cost of weaker incentives for individual effort. Of course, in this case it is possible to incorporate both narrow and broad measures into an employee's compensation, and the firm must consider how the relative weights on the two measures will affect the employee's on-the-job decisions.

Whatever measures are used in explicit incentive contracts, it is almost always the case that direct monitoring and subjective evaluation are used in tandem with the explicit contract. The role of such monitoring is often to offset the risk and multitask problems associated with the performance measures in the explicit contract. Since monitoring consumes valuable managerial resources, firms should also consider how the choice of performance measures will affect what activities will need to be directly monitored. To build on our discussion of relative and absolute performance measures, if it is easy for the firm to monitor for actions taken by one employee that are intended to reduce the performance of another, this favors the use of relative measures. The firm can use the information gained from its monitoring to reduce the compensation of any employee who engages in this activity. If, on the other hand, it is easy for the firm to gain information regarding the common random factors affecting employees' performance, these random factors can be filtered through monitoring without relying on relative comparisons.

◆ ◆ ◆ ◆ ◆ DO PAY-FOR-PERFORMANCE INCENTIVES WORK?

Finally, we review recent evidence on the question of whether pay-for-performance incentives work. This question can receive either of two answers, depending on the meaning of the word "work." If this question is taken to mean "Do pay-for-performance incentives in firms affect employees' actions?" the answer appears to be an unqualified yes. However, if the question is taken to mean "Does implementation of pay-for-performance incentives always increase a firm's profits?" the evidence is less clear.

There is ample recent evidence suggesting that employees do appear to consider the effects on their compensation when making decisions.[30] One series of studies has examined simple jobs for which measures of on-the-job performance are easily available. As discussed in Example 14.2, Edward Lazear has documented large increases in employee productivity after Safelite Glass Corporation implemented a piece-rate-based compensation system. Harry Parsch and Bruce Shearer conducted a similar analysis using payroll records from a tree-planting firm in British Columbia. They estimate that tree planters were 22.6 percent more productive when paid on a piece-rate basis as compared to a fixed wage.[31]

For complex jobs, it is somewhat more difficult to assess whether the use of incentive compensation increases productivity. Researchers have instead offered evidence suggesting that pay-for-performance incentives do improve performance *along measured dimensions*. Martin Gaynor, James Rebitzer, and Lowell Taylor, for example, have studied incentives for physicians in an HMO network.[32] They estimate that under the HMO's contract, a physician's pay increases by 10 cents for every $1.00 reduction in medical expenditures. They find that implementation of these cost-sensitive contracts led to a reduction in medical expenditures of 5 percent. They also show that linking pay to measures of quality led to improvements along these quality dimensions. Note, however, that it is not straightforward to conclude from this study that HMO incentives improve the overall provision of health care. "Quality" is difficult to measure, and it is hard to rule out the possibility that the cost reductions and improvements in measured quality come at the expense of quality on unmeasured dimensions.

Related research verifies a prediction of the multitask principle by showing that pay-for-performance will often *reduce* performance on unmeasured (and therefore unrewarded) dimensions. A number of studies have shown that when job placement agencies are rewarded on the basis of their success in placing trainees, they tend to focus their resources on the most qualified candidates at the expense of those in greater need of assistance.[33] In a study of data from an Australian survey of nonsupervisory employees, Robert Drago and Gerald Garvey found that employees help each other less and exert more individual effort when individual-based promotion incentives are strong.[34]

This second set of studies involving complex jobs illustrates why it is difficult to answer the question of whether the use of pay-for-performance incentives increases profits. In cases in which jobs are simple enough for productivity to be measured directly, it is possible to link pay-for-performance to increases in profits. In more complex settings, however, establishing this link is more problematic, for two reasons. First, comparing the profitability of firms offering pay-for-performance incentives to those that do not offer such plans is unlikely to offer a satisfactory answer to the question of whether incentives increase profits. If firms elect different means of compensating employees, it is likely that the sets of performance measures available within the firms are different, and hence that the production technologies used by the firms are different. It is therefore difficult to attribute any differences in profitability across firms to the use of pay-for-performance incentives.

Second, it is relatively easy to find examples in which pay-for-performance compensation plans have had destructive effects. According to our earlier discussion, basing pay on specific measures of performance is useful only if the performance measures are sufficiently good. The performance measures must not be subject to considerable randomness, must not reward activities that the firm does not want employees to pursue, and must not omit activities that the firm does want employees to pursue. Given the complexity of many jobs in a modern economy, the problem of devising good performance measures is difficult, and managers do make mistakes. As our discussion of Lantech shows, well-intentioned incentive compensation plans sometimes have unanticipated side effects.

CHAPTER SUMMARY

◆ Economists use the *principal/agent framework* to analyze firms' interactions with their employees. An agent is hired by a principal to take actions or make decisions that affect the payoff received by the principal.

◆ Problems arise in agency relationships when the action taken by the agent or the information available to the agent cannot be used as the basis for an incentive contract. In these cases, the principal cannot reward the agent directly for the actions he or she undertakes, and hence must rely on other measures of performance to provide incentives.

◆ Employees respond to pay-for-performance incentives by taking actions that maximize their personal net benefits. That is, they compare the personal benefits from their actions to the personal cost. The employee takes the value-maximizing action only if he or she receives the *full* marginal benefit of that action.

◆ Paying for performance is costly if the measures of performance are poor.

◆ If a performance measure is affected by random factors, linking pay more closely to performance places more risk on an employee. Since employees are risk averse, they dislike jobs that involve risky pay, and the firm must compensate the employee for bearing this risk. This makes provision of incentives expensive and means that there is a tradeoff between risk and incentives.

◆ Performance measures may also fail to reflect activities that the firm wants the employee to pursue. According to the multitask principle, stronger incentives will cause employees to focus more on activities that are measured at the expense of activities that are not measured.

◆ Performance measures may also reflect activities that the firm does not want the employee to pursue. Here, stronger incentives will result in employees engaging in more of these counterproductive activities.

◆ Selecting from among performance measures often involves trading off these costs against each other. Frequently, measures that incorporate all aspects of performance will expose employees to considerable risk, while less risky measures will omit valuable aspects of the job.

◆ Evidence on pay-for-performance suggests that employees respond to incentives by increasing performance along measured dimensions.

QUESTIONS

1. Using your own experience, if possible, identify three types of hidden information that could affect an agency relationship. Identity three forms of hidden action as well.

2. Suppose that you were granted a "risky job" of the type examined in this chapter. The job pays $40,000 with probability $1/2$ and $160,000 with probability $1/2$. What is your certainty equivalent for this risky payoff? To answer this question, compare this risky job to a safe job that pays $100,000 for sure. Then reduce the value of the safe job in $1,000 increments until you are indifferent between the safe job and the risky job. What is your certainty equivalent for a job paying $10,000 or $190,000, each with equal probability?

3. In the United Sates, lawyers in negligence cases are usually paid a contingency fee equal to roughly 30 percent of the total award. Lawyers in other types of cases are often paid on an hourly basis. Discuss the merits and drawbacks of each from the perspective of the client (i.e., the principal).

4. Suppose that a firm offers a divisional manager a linear pay-for-performance contract based on the revenues of the division the manager leads. The manager's pay is given by

$$\text{Pay} = F + \alpha \text{ Revenue}$$

where F is a fixed yearly salary and α is the fraction of the division's revenue that is paid to the manager. Suppose that the demand for this type of divisional manager increases, meaning that the firm has to increase this manager's pay in order to retain her. Should the firm do this by increasing the salary F, the commission α, or both? Explain.

5. Regulated firms, such as electric utilities, typically have limited discretion over the prices they charge. Regulators set prices to guarantee a fixed return to the firm's owners after gathering information about operating costs. Studies of executive pay practices have

consistently shown that the compensation of utility CEOs is significantly less sensitive to the firm's performance than that of nonutility CEOs. Explain why, using the tradeoff between risk and incentives.

6. Firms often use quotas as part of compensation contracts for salespeople. A quota-based contract may stipulate, for example, that the salesperson will receive a $10,000 bonus if yearly sales are $1 million or more and no bonus otherwise. Identify actions a firm probably does not want pursued that the employee will be motivated to pursue under such a contract.

7. Though in principle it is feasible for business schools to write explicit pay-for-performance contracts with professors, this is rarely done. Identify drawbacks of the following performance measures for this job:

   • Number of research articles published

   • Students' ratings of professors' courses

   • Dollar value of research grants won

   • Starting salaries of students after graduation

8. Suppose that Minot Farm Equipment Corp. employs two salespeople. Each covers an exclusive territory; one is assigned to North Dakota and the other to South Dakota. These two neighboring states have similar agricultural economies and are affected by the same weather patterns. Durham Tractor Co. also employs two salespeople. One works in North Carolina, and the other is assigned to Oregon. Farm products and methods vary considerably across these two states. Each firm uses the dollar value of annual sales as a performance measure for salespeople. Which of the firms do you think would benefit most from basing pay on its salespeople's relative performance? Why?

9. Consider a potential employee who values wages but also values the opportunity to pursue non–work-related activities. (You may think of these activities as relating to family obligations, such as child care.) Suppose that other jobs available to this employee pay $100 per day but require him to work at the company's facility, effectively eliminating his ability to pursue nonwork activities. Ignore "effort" for the purposes of this problem and assume that the only agency problem pertains to how the employee allocates his time. Suppose that if the employee allocates all of his time in a day to "work," he creates $150 worth of value (gross of wages) for the firm. The employee may also have access to two forms of "nonwork" activities: (1) a high-value nonwork activity (think of unexpected child care needs) and (2) a low-value nonwork activity (think of leisure—playing video games or watching TV). The employee values the ability to complete the high-value nonwork activity at $200 and the ability to complete the low-value nonwork activity at $50.

   a. Suppose first that the low-value nonwork activity does not exist and that the high-value nonwork activity exists with probability 0.10. (*Interpretation:* There is a 10 percent chance that the employee will need to perform an important child-care duty each day.) Suppose that your firm is considering offering this employee a telecommuting job. Assume here that if the employee telecommutes and the high-value activity arises, he spends all his time on this activity and creates no value for the firm that day. If the high-value nonwork activity does not arise, he spends all his time working on behalf of the firm. What daily wage should you offer? What will your profits be? Is your firm better off than if it offered the employee a nontelecommuting job? Why?

   b. Suppose now that the low-value nonwork activity does exist. Unlike the high-value activity (which only arises with some probability), the low-value activity is always present. Suppose also that the firm cannot pay this employee based on individual performance because the available performance measures are of insufficient quality. Suppose that your firm offers the telecommuting job you described in part (a). According to the multitask principle, how will the employee spend his time? Are your profits higher offering the telecommuting job or the nontelecommuting job?

c. Now suppose that the firm does have access to a good measure of individual performance. It can make pay contingent on whether the employee works on the firm's activity. Which job (telecommuting or nontelecommuting) and compensation arrangement (fixed, or fixed plus some variable dependent on output) will maximize the firm's profits? Comment on the types of jobs in which one might expect to see firms offering telecommuting.

10. Oil companies such as British Petroleum and Royal Dutch Shell sell gasoline through their own branded gas stations. In some cases, these companies own their gas stations. In others, the stations are owned by local franchises. How might the following factors affect the choice of corporate versus local ownership?

a. The gas station also does a lot of automotive repairs.

b. The gas station is located on an interstate highway.

c. The gas station has a large convenience store.

ENDNOTES

[1]Quoted in "3M 1 GE 5 ?," *Fortune*, August 12, 2002.

[2]Womack, James P., Daniel T. Jones, and Daniel Roos, *The Machine That Changed the World*, New York, Harper Perennial, 1990.

[3]"Bronx Network Succeeds with Pay System Based on Visits," *Physician Compensation Report*, October 2001.

[4]To derive this, we differentiate the employee's objective with respect to e and find the value of e at which the resulting quantity is equal to zero. This yields $10 = e - 40$, or $e = 50$.

[5]Here, we have calculated the employee's commission payment ($14,000) less effort costs $(1/2 (100)^2 = \$5,000)$ as equal to $9,000. Hence, even if the employee is required to pay the firm $8,000 in order to take the job, the employee will be indifferent between this job and other jobs available in this labor market.

[6]This example is drawn in part from Lafontaine, F. and K. Shaw, "The Dynamics of Franchise Contracting: Evidence from Panel Data," *Journal of Political Economy*, 107, 1999, pp. 1041–1080.

[7]Quoted in "Franchising Creates a Powerful New Class," *Wall Street Journal*, May 21, 1996.

[8]"Kazi Foods Acquires Hawaii Burger Kings," *Pacific Business Journal*, July 5, 2002.

[9]"Cloning Success: Franchising Can Pay Off—If You Have the Right Concept and a Good Strategy," *Wall Street Journal*, June 14, 1999.

[10]"Beauty Chain Receiving Facelift," *China Daily*, June 20, 2005.

[11]This example is drawn from Lazear, E., "Performance Pay and Productivity," *American Economic Review*, 90, 2000, pp. 1346–1361.

[12]Recall that the *expected value* of a random variable is the probability-weighted sum of the possible outcomes. Suppose that the random variable $\tilde{x}$ has possible outcomes given by $(x_1, \ldots, x_n)$. Let the probability that outcome x_i occurs be p_i, and suppose that $\sum_{i=1}^{n} p_i = 1$. The expected value of $\tilde{x}$, $E(\tilde{x})$, is equal to $\sum_{i=1}^{n} p_i x_i$.

[13]If you think you prefer the risky job, consider the following thought experiment. Suppose that you and a friend each take the safe job. You can easily convert these two safe jobs into two risky jobs by betting $60,000 on a coin flip at the end of the year. Would you be willing to do this? Note that it would be easy for people to inject randomness into their wealth in this way, but we rarely observe anyone doing so. This suggests that most people do indeed dislike large random fluctuations in their wealth.

[14]Quoted in P. G. M. Dickinson, *The Sun Insurance Office, 1710–1960*, London, Oxford University Press, 1960.

[15]See Holmstrom, B. and P. Milgrom, "Aggregation and Linearity in the Provision of Intertemporal Incentives," *Econometrica*, 55, 1987, pp. 308–328, and Holmstrom, B. and P. Milgrom, "Multitask Principal-Agent Analyses: Incentive Contracts, Asset Ownership and Job Design," *Journal of Law, Economics & Organization*, 7, 1991, pp. 524–552.

[16]"A Soft Sell for Troubled Times: Retailing's Elite Keep the Armani Moving Off the Racks," *New York Times*, December 22, 2001.

[17]Recall that the variance of a random variable is a measure of spread or dispersion. If the random variable has expected value, the variance of $\tilde{x}$ is given by $E[\,(\tilde{x} - \bar{x})^2\,]$. If values of $\tilde{x}$ that are far above or below $\bar{x}$ are very unlikely, $\tilde{x}$ will have a low variance. If, on the other hand, such values are very likely, $\tilde{x}$ will have a high variance.

[18]This specification of the employee's certainty equivalent is useful for expositional purposes, but it does oversimplify preferences somewhat. In particular, the specification ignores the possibility that an individual may become less risk averse as he or she becomes wealthier.

[19]The marginal cost of effort is the first derivative (or slope) of the cost function with respect to e. The cost function is $\frac{1}{2}\,(e - 40)^2$, which has derivative $(e - 40)$. To find the value of e for which marginal benefit to marginal cost, we have

$$100\alpha = e - 40$$

which yields $e = 40 + 100\alpha$

[20]Note that if the variance of sales is 10,000, the standard deviation of sales is $100.

[21]"Level 3 Communications Begins Trading on NASDAQ," *PR Newswire*, April 1, 1998.

[22]Aggarwal, R. and A. Samwick, "Executive Compensation, Relative Performance Evaluation, and Strategic Competition: Theory and Evidence," *Journal of Finance*, 54, 1999, pp. 1999–2043.

[23]Even this statement must be qualified somewhat. Salespeople are frequently asked to perform non–sales-related tasks such as stock-taking. Sales commissions provide little incentive for this task, and retail salespeople are frequently paid hourly wages for this type of work.

[24]This example is discussed in Holmstrom and Milgrom (1991)

[25]Note, however, that teaching to the test does happen in practice. According to *Catalyst*, an independent publication assessing public school reform in Chicago, some schools have "narrowed their curriculum in the pursuit of (standardized test) gains. At one South Side elementary school, the principal told her faculty to cut science, social studies, and writing from the curriculum and 'just prepare for the test,' an eighth grade teacher reports." See "Accountability Impact Both Positive, Negative," *Catalyst: Voices of Chicago School Reform*, October 2000.

[26]See "Incentive Pay Can Be Crippling," *Fortune*, November 13, 1995.

[27]Many attempts are under way to reform public schools, and many of these make at least some use of standardized test scores to measure performance. In Chicago, for example, three elementary schools were closed in June 2002, in part for failing to improve students' scores. Teachers and administrators from the closed schools were not guaranteed jobs elsewhere in the system. See "Staff at Closing Schools on Their Own," *Chicago Sun Times*, April 14, 2002.

[28]Dranove, David, et al., "Is More Information Better? The Effect of Report Cards on Health Care Providers," *Journal of Political Economy*, 2003, pp. 555–588.

[29]To illustrate, consider a setting in which two salespeople's individual performance measures depend on their effort, their individual luck, and the condition of the local economy. Suppose that employee A's individual performance is $e_A + \bar{\epsilon}_{A1} + \bar{\epsilon}_2$, where $\bar{\epsilon}_{A1}$ is a random variable representing individual luck and $\bar{\epsilon}_2$ is a random variable representing the condition of the local economy. Suppose similarly that employee B's individual performance is $e_B + \bar{\epsilon}_{B1} + \bar{\epsilon}_2$, and that $\bar{\epsilon}_{A1}$ and $\bar{\epsilon}_{B1}$ are independent. In this case, the total variation in employee A's performance is $\bar{\epsilon}_{A1} + \bar{\epsilon}_2$. This is positively correlated with the variation in employee B's performance because $\bar{\epsilon}_2$ affects both. If the firm uses the *difference* between the employees'

individual output as a performance measure, employee A's pay will depend on $e_A - e_B + \bar{\epsilon}_{A1} - \bar{\epsilon}_{B1}$. If the variance of $\bar{\epsilon}_2$ is large relative to that of $\bar{\epsilon}_{A1}$ and $\bar{\epsilon}_{B1}$, this relative measure exposes employees to less risk than does the absolute measure.

[30]This discussion draws from a survey article written by Candice Prendergast. See "The Provision of Incentives in Firms," *Journal of Economic Literature*, 37, 1999, pp. 7–63.

[31]Parsch, H. and B. Shearer, "Piece Rates, Fixed Wages, and Incentive Effects: Statistical Evidence from Payroll Records," *International Economic Review*, 41, 2002, pp. 59–92.

[32]Gaynor, M., J. Rebitzer, and L. Taylor, "Physician Incentives in Health Maintenance Organizations," *Journal of Political Economy*, 2004, pp. 915–932.

[33]See, for example, Anderson, K., R. Burkhauser, and J. Raymond, "The Effect of Creaming on Placement Rates under the Job Training Partnership Act," *Industrial and Labor Relations Review*, 46, 1993, pp. 613–624, and Heckman, J., C. Heinrich, and J. Smith, "Assessing the Performance of Performance Standards in Public Bureaucracies," *American Economic Review*, 87, 1997, pp. 389–395.

[34]Drago, R. and G. Garvey, "Incentives for Helping on the Job: Theory and Evidence," *Journal of Labor Economics*, 16, 1998, pp. 1–25.

INCENTIVES IN FIRMS

15

*F*or many salespeople, pay consists of a salary plus a sales-based commission. Chief executive officers typically receive salary plus stock or options, a form of compensation that links their pay directly to the value of the firm. However, jobs like these—in which pay is determined by a preset formula linked to a numerical measure of performance—are the exception rather than the rule. For many (perhaps most) jobs, basing pay exclusively on a measure like sales or firm value would be counterproductive. Instead, firms rely on other means to motivate employees.

In this chapter we broaden our analysis of agency and incentives. We pose the following central question: how do firms provide incentives when explicit, pay-for-individual-performance contracts are not feasible? We survey the many different mechanisms that firms use to provide incentives in this case, outline the economic reasoning underlying each of these mechanisms, and discuss conditions under which each might be most advantageous.

We proceed by first discussing the role of implicit incentive contracts in mitigating the costs of explicit incentive contracts. We consider the use of subjective performance evaluation and describe properties of promotions and threat of termination as incentive mechanisms. We then discuss how firms provide incentives in cases in which employees work together in teams. Next, we describe how employees' actions may be guided in part by career concerns. Finally, we focus on how incentives and decision making in firms are linked, and argue that managers must examine ways of motivating good decisions as part of determining how to delegate effectively.

IMPLICIT INCENTIVE CONTRACTS ◆ ◆ ◆ ◆ ◆

In this section we discuss how firms provide incentives using implicit contracts. The primary advantage of implicit incentive contracts over explicit incentive contracts is the range of performance measures that can be incorporated. Recall from Chapter 14 that the key property of an explicit incentive contract is that it can be enforced by an outside third party, such as a judge or arbitrator. Because of this, any performance measures incorporated into such contracts must be verifiable; that is, the third party must be able to determine what value was taken by the performance measure. If a performance measure is unverifiable, the judge or arbitrator will be unable to determine whether the contract's terms were met and hence will be unable to enforce it.

Most of the performance measures discussed in Chapter 14 are likely verifiable. Consider, for example, the fraction of a division's sales coming from new products, the number of patients seen by a physician, or the dollar value of goods sold by a salesperson. Assuming that the firm is able to implement reliable internal control systems, each of these measures (at some small cost, perhaps) can be obtained by an outside third party, which can then determine whether the terms of the contract were met. For many jobs, the available verifiable performance measures are imperfect in some way. In Chapter 14 we described three potential ways in which performance measures can be imperfect. (1) The measures may be affected by random factors beyond the employee's control; (2) they may reward activities that the firm does not want the employee to pursue; or (3) they may fail to reward activities that the firm does want the employee to pursue. As an example of a situation with imperfect verifiable performance measures, consider the problem of motivating an employee to share knowledge with other employees. Any time spent codifying and communicating knowledge is, presumably, time taken away from other responsibilities. Hence, according to the multitask principle, employees will tend to ignore this activity if it is not directly rewarded.

But how can a suitable measure of an employee's knowledge-sharing efforts be devised? Firms could base compensation on the number of reports written or the number of suggestions made, but this would clearly motivate employees to write reports or make suggestions even if the information contained therein is of limited value. Ideally, firms would like to write incentive contracts that reward employees for sharing valuable information but not reward them for sharing useless information. The difficulty here is that an outside third party, such as a judge or arbitrator, will not easily be able to determine whether any specific piece of information is valuable to the firm. Hence, any explicit contract based on whether the employee shares valuable information will not be enforceable.

It may, however, be very easy for an employee's supervisor to recognize valuable information when it is shared. The supervisor's assessment can therefore be used as a performance measure in an implicit incentive contract. A firm, perhaps as part of a knowledge management initiative, may announce to an employee, "Your bonus, raise, or promotion depends in part on whether your supervisor believes your information-sharing efforts were good, satisfactory, or poor." As long as there is general agreement between the firm and the employee as to what constitutes valuable information, such an approach can improve on explicit contracts. E-Land, a South Korean fashion retailer, provides an example. While suffering through a severe business slump in late 1998, the firm began asking its employees to post useful information on its intranet. The quality of these tidbits, collected on an employee's "knowledge resume," figures prominently in promotion and bonus decisions.[1] The firm credits this practice with large increases in productivity. Its revenues increased by 21 percent in 2001, and it is now viewed as a market leader.

Although this approach may link rewards more directly to the sharing of valuable information, what mechanism serves to enforce the contract? That is, what is to keep the firm from simply claiming that the employee's information-sharing efforts were poor, and pocketing the funds earmarked for bonuses or raises?

A firm that reneges on its current promises may find that its employees expect it to renege on future promises. If this is so, employees will not be willing to exert effort to achieve good performance. Thus, a firm that goes back on its promises will profit in the short term by saving the funds earmarked for bonuses and raises, but it will lose in the longer term because the emloyees will not be willing to put forth their full effort. To put this another way, reneging on an implicit contract may cost the firm its reputation as a good employer.

Firms using implicit contracts must therefore take special care to ensure that employees perceive the firm to be acting in accordance with those contracts. Firms should try to verify that performance standards are applied consistently across the organization and should communicate clearly with employees in the event economic conditions preclude the payment of promised bonuses or raises.

Subjective Performance Evaluation

As E-Land's example demonstrates, one advantage of implicit contracts is that they allow firms to use subjective assessments as performance measures. Firms implement subjective performance evaluation in a variety of ways. Some perform *360-degree peer reviews*, in which an employee's supervisor, coworkers, and subordinates are all asked to provide information regarding that employee's performance over a period of time. Others use *management by objective systems* whereby an employee and a supervisor work together to construct a set of goals for the employee. At the end of some specified period, the supervisor and the employee meet to review the employee's performance on the preset goals. The employee's performance assessment depends not just on whether the goals were reached but also on the presence of other factors that may have made them unexpectedly easy or difficult to attain. Still other firms implement *merit rating systems*, in which employees are given numerical scores. Often these systems give supervisors a fixed pool of points to be allocated among employees. The common thread among all these systems is that firms use judgments made by other employees (supervisors and, in some cases, others) in assessing performance.

Incorporating subjective assessments of employee performance into the compensation process has important potential advantages, but there are two costs to consider. First, supervisors may find it personally unpleasant to reward some employees but not others. To avoid making sharp distinctions among subordinates, supervisors may give all their subordinates an average (or even above-average) grade. This effect, known as *ratings compression*, weakens incentives; if all employees receive the same grade all the time, there is little reason to strive for a high mark.

This raises the question of how the firm can provide incentives for supervisors to provide good evaluations. Some have experimented with forced rankings systems, in which evaluators are required to grade employees on a curve. Sun Microsystems, for example, requires supervisors to rate 20 percent of employees as superior, 70 percent as Sun standard, and 10 percent as underperforming.[2] Although this approach counteracts supervisors' tendency to rate everyone as average or better, firms must be careful to apply evaluation criteria fairly. Since 1999, Microsoft, Ford Motor Company, and Conoco, among others, have been sued by employees who have alleged that poor evaluations reflect supervisors' biases rather than their own performance.

Second, subjective assessments of performance are subject to influence activity. Subordinates may attempt to affect their evaluations by establishing good personal relationships with supervisors. Although such relationships may be valuable to a certain extent, employees may choose to spend too much time developing them.

Employees may also lobby, hide information, or gain "face time." Chris Congdon, a computer support specialist at Ford, says that he was able to increase his ranking by regularly e-mailing computing-related news articles to all members of his department. This, he claims, increased his visibility to supervisors, even though the articles were of little value to computer users.[3] Where possible, firms may try to limit influence activity by restricting access to decision makers. This remedy is difficult to apply in this case, since supervisors must interact closely with employees in order to make good subjective evaluations. Thus, when assessing the efficacy of subjective performance measures, it is important to weigh the costs against the benefits. A good performance measure has limited noise, reflects all the activities a firm wants its employees to undertake, and reflects no activities the firm does not want them to undertake. As we have seen, subjective measures can cause employees to work to raise their visibility to supervisors, which, presumably, the firm does not value. Similarly, subjective measures can be noisy, especially if a supervisor is responsible for many employees and therefore has somewhat limited interaction with each. Various types of subjective measures can be analyzed and weighed against each other in much the same way as the nonsubjective measures discussed in Chapter 14.

Promotion Tournaments

One important way in which subjective evaluations are used in determining payoffs to employees is through promotions. In most firms, promotions involve marked increases in wages, which means that employees have strong incentives to take actions that will increase their likelihood of being promoted. Promotion criteria are, however, not typically written down as part of an explicit contract. Instead, there is a general understanding between the firm and its employees as to what sorts of actions will lead to promotion. Firms usually offer promotions to employees whose performance in lower-level jobs is especially good or to employees who demonstrate skills that are valuable in higher-level jobs.

As Edward Lazear and Sherwin Rosen have pointed out, promotion-based incentives often take the form of a tournament.[4] In a tennis, golf, or football tournament, a set of players or teams competes to win a prize. In a *promotion tournament*, a set of employees competes to win a promotion. Consider the case of a bank that employs two senior loan officers. One of the two officers will be promoted to vice president, and the promotion will take place in approximately a year's time. If the duties of a vice president are somewhat similar to those of a senior loan officer, it may be sensible for the bank to promote the loan officer who turns in the best performance in that job.

Suppose that the salary paid to senior loan officers is w. As part of the promotion, the winning loan officer receives a raise that increases his salary to w^*. The losing loan officer remains with the firm as a loan officer but receives no raise. Hence, the prize that accompanies the promotion is the wage differential $w^* - w$.[5] Given the firm's promotion policy, the first officer can increase the likelihood of being promoted to vice president by increasing his effort level. Let the probability that officer 1 is promoted, given his effort choice, be $p(e_1)$, and suppose that the cost to officer 1 of making effort choice e_1 is $c(e_1)$.

Therefore, the first loan officer will select his effort so as to maximize

$$p(e_1)(w^* - w) - c(e_1)$$

The loan officer chooses an effort level by making a cost/benefit comparison. The marginal benefit of effort comes from the fact that an increase in effort results in the increased probability of winning the promotion. The increase in the probability of winning times the value of winning is the marginal benefit of effort. In selecting his or her effort level, the first loan officer will equate the marginal benefit of effort to the marginal cost.[6]

Recall that in our discussion of commission-based pay in Chapter 14, we found that a principal can affect the marginal benefit of effort by increasing the commission rate. What tools can the firm use to affect an agent's effort choice in a tournament? Here, the firm can increase the marginal benefit of effort by increasing the wage differential $w^* - w$. That is, by increasing the size of the prize, the firm can induce employees to work harder to earn it. To use a sports analogy, tennis players may value a singles championship at Wimbledon more highly than a championship at any other tournament; if so, they will exert more effort to win there than at any other event.

Just as firms can select the commission rate that maximizes profits, they can select the profit-maximizing prize. Increasing the size of the prize in a tournament has effects similar to those of increasing the commission rate in a pay-for-performance contract: a larger prize causes the employee to work harder, but it also causes him or her to bear more risk. The optimal prize, like the optimal commission rate, balances risk against incentives. If the firm chooses to increase the size of its prize, it should do so by both increasing w^* and reducing w. To see why it should adjust both, note that a potential employee will take into account both wages in making decisions about where to work. Just reducing the senior loan officer's wage, w, would make this job less attractive to potential employees and thus make it harder to fill. Just increasing w^* makes the senior loan officer's job more attractive (since the promotion prospects attached to this job are more attractive) and means that the firm can reduce w somewhat and still hire senior loan officers.

Given this formulation, we can identify three important properties of promotion tournaments:

1. As we have already shown, employees' effort levels increase as the difference between the vice president and senior loan officer's salaries increases.
2. If the bank adds competitors to the tournament, it can maintain the same incentives for effort simply by increasing the size of the prize. To illustrate this point, consider the effect of adding a third senior loan officer to the tournament. This presumably reduces the likelihood that the first officer will win, for now the officer must outperform *both* loan officer 2 *and* loan officer 3 to earn the promotion. The firm can offset this reduction in officer 1's marginal benefit of effort by increasing w^* or reducing w, thus making winning more valuable.
3. Sherwin Rosen has shown that if there are successive rounds of promotion tournaments, the wage differentials between levels must increase in order to maintain the same incentives for effort.[7] Consider adding another round to the tournament described earlier. Suppose that if a senior loan officer is promoted to vice president, the officer then participates in another tournament, which may result in eventual promotion to chief executive officer (CEO). If a senior loan officer is not promoted to vice president, he or she cannot subsequently become CEO. Accordingly, part of the prize associated with being promoted to vice president is the right to compete for the CEO position. If the firm wants to motivate the same effort level from vice presidents as from senior loan officers, the CEO/vice president wage differential must be larger than the vice president/senior loan officer wage differential.

Promotion tournaments have both advantages and disadvantages. In deciding whether to use tournaments to provide incentives, a firm must consider the extent to which these factors apply to its specific situation. Advantages of using tournaments for incentives include the following:

- Tournaments circumvent the problem of supervisors who are unwilling to make sharp distinctions between employees. To see why, consider a supervisor who controls a bonus pool that can be divided among a set of subordinates. If the supervisor finds it costly to differentiate among subordinates, he or she may elect to distribute the bonus pool roughly equally. This means that the difference between the bonuses paid to top and bottom performers will be small, and incentives to be a top performer will be weak. Since a promotion is an indivisible reward, the difference between the payoffs received by top and bottom performers is necessarily large, and incentives to be a top performer are strong. This reasoning suggests that any "winner-take-all" reward can serve to counteract compression in subjective evaluations.

- Tournaments are a form of relative performance evaluation. Because only the relative ranking of competitors affects who gets the prize, any common random factors that affect performance are netted out. If bank loan officers are evaluated in part on the profitability of their loan portfolios, the quality of the local economy will affect both. However, since the promotion goes to the officer who achieves the best performance, the quality of the local economy will not affect the payoffs to either officer.

Potential disadvantages of tournaments include the following:

- A conflict exists between providing incentives for good performance in lower-level jobs and selecting the best person for a higher-level job. In our example involving bank loan officers, it could easily be the case that the employee who achieves the best performance as a senior loan officer is not the employee who holds the greatest promise as a vice president. This may be especially likely if the lower- and higher-level jobs require markedly different skill sets.

- As discussed in Chapter 14, relative performance evaluation rewards employees for taking actions that hamper the performance of other employees. Hence, firms need to consider whether such actions can be monitored and discouraged before implementing tournament-based incentives.

A study by George Baker, Michael Gibbs, and Bengt Holmstrom has confirmed the link between promotions and wage growth.[8] They obtained confidential personnel records from a large U.S. firm and found that employees received substantial increases in pay (5 to 7 percent, depending on level) when they were promoted. Notably, they report that promotions did not appear to be the only factor determining variations in wages. That is, unlike the tournament model we have sketched here, it did not appear that all employees at lower levels earned the same wage, with wage increases coming only with promotions. These findings suggest that firms may use tournaments in conjunction with merit-based raises within job ranks.

Other researchers have studied intrafirm wage differentials for evidence of tournament effects. Brian Main, Charles O'Reilly, and James Wade, for example, found that wage differentials increase with rank, as one would expect if tournaments consist of successive rounds of elimination. They also found that the difference in salary between chief executive officers and corporate vice presidents is larger in firms that

EXAMPLE 15.1 PROMOTION TOURNAMENTS AT GENERAL ELECTRIC

On November 28, 2000, Jeffrey Immelt was named president and chairman-elect of General Electric Company (GE), succeeding Jack Welch. Immelt, who had previously led GE Medical Systems, was chosen by the firm's board from a field of three candidates that also included GE Power Systems chief Robert Nardelli and GE Aircraft Engines head James McNerney. The three had each worked for GE for more than 15 years, and each had been very successful in a number of roles.[11]

The firm conducted a rather public "horse race" among the three candidates. Welch announced in 1996 that by the summer of 2000 he intended to identify three candidates for the top job. Although the firm never publicly identified the candidates, press accounts tabbing the trio as the main contenders appeared as early as mid-1999. In selecting Immelt, Welch lauded the new CEO's team-building skills and technological background, and hoped that Immelt—only 44 when named as Welch's successor—would be able to run the firm for 20 years or more.

Immelt received a substantial boost in pay to match his new responsibilities. According to the firm's March 8, 2002, proxy statement, Immelt's salary plus bonus in 2001 amounted to $6.25 million, a 78 percent raise over his 2000 salary-plus-bonus figure of $3.5 million.

Nardelli and McNerney were disappointed, but their talents were quickly put to good use elsewhere. Within a week of Immelt's succession, Nardelli was hired as CEO of Home Depot, while McNerney took the top job at 3M. According to their firms' 2001 disclosures to the Securities and Exchange Commission, Nardelli was paid about $6 million in 2001, and McNerney earned nearly $4 million. To retain these managers, General Electric would presumably have had to offer comparable compensation packages—rather high prices to pay for mere "management team" members. Anticipating the departure of the tournament's losers, the firm designated successors at its Medical Systems, Power Systems, and Aircraft Engines divisions in June 2000, well in advance of the final decision.

Welch himself had been chosen for the post of CEO at General Electric in a very similar process that unfolded 21 years earlier. In August 1979, then-CEO Reg Jones announced a three-man race between Welch, Ed Hood, and John Burlingame. Just over a year later, in December 1980, Jones recommended to GE's board that Welch take over as CEO. Unlike the later succession race, both Hood and Burlingame stayed with the firm in the position of vice chairman. Burlingame remained at GE until 1985, while Hood remained a director until 1993.

---

have more vice presidents. If more VPs mean more competitors in the CEO tournament, firms may set a larger prize in order to maintain effort incentives.[9] Tor Eriksson obtained similar findings using a broad sample of 2,600 executives at 210 Danish firms between 1992 and 1995.[10]

Efficiency Wages and the Threat of Termination

Another way in which firms can link employees' rewards to performance is through the threat of firing. Like tournaments, firing-based incentives are usually implicit; firms do not often write contracts with employees stating that the employee will be fired if some easily measurable aspect of performance is below a preset standard. Instead, firms offer continued employment to those employees whose performance is "satisfactory," where the meaning of this term is usually understood by both parties but not carefully defined. To study termination-based incentives, we sketch a simple model in which an employee must decide whether to work hard. Suppose that the cost to the employee of working hard is $50; this means that the employee will work hard if and only if doing so raises her expected pay by at least $50. If, on the one hand, the employee works hard, the probability that the firm will find her performance to be satisfactory is 1. If, on the other hand, the employee does not work hard, the firm is able to detect this lack of effort with probability p, where $p < 1$. If the firm discovers that the employee has not worked hard, the employee's performance is judged to be unsatisfactory and she is fired.

If the employee keeps the job, she earns wage w; if the employee is fired, she seeks out her next-best employment opportunity, which pays w^{**}.[12] In deciding whether to work hard, the employee compares the net payoff from working hard to the net payoff from shirking (that is, choosing not to work hard). If she works hard, she incurs effort costs of $50 but gets to keep the job. In this case her expected payoff is

$$w - \$50$$

If the employee shirks, she incurs no effort costs. Shirking is detected with probability p, and in this case the employee earns the next-best wage, w^{**}. If shirking is not detected, the employee keeps the job and earns w. Her expected payoff is therefore

$$pw^{**} + (1 - p)w$$

The employee will choose to work hard if

$$w - \$50 > pw^{**} + (1 - p)w$$

or, equivalently, if

$$p(w - w^{**}) > \$50$$

This last inequality has a highly intuitive interpretation. On the left-hand side, $w - w^{**}$ is the cost associated with being fired. It is the difference between the value to the employee of the current job and the value of the next-best job. The variable p is the probability of being fired if the employee shirks. Hence, $p(w - w^{**})$ is the expected cost incurred by the employee if she decides to shirk. On the right-hand side, $50 is the cost to the employee if she decides to work hard. The inequality states that the employee will work hard if the expected cost of shirking is greater than the cost of working hard. What tools does the firm have to affect the employee's actions? As one might expect, the firm can more easily motivate hard work if it detects shirking more often. That is, if p is higher, the expected cost of shirking is higher, and this tips the employee's cost/benefit tradeoff in the direction of hard work. However, this model also identifies a second way for the firm to affect the employee's actions. Firms can increase the expected cost of shirking by *raising the employee's wage*, w. That is, by making the job more valuable, the firm can motivate an employee to take actions (such as working hard) that enable him or her to keep the job.

Carl Shapiro and Joseph Stiglitz refer to a wage that is high enough to motivate effort as an *efficiency wage*.[13] They use this idea to explain how having a pool of unemployed workers in a labor market serves to provide incentives for those who are employed. If, on the one hand, all firms offer a wage w and fired workers can easily find new employment at this wage, then w^{**} is close to w. This means that being fired involves no loss to the worker and hence has no incentive effects. If, on the other hand, being fired means a long and costly spell of unemployment, the prospect of being caught shirking will provide an incentive to work hard.

It is not difficult to find cases of firms paying what appear to be above-market wages. In one well-known example, on January 5, 1914, the Ford Motor Company announced an increase in workers' wages from $2.30 per day to $5. The "Five-Dollar Day," as it became known, was introduced in tandem with adoption of the eight-hour workday and an increase in the number of work shifts from two to three. Henry Ford told reporters that his plan was "neither charity nor wages, but profit sharing and efficiency engineering."[14] According to Ford's later statements, the firm found that the change in wage policy improved both the discipline and efficiency of its workforce. Ford workers did not dare risk their jobs—there were no alternatives anywhere near as attractive. These effects are consistent with the view that the increase in wages raised the value of a Ford job to employees, making efforts to keep the job more valuable.[15] This observation may also help explain why some firms offer nonwage benefits that potential employees see as especially attractive. Consider, for example, firms that appear on lists such as *Fortune* magazine's "Top 100 Companies to Work For." These firms' employee-friendly policies may increase employees' effort by making these jobs especially valuable.

One important implication of efficiency wages is that high wages and monitoring are substitutes for each other. That is, if it is costly for the firm to monitor workers, the firm can instead provide strong termination-based incentives by making employees' jobs valuable. Monitoring may be costly if it requires firms to hire supervisors or develop management information systems. This suggests that high efficiency wages are most useful in cases in which it is difficult for the firm to observe the employee's actions. A study by Erica Groshen and Alan Krueger examines the relationship between the wages of staff nurses and the number of supervisory workers.[16] Consistent with the efficiency wage explanations, they found that wages tend to be lower when more supervisors are present.

The logic of efficiency wages also suggests that the firm's legal environment can have a significant effect on its pay policies. In the United States, for example, employment relationships have historically been governed by the doctrine of at-will employment. This means that both the employer and the employee are free to end the relationship at any time and for any reason.[17] In contrast, in continental Europe many nations place significant restrictions on firms' ability to fire workers. In Italy, an employee who is fired has the right to appeal the firm's decision to a judge. If the judge overturns the firing, the firm is required to place the employee back on the payroll, pay him or her the wages lost during the period of the litigation, and pay a fine to the nation's social security system.[18]

These different legal regimes may have significant consequences for the efficacy of termination-based incentives. Note that the required magnitude of an efficiency wage depends crucially on the probability of being fired conditional on exerting low effort. If p is high, shirking can be unattractive to the employee even if $w - w^{**}$ is small. If p is low, $w - w^{**}$ must be large in order to make shirking unattractive. If, on the one hand, it is not difficult for firms to fire workers who are caught shirking, a low-efficiency wage will be sufficient to induce high effort. On the other hand, if there are restrictions on firms' abilities to fire workers, the probability of being fired even if caught shirking may be low. In this case, the firm would need to pay a very high efficiency wage in order to induce workers not to shirk. Firms may need to abandon efficiency wages and termination-based incentives altogether and instead focus on other means of providing incentives.[19]

◆ ◆ ◆ ◆ ◆ INCENTIVES IN TEAMS

Often firms find that the most effective means of production involves asking a group of employees to work together. Consider, for example, the development of the Scorpio, a new sport-utility vehicle designed by Mahindra & Mahindra, India's largest seller of utility automobiles. The firm practiced what it calls Integrated Design and Manufacturing (IDAM), splitting a 120-person development staff into 19 cross-functional teams. Each team, which combined marketing and engineering professionals, tried to find ways of meeting marketing aims while keeping manufacturing costs low. Team leaders were made accountable for guaranteeing that targets were met. Mahindra & Mahindra credits the IDAM method with keeping design costs under control; the firm claims that it spent just 6 billion rupees ($120 million) to design the Scorpio, compared to the 17 billion rupees rival Tata Engineering spent on the Indica passenger car.[20] Examples such as this have become common throughout the world in recent years.

Achieving the full benefits of team production requires rewarding individuals for how the team performs as a whole. Note that Mahindra & Mahindra could, in principle, have attempted to separately identify each team member's contribution toward the final Scorpio design. The firm could have rewarded design engineers for improvements that resulted in lower manufacturing costs, and could have rewarded marketing executives for innovations that increased the vehicle's market appeal. This approach would have led to problems, however, if a marketing executive had proposed a new product feature that increased manufacturing costs. If design engineers care only about the cost of manufacturing the new product, they may resist endorsing the new feature, even if it will increase the product's revenue by more than the increase in cost. This problem is especially severe if only the design engineers can determine the increase in manufacturing costs associated with the new feature. The engineers may overstate the effect of the feature on costs in order to block its adoption.

Of course, the firm is best off if the employees work together to determine whether the expected increase in revenue associated with the new feature is larger than the expected increase in manufacturing costs. If performance is measured at the individual level, however, there is little incentive for the employees to combine their knowledge to make the decision that is best overall. Measuring performance by the overall profits generated by the new product eliminates this problem and motivates all parties to work together.

In order to realize this important benefit, however, firms must develop ways to combat the costs of team-based performance measures. To illustrate these costs, consider a design engineer working as part of a six-person team to design part of a new automobile. Suppose that all team members are evaluated on whether their design meets certain marketing objectives and cost targets. The team will split a bonus of $1,000 if the targets are met, but it will receive no additional compensation if targets are not met.

Suppose that the design engineer gets an idea for an alternative design for the vehicle part. The engineer believes the alternative design will reduce manufacturing costs substantially and therefore will increase the likelihood of meeting design targets from 40 to 70 percent. Although the idea seems promising, it will take considerable time and effort for the design engineer to work out all the details. Will the engineer be willing to exert the effort necessary to fully develop this idea?

In making this decision, the engineer will weigh the costs against the benefits. If the engineer develops the idea, the likelihood of the team's success in meeting targets goes up by 30 percentage points, which means that the expected bonus paid to the team increases by $300. This bonus is split among the six team members, so developing the idea causes the design engineer's expected bonus to increase by $50.

If the cost, in terms of time and effort, to the design engineer of working out the idea's details is less than $50, the engineer will likely be willing to do so. Note, however, that the overall payoff to the team—that is, the sum of the increase in expected bonus to all team members—is $300 if the idea is pursued. If the cost of pursuing the new idea is less than $300 but greater than $50, the team would be better off if the new idea is pursued, but the design engineer will not be willing to do so.

The key insight here is that team-based performance measures mean that the benefits from an individual's actions are *shared* with the entire team. Hence, if there are n members in the team, the individual taking the action receives just $1/n$ of the benefit. Consider, then, any actions with the following two properties:

1. Total benefit to team from action > total cost of action.
2. Total cost of action > $(1/n)$ * total benefit to team from action.

Actions with property (1) are value-creating actions in that the total benefit is greater than the total cost. However, since the individual undertaking the action compares this cost to the *personal benefit*, actions with property (2) may not be undertaken. The mismatch between the total benefit to the team and the personal benefit to the design engineer means that the design engineer's effort choices may not be the ones that maximize overall welfare.

This effect is known as the *free-rider problem*, although this name may be something of a misnomer. The phrase suggests that one team member may elect not to work and instead try to get a "free ride" on the efforts of his or her teammates. The problem is even worse than the phrase suggests, however, since it affects not just one but *every* team member. Because every team members receives $1/n$ of the total benefit from his or her actions, every team member will elect not to undertake actions that satisfy properties (1) and (2). The risk, then, is not simply that one team member will fail to take valuable actions but that *all* team members will fail to take valuable actions.

While our example makes use of a bonus based on a verifiable performance measure, free-rider problems are present even if team performance is used as an input into a subjective performance evaluation system. Suppose that a marketing executive's raise, bonus, or promotion depends on a supervisor's subjective assessment of the quality of the marketer's joint work with the design engineer. The design engineer's efforts will affect the performance evaluations of both employees. In making an effort choice, however, the design engineer may fail to take into account the effect of his or her actions on the marketer's raise or promotion.

The free-rider problem can be exacerbated by the multitask principle. Suppose, for example, that a design engineer pursues two tasks. The first is a solo project in which the engineer works to design parts for a new vehicle without input from marketing. The second is the team-based project described earlier. The design engineer receives the full benefit associated with any actions toward the first task but shares the benefit associated with the second task with team members. If the design engineer must decide how to spend his or her time, the weaker incentives associated with the team-based task may lead to a focus on the individual-based task at the expense of the team-based task.

Researchers studying the free-rider problem have focused on professional partnerships. Partnership arrangements are common in law, accounting, medicine, and consulting. Such firms typically pool the profits generated by each partner's activities and divide this pool among the partners according to some predetermined sharing rule. Sharing rules vary across firms and industries, with some firms dividing the pool equally (so that each partner receives share $1/n$ of the total) and others awarding somewhat larger shares to partners who are more productive or more senior. Regardless of the particular sharing rule, it is always the case that some fraction of the profit generated by an individual is captured by the other partners. This means that the personal benefit from effort is always lower than the total benefit, raising the possibility that partners will provide too little effort. Martin Gaynor and Mark Pauly demonstrated this effect in their study of medical practices. They found that increases in the size of partnerships led to reductions in individual productivity.[21] Similarly, a study of law firms by Arleen Leibowitz and Robert Tollison revealed that larger firms were less able to contain costs than smaller ones.[22] Firms can mitigate the free-rider problem in a number of ways. First, they can keep teams small. Property (2) suggests that as the number of team members (n) increases, effort incentives become weaker.

Second, firms can allow employees to work together for long periods. Repeated interaction allows team members to make their current actions depend on what other members have done in the past. Thus, if one member fails to contribute to the team's goals today, others can punish the miscreant in the future. Punishments can take the form of peer pressure, social isolation, or simply refusing to help that individual.

The addition of future periods of interaction to a team-based incentive problem changes the nature of each individual's decision. Recall that an individual within a team makes an action choice based on a cost/benefit comparison. If the personal benefit from an action (which, as we have shown, is only $1/n$ of the total benefit) is greater than the personal cost, the individual will take the action. In a repeated interaction, failure to take an action today can result in future punishments. Hence, an extra *benefit* to an individual of taking a value-creating action today is that future punishments are avoided. This additional benefit helps tip the cost/benefit balance in a direction that favors value-creating actions. However, as Margaret Meyer has pointed out, stable teams have the potential drawback of making it difficult for firms to learn about employees' abilities.[23] Suppose, for example, that a design engineer works repeatedly with the same marketing executive and the resulting products are highly successful. If the firm seeks to identify high-ability employees in order to promote them to positions with greater responsibility, how can it identify which of the two employees is ready to be promoted? The team's success could be due to high ability on the part of either of its members, or both. If a design engineer works with a variety of different marketing executives, it may be easier for the firm to identify high performers. If there are large long-run benefits associated with identifying high-potential individuals, the firm may institute regular rotations of team assignments, even though this could hamper team performance in the short run.

Third, firms can attempt to structure teams so that their members can monitor one another's actions. The benefits of repeated play described earlier can be obtained only if team members are able to identify other members who fail to take actions that further the team's objectives. Mark Knez and Duncan Simester illustrated this point in their study of team-based incentives at Continental Airlines.[24] In 1995, the firm offered each hourly worker a $65 bonus for every month in which the firm ranked among the top five in the industry in on-time arrivals. Although this scheme would appear to suffer from severe free-rider problems, Knez and Simester found that

EXAMPLE 15.2 STOCK OPTIONS FOR MIDDLE-LEVEL EMPLOYEES

3Com Corporation, a manufacturer of networking equipment headquartered in Santa Clara, California, employs more than 4,500 people worldwide. According to the firm's web site, 3Com has a policy of granting stock options to all newly hired employees. A stock option is a contract that allows the employee to purchase a share of the firm's stock at a specified price (the exercise price) at any time up until a preset expiration date. Option grants to employees typically come with a vesting period, which means that the employee cannot exercise the option immediately but must wait until the vesting period is over. Thus, at any point after the end of the vesting period but before the expiration date, the employee can exercise the option and, if he or she wishes, immediately sell the shares, pocketing the difference between the stock price and the exercise price. Since the options are worth more if the stock price is higher, the employee has ample reason to care about the firm's overall performance.

Two recent surveys shed light on firms' option-granting decisions. The Bureau of Labor Statistics, an office of the U.S. Department of Labor, surveyed a random sample of establishments in the United States, asking whether, and if so to whom, they granted stock options. Just 1.4 percent of U.S. business establishments granted stock options to nonexecutive employees in 1999. A second survey, conducted by the National Center for Employee Ownership (NCEO), questioned only firms that elect to grant options to middle- and lower-level employees. At those firms, option grants tended to have the following characteristics: (1) Options were typically granted "at-the-money," meaning that the exercise price was set at the market price on the date of the grant; (2) the options typically expired after 10 years; and (3) they became fully vested after four years. Option grants made up a fairly large fraction of overall compensation at the NCEO survey firms. At one medium-sized

firm, newly hired middle managers were paid an annual salary of $70,000 but received option grants potentially worth $224,000. If the firm planned to replenish the employee's options every four years, options accounted for 44 percent of the employee's overall compensation.

This grant had a large value, but the incentive effects associated with it were quite small. Because the firm had a large number of shares outstanding, the grant comprised only 0.066 percent of the firm's outstanding shares. This means that if the middle manager took an action that caused the value of the firm to increase by, say, twice his or her annual salary, the value of the option package would increase by at most 0.066 percent of $140,000, or just $92.

Given that the price of the firm's shares could go up or down, this form of compensation injected considerable risk into the employee's pay. If the firm's share price falls below the exercise price (which it could do, even if the employee's performance is good), the options may be worth nothing. On the other hand, if the firm is very successful (which it could be, even if the employee's performance is poor), the options could be worth considerably more than the initial figure of $224,000.

Paul Oyer and Scott Schaefer have shown that, even assuming a fairly risk tolerant employee, the risk premium associated with this option grant is around $40,000.[26] This figure led them to question whether stock option packages are effective incentive mechanisms. Wouldn't the firm be better off, they asked, using subjective performance evaluations to determine which middle managers take actions that lead to large increases in the value of the firm? The firm could then offer raises of $1,000 (or more) to managers who take actions that result in large increases in the firm's value. This would provide *stronger* effort incentives without causing employees' compensation to move up and down with the firm's share price.

Continental's on-time arrival rates increased at airports where the system was implemented. They argued that an important aspect of Continental's success was the division of the firm's employees into autonomous work groups at each airport location. Members of these groups could easily observe one another's actions, and such monitoring benefited the firm in two ways. First, sources of delay were quickly discovered, and employees were motivated to offer help in clearing the bottlenecks. Second, if the delay was due to poor performance by one team member, the other members could act to punish the offender by challenging that person publicly or reporting him or her to management. These benefits could not have been achieved had employees been unable to observe one another's actions.

◆ ◆ ◆ ◆ ◆ CAREER CONCERNS AND LONG-TERM EMPLOYMENT

Eugene Fama has argued that, for some jobs, important incentives are provided by employees' career concerns.[26] If employees can regularly "test the market" for their skills, their current actions may affect their future market value. Employees therefore will select current actions with an eye toward keeping their market value high. Investment bankers, mutual fund managers, and professional athletes are examples of employees whose actions may be driven in part by a desire to keep their future prospects bright.

From the firm's perspective, employees' career concerns may either simplify or complicate the problem of providing incentives, depending on the circumstances. Consider, for example, the problem of providing incentives to professional athletes in team sports. Explicit pay-for-performance contracts would clearly lead individual athletes to take actions that do not further the interests of the team. For example, paying soccer forwards according to the number of goals scored would encourage these athletes to take excessive risks in attempting to score, leaving the team vulnerable to counterattack. A forward's market value, however, will likely depend on whether potential employers believe that the forward has sufficiently good judgment. Hence, a player whose actions are driven by concern for this market value will attempt to exhibit good judgment in pressing attacks. The presence of career concerns here helps alleviate problems associated with explicit incentive contracts. As Example 15.3 illustrates, career concerns can also cause employees to take actions that may not be in the firms' interests, thus exacerbating incentive problems.

One important property of incentives based on career concerns is that they wane as the employee nears the end of his or her career. Robert Gibbons and Kevin Murphy demonstrated this effect in a study of chief executive officers.[27] They found that firms linked pay more and more closely to firm performance as CEOs neared retirement age. This suggests substitution toward explicit incentives as the implicit incentives provided by career concerns diminish. Sports teams appear to be aware of this effect as well, as they often attempt to incorporate more explicit performance measures in contracts with athletes whose career concerns are limited. In 1997, for example, the Chicago White Sox signed 29-year-old baseball star Frank Thomas to a nine-year contract for around $10 million per season. Since it is rare for players to compete past their late 30s, this contract was likely to be the last one of Thomas's career. The team insisted that the deal include a clause allowing it to reduce the player's pay if he failed to be named to the All-Star Team, win the league's Silver Slugger

EXAMPLE 15.3 CAREER CONCERNS OF MUTUAL FUND MANAGERS

Mutual fund companies typically hire managers to make investment decisions for their funds. For index funds (i.e., funds that aim to match the return on a stock index like the S&P 500 or the Wilshire 5000), there are relatively few decisions to make. These managers simply aim to buy and sell shares in the right proportions to keep their holdings in line with the index. Actively managed funds, however, give managers considerable discretion over what stocks to hold. Funds often specialize in a certain class of stocks by stating an objective such as growth or income. Managers are given a free hand to choose stocks that fit the fund's objective.

Judy Chevalier and Glenn Ellison studied how career concerns might affect fund managers' portfolio allocation decisions.[29] They argued that career concerns are likely to be most important for young fund managers. To see why, consider a fund manager who suffers through a year in which his fund performs poorly. If that manager has a long track record of good performance, the fund company is likely to attribute the poor year to bad luck rather than to lack of ability on the part of the manager. If, on the other hand, the manager is new to the job, the firm may attribute the low returns to poor choices on the part of the manager and fire him.

To examine this issue, Chevalier and Ellison collected data on fund performance and fund manager characteristics. They found that mutual fund managers are frequently fired and that firing usually follows a period in which the manager's fund performs poorly relative to other funds with the same objective. They also found that the probability of being fired increases much more quickly with poor relative performance for young managers than for older managers.

This set of facts means that incentives are especially strong for young fund managers to avoid poor relative performance. One way young managers can do this is by choosing to hold similar portfolios to those of other funds within the same objective class. By "following the herd," a young manager can reduce the likelihood of performing badly while comparable funds perform well, and thus reduce the likelihood of being fired.

Chevalier and Ellison found strong evidence that young fund managers do exactly this. To measure herding behavior, they computed the fraction of each fund's holdings that are allocated to stocks from each of 10 industries. They then compared these fractions across funds within an objective class to see which managers were acting in concert with others and which ones were striking out on their own. To illustrate their result, suppose that the typical growth fund placed 20 percent of its assets in shares of telecommunications firms. Chevalier and Ellison found that young managers were far less likely to decide to place 10 or 30 percent of their fund's assets in telecom shares. Instead, they tended to allocate their assets in a pattern very comparable to that selected by others. Older managers, for whom career concerns are less salient, were more likely to make bold allocations that depart from the herd.

How are a fund's investors affected? Investors choosing actively managed funds presumably want managers to gather information and use it to try to earn high returns. It appears, however, that young fund managers' career concerns make them less willing to make bold allocation decisions based on information that is uniquely their own.

award, or finish among the top 10 in voting for the league's Most Valuable Player award.[28] Unfortunately for Thomas, he suffered through poor seasons in 2001 and 2002, and the team elected to invoke this clause.

The presence of career concerns can have important implications for employees' choices about what types of skills to acquire. An employee whose aim is to increase her value to alternative employers will be unwilling to invest in acquiring skills that are of value only to her current employer. Employees who believe that they may change jobs in the future may thus be willing to invest in general-purpose human capital—that is, in skills that will be of use to a broad range of employers—but may not be willing to invest in human capital that is specific to their current employer. Examples of general-purpose human capital include skill at structuring mergers, constructing investment portfolios, or shooting a basketball. Firm-specific skills include knowledge of a firm's proprietary internal computer systems, relationships with the firm's clients, and relationships with other employees.

Firms therefore face choices in structuring internal career paths and job promotion ladders. If a firm wants to make use of career concerns coming from external employment opportunities to provide incentives, it will have difficulty encouraging employees to invest in unique skills. If, however, the firm needs employees to invest in skills that are not valued elsewhere, it will need to reward them for investing in those skills and ensure that they will not find it in their best interests to seek outside employment later.

Firms that are interested in motivating employees to develop firm-specific skills have typically accomplished this by offering long-term employment relationships. As an example, until 1990 IBM was well known for offering a guarantee of lifetime employment. The firm offered a relatively low starting salary but increased compensation rapidly with seniority. By the end of a career, the employee was typically earning far more than he or she could have made outside the firm. Long-term employment arrangements that are combined with backloaded compensation (that is, compensation that is relatively low compared to market wages at the beginning of a career but high at the end) have two useful properties. First, they encourage employees to invest in firm-specific skills. If employees are likely to stay with a firm for a long time, they are less bothered by the fact that the value of firm-specific skills will be lost if they must change employers.

Second, the backloaded compensation can act as an efficiency wage. To illustrate, consider a firm that offers salaries that are $10,000 below market to young employees but $10,000 above market to older employees who started their careers with the firm. This firm has the same expected wage costs as a firm that offers market salaries to all employees, and employees have the same expected career earnings. Now consider a young employee who is caught shirking and is fired. This employee loses the chance to earn an above-market salary later in his or her career and forfeits the $10,000 premium as a result. By increasing the difference between what the employee earns in the current job and what he or she earns in the next-best job, the firm provides stronger incentives for the employee to work to keep the job.

◆ ◆ ◆ ◆ ◆ INCENTIVES AND DECISION MAKING IN ORGANIZATIONS

Finally, we consider the link between incentives and decision making in firms. Michael Jensen and William Meckling observed that firms must often respond to information they receive.[30] One key problem in organization, therefore, is determining *who should decide* on the appropriate response to a given piece of information. Should it be the person who receives the information, or should the person receiving the information pass it to another individual, who then decides?

As a concrete example, consider a manufacturing setting in which a line worker observes a high rate of defects. Should the firm instruct the line worker to stop the production process and seek to identify and solve the problems himself? Or should the firm instruct the worker not to stop the line but instead to phone a supervisor, who then decides what to do? In one scenario, the firm delegates the decision of whether to stop the line to the employee; in the other, the firm asks the employee to transmit information to a different person in the firm.

Jensen and Meckling argued that when information is difficult to communicate or when the value of information depreciates quickly, firms can benefit from delegating decisions to the individual who receives the information. They pointed out, however, that this can be done only if that individual can be motivated to make the *correct* decision. That is, decision making can be delegated to the individual receiving information only if the firm can effectively reward good decisions and penalize bad ones. This reasoning suggests that the problems of delegating and providing incentives are linked. If firms elect to empower employees to make certain decisions, they must first consider whether employees will be motivated to make the right decisions.

As one example, we discuss Masahiko Aoki's comparison of manufacturing jobs in the United States and Japan during the 1980s.[11] At the time, American manufacturing was notable for its sharp job demarcations; that is, most employees were expected to perform extremely narrow tasks. Aoki wrote, "Operating workers are normally not responsible for coping with unexpected emergencies, as is evident from a long-standing custom at the American factory that prohibits the workers from stopping the production line on his or her own initiative, *even when an event takes place that makes it desirable*" [italics added]. In contrast, manufacturing workers in Japan were empowered to make many decisions in response to shop-floor contingencies. Employees were frequently asked to solve problems themselves or as part of a group of production workers. Furthermore, Aoki wrote, "individual workers are authorized to stop a production line when necessary."

Why would American firms restrict employees from making these decisions? Clearly, communicating problems to specialists can lead to costly delays in effecting a remedy. Why restrict employees from taking what may be obvious steps to fix a problem? Aoki's discussion of human resource practices in the two nations yields an answer. In the United States, unions negotiated wage scales with firms, and these scales were tied rigidly to seniority rather than to an individual employee's on-the-job performance. In contrast, the Japanese firm "evolved a system of individual incentive schemes with which to evaluate and reward its employees over a long-term basis. . . . This system has three important elements: (1) the wage system, which combines seniority and merit rating, (2) internal promotion discriminately applied to employees on the basis of merit rating, and (3) a lump sum payment at the time of separation" (Aoki, 1988).

In the United States, it was difficult for firms to provide incentives for employees to make good decisions. Had control over the production line been delegated to workers, a firm would have had no way to ensure that the line stopped when (and *only* when) it was in the firm's interest for this to happen. Firms responded to their inability to vary wages in response to performance by choosing not to delegate this decision.

In contrast, Japanese firms provided incentives in several ways. Subjective evaluations affected raises and promotions through the merit rating system. The lump-sum payment at separation operated as a form of backloaded compensation, yielding an efficiency-wage effect. Through these means, firms rewarded employees who took

EXAMPLE 15.4 TEAMS AND COMMUNICATION IN STEEL MILLS

As the final step in production, sheet steel is subjected to various processes on what is called a finishing line. Typically, coils of sheet steel weighing up to 12 tons are unrolled at the line's entry point. A finishing line processes the unfinished steel by cleaning, heating, stretching, softening, or coating it. At the end of the line, the treated steel is coiled again for shipment to customers.

Jon Gant, Casey Ichniowski, and Kathryn Shaw argue that steel finishing lines offer an especially useful place to study the impact of team-based incentives on productivity. The production methods used on finishing lines do not vary significantly from one firm to another. This process is extremely capital intensive, so a line's profitability depends crucially on the amount of time it is operating correctly. If a line is shut down for repairs, or if it is producing defective steel that cannot be sold to customers, the firm's bottom line suffers. Hence, the key task for operators, maintenance workers, and managers is to identify and solve problems as quickly as possible.[32]

Lines also make markedly different choices with regard to their human resource management policies. Gant and colleagues place lines in two categories: involvement-oriented and control-oriented. Involvement-oriented (IO) lines tend to have broadly defined jobs, work teams, screening of potential employees, incentive pay based on output quality, and skills training. Control-oriented (CO) lines have adopted few of the policies characteristic of IO lines; they run their processes with limited worker–manager communication and less worker involvement.

The authors visited a number of finishing lines and conducted surveys of all employees.

They found that the levels of intra-crew communication were dramatically higher at IO lines than at CO lines. In IO line crews, the average crew member communicated regarding operational issues with 70 to 80 percent of other crew members. At CO lines, these figures were much lower, averaging less than 20 percent.

The IO lines' higher levels of communication meant that crew members were able to share information and identify problems more quickly. As an example of how this increased communication might help, Gant and colleagues described a CO line where sheets of steel were shifting from side to side as they passed through the equipment. This caused sheets to crumple at the edges, leading to a high rate of defective output. A team of engineers and managers was created to fix the problem but was unable to identify the cause for some time. The problem was finally resolved after an hourly worker noticed a piece of equipment that appeared to be in the wrong location. By chance, this employee mentioned the problem to others, and a fix was immediately found. The authors argue that regular communication among all employees working on the line would have led to speedier resolution of the problem.

Gant and colleagues attribute the increased communication at IO lines to the broader job design and the output-based incentives. Broader jobs and frequent job rotation mean that employees have a wider perspective on the line's operations. Incentives based on team output give a strong incentive to combine knowledge and communicate to solve problems. Increased communication, it appears, does translate into higher productivity; IO lines have longer operating times and higher yields (that is, lower rates of defects) than CO lines.

actions that benefited the firm and punished those who took actions that did not benefit the firm. This meant that firms could effectively delegate more decisions to employees.

Aoki's analysis raises the question of why the American and Japanese firms differed so much in their ability to provide incentives to employees. Economic historian Chiaki Moriguchi identifies one possible answer by tracing the history of American and Japanese manufacturing industries from 1910 through 1940.[33] She finds that human resource practices in the two nations were very similar in the period prior to the Great Depression. Implicit contracts, she argues, became more and more prevalent in both nations beginning around 1920.

The Depression, which was much more severe in the United States than in Japan, marks the point at which human resource management trends begin to differ. American firms, devastated by the economic slowdown, were unable to follow through on promises they had made as part of their implicit contracts. This destroyed employees' trust in the firms' future promises and led the employees, through their unions, to demand that pay scales be incorporated into explicit contracts. With wages now set in union negotiations, firms lost the ability to link pay to individual performance and therefore had to rethink what kinds of decisions could be profitably delegated to lower-level workers. Although Japan's economy did shrink during the 1930s, Japanese firms were able to maintain employees' trust and thus continued to make use of implicit incentive contracts. As a result, they were able to develop the manufacturing methods outlined by Aoki.

Notably, changes in U.S. manufacturing since 1985 have centered on making better use of knowledge possessed by shop-floor employees. Innovations such as total quality management and just-in-time production require that decision-making authority be delegated to line workers. An important point is that these organizational changes must be paired with changes in incentive policies in order to encourage employees to make decisions with the firm's interests in mind.

Developments at Westinghouse Air Brake's Chicago facility offer an illustration.[34] The plant, which manufactures parts for locomotive brakes, adopted a continuous improvement plan in 1991. As part of this program, the firm instituted team-based bonuses linked to whether the plant as a whole meets production quotas. For every day the plant hits its target, each member of the nonunionized workforce receives a bonus of $1.50 per hour. The bonuses encourage employees to work together to identify problems and to make suggestions that improve overall efficiency. The company claims that the organizational changes have increased production by a factor of 10 since 1991, saving jobs that might otherwise have been moved to locations with lower labor costs.

CHAPTER SUMMARY

◆ For many jobs, firms can improve on explicit incentive contracts by using implicit incentive contracts. This is true when the available verifiable performance measures are noisy, reward activities that the firm does not want employees to pursue, or fail to reward activities that the firm does want employees to pursue.

◆ Implicit incentive contracts allow firms to make use of performance measures that cannot be verified by external enforcement mechanisms such as judges or arbitrators. Implicit incentive contracts are enforced through the use of reputation. A firm that fails to follow through on promises made as part of an implicit contract will lose its reputation as a good employer, and employees will not respond to future incentives based on implicit contracts.

◆ Often firms use supervisors' subjective assessments of employees' actions as performance measures in implicit contracts. If supervisors find it difficult to make sharp distinctions among employees, all employees might end up with similar evaluations. This weakens incentives to be a top performer.

◆ Strong incentives can be provided through the use of promotion tournaments. The strength of incentives provided by tournaments depends on the size of the prize—that is, on the difference between the wages earned by the tournament's winner and losers.

◆ Firms can also provide incentives by threatening to fire underperforming employees. The strength of these incentives depends on the value of the job to employees. Firms that pay efficiency wages make their jobs more valuable to employees and thus increase incentives for effort.

◆ Firms can motivate employees to work together by using team-based performance measures. Such measures can suffer from free-rider problems, however. Firms can combat free-rider problems by keeping teams small, allowing employees to work together repeatedly, and making sure employees working together can observe one another's actions.

◆ Incentives are also provided through employees' career concerns. If employees expect to test their market value in the future, their actions will be guided in part by concern for keeping this market value high.

◆ When delegating decisions to employees, firms must ask whether employees will be motivated to make correct decisions. The problems of allocating decisions within firms and providing incentives to employees therefore are linked.

QUESTIONS

1. Implicit incentive contracts can be somewhat difficult to communicate to a firm's employees. Often firms will make available a set of rewards (raises, bonuses, or promotions) to employees with "good" performance, but what constitutes good performance is never explicitly defined. As part of the job-interview process, potential employees often spend many hours talking to a large number of the firm's employees. Although this practice helps the firm gain information about the potential employee, information about the firm is also transmitted to the potential employee. Explain, using your own experience if possible, what questions job applicants ask of interviewers and how this may inform them about important aspects of firms' implicit incentive contracts.

2. What kinds of value-creating actions might not be reflected in subjective performance evaluations by an employee's supervisor? Explain how 360-degree peer reviews might mitigate this problem. What are some potential drawbacks associated with 360-degree peer review as a performance measure?

3. Giganticorp, a large conglomerate, has just acquired Nimble, Inc., a small manufacturing concern. Putting yourself in the shoes of Nimble's employees, what concerns do you have about the implicit incentive contracts that governed your relationship with Nimble before the merger? Now place yourself in the position of Giganticorp's merger integration team. How might concern about implicit incentive contracts affect your dealings with Nimble's employees?

4. According to Example 15.1, the 2001 salary and bonus for the "winner" of General Electric's CEO tournament, Jeffrey Immelt, was just slightly larger than that of the "loser," Robert Nardelli. Does this small monetary prize mean that the incentives to win were muted? Why or why not?

5. Suppose a firm announces that it is giving a $1 million raise in salary to the CEO effective immediately. In addition, it will keep the CEO's salary higher by $1 million even *after* the current CEO leaves office. Thus, all future CEOs will benefit from this raise as well. Describe the effects of this plan on the tournament-based effort incentives for the firm's non-CEO employees.

6. A firm faces a choice between two ways of making it costly for an employee to shirk. It can invest in technology that makes it easier to detect shirking, or it can raise the employee's

salary. Let the employee's salary in his or her next-best job be $40,000, and suppose that the cost to the employee of working hard is $5,000. If the firm invests $X in the monitoring technology, the probability that the firm will find out if the employee shirks is given by (square root of (x/5000)). Assume that the firm wants to motivate the employee to work hard.

    a. What wage should the firm offer, and how much should it invest in the monitoring technology in order to minimize its total expenditure?

    b. How should the firm adjust wages and monitoring investments if the monitoring technology becomes more effective? Compute the firm's wage and monitoring expenditure, assuming that the probability of catching the employee shirking is 2 * (square root of (x/5000)).

7. After the fall of the Berlin Wall in 1989, hundreds of thousands of East Germans migrated to West Germany. This led to a significant increase in labor supply in the West. How would you expect an increase in labor supply to impact a firm's ability to use efficiency wages?

8. Offer examples (from your own experience, if possible) of three skills that qualify as general-purpose human capital and three skills that qualify as firm-specific human capital. Explain why for each.

9. Two young partners at the consulting firm MacKenzie and Co. (call them Bob and Doug) leave the firm to set up their own partnership. They agree to maintain the partnership for one year and to split the profits 50/50. Profits depend on the partners' actions, as follows. If both work hard, the new firm will make profits of $1,500,000. If one of the consultants works hard while the other shirks, the firm's profits will be $1,150,000. If Bob and Doug both shirk, they will make profits of $700,000. Each partner is willing to work hard only if doing so earns him an additional $250,000 in a year. Draw this "partnership game" in matrix form (using ideas from the Economics Primer). Does this game have dominant strategies? What is the Nash equilibrium? Is this partnership game a prisoners' dilemma? What is the relationship between the prisoners' dilemma game and incentives in teams?

10. Consider a monopolist firm that consists of two functional divisions. The manufacturing division produces the firm's product, and the actions of the managers in manufacturing have a large effect on the firm's costs. The sales division markets and sells the firm's product, and the actions of the managers in sales have a large effect on the firm's revenues.

    a. Explain why the firm may want to use its revenue instead of its profit as a performance measure for the sales managers. Explain why measures of cost might be preferred to measures of profit for motivating manufacturing managers.

    b. If the firm rewards sales managers on the basis of revenues, can it delegate decisions over prices and quantities to these managers? If the firm did delegate these decisions, what price would the sale managers choose to charge for the firm's product?

    c. Suppose that because sales managers are in constant contact with customers, they have the most accurate information about current demand for the firm's product. What performance measure should the firm use if it is essential to delegate pricing decisions to achieve quick price responses to changes in market demand? Use your discussion to identify the cost to the firm of delegating this pricing decision.

ENDNOTES

[1]"Knowledge Management Sweeping Korea's Corporate Landscape," *Korea Herald*, June 22, 2002.

[2]"Rank and File Attrition Isn't Working, So Best-to-Worst Grading is Gaining," *Time*, June 18, 2001.

[3]"More Firms Cut Workers Ranked at Bottom to Make Way for Talent," *USA Today*, May 30, 2001.

[4]Lazear, E. and S. Rosen, "Rank Order Tournaments as Optimal Labor Contracts," *Journal of Political Economy*, 89, 1981, pp. 841–864.

[5]Promotions typically confer prestige and other benefits, such as (perhaps) a corner office. To the extent that employees value these additional aspects of promotions, the wage differential will understate the true value to an employee of winning a promotion tournament.

[6]Our discussion here omits a subtle aspect of tournament theory. Because it is the best loan officer who earns the promotion, the probability that loan officer 1 will win the tournament depends not just on his own effort but also on that of the second loan officer. Officer 1's optimal effort choice therefore may depend on the effort choice made by officer 2. The simultaneous choice of efforts by competitors in a tournament is conceptually similar to the simultaneous choice of quantities by Cournot duopolists. Lazear and Rosen derived reaction functions for tournament competitors and solved for the Nash equilibrium of this game.

[7]Rosen, S., "Prizes and Incentives in Elimination Tournaments," *American Economic Review*, 76, 1986, pp. 921–939.

[8]Baker, G., M. Gibbs, and B. Holmstrom, "The Wage Policy of a Firm," *Quarterly Journal of Economics*, 109, 1994, pp. 921–956.

[9]Main, B., C. O'Reilly, and J. Wade, "Top Executive Pay: Tournament or Teamwork? *Journal of Labor Economics*, 11, 1993, pp. 606–628.

[10]Eriksson, T., "Executive Compensation and Tournament Theory: Empirical Tests on Danish Data," *Journal of Labor Economics*, 17, 1999, pp. 262–280.

[11]See "Running the House That Jack Built," *Business Week*, October 2, 2000.

[12]The wages w and w^{**} in this model can be interpreted rather broadly. The wage w, for instance, can be viewed as the net present value of the employee's future employment prospects conditional on retaining her current job today. The wage w^{**} can be interpreted as the net present value of future employment prospects conditional on being fired from the current job. Many factors could cause w^{**} to be less than w; firing may result in a long and costly period of unemployment, a black mark on a resume, or a lower-paying next job.

[13]Shapiro, S., and J. Stiglitz, "Equilibrium Unemployment as a Discipline Device," *American Economic Review*, 74, 1984, pp. 433–444.

[14]Quoted in Allan Nevins, *Ford: The Times, The Man, The Company*, New York, Charles Scribner's Sons, 1954. See also Raff, D. and L. Summers, "Did Henry Ford Pay Efficiency Wages?" *Journal of Labor Economics*, 5, 1987, pp. 57–86.

[15]The concept of efficiency wages is not the only way to account for the observation that raising wages increased productivity. The Five-Dollar Day may have allowed Ford to attract more highly qualified workers, although the very simple tasks assigned to workers on Ford's assembly line suggests that attracting skilled workers was not essential to Ford's success.

[16]Groshen, Erica and Alan Krueger, "The Structure of Supervision and Pay in Hospitals," *Industrial and Labor Relations Review*, 43, Feb 1990, 1345–1465.

[17]Since the mid-1960s, the U.S. Congress has enacted a number of laws that restrict at-will employment by barring employers from discriminating on the basis of race, age, sex, and disability in making certain employment decisions. See Steiber, J., "Recent Developments in Employment-at-Will," *Labor Law Journal*, 36, 1985, pp. 557–562, or Donohue, J. and P. Siegelman, "The Changing Nature of Employment Discrimination Litigation," *Stanford Law Review*, 43, 1991, pp. 983–1033.

[18]This discussion is taken from Ichino, A., M. Polo, and E. Rettore, "Are Judges Biased by Labor Market Conditions?" *European Economic Review*, 47, 2003, pp. 913–944.

[19]High unemployment rates in continental Europe—9.5 percent in Italy in 2001—may be related to these restrictions on firms' abilities to fire. The efficiency wages model suggests that if p is low, $w - w^{**}$ must be large in order for the threat of termination to provide incentives. One way in which w^{**} can be low is if termination leads to a very long spell of unemployment, as would likely be the case if there is a large pool of unemployed workers in the economy.

[20]"Will This Machine Change M&M?" *Business Today*, July 21, 2002.

[21]Gaynor, M. and M. Pauly, "Compensation and Productive Efficiency in Partnerships: Evidence from Medical Group Practice," *Journal of Political Economy*, 98, 1990, pp. 544–573.

[22]Leibowitz, A. and R. Tollison, "Free Riding, Shirking, and Team Production in Legal Partnerships," *Economic Inquiry*, 18, 1980, pp. 380–394.

[23]Meyer, M., "The Dynamics of Learning with Team Production: Implications for Task Assignment," *Quarterly Journal of Economics*, 109, 1994, pp. 1157–1184.

[24]Knez, M. and D. Simester, "Firm-wide Incentives and Mutual Monitoring at Continental Airlines," *Journal of Labor Economics*, 19, 2001, pp. 743–772.

[25]Oyer, P. and S. Schaefer, "Why Do Some Firms Give Stock Options to All Employees? An Empirical Examination of Alternative Theories," *Journal of Financial Economics*, 76, 2005, pp. 99–133.

[26]Fama, E., "Agency Problems and the Theory of the Firm," *Journal of Political Economy*, 88, 1980, pp. 288–307.

[27]Gibbons, R. and K. J. Murphy, "Optimal Incentive Contracts in the Presence of Career Concerns: Theory and Evidence," *Journal of Political Economy*, 100, 1992, pp. 468–505.

[28]Note that had the team contracted on, say, whether Thomas hit 30 home runs, Thomas might have been motivated to ignore other valuable activities in pursuit of the home run goal. The performance measures actually included in Thomas's contract, though verifiable, are all based on voting by fans, other teams' managers, or sportswriters. This means that Thomas likely had little incentive to alter his actions in subtle ways to achieve these targets.

[29]Chevalier, J. and G. Ellison, "Career Concerns for Mutual Fund Managers," *Quarterly Journal of Economics*, 114, 1999, pp. 389–432.

[30]Jensen, M. and W. Meckling, "Specific and General Knowledge, and Organizational Structure," in Werin, L. and H. Wijkander (eds.), *Contract Economics*, Cambridge, MA, Blackwell, 1992.

[31]Aoki, M. *Information, Incentives and Bargaining in the Japanese Economy*, Cambridge, Cambridge University Press, 1988.

[32]This example is drawn from Gant, J., C. Ichniowski, and K. Shaw, "Working Smarter by Working Together: Connective Capital in the Workplace," working paper, Stanford University, 2003.

[33]Moriguchi, C., "Implicit Contracts, the Great Depression, and Institutional Change: The Evolution of Employment Relations in U.S. and Japanese Manufacturing Firms, 1910–1940," *Journal of Economic History*, 63, 2003, pp. 625–665.

[34]"Rust-Belt Factory Lifts Productivity and Staff Finds It's No Picnic," *Wall Street Journal*, May 18, 1999.

16

STRATEGY AND STRUCTURE

Until the early 1980s, the Pepsi-Cola Company comprised three divisions that reported to corporate headquarters. Pepsi USA created marketing campaigns—the famous "Pepsi Challenge" was its brainchild. The Pepsi Bottling Group (PBG) bottled and distributed the product in local markets in which Pepsi chose not to use independent bottlers. PBG was also responsible for local marketing campaigns. The Fountain Beverage Division (FBD) sold to fast-food outlets, restaurants, bars, and stadiums.

This structure created several problems. It made it difficult for Pepsi to negotiate with regional and national retailers, such as Piggly Wiggly and Wal-Mart. Pepsi USA and PBG often ran competing (and sometimes conflicting) promotional campaigns. Employee backgrounds, characteristics, and compensation also varied across divisions, with workers in PBG and FBD resenting the high salaries and high profiles of the Pepsi USA employees. To resolve these problems, Pepsi reorganized its beverage operations in 1988. Pepsi USA, PBG, and FBD ceased to exist. Sales and account management responsibilities were decentralized among four geographic regions. Decisions about national marketing campaigns, finance, human resources, and corporate operations, including trucking and company-owned bottlers, were centralized at headquarters and handled nationally. But this reorganization did not solve Pepsi's coordination problems for long. Negotiations with national accounts often had to pass through several layers of management before a final decision could be reached, resulting in the loss of important accounts, notably Burger King. Conflicts between national and local promotional campaigns continued to arise. So in 1992, Pepsi reorganized again. This time, marketing and sales campaigns were further centralized, and responsibility for a given retail outlet was delegated to a single salesperson.

Throughout these two reorganizations, Pepsi enjoyed popular products, a motivated workforce, strong stock price performance, and a benign competitive environment. Even so, the firm's top managers believed that these favorable factors could not guarantee continued success and that to remain profitable, Pepsi needed to reorganize. Ample general evidence supports Pepsi's view that technology, product mix, and market position do not fully account for a firm's performance. Richard Caves and David Barton found that firms in the same industry, with similar technologies and labor forces, often have substantially different levels of productivity.[1] While some of the reasons for differences in performance are idiosyncratic and do not lend themselves to general principles (e.g., the role of Bill Gates in attracting talent to Microsoft), others can be generalized. We have previously discussed, for example, the importance of appropriately applying resources and capabilities to the competitive environment.

In this chapter, we consider *organizational structure*. Organizational structure describes the arrangements, both formal and informal, by which a firm divides up its critical tasks, specifies how its managers and employees make decisions, and establishes routines and information flows to support continuing operations. Structure also defines the nature of agency problems within the firm–who has authority for which decisions, who controls information regarding which activities, and whose goals are aligned or not aligned regarding an activity and its outcomes.

Does it matter how a firm is organized? Are some structures better than others? We argue that the way a firm organizes does matter and is fundamental to its success in implementing its strategic choices. This is because structure enables managers to link a firm's resources and capabilities with the opportunities that managers perceive in their business environment. This implies that an optimal structure will permit the firm to create the most value in implementing its strategic choices.

Although there may be many ways in which a firm can marshal its resources to respond to environmental conditions, some will be more effective than others, others will require less effort and fewer resources than others, and still others will be more sustainable over a longer time frame. How the firm organizes to implement its strategies makes a difference. An appropriate structure provides workers with the information, coordination, and incentives needed to implement strategy so as to create the most value possible. This makes the ability to organize in pursuit of strategic goals a critical capability for a firm.

In his classic set of case studies, *Strategy and Structure*, Alfred Chandler argued these same ideas in making the case that the founding top managers of large industrial firms structured their firms to best allow them to pursue their chosen business strategy—or, simply put, that *structure follows strategy*.[2] This theme, which we believe is applicable to firms of all sizes, is the starting point for our discussion in this chapter.

The growth of the Internet, the spread of globalization, changing workforce demographics, and other factors have led some observers to question whether organization structure has the same importance for firms that it once did. Traditional divisional structures that were once the hallmark of large corporations are being scaled back and even dropped in favor of either more complex matrix structures or less elaborate and more flexible structures. Although such skepticism is certainly reasonable, any particular organizational structure, especially in a world of professional "free agents," entrepreneurial start-ups, and technologically driven "virtual" firms, we remain convinced of the importance of structure–that firms must organize (and reorganize) so as to maintain the linkages between their firm's evolving resources and capabilities and the changing contexts in which they must be put to work.

Before further developing the link between strategy and structure, it is helpful to introduce some basic concepts behind any complex organization and then describe some of the major organizational forms that tend to arise.

◆ ◆ ◆ ◆ ◆ AN INTRODUCTION TO STRUCTURE

Before demonstrating the link between strategy and structure, it is helpful to introduce some basic concepts and describe the major kinds of organizational forms.

Individuals, Teams, and Hierarchies

Simple tasks performed by a small group of people can be structured in several ways:

- *Individually.* The members of the work group are paid based on individual actions and outcomes.

- *Self-managed teams.* A collection of individuals work together to set and pursue common objectives. Individuals are rewarded, in part, on team performance.

- *Hierarchy of authority.* One member of the group specializes in monitoring and coordinating the work of the other members.

Organizing by individuals or teams involves a host of issues already discussed in Chapters 14 and 15. Most firms, even small ones, combine these simple arrangements in some way. An employee may do some tasks individually and others in a team. The extent to which an authority relationship enters into small-group arrangements also varies among firms, with some resembling a collection of independent workers, a common situation in professional service firms. At the other extreme, some organizations, such as police agencies, may closely resemble military models of hierarchy. A work group may organize some activities around individuals and others around the group, while a supervisor may monitor the activities and outputs of both groups and individuals.

The appropriateness of each way of organizing tasks in small groups varies according to circumstances. Treating the workers as self-managing individuals is most appropriate when their tasks do not require coordination, for example, in a social service agency in which staff interact with clients on a case-by-case basis and where coordination may be restricted by privacy considerations. When coordination is necessary, say because the work involves design attributes or relationship-specific investments, then organizing by teams or hierarchy is more appropriate.

Group self-management is more appropriate than a hierarchy when work outcomes benefit from frequent group interaction and group incentives (such as from information sharing or from increased motivation and group support) and when the costs of group coordination do not detract from other group outcomes. Organizing by self-managing groups, however, makes it difficult to monitor and control individual outputs and align individual incentives with the firm. Armen Alchian and Harold Demsetz raise these issues about groups and hierarchies in explaining why firms exist.[3] Beyond a certain size, group self-management becomes too costly, and some form of hierarchy is necessary to maintain and evaluate the group as well as reduce agency problems that occur when individuals try to influence firm decisions for their private benefit. How much control is introduced depends on the extent of agency problems and the time and effort needed to control them. These comprise the *influence* costs that we discussed earlier.

Although most everyone is familiar with these issues in organizing small firms or work groups, this level of organizing is seldom of strategic importance, especially when compared to the investments firms make to achieve large-scale or serve extended markets. These simpler strucctures can be readily changed and affect small numbers of individuals at a given time. Of much greater importance are the organizational schemes used in larger firms that affect considerable numbers of people and govern the allocation of significant organizational assets. These are *complex hierarchies*, which involve organizing large numbers of groups within extensive and potentially overlapping schemes. These organizational assets can be of strategic significance.

Complex Hierarchy

Large firms require *complex hierarchies*—that is, the structure of the firm involves multiple groups and multiple levels of groupings. Complex hierarchy arises from the need not just to organize individuals into groups, but to organize groups into larger groups. This process quickly becomes complicated and involves two related problems:

1. *Departmentalization*
2. *Coordination of activities* within and between subgroups to attain the firm's objectives

Most organization designs combine solutions to departmentalization and coordination problems under the specific conditions a firm faces.[4]

Departmentalization

Departmentalization involves the partition of the organization into different groups and sets of groups. It may occur along several dimensions: tasks (or functions), inputs, outputs, geography, and time of work.

Departmental schemes can get quite complicated. For example, when large industrial firms initially formed around 1900, the fundamental groupings of their structures came from the existing structures of companies that merged together to form these giants. These hodgepodge structures were not conducive to efficiency within the successor firm and thus required subsequent rationalization along one of the dimensions listed above. At its most basic level, departmentalization represents the choices of managers regarding the appropriate division of labor in the firm. Samples of departments organized around common tasks or functions include accounting, marketing, and production. Other grouping schemes can focus on criteria related to the firm's inputs and outputs. Examples of these schemes include the Pepsi Bottling Group and Fountain Beverage Division that we discussed earlier. Departments and divisions can also be organized around locations, such as with regional sales offices or service centers. There can even be time-based groupings which would reflect different priorities in organizational activities at different times of the week or some other cycle of activities. This could be an issue with 24-hour call centers, where employees may deal with people in different parts of the world, depending on the shifts they work. Another example would be organizing staff on the basis of short-term versus long-term project commitments in a contract engineering firm.

Deciding how to organize tasks within a firm reflects the choices of managers regarding what activities are to be done and their relative importance. Departmentalization is thus also associated with the choice of a firm's boundaries. For example, diversification into new businesses will be reflected in an expansion in the set of a corporation's divisions, departments, and other groups. A decision to outsource a significant function will lead to a contraction of a firm's structure; this removes the individuals and activities associated with that function from the organization, placing it outside the firm's boundaries. We discussed decisions about the firm's boundaries in earlier chapters, and the results of boundary choices will be apparent in the contours of a firm's structure.

Choosing the dimensions along which to organize departments always involves tradeoffs. For example, organizing by task may lead to greater consistency in a firm's purchasing, manufacturing, and sales operations, but may detract from the firm's ability to respond to customer demands in different locations. How authority for different types of decisions is located within a structure should thus give some indication of how the firm's managers prioritize those decisions.

In general, when selecting organizing dimensions, managers should consider economies of scale and scope, transactions costs, and agency costs. A firm should combine workers or teams into a department when their activities involve economies of scale or scope. For example, if a multiproduct firm can achieve significant scale economies in research and development, then an organizational structure that included a companywide research department would be more efficient than dispersing R&D personnel throughout a number of independent product groups. Workers and teams should also be organized into departments when significant relationship-specific assets cut across them and thus necessitate a more general grouping scheme.

Environmental constraints may also be operative, determining which activities are included within a firm's structure and which are not. For example, U.S. antitrust policy in the early twentieth century may have limited the ability of firms to acquire R&D capabilities from the marketplace and may have hastened the growth of internal R&D capabilities that need to fit with the firm's structure. The approval of some mergers may require the divestment of units within the merging firm that may pose a threat to competition after the combination.

Finally, the choice of an organizing dimension has implications for agency costs, such as we discussed in Chapter 14. For example, measuring the performance for a firm of functional departments, such as finance and purchasing, can be difficult. Moreover, because of the weak linkage with overall firm performance, individuals in these departments are likely to think of their performance in terms of functional excellence rather than overall firm success. This makes it hard to evaluate and reward department managers, which further increases agency costs inside the firm.

Coordination and Control

Once groups have been identified and organized, the interrelated problems of coordination and control arise. *Coordination* involves the flow of information to facilitate subunit decisions that are consistent with each other and with organizational objectives. *Control* involves the location of decision-making and rule-making authority within a hierarchy. Coordination and control involve issues of technical and agency efficiency discussed in Chapter 14. They influence technical efficiency because decision makers need access to low-cost, accurate, and timely information, while assuring that the firm takes full advantage of economies of scale and scope in production. For example, poor coordination between the Pepsi Bottling Group and Pepsi USA resulted in technical inefficiencies when the two divisions failed to economize on marketing and sales efforts. This suggests that decision rights should be allocated so that individuals with the best and most timely information are empowered to make decisions, provided of course that the decision maker's goals are aligned with those of the firm.

Coordination and control also affect agency efficiency because structures designed for similar tasks may differ in the opportunities they offer managers to pursue personal or unit objectives that are inconsistent with the firm's objectives. By allocating decision rights throughout a hierarchy, a firm's managers designate a legitimate basis of authority that they perceive will best support overall firm objectives. In the next chapter, we will discuss formal authority and its relationship to other bases of power and influence.

There are two alternative approaches for developing coordination within firms.[5] The first emphasizes *autonomy* or *self-containment*, whereas the second emphasizes strong *lateral relations*. When firms organize using autonomous work units, unit managers control information about operating decisions, and the flow of information between units is minimal. Unit managers provide summary financial and accounting data, including profit data when available, to headquarters. Operating information remains within the units.

A common approach to self-containment is to organize into separate product groups, each of which contains the basic business functions of manufacturing and sales and would be capable of existing by itself in the marketplace. These autonomous groups, often called *profit centers*, are controlled on the basis of a target profit goal. Managers in autonomous groups are rewarded for meeting or exceeding a profit goal and punished for failing to meet it. Managers in autonomous divisions may have limited interactions with their counterparts in other units. Diversified firms, such as Procter & Gamble and Johnson & Johnson, make frequent use of profit centers. When groups focus on other performance measures besides profit, such as cost, revenue, or investment goals, they are called *responsibility centers*. Research programs at pharmaceutical companies often make use of responsibility centers and base their performance judgments on such criteria of research productivity as patents and research publications.

The alternative to self-contained groupings is the development of strong lateral relations across units. Lateral relations make sense when realizing economies of scale or scope requires close coordination of the activities of work groups. Lateral relations can be informal, such as with ad hoc or temporary teams or liaisons, or they can be formalized within the firm's structure. An example of a formal attempt to foster lateral relations is the *matrix organization*, in which employees are subject to two or more sets of managers at once. This occurs, for example, when an engineer reports both to a research and development department and a project office, or when a salesperson reports both to the head of sales for a particular product and to a regional manager. We discuss matrix organizations in more detail in the next section.

A firm's authority is often allocated in terms of *centralization* versus *decentralization*. As some decisions come to be made by senior managers, the firm is said to be more centralized regarding those decisions. Conversely, as certain decisions are made at lower levels, the firm becomes more decentralized regarding those decisions. Centralization and decentralization often are considered alternatives—a firm is seen as either one or the other. The situation in real firms is more complicated in that most firms are centralized on some dimensions and decentralized on others. For example, a firm may delegate considerable operating authority to division managers (decentralization). Senior managers in the firm, however, will likely retain authority to review division performance and make decisions regarding the career advancement of division managers (centralization).

Types of Organizational Structures

There are four basic structures for large organizations.[6]

1. The unitary *functional* structure (often called the U-form)
2. The *multidivisional* structure (often called the M-form)

3. The *matrix* structure
4. The *network* structure

Traditional discussions of organizational structure have focused on the first three structures, which are the most widely used ones in practice. The network structure represents a recent development that emphasizes contracting rather than internal organization.

Functional Structure (U-form)

Figure 16.1 represents the unitary functional structure or U-form. The term *unitary functional* refers to the fact that in this structure a single department is responsible for each of the basic business functions (e.g., finance, marketing, production, purchasing) within the firm. A division of labor that allows for specialization of basic business tasks characterizes this structure. As a firm grows, new tasks can be added to the structure or existing departments can be subdivided without jeopardizing the logic of the structure. An example of this structure was Cray Research around 1980, which maintained companywide departments of finance, marketing and sales, hardware research and development, and software research and development. The component groups or units in the functional structure are called *departments*. A functional division of labor in the firm makes each department dependent on direction from central headquarters. Such departments probably could not exist outside of the firm except as contract vendors to a firm that independently secures the other functions. Individuals grouped within a common department will share similar backgrounds, norms of behaviors, goals, and performance standards. This promotes performance within the department but makes coordination with other departments difficult. This is why firms organized along functional lines tend to centralize their strategic decision making.

The functional structure developed when firms began to grow bigger and become more specialized in the nineteenth century. From its inception, it has been a structure suited to relatively stable conditions in which operational efficiency is valued. Even so, large firms were slow to adopt the functional structure. The early growth of large firms that we discussed in Chapter 1 was characterized by loose combinations of formerly independent firms, often still run by their founders. These combinations failed to coordinate leadership and generally did not combine work groups performing

FIGURE 16.1
SAMPLE CHART OF A FUNCTIONAL ORGANIZATIONAL STRUCTURE

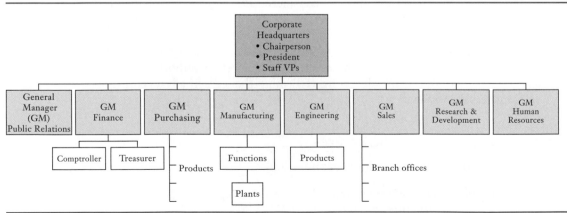

similar tasks into companywide departments. Rather, they resembled alliances or associations of equals. (U.S. Steel looked this way when it became the first billion-dollar firm in 1901.)

Functional organization in large firms developed when managers realized that firms that rationalized their activities along functional lines could outperform those competitors that did not. The widespread adoption of the functional structure among large firms occurred during the first merger wave that took place in the 1890s. In addition, older firms, such as Standard Oil and the Union Pacific Railroad, were also further rationalized around this time. A similar process of rationalization took place recently among large European firms with the advent of European economic integration.

Multidivisional Structure (M-form)

Figure 16.2 shows the divisional (or multidivisional) structure. It encompasses a set of autonomous divisions led by a corporate headquarters office, which is assisted by a corporate staff that provides information about the internal and external business environment. Rather than organizing by function or by task, a multidivisional structure organizes by product line, related business units, geography (e.g., by region), or customer type (e.g., industrial versus consumer versus government products). *Divisions* are groupings of these interrelated subunits. The subunits that comprise a division could be functionally organized departments or even other divisions, which in turn can be composed of functionally organized departments.

Oliver Williamson, who coined the distinction between M- and U-forms, argues that the M-form develops in response to problems of inefficiency and agency that arise in the functionally organized firm as it increases in size and operating complexity. Relative to a functional structure, the M-form improves efficiency by a division of labor between strategic and operational decisions. Division managers focus on

FIGURE 16.2
SAMPLE CHART OF A MULTIDIVISIONAL STRUCTURE

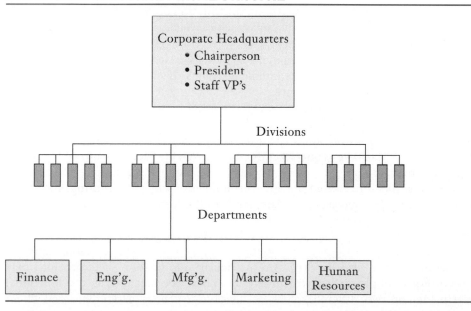

operational issues, while strategic decisions are left to top managers and corporate staff. The M-form reduces agency problems within the firm because it fosters an internal capital market, in which division managers compete for discretionary corporate funds on the basis of their results. Corporate staff, using strategic controls, promotes corporate goals by monitoring division performance and advising managers on how to align their activities with corporate goals. A strong corporate staff is important for the M-form, and its absence leads to a weaker *holding company* form that generates less value from organizing unrelated units.

The divisional structure developed in response to problems with the functional structure in large, diversified firms. As firms diversify across geographic or product markets, they have to coordinate different functional areas within each market. For example, geographically diversified firms, such as McGaw Cellular Communications or Waste Management, run what amount to autonomous businesses in distinct geographic markets. A divisional structure organized along geographic lines allows these firms to coordinate production, distribution, and sales functions within their different markets, each of which may face unique competitive conditions.

The divisional structure also solves another problem of large organizations: the desire to reduce agency costs by closely linking individual pay to performance. Authority for operating decisions is generally decentralized to division managers, who are held accountable for their divisions' performance. A simple example of this occurs in retailing. In a chain of retailers, such as Piggly Wiggly, Wal-Mart, or Macy's Department Stores, each store is, in effect, its own division, with profits calculated on a store-by-store basis. This provides top management with a simple measure of store performance, which they can then use to evaluate store managers and reward good performance.

As we discussed in Chapter 15, the lower the "white noise" or "measurement error" in the performance measure used in pay-for-performance schemes, the less susceptible it is to covert manipulation by managers, and the more effective the pay-for-performance scheme will be in motivating managerial effort and reducing agency costs. The divisional structure clearly measures how much the performance of each division contributes to overall corporate success: divisional profits and losses. Equally clear and nonmanipulable measures of the contribution of departmental performance to overall corporate success are often unavailable, which is why functional structures have tended to focus on operational efficiency rather than on profitability. This could change, however, with the development of activity-based accounting systems that enable top management to evaluate middle managers. If so, it may weaken an agency justification for a divisional structure.

Divisions are often subdivided into functional areas. For example, each of the regional divisions of Waste Management has marketing, service, and finance departments. A functional organization also can be analyzed and reorganized along divisional lines. For example, IBM recently reorganized its sales organization from a geographic to an industry-focused structure. The rationales for these subdivisions are as stated earlier—to take advantage of economies of scope, monitoring, and evaluation, at lower, albeit more appropriate, levels of the firm.

Matrix Structure

Figure 16.3 illustrates the matrix structure: The firm is organized along multiple dimensions at once (usually two). Any particular combination of dimensions may be used. For example, matrix structures can include product groups and functional departments or two different types of divisions (such as geographic and client

FIGURE 16.3

A MATRIX ORGANIZATION STRUCTURE
WITH PROJECT AND FUNCTION DIMENSIONS

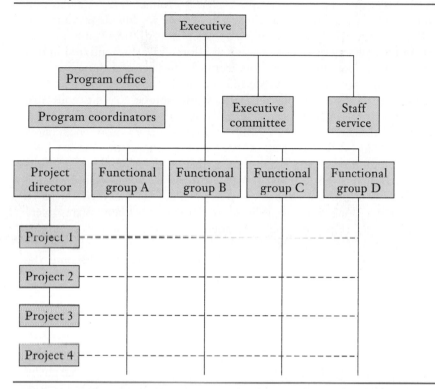

Source: Adapted from McCann and Galbraith, 1980.

divisions). Individuals working at the intersections of the matrix (usually middle managers) report information to two hierarchies and have two bosses. For example, the Pepsi matrix that was created in the late 1980s was organized along geographic and functional lines. Area manufacturing managers simultaneously reported to regional general managers (geographic-based divisions) and a national senior vice president for operations (functional-based divisions). Although the matrix may extend throughout the entire firm, some level is often organized according to a matrix while the rest of the organization is not. Thus, Pepsi's national marketing group remained outside of the matrix. At the same time, area-manufacturing managers reported to two bosses. Individuals reporting to these area managers, however, had just one boss and thus were not part of the matrix.

A matrix is valuable when economies of scale or scope or agency considerations provide a compelling rationale for organizing along more than one dimension simultaneously or when some important issues, such as regulatory or environmental issues, are not well addressed by the firm's principal organizing approach. For example, Pepsi believed that national coordination of manufacturing helped achieve scale economies in production, justifying organization along functional lines, while regional coordination increased Pepsi's effectiveness in negotiating with large purchasers, justifying organization along geographic lines. The demands of competing dimensions must be roughly equivalent and difficult to address sequentially. If one dimension was

EXAMPLE 16.1 ABB's MATRIX ORGANIZATION[7]

Asea Brown Boveri (ABB) is a large global producer of heavy capital equipment, such as turbine generators and railway engines. It was formed in 1988 when ASEA of Sweden merged with Brown Boveri of Switzerland. Soon after the merger, ABB's senior management concluded that to be more responsive to customer needs in different parts of the world, ABB's organization would have to be decentralized and made flexible to local conditions. ABB was thus reorganized. The reorganization resulted in a matrix structure in which ABB's 1,300 local business units (e.g., its railway engine division in Norway) were organized along two dimensions: products and geography. On the product dimension, ABB created 65 business areas (BAs), each responsible for one of ABB's product lines. On the geography dimension, ABB created countrywide organizations. At the intersection of a matrix were local business units, each responsible for a particular product line within a particular country. The head of each local unit was subject to "dual reporting." That is, the manager for a particular product line in a given country would report to both the worldwide business area manager for that product line and to the head of the countrywide organization for that country.

Some of the immediate successes that arose from ABB's restructuring were reductions in manufacturing costs through rationalizing production operations and improving new product development through better targeting of R&D funding. The BAs organized themselves according to a "lead center" concept. Under this concept, for each product line, one location was chosen to provide worldwide product leadership and support. All R&D and process improvement efforts were concentrated in this location, from which successful strategies were transferred to other locations. Each lead center became the single source for the collective knowledge within each of ABB's product lines.

ABB's matrix structure also encouraged healthy competition among the various geographic units that made up a BA. The units that provided the most efficient manufacturing facilities were retained to cater to the BA's worldwide requirements. These plants were then expanded to achieve global-scale production levels, thereby giving them scale efficiencies. This helped the company become the leader in almost all the product groups it competed in. Inefficient plants were shut down or sold.

ABB encountered one serious problem with its matrix structure, however. Because the structure essentially requires multiple reporting, important decisions had to be taken by multimember teams from all over the world. This slowed down decision making. To overcome this, ABB embarked on an ambitious internal mail and information system based on Lotus Notes. This system allowed managers to freely communicate, exchange files and data, and thus make decisions more quickly. With over 70,000 users around the world, ABB's Lotus Notes network became a backbone for reporting and decision making within the organization.

clearly more important, then the preferred structure would be multidivisional, with the dominant dimension being "higher" in the firm's structure than the other. Similarly, if demands can be sequenced, then it may be possible to address big issues early on and at a high position in the hierarchy. Less important issues can be addressed later on temporally and further down in the hierarchy.

A matrix also permits economizing on scarce human resources. For example, a firm that produces industrial controls for continuous-flow manufacturing environments (oil refining, chemical processing, flour milling) may find that a structure using product groups based on customer type (e.g., an oil industry group or a chemical industry group) maximizes the effectiveness of its product development, marketing, and servicing efforts. To develop new applications for existing products and designs for new products, however, a firm's chemical and electrical engineers must develop sufficient firm-specific, product-specific, and customer-specific know-how. Because recruiting and training good engineers is costly and because the engineers benefit from interaction and collaboration with one another, it may be neither possible nor desirable for the firm to maintain a separate engineering department within each product group. A matrix structure in which engineers are part of a companywide engineering department but also report to product groups may allow the firm to economize on scarce human resources while also encouraging its engineers to develop product-specific and customer-specific know-how.

A disadvantage of a matrix structure is that employees can find themselves torn between two lines of authority. If a conflict develops in a matrix between the demands of an area manager and a product manager over a salesperson's obligations toward a major client, the hierarchy does not dictate which manager would prevail, since they share the same level within the firm. This would not happen in functional or divisional organizations. Settling a conflict such as this would require discussion and negotiation between affected individuals on the merits of each case. Although such conflicts can be costly, the assumption behind the matrix is that the firm addresses sufficient numbers of problems with such quality requirements to make a confrontational structure cost-effective. While conflict is expected in matrix structures, if it occurs too frequently, or if conflicting parties fail to resolve their differences and instead pass their conflict further up the hierarchy, then the matrix quickly becomes dysfunctional.

Matrix or Division? A Model of Optimal Structure

The potential for managerial conflict in balancing the demands of matrix dimensions raises the issue of when a matrix structure is preferable to another structure. David Baron and David Besanko developed an economic model of shared incentive authority to address this question. They focus on firms that face organizing demands on both product and geographic dimensions.[8] The optimal structure to use emerges from the interplay of spillovers within product lines and within geographies and the interrelationships among multiple activities that local units perform.

Baron and Besanko see two considerations driving structural choice. The first is whether demand-enhancing activities, such as advertising or product promotion, and cost-reducing activities, such as downsizing or production rationalization, are profit complements or substitutes. Demand-enhancing and cost-reducing activities are complements when an increase in the level of one activity increases the marginal profitability of the other. For example, this would occur when managers redesign their products and in the process also reduce their defect rates. Demand-enhancing and cost-reducing activities are substitutes when an increase in the level of one activity reduces the marginal profitability of the other. This would occur, for example, when managers allocate scarce resources (e.g., managerial attention to control costs) to some products at the expense of others.

The second consideration driving structural choice is whether spillovers of know-how are positively or negatively correlated. Spillovers refer to the transfer of knowledge within the firm that occurs when a given activity is performed. The spillovers that are available to a firm in a given situation depend on the firm's capabilities at that time. Spillovers in two activities are positively correlated if they both primarily benefit a single dimension. For example, this would occur if the introduction of a new product in one market helps the firm produce or sell the product in other markets. They are negatively correlated if spillovers in one activity benefit one dimension (e.g., products) while spillovers in a second activity benefit the other dimension (e.g., geography).

The problem for top managers in a decentralized multiproduct, multilocation firm is to shape the incentives for local managers so that they perform appropriately on product and geographic dimensions. Doing this counteracts the free-rider problem that arises when local managers fail to internalize the benefits that their activities generate for the rest of the firm. The choice of an appropriate organization design can shape local managers' incentives to perform optimally.

Baron and Besanko identify the conditions in which a matrix structure is never optimal and those conditions in which a matrix can be optimal. A matrix will never be optimal when spillovers are positively correlated and activities are profit complements. When activities are profit complements but spillovers are negatively correlated, a matrix may be optimal if spillovers do not disproportionately favor one dimension over another. If activities are profit substitutes and spillovers are positively correlated, then a matrix can be optimal if the activities are strong substitutes. Otherwise, a product or geographic structure is optimal. Finally, if spillovers are negatively correlated and activities are profit substitutes, a matrix will be optimal if spillovers are strongly product-specific in one activity and strongly specific to geography in the other activity.

To see if (and how) real global firms acted consistently with their model, Baron and Besanko looked at how Citibank reorganized as it adopted a global approach to its business that required a balance between product and local market demands.[9] They examined the formation of the Global Relationship Bank (GRB) in 1994 and the creation of the Global Markets unit in 1997 to bridge between the GRB and Emerging Market units within Citibank. They concluded that Citibank's reorganizations were consistent with a need to balance customer and geographic orientations within a global framework.

Network Structure

Figure 16.4 represents the network structure. The basic unit of design in the network structure is the worker rather than the specified job or task. Workers, either singly or in combination, can contribute to multiple organizational tasks or can be reconfigured and recombined as the tasks of the organization change. At a more aggregated level of analysis, networks develop from the patterned relationships of organizational

FIGURE 16.4
THE SPIDER'S WEB ORGANIZATION—AN EXAMPLE OF A NETWORK

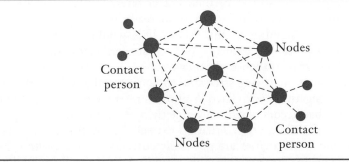

The figure shows a network organization structure based on communications patterns.

Source: Adapted from J. B. Quinn, *Intelligent Enterprise*, 1992, pp. 120–129.

subunits. Networks of small autonomous firms can even approximate the behavior of larger firms, earning them the name "virtual firms."

Groups in a network are organized into cross-cutting teams on the basis of task, geography, or customer, but relationships between work groups are governed more by the often-changing implicit and explicit requirements of common tasks than by the formal lines of authority that characterize other structures, although the structure includes both formal and informal linkages among members.[10] A network is preferable to other structures when the substantial coordination costs of employing it are less than the gains in technical efficiency and cooperation. The Japanese *keiretsu* structure discussed earlier is a type of network in which informal ties between members also facilitate coordination and reduce agency problems. The interrelationships among firms in the biotechnology industry provide an example of network structures that facilitate information flows. Such flows are necessary because these technologies have applications in such diverse areas as seeds, pharmaceuticals, and beer. Observers have seen these networks as a principal reason for the industry's historically high level of new product development.[11]

Network structures are becoming more popular as their organizational costs decline. The spread of the Internet has provided an infrastructure with which networks can form and continue operating at a much lower cost than for more traditional relationship-based infrastructures or for more dedicated but less flexible coordination schemes such as Electronic Data Interchange (EDI). In this sense, networks have always been possible modes of organizing but have been too costly to rely on in most business environments. There are exceptions, of course. For example, the world diamond industry has long been characterized by extensive informal networks that routinely handle large amounts of expensive product, relying almost solely on interpersonal trust.

Modular organization is a type of network structure that involves relatively self-contained organizational subunits tied together through a technology that focuses on standardized linkages. Most of the critical activities for a modular subunit are contained within that unit, and links with the broader organization are minimized. Modularity is most common in those industries characterized by heterogeneous production processes in terms of both inputs and outputs. Firms in these industries require the flexibility provided by modular organization. The degree of industry technological change also influences the possibilities for modular organization, since the structure facilitates adaptation to such change.

Although modular organization may limit some opportunities for scope economies, it also helps networks to grow by fostering the piecemeal modification of the network through the addition or subtraction of subunits without significant disruption to other relationships. This also increases the opportunities for innovation within subunits. Finally, networks, especially modular ones, grow as actors gain experience in organizing around a common set of standards that permit the combination of complementary products around tight interunit linkages but without the need for common ownership. The overall effect of these changes is to increase the possibilities for cooperative action in networks by reducing search, monitoring, and control costs for network actors without significantly increasing the transactions costs of interactions.

Why Are There So Few Types?

The preceding discussion suggests a relatively small number of structural types from which a would-be organization designer might choose. Although experts might differ on particular entries, the idea that there are only a few basic types of structures is a common one among academics, consultants, and managers. At first glance, this might seem strange. Given the size and complexity of large firms, one might suspect that there could be a very large number of design variables and many ways to organize. This suggests that firms would come to idiosyncratic organizing solutions to meet their particular needs and thus produce a variety of structures. Yet this does not seem to happen.

One reason for the limited range of types might be imitation. As large, successful, and visible firms reach solutions regarding how they should organize, other firms may see what they do and imitate them. Indeed, as we have already mentioned, it was not uncommon to hear about the "General Motors" model or multidivisional organization. This may have some value, but it is hard to see how a small number of firms are so widely imitated across industries as to justify a small set of general types. Imitation also fails to explain how these types are identified by pathbreaking firms in the first place.

John Roberts suggests that the reasons for the limited range of structural types may be more fundamental.[12] While a large number of design variables are available, choices from among these variables are not independent of each other. Structural variables and related change activities are interdependent and thus may share *complementarities*, such that doing more of some design variables will increase the returns to managers doing more with other related variables. For example, organizing to pursue a product differentiation strategy based on product quality will be associated with lower volume performance, specialized staffing, frequent product redesign, and higher prices. Design variables may also be interdependent as *substitutes*, such that doing more of some activities reduces the value from doing more of others.

The ways in which organizational design variables are interdependent will determine the general types of structural types that emerge. Complementarities among choice variables will result in a set of variables having a greater overall value than can be obtained from changing the particular change variables in isolation of the others. In such circumstances, it could even be that changes in any one design variable will not contribute to firm performance and could even detract from it. This suggests that organization design choices will tend to cluster together, that a "mix and match" approach will not prove feasible and that intermediate positions between structural types will not promote effectiveness and may actually reduce effectiveness, relative to a choice of one clear type or another. Roberts refers to these ideas as the *nonconvexity* of the organization design choice set and the *nonconcavity* of organizational performance.

◆ ◆ ◆ ◆ ◆ STRUCTURE–ENVIRONMENT COHERENCE

Knowing that a structure is coherent is a first step toward solving the organizational design problem. It is also necessary for managers to determine whether a structure is appropriate for them. A coherent structure will destroy rather than create value if it fails to enable the firm to apply its resources and capabilities to opportunities within its business environment. Thus, the optimal organizational structure for a firm depends on the environmental circumstances it faces. For example, a functional structure may work well for a manufacturer of supercomputers, such as Cray Research, but would probably work poorly for a large bank, such as Chase.

The idea that there is no uniformly "best" structure for all firms in all circumstances is an old one that focuses on environmental contingencies. Some contingency-based research has examined how environmental characteristics may be associated with structural characteristics of firms without considering the product market choices that a firm might make. The idea is that any firm working in such an environment would have to adapt its design to address environmental demands. This work has focused on two sets of envirnmental factors that may influence the relative efficiency of different structures: (1) technology and task interdependence and (2) information processing.

Technology and Task Interdependence

Technology generally refers to the base of scientific knowledge underlying what a firm does, as well as the general state of know-how behind the application of scientific knowledge to specific products and services. While many firms do invest in their own R&D to enhance their competitive positioning, most firms must take their technology as exogenous, at least in the short term. That the characteristics of a firm's knowledge base will influence the structural type that it adopts is clear. A firm employing a well-known and mature technology, for example, will almost certainly organize differently from a firm working with a rapidly evolving and less well-known technology, the first being likely to adopt a structure conducive to more stable, more standardized, and higher volume production, while the second will need flexibility, responsiveness to change, and specialist staff resources and other attributes helpful in more turbulent environments.

As the characteristics of the firm's technology change, its structure will also need to change to accommodate new coordination needs. For example, if a firm's technology changed to permit increased production volume and more routine handling of raw materials, its coordination needs would also change. The firm's structure would need to change to accommodate the increased volume of activities that the firm would have to perform and the increased number of decisions that it would have to make to handle that volume. For example, this might require a new division with purchasing responsibilities.

James Thompson argues that technology determines the degree of *task interdependence*—the extent to which two or more positions depend on each other to do their own work.[13] Thompson defines three modes of task interdependence: reciprocal, sequential, and pooled. *Reciprocal interdependence* exists when two or more workers or work groups depend on each other to do their work. *Sequential interdependence* exists between two or more workers, positions, or groups when one depends on the outcomes of the others, but not vice versa. For example, this situation would occur if an upstream manufacturing unit produced inputs that were critical for the success of a downstream sales or assembly unit. Finally, *pooled interdependence* exists when two or more positions are not directly dependent on each other but are associated through their independent contributions to the success of the firm. For example, line units in different product divisions may have little or no relationship with each other short of being parts of the same corporation. This distinction suggests that organization design processes that successively group individuals to coordinate their activities and utilize their shared resources. Positions and tasks that are reciprocally interdependent should be grouped together first, since they are the most costly to coordinate. Next, positions that are sequentially dependent, such as positions at different points of the value chain, may be grouped together. Finally, positions having pooled interdependence need only be linked by a common affiliation.

As technology changes, so may the basis for competition in an industry by changing the industry's core assets.[14] This in turn will alter task interdependence within firms and possible changes in the appropriate structures for affected firms. Advances in computers and telecommunications weaken reciprocal and sequential interdependence among many positions and reduce the costs of coordinating activities among individuals and groups within the firm or with partners in other firms. Using faxes, personal computers, and "groupware" computer software, engineers and product specialists located on different continents can coordinate the design of a new product even while few managers of such a team ever meet face to face. With such technology, a small investment research firm can provide analysis to subscribers from Chicago and distribute it globally to subscribers out of New York, while the firm's marketing agent could reside in Puerto Rico and its publicist in Phoenix. Neither of these arrangements would have been possible 20 years ago. This reduction in the costs of coordination reduces the need for members of a team to be in the same part of the firm's formal organization or even to be part of the same firm. (We also note that virtual firms appear to suffer from diseconomies of scale if they attempt to grow too large, since relationships among members become very complex and costly to coordinate above a fairly small number of individuals.)

Efficient Information Processing

Jay Galbraith presents an argument for organization design based on information processing.[15] He argues that work groups can normally operate independently and can manage themselves by work rules that become increasingly routine. Administrative hierarchy (i.e., bosses, supervisors) develops to handle "exceptions": decisions that cannot be easily made by applying standard organizational routines. Successively higher levels of organization are needed to handle more difficult types of exceptions. Decisions at the top of an organization are presumably the most difficult and least routine of all—that is, strategic decisions. This implies that structural change occurs in response to changes in the amount, complexity, or speed of information processing that a firm must undertake. As work groups are forced to process more information or act more quickly, existing routines become strained, and some adjustment, either in additional supervision or some cross-cutting team arrangement, is needed. For example, marketing decisions that may be routine in an industry with stable demand, high entry barriers, and a few well-known domestic competitors become less routine as the market becomes more globalized or as changes in technology destroy entry barriers. Effective pricing and promotion decisions may now require keeping track of foreign competitors and monitoring demand conditions in an increasingly segmented market. These new demands might overwhelm standard operating procedures developed in an earlier and more stable era.

Luis Garicano models the influence of information processing on organization design and achieves a result consistent with Galbraith's work.[16] He proposes a production function that requires time and knowledge as inputs about production problems and in which problems differ according to their difficulty and the frequency. Workers can acquire and communicate knowledge about solutions to problems. Garicano finds that an optimal organization design involves dividing workers into production workers and problems solvers who specialize in dealing with more difficult and/or infrequent problems. His results are consistent with a pyramidal structure in which the human capital of workers increases as the number of workers at a level decreases. His results imply that a decrease in the cost of acquiring or transmitting knowledge increases the average span of control and may reduce or increase the number of organizational levels through scale effects.

The reorganization of Pepsi in 1988 illustrates how demands for faster information processing driven by changes in the external business environment can overwhelm a hierarchy. For Pepsi, a key change was the emergence of large regional supermarket chains. These often operated in territories that encompassed several different regional offices within the Pepsi Bottling Group, while Pepsi's existing structure gave nobody regionwide authority over pricing. When faced with requests for promotions or special pricing deals by a supermarket chain, executives at Pepsi often disagreed over the appropriate strategy to follow. Their disputes were then funneled up the hierarchy to Roger Enrico, then the head of Pepsi USA, who was forced to become involved in region-level pricing and promotion decisions. Not surprisingly, this impaired Pepsi's ability to respond and put it at a competitive disadvantage in a market that demands nimble responses to fast-changing circumstances. Part of the reason Pepsi chose a geographically oriented matrix when it reorganized was to clarify the lines of authority in pricing and promotion decisions. The new structure created the position of area general manager, who had final authority for operational decisions (including pricing and promotions) within areas that were roughly the size of the territories of the large supermarket chains.

Arthur Stinchcombe emphasizes the role of organizational structure in promoting more efficient *information retrieval*.[17] He argues that firms should be structured to facilitate the efficient retrieval of information in the varied conditions faced by the firm on a regular basis. For example, a pharmaceutical firm might want an independent R&D department capable of rapid interaction with medical school faculty, an important source of new product development. Different levels of structure can deal with different informational needs. For example, information about labor costs or demand may be highly local. If local work groups control these factors, they will have the proper incentives to gather information. Dealing with federal regulations, however, should be the responsibility of a work group with a broader scope. Stinchcombe also argues that firms should internalize activities (rather than rely on market coordination) when information from them is critical. It is important for firms to be "where the news breaks, whenever it breaks," since rapid information processing facilitates effective adjustments.

Bruce Kogut and Udo Zander pursue a knowledge-based view of the firm and make a similar argument for the superiority of organizational structure in processing information relative to market alternatives.[18] Their focus is on the *multinational corporation*, a variant of the multidivisional structure whose units cross national boundaries. They argue that this structural form is superior at transferring specific types of knowledge across national boundaries rather than as a means for internalizing transactions in the face of market failure. Their focus is on tacit knowledge that is complex, difficult to codify, and difficult to teach. They hypothesized that the more a firm's projects were characterized by tacit knowledge, the more likely the firm was to internalize those projects. They found modest support for this hypothesis in their study of 20 innovative Swedish firms and 45 total innovations.

These arguments are also related to the discussion in Chapter 4 about how firms may integrate upstream to obtain better information about input availability and prices. As innovations in computers, telecommunications, and financial markets have reduced the costs to firms of information gathering, this rationale has become less important in choosing an organizational structure, depending on whether innovations weaken a firm's existing competencies or its basis for obtaining better information through vertical integration.

EXAMPLE 16.2 ORGANIZATIONAL STRUCTURE AT AT&T

Robert Garnet examined the growth of the Bell System between 1876 and 1909, during the early years of the firm when neither its monopoly status nor its corporate survival could be taken for granted.[19] Garnet's study illustrates the relationship between a firm's structure and its environmental contingencies factors, such as size and market turbulence. One of his conclusions was that as the volume of its activities increased, the firm needed to reorganize to meet the increased informational demands. AT&T faced this situation during these years. Between 1885 and 1920, the Bell System went from fewer than 2,000 central offices with 25,000 employees to nearly 6,000 offices and 240,000 employees. In the aftermath of this growth, Bell needed substantial reorganization.

Garnet also came to the conclusion that as AT&T's environment became more volatile, for example, because of increased competition, it needed to reorganize to promote rapid processing of information. AT&T faced increased competition during its early period. Its initial patents expired in 1894, after which new competitors entered local markets. The changes made by AT&T in its organization structure are consistent with the need for firms to organize in a manner consistent with environmental pressures. When the firm was first consolidated around 1880, it was a loose affiliation of Bell Company interests and licenses, held together not by formal structure, but by the terms of licenses and by partial equity ownership of licenses by the Bell Company. By 1884, this structure was obsolete and inefficient, and attempts were made to tighten leases, improve accounting controls, and consolidate the firm. Despite these efforts, the company's earnings continued to decline.

By 1890, the first significant organization structure was proposed, largely along territorial lines. Corporate accounting procedures were also revised in 1891. Another major reorganization occurred at AT&T in 1909, this time focusing on operating companies that were organized on state lines and that were subject to overall control by AT&T corporate headquarters. Each operating company was internally organized along functional lines. This reorganization occurred, coincidentally, at the lowest ebb of corporate performance before the Kingsbury Commitment, a 1913 agreement between AT&T and the U.S. Department of Justice that secured the firm's dominant market position in exchange for a commitment to allow competitors to interconnect with the AT&T system. AT&T corporate headquarters was also reorganized along functional lines in 1912. These reorganizations are consistent with a contingency view. The functional structure improved the operating companies' ability to handle the increased volume of operations that developed during this period. The new headquarters structure fostered a division of labor between operating companies and headquarters and allowed the firm to expand as the Bell system grew.

◆ ◆ ◆ ◆ ◆ STRUCTURE FOLLOWS STRATEGY

Understanding the relationship between structure and environmental factors, such as technological requirements or exogenous demands for information processing, is a necessary part of explaining how a firm organizes. It is not sufficient for understanding a firm's structural choices, however, because although many factors may affect a firm's structure in a given situation, only a few will be critical. We need to know which factors the firm's managers have seen as critical in their decisions. This requires considering the relationship between the firm's strategy and its organization structure.

In his classic work, *Strategy and Structure*, Alfred Chandler first articulated how firms' strategic choices influence their structures.[20] Based on case studies of firms such as DuPont, General Motors, Standard Oil of New Jersey (which has become ExxonMobil), and Sears, Chandler concluded that changes in organization structure were driven by changes in strategy, which, in turn, were associated with changes in the external conditions firms faced. In short, Chandler's thesis is that *structure follows strategy*.

Chandler's basic argument runs as follows. In the late nineteenth century, developments in the technological and market infrastructures (which we describe in Chapter 1) created opportunities for achieving unprecedented economies of scale and scope in various industries, such as tobacco, chemicals, light and heavy machinery, and meatpacking. Firms such as American Tobacco, DuPont, McCormick Harvesting Machine Company (which became International Harvester), and Swift responded by investing in large scale production facilities and internalizing activities, such as sales and distribution, that independent companies had previously performed for them. They also invested in the development of managerial hierarchies. The first structure typically employed by these early hierarchical firms was the U-form, which permitted them a specialized division of labor that facilitated economies of scale in manufacturing, marketing, and distribution.

The firms that were the first in their industries to invest in large-scale production facilities and develop managerial hierarchies expanded rapidly and often dominated their industries. But most of the early growth of these firms was within a single line of business or occurred within a single market. Shortly after 1900, however, this began to change. Some firms, such as Singer and International Harvester, aggressively expanded overseas. Indeed, by 1914, the largest commercial enterprises in Russia were Singer and International Harvester. Others, such as DuPont and Procter & Gamble, diversified their product lines. This shift in strategy revealed shortcomings in the U-form. According to Chandler, the attempt by the top management of the newly diversified firms to monitor functional departments in the U-form structure led to administrative overload and motivated managers to experiment with alternative organizational structures.

The multidivisional structure, or M-form, that emerged after 1920 was a response to the limitations of the U-form in larger diversified firms. The M-form removed top managers from involvement in the operational details of departments, allowing them to specialize in strategic decisions and long-range planning. Division managers monitored the operational activities of the functional departments that reported to them and were rewarded on the basis of divisional performance. As we discussed, divisional contributions to corporate success are easier to measure than the contributions of functional departments. This made running divisions as profit centers and basing rewards for division managers on division profit-and-loss statements effective ways to motivate division managers.

Although corporate structures have evolved since the days of the M-form, the principle that structure follows strategy still applies. The network structure of the clothing manufacturer Benetton provides a clear example. Benetton's generic strategy is to differentiate itself from its competitors based on unique color combinations and bold designs. Its formal structure is functional, although it outsources many of its traditional functions. The organization operates not just through internal coordination, but through active external coordination of a network of suppliers and distributors. Top management maintains direct lines of communication with storeowners to exchange information about customer demands. Benetton also works with several

EXAMPLE 16.3 STRATEGY, STRUCTURE, AND THE ATTEMPTED MERGER BETWEEN THE UNIVERSITY OF CHICAGO HOSPITAL AND MICHAEL REESE HOSPITAL

The idea that strategy follows structure has implications for mergers between firms that have pursued different strategies. In melding two such organizations together, issues relating to the control of assets and resources frequently arise. As we saw earlier, the allocation of rights of control of assets is a key determinant of how efficiently a vertical chain or a partnership of two organizations performs. Inside an organization, structure determines the basic rights to control the firm's assets. Thus, organizational structure can critically affect the success of a merger.

The attempted merger between the University of Chicago Hospital and the Michael Reese Hospital provides an example in which the control of assets and resources was a key issue in the attempted integration of the two organizations. The University of Chicago Hospital is on the campus of a leading research university, which led the hospital to pursue a strategy based on a reputation for providing state-of-the-art medicine. Indeed, advertisements for the hospital celebrated the research accomplishments of its medical staff. Consistent with this strategy, most physicians had faculty appointments in the university's medical school, and faculty were evaluated on the basis of their research. Physician salaries were based more on their academic standing than on the patient revenues they brought to the hospital.

The University of Chicago Hospital's nearest competitor on the city's south side was the Michael Reese Hospital. This hospital also had a long history of quality care, with special emphases on community service and close relationships between medical staff and patients. The medical staff was organized according to a traditional scheme—staff members were identified by clinical areas but billed patients for their services independently of the hospital's billings. In other words, physicians were rewarded exclusively for providing patient care.

The two hospitals sought to merge in 1985. The merger would allow them to consolidate and reallocate some services and possibly avoid price and nonprice competition in their shared markets. Anticipating a potential conflict between medical staffs over resources and authority to set policy, the two hospitals attempted to negotiate an organizational structure before they merged. As it turned out, they could not develop an agreeable structure to manage their surgical departments as an integrated unit. University physicians refused to be evaluated on the basis of clinical care, while Reese physicians refused to be thought of as research faculty. Unable to coordinate this vital area and fearful that economies in surgery would not be realized, the hospitals called off the merger.

suppliers who can rapidly fill orders for undyed wool and cotton sweaters. Benetton's network structure, built around functional areas, enables it to rapidly tailor its product line to meet ever-changing consumer tastes.

A similar network structure developed in SAP AG, a German firm that is one of the world's largest software producers and the leading producer of real-time, integrated applications software for client/server computing. The company has grown rapidly (sales revenues grew nearly 400 percent between 1991 and 1995 to DM 2.7 billion), while its founders have been intent on SAP remaining largely a product development firm with a flat organization structure. To do this, SAP managers decided not to expand into related but different lines of business, such as training and implementation consulting, even though meeting customer needs during implementation would

EXAMPLE 16.4 SAMSUNG: REINVENTING A CORPORATION[21]

Major environmental shifts often force firms to reassess strategies and restructure their organizations. The Samsung business group provides an example of how to reinvent a corporation when faced with the hostile market forces that Asian firms must increasingly endure. Samsung was founded in 1938 as a general trading store, exporting fruit and dried fish to Japanese-occupied Manchuria. It has since become the largest South Korean business group, or *chaebol*, at $54 billion in sales in 1995. Samsung operates in such diverse industries as aerospace, chemicals, and finance, but is best known as the world's largest maker of leading-edge computer memory chips.

Samsung's rise to prominence was based on strong support from the Korean government, inexpensive labor, and an authoritarian culture. As a result, Samsung's strategy from the 1960s until the mid-1980s was based on using cheap labor to produce lower-quality products at low prices. By also producing large volumes, Samsung reaped economies of scale and thus captured comfortable margins, which also enabled it to enter a variety of businesses with great success.

In the late 1980s, however, a combination of factors impaired Samsung's historical sources of competitive advantage and caused its managers to reevaluate strategies that had brought the company such success for over two decades. South Korean wages began to rise, and workers began to unionize and strike, causing labor instability. Samsung does not have unions because it pays high wages. Even so, the general labor climate has become less friendly. The value of the South Korean currency, the won, had also appreciated, making South Korean exports more expensive. In addition, increased global competition has further eroded Samsung's competitive positioning.

In response, Chairman Lee Kun-Hee has launched a sweeping remake of Samsung's culture, including a restructuring of operations. Lee has radically decentralized decision making and encouraged individuality in a company that was known for its rigid hierarchy and subservience to authority. Managers who are not able to assume such responsibility are fired. To encourage individuality, Lee has initiated training programs and other innovative techniques. For instance, each year Samsung sends 400 managers abroad, fully subsidized, for 12 months to do whatever they want. The only requirement is that when they return, they must show proficiency in the host country's language and culture. In addition to reinventing Samsung's culture, Lee has consolidated groups in related businesses and specialized in more capital- and technology-intensive industries. Samsung has also tried to shift from being a low-quality, low-cost producer to producing higher-quality goods. Lee wanted to pursue high-quality, high-tech markets and compete on an equal basis with leading American, Japanese, and European firms.

This shift in culture and operations forced Samsung to be at the leading edge in innovation and productivity. The firm traditionally adopted its technology from more advanced firms, but Lee instituted massive R&D spending to make Samsung more self-sufficient. Furthermore, Lee has automated plants and even moved some plants to Mexico to save labor costs. Samsung has transformed itself in response to major changes in both global markets and South Korea. One sign that Lee's programs are working is that Samsung won IBM's seal of approval as a supplier, resolving many doubts about its ability to provide quality products.

be critical for growth. To accomplish its growth objectives, SAP has developed a network organization of partners, who perform 80 to 90 percent of the consulting implementation business generated by SAP products. Partners range from major consulting firms, such as Accenture and CSC Index, to hardware manufacturers, such as IBM, HP, and Sun Microsystems, to software and chip manufacturers, such as Oracle,

Microsoft, and Intel. Relationship managers for these partnerships play an important role in SAP's corporate structure.

Strategy, Structure, and the Multinational Firm

The idea that structure follows strategy has been applied to firms that compete internationally.[22] As multidivisional firms became larger, they were more likely to expand their operations overseas. These firms initially created "international divisions" to manage their foreign activities. As foreign business grew, however, this structure increasingly failed to coordinate foreign operations that, in effect, duplicated the activities of the domestic firm in multiple markets. This led to reorganization into multinational firms, characterized by separate divisions for different countries (or regions, if national markets were sufficiently similar or if the volume of business in a particular area was small). Growing multinationals faced pressures for coordination across countries and specialization within countries, especially firms with technologies that permitted substantial scale and scope economies. This led to global strategies that viewed the world as the firm's market. This represented a shift away from the firm's home market as the locus for its strategy. Firms that pursued this strategy reorganized to promote scale economies in global production and distribution.

The final step in the structural development of these multinational firms occurred when managers at corporate headquarters learned to balance responsiveness to local conditions with centralization to achieve global economies. This transnational strategy is associated with flexible organizations that combine matrix and network structures in ways that permit a great variety of organizational designs. Recent research has focused on the variety of structures that can emerge within internally differentiated multinational firms. A parallel interest of this work has been in the processes used to manage corporate activities. This supports the idea of corporate management as focusing on the interactions among business units and groups, rather than on their particular product market strategies.

Structure, Strategy, Knowledge, and Capabilities

Thomas Hammond argues that structure influences strategy because critical knowledge and decision-making capabilities in large firms are dispersed throughout the firm rather than concentrated in top managers.[23] This means that a firm's structure determines how and in what order lower-level decision makers come together to contribute their information to corporate decisions. Structure sets the agenda for top managers in making strategic decisions, since it determines which options are considered for a decision, which options are to be compared, and in what order comparisons are to be made. This view of structure is related to the knowledge-based view of the firm, which argues that organizations not only reduce costs but provide enhanced abilities to generate and manipulate new knowledge to use as a strategic capability.[24]

Organizational structure can also bias the information that flows up through the hierarchy to top managers. The perspectives of lower-level decision makers, while providing the information critical for strategic decisions, may also be systematically biased according to the requirements of their positions within the firm. For example, manufacturing, sales, and research personnel often differ in their time frames (e.g., short-run versus long-run orientations) and their responsibilities to the organization. This means that the top management team, through its composition and

EXAMPLE 16.5 TRANSNATIONAL STRATEGY AND ORGANIZATION STRUCTURE AT SMITHKLINE-BEECHAM[25]

SmithKline-Beecham, a transnational pharmaceutical firm that was created in 1989 by the merger of the American firm SmithKline-Beckman and the British firm Beecham, illustrates the interaction of strategy and structure in global markets. A merger with Beecham was attractive to SmithKline for several reasons. SmithKline depended on a few products (primarily the ulcer drug Tagamet) for much of its sales. It was vulnerable to losing market share to generic drugs and was open to a takeover because it had overdiversified. SmithKline-Beckman and Beecham also had several complementary product lines. Beecham was strong in consumer health products and self-medications, whereas SmithKline was stronger in prescription drugs. The two firms also had potential synergies in their scientific competencies and new product development schedules. This merger created a firm with a combined annual research and development budget of over $750 million. Finally, the firms had complementary geographic markets: Beecham was strong in Europe; SmithKline in the United States and Japan.

SmithKline might have been able to expand into new products and markets and develop additional scientific competencies either through internal development or through hybrid organizational arrangements, such as strategic alliances and joint ventures. But its managers felt that internal product development and market expansion would have been too slow to be of much practical value in the increasingly competitive global pharmaceuticals market. And while it did experiment with strategic alliances and joint ventures, SmithKline found both experiences to be unsatisfactory. Alliances were too loose to provide incentives for the allied firms to cooperate with each other, and the autonomy of the partners in their joint ventures led to governance and incentive problems. Given the complex synergies that motivated the merger, determining an organizational structure for the combined firm was a significant issue. Henry Wendt, the CEO after the merger, summed up the problem: "Neither form of organization structure (product or geography) simultaneously captures the kinds of global-local synergies of skills, scale, and scope now considered necessary by aggressive transnational companies."

SmithKline-Beecham eventually adopted a flexible matrix structure that comprised "modified matrix-based multifunctional teams." This structure combines both centralized functional structures with local autonomy. The flexible matrix emphasized strong local management teams, with responsibility for customer-focused functions, including sales, marketing, and product design. In addition to local decision-making autonomy, the structure allows global efficiencies to be pursued at the corporate level by functional groups, such as manufacturing, information technologies, and research and development.

decision processes, bears the additional burden of compensating for lower-level biases.

Structure also provides the rules for resolving implementation disputes. However, the rules for dispute resolution provided by a given structure may be inconsistent with the requirements of the firm's strategy. For example, if a strategy requires that employees perform their tasks and represent themselves to customers consistently, then disputes among employees should be referred up the hierarchy, so that a consistent approach can be developed. A structure that provides incentives to employees to use the hierarchy for resolving disputes would be consistent with this strategy. On the other hand, if a strategy required the timely use of localized knowledge by

EXAMPLE 16.6 WINGSPANBANK.COM: A NETWORK ORGANIZATION[27]

WingspanBank.com was launched on June 24, 1999, as an Internet-only banking venture of First USA, a credit card subsidiary of Bank One, one of the largest bank holding companies in the United States. The intent of the venture was to create a virtual bank that could offer a full array of banking services, with one-stop shopping available on a "24/7" basis, on the Internet. The new bank would offer customers an experience driven by two principles: (1) a single application to access any of the bank's products and (2) a single log-on from which customers could access any of their accounts.

Industry observers and practitioners had long noticed a trend toward moving customers to lower cost channels, such as automated teller machines (ATMs) and telephone banking. With the increased competition in the business brought about by deregulation and the increased availability of tools and facilitating infrastructure, Internet banking was viewed as the wave of the future, a line of business that could be profitable and scalable, provided that first-mover advantages were obtained.

Dick Vague, the First USA CEO who spearheaded the project, saw a need to move quickly and independently of the Bank One system. To do this, he put together a project development team of over 30 different organizations to provide the needed components of the venture. WingspanBank was to be a network organization, with First USA (and Bank One) playing the role of the aggregator, which integrated vendor services together seamlessly for consumers and which in turn would own the relationship with consumers. Among the partners on the project were IBM Global Services, McKinsey, Sanchez Computer Associates, and DLJ Direct, along with a host of specialized technical and banking service providers. Because of the project's complexity, the demanding customer requirements, and the need for rapid growth, profitability goals were subordinated to four more immediate operational goals: acquiring new customers, cross-selling products, maintaining site integrity, and providing excellent customer experiences.

The implementation of WingspanBank proved to be an example of "winning battles, but losing wars." The bank provided the wide range of services to consumers that it had promised, even though savings accounts and money market accounts were not provided. The bank was positively viewed by industry experts and won a number of awards in 1999, including "#2 Overall Internet Bank," "#1 Online Bank for Retail Customers," and "#1 Banking Site Best of the Web." Nevertheless, customer growth had not gone as planned. WingspanBank reported having 144,000 accounts by March 31, 2000 (versus expectations for 500,000 new accounts). New customers had been expensive to obtain, with the bank's nationwide advertising campaign costing $110 million. This translated into a cost per account of over $1,000 (versus $400 expected costs). The accounts that were established were smaller than expected.

Part of the difficulty appears to be that WingspanBank's developers focused on the technical details of their plan without considering the soundness of their strategy. It is difficult for even a well-crafted network to overcome such a shortcoming. Customers proved very amenable to using Internet banking, provided they already had a relationship with their bank. Major established banks, like Wells Fargo, that linked Internet services to their existing branch structures added millions of customers. Even Bancone.com, the sister site to WingspanBank, had 500,000 customers by the end of 1999, without the large marketing budget of WingspanBank. Not surprisingly, customers proved very reluctant to place significant amounts of their savings in Internet bank accounts. During the 1999–2000 period, for example, over 3.2 million customers opened on-line accounts, while another 3.1 million closed such accounts. These factors led to WingspanBank being consolidated on a single platform with Bancone.com. The unprofitable venture was eventually closed in 2001. Bank One is part of the new bank JPMorgan Chase created on July 1, 2004 upon completion of the holding company merger between JPMorgan Chase & Co. and Bank One Corporation. The Bank One retail brand is now known as Chase.

employees, then approaches that consistently referred problems up the hierarchy would be inconsistent with the strategy and would probably increase rather than decrease the firm's implementation costs.

Structure as Routine and Heuristic

Richard Nelson and Sidney Winter, proponents of evolutionary economics, view the actions of firms as the result of a complex set of behavior patterns, or *routines*.[26] These routines evolve as the firm develops in response to changes in its external environment. Routines simplify the complexity of the information a firm receives from its environment and constitute its "learning by doing." As the firm encounters problems, it experiments by varying current routines until it obtains a satisfactory result. When that occurs, the organization "remembers" the solution by continuing to perform the routine in the future. In this sense, an organization's routines form the basis of its distinctive competencies. A firm's routines can also concern conflict resolution and governance. As the firm develops, it also encounters problems with conflict resolution, incentives and motivation, and control. Satisfactory solutions to these problems are retained in routines, while unsatisfactory activities are eventually changed. Thus, routines represent "truces" among contending parties within the firm.

Nelson and Winter offer two views of the strategy–structure relationship that differ from Chandler's perspective. The first is a "bottom-up" view, in which strategy and structure evolve from local interactions of the firm with its environment rather than from top managers formulating and implementing a comprehensive reorganization. This suggests that the relationship of the firm to its environment, as well as the current patterns of interpersonal relationships generally referred to as the firm's "structure," are both the cumulative result of a long series of adaptations.

A second view of the strategy–structure relationship that Nelson and Winter present considers how managers make decisions. Strategy and structure are examples of high-level *heuristics*: principles or guideposts that reduce the average time spent by decision makers in addressing difficult and unusual problems. In this sense, strategy is a set of principles or decision guidelines that managers use to foster a firm's survival and profitability. Similarly, structure is a set of principles or guidelines for coordinating a firm's decisions in a manner consistent with its activities in the environment. In making strategic decisions, top managers will be bound by their routines and will either maintain prior decisions or incrementally modify them. Current decisions about strategy and structure will be constrained by past decisions. In this sense, strategy can follow structure just as easily as structure follows strategy.

CHAPTER SUMMARY

◆ Organizational structure concerns the arrangements, both formal and informal, by which a firm divides up its critical tasks, specifies how its managers and employees make decisions, and establishes routines and information flows to support operations so as to link opportunities in the environment with its resources and capabilities.

◆ If a firm's strategy is to be carried out, or *implemented*, individuals working within the firm must know about the strategy and its operational requirements for tasks and their coordination. A firm's structure reflects the ways in which the firm solves problems of information and coordination implied by its strategic decisions.

◆ Coordinating people and tasks is difficult even when everyone cooperates. Problems of incentives and controls further complicate the problem of coordinating cooperative agents to carry out the firm's strategy.

◆ Organization design typically involves two steps. First, simple tasks performed by simple work groups need to be organized. Second, work groups and their activities must be linked together into complex hierarchies.

◆ Simple tasks performed by small work groups can be structured in three ways: (1) *individually*—members of the work group are treated as if they were independent and receive incentives based on individual actions and outcomes; (2) *self-managed teams*—a collection of individuals, each member of which works with others to set and pursue common objectives, with individuals rewarded, in part, on the basis of group performance; and (3) *hierarchy of authority*—one member of the group monitors and coordinates the work of the other members.

◆ Large firms often require *complex hierarchies*, by which is meant a structure that involves multiple groups and multiple levels of groupings. Complex hierarchy arises when there is a need to organize simple work groups together into larger groups.

◆ Complex hierarchy involves two problems: (1) *departmentalization* and (2) *coordination and control of activities*.

◆ Departmentalization identifies formal groupings within the organization. These may be organized along a number of dimensions: common tasks or functions, inputs, outputs, geographic location, and time of work.

◆ Once groups have been identified and organized, problems of coordination and control arise. *Coordination* involves the flow of information to facilitate subunit decisions that are consistent with each other and with organizational objectives. *Control* involves the location of decision-making rights and rule-making authority within the hierarchy.

◆ There are two alternative approaches for developing coordination within firms. The first emphasizes *autonomy* or *self-containment* of work units, so that coordination needs across units are reduced. The second approach emphasizes the importance of strong *lateral relations* across work groups.

◆ The allocation of authority within the firm is typically considered in terms of *centralization* versus *decentralization*. As decisions are made at higher levels within a firm's hierarchy, the firm is said to be more centralized regarding those decisions. Conversely, as certain decisions are made at lower levels, the firm is more decentralized regarding those decisions.

◆ Four basic types of structure for large organizations can be identified: (1) the unitary *functional* structure (often called the U-form); (2) the *multidivisional* structure (often called the M-form); (3) the *matrix* structure; and (4) the *network* structure.

◆ The functional structure, or U-form, allows a specialization of labor to gain economies of scale in manufacturing, marketing, and distribution.

◆ The multidivisional structure, or M-form, creates a division of labor between top managers and division managers that removes top managers from involvement in the operational details of functional departments and divisions and allows them to specialize in strategic decisions and long-range planning. Division managers in the M-form firm monitor the operational activities of the functional departments that report to them and are rewarded on the basis of overall divisional performance.

◆ Matrix structures involve overlapping hierarchies and are necessary in situations where there are conflicting decision demands and severe constraints on managerial resources.

◆ The network structure focuses on individuals rather than positions and is the most flexible of the structural types. Recent developments in networking technologies and modular product designs have greatly expanded the potential applications of network organizations.

◆ Only a limited number of structural forms are efficient because the characteristics of structures share complementarities. Thus, it is difficult to mix and match structural types, and performance may decline if mixing is attempted.

◆ The best organizational structure for a particular firm depends on the specific circumstances it faces, although managers may differ on the environmental situation facing the firm or how the firm should organize to address it.

◆ Researchers have focused on two factors that affect the relative efficiency of different organizational structures: (1) technology and task interdependence and (2) information flows.

◆ Many plausible contingencies may affect a firm's structure at any given time. Those factors addressed by the firm's strategy will be the most important in determining an appropriate structural choice for the firm.

◆ The thesis that structure follows strategy has been applied to firms that compete internationally. Multinationals have discovered the need to balance responsiveness to local conditions with centralization to achieve global economies. This is the transnational strategy, and it is becoming associated with flexible organizations that combine matrix and network structures.

QUESTIONS

1. A team of six individuals must fold, stuff, seal, and stamp 250 preaddressed envelopes. Offer some suggestions for organizing this team. Would your suggestions differ if the team was responsible for processing 2,500 envelopes? for assembling 250 personal computers? Why would you change your recommendations?

2. Consider a firm whose competitive advantage is built almost entirely on its ability to achieve economies of scale in producing small electric motors that are used by the firm to make hair dryers, fans, vacuum cleaners, and food processors. Should this firm be organized on a multidivisional basis by product (hair dryer division, food processor division, etc.), or should it be organized functionally (marketing, manufacturing, finance, etc.)?

3. What types of structures would a firm consider if it was greatly expanding its global operations? What types of organizing problems would it be most likely to encounter?

4. In the 1980s, Sears acquired several financial services firms, including Allstate Insurance and Dean Witter Brokerage Services. Sears kept these businesses as largely autonomous divisions. By 1994, the strategy had failed, and Sears had divested all of its financial services holdings. Bearing in mind the dictum that structure follows strategy, identify the strategy that Sears had in mind when it acquired these businesses, and recommend a structure that might have led to better results.

5. Matrix organizations first sprang up in businesses that worked on scientific and engineering projects for narrow customer groups. Examples include Fluor, which built oil refineries in Saudi Arabia, and TRW, which supplied aerospace equipment to NASA. What do you suppose the dimensions of the matrix would be in such firms? Why would these companies develop such a complex structure?

6. It is sometimes argued that a matrix organization can serve as a mechanism for achieving *strategic fit*—the achievements of synergies across related business units resulting in a combined performance that is greater than units could achieve if they operated independently. Explain how a matrix organization could result in the achievement of strategic fit.

7. Is it possible to organize too much or too little to meet the needs of the environment? This would be a case of *strategic misfit*. How would you know if a misfit has occurred? Think of an example of misfit caused by an inappropriate organization design. Explain how a firm's structure could systematically increase its costs and place it at a strategic disadvantage.

8. Internet entrepreneurs worked hard to get their venture to the point of a successful initial public offering (IPO), but many discovered that their organizational issues changed and became more daunting after the IPO than they were before it and were just working to accommodate rapid growth. Explain why "going public" might put such a stress on a small firm's structure.

9. The "#1 or #2; Fix, Sell, or Close" rule was one of the most memorable aspects of Jack Welch's corporate strategy at GE. (Business units needed to achieve a #1 or #2 market share; if not, they had to fix, sell, or close the unit.) In the 1990s, however, this rule was changed to focus on smaller (10 to 15 percent) market share requirements but a requirement that business unit managers demonstrate significant growth potential. What impact did this change in corporate strategy have on the organization design of business units?

10. Many of the most pressing organizational issues attracting public attention seem to concern government agencies, especially those with responsibilities for preventing man-made disasters and attacks or responding to natural ones, such as hurricanes. How do the organizational design issues facing large firms compare with those facing rapid response public agencies such as FEMA or the EPA?

11. Although most managers might agree that firms should organize appropriately to their environmental conditions, they might easily differ on what environmental conditions a firm was facing and what an appropriate response to those conditions might entail. Explain the manager's role in developing a fit with the firm's environment.

12. The Lincoln Electric Company is a longtime maker of welding equipment in Cleveland, Ohio, whose industry performance has been legendary. Its operations have focused on its well-known piece-rate incentive system that permits it to gain significantly greater utilization of its capital assets than competitors, with a resulting competitive advantage on costs. In the mid-1990s, however, Lincoln experienced some difficulties in establishing new facilities outside of the United States and ended up modifying its organizational system when it opened facilities in Asia. What factors might contribute to the difficulties that even a well-managed firm might face in transferring its management and production systems to international locations?

ENDNOTES

[1]Caves, R. and D. Barton, *Efficiency in U.S. Manufacturing Industries*, Cambridge, MA, MIT Press, 1990, pp. 1–3.

[2]Chandler, A. D., *Strategy and Structure*, Cambridge, MA, MIT Press, 1962.

[3]Alchian, A. and H. Demsetz, "Production, Information Costs, and Economic Organization," *American Economic Review*, 62, 1972, pp. 777–795.

[4]The classic statement of these two problems is in March, J. and H. Simon, *Organizations*, New York, Wiley, 1958, pp. 22–27. For a review of research on these problems, see McCann, J. and J. R. Galbraith, "Interdepartmental Relations," in Nystrom, P. C. and W. H. Starbuck, *Handbook of Organizational Design*, 2, New York, Oxford University Press, 1981, pp. 60–84.

[5]This distinction is taken from information processing approaches to organization design. For a review, see McCann and Galbraith (1981). A similar distinction between informational decentralization and informational consolidation is sometimes made in economic analyses of organization structure. See Baron, D. and D. Besanko, "Information, Control, and Organizational Structure," *Journal of Economics & Management Strategy*, 1, Summer 1992, pp. 237–276.

[6]The network structure described in the first section is an alternative that relies on external contracting relationships.

[7]We would like to thank Suresh Krishna for developing this example.

[8]Baron, D. P. and D. Besanko, "Shared Incentive Authority and the Organization of the Firm," unpublished mimeo, Northwestern University, Department of Management and Strategy, July 1997.

[9]Baron, D. P. and D. Besanko, "Strategy, Organization, and Incentives: Global Banking at Citicorp," unpublished mimeo, Northwestern University, Department of Management and Strategy, April 1998.

[10]For an extended discussion of the network organization, see Baker, W. E., "The Network Organization in Theory and Practice," in Nohria, N. and R. G. Eccles, *Networks and Organizations*, Boston, Harvard Business School Press, 1992, pp. 397–429.

[11]For studies of interfirm networks that focus on Japanese and biotechnology examples, see Nohria, N. and R. G. Eccles (eds.), *Networks and Organizations*, Boston, Harvard Business School Press, 1992, pp. 309–394. For a detailed study of Monsanto's network efforts to develop and commercialize its biotechnology products, see Charles, D., *Lords of the Harvest*. Cambridge, MA, Perseus Publishing, 2001. For a general approach to network analysis that includes relations within and between firms, see Burt, R. S., *Structural Holes*, Cambridge, MA, Harvard University Press, 1992.

[12]Roberts, J. *The Modern Firm: Organizational Design for Performance and Growth*. Oxford, Oxford University Press, 2004, pp. 32–67.

[13]Thompson, J. D., *Organizations in Action*, New York, McGraw-Hill, 1967.

[14]McGahan, A. M., *How Industries Evolve*. Boston, Harvard Business School Press, 2004.

[15]Galbraith, J. R. and R. K. Kazanjian, *Strategy Implementation: The Role of Structure and Process*, 2d ed., St. Paul, MN, West Publishing, 1986.

[16]Garicano, L., "Hierarchies and the Organization of Knowledge in Production," *Journal of Political Economy*, October 2000.

[17]Stinchcombe, A. L., *Information and Organizations*, Berkeley, University of California Press, 1990.

[18] Kogut, B. and U. Zander (1993) Knowledge of the firm and the evolutionary theory of the modern corporation. *Journal of International Business Studies*, pp. 625–645.

[19]Garnet, R. W., *The Telephone Enterprise: The Evolution of the Bell System's Horizontal Structure, 1876–1909*, Baltimore, MD, Johns Hopkins University Press, 1985.

[20]Chandler, *Strategy and Structure*.

[21]This example is based on materials from four sources: "Samsung's Radical Shakeup," *Business Week*, February 28, 1994, pp. 74–76; "Samsung: Korea's Great Hope for High Tech," *Business Week*, February 3, 1992, pp. 44–45; "Good to Be Big, Better to Be Good," *The Economist*, August 18, 1990, pp. 7–10; "Samsung: South Korea Marches to Its Own Drummer," *Forbes*, May 16, 1988, pp. 84–89.

[22]For examples of these applications, see Stopford, J. and L. Wells, *Managing the Multinational Enterprise*, London, Longmans, 1972; Yoshihara, H., "Towards a Comprehensive Concept of Strategic Adaptive Behavior of Firms," in Ansoff, H. I., R. P. Declerck, and R. L. Hayes (eds.), *From Strategic Planning to Strategic Management*, New York, Wiley, 1976, pp. 103–124; and Galbraith, J. R. and R. K. Kazanjian, *Strategy Implementation*, 2d. ed., St. Paul, MN, West Publishing, 1986, pp. 128–144.

[23]Hammond, T. H., "Structure, Strategy, and the Agenda of the Firm," in Richard P. Rumelt, Dan E. Schendel, and David J. Teece (eds.), *Fundamental Issues in Strategy: A Research Agenda*. Boston, Harvard Business School Press, 1994, pp. 97–154.

[24]For discussions of this view of the firm, see Kogut, B. and U. Zander, "Knowledge of the Firm, Combinative Capabilities, and the Replication of Technology," *Organization Science*, 3, 1992, pp. 383–397; Grant, R. "Towards a Knowledge-based Theory of the Firm," *Strategic Management Journal*, 17, 1996, pp. 109–122.

[25]This example is based on material in Wendt, H., *Global Embrace*, New York, HarperBusiness, 1993, chaps. 2 and 6.

[26]Nelson, R. R. and S. G. Winter, *An Evolutionary Theory of Economic Change*, Cambridge, MA, Belknap, 1982.

[27]This example was based on *WingspanBank.com (A)* (HBS Case #9-600-035) and *WingspanBank.com (B): Should This Bird Fly?* (HBS Case #9-601-071).

ENVIRONMENT, POWER, AND CULTURE

17

$t$hroughout the book, we have offered guidance to managers seeking to be responsive to their economic environments. Thus, Chapter 3 details the economic factors affecting the decision to outsource, while Chapter 7 provides a competitive framework for firms considering whether to sink investments in new technologies. In this chapter, we examine several aspects of managerial decision making that are not traditionally included in economic analyses of strategy. In particular, we examine the social context of firm behavior—the nonmarket, noncontractual relationships and activities that are essential to business. In this analysis, we observe that the social context of business forms the foundation for economic transactions by providing managers with the order and predictability needed for ongoing business activity.

THE SOCIAL CONTEXT OF FIRM BEHAVIOR ◆ ◆ ◆ ◆ ◆

The most visible example of a firm's social context is regulation, both formal and informal. Formal regulations—those written and enforced by government officials—are necessary to enforce contracts and assure the smooth functioning of markets. Regulations cover such key areas of strategy as contracting, employment practices, pricing, entry-deterring behaviors, and exclusive dealing in the vertical chain. Compliance with regulations is not just a matter of enforcement and compulsion. Compliance also gives firms a recognized legitimacy and the right to compete.

Firms are also subject to informal regulations that emerge from the cultural/cognitive order of the market. Firms in the same market situation will likely operate within a set of shared general understandings and values regarding customers, competitors, products, and other aspects of a business. This need not imply collusion or lock-step consistency, but only a shared common understanding about the business on the part of firms competing in that business. Although managers can agree on their general tasks and missions in an industry setting, they still can differ sharply on how to perform those tasks to best satisfy consumer needs and generate profits. These shared understandings may stem from a common history, or from common regulatory and technological constraints, but they also can change. Disagreements about what were thought to be consensual matters may signal the emergence of new opportunities for competitive advantage in an industry. A reexamining of formerly implicit assumptions about competition in a particular industry setting may have the same effect.

Social context also involves shared norms about which types of activities are seen as legitimate and which as illegitimate. In some industries (aerospace, biotechnology), formal contracting is common, whereas in others (diamonds), large transactions often occur on the basis of a handshake. Universities do not try to hire away each other's faculty after May 1, so as to permit each school to schedule the next year's classes. The dealers for a particular automobile manufacturer trade cars among each other whenever a customer in town A wants a particular car that the dealer in town B has in the showroom. The latter agreements are not governed by contracts, but they are seldom breached.

Behavioral norms can develop around such areas as pricing, customer service, product design, research or advertising expenditures, dispute resolution, merger and acquisition activity, and restructuring. These norms reflect the habits and "ways of doing business" that develop in an industry over time and come to be taken for granted until times of industry change. Although these norms seldom have the status of formal regulations or laws, they often are important to industry participants and, once established, change slowly. Social context includes both the context in which firms act and the context in which managers make decisions. This permits a distinction between *external* and *internal* contexts. Internal context concerns the political and cultural environment within a firm that affects how managers and employees behave. Of course, the behavior of managers and employees is also formally regulated. This was discussed in Chapter 16 in terms of organizational structure. We consider internal context first and complete the chapter by considering external context.

◆ ◆ ◆ ◆ ◆ INTERNAL CONTEXT

Just as firms operate within an external environment of other firms that constrains and guides their behavior, they are also subject to an internal social context that constrains and guides managers in making and implementing strategic decisions. Internal context is influential where formal rules and contracts are either infeasible or too costly. We emphasize two aspects of internal context: power and culture.

Firms embody a complex array of goals. In pursuing them, individuals link their activities and rewards to those of the groups and subunits to which they belong, and ultimately to the firm. The performance of individuals thus ultimately determines the performance of the firm, although this requires coordination with other individuals and groups. Environmental uncertainty, along with the complexity of goal and reward structures, makes conflicts likely over what goals to pursue as well as how and when to pursue them. An individual may be tempted to pursue his or her own goals, even to the detriment of the firm, provided the incentive to do so is sufficiently high. When individuals rise to top management positions, their goals can become the firm's goals.

One would think that a control system could be designed to integrate individual behaviors into unified organizational action. As we have observed in the previous three chapters, however, this seems unlikely. Because of the limitations of formal structures and controls, many activities and interactions both within and between organizations must occur outside of their scope. Managers from different units may need to cooperate but are not required to do so. Managers from different firms may need to coordinate over matters that may be much more important to some of them than to others. It is in situations of chronic goal conflict, where formal authority is lacking, formal controls are inadequate, and cost-effective contracts are difficult to fashion, that *power* and *culture* become important. While power and culture are inter-related, we discuss them separately in this chapter.

POWER

Because power and related terms are so widely used by both academics and business practitioners, the meanings associated with them are often confusing. We take *power* to be an individual actor's ability to accomplish his or her goals by using resources obtained through *noncontractual exchange relationships*. By this we mean exchanges of goods, services, or promises on terms that take place outside of tra-ditional economic markets and that are not enforceable in court. For example, some-one in need of emergency assistance may receive help from an individual and have little to offer that particular individual in return immediately. The individual provid-ing assistance may never have need of reciprocation in kind. Nevertheless, there may still be an implied promise that the favor would be returned if needed. The terms of the agreement are not specified, since it is not known in advance when or how the favor can be best returned. A failure to provide future assistance when requested would not give cause to legal action either, because there was no contract. Still, one can consider such an arrangement as an exchange whose obligations many people would fulfill out of a felt need to reciprocate.

Power is not the same as *authority*, which stems from the explicit contractual decision-making and dispute-resolution rights that a firm (or some other source) grants to an individual. A manager may exercise power by redirecting the activities of other actors away from their immediate goals and toward accomplishing the manager's own goals. Others follow, not because they are contractually obligated to do so (i.e., from authority), but because they perceive it is in their best interest to do so. In this sense, power is the ability to get things done in the absence of contracts. *Influence*, a related term, refers to the exercise or use of power in a given situation by an individual. The influence a person has over others is thus an effect of his or her broader power.

Power exists at many levels in a firm. Individual managers, such as the CEO, may be powerful relative to their peers on the management team. It is also common to dis-cuss power at the department or group level. In universities, academic departments continually vie with each other for budgetary resources and view their success in obtaining such resources as evidence of their power, which may stem from their popu-larity with students, the research productivity of their faculty, or their success in secur-ing government and foundation grants. Firms can also exercise power in their product markets, in other factor markets (such as for raw materials or labor), or in relations with suppliers, competitors, or other actors or groups that operate in the firm's broader environment. For example, Disney may obtain a more favorable distribution of a new animated film than would a rival studio. It would also have power in nego-tiations with toy companies seeking to develop products based on Disney characters.

The Sources of Power

Power is often exerted in an economic market, as when a firm with a patent for a popular new drug uses its market power to set a high price–cost margin. Our interest here is in power that cannot be exerted in the market (i.e., that cannot be easily priced). Individuals attain this power when they possess resources that others value but are not readily bought and sold in a market. This would include the power to control the allocation of resources within firms, where internal markets for such resources are virtually nonexistent.

One way to look at the sources of power is in terms of power bases—attributes of the actor or resources that help the actor gain power. Power can stem from an individual's position within a hierarchy. This is known as *legitimate power* or *formal power*. An individual who possesses formal power has reason to expect compliance, at least on those matters that are of moderate or little importance to others. Chester Barnard uses the term *zone of indifference* to define the set of issues over which the powerful individual with formal authority usually prevails.[1] Power can also stem from an ability to grant rewards or administer punishments, or from the possession of specialized knowledge valued by other actors. Finally, power can be based on one's favorable position within a social order, due to status, image, or reputation. For example, an individual with a well-known history of winning in prior conflicts will have reputation-based power that could lead potential adversaries to comply with future demands without a struggle. Of course, this may be put at risk by significant or poorly timed failures. This last type of power is rooted not only in individuals and their attributes, but also in the relationships that develop among individuals as they participate in networks of tasks, exchange, or information sharing.

Relational views of power are often based on *social exchange*. Social exchange is a transfer between two or more parties of resources, or rights to control resources, that occurs outside of a market.[2] Power arises in future social exchange as a result of persistent inequalities in past social exchanges between actors.

To illustrate how power might arise out of social exchanges, suppose that actors A and B are exchange partners. If an acceptable exchange occurs between them, their transaction is complete. Suppose, however, that they cannot complete an exchange in a mutually acceptable manner, and as a result, A provides more of value to B than B can provide to A in return. B, in effect, "owes" A the deficit of the exchange. Unless it is explicitly considered as such, this is not a formal debt, and A cannot sue B to recover the deficit. As B's deficit to A increases over successive exchanges, B is said to be increasingly dependent on A. Conversely, A is said to have power over B to the extent that B is dependent on A. The dependence of B on A is mitigated to the extent that A depends on B for some other matter or in some other set of exchanges.

A professional situation in which such a pattern could develop would be in the requesting of advice by a junior employee from a senior colleague on some matter important to the junior employee's work assignment but not an immediate concern of the senior colleague. How does the junior repay the senior colleague for providing assistance? Sometimes deference and respect from the recipient of help might suffice. In settings where such exchanges are beneficial, firms may promote norms among employees, encouraging such cooperative behavior and even sanctioning individuals who refuse requests for assistance.

How does this view of social exchange differ from the economic exchanges with which we have been concerned in other chapters? If both parties agree to participate, why are power relationships any different from other exchanges? In voluntary exchanges, why would an actor like B choose to become dependent on another actor like A and presumably commit future resources to A's discretion? Why would A provide resources in the present in return for the uncertain future obligations of B? After all, despite B's "debt," A cannot use formal means, such as the courts, to force compensation from B. One could argue that an individual choosing a dependence relation lacks a better alternative. The resources controlled by the other party may be important to the future of the firm, there may be no clear substitutes or alternative sources, and/or it may be too costly to write a formal contract. This is the *resource dependence* view of power, expressed by Jeffrey Pfeffer.[3] Individuals and firms seek to gain power by reducing their dependence on other actors, while increasing the dependence of others on them. This is analogous to the efforts by firms to avoid supplier power by securing multiple supply channels and to achieve market power by selling to customers who have few alternatives.

Resource dependence helps explain why firms benefit from asymmetric social exchange, but it does not clarify why individuals willingly give up resources today in exchange for an uncertain future response. One explanation is that, on the merits of the exchange itself, it is beneficial to the actor providing resources to trust the other party. Once trust has been established by repeated interactions, similar exchanges will seem less risky. Conversely, A may value what it expects B to provide so highly that A is willing to tolerate the chance that B will not reciprocate. The willingness of an actor to provide resources in exchange for unspecified future consideration may also be based on more generally held norms of reciprocity that are part of the culture in which both actors operate.

Along with the idea that actors will work to reduce their dependency on others, the resource-dependence view also identifies which individuals in a firm are likely to attain power. Specifically, individuals who control critical resources will accumulate power. Those who help the firm cope with problems that pose major threats to it will come to exercise the most power within the firm. Examples can be seen in firms where members of a critical occupational or professional group gain control (petroleum engineers in oil companies), where individuals with links to key regulators or stakeholders gain control (lawyers in regulated businesses), or where individuals with unique and valuable skills gain control (surgeons in teaching hospitals).[5] These sources of power may be clear in theory, but they are difficult to identify and manage in practice.

Structural Views of Power

A firm's structure, or some broader structure within which an actor operates, may also serve as a source of power. Those who occupy certain critical locations within that structure have more power. Often the most powerful individuals in a firm occupy multiple key positions. For example, the chairman and CEO of a firm, such as Jeff Immelt at GE, likely has more power than would be the case if he occupied only one of those top positions. We have already discussed the formal authority or position power that designated managers have in a firm owing to their positions. There are other types of structurally based power that are less direct but potentially as important.

As we saw in Chapter 16, organization structure involves the information network operating within a firm and the network of informal social relationships that develops among the firm's employees, customers, suppliers, and other stakeholders. These networks can both support and impede the power of their participants. Having a prominent position within informal networks of importance to a firm can give an individual

EXAMPLE 17.1 THE SOURCES OF PRESIDENTIAL POWER

One of the most famous studies of the bases of power was *Presidential Power*, Richard Neustadt's 1960 examination of how Franklin Roosevelt, Harry Truman, and Dwight Eisenhower dealt with power and influence during their administrations. The book was widely read at the beginning of the Kennedy administration and has remained important to sitting presidents, their staffs, and policy analysts.[4]

The important issue for Neustadt is the conflict between the image of the president as powerful and the reality of the presidency as institutionally weak. Presidential power does not consist of the president taking direct action on some front, such as Truman's recall of General Douglas MacArthur or his seizure of the steel mills in 1952, or Eisenhower's decision to send troops to Little Rock, Arkansas, in 1957 to assist in desegregation. These command decisions were more exceptions than typical uses of power. Nor did any of them solve the president's policy problems. Instead, they used up scarce presidential power and, at best, allowed the president and others involved in the situation more time to search for a lasting solution. Neustadt suggests that decisions made by command or fiat are more likely to be evidence of a lack of power than of its effective use. In a given situation, however, there may have been no other choice than to command. For example, whatever problems Truman encountered in recalling MacArthur, the cost of not recalling him and thus allowing civilian authority to be flouted would probably have been higher.

Presidential power is the ability to influence the people who make and implement government policies. It has three sources. The first is the bargaining advantage that comes with the office that enables the president to persuade others to work in his interest—the formal powers and authority of the president. The second source is professional reputation, which comprises the expectations of professional politicians, bureaucrats, and others in the political community regarding the president's power and his willingness to use it. This is related to the ability to control the votes of Congress on key issues. Once the president loses control of a majority in Congress, he cannot guarantee that his programs will be enacted and will lose

power as a result. A third source of presidential power is his prestige among the public, specifically how the political community assesses his support among different constituencies and the consequences that failure to support the president will have for politicians.

Although the political situations facing the president of the United States are different from those facing the CEOs of large firms, Neustadt's three sources are consistent with those discussed earlier. The formal powers of the job, whether stemming from the Constitution, laws, or customs, along with the institutional routines that have grown up around it, provide a basis for incumbent power, a basis that can be used well or poorly. Professional reputation in a firm refers to how observers expect the powerholder to act in a given situation, based on their accumulated experience with the powerholder. Finally, prestige for politicians is analogous to control over critical resources. For the president and professional politicians, that resource is public sentiment, which translates into votes.

Looking back to 1990, in light of the six presidents who had served since *Presidential Power* was first published, Neustadt saw little reason to change his fundamental conclusions. For example, the experience of Nixon and Watergate, on the one hand, and Johnson and Vietnam, on the other, showed the importance of credibility and perceived legitimacy for both public prestige and professional reputation. Similarly, although Neustadt still emphasizes the importance of political skills for the president, the experiences of Johnson and Nixon also emphasize the relevance of individual temperament for success in office. The president needs to be patient enough to tolerate a complex political system that rarely allows him to successfully implement major policy initiatives immediately. Neustadt still sees political skills and experience as crucial for success in office. (The presidency is no place for amateurs.) Political skills and experience, however, though necessary to success in the presidency, are not sufficient. Both Nixon and Johnson were highly experienced in elective office and possessed formidable political skills, yet their sense of power led both of them to support policies that ultimately dissipated their power and impaired their effectiveness.

holding that position power that will enhance his or her formal authority and make it easier to influence organizational outcomes. Individuals holding minor or marginal positions within informal networks will likely find their power limited relative to those holding more central positions.

Ronald Burt provides a general version of how structural power can be conferred by positions in network structures in his theory of structural holes.[6] *Structural holes* are relationships in social networks in which one actor is the critical link between individuals or entire groups of actors. To associate with each other, these individuals or groups must go through the actor who spans the structural hole. The presence of a structural hole allows the individual who can span the disparate groups (or "span the hole") to use the control of information or resource flows as a source of power. The elimination of a structural hole, such as when representatives of the two previously separate groups begin interacting regularly on their own, eliminates the dependence of the two groups on the focal individual, eliminating his or her power.

Providing a valued relationship between two unconnected actors or groups of actors provides a basis for power accruing to individuals employing what Burt calls a *tertius gaudens* (happy third) strategy. The tertius is the "third who benefits," and the strategy involves spanning a structural hole and bargaining with the parties on either side for the most favorable terms. This occurs when an actor is the third between two parties in the same relationship, such as a broker in a buyer–seller relationship. It can also occur when an actor is the third between two parties in two or more relations with conflicting demands. An example would be employees who work in the same firm but on different projects and who must compete for scarce time with their manager.

The potential for those spanning structural holes to accumulate power can prompt concerns among other members of the network. One way to address this is to reconfigure networks to reduce the number of structural holes. Depending on the costs of forging redundant or duplicate connections, this may be infeasible or inefficient for many networks. It may pay to have specialized network actors, even if there is a potential for them to abuse their positions. Another way to limit abuses by those spanning structural holes is through the development of regulations and norms governing such actors. Roberto Fernandez and Roger Gould found this in their study of the influence of five types of brokerage positions on decision making on national health policy.[7] They identified a "paradox of power" in which brokers had to appear neutral in decision processes. This suggests that holding key network positions can augment one's power as long as that power does not benefit personal interests. The recent indictment and conviction of Arthur Andersen for its role in the Enron bankruptcy shows the importance that norms of appropriate behavior have for critical network actors such as auditors. Even though Andersen's conviction was recently set aside, that is of little solace for the thousands of employees and retirees who were adversely affected by the firm's demise.

Do Successful Organizations Need Powerful Managers?

Unless employee relationships can be completely governed by incentive contracts, a manager must possess some power in order to be successful. But the presence of a powerful manager does not guarantee success. A manager might use power for personal interests that significantly diverge from those of the firm. Consider how the power that accrued to Kenneth Lay, Jeffrey Skilling, and Andrew Fastow from their initial successes at Enron, and Enron's soaring share price, ultimately worked against the firm's shareholders, bondholders, and employees.

EXAMPLE 17.2 POWER AND POOR PERFORMANCE: THE CASE OF THE 1957 MERCURY

While power may be useful in getting things done, it can also be dysfunctional if it helps the wrong programs to be accomplished—that is, if it is used to circumvent the checks and balances that are necessary to evaluate the market feasibility and cost effectiveness of any effort. An example of this occurred with the development of the 1957 Mercury. Called the "Turnpike Cruiser" by Ford managers and a "steel cartoon" by its critics, the model was introduced to great fanfare but failed to make good on its high costs and lofty sales projections. Overall, Ford lost an estimated $369 on every 1957 Mercury it sold, and the car proved a harbinger of even greater problems that came with the now-infamous Edsel. In his group history of the careers of the "Whiz Kids" at Ford, John Byrne provides an example of the functions and dysfunctions of power in the career of the Whiz Kid responsible for the new Mercury, Francis "Jack" Reith.[8]

Reith had a number of power bases from which to push the development of the new Mercury. First, he was a dynamic and almost charismatic leader, who drove his subordinates but inspired considerable admiration in the process. He was also highly intelligent and effective at persuading others to follow his direction. Reith had a considerable track record since he joined Ford in 1946. Most recently, he had received credit for the successful turnaround and sale of Ford's subsidiary in France. On the basis of this success, Reith enjoyed the support of his superiors, Lewis Crusoe and Henry Ford II. He also gained standing from his association with the Whiz Kids, who had nearly all distinguished themselves at Ford and who were clearly recognized as a group as well as individually. Finally, Reith had position power, in that he was promoted to the head of the Mercury division once his 1957 plan had been approved.

Reith saw the 1957 Mercury as part of a larger plan by which Ford could contend with General Motors for leadership in automobiles through a major expansion of an existing make (Mercury) and the introduction of an entirely new one (the Edsel). Reith's boss, Lewis Crusoe, promised him his support (and the top job) at Mercury, if the plan could be approved by the board of directors. In preparing for that board meeting, Reith used all of his bases of power effectively.

He was perhaps too effective. There were doubts about the initiative in several quarters. The plan promised too much (a 54 percent sales increase). It required a larger expansion of the dealer network than Ford had ever anticipated. The projected expenses of the project were staggering and, in effect, required a large increase in market share to justify the project. As one executive remembered, "the numbers were totally unrealistic. They had to be. It was the only way to justify the plan" (Byrne, p. 225). The estimated price for the project was equal to the company's total profit before taxes the previous year ($485 million).

These doubts were not raised, however, because Reith's colleagues, whose job it was to ask difficult questions about projects, failed to do so in this case out of deference to their friend. When questions were raised, Reith and Crusoe jointly overpowered the opposition. Much of this persuasion was based on fear, intimidation, and concern for the career consequences of resistance. The norm for rational project analysis that the Whiz Kids had introduced to Ford was forgotten in the process of securing project approval.

The failure of the car, which ended Reith's career at Ford, was due in part to the flawed decision processes described above that allowed Reith to push through his initiative at the expense of critical analysis. Reith and his managers, however, also failed to pay attention to market research, which indicated increased consumer interest in safety and decreased interest in the stylistic flourishes that characterized the car. Instead, the 1957 Mercury was based on managerial intuitions about consumer preferences for stylish cars rather than on data. The car also suffered from numerous quality and safety problems. In making this error, however, Reith was not alone. The year 1957 was a strong one for the Volkswagen, a small, simple car that focused on economy. It was also the first year in which consumers' interest in automobile safety and quality increased. Many managers in Detroit missed this shift in the market, which would lead to further problems for the industry in the 1960s and 1970s and beyond.

A major purpose of corporate governance is to rein in the power of CEOs. The CEO is the agent of the shareholders by way of the board of directors. In the presence of agency costs arising from hidden actions, hidden information, and related problems, a powerful manager may divert information and resources toward personal goals. Clearly, power is a two-edged sword whose effects can be positive or negative for firms. We expect that the accumulation of power will be helpful or harmful according to the following conditions:

Accumulation of power is helpful when

1. There are high agency costs in coordinating managers and lower-level workers.
2. The firm's environment is relatively stable.

Accumulation of power is harmful when

1. There are high agency costs in coordinating among levels of upper management.
2. The firm's environment is relatively unstable.

The Decision to Allocate Formal Power to Individuals

Thus far, our discussion has skirted a critical issue: Why should the firm grant formal authority to individuals who already wield great power by virtue of their control over key resources? When should power not be allocated to such individuals? The choice to internalize is made in part because transactions costs make dispute resolution in markets too costly. Firms internalize decisions when fiat and administrative discretion are more efficient ways of settling disputes. However, this does not indicate who should be allowed to exercise that authority and discretion.

A first answer is that *knowledgeable* individuals should receive power. If formal power is to be used effectively, then its holders should be informed about the policies they will need to approve and the disputes they will need to resolve. That knowledge forms an important basis for authority and power has been recognized since the earliest writings on bureaucratic organizations.[9] The duly authorized decision maker need not be the most knowledgeable individual in the firm. In some settings (e.g., research laboratories), it would be inefficient to make the most knowledgeable individual the manager, since that individual would be most useful to the firm as a generator of knowledge rather than as a resolver of disputes. The knowledge base of the decision maker is often an issue for managers who come from outside of the firm. Outside managers can bring considerable knowledge of their industry and functional areas, but will lack detailed knowledge of their new firms and the specific businesses pursued by those firms.

A second basis for allocating authority concerns managerial motivations and interests. Holdup can occur for a firm when noncontractible contingencies arise and the firm has made relationship-specific investments with managers whose interests diverge from those of the firm. This makes holdup an ever-present problem, since much of managerial decision making is inherently noncontractible. The threat can be mitigated by tying managerial compensation to firm profits, such as through substantial bonuses. But these have their limitations, as discussed in Chapters 14 and 15.

If those who wield power in the firm are also necessary for the effective control and allocation of its critical resources, then the firm is vulnerable to their departure, especially to join the competition. This implies that firms should invest in and allocate power to those individuals who are more likely to stay with the firm. Excessive turnover of key decision makers not only takes critical knowledge out of the firm, but also

EXAMPLE 17.3 GARY WENDT AT CONSECO[10]

The story of Gary Wendt at Conseco provides an example of how knowledge and motivation interact with managerial power. Conseco is an Indiana-based insurance firm that had been struggling with the effects of poor acquisitions and managerial excesses at the time Wendt arrived amid much fanfare in 2000. Wendt joined the firm after a distinguished career at GE, where he is credited with building up GE Capital, which fueled much of the parent firm's profitability growth in the 1990s. He thus brought considerable knowledge of the finance industry and a solid reputation as a successful manager and builder of businesses in a great company. It was unclear, however, that he had the skills to manage a turnaround such as Conseco required.

Before taking the Conseco job, Wendt negotiated a substantial compensation that was only loosely tied to Conseco performance. It included a $45 million signing bonus, an $8 million bonus that could be collected after two years, and a retirement annuity of $1.5 million per year that was expected to cost the firm at least $22 million. This means that upward of $70 million of Wendt's compensation was guaranteed in advance.

Wendt collected his bonus on schedule in July 2002. Around the same time, however, A.M. Best, an insurance rating agency, cut Conseco's rating to B11, which would make it difficult to sell some types of insurance. Conseco's stock price, which had risen to a peak value over $20 under Wendt, soon fell to 34 cents. During his first two years, the firm reported one profitable quarter and six unprofitable ones, with total reported losses of $1.37 billion. By August 2002, Wendt admitted that restructuring efforts had been unsuccessful and began to discuss the potential for a Chapter 11 bankruptcy filing. Wendt is an example of a powerful manager, a "big name," hired from the outside to save the firm. One wonders, however, whether his knowledge and motivation were right for the job. Conseco was in serious trouble before Wendt arrived. Still, analysts wonder whether his efforts to grow the firm out of its troubles rather than sell its core businesses to raise cash were appropriate for the situation in which Conseco found itself. Moreover, Wendt's guaranteed compensation raises questions about how much financial risk he wished to bear in pursuing this strategy and how hard he would work toward implementing it. His professional reputation was clearly at risk.

paralyzes its strategic decision-making processes so that managers who remain have difficulties operating effectively. Julio Rotemberg argues that firms may actually prefer to give decision makers power rather than higher wages as a way of reducing turnover. Power may be thought of as a firm-specific asset—the decision maker may get better pay elsewhere but might not achieve comparable levels of power and influence.[11]

◆ ◆ ◆ ◆ ◆ CULTURE

Although the profitability of a firm is linked to its efficiency, its resource endowment, its competitive strategy, and its positioning, it is also a function of the firm's *culture*. A firm's culture is a set of values, beliefs, and norms of behavior shared by its members that influences employee preferences and behaviors. It also involves the special mindsets, routines, and codes that shape how members view each other and the firm. It thus sets the context in which relations among members develop, and it provides the basis for implicit contracts between them.[12] Culture represents the behavioral guideposts and evaluative criteria in a firm that are not spelled out by contract but still constrain and inform the firm's managers and employees in their decisions. As David Kreps explains, "culture...gives hierarchical inferiors an idea *ex ante* how the firm will 'react' to circumstances as they arise—in a very strong sense, it gives identity to the organization."[13]

Culture and Performance

An obvious concern for managers is whether a firm's culture affects its performance. It is difficult to directly link the two. Culture may be associated with performance without necessarily causing that performance. For example, until IBM experienced problems in the late 1980s, it was thought to have a strong culture, combining customer service, employee development, and highly demanding professional standards. However, IBM's history of persistently high earnings and market leadership, as well as its strong competitive practices, may have provided an environment in which a strong culture could develop. It is unclear whether the culture caused IBM's high performance or vice versa.

The link between culture and performance may be indirect. Once a set of strong norms develop around an activity, their existence may constrain the freedom of management in directing that activity. For example, managers accustomed to unit autonomy and individual accountability may find it difficult to cooperate with other managers on activities that require cooperation and joint action. They may also have difficulties with the exercise of centralized authority by corporate managers. At the same time, the presence of strong norms, such as for individual or group accountability, may also aid the work of managers, provided that the norms support the firm's strategies. For example, the famous piece-rate system used by the Lincoln Electric Company is dependent for its success on supportive norms for individual achievement and accountability, coupled with strong supervision by management and appropriate organizational policies. This interlocking of culture, structures, practices, and people provides an example of the multidimensional nature of organization design and its influence on performance. John Roberts develops these links further in terms of a PARC, referring to *people* interacting with organizational *a*rchitecture, *r*outines, and *c*ulture.[14]

Jay Barney identifies the conditions under which culture can be a source of sustained competitive advantage.[15] Culture first must be valuable for the firm. Something about the firm's culture and values must be linked to the value the firm creates for customers. Culture must also be particular to the firm. If the culture is common to most firms in the market, so that it reflects the influence of the national or regional culture, then it is unlikely to lead to a relative competitive advantage, since most of the firm's competitors will share the same cultural attributes. This changes, of course, if a firm with a distinctive national or regional culture that supports performance diversifies internationally and begins competing with foreign firms, whose cultures are not as supportive. The experience of Japanese automakers entering the U.S. market provides an example of this, and the success of firms like Honda has often been attributed to the cultural attributes of Japanese firms. Finally, culture must be inimitable. If aspects of a firm's culture are easy to imitate, other firms will begin to do so, which will soon nullify any advantage for the firm where the culture first developed.

What does it mean for a culture to be imitable? The influence of culture on a firm is likely to rest on tacit factors that are not easily described and that represent the accumulated history of the firm much better than does a simple description. The complexity that makes a culture difficult for others to imitate also makes it difficult for managers to modify the culture of their own firms to significantly improve performance. Firms like Lincoln Electric, for example, have experienced troubles in opening new plants and attempting to replicate their own system, which suggests that competitors will have an even harder time. Barney even suggests a tradeoff between the degree to which a culture is manipulable and the amount of sustained value that a firm can obtain from it. A culture that is manipulable is not likely to be linked to the fundamental resource commitments of the firm that form the basis for sustained competitive advantage. Rather, it is more likely to be common to several firms, more easily imitable, and hence less valuable.

Culture creates value for firms in three ways. First, culture reduces information processing demands on individuals within the firm. Second, it complements formal control systems and reduces the costs of monitoring individuals. Third, it shapes the preferences of individuals toward a common set of goals. This reduces negotiation and bargaining costs and fosters cooperation that would be difficult to achieve through more explicit means. We discuss these properties in more detail below.

Culture Simplifies Information Processing

A culture's values, norms of activity, and accompanying signals focus the activities of employees on a limited set of activities and arrangements. This frees employees from the need to continually negotiate what their tasks will be within the firm. In effect, each employee knows his or her role in the firm. A strong culture may thus reduce the costs of decision making and permit a specialization of effort. It also helps standardize the ways in which employees, customers, and other stakeholders interact.

An example of how culture can help focus activities is the case of Cray Research.[16] Founded by Seymour Cray in 1976, Cray had designed some of Control Data's first supercomputers and had become well known for its innovations in the development of supercomputers. The culture of the firm was an important part of its reputation. This culture stressed decentralized decision making, and Seymour Cray was more likely to be found on a surfboard than in his office making executive decisions. Starting in 1978, however, Cray grew at a phenomenal rate. Cray needed to ramp up production while continuing to innovate. The number of Cray employees grew five times between 1978 and 1983, from 321 to 1,551. During that same period, total revenue grew from $17 million to nearly $170 million. However, the structure of the firm remained fairly simple and nonbureaucratic. Cray and other top managers gave their young engineers the same freedom to innovate; in return, the engineers enjoyed the same work environment that could be found in smaller firms. This allowed Cray to continue to increase the computational power of its supercomputers and keep ahead of the competition.

Culture Complements Formal Controls

Culture, as a set of collective values and behavioral norms, serves as a control within organizations. Culture controls the activities of employees on the basis of their attachment to the firm rather than on the basis of incentives and monitoring. Individuals who value belonging to the culture will align their individual goals and behaviors to those of the firm. If culture serves this function in a firm, then individual activities will be controlled more efficiently than they will be through formal control systems. This efficiency can be attributed to individuals controlling themselves, monitoring costs being reduced, and opportunism being held to a minimum (since worker interests are more aligned with the firm).

EXAMPLE 17.4 CORPORATE CULTURE AND INERTIA AT ICI

Andrew Pettigrew provides an example of how cultural inertia can stymie organizational adaptation in his case studies of Imperial Chemical Industries (ICI), the leading British chemical manufacturer.[17] In 1973, ICI was the largest manufacturing firm in Great Britain. It had possessed a strong and homogeneous culture for the nearly 50 years it had existed. Sales growth in 1972 was strong in chemicals, at twice the national growth rate for manufacturing. ICI had also been successful at new product development, with half of its 1972 sales coming from products that had not been on the market in 1957.

Strong threats to ICI's continued success developed in its business environment in the 1970s. These threats included overcapacity in its core businesses, threats of both inflation and recession in the British domestic economy, and import threats from Europe and North America. These pressures substantially affected ICI's profitability in 1980, when its profit totals and profitability ratios were halved. Several years of consistently poor performance followed. In the five years between 1977 and 1982, ICI cut its domestic workforce by nearly one-third.

Individuals within top management had been recommending changes in the structure and governance system of ICI to allow it to better adapt to changed economic and political conditions since at least 1967, when they were raised by a single individual during a board election and ignored. A board committee on the need for reorganization had been set up in 1973 and issued a report calling for extensive organizational changes within ICI. The report encountered extreme political opposition from the start and, in the words of an executive director, "sank at the first shot." These calls for reorganization and strategic change were not adopted by ICI until 1983, when the firm had already experienced several years of poor performance.

Pettigrew's analysis of this history highlights the culture of conservatism and the "smoothing" of problems that dominated ICI at this time. These aspects of its culture were functional during prosperous and stable times, but were dysfunctional during environmental shifts. Individuals who had benefited from the prior success of the firm were able to block initiatives, while external stimuli that could move management to action, such as poor performance, were not forthcoming until 1980. As management and board members changed during the 1970s, however, the culture also changed, so that management became more receptive to new ideas. Despite the best efforts of individuals who saw the need for change, the culture constrained the firm and kept its managers from deciding on change until conditions were present. The culture of ICI, which had benefited the firm during its first 50 years, kept it from adapting in the late 1970s.

For an example of how culture complements more formal processes, consider the information-sharing needs in major global consulting firms, such as McKinsey and Company. These firms rely on intellectual assets that need to be circulated throughout the firm and continually replenished. These firms, in securing new business, must develop their practices by drawing on the capabilities and experiences of consultants throughout the firm to identify and market new products. At any given time, however, most of the human capital of these firms is already committed to a complex set of projects at any given time. In addition, the complexity of these firms makes any strictly formal systems for organizing the potential inputs to typical projects highly complex. Firms take different approaches to managing their intellectual assets, including complex matrix structures and the development of specialist positions. McKinsey, however, is able to use its strong culture, which includes norms of reciprocity, to help address this problem without undue dependence on formal structures and processes.

It is a valued part of the firm's culture that assistance is provided to projects when requested and wherever possible from those in a position to help anywhere in the world.

Culture Facilitates Cooperation and Reduces Bargaining Costs

Gary Miller argues that culture mitigates the detrimental effects of power dynamics within firms by creating "mutually reinforcing" norms.[18] These permit mutually beneficial cooperative activities to emerge that would not be likely among self-interested actors outside the organization. Miller builds on the work of David Kreps, who examines the problems of securing cooperative outcomes in repeated games. Both Miller and Kreps are interested in the implications of a result called the *folk theorem*.

The folk theorem concerns the possibilities for achieving an equilibrium result in repeated play of games, such as the prisoner's dilemma (discussed in the Economics Primer). Its general result is that many equilibria are possible in infinitely repeated games. Some can be conflictual, combining expectations of opportunistic behavior with threats of strong retaliation if the other player responds inappropriately. The result of the folk theorem implies that it may not be possible to arrive with certainty at a cooperative organizational arrangement—cooperation is only one of many possible arrangements. In addition, even if cooperation was possible, the costs of reaching it, in terms of the haggling costs involved in choosing one arrangement over other possible ones, are likely to be high.

Miller argues that attempts to solve organization problems through contracts, incentives, and formal controls will entail large influence costs. The problem with hierarchical organization is that, although it mitigates transactions costs associated with market coordination of economic activity, it creates dilemmas of its own. These dilemmas cannot be resolved by recourse to formal governance mechanisms or by increased controls over employees. Building on the ideas of Kreps, Bengt Holmstrom, and others, Miller argues that any hierarchical organization will have serious principal–agent problems built into its structure. A "machine" model of organization is likely to self-destruct.

Most real organizations arrive at some acceptable organizational arrangements, despite these problems. To account for this, Kreps suggests that norms and social conventions may provide a focus for actors around which a consensus can form. This set of norms and conventions is the organization's culture. Kreps states that corporate culture is "the means by which a principle [of group decision making] is communicated to hierarchical inferiors." It says "how things are done and how they are meant to be done" in the firm.

Miller argues that a firm's culture resolves these problems if its norms stress cooperation and not conflict. A cooperative culture modifies individual expectations and preferences and allows actors to expect cooperation from others. These mutually reinforcing values and norms allow firms to fashion solutions to agency problems that would not be possible in a market. Miller is ambiguous about the ability of management to intentionally influence a firm's culture. On the one hand, he argues that managers can exercise leadership that fosters cooperation rather than conflict among employees. On the other hand, a cooperative culture is also likely to be fragile, so that attempts to modify it to gain advantage could backfire and result in employees becoming more uncooperative. Cultivating and using power and influence may be more feasible for managers than cultivating culture, even though a cooperative culture may be more desirable.

EXAMPLE **17.5** POLITICS, CULTURE, AND CORPORATE GOVERNANCE

Analyses of laws governing corporate governance in such areas as the board of directors, executive pay, and tender offers, have emphasized how management practices contribute to the efficiency of firms by attenuating principal–agent problems and reducing their costs for owners. Because of this, corporate law has been seen as the set of governance principles that has evolved over years of corporate trials and that constitutes the starting point in determining how firms govern themselves. Gerald Davis and Tracy Thompson argue that economic explanations are incomplete and neglect the influence on governance changes of actors in the political and cultural environment of the firm.[19] The political environment is important because the laws and regulations governing corporate activities, while of economic significance, are the products of political bodies, such as legislatures and regulatory agencies. The cultural environment is important because the attitudes and values of the general public on a given issue can be a source of legitimacy for political actors and will thus influence how they regulate firms.

Davis and Thompson provide an example of the importance of explanations incorporating power and culture in their discussion of the controversy in the early 1990s over "runaway executive pay." On its economic merits alone, it appeared that shareholders had at best weak incentives to pursue the issue. While the average U.S. CEO made 85 times the pay of a typical factory worker (versus 17 times in Japan), the dollar amounts that were paid to these executives were so small, relative to the overall value of the firm, that they had little or no effect on corporate performance. (There would still have been no effect if overpaid executives had given back their entire salaries to their firms.) While it was plausible that linking executive pay to corporate performance would help the firm's share price, it was far from clear that this actually happened. Regardless of its economic merits, however, the issue of CEO pay took on national political significance, in that it received extensive media coverage, many politicians raised the issue, and several pieces of legislation limiting executive pay were introduced in Congress.

Shareholder activists and institutional investors seized upon the political attention given to the CEO pay issue at the national level (that of the SEC), where they were relatively better organized and prepared to lobby. They pursued proxy reform indirectly, through a focus on CEO pay as one instance of a broader failure of management accountability. The apparent affront to national values and sensitivities caused by excessive CEO pay gave activists the opportunity to move proxy reform from the state government level, where they had little power, to the SEC, where they enjoyed greater power. This allowed the SEC to take up proxy reform at a national level. By the end of 1992, this campaign had succeeded in expanding the power of large shareholders, as evidenced by their greater participation and influence in corporate governance. This influence extended down from the national political domain to individual firms. Negative publicity and pressure on such large firms as ITT, W. R. Grace, and Ryder led to changes in executive compensation systems that more tightly linked pay to corporate performance.

Changes in the firm's larger political and cultural context also affect the incentives that top managers employ. As the incentives and compensation of top managers are better aligned to firm performance, follow-up changes in the rest of the firm may involve substantial reorganization, decentralization of decision making, and the increased use of market-based performance incentives. These in turn will prompt changes in norms and values, leading the firm to develop a culture aligned to shareholder value. Michael Useem describes how these changes affected the cultures inside firms and how managers in firms that realigned themselves toward shareholder value used their control over organizational architecture, symbols, and vocabulary to support realignment.[20]

Some firms resist reorganization, and a near-crisis atmosphere may develop among employees. In such situations, culture is inertial rather than supportive of change. Other firms react much more positively. The 1990 reorganization of Hewlett-Packard both maintained the firm's culture and improved shareholder value. While the reorganization eliminated thousands of positions in a firm that had prided itself on not laying off employees, the aggressive management approach of CEO John Young managed to retain the firm's innovative culture and significantly increase performance until he retired.[21]

Culture, Inertia, and Performance

Culture can also impair firm performance. Examples of an apparent negative association between culture and performance are nearly as common as those showing a positive one. In fact, sometimes the same firm provides examples of both. For example, IBM was seen as recently as 1986 as a powerful exemplar firm that was admired for its management depth and corporate culture. Yet less than 10 years later, obituaries were being written for IBM and its inertial culture.

If performance is related to its culture, it is because the firm has made investments and oriented its business toward environmental conditions that affect operations in predictable ways. In making their investments, managers must correctly anticipate how the conditions facing the firm affect its operations. This suggests a contingency logic, so that when the firm's strategy "fits" with the demands of its environment, then the culture that develops out of a firm's activities can support the direction of the firm and make it even more efficient, through greater focus and the reduction of haggling costs.

The values of a firm's culture must be consonant with the values required by its strategic choices, and poor fit could develop for a variety of situations. Simple growth, by increasing formality and bureaucracy, could ruin the culture of a start-up venture that stressed innovation and entrepreneurship. Conversely, a cultural misfit could occur when the values of a firm culture stressed routines, efficiency, and stability, while the firm's environment changed in ways requiring innovative, entrepreneurial, and flexible responses. Another type of value conflict could occur if a firm that had been a long-standing practitioner of a cost-based strategy suddenly changed direction and diversified, attempting to pursue a differentiation strategy. Conflict could also occur if a firm pursuing a given strategy acquired a firm committed to a very different strategy. This is the "culture clash" problem of merger integration.[22]

When the environment changes and firms must adapt to survive, a culture that was once a source of competitive advantage can instead impair performance. In an unfavorable environment, an unmanageable culture can become a source of inertia or a barrier to change. Executives with long tenure may have learned their jobs during prosperous times and thus be poorly equipped to handle change. Internal politics may allow threatened parties to block change. The terms of managers and directors, the rules by which they are chosen, and the procedures by which they operate may be designed conservatively to frustrate rather than permit change.

◆ ◆ ◆ ◆ ◆ EXTERNAL CONTEXT, INSTITUTIONS, AND STRATEGIES

How does social context influence managerial decisions outside of the formal boundaries of the firm, where managerial authority cannot be used to resolve disputes? The interactions of the firm, its competitors, and related organizations often appear to be less fluid and freewheeling than theories of competition might suggest. All firms are subject to some governmental regulation. As firms get bigger, they are subject to more regulatory oversight for environmental concerns, employment activities, new product development and testing, and interactions with competitors. Power and dependence relationships among firms, once established, appear to change slowly, barring some major discontinuity. Managers often acknowledge industry norms and traditions, the maintenance of which they see as valuable. Resistance to change on such matters as the adoption of new technologies and changes in work practices is fairly common. The behavior of top managers in an industry sometimes appears strongly oriented more toward winning peer approval and respect for themselves and their firms than toward maximizing shareholder wealth.

Even in the absence of formal rules and regulations or special government action, groups of firms frequently develop codes of acceptable conduct, conform to those codes, and exert pressures on other firms to conform likewise. Economically, this would fall into oligopoly behavior, but the group activity often appears to involve more than oligopoly models might suggest. Although this is apparent in commodity cartels, such as the diamond business, it is also common in high-technology industries, where consortia of firms develop around a set of standards.[23] It is also apparent in established industry sectors among major competitors or between competitors and the supply chain partners.[24] While firm behaviors can often seem inertial in these industries, at other times changes in firm behavior can occur rapidly and often spread very quickly by diffusion across a variety of industries and sectors.

Sociologists study these aspects of firm behavior by focusing on *institutions*, which are relatively stable organizational arrangements, often possessing a distinct identity within the broader social context, that help bring order to sets of economic trans-actions. Institutions can involve the formal regulation of firms, whether by govern-ment agencies or other nongovernmental regulatory organizations. They can also be less formal and involve ongoing power–dependence relationships between firms that come to be taken for granted. Finally, similar to how we discussed a firm's culture earlier in this chapter, institutional arrangements may embody general patterns of values, beliefs, and behavioral norms that motivate and stabilize affected firms.[25]

Firms are not solely reactive to the demands of their external environment. In some circumstances firms can influence their external contexts to their advantage. Large and successful firms, such as Microsoft, may be able to influence regulation, drive industry innovation, discipline their buyers and suppliers, and even modify industry culture on their own terms, at least somewhat. Even smaller firms, often in conjunction with competitors and media organizations, may jointly lobby regulators and cooperate with government agencies to bring about favorable regulatory or environmental changes or just oppose the actions of strong competitors (Wal-Mart, for example).

Institutions and Regulation

In a firm's external environment, there remain rules to be followed and penalties that those firms may suffer for noncompliance. The coercive enforcement side of regu-lation must be minor, however, since rules based largely on the threat of force are unli-kely to be widely accepted and valued, and monitoring and enforcement are costly. Regulations must also be seen as legitimate to be effective. They constitute the "rules of the game" that provide a common basis for all participants in an industry or sector.[26]

Outside of the firm, however, enforcement is the job of regulatory agencies (mostly but not exclusively governmental) rather than the firm's own hierarchy. The regulatory function may be formally designated or may be informal in a given set-ting. Formal regulations are often accompanied in practice by a variety of informal codes, whose purpose is to help firms manage the gaps in the official rules. As the Enron case in the Introduction illustrates, gaps in formal rules are also opportunities for manipulation. Many institutions make laws and rules to govern firm behavior and punish violators with sanctions. Government institutions, ranging from Congress to special regulatory agencies to law enforcement agencies, serve this function. So do a variety of quasi-public and professional groups, such as professional and trade associations, professional standards organizations, and even some private organizations. It is also possible for groups of firms to self-regulate on important aspects of joint behavior. This is unusual, however, although it is becoming more common in such activities as standards-setting by technology firms.

We know that regulatory activity has huge influences on the strategic behavior of firms. Court decisions have defined the types of structures that firms may employ as they grow and diversify. Justice Department policies and standards, along with the courts, have constrained how firms can behave, how they acquire knowledge from their environment, what types of mergers can be made, and what limits can be placed on corporate decisions and influence activities. Tax regulations can alter the course of whole sets of corporate activities, ranging from charitable donations to the securing of advice on corporate control transactions.

Regulation imposes costs on firms. These include the direct costs of compliance, the increased business costs due to noncompliance (for example, the costs of borrowing with a poor rating from a rating agency), the costs of strategic options that must be forgone because of regulations, the higher prices for goods that consumers pay, along with other potential distortions to a market that may result from the imperfections of a given regulatory regime. If a firm, often jointly with others, pursues what David Baron calls a "nonmarket" strategy that attempts to shape legislation through lobbying, then the costs of such a strategy must also be considered.[27] As the example of Enron shows, such a strategy can be wildly successful, at least for a time, but is also expensive and risky. Regulations may strategically advantage regulated firms. For example, they can restrict entry, which allows industry incumbents to enjoy greater scale and reduced price competition. By responding to the complaints of incumbents, regulatory agencies may raise the costs for rivals by forcing them to respond to complaints and to pay any penalties that are awarded. Regulations can also limit innovations that injure the capabilities of incumbents, while focusing competition on those aspects of the business at which incumbents excel. These factors will tend to increase both profitability and predictability for a stable regulatory regime. Industry-specific regulatory agencies may actually protect incumbents and come to associate with their economic interests. In times of significant change, however, such as from technological innovations or increased global competition, protective regulations are more likely to impede the ability of incumbents to adapt.

The strategic implications of regulations for firms are complicated by the fact that regulatory organizations are seldom neutral third parties but instead are pursuing their own strategies, using their regulatory power to do so. David Dranove provides an example of this when he discusses how in the 1990s program managers at Medicare and Medicaid, which were originally intended as hands-off federal health insurance programs, used their discretion and their resources to pursue the objectives of cost containment and quality control. These same goals were being pursued by private managed-care organizations at the same time.[28]

Interfirm Resource Dependence Relationships

Firms develop relationships with other firms and organizations in their environment, whether competitors, buyers, suppliers, complementors, or noneconomic organizations. Asymmetries in information, resources, capabilities, and other factors often characterize these relationships and lead to the development of power/dependence relationships. Resource-dependence arguments can easily apply to organizations and industries as well as individuals. For example, shipments between industries may indicate the relative dependence of firms in one industry on those in another. If one industry is a net importer from another, a dependency relationship may emerge, especially if the inputs are of critical importance and not otherwise available.

Firms suffering from dependence relationships with buyers or suppliers can take action to reduce their dependence through vertical integration, long-term contracting, or joint ventures and alliances. Several studies have documented such effects.[29] Jeffrey Pfeffer documented how asymmetric power relations between buyers and sellers were associated with vertical mergers. Menachem Brenner and Zur Shapira found that asymmetric trading was positively associated with vertical mergers, while mutual trading was inversely associated. In a 1997 study, Sydney Finkelstein replicated Pfeffer's original study, but only weakly, showing that, although resource dependence contributes to our understanding of vertical mergers, it is not the dominant explanation proposed by Pfeffer.

There are other bases around which resource dependence relations might develop to organize an industry or sector. For example, in developing economies, a chronic shortage of capital along with profound market imperfections may discourage foreign investment. In such situations it is not surprising to see the development of business groups, often around a central trading family with a strong name or a large financial institution. These groups serve as intermediary structures between governments and markets, and are common in Japan, Korea, India, and other Asian nations.

Burt's ideas on structural holes also apply to relations among firms in an industry. If a firm could obtain a central position relative to other firms in the industry, it would be in a position to charge for access or assistance or gain other benefits from its favored position. Once again, Enron provides an example. Part of Enron's business strategy was to take a central position in newly deregulated resource markets. To this end, Enron made initial investments in slack capacity that it needed to guarantee that market would function. Once confidence in the market was established, Enron could dispose of those slack assets and register an extraordinary profit. Enron's central position was further strengthened with such activities as EnronOnline, which provided the firm with information on both sides of the transactions it facilitated.

Sometimes important industry resources can be intangible. Status and reputation are two such resources. Achieving a strong and positive reputation or a high status within an industry may reduce the costs to a firm of establishing its presence to customers, negotiating with rivals, or securing the cooperation of partners. Firms possessing such assets will want to maintain them, while smaller and less established firms will want to associate with high-status firms to benefit from their standing. This interaction can provide a basis for associations among firms. For example, Joel Podolny studied the groupings that arose among investment banks around the issuance of new securities. High-status firms, as listed on the "tombstone" announcements of an issue, provided the basis around which consortia of banks would form. The role of a bank in a given deal, and its compensation, were determined by its position in the status ordering.[30]

Lowered reputation and status may stem from poor performance. It could also derive from passing crises, such as the withdrawal of a product for safety reasons, such as with Merck and its Vioxx drug. It could also stem from widely perceived excessive price increases, such as occurs regularly with petroleum firms following political crises or natural disasters such as Hurricane Katrina. Firms could also become tainted by the involvement of top managers in major scandals, such as with Tyco and Dennis Kozlowski.

EXAMPLE 17.6 INSTITUTIONS AND CULTURE: THE EBAY IPO[31]

The rapid growth of entrepreneurial firms places great strains on the informal and adaptive culture that frequently characterizes the early history of start-ups. With growth, there are too many transactions to be handled informally and too many employees to be recruited, managed, and paid informally. Everyone ceases to know everyone else in the firm by name. Formal structures and professional managers are needed to avoid the onset of chaos and respond to everyday demands without losing the entrepreneurial vision that originally motivated the start-up. The culture of the firm quickly becomes more bureaucratic and impersonal, while initial employees feel a sense of loss. Even the founders are eventually replaced by professionals. When growth is accompanied by institutional change, the stresses on culture are even greater, since the firm and its managers must comply with new rules, exhibit new behaviors, respond to new constituencies, pursue new objectives, and keep new sets of records. This is particularly the case when a firm "goes public" with an Initial Public Offering (IPO) of shares that then begin to trade in public markets.

The 1998 IPO of eBay showed these stresses and strains. Pierre Omidyar, a computer engineer, started the firm in 1995. The intent was to provide a space where buyers and sellers could transact securely. EBay charged sellers a small fee to list items for sale, and sellers paid a commission for items that sold. The firm was an instant success, making money its first month and every month afterward. By 1998, it was one of the few Internet firms to consistently show a profit. We have already mentioned eBay in Chapter 12 as an example of a firm benefiting from network effects, because it has more buyers and sellers by far than its competitors. At the time of its IPO, these network effects were already apparent. EBay was one of the most visited sites on the Internet, serving about 1 million browsers and featuring over 600,000 items for sale. In 1997, eBay made $874,000 on revenue of $5.74 million. The IPO was a startling success, with 3.5 million shares offered and initial price of $18. Soon afterward, however, the price surged to $54 and closed around $47 on the first day of trading. At the height of the day's activities, eBay was valued at nearly $2 billion.

Even granting the financial success of the IPO, many of the people associated with the firm felt that the IPO had fundamentally changed it for the worse. Although eBay benefited from network economies once it had grown large, it could not rely on them to start with. Like other Internet businesses, the firm focused on building a community with its users, through such vehicles as chat rooms, newsletters, reputational rankings, extensive courting of user input, and other activities. These actions, along with efforts to ensure the integrity of transactions, were a distinctive part of eBay's early history. Success in these efforts guaranteed a devoted user base that stayed with the firm and promoted eBay and even trained new users. In addition, the active exchange of information with users helped improve eBay's operations and let the firm excel at customer service, all of which in turn helped it to grow even further.

When the eBay IPO finally occurred, however, users were not included. Several reasons were offered for the omission. Some claimed legal restrictions as a reason. Others mentioned the fear that the IPO might fail and actually harm users. Still others noted how eBay's managers became billionaires following the IPO. Regardless of the reasons, the failure to follow through on initial expectations was a bone of contention within the firm long after the IPO, and long-time employees and users saw it in terms of the violation of the firm's community culture. Although some of these complaints might be expected with the growth and professionalization of a start-up venture, concerns about maintaining the initial distinctive culture of a start-up seem to have been important for the founders of Google in the quirky structuring of their 2004 IPO.

Institutional Logics: Beliefs, Values, and Behavioral Norms

There is a broader cognitive and cultural environment into which firms must fit. Although firms have their own cultures that vary in strength, they are also part of a large macro-culture that affects a wider set of firms and can differ in content significantly from corporate culture. Firms also act within a broader scientific and technological context that strongly influences what products and services firms offer, the performance standards that offerings must meet, and the rate of technical or market change that an industry or sector undergoes. Analogous to what we discussed for corporate culture, the institutional environment of firms also involves shared beliefs about the world, shared values about what is important, and norms about appropriate and inappropriate behaviors.

As firms in an industry or sector interact over time, they tend to develop shared conceptions about the nature of the business, how they serve customer needs, the most effective ways to conduct their operations, and other matters. The extent to which these common beliefs develop will be influenced by the stability of the industry's environment and its relationships to other industries. Sectors with long and fairly continuous histories (for example, higher education) will develop stronger sets of common beliefs than sectors subject to continual regulatory and technological change or constant combination with other sectors (for example, entertainment). Out of these common beliefs come common ideas and practices regarding what managers should do, how changes should occur, how business should be transacted, and what types of innovations are worthwhile. These interrelated beliefs, values, material practices, and norms of behavior that exist in an industry at any given time are referred to as *institutional logics*.

What is the strategic value of institutional logics for particular firms? Paradoxically, to the extent that they are stable, institutional logics have little strategic importance since they concern what firms take for granted. If firms share an institutional logic, then that logic does not provide a basis for relative advantage among the firms. Competitive advantage must come on some other dimension. In this sense, institutional logics are valuable because they lower the costs for firms of adapting to their environments.

What if not all the firms in an industry or sector share the institutional logic? There may be strategic advantage to be had in such situations, since some firms will not take the institutional logic for granted and will thus think about how to take advantage of the acquiescence of other firms. This could occur as a result of new entry into an industry from another industry or from a foreign market. It could also result from industry consolidation that brings together formerly distinct industry subgroups and forces firms to examine where their respective institutional logics differ. It could also stem from industry change that forces incumbents to alter their routines and develop new logics.

When common beliefs about an industry are disrupted, then most everything else about the industry becomes open to reconsideration by incumbents and eventual change. For example, the deregulation of natural gas pipelines disrupted commonly held ideas about how to do business and actually made it difficult for incumbent firms to be profitable by following industry norms. To respond to this, Enron's Kenneth Lay brought in McKinsey consultants, who changed their ideas of how to compete in the industry by applying ideas that were common in finance and banking to energy markets. The firm's initial success with this experimentation led to a redefinition of the energy business and how to strategize about it, changes in what managers did and how they were rewarded, and changes in which practices were valued by incumbent managers and which were not.

It is sometimes possible to link changes in industry logics to specific external stimuli, such that some event can be seen as the cause of industry change. In other situations, however, changes in institutional logics occur as a result of multiple stimuli, without a clear external push. In these conditions, the institutional logics may appear to change independently of external stimuli and then lead to further changes in the practices of incumbent industry firms.

Patricia Thorton and William Ocasio conducted a detailed study of how institutional logics changed in the higher-education publishing industry.[32] This niche within the publishing industry developed around supplying textbooks to college and university students. Thorton and Ocasio documented the presence of a traditional logic, what they term an "editorial logic" in the business. This logic included a view of publishing as a profession, with legitimacy based on personal reputation and rank in the firm's hierarchy, authority that centered on founding editors, a focus on increasing sales, and a strategy of organic growth. This was summed up as a system of "personal capitalism."

In the early 1970s, the logic of the business changed owing to a number of causes, including changes in firm ownership, changes in technology, the introduction of "professional" management into the business, and other factors. The new logic was called a *market logic*. It included a view of publishing as a business, with legitimacy based on market position and financial performance, authority that centered on a professional CEO, a focus on increasing profits, and a strategy of growth through acquisitions and channel expansion. This was summed up as a system of *market capitalism*.

Are changes in industry logics good or bad? That depends on whom you are asking and what is meant by good or bad. Institutional research has shown how these reference points themselves change as industry changes affect common beliefs and values. Values that were nonnegotiable at one time may become less important at another. Stakeholder groups may rise or fall in importance as an industry evolves. For example, debates about the consequences of health-care reform need to specify whether the focus is on the patient, physicians, shareholders, or the general public. One also needs to be clear about whether the performance variable of interest is quality of care, costs, timeliness, or some combination of outcomes.

Do industry logics drive change in industry practices, or do they result from changes in practices? Is the belief system in an industry a byproduct of industry economics, or does it shape those economics? The answer is probably a bit of both. On the one hand, as industry participants experiment with new products and services, some prove more successful than others and come to be adopted. Once they are adopted, common beliefs develop around recognition of the benefits of the new products and services. At the same time, the industry or the society at large may have long-standing beliefs regarding such matters as the importance of research and development, opposition to government intervention, the value of individual initiatives, the fostering of family values, the need for public education, and so on. The stronger these beliefs, the more possible it is that they may constrain experimentation in an industry and influence the judgments made regarding products and services.

Heather Haveman and Hayagreeva Rao came to this conclusion after studying the evolution of the thrift industry in California.[33] They examined the different forms of these early savings institutions, forerunners of S&Ls, that developed during the end of the nineteenth century up through 1920, along with the parallel development of the institutional logics for thrifts. They found that these institutions developed in part as a result of experimentation and technical problem solving. They also developed under the influence of more macro pressures of large population growth and the development of values of bureaucracy and voluntary effort associated with Progressivism, in opposition to the less formal and more collective values characterizing early thrift plans. Individuals attempting to develop thrift institutions had to balance needs for technical efficiency and professional management in their plans with pressures for institutional legitimacy that pushed them toward conformity with prevailing ways of organizing plans.

CHAPTER SUMMARY

◆ Firms act within a broader social context that constrains how their strategic decisions are made and implemented. The culture and power relations within a firm comprise its internal social context, which influences how its managers make and implement decisions. The external social context of the firm includes its regulatory environment, its resource-dependence relationships, and its institutional domain.

◆ *Power* refers to an individual actor's ability to accomplish his or her goals by means of resources obtained through *noncontractual exchange relationships*.

◆ In the *resource dependence* view of power, individuals and firms seek to gain power by reducing their dependence on other actors, while building the dependence of other actors on them through the control of critical information and resources.

◆ Power is also embodied in important structures within firms or in the broader business environment. Particular positions permit the control of resources, information, and access and thus give their incumbents power and influence.

◆ Power can help or hurt a firm's performance. It is helpful when there are high agency costs between managers and lower-level workers and when the firm's environment is stable. It is harmful when there are high agency costs between levels of upper management and when the firm's environment is unstable.

◆ Formal power should be allocated to managers on the basis of their value to the firm, the costs of replacing them, and the likelihood that they will tend to act in a manner consistent with the firm's objectives.

◆ *Culture* is a set of collectively held values, beliefs, and norms of behavior among members of a firm that influences individual employee preferences and behaviors on the job. It frees them from the need to renegotiate their tasks, reduces their costs of making decisions, and permits more specialization of effort.

◆ Culture controls the activities of employees on the basis of their attachment to the firm, rather than on the basis of individual incentives and monitoring. It mitigates power dynamics by creating "mutually reinforcing" norms that permit the emergence of mutually beneficial activities that would not be likely in the marketplace.

◆ When a firm's strategy "fits" with the demands of its environment, then its culture supports the direction of the firm and its policies, making it more efficient. When the environment changes, however, and requires firms to adapt to changes, culture is more likely to be inertial and lead to maladaptive firm behavior.

◆ Firm behavior in the external environment is governed by rules and regulations that are supported by accepted behavioral norms as well as more formal sanctions. Regulations provide a common basis for action by all participants in an industry or a sector.

◆ Enforcement of rules and norms in the environment is typically the job of regulatory agencies or peer organizations rather than the firm's own hierarchy. Government institutions, ranging from Congress to special regulatory agencies to law enforcement agencies, serve this regulatory function, as do a variety of quasi-public and professional groups, such as professional and trade associations, professional standards organizations, and even some private organizations.

◆ Regulation imposes costs on firms, including the direct costs of compliance, the indirect costs of forgone activities, and the costs of influencing regulators. Regulations may also strategically advantage regulated firms, by restricting entry and allowing incumbents to enjoy greater scale and reduced price competition. Regulations can also limit innovations that injure incumbents, while focusing competition on those aspects of the business at which incumbents excel.

◆ Firms develop power-dependence relationships in their environment that are characterized by asymmetries in information, resources, capabilities, and other factors.

◆ Firms enter into cooperative relationships through long-term contracts, mergers and acquisitions, or strategic alliances and joint ventures, to manage these dependence relationships with other organizations and reduce environmental uncertainty.

◆ There is a broader social and cultural environment into which firms must fit. While firms have their own cultures, they are also part of a large macroculture that affects a wider set of firms and can differ significantly from corporate culture.

◆ Firms also act within a broader scientific and technological context that strongly influences what products and services firms offer, the performance standards that offerings must meet, and the rate of change that an industry or sector undergoes.

◆ Analogous to corporate culture, the institutional environment of firms also involves shared beliefs about the world, shared values about what is important, and norms about appropriate and inappropriate behaviors.

◆ These interrelated beliefs, values, material practices, and norms of behavior that exist in an industry at any given time are referred to as *institutional logics*.

◆ It is sometimes possible to link changes in industry logics to specific external stimulus. In other industries, however, changes in industry logics occur as a result of multiple stimuli, without a clear external cause, and still significantly influence firms.

QUESTIONS

1. How does the resource-dependence view of power differ from the market-imperfections perspective of transactions-cost economics?
2. When might it not be reasonable to remedy a power differential with a critical buyer or supplier?
3. Power often accrues to individuals who are very effective in their jobs or to firms that enjoy sustained high performance? If this is so, how is power different from basic competence, efficiency, or performance?
4. Major professional schools are highly competitive, and most applicants do not get past the admissions process. That makes admissions a critical gatekeeper function for these schools. Given that, why don't admissions officers enjoy higher status and power among the faculty and staff of professional schools?
5. How might a favorable location within the interpersonal networks within a firm help an individual acquire and maintain additional bases of power?
6. How would you go about identifying the powerful people within your organization? What indicators would you look for? From what types of problems would these indicators suffer?
7. All firms operate within an institutional environment of some kind. How do the common beliefs, values, and norms of behavior that characterize the institutional environment affect

the ability of firms to pursue sustainable strategies? Are institutional influences always constraining, or can they ever promote competition and innovation?

8. Discuss the idea of structural holes in the context of competitive strategy. How can you link network advantage to value creation and competitive advantage for firms enjoying favorable positions?

9. Every firm has a culture, but not all cultures are relevant for a decision maker or analyst. Under what conditions is it important to pay attention to culture? When is it less important to analyze the influence of culture?

10. Why is firm growth often antithetical to the maintenance of a stable corporate culture?

11. How can powerful individuals influence a firm's culture? Do "superstar" CEOs really exert the influence on firms that the popular business press claims for them? How much does the leader matter in a firm with a long history and a strong corporate culture?

12. The more manageable a firm's culture is, the less valuable it will be for the firm. Agree or disagree—and explain.

13. Visitors to China are sometimes puzzled by the combination of a very strong central government and a very competitive economic system. What is the connection between the strength of government agencies and the type of market activities that develop within that regulatory context?

ENDNOTES

[1] Barnard, C., *The Functions of the Executive*, Cambridge, MA, Harvard University Press, 1938, pp. 167–171.

[2] For the principles of social exchange, see Coleman, J. S., *Foundations of Social Theory*, Cambridge, MA, Belknap, 1990, chap. 2.

[3] Pfeffer, J., *Managing with Power: Politics and Influence in Organizations*, Boston, Harvard Business School Press, 1992; Pfeffer, J., *Power in Organizations*, Marshfield, MA, Pitman, 1981.

[4] The material for this example is taken from Neustadt's 1990 revision. See Neustadt, R. E., *Presidential Power and the Modern Presidents*, New York, Free Press, 1990.

[5] This variant of the resource-dependence approach is the *strategic contingencies view* of power. See Hickson, D. J., C. R. Hinings, C. A. Lee, R. E. Schneck, and J. M. Pennings, "A Strategic Contingencies Theory of Intraorganizational Power," *Administrative Science Quarterly*, 16, 1971, pp. 216–229.

[6] Burt, R. S., *Structural Holes: The Social Structure of Competition*, Cambridge, MA, Harvard University Press, 1992.

[7] Fernandez, R. M. and Gould, R. V., "A Dilemma of State Power: Brokerage and Influence in the National Health Policy Domain," *American Journal of Sociology*, 99, May 1994, pp. 1455–1491.

[8] Byrne, J. A., *The Whiz Kids*, New York, Currency Doubleday, 1993. The Whiz Kids were a group of academics and operations analysts, including Reith, Charles Thorton, Robert McNamara, and Arjay Miller, who distinguished themselves in operations analysis for the Army Air Force in World War II and later joined the management of Ford as a group in early 1946. Most rose to senior positions within Ford, and two, McNamara and Miller, rose to its presidency.

[9] Weber, M., *Economy and Society*, Vol. 1, Berkeley, University of California Press, 1978, pp. 212–226.

[10] "Conseco's Turnaround Hopes Are Fading," *Wall Street Journal*, August 8, 2002, p. B3. "Conseco Recovery Efforts Fail: A Bankruptcy Filing Is Possible," *New York Times*, August 10, 2002, pp. B1, B14.

[11]Rotemberg, J. J., "Power in Profit-Maximizing Organizations," *Journal of Economics and Management Strategy*, 2, 1993, pp. 165–198.

[12]Roberts, J., *The Modern Firm*. Oxford, Oxford University Press, 2004, p. 18.

[13]Kreps, D. M., "Corporate Culture and Economic Theory," in Alt, J. and K. Shepsle (eds.), *Perspectives on Positive Political Economy*, Cambridge, UK, Cambridge University, 1990.

[14]Roberts, *The Modern Firm*, pp. 41–44; 260–262.

[15]Barney, J. B., "Organizational Culture: Can It Be a Source of Sustained Competitive Advantage?" *Academy of Management Review*, 11, 1986, pp. 656–665.

[16]Information in this example comes from Cray Research, Inc. (HBS #385-011).

[17]Pettigrew, A. M., *The Awakening Giant: Continuity and Change at ICI*, Oxford, UK, Blackwell, 1985, chap. 10, pp. 376–437; Pettigrew, A. M., "Examining Change in the Long-Term Context of Culture and Politics," chap. 11 in Johannes M. Pennings and Associates, *Organizational Strategy and Change*, San Francisco: Jossey-Bass, 1985, pp. 269–318.

[18]Miller, G. J., *The Political Economy of Hierarchy*, Cambridge, UK, Cambridge University Press, 1992, chap. 10; Kreps, D. M., *A Course in Microeconomic Theory*, Princeton, NJ, Princeton University Press, 1990, chap. 14.

[19]Davis, G. F. and T. A. Thompson, "A Social Movement Perspective on Corporate Control," *Administrative Science Quarterly*, 39, 1994, pp. 141–173.

[20]Useem, M., *Executive Defense: Shareholder Power and Corporate Reorganization*, Cambridge, MA, Harvard University Press, 1993, chap. 3.

[21]Yoder, S. K., "A 1990 Reorganization at Hewlett-Packard Is Already Paying Off," *Wall Street Journal*, July 22, 1992, pp. A-1, A-10.

[22]For a discussion of cultural clash issues in acquisitions, see Haspeslagh, P. C. and D. B. Jemison, *Managing Acquisitions: Creating Value Through Corporate Renewal*. New York, Free Press, 1991. For a general discussion of these conflicting sets of values, see March, J. G., "Exploration and Exploitation in Organizational Learning," *Organizational Science*, 2, 1991, pp. 71–87.

[23]See Spar, D. L., *The Cooperative Edge*. Ithaca, NY, Cornell University Press, 1994, for a discussion of private regulatory structures in cartels. See Shapiro, C. and H. R. Varian, *Information Rules*, Boston, Harvard Business School Press, 1999, for a discussion of collective standard-setting activities in information businesses.

[24]Shanley, M. and M. Peteraf, "Vertical Group Formation: A Social Process Perspective, " *Managerial and Decision Economics*, 2004, pp. 473–488.

[25]Scott, W. R., *Institutions and Organizations*, 2d ed., Thousand Oaks, CA, Sage, 2001.

[26]North, D. C., *Institutions, Institutional Change, and Economic Performance*, Cambridge, UK, Cambridge University Press, 1990.

[27]Baron, D. P., *Business and Its Environment*, 3d ed., New York, Prentice-Hall, 2000.

[28]Dranove, D., *The Economic Evolution of American Health Care*, Princeton, NJ, Princeton University Press, 2000, pp. 61–64.

[29]Pfeffer, J., "Merger as a Response to Organizational Interdependence," *Administrative Science Quarterly*, 17, 1972, pp. 382–394; Brenner, M. and Z. Shapira, "Environmental Uncertainty as Determining Merger Activity," chap. 3 in W. Goldberg (ed.), *Mergers*, New York, Nichols Publishing, 1983, pp. 51–65; Finkelstein, S., "Interindustry Merger Patterns and Resource Dependence: A Replication and Extension of Pfeffer (1972)," *Strategic Management Journal*, 18, 1997, pp. 787–810.

[30]Podolny, J., "A Status-based Model of Market Competition," *American Journal of Sociology*, 98, 1993, pp. 829–872.

[31]Materials for this example came from Cohen, A., *The Perfect Store: Inside eBay*, New York: Little, Brown, 2002.

[32]Thorton, P. H. and W. Ocasio, "Institutional Logics and the Historical Contingency of Power in Organizations: Executive Succession in the Higher Education Publishing Industry, 1958–1990," *American Journal of Sociology*, 105, 1999, pp. 801–843.

[33]Haveman, H. A. and H. Rao, "Institutional and Organizational Coevolution in the Thrift Industry," *American Journal of Sociology*, 102, 1997, pp. 1606–1651.

18

STRATEGY AND
THE GENERAL MANAGER

◆ ◆ ◆ ◆ ◆ **INTRODUCTION**

"The last thing IBM needs right now is vision."—Louis Gerstner, CEO of IBM

"It's an accountant's answer, not a leader's."—Robert Galbreath of Philip Crosby Associates, commenting on Gerstner's statement.

"Being a visionary is trivial. Being a CEO is hard. All you have to do to be a visionary is to give the old 'MIPS to the moon' speech. That's different from being the CEO of a company and seeing where the profits are."—Bill Gates, CEO of Microsoft[1]

What is the role of the CEO? Is the CEO a problem solver or a visionary? We believe that a successful manager must be both. Managers must manage a firm's internal and external relations, but must also establish a profitable and defensible position in fierce markets. Upon his retirement in 2002, Gerstner was rightly credited with a remarkable 10-year turnaround at IBM that focused not on vision but on cutting prices and costs, streamlining operations, and exiting poorly performing businesses. Like Gerstner, Bill Gates has skillfully managed vertical relations, market competition, and innovation within Microsoft. But he also had the vision from the beginning to understand that a large installed base of DOS-based personal computers would create a first-mover advantage permitting DOS to become the industry standard and Gates to become a multibillionaire. The 2001 retirement of Jack Welch, after a legendary career, has raised similar issues about what it is that effective CEOs and general managers do and what balance of skills and qualities will make them more effective. Although most general managers (GMs) will not realize the same financial rewards as Gates or Welch, they will face similar strategic problems and will need to strike a balance among multiple roles that they are called on to play while leading their businesses.

Whereas the retirements of CEO superstars Gerstner and Welch stirred debate about what constitutes general management excellence, other recent executive departures, such as those of Tyco's Dennis Kozlowski, Enron's Kenneth Lay and Jeffrey Skilling, and WorldCom's Bernard Ebbers, moved discussions on the role and importance of general managers in altogether different directions. These executives left under suspicion of improper or even criminal behavior. They left behind firms that were in financial ruin, while shareholders and retirees saw their pensions reduced. They also left regulators scrambling for legal and regulatory responses to executive misbehavior (such as the Sarbanes-Oxley Act of 2002). The uproar created by these scandals all but drowned out discussions of CEO excellence and brought to the surface issues of trust, conflicts of interest, legality, and fairness that have not been raised as strongly since the Progressive movement of the early twentieth century and the Great Depression. As if the scandals were not enough, even legendary CEOs who managed to avoid scandal, such as Michael Eisner at Disney, found themselves unable to maintain their power and rest on their past laurels while the current performance of their firms languished. Eisner ended up leaving Disney in 2005 after more than 20 years at its helm in a conflict that sparked debates about limiting the power and circumscribing the roles of future leaders at Disney.[2]

This chapter describes the many tasks general managers confront and the different decision-making roles they have to perform. The GM has comprehensive decision-making responsibilities for one or more business units within a firm. John Kotter found seven types of general management positions in his comparative case studies of managers, ranging from corporate CEOs to division managers to operations and product market managers in profit centers.[3] While most firms are led by a single CEO, the roles exercised by the top manager vary and a top management team is often more important for exercising general management responsibilities for the firm on a collective basis.

A HISTORICAL PERSPECTIVE ON THE GENERAL MANAGER

The GM position has interested business observers ever since the growth of the first large firms. Alfred Chandler notes that the first references to managers appeared in the early journals of railroad engineers, reflecting both the growing complexity of railroad operations and the role of the railroads in fostering the growth of large firms. As these firms, such as U.S. Steel, developed around 1900, the general manager's administrative expertise facilitated internal coordination and helped reduce the risks of marketplace decisions. Managers became the "visible hand" that replaced the "invisible hand" of the market in making decisions for the firm.[4]

As managers became more important, interest in them grew among observers, students, and even critics of business. General management classes in leadership and business policy have figured prominently in MBA curricula since the first MBA programs were developed shortly after 1900. Classic essays on the important role of the general manager, by such authors as Chester Barnard, Philip Selznick, Mary Parker Follett, and Alfred Sloan, remain in print today.[5] Critics of the large corporation have focused on the increasing power of managers, coupled with their lack of accountability to shareholders, as threats to social and economic stability.[6] The link between the general manager and the firm's strategy has persisted in current research. This is due in part to the enormous influence of the Business Policy group at the Harvard Business School, which developed the concept of strategy as a "simple practitioner's theory" of general management (i.e., strategy is synonymous with what general managers do).[7]

Despite this interest, we still know little about general managers, leadership, and related issues. Although most scholars suspect that general managers are important for their firms, they are much less clear on how they are important. Theories of management have been superficial and prescriptive, while evidence on managerial behaviors has been sparse and difficult to interpret. Warren Bennis, in reviewing research on strategy and leadership, concludes that "never have so many laboured so long to say so little."[8] It is only recently that researchers have obtained sufficient data to begin explaining managerial behavior, especially the behaviors of general managers.

◆ ◆ ◆ ◆ ◆ WHAT DO GENERAL MANAGERS DO?

At the conclusion of a book on the economic principles underlying strategic decisions, it is reasonable to ask if there are any principles regarding the tasks and roles of the individuals who make strategic decisions—the general managers of a firm and its business units. If the general manager's tasks could be simply mapped onto a series of economic decisions, then understanding the GM position would not be difficult. There would also be little to say above and beyond what we have already discussed in earlier chapters. Problems with the GM position arise because a manager must make whole sets of decisions simultaneously or else decide how to sequence them. Some important studies on the decision processes of actual GMs have raised this issue in terms of *incremental* decision making.[9] Moreover, the decisions that present themselves to general managers are seldom typical, since these would be covered by existing policies and procedures and thus would be fairly routine. General managers get to face the unusual decisions, the exceptions to the routines. This complicates our view of the GM position and motivates our search for managerial roles.

In discussing GMs, we assume that general managers control their firms and business units. We do so for analytical simplicity. In reality, top management teams often perform most of the tasks we ascribe to individual GMs. Employing a top management team allows for a full delineation of top management roles without placing all complex top management decisions in a single individual. Concentrating all decision authority for a complex firm in the hands of a single individual would be highly stressful for the individual and inefficient for the firm, whose complexity would overwhelm the abilities of even the most capable managers taken singly. Research on top management teams has been growing, and its findings parallel those of studies of general managers.[10] In addition, understanding top management teams requires understanding the behavioral processes by which these teams operate, such as dividing up managerial responsibilities among team members, communicating team results, settling disputes, and avoiding negative groups dynamics (i.e., "groupthink").

In the remainder of this chapter, we discuss the tasks and roles of general managers. We then consider the many tensions among these roles that make the GM position so difficult. We conclude by noting that, just as the definition of the firm changes in response to history and changing business conditions, so also the definition of the GM evolves and does not describe the same combination of tasks from one era to the next.

Case Studies of General Managers

Henry Mintzberg's case studies were among the first to show how the behavior of managers differed from both common perceptions and general prescriptions. He found that, rather than being reflective and systematic, the behavior of effective managers was characterized by brevity of interactions, discontinuity of action, and lack of reflection. Rather than favoring written, aggregated, and well-analyzed quantitative information, managers tended to strongly prefer informal, disaggregated, and verbal media for communicating and obtaining information. Mintzberg was one of the first to show that the management profession was a craft rather than a science.[11] Managers organize their work according to informal roles, including interpersonal roles, such as being a leader; informational roles, such as being the spokesperson for the firm or one of its units; and decisional roles, such as being a negotiator or someone who handles disturbances. Managers rely on intuition and judgment to make their decisions.

John Kotter also looked at managerial roles. His detailed case studies of GMs show the variety of ways in which general managers adjust to the fluid surroundings in which they must accomplish their tasks.[12] He comes to three general conclusions. First, GMs do not follow a purely analytical approach of goal setting, analysis, and execution. Rather than plan and implement in a linear manner, effective general managers build agendas for their businesses and then work to accomplish them. Managers are rational, but they are also flexible in how they pursue their goals and opportunistic in taking advantage of situations permiting progress toward their goals.

Kotter also finds that effective general managers must build extensive interpersonal networks to get the information necessary to accomplish their agendas. Viewing managers as key players in dense interpersonal networks is reasonable, given the internal complexity of large firms, the range of supplier and product markets these firms serve, and the types of decisions managers must make. This view of GMs as builders of relationship networks also has been developed by John Gabarro, who studies how successful GMs develop at the beginning of their tenure with a firm, and Hermine Ibarra, who considers successful GM networking strategies.[13] It also is consistent with the structural hole argument of Ron Burt (discussed in Chapter 17) that managers gain power by occupying critical network positions and suggests that managers embedded in networks can transfer value and resources from one set of relationships to others.[14]

Kotter's third conclusion is that managerial effectiveness takes time to develop. In part, effectiveness is a simple matter of learning through problem solving and applying that experience to new but related problems. Critical interpersonal networks also take time to develop. For example, knowledge of the key decision makers or new product development practices in one firm will be less valuable if the manager possessing that knowledge moves to another employer. If management capability is an asset, it is often highly firm-specific. This goes against the conventional wisdom taught in many MBA programs that management skills are generic and highly portable from firm to firm.

The Roles of the General Manager

In bringing value to the firm, the GM plays many roles. First, the GM is an *entrepreneur* who makes and changes the fundamental position of the firm in its markets. The GM is also an *organizer/implementor*, who establishes a division of labor in the firm and coordinates the allocation of decision-making rights. Related to this role, the GM is a *contractor*, who balances inducements and contributions in formal agreements with employees, buyers, suppliers, and other key stakeholders. Since there are limits to the possibilities for contracting within the firm, the GM also must be a *powerholder*, who uses varied bases of influence, and a *facilitator*, who uses interpersonal skills to build relationships and secure agreements even in the absence of formal contracts. Along with coordinating action within the firm, the GM is also a *competitor*, who adapts the firm's activities to those of other firms in the industry. The GM must be an effective *adapter*, who readjusts the firm's assets and commitments in response to significant changes in business conditions. Finally, while the GM is fulfilling one of more of the above roles, it is important to remember that the GM serves others (unless the manager is also the owner). Business managers work for group managers. Even top managers work for the shareholders (via the board of directors). This means that the GM must fulfill the additional role of being an accountable *agent*.

The General Manager as Entrepreneur

The managerial role of defining how the firm creates and sustains value is analogous to the entrepreneurial function of management. Just as entrepreneurs choose where to commit the capital of their investors and how best to manage those investments, so GMs choose how best to commit the capital of owners and to position the firm in its product markets to create value on a sustainable basis. The sheer size of large firms ensures that GMs will make many of these important decisions. The large amount of fixed strategy-specific assets that these decisions require ensures that the decisions made by GMs will commit the firm to a strategic position with long-term implications for its performance.

While the entrepreneur role is critical for the firm, many new GMs find that their firms are already committed to an extensive set of value-creation opportunities, by virtue of its history, sunk investments, and long-term relationships. This is not a problem in stable environments, as GMs will have plenty of other issues to which they must attend. If competitive conditions change unexpectedly, however, firms may be vulnerable to competitors that are not constrained by prior investments and commitments. This is a common occurrence in industries undergoing deregulation and suggests that GMs in such situations face serious challenges in defining how their firm creates value.

Preexisting constraints may limit a manager's freedom to create new strategies, but they do not render the value-creation function altogether moot. Rather, these constraints increase the pressures on GMs to identify and exploit opportunities for value creation. Indeed, it is when environmental challenges are great and institutional constraints are high that it is most important to find new opportunities for value creation.

The General Manager as Organizer/Implementor

Chandler's dictum that structure follows strategy (discussed in Chapter 16) implies that GMs organize their firms to best implement their strategic choices. As we discussed in Chapter 11, for example, a choice of a competitive position highlighting cost advantage will be associated with such implementation choices as standardized products, mass-production facilities, and a traditional management style. A position favoring benefit advantage, however, will be associated with customized products and tradeoffs between scale and flexibility in production.

The organizer/implementor role involves several generic decisions. The first is how best to coordinate information and resource flows within the firm around its strategic choices. This is akin to Galbraith's idea of organizational design based on efficient information processing (discussed in Chapter 16). This role also involves decisions regarding which organizing dimensions are most important, which types of activities need the most coordination, which coordination needs take priority in general, and how to resolve specific coordination conflicts that may arise. Another aspect of this role is delegation—specifically deciding who should have decision-making rights over which of the firm's decisions, along with what type of incentive scheme will motivate them and how their performance should be evaluated (discussed in Chapter 15).

Decisions concerning implementation are not just derivative from the firm's strategy. Implementation often requires information that is unavailable until after strategic decisions have been made. For example, this can involve carefully matching people to organizational resources to enable the firm to deal with implementation problems. Mismatches can lead to suboptimal responses to problems. More importantly, they can threaten the entire strategy. Merger integration is a situation in which the costs of implementation failures can be high. For example, a merger whose strategy was based on specialized human capital in the acquired firm could be implemented in ways that alienated key individuals in the acquired firm and drove them to leave. Incomplete or haphazard changes in incentive schemes could do this as well. The managers in charge might not even know there was a problem until their key employees had left the firm.

The choices that managers make in implementing their strategies also commit the firm to courses of action. Implementation can promote inertia through large investments in sunk assets, training and human resource development, or critical relationships with other actors that impede the firm's flexibility and responsiveness to environmental changes. Implementation choices also constrain the future strategic choices of the general manager, especially if the GM had to publicly commit to decisions or expend scarce political/social capital to secure the agreement of others.

The General Manager as Contractor

Managers are contractors, both inside and outside the firm. The importance of external contracting, such as with supply chain partners, is clear. As the transactions costs of securing activities through the market increase, it becomes increasingly worthwhile to internalize these activities inside the firm. We discussed this subject in Chapter 3, in terms of "make-or-buy" decisions. In dealing with employees and other stakeholders, a contracting perspective is also relevant, even if most employees do not work with an explicit employment contract. The reason is that interactions akin to the contract negotiation can occur in a wide range of relationships. We discussed this in Chapter 17 in terms of social exchange and power-dependence relationships. In these situations, the managerial role as contractor is clear—to get the best deal and spell out the terms of an agreement as completely as possible. The management literature has often underemphasized the importance of contracting within the firm, although as we discussed in Chapter 14, research on principal–agent relationships has not neglected it.

The General Manager as Powerholder

As we discussed in Chapter 17, important activities occur within the firm for which cost-effective contracts cannot be easily developed. In these situations, GMs can use their power to complement their formal authority so as to secure the cooperation of all the parties necessary for an activity to succeed.

In exercising their power, however, GMs also must consider the costs. The goals of managers will only rarely be fully aligned with those of the firm, and conflicts will often arise among managers who implement different aspects of a firm's strategy. In such situations, the use of power by a manager may hinder firm performance by impeding the achievements of other managers. In addition, GMs are not immune from the temptation to pursue strictly personal goals. In such circumstances, power will detract from firm performance. The overall costs of using power and its net effect on firm performance will be clear only in specific situations. Nevertheless, the recent fate of such flamboyant power-wielding CEOs as Dennis Kozlowski, Michael Eisner, or "Chainsaw Al" Dunlap is instructive regarding whether too much executive power is a good thing. It is instructive that recent prescriptive approaches to strategy featuring CEOs have tried to fashion roles that soften the pursuit of individual glory in favor of firm goals.[15]

The General Manager as Facilitator

GMs often need the cooperation of others, yet they can neither contract for that cooperation nor bring their power and influence to bear to obtain it. One example would occur when one manager needs the cooperation of another manager with comparable authority in the firm. Other examples would occur when the success of an activity depends on efforts by crucial employees, but where the manager cannot monitor what the employees actually do, where the employees can legitimately refuse to provide such effort, and where the manager cannot provide sufficient tangible incentives to the employees. In these situations, the GM's role is to persuade and shape the impressions and preferences of others to increase the chances of obtaining their cooperation. These activities are often associated with building an organization culture, which we discussed in Chapter 17. Although this role appears to focus more on intangibles and "softer" activities than other roles, skills at facilitation are likely among the most valuable that a manager can possess, since they address some of the most difficult situations that managers must face.

Benjamin Hermalin considers facilitation in terms of two problems that managers face in securing cooperation from others.[16] First, a manager must convince potential followers that it is in their interest to follow—that they will gain from cooperating and contributing to unit performance. This involves transmitting more information to potential followers than they already possess. Second, a manager must convince followers that they are not being misled, that is, that the leader is truthful. Potential followers may believe that a manager has an incentive to mislead them to get them to work harder.

Managers can employ two methods to convince others that they are not being misled. The first is to lead by example. A manager can work long hours and thus convince others that it is worthwhile for them to do so too. The second way is lead by sacrifice. A manager may offer gifts or other side payments to followers to gain their cooperation. This sacrifice is convincing not because of the worth of the side payments to their recipients but because the payments signal the manager's true beliefs regarding the value of an activity. Hermalin models this choice between leading by example and leading by sacrifice and finds that leading by example is the best way of signaling the quality of information to potential followers. Leading by sacrifice may still be necessary if leading by example is not possible.

GMs also facilitate cooperation by building relationships with key individuals inside their firms and within their broader business environments. A manager who is embedded within a network of relationships is better able to resolve disputes over particular transactions because the parties value maintaining a relationship. John Kotter sees relationship-building as a central activity of general managers. In emerging or newly deregulated markets, relationships may be crucial for success because the legal and institutional infrastructure may not be sufficiently developed to permit the cost-effective governance of transactions. In Eastern European countries, following the end of Communist rule, for example, concepts of contract and fiduciary obligation were underdeveloped. Western firms entering those markets needed to do so on the basis of long-standing relationships with government and business leaders rather than on specific guarantees that may not have been upheld in a contracting dispute.

Where such a situation exists, firms that are first to enter the market have the potential to build first-mover advantages through relationships with key actors. Gary Miller advances this culture- and relationship-building view of how managers facilitate cooperation as a complement to their use of incentives, controls, and formal structure.[17] By engaging in these nonpecuniary motivational activities, managers shape expectations of how activities within the firm will be conducted, how managers will work with employees, and how disputes will be resolved. By shaping expectations, managers limit the range of activities open to employees and reduce the chances that noncooperative norms develop.

The facilitation role is increasingly extending to interfirm relationships. As we discussed in Chapter 10, complementor relationships are becoming increasingly common in a variety of industries. This means that general managers are increasingly having to cooperate with their counterparts in other firms, including firms with which they normally compete. This is common, for example, in industries driven by the need to develop common sets of standards regarding new technologies, such as in mobile phones, personal computers, software, and Internet businesses.

The General Manager as Competitor

As the manager of a business unit that competes in a market, the GM must take into account the activities of competitors who are trying to gain a competitive advantage. GMs must understand the nature of competition in their served markets. They must gather and analyze information about competitors, anticipate their reactions to possible moves, and determine how best to modify their unit's strategic activities on the basis of expected interactions. Interactions with competitors can be direct or indirect and can be as limited as evaluating their observed activities without any explicit, implicit, or tacit collusion. The activities associated with this role typically occur during product market interactions, but can involve other settings, such as at trade association meetings. The role of competitor is only infrequently discussed in detail in general management writings.[18] Yet documents produced in hundreds of antitrust cases reveal the importance that managers ascribe to their role of actively coping with competitors.

The General Manager as Adapter

Managers' decisions are often specific to the business conditions in hand. Significant changes in the business environment may lead GMs to reassess their basic decisions regarding the horizontal and vertical boundaries of the firm and their strategic position. For example, this could occur as managers in basic metals industries, such as steel and aluminum, discover that the market conditions that made extensive vertical integration reasonable during the early history of these industries have changed. Vertically integrated firms may now be inertial and unresponsive to conditions in world metals markets that have become more competitive.

If fundamental environmental changes occur, then the firm may need to redefine itself to survive. The GM can begin this process by directing discretionary resources. More often, however, major change requires making new, costly, and risky sunk investments, changing relationships, and getting out of past commitments. Such fundamental reorientation may be possible, but it is likely to be painful, as whole categories of assets and employees that were once valuable must be let go.

The GM will not only need to decide whether a fundamental reorientation and restructuring is necessary, but will also need to facilitate the cooperation of the firm's employees and stakeholders if the reorientation is to be effective. Those workers who remain after their firm restructures will often find that their position has been greatly altered. Workers who are now critical to the value-creation activities of the firm may find their positions enhanced. Other workers, however, will find themselves increasingly relegated to a peripheral and tenuous role in the firm and will see themselves as increasingly vulnerable to future cutbacks and restructurings.

The General Manager as Agent

As general managers perform all of the aforementioned roles, they are doing so on behalf of someone else. Unit and subunit managers report to an overall GM. That GM in turn reports to a division or group GM. At the top of the firm's hierarchy, the CEO and his or her management team are responsible to the board of directors and shareholders. The inherent tension between pursuing one's own interest while working as an agent for someone else is exacerbated by the GM's power and knowledge. The actors to whom GMs are accountable are often in a poor position to disagree with managers about the terms of their work. As managers become more knowledgeable and powerful, the potential for agency problems will grow. The temptation to excess may become too strong to resist, especially in high-growth and speculative market environments.

Only a small number of executives violate their responsibilities to shareholders to such an extent that it attracts negative publicity and legal actions. Only a small number of firms fail and are forced to seek bankruptcy protection. One is tempted to claim that corporate governance systems are working and that few changes are needed. Yet, the consequences of a small number of failures such as those at Enron, WorldCom, Comdisco, Adelphia, and others can be catastrophic. Enron's bankruptcy involved the destruction of share price value for a firm once valued at $80 billion. WorldCom's bankruptcy was even larger, surpassing $100 billion. Along with the destruction of shareholder value, bondholders were hurt and thousands of employees lost jobs. Thousands of other individuals saw their retirement plans destroyed or sharply reduced in value due to the drop in company stock price. Trust in many other companies was shattered. While most GMs perform the role of agent well, the consequences of failure can be devastating for those not responsible but still affected by managerial misbehavior. The recognition of these consequences is what is driving proposals for governance reform, the activities of prosecutors such as Eliot Spitzer, and new legislation, such as the Sarbanes-Oxley Act of 2002.

The Tensions of Managerial Work

Only some of the managerial roles that we have discussed are present at any given time. Which roles are relevant in a situation can also vary according to the GM's level with the larger organization. Some tensions among many of these roles are also inherent, however. These tensions can be managed but probably never totally eliminated.

One tension concerns routines. Some parts of the firm can be routinely managed, with clear goals, tasks, and outcomes, an effective incentive system, and ample information flows. The job of the GM for these tasks is to administer clearly defined systems. For other decisions, however, the task is harder. For example, GMs may have difficulty integrating disparate functions at the firm level because these functions differ in their tasks, their goals, their time span for results, and even the complexity of their language. The tension arises when managers attempt to impose a similar set of routines across disparate functions or across a diversified set of business units.

The problem of managing individuals from different functional areas—manufacturing, sales, and research and development (R&D)—under a single set of policies and procedures provides a classic example of this tension. While each function may be manageable and possess characteristics with sufficient routines to allow the development of administrative procedures, the functions differ in which of their characteristics are manageable and what values to attach to a set of results. Manufacturing has a well-defined set of tasks, a short-term time frame, and unambiguous results, whereas R&D has less-defined tasks, a long-term time frame, and more ambiguous results (although potentially more valuable for the firm). The sales function differs from both manufacturing and R&D on these dimensions. It has a longer time frame than manufacturing but a shorter one than R&D. It has less ambiguous results than R&D, but is also less clear than manufacturing on the most efficient means to achieve its goals. To be effective, the GM must both administer each function and integrate the functions, so that the firm can coordinate how its product reaches its customers and how it develops new products. This integration function is often less routine and more sporadic, reactive, and unpredictable than are the tasks associated with particular functions. Yet the GM must perform both types of tasks.

In addition to routine and nonroutine internal tasks, the GM also must respond to unpredictable market demands, as would any other market participant. Marketplace demands become further complicated if the GM has to jump additional internal hurdles set by the firm's capital budgeting and planning systems. The policy instituted by General Electric under Jack Welch—that business units be number one or two in their respective markets or risk being sold off—is an example of how corporate management can attempt to intensify the market pressures that GMs face and thus motivate them to greater effort. That such pressures are not always successful is shown by Welch's eventual modification of the "No. 1 or No. 2" strategy in response to the recognition that clever managers can game the system and propose a market definition that was sufficiently limited to guarantee their success and not require them to stretch.[19]

Corporate-level GMs face their own variant of this tension with their subsidiary managers. On the one hand, if they fail to intervene with divisions, they risk being seen as unnecessary and ineffective. If divisions do not need corporate guidance, then what purpose does corporate management serve? On the other hand, intervening with division management may harm corporate performance by hurting the ability of divisions to respond to markets. Corporate GMs also face their own integration problems in getting staff units to work together for the firm rather than to justify particular projects or groups.

Although some parts of the GM's tasks appear ordered, the overall demands of this job make it appear disorganized and reactive. Nowhere is this tension for GMs between routine and disorder more apparent than in formal strategic planning processes, such as those popularized by General Electric (and ended by Jack Welch), that attempted to make strategic decision making more routine and to control even the most nonroutine aspects of the business environment. Henry Mintzberg emphasizes this tension in his critique of strategic planning systems.[20]

A second tension faced by a GM is the need to adopt different (and potentially conflicting) perspectives, according to the particular managerial role that he or she is playing. For example, relative to the board of directors and the shareholders, the GM is an agent whose ultimate objective is to maximize shareholder value. However, the GM can also act like a principal in relationships with employees and in contractual relationships with actors outside the firm.

This tension in the GM's role relative to owners and other stakeholders is recognized in writings about top managers. Gordon Donaldson and Jay Lorsch, in their study of top management decisions, show how the GM can perceive owners as but one of the many stakeholder constituencies that must be accommodated when managing the firm.[21] Chester Barnard's inducement-contribution framework also suggests that owners, suppliers of capital, are one group among several stakeholders of the firm and that the firm's success depends on balancing the demands of many different stakeholders.[22] David Hickson and his colleagues document how strategic decisions are characterized by the involvement of numerous parties inside and outside firms. The more parties involved, the greater the likelihood of serious conflicts of interest among them.[23]

The problem with the tension caused by GMs performing multiple tasks to different constituencies is that, without careful management and design in advance, the effort the GM provides will likely be a function of the relative costs and benefits for the GM of attending to particular tasks. This may well differ from the importance of particular tasks to the firm overall. One way to address this tension and unify conflicting perspectives is to employ a common metric for performance that is relevant for different perspectives. The use of stock price as the fundamental indicator of companywide performance is a popular choice for a common metric. Once again, GE under Welch sets the example for this, with stock price providing the basis for managerial incentives throughout the firm. Whether relying on share price fully resolves the problem of multiple perspectives is doubtful, however, since individuals own different numbers of shares, receive their shares for different reasons (performance versus investment, for example), and differ in how constrained they are in buying and selling shares.

Some of these conflicts are fundamental and not likely to be easily resolved any time soon. For example, adding a significant customer service component (perhaps including an Internet capability) to normal sales and distribution activities may require informing customers about the entirety of products and services available, including those from competitors. Providing good service may involve directing some customers away from your offerings. Similarly, enhancing your own business reach through the development of web-based sales capabilities may bring a firm and its managers directly into conflict with its current suppliers and distributors. There may be no easy answers to such conflicts short of hard negotiations and profit sharing.

A third tension is between the GM's implementor and adapter roles. As discussed in Chapters 7 and 12, implementing a firm's strategy often requires investments in sunk strategic assets that commit the firm to a long-term course of action. Commitment, however, presumes some stability in the firm's strategic environment, so that it can persist in its strategic activities long enough to recoup its investments. Managers are all too aware, however, that the business environment changes regularly and that their firms need to be sufficiently flexible to respond to these changes. Thus, the firm's need to commit to a strategy often conflicts with its need to maintain flexibility in order to respond to environmental pressures and uncertainties.

For GMs in charge of subunits, a further tension exists between firm and subunit objectives. A division of labor inside the firm that creates subunits runs the risk that managers of those units will work to maximize subunit performance at the expense of overall firm profitability. For multidivisional firms, the delegation of operational authority to divisional managers compounds the problem. This means that for product market decisions, the divisional GM is independent, while still remaining just one component of corporate profit objectives. These tensions can become acute when, as in corporate portfolio strategies, the division manager may be called upon to limit the expansion of his or her own division to cross-subsidize the activities of other divisions.

Changing Definitions of Managerial Work

The nature of managerial work is defined by the nature of the firms in which managers work. Since the nature of the firm has changed greatly over the last century, it is not surprising that the nature of the GM's job has also changed, no doubt frustrating the efforts of observers who seek to neatly characterize it. Writings about GMs have frequently emphasized the changing nature of managerial work, to the point where the rhetoric of change has become part of a manager's tasks, even when a manager is working in a period of relative stability rather than one of dramatic change.

When managers first became prominent, large vertically and horizontally integrated firms were new and had developed in response to the inability of existing markets to handle the requirements of firms that had to produce and distribute large-volume production to a mass market. Under these conditions, the manager was seen as a visible hand that substituted for the market and whose job required much more administration than market coordination. As firms grew larger and more diverse, however, they also became more difficult to administer and control routinely. Firms responded by introducing the M-form, whose structure included decentralized decision making, profit-based controls of business unit managers, and a division of labor between corporate managers, divisional managers, and corporate support staff. These changes exacerbated the already-difficult problems of coordination across business units and among corporate GMs and introduced market-based decision-making criteria into subunit managers' behaviors.

As conditions changed again in the 1990s, with the global expansion of firms, the general increase in rivalry in many industries, and changes in telecommunications and data processing that have made it possible to communicate more quickly with more people, the tasks of managers have changed further. Christopher Bartlett and Sumantra Ghoshal see these changes in terms of a shift from corporate strategy to corporate purpose.[24] By corporate purpose, Bartlett and Ghoshal mean that managers must increasingly integrate strategy and operations at much lower levels within the firm than had previously been the case. This approach combines managerial roles of value creation, implementation, and facilitation in ways that were less common in the strategy–structure approach to managing the multidivisional firm. Instilling a corporate purpose ensures that lower-level managers, who increasingly work in diverse markets around the globe, can effectively address local market issues and remain linked to corporate objectives. By internalizing corporate purpose in its employees, firms can achieve a degree of integration that would not be possible under more formalized integration approaches.

Changes in business conditions that require adaptation by managers are often limited to particular sectors or geographic areas. In deregulated industries, managers are being forced to obtain market-related skills, as traditional restrictions on entry are eliminated and new rivals emerge. In different geographic areas, political changes are forcing similar adjustments by managers. Changes in Eastern Europe, following the fall of communism in 1989, provide good examples. In these countries, governmental infrastructures were obsolete and unsuitable for changed economic conditions. This prompted large-scale experimentation throughout the region, both in the governmental sphere, where formerly state-owned enterprises were privatized and a commercial and legal infrastructure was developed, and in the new private sector, where new forms of organization in manufacturing, distribution, and human resources also emerged. While culture and history may affect managerial needs in these emerging markets, such as with the bureaucratic culture developed under 50 years of communism, the problems of management development in these areas are similar in many ways to the general managerial challenges facing Western firms.

General management roles are also being shaped by the changing demographic profile of the workforce in industrialized nations. The aging of the baby-boom generation, the increased entry of women into the workforce, and related factors have made it more difficult for firms to employ the incentives and controls that had been effective with managers after World War II. Good managers are increasingly turning down promotions, transfers, and increased responsibilities in an effort to balance work and family issues. At the same time, competition and the development of niche markets has made it more important to hire and retain specialized employees precisely at the time when these employees are likely to become increasingly scarce, owing to demographic changes and other macro developments. These issues are requiring firms to provide child care and related services if they hope to retain the talented managers that are increasingly critical resources in contemporary markets.[25]

CHAPTER SUMMARY

◆ The general manager (GM) fulfills an integrative role in making strategic decisions for his or her firm. The GM balances the various decision needs of the firm to decide how a set of decisions should be made together.

◆ The general manager is both a problem solver and a visionary. As a problem solver, the GM defines and manages the boundaries of the firm, sets a competitive strategy, and oversees the firm's internal incentives, culture, and structure. As a visionary, the GM identifies a sustainable position for long-term success.

◆ GMs use both formal and informal means to accomplish objectives. While relying on qualitative analyses as much as or more than quantitative analyses, they also rely on formal agendas and information networks.

◆ GMs may play one or more of several roles: entrepreneurial, organizer/implementor, contractor, facilitator, competitor, and adapter. Tensions arise when these roles require conflicting actions.

◆ General managers have had to change their roles in response to changing technological, regulatory, and competitive conditions.

◆ Regardless of their changing and varied roles, GMs remain agents of shareholders, accountable to them and to other stakeholders for the conduct of the firm's business.

ENDNOTES

[1]Miller, M. and L. Hays, "Gerstner's Nonvision for IBM Raises a Management Issue," *Wall Street Journal*, July 29, 1993, p. 131.

[2]Stewart, J., *Disney War*, New York, Simon & Schuster, 2005.

[3]Kotter, J., *The General Managers*, New York, Free Press, 1982, pp. 22–27.

[4]Chandler, A., *The Visible Hand*, Cambridge, MA, Belknap, 1979.

[5]Barnard, C., *The Functions of the Executive*, Cambridge, MA, Belknap, 1938; Selznick, P., *Leadership and Administration*, Berkeley, University of California Press, 1957; Graham, P. (ed.), *Mary Parker Follett: Prophet of Management*, Boston, Harvard Business School Press, 1995; Sloan, A., *My Years with General Motors*, Garden City, NY, Doubleday, 1964.

[6]Berle, A. and G. Means, *The Modern Corporation and Private Property*, New York, Macmillan, 1932.

[7]See Bower, J., C. Bartlett, C. Christensen, A. Pearson, and K. Andrews, *Business Policy: Text and Cases*, 7th ed., Homewood, IL, Irwin, 1991, p. ix.

[8]Bennis, W. and B. Nanus, *Leaders: The Strategies for Taking Charge*, New York, Harper & Row, 1985, p. 4.

[9]Quinn, J., *Strategies for Logical Incrementalism*, Homewood, IL, Dow Jones/Irwin, 1980.

[10]Hambrick, D. C., "Top Management Groups: A Conceptual Integration and Reconsideration of the 'Team' Label," in Staw, B. M. and L. L. Cummings (eds.), *Research in Organizational Behavior*, 16, 1994, pp. 171–214; Miller, C., L. Burke, and W. Glick, "Cognitive Diversity Among Upper-Echelon Executives: Implications for Strategic Decision Processes," *Strategic Management Journal*, 19, 1998, pp. 39–58.

[11]Mintzberg, H., *The Nature of Managerial Work*, New York, Harper & Row, 1973; for a shorter summary, see Mintzberg, H., "The Manager's Job: Folklore and Fact," *Harvard Business Review*, July–August 1975, pp. 49–61.

[12]Kotter, J., *The General Managers*, New York, Free Press, 1982, pp. 60–79.

[13]Gabarro, J. J., "When a New Manager Takes Charge," *Harvard Business Review*, May–June 1985, pp. 110–123; Ibarra, H., "Structural Alignments, Individual Strategies, and Managerial Action: Elements Toward a Network Theory of Getting Things Done," in Nohria, N. and R. G. Eccles (eds.), *Networks and Organizations: Structure, Form, and Action*, Boston, Harvard Business School Press, 1992, chap. 6.

[14]Uzzi, B. and J. Gillespie, "Knowledge Spillover in Corporate Financing Networks: Embeddedness and the Firm's Debt Position," *Strategic Management Journal*, 23, 2002, pp. 595–618.

[15]See the idea of "Level 5 Leadership" in Collins, J., *Good to Great*, New York, Harper Business, 2001, p. 17.

[16]Hermalin, B. E., "Toward an Economic Theory of Leadership: Leading by Example," *American Economic Review*, 88, 1998, pp. 1188–1206.

[17]Miller, G. J., "Managerial Dilemmas: Political Leadership in Hierarchies," in Cook, K. S. and M. Levi (eds.), *The Limits of Rationality*, Chicago, University of Chicago Press, 1990.

[18]For example, in his memoirs, former GE CEO Jack Welch says virtually nothing about specific competitive considerations facing particular business units and how they affected his decisions regarding those units. See Welch, J., *Jack: Straight from the Gut*, New York, Warner Business Books, 2001.

[19]Welch, J., *Jack: Straight from the Gut*, New York, Warner Business Books, 2001, pp. 201–202.

[20]Mintzberg, H., *The Rise and Fall of Strategic Planning*, New York, Free Press, 1994, pp. 380–396.

[21]Donaldson, G. and J. Lorsch, *Decision Making at the Top*, New York, Harper & Row, 1983.

[22]Barnard, C., *The Function of the Executive*, Cambridge, MA, Belknap, 1938.

[23]Hickson, D. J., R. J. Butler, D. Cray, G. R. Mallory, and D. C. Wilson, *Top Decisions: Strategic Decision Making in Organizations*, San Francisco, Jossey-Bass, 1986, pp. 42–54.

[24]Bartlett, C. A. and S. Ghoshal, "Changing the Role of Top Management, Beyond Strategy to Purpose," *Harvard Business Review*, November–December 1994, pp. 79–88.

[25]For an excellent discussion of these issues, see Bailyn, L., *Breaking the Mold: Women, Men, and Time in the New Corporate World*, New York, Free Press, 1993; also see Arthur, M. B. and D. M. Rousseau (eds.), *The Boundaryless Career: A New Employment Principle for a New Organizational Era*, New York, Oxford University Press, 1996; for a discussion of demographic issues, see Drucker, P., *Management Challenges for the 21st Century*, New York, HarperCollins, 2001.

GLOSSARY

accommodated entry Entry is accommodated if structural entry barriers are low, and either (a) entry-deterring strategies will be ineffective, or (b) the cost to the incumbent of trying to deter entry exceeds the benefits it could gain from keeping the entrant out

activity-cost analysis A method of assigning costs that views the firm as a set of value-creating activities and then assigns costs accordingly. Templates such as Porter's value chain or the McKinsey Business System Framework can be used to identify the relevant activities for this analysis

agency costs Costs associated with slack effort by employees and the costs of administrative controls designed to deter slack effort

agency efficiency Agency efficiency refers to the extent to which the exchange of goods and services in the vertical chain has been organized to minimize the coordination, agency, and transactions costs

agency theory A theory that examines the use of financial incentives to motivate workers

agent One to whom responsibility has been delegated

arm's-length market transaction A market transaction in which autonomous parties exchange goods or services with no formal agreement that the relationship will continue in the future

asymmetry requirement A requirement for entry barriers to be present. The incumbent must have incurred sunk costs that the entrant has not

attribute-rating method Technique for estimating benefit drivers directly from survey responses and then calculating overall benefits on the basis of attribute scores

autonomous work units Business units in which the unit managers control information about operating decisions, and in which the flow of information between units is minimal

backloaded wages Wages which are below productivity early in the employee-employer relationship, but which exceed productivity with seniority

backward integration An organizational arrangement in which a downstream firm owns the assets of an upstream firm, so that the downstream firm has control over both operating decisions

barriers to entry Factors that allow incumbent firms to earn positive economic profits by making it unprofitable for newcomers to enter the industry

benefit advantage One of the major strategies to achieve a competitive advantage. When pursuing a benefit advantage, firms seek to attain a higher perceived benefit while maintaining a cost that is comparable to competitors

benefit drivers Attributes of a product that form the basis on which a firm can differentiate itself, including: the physical characteristics of the product itself; the quality and characteristics of the services or complementary goods the firm or its dealers offer for sale; characteristics associated with the sale or delivery of the good; characteristics that shape consumers' perceptions or expectations of the product's performance or its cost in use; and the subjective image of the product

blockaded entry   A condition where the incumbent need not undertake any entry-deterring strategies to deter entry

bounded rationality   Limits on the capacity of individuals to process information, deal with complexity, and pursue rational aims

broad coverage strategy   A targeting strategy that is aimed at serving all segments in the market by offering a full line of related products

bureaucratic control   Control that is characterized by much greater specialization of organizational roles and tasks, short-term employment, individual responsibility, and individual decision making

buyer power   The ability of individual customers to negotiate purchase prices that extract profits from sellers

capabilities   Clusters of activities that a firm does especially well in comparison with other firms

career concerns   If employees can regularly "test the market" for their skills, then their current actions may affect their future market value. Employees therefore will select current actions with an eye on how they affect their career

causal ambiguity   A term coined by Richard Rumelt to refer to situations in which the causes of a firm's ability to create more value than its competitors are obscure and only imperfectly understood

certainty equivalent (of a gamble)   Payment which must be offered to a risk averse individual to willingly accept the gamble

channel-stuffing   In a multidivisional firm, practice where orders from other parts of the company are rushed to be filled at the end of each month

competitive advantage   The ability of a firm to outperform its industry, that is, to earn a higher rate of profit than the industry norm

complementarities   Synergies among organizational practices, whereby one practice is more effective when others are in place

complete contracts   Stipulates each party's responsibilities and rights for each and every contingency that could conceivably arise during the transaction

complex hierarchy   Involves multiple groups and multiple levels of groupings. Complex hierarchy arises from the need not just to organize individuals into groups, but to organize groups into larger groups

conflicting out   When a potential client approaches a professional services firm with new business, it may be concerned that the firm is already doing business with one or more of its competitors. The firm may lose this potential business because it is conflicted out

conjoint analysis   A set of statistical tools used by market researchers to estimate the relative benefits of different product attributes

constant returns to scale   Indicates that average costs remain unchanged with respect to output

consumer surplus   The perceived benefit of a product per unit consumed minus the product's monetary price

contingency theory   An idea which posits that there is no uniformly "best" organizational structure for all firms in all circumstances. Contingency theory has focused on three factors that may affect the relative efficiency of different structures: (1) technology and task interdependence, (2) information flows, and (3) the tension between differentiation and integration

control   The location of decision-making rights and rule-making authority within a hierarchy

cooperative pricing   Refers to situations in which firms are able to sustain prices in excess of those that would arise in a noncooperative single-shot price or quantity-setting game

coordination   The flow of information within an organization to facilitate subunit decisions that are consistent with each other and with organizational objectives

corporate culture   A set of collectively held values, beliefs, and norms of behavior among members of a firm that influences individual employee preferences and behaviors

cospecialized assets   Assets that are more valuable when used together than when separated

cost advantage   One of the major strategies to achieve a competitive advantage. When pursuing a cost advantage, firms seek to attain lower costs while maintaining a perceived benefit that is comparable to competitors

cost drivers   The basic economic forces that cause costs to vary across different organizations

cost of capital   The rate of return just sufficient to induce investors to provide financial capital to the firm

creative destruction   When quiet periods in markets are punctuated by fundamental "shocks" or "discontinuities" that destroy old sources of advantage and replace them with new ones

cross-price elasticity of demand   Given two products x and y, the cross-price elasticity of demand measures the percentage change in demand for good y that results from a 1 percent change in the price of good x

cube-square rule   As one increases the volume of a vessel (e.g., a tank or a pipe) by a given proportion, the surface area increases by less than this proportion. A source of scale economies

customer specialization   A targeting strategy in which the firm offers a variety of related products to a particular class of consumers

departmentalization   The division of an organization into formal groupings

deterred entry   Occurs when an incumbent can keep an entrant out by employing an entry-deterring strategy

differentiation advantage   One of the major strategies to achieve competitive advantage. When pursuing a differentiation advantage, firms seek to offer a higher perceived benefit while maintaining costs that are comparable to competitors

direct competitor   When firms are direct competitors, the strategic choices of one directly affect the performance of the other

direct labor costs   The costs of labor that are physically traceable to the production of the finished goods

direct materials costs   The costs of all materials and components that can be physically traced to the finished goods

diseconomies of scale   Indicates that average costs increase as output increases

disruptive technologies   Class of technologies that has higher B-C than their predecessors, but does so through a combination of lower B and much lower C

division of labor   Refers to the specialization of productive activities, such as when a financial analyst specializes in the analysis of startup biotech companies

dominant strategy   A strategy that is the best decision for the firm, no matter what decision its competitor makes

dynamic capabilities   Ability of a firm to maintain and adapt the capabilities that are the basis of its competitive advantage

dynamic efficiency   The achievement of long-term growth and technological improvement

early-mover advantages   Once a firm acquires a competitive advantage, the early-mover advantage increases the economic power of that advantage over time. Sources of early-mover advantages

include: the learning curve, brand name reputation when buyers are uncertain about product quality, and consumer switching costs

economic profit   A concept that represents the difference between the profits earned by investing resources in a particular activity, and the profits that could have been earned by investing the same resources in the most lucrative alternative activity

economies of scale   Indicates that average costs decrease as output increases

economies of scope   Cost savings that the firm achieves as it increases the variety of activities it performs, such as the variety of goods it produces

efficiency effect   Refers to the fact that the benefit to a firm from being a monopolist as compared with being one of two competitors in a duopoly is greater than the benefit to a firm from being a duopolist as compared with not being in the industry at all

efficiency frontier   Shows the lowest level of cost that is attainable to achieve a given level of differentiation, given the available technology

efficiency wage   A wage payment made to an agent that exceeds his opportunity cost of working. The extra payment is made to discourage the agent from shirking

exclusive dealing   A practice whereby a retailer agrees to sell only the products made by one manufacturer

experience good   A product whose quality can be assessed only after the consumer has used it for a while

explicit incentive contract   Incentive contract that can be enforced by an outside third party such as a judge or an arbitrator

five-forces analysis   A method, developed by Michael Porter, which systematically and comprehensively applies economic tools to analyze an industry in depth. The five forces are internal rivalry, entry, substitute and complement products, supplier power, and buyer power

fixed costs   Costs that must be expended regardless of total output

focal point   A strategy so compelling that it would be natural for a firm to expect all others to adopt it

focus strategy   A targeting strategy that concentrates either on offering a single product or serving a single market segment or both

folk theorem   An idea that concerns the possibilities for achieving an equilibrium result in repeated play of games, such as the prisoner's dilemma. Its general result is that many Nash equilibria are possible in infinitely repeated games

forward integration   An organization arrangement in which an upstream firm owns the assets of a downstream firm, so that the upstream firm has control over both operating decisions

franchising   A business format franchise agreement allows one firm (referred to as the franchisee) to use the trade name and business plan of another firm (the franchisor) for a specified period of time

free-rider problem   Problem that affects teams. Because every team member receives only a fraction of the total benefit from his actions, every team member will elect not to undertake actions that would be in the best interests of the entire team

game theory   The branch of economics concerned with the analysis of optimal decision making when all decision makers are presumed to be rational, and each is attempting to anticipate the likely actions and reactions of its competitors

geographic specialization   A targeting strategy in which the firm offers a variety of related products within a narrowly defined geographic market

hedonic pricing   Uses data about actual consumer purchases to determine the value of particular product attributes

Herfindahl index   The sum of the squared market shares of all the firms in a market

hidden action   Situations in which aspects of the agent's action that are important to the principal cannot be observed

hidden information   Situations in which aspects of the productive environment that are important to the principal cannot be observed

hierarchy of authority   An organizational arrangement in which one member of a group specializes in monitoring and coordinating the work of the other members

holdup problem   A problem that arises when a party in a contractual relationship exploits the other party's vulnerability due to relationship-specific assets. For example, a seller might attempt to exploit a buyer who is dependent on the seller by claiming that production costs have risen and demanding that the price be renegotiated upward

horizontal differentiation   Differences between products that increase perceived benefit for some consumers but decrease it for others

human capital theory   A theory, developed by Gary Becker, which suggests that workers might accept very low wages early in their careers if they receive on-the-job training that enhances their productivity and job opportunities later on

implicit incentive contract   Contract based on information that cannot be observed by courts or arbitrators

indifference curve   The set of price-quality combinations that yields the same consumer surplus to an individual

indirect competitor   When firms are indirect competitors, the strategic choices of one also affect the performance of the other, but only through the strategic choices of a third firm

indirect labor costs   Salaries of production workers whose efforts usually are not directly traceable to the finished good, including personnel, quality-control workers, and inspectors

influence costs   A concept, developed by Paul Milgrom and John Roberts, which denotes the costs of activities aimed at influencing the distribution of benefits inside an organization

institutional logics   Interrelated beliefs, values, material practices, and norms of behavior that exist in an industry at any given time

internal capital markets   Used to describe how firms allocate financial and human resources to internal divisions and departments

internal rivalry   Competition for share by firms within a market

isolating mechanisms   A term coined by Richard Rumelt which refers to economic forces that limit the extent to which a competitive advantage can be duplicated or neutralized through the resource-creation activities of other firms

joint venture   A particular type of strategic alliance in which two or more firms create, and jointly own, a new independent organization

key success factors   The skills and assets a firm must possess to achieve profitability in a given market

learn-to-burn ratio   The ratio of the "learn rate"—the rate at which new information is received by a firm that allows it to adjust its strategic choices, and the "burn rate"—the rate at which a firm is investing in sunk assets to support its strategy

learning curve   An idea that refers to the cost advantages that flow from accumulating experience and know-how

legitimate power   Formal authority one receives by occupying a high-ranking position

leveraged buy out   Transaction in which a company is purchased not by another firm, but by a group of private investors, often with the assistance of incumbent management

limit pricing   The practice whereby an incumbent firm can discourage entry by charging a low price before entry occurs

M-form   *See multidivisional structure*

make-or-buy decision   The decision of a firm whether to perform an upstream, downstream, or professional supporting activity itself or to purchase it from an independent firm

manufacturing overhead   All the costs associated with manufacturing other than direct labor and indirect materials

marginal cost   Refers to the rate of change of total cost with respect to output

margin strategy   Strategy by which a firm maintains price parity with its competitors and profits from its benefit or cost advantage primarily through high price-cost margins, rather than through a higher market share

market definition   The process of identifying the market or markets in which a firm competes

market for corporate control   An idea, first proposed by Henry Manne, which states that control of corporations is a valuable asset that exists independently of economies of scale and scope. If this is so, then a market for this control exists and operates such that the main purpose of a merger is to replace one management team with another

market segment   A group of consumers within a broader market who possess a common set of characteristics

market structure   The number and size distribution of the firms in a market

matrix organization   An organizational form in which employees are subject to two or more sets of managers at once

merchant coordinators   Independent firms that specialize in linking suppliers, manufacturers, and retailers

minimum efficient scale   The smallest level of output at which economies of scale are exhausted

monopolistic competition   A theory of competition for markets in which there are many sellers and each seller is slightly differentiated from the rest

monopsonist   A firm that faces little or no competition in one of its input markets

most favored customer clause   A provision in a sales contract that promises a buyer that it will pay the lowest price the seller charges

multidivisional structure   An organizational form that is comprised of a set of autonomous divisions led by a corporate headquarters office, assisted by a corporate staff that provides information about the internal and external business environment. Rather than organizing by function or by task, a multidivisional structure organizes by product line, related business units, or customer type

multitask principle   Principle stating that when allocating effort among a variety of tasks, employees will tend to exert more effort toward those tasks that are rewarded

N-firm concentration ratio   The combined market share of the N largest firms in a market

Nash equilibrium   Indicates an outcome of a game where each player is doing the best it can, given the strategies of all of the other players

net present value (of an investment)   The present value of the cash flows the investment generates minus the cost of the investment

network externality   Refers to a situation where, when additional consumers join a "network" of users, they create a positive external benefit for consumers who are already part of the network

network structure   An organizational form in which work groups may be organized by function, geography, or customer base, but where relationships between work groups are governed more by often-changing implicit and explicit requirements of common tasks than by the formal lines of authority that characterize other structures

niche strategy   A targeting strategy in which the firm produces a single product for a single market segment

noncompete clause   A clause that states, should an individual leave a firm, he or she may not directly compete with it for several years

numbers-equivalent   The number of equal-sized firms that can generate a given Herfindahl index in a market. The numbers-equivalent is also equivalent to the reciprocal of the Herfindahl index

oligopoly   A market in which the actions of individual firms materially affect industry price levels

opportunity cost   A concept which states that the economic cost of deploying resources in a particular activity is the value of the best foregone alternative use of those resources

option value   The expected net present value that arises when a firm leaves itself with options that allow it to better tailor its decision making to the underlying circumstances it faces

organizational structure   Describes how a firm uses a division of labor to organize tasks, specify how its staff performs tasks, and facilitate internal and external information flows. Structure also defines the nature of agency problems within the firm

overserve   A broad-coverage competitor overserves a customer group when it offers costly product attributes that customers in that group do not especially value

own-price elasticity of demand   The percentage change in a firm's sales that results from a 1 percent change in its own price

patent race   A term used to characterize the battle between firms to innovate first

path-dependence   A process shows path-dependence if past circumstances could exclude certain evolutions in the future

pay-for-performance   Contract by which the value of the compensation depends on the measured performance of the employee

perceived benefit   The perceived gross benefit of a product minus the user cost of the product and minus any purchasing and transactions costs

percentage contribution margin   The ratio of profit per unit to revenue per unit on additional units sold

perfectly contestable market   A market in which a monopolist cannot raise price above competitive levels because of concern over possible entry

performance measure   Piece of information on which an incentive contract (explicit or implicit) can be based

performance standard   The output that a hardworking agent can be expected to produce

perpetuity   A level cash flow received each year forever

piece-rate contract   A contract that pays a fee for each unit of output

pooled interdependence   Exists when two or more positions are not directly dependent on each other, but are associated through their independent contributions to the success of the firm

predatory act   Entry-deterring strategies that work by reducing the profitability of rivals

predatory pricing   The practice of setting a price with the objective of driving new entrants or existing firms out of business

price elasticity of demand   The percentage change in quantity demanded brought about by a 1 percent change in price

principal   One who delegates responsibility to another, known as the agent

private information   A firm's *private information* is information that no one else knows. It may pertain to production know-how, product design, or consumer information

process reengineering   A management philosophy which advocates that firms should not take the existing configuration of activities and processes for granted, but rather should start from scratch and redesign the chain of activities to maximize the value that can be delivered

product performance characteristics   A product's performance characteristics describe what it does for consumers. Though highly subjective, listing product performance characteristics often clarifies whether products are substitutes

product specialization   A targeting strategy in which the firm concentrates on producing a single type of product for a variety of market segments

profit center   Autonomous groups within a firm whose managers are rewarded on the basis of a target profit goal

promotion tournament   Situation in which a set of employees competes to win a promotion

quasi-rent   An amount equal to the difference between (a) the revenue a seller would actually receive if its deal with a buyer were consummated according to the original terms of the implicit or explicit contract, and (b) the revenue the seller must receive to be induced not to exit the relationship after it has made its relationship-specific investments

real option   A real option exists when a decision maker has the opportunity to tailor a decision to information that will be received in the future

regression analysis   A statistical technique for estimating how one or more factors affect some variable of interest

regression to the mean   A process shows regression to the mean if its shocks are not persistent over time.

related acquisition   A purchase of one firm by another, where both firms are active in similar lines of business

relationship-specific asset   An investment made to support a given transaction

rent   An amount equal to the difference between the revenue a seller receives in a transaction and the minimum amount it must receive to make it worthwhile for it to enter into a relationship with the buyer

replacement effect   A phenomenon whereby, despite equal innovative capabilities, an entrant is willing to spend more to develop an innovation.

The reasoning behind this phenomenon is that through innovation the entrant can potentially replace the monopolist in the industry; however the monopolist can only "replace" itself

reservation price The maximum monetary price the consumer is willing to pay for a unit of a product or service

residual rights of control All rights of control that are not explicitly stipulated in a contract

resource-based theory of the firm A framework used in strategy based on resource heterogeneity; It posits that for a competitive advantage to be sustainable, it must be underpinned by resource capabilities that are scarce and imperfectly mobile, which means that well-functioning markets for the resources and capabilities do not or cannot exist

resource dependence (view of power) Theory in which individuals and firms seek to gain power by reducing their dependence on other actors, while increasing the dependence of other actors on them

resource deployment strategy A perspective on power, developed by Edward Laumann and David Knoke, which looks at power from the standpoint of the actor providing resources

resource mobilization strategy A perspective on power, developed by Edward Laumann and David Knoke, which looks at power from the standpoint of the recipient of resources

resources Firm-specific assets such as patents and trademarks, brand-name reputation, installed base, and organizational culture. Resources can directly affect the ability of a firm to create more value than other firms, and can also indirectly impact value-creation because they serve as the basis of the firm's capabilities

responsibility center A self-contained group that focuses on other performance measures besides profit, such as cost, revenue, or investment goals

risk averse Describes an agent who prefers a sure thing to a gamble of equal expected value

risk neutral Describes an agent who is indifferent between a sure thing and a gamble of equal expected value

risk premium An extra payment above and beyond the expected outcome of a gamble which must be offered to a risk-averse individual to willingly accept the gamble

risk-sharing contract A contract that guarantees an agent some payment, but provides enough incentive so that the agent does not shirk

search goods Goods whose quality is relatively easy to evaluate before purchase

self-managed team A collection of individuals, each member of which works with others to set and pursue some common set of objectives

sequential interdependence Exists between two or more workers, positions, or groups when one depends on the outcomes of the others, but not vice versa

share strategy Strategy by which a firm exploits its benefit or cost advantage through a higher market share rather than through high price-cost margins

short run The period of time in which the firm cannot alter key choices of interest (such as price or capacity)

SIC code Standard Industrial Classification (SIC), as defined by the U.S. Bureau of the Census. SIC codes identify products and services by a seven-digit identifier, with each digit representing a finer degree of classification

social exchange A transfer between two or more parties of resources, or rights to control resources, that occurs outside the terms of a market context

soft commitment A commitment made by a firm such that, no matter what its competitors do, the firm will behave less aggressively than if it had not made the commitment. Thus, in a Cournot game a soft commitment will cause the firm to produce relatively less output, while in a Bertrand game a soft commitment will induce the firm to charge a higher price than if it had not made the commitment

SSNIP criterion According to the DOJ, an analyst has identified all of the competitors of a given firm if a merger among those firms would facilitate a *small but significant nontransitory increase in price*

stakeholders Shareholders, employees, and others with a stake in the firm

static efficiency The optimal allocation of society's resources at a given point in time

strategic alliance An agreement between two or more firms to collaborate on a project or to share information or productive resources

strategic commitments Decisions that have long-term impacts and that are difficult to reverse

strategic complements Two or more products whose reaction functions are upward sloping with respect to the actions taken by one another

strategic intent An idea, developed by Gary Hamel and C. K. Prahalad, which means a fundamental focus of a firm's strategy that commits it well beyond its current resource profile

strategic stretch An idea, developed by Gary Hamel and C. K. Prahalad, which combines commitment to the firm's ambitions with the flexibility to change with circumstances

strategic substitutes Two or more products whose reaction functions are downward sloping with respect to the actions taken by one another

structural hole A relationship in a social network in which one actor is the critical link between individuals or entire groups. The presence of a structural hole allows the individual who can span the hole to use the control of information or resource flows to his or her own advantage

stuck in the middle The idea—argued by Michael Porter—that firms which attempt to pursue both a cost advantage and differentiation advantage simultaneously will be ineffective, providing both a lower perceived benefit to consumers than those firms that pursued a differentiation advantage and incurring higher costs than those that pursued a cost advantage

structure (of a market) The number and characteristics of the firms that compete within a market

subgame perfect Nash equilibrium An outcome of a game where each player chooses an optimal action at each stage in the game that it might conceivably reach and believes that all other players will behave in the same way

sunk cost effect A phenomenon whereby a profit-maximizing firm sticks with its current technology or product concept even though the profit-maximizing decision for a firm starting from scratch would be to choose a different technology or product concept

sunk costs Costs that have already been incurred and cannot be recovered

supplier power The ability of input suppliers to negotiate prices that extract profits from their customers

sustainable competitive advantage A competitive advantage that persists despite efforts by competitors or potential entrants to duplicate or neutralize it

switching costs Refers to costs incurred by buyers when they switch to a different supplier

tactical decisions Decisions that are easily reversed and where impact persists only in the short run

tapered integration A mixture of vertical integration and market exchange in which a manufacturer produces some quantity of an input itself and purchases the remaining portion from independent firms

targeting Refers to the selection of segments that the firm will serve and the development of a product line strategy in light of those segments

task interdependence Extent to which two or more positions depend on each other to do their own work

technical efficiency The degree to which a firm produces as much as it can from a given combination of inputs. A broader interpretation is that technical efficiency indicates whether the firm is using the least-cost production process

termination-based incentives Implicit contract in which incentives come from the threat by the employer to fire the employee if some easily measurable aspect of performance is below a preset standard

tertius gaudens Providing a valued relationship between two unconnected parties (actors or groups of actors). The tertius is the "third who benefits," and the strategy involves spanning a structural hole and bargaining with the parties on either side for the most favorable terms

throughput The movement of inputs and outputs through a production process

tit-for-tat strategy A policy in which a firm is prepared to match whatever change in strategy a competitor makes

total cost function Represents the relationship between total cost and output, assuming that the firm produces in the most efficient manner possible given its current technological capabilities

total quality management A management philosophy which teaches that firms can lower their costs and maintain or increase quality by improving the efficiency of their production processes

tough commitment A commitment made by a firm such that, no matter what its competitors do, the firm will behave more aggressively than if it had not made the commitment. Thus, in a Cournot game a tough commitment will cause the firm to produce relatively more output, while in a Bertrand game a tough commitment will induce the firm to charge a lower price than if it had not made the commitment

tournament Competition among workers to outperform one another to earn rewards and move up the hierarchy of the firm. Arises when individuals are ranked relative to one another and when the hardest-working and most able workers are promoted

transactions costs A concept, developed by Ronald Coase, which denotes the costs to using the market—such as costs of organizing and transacting exchanges—which can be eliminated by using the firm

U-form *See unitary functional structure*

umbrella branding The practice of offering a broad product line under a single brand name. A source of scope economies

underserve A broad-coverage competitor underserves a customer group when it offers insufficient levels of product attributes that customers in the target set especially value

uniform delivered pricing A single delivered price that a seller quotes for all buyers and in which the seller absorbs any freight charges itself

uniform FOB pricing A price that a seller quotes for pickup at the seller's loading dock, and the buyer absorbs the freight charges for shipping from the seller's plant to the buyer's plant

unitary functional structure An organizational form in which there is a single department responsible for each of the basic business functions within the firm. This structure is characterized by a division of labor that allows for specialization of the basic tasks that a business performs. Each department depends on direction from central headquarters and probably could not exist autonomously outside the firm except as contract vendors to a firm that independently secures the other functions

unrelated acquisition A purchase of one firm by another, where the two firms are active in different lines of business

value-added analysis The process of using market prices of finished and semifinished goods to estimate the incremental value-created by distinctive parts of the value chain

value chain A concept, developed by Michael Porter, which describes the activities within firms and across firms that add value along the way to the ultimate transacted good or service

value-created The difference between the value that resides in a finished good and the value that is sacrificed to produce the finished good

value net The firm's "value net" which includes suppliers, distributors, and competitors whose interactions can enhance total industry profits, and the profits of each member of the net

variable costs Costs, such as direct labor and commissions to salespeople, which increase as output increases

vertical chain The process that begins with the acquisition of raw materials and ends with the distribution and sale of finished goods

vertical differentiation Distinction of a product that makes it better than the products of competitors

vertically integrated firm A hierarchical firm that performs many of the steps in the vertical chain itself

winner's curse The firm that wins the bidding war for an input may be overly optimistic about its value. Unless it accounts for the possibility of overoptimism, the winning bidder may end up overpaying for the asset

zone of indifference The set of issues over which a powerful individual usually prevails

NAME INDEX

Adams, Walter, 73, 311, 427, 435, 451
Aggarwal, Rajesh, 470–471, 485
Ainsworth, Megan, 284
Akerlof, G., 285
Alchian, Armen, 512, 538
Alt, J., 134, 566
Altman, Rory, 284
Amaran, M., 248
Ambrose, S. E., 73
Amihud, Yakov, 175, 187
Anderson, E., 162
Anderson, Eric, 143
Anderson, K., 486
Andrews, K., 8, 581
Ansoff, H. I., 539
Aoki, Masahiko, 503–505, 509
Arnstein, Edward, 284
Arrow, Kenneth, 436, 452
Arthur, M. B., 428, 581
Ashenfelter, O., 187
Astor, John Jacob, 45
Avery, Chris, 174, 187
Axelrod, Robert, 260, 284
Azoulay, Pierre, 134

Bailyn, L., 581
Bain, Joe, 289–290, 310, 311
Baker, David, 284
Baker, George, 151, 492, 508
Baker, W. E., 539
Baldwin, C. Y., 73
Barad, Jill, 404–405
Barnard, Chester, 565, 569, 578, 580, 581
Barnett, D. F., 73
Barney, Jay, 415, 427, 551
Barney, J. B., 566
Baron, David, 521, 539, 558, 566
Bartlett, Christopher, 579, 581
Barton, David, 161, 511, 538
Baumgardner, J., 104
Baumol, William, 296, 311
Bazerman, Max, 172, 186
Beard, D., 427
Beard, P., 73
Behr, Rafael, 452
Bell, Alexander Graham, 439

Beniger, J. R., 50
Benkard, C. L., 104
Benkard, Lanier, 96–97, 327, 340
Bennis, Warren, 570, 581
Berger, Philip, 180, 188
Berle, Adolph, 173, 186, 581
Bertrand, Joseph, 213–217, 221
Besanko, David, 270, 284, 395, 521, 538, 539
Best, M., 186
Bettis, Richard, 167, 186, 187
Beyer, J. M., 452
Binzen, P., 396
Blasi, J. R., 73
Bliss, Richard, 187
Bliss, Richard T., 175
Blumenstein, R., 248
Borenstein, Severin, 162, 296–297, 311
Bower, J., 581
Boycko, M., 73
Brandenberger, Adam, 312–313, 318–319
Brander, J., 248
Branson, Richard, 412
Brealey, R. A., 39
Brenner, Menachem, 559, 566
Bresnahan, Timothy, 218, 222, 419
Brock, Gerald, 416, 428
Brown, C., 104
Brown, Christopher, 284
Brown-Humes, Christopher, 452
Browning, L. D., 452
Brush, Thomas, 167, 186
Bulow, J., 248
Burgelman, R. A., 452
Burke, L., 581
Burkhauser, R., 486
Burlingame, John, 493
Burnett, Leo, 109
Burrows, John, 44–45, 46
Burt, Ronald, 539, 547, 565, 571
Butler, R. J., 581
Byrne, John, 548, 565

Campa, Jose, 181, 188
Capon, Noel, 180, 187
Capps, C., 221

Card, D., 187
Cardinal, Laura, 180, 188
Carnegie, Andrew, 53
Carpenter, G. S., 428
Carroll, P., 396
Case, Stephen, 93, 105, 175
Cassano, James, 167, 186
C'Aveni, R., 451
Caves, Richard, 161, 511, 538
Chamberlin, Edward, 203, 207, 221, 254, 283
Chandler, A. D., Jr., 161
Chandler, Alfred, 8, 53, 54, 72, 73, 511, 529, 538, 569, 580
Charles, D., 539
Chatterjee, Sayan, 183, 188
Chen, Ming-Jer, 228, 247
Cherry, Andrew, 284
Chevalier, Judy, 174, 187, 188, 501, 509
Chodorow, Jeffrey, 305
Christensen, Clay, 432, 451, 581
Christensen, H. K., 187
Citron, Jeffrey, 399
Clark, Jim, 153
Clark, K., 73
Clark, K. B., 452
Clark, Kim, 445
Clark, R., 162
Coase, Ronald, 123, 135
Cochran, T. C., 72, 73
Cockburn, I., 89, 104, 362, 395, 433, 451
Cockenboo, L., 104
Cohen, A., 305, 566
Colberg, S., 248
Coleman, J. S., 565
Collins, J., 581
Collins, Jim, 3, 8
Comment, Robert, 164, 186
Connelly, John, 115
Cook, K. S., 581
Cooper, Thomas, 274, 284
Cortada, J. W., 73
Cournot, Augustin, 209–212, 211, 215
Courtney, Hugh, 241, 249
Crandall, R. W., 73
Craw, Chip, 284
Crawford, Fred, 369, 395

592

SUBJECT INDEX

corporate control market and, 177–179

corporate governance problems and, 175–177

diversification discount, 181

diversified firm performance, 179–183

economies of scale and scope and, 167–168

efficiency based reasons for, 167–173

history of, 163–166

internal capital markets and, 170–171

long-term performance and, 181–183

managerial reasons for, 173–179

in modern business, 58–59

operating performance studies, 179–180

potential costs of, 172–173

shareholder's portfolios and, 171

stock market response to, 181

transaction costs and, 168–170

undervalued firms and, 171–172

valuation and event studies, 180–181

Divided technical leadership, 419

Division of labor, 82, 83

Divisional structure, 517–518

DKB, 158

Dominant-business firms, 164

Double marginalization, 130–131

Dow Chemicals, 261

Dow Corning, 59

Downstream industries, 317–318

Dr. Pepper, 197

Dumping, 306

DuPont, 53, 294

Dynamic capabilities, evolutionary economics and, 443–445

Dynamic pricing rivalry. *See also* Cooperative pricing

Bertrand model and, 251–252

competitor responses and, 254–256

coordination and, 257–260

Cournot model and, 251–252

folk theorem and, 257

intuition and, 252–254

misreads and, 260–262

tit-for-tat pricing and, 254–257, 260

Dynamics, firm, 7–8

Early-mover advantages, 408–409

buyer switching costs, 416–417

dominant standards, 421

learning curve, 415

market competition, 420–421

network effects, 417–418

reputation and buyer uncertainty, 415–416

standards, 418

Early-mover disadvantages, 421–422

eBay, 182–183, 418, 560

Economic costs *vs.* accounting costs, 19–21

Economic modeling, 2–3

Economic profit

versus accounting profit, 20–21, 110

within and across industries, 347–348

competitive advantage and, 346–350

net present value and, 21–23

Economies of density, 81, 388

Economies of model volume, 388

Economies of scale and scope, 14. *See also* Diseconomies of scale

in advertising, 86–89

alternative technologies and, 79–81

capital intensive production and, 82

complementarities and strategic fit, 90–91

cube-square rule, 85

definition of scale, 75–76

definition of scope, 76–77

departmentalization and, 514

diversification and, 167–168

division of labor and, 82–84

entry and, 316

hub-and-spoke networks and, 81

as impediments to imitation, 411–413

indivisibilities and, 78–84

industry entry and, 292–294

inventories and, 84–85

learning curve and, 99–100

long-run, 80

market structure and, 218–219

physical properties of production and, 85

product-specific fixed costs and, 78–79

in purchasing, 86

in research and development, 89

short-run, 80

specialization and, 82

vertical integration and, 139

Economizing, 136–137

EDS, 59, 109

Efficiency effect, 436–437

Efficiency wages, 493–496

Elastic demand, 25

Electric utility industry, vertical integration and, 142–143

Electronic component industry, vertical integration and, 143

Electronic data interchange (EDI), 523

Eli Lilly, 107

Embedded ties, 156

Emerging markets, infrastructure in, 62–64

EMI, 89, 421

Emirates Air, 293

Employee discount price war, 255

Enron, 4–5, 69, 558, 559

Enterprise Rent-A-Car, 361, 383

Entertainment Arts, 438

Entrepreneur, general manager as, 572

Entrepreneurship, 430–431

Entry and exit

accommodated entry, 289

analyzing entry conditions, 289–291

antitrust laws and, 292

asymmetries and, 291

Bain's typology, 289

barriers to entry, 289–295

barriers to exit, 295–296

basic concepts of, 288–296

blockaded entry, 289

capacity expansion and, 304–305

Chicago hospital market analysis, 322–323

commercial airframe manufacturing analysis, 326–327

deterred entry, 289

economies of scale and scope and, 292–294

entry-deterring behavior, 308–309

entry-deterring strategies, 296–306

erosion of profits and, 316

essential facilities doctrine, 292

exit-promoting strategies, 306–308

facts about, 287–288

hit-and-run entrants, 296

industry analysis and, 316

judo economics and, 305–306

limit pricing and, 297–301

marketing advantages of incumbency, 295

patents and, 292

predatory pricing and, 301–304

professional sports analysis, 331–333

puppy-dog ploy and, 305–306

resource control and, 291–292

structural entry barriers, 291

sunk costs, 296

survey data, 308–309

wars of attrition and, 306–308

Epson, 268

Essential facilities doctrine, 292

Event studies, 180–181

Evolution of modern business. *See also* Emerging markets

world in 1840, 44–52

communications, 47–48

doing business in, 44–45

finance, 48

government, 51–52

production technology, 48–51

transportation, 46–47

world in 1910, 52–58

communications, 55–56

doing business in, 52–55

Price (*cont.*)
brand-level *vs.* industry-level,
26–27
conditions causing competition in, 315
cooperative pricing and sensitivity,
270
discrimination by suppliers, 318
elasticity of demand, 24–28, 315,
371–372
exploiting competitive advantage
through, 371
industry profits and, 315
intensity of, 198
leadership, cooperative pricing and, 273
limit pricing, 302–304
most favored customer clauses, 274
predatory, 301–304, 306–308
pricing decisions, 29–31
relationship with concentration,
217–218
sensitivity, demand curve and, 24–25
umbrellas, 268
uniform delivered prices, 274–275
wars, 306–308
Primerica, 165
Principal/agent framework, 455–464.
See also Incentive contracts;
Performance measures
Principles, need for, 3–6
Private information, leakage of,
122–123
Process issues, in vertical mergers,
147–148
Process reengineering, 390
Procter & Gamble, 169–170, 515
Product features, price sensitivity and, 26
Product life cycle, 97–98
Product market share, vertical
integration and, 140
Product performance characteristics,
competition and, 193
Product specialization strategy, 383
Production, physical properties of, 85
Production technology
in 1840 business world, 48–51
in 1910 business world, 55
in today's business world, 61–62
Professional sports analysis
buyer power, 335
entry, 331–333
internal rivalry, 329–331
market definition, 329
substitutes and complements,
333–334
supplier power, 334–335
Profit centers, 515
Profit-maximization hypothesis, 29
Profitability, 19–23. *See also* Costs;
Sustainable competitive advantage
economic profit *vs.* accounting
profit, 20–23

economic *vs.* accounting costs,
19–21
extracting from cost and benefit
advantages, 368–372
industry and business unit effects,
348–350
monopolistic competition and, 206–
207
net present value, 21–23
persistence of, 400–403
Promotion tournaments, 490–493
PSCO, 290
Puppy-dog ploy, 305–306
Purchasing, economies of scale and
scope in, 86

Quaker Oats, 35, 59, 232, 294
Quality competition, 276–282
among U.S. health plans, 278
in competitive markets, 277–279
marginal benefits of improving
quality, 280–282
marginal cost of increasing quality,
280
sellers with market power and,
279–282
Quasi-rents, 123, 124–126
Queuing theory, 85

Railroads, growth from 1840 to 1890,
50
Ratings compression, 489
Raw materials, as barrier to entry, 316
RCA, 59, 429
Real options, 240–242
Reciprocal interdependence, 525
Regression analysis of cost functions,
102–103
Regression to the mean, 400
Regulations, 541–542, 557–558
Related industries, global competitive
advantage and, 447–448
Relatedness, 164, 410
Relationship-specific assets, 123–124
dedicated assets, 124
forms of, 123–124
fundamental transformation, 124
human asset specificity, 124
physical asset specificity, 124
site specificity, 123
Relationship-specific investments, 126
Renegotiation, holdup problem and,
128–129
Rents, 124–126
Replacement effect, 436
Republic Steel, 57
Reputation
early-mover advantages and,
415–416
as intangible resource, 559
for toughness, 304

Research and development (R&D). *See
also* Innovation
in biotechnology sector, 438
capital allocation for, 439
correlated research strategies, 443
departmentalization and, 514
economies of scale in, 89
government encouragement of, 62
patent races and, 439–441
riskiness of, 441–443
technology choices, 441–443
Reservation price method, 391
Residual rights of control, 143–147
Resource-based theory of the firm,
403–406
Resources
control of as entry barrier, 291–292
cospecialized, 406
imperfectly mobile, 405–406
power and dependence on, 545
scarce, 405–406
spreading too thin, 92
value creation and, 360–363
Responsibility centers, 515
Restructuring, general manager and,
575–576
Return on invested capital (ROIC),
423–424
Revenue
marginal revenue function, 27–29
total revenue function, 27–29
Revenue destruction effect, 212, 315
Rising star product, 97
Risk, incentives and, 469–474
Risk adversity, 116
Risk-neutral decision makers, 465
Risk premium, 467
Risk sharing, performance-based pay
and, 465–469
Rivalry, global competitive advantage
and, 448
RJR, 260, 269
Routines, actions of firms and, 535
Russian privatization program, 66

Safelite Glass Corporation, 464
Safeway, 346
Sales orders, price competition and,
315
Sales revenues, demand and, 23–29
Samsung, 88, 209–213, 531
Sanwa, 158
SAP AG, 530
Sarbanes-Oxley Act, 61
Scale
exploitation of, 113–117
as impediment to imitation,
411–413
vertical integration and, 140
Scarce resources, 405–406
Scope economies, 53

Keebler
Kellogg
Kentucky Fried Chicken
Kirin
KKR
KLM
KLM Royal Dutch Airlines
Kmart
Kodak
Kohls
Kraft
Kroger
Kubota

Lear
Lego
Levelor Blinds
Lexus
Lidl
Liggett and Myers
Lincoln Electric Company
Lionel Corporation
Loblaw Companies Limited
Lockheed
Louisiana-Pacific
Lowes
Lubrizol
LucasVarity
Lucent

Macy's Department Stores
Mahindra & Mahindra
Malt-O-Meal
Marathon Oil Corporation
Martha Stewart
Matsushita
Mattel
Maxwell House
Maytag
Mazda
MBNA America
MCC (Microelectronics and
    Computer Technology
    Corporation)
MCI
McCormick Harvesting Machine
    Company
McDonald's
McDonnell Douglas
McGaw Cellular Communications
McIlhenny
McKinsey & Associates
Medicaid
Medicare
Mercado Libre
Mercedes
Merck

Merrill Lynch
MGA Entertainment
MGM
Michael Reese Hospital
Micron
Microsoft
Midas Muffler
Millenium Pharmaceuticals
Miller Brewing Company
Mintek
Mitsubishi
MLB
Molson Coors
Montefiore Ambulatory Care
    Network
MosaidTech.
Motorola
MSN
MTV
Musicland

Nabisco
Nan Ya Plastics
National
National Football Leauge
Natural Beauty Salon
Navistar
NBA
NEC
Neiman-Marcus
Nestle
Netscape
New Line Cinema
New York Times
Newbridge Networks
Newport Golf
NFL
NHL
Nickelodeon
Nike
Nine West
Nintendo
Nokia
Nordic Mobile Telephone
Nortel Networks
North Star
Northwest Airlines
Nucor

Oak Technology
Ocean Spray
OfficeMax
Olicom A/S
Omnicom Group
Opti Computer
Oracle-Peoplesoft
OshKosh B'Gosh

Paccar
Packard Bell
Pampers
Panamco
Panasonic
Patek Philippe
Paypal
Peapod
Penn Central
Pennsylvania Railroad
People's Express
Pepsi-Cola
Petco.com
petfooddirect
Petopia
Pets.com
Petsmart.com
Petstore.com
Pfizer
Pfizer Health Solutions
Pharmacia
Phelps Dodge
Philip Morris
Philips
Pickwick International
Piggly Wiggly
Pioneer
Pittsburgh Brewing Company (PBC)
Polar
POSCO
Post
Pratt-Whitney
Primerica
Procter and Gamble
Procter and Gamble-Gillette
Providian
Prudential

Qantas of Australia
Quaker Oats
Quality Semiconductor
Qwest

Railway Mail Service
Ralston Purina
Ramtron International
Rand Corporation
Random House
RCA
REM Eyewear
Remington Rand
Republic Airlines
Republic Steel
Revlon
Ricoh
Rite Aid
RJR